This collection of essays includes studies of women's political writings from Christine de Pizan to Mary Wollstonecraft and explores in depth the political ideas of the writers in their historical and intellectual context.

The volume illuminates the limitations placed on women's political writings and their broader political role by the social and scholarly institutions of early modern Europe. In so doing, the authors probe legal and political restraints, distinct national and state organization, and assumptions concerning women's proper intellectual interests. In this endeavor, the volume explores questions and subjects traditionally ignored by historians of political thought and little considered even by current feminist theorists, groups who give slight attention to women's political ideas or place women's writings within the social and intellectual structures from which they emerged and which they helped to shape.

Women writers and the
early modern British political tradition

Women writers and the early modern British political tradition

Edited by

Hilda L. Smith

University of Cincinnati

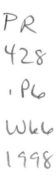

PR
428
.P6
W66
1998

Published in association with the Folger Institute, Washington, D.C.

PUBLISHED BY THE PRESS SYNDICATE OF THE UNIVERSITY OF CAMBRIDGE
The Pitt Building, Trumpington Street, Cambridge CB2 1RP, United Kingdom

CAMBRIDGE UNIVERSITY PRESS
The Edinburgh Building, Cambridge CB2 2RU, United Kingdom
40 West 20th Street, New York, NY 10011–4211, USA
10 Stamford Road, Oakleigh, Melbourne 3166, Australia

First published 1998

Printed in the United Kingdom at the University Press, Cambridge

Typeset in Plantin 10/12 pt [CE]

A catalogue record for this book is available from the British Library

Library of Congress Cataloguing in Publication data
Women writers and the early modern British political tradition / edited
by Hilda L. Smith.
     p.   cm.
Includes bibliographical references and index.
ISBN 0 521 58509 0
1. English literature – Early modern, 1500–1700 – History and criticism.
2. Politics and literature – Great Britain – History – 16th century.
3. Politics and literature – Great Britain – History – 17th century.
4. English literature – Women authors – History and criticism.
5. Great Britain – politics and government – 1485–1603.
6. Great Britain – Politics and government – 1603–1714.
7. Women and literature – Great Britain – History.
8. Women in politics – Great Britain – History.
9. Political science – Great Britain – History.
10. English literature – Political aspects.
I. Smith Hilda L., 1941– .
PR428.P6W66 1998
820.9′358 – dc21 97–33409 CIP

ISBN 0 521 58509 0 hardback

Contents

Contributors

ANNA BATTIGELLI is associate professor of English at the Plattsburgh State University of New York. She is book review editor for *1650–1850: Ideas, Aesthetics, and Inquiries in the Early Modern Era* and has published articles on seventeenth-century literature. Her intellectual biography of Margaret Cavendish, *A Strange Enchantment: Margaret Cavendish and the Exiles of the Mind*, is forthcoming.

BERENICE A. CARROLL is professor of political science and director of Women's Studies at Purdue University. She is author of *Design for Total War: Arms and Economics in the Third Reich*, editor of *Liberating Women's History: Theoretical and Critical Essays*, and author of numerous other works. Her work on women's social and political thought includes studies of Mary Beard (1972) and Virginia Woolf (1978) and the essay, "The Politics of Originality: Women and the Class System of the Intellect" (1990). She has also recently completed *Women's Social and Political Thought: An Anthology*, in collaboration with Hilda L. Smith.

WENDY GUNTHER-CANADA is assistant professor of government and public service at the University of Alabama at Birmingham. She has published essays in the collection *Feminist Interpretations of Mary Wollstonecraft* (1996) edited by Maria Falco. She has recently completed a manuscript, "Rebel Writer: Mary Wollstonecraft's Challenge to Political Theory."

SARAH HANLEY recently a Guggenheim Fellow, and a Camargo Foundation Fellow, is professor of history, the University of Iowa, Iowa City, and director of the Society for French Historical Studies. Her most recent publications include the opening chapter, "Loi Salique (Salic Law)" in the *Encyclopédie historique et politique des femmes*, and the article, "Social Sites of Political Practice in France: Lawsuits, Civil Rights, and the Separation of Powers in Domestic and State Government, 1500–1800," *American Historical Review*; and her forthcoming book, *State Building in Early Modern France: Law, Litigation, and Local Knowledge.*

JANE S. JAQUETTE is B. H. Orr Chair in the liberal arts, professor of politics and chair of the Department of Diplomacy and World Affairs at Occidental College in Los Angeles. She has written extensively on issues of comparative women's political participation and democracy, and is finishing a book on gender and political realism in the work of Machiavelli and Hobbes.

CAROLE PATEMAN is professor of political science at the University of California, Los Angeles, and adjunct professor at the Research School of Social Sciences, Australian National University. Her publications include *Participation and Democratic Theory, The Problem of Political Obligation* and *The Sexual Contract.* She was President of the International Political Science Association 1991–94, and is a Fellow of the American Academy of Arts and Sciences.

J. G. A. POCOCK is professor emeritus of history at the Johns Hopkins University. Author of numerous books and articles on aspects of the history of political thought and of revolutionary England, including *The Ancient Constitution and the Feudal Law: A Study of English Historical Thought in the 17th Century, The Machiavellian Moment: Florentine Political Thought and the Atlantic Republican Tradition,* and editor of *The Varieties of British Political Thought, 1500–1800.* Also a founder of the Center for the History of British Political Thought, he serves on its steering committee. His current interests include eighteenth-century historiography, especially Edward Gibbon.

GORDON SCHOCHET is professor of political science at Rutgers University. A founding member of the Center for the History of British Political Thought and currently a member of its steering committee, he has edited its six-volume *Proceedings.* The author of *Patriarchalism in Political Thought* and the forthcoming *Rights in Contexts: the Political and Historical Construction of Moral and Legal Entitlements,* as well as numerous articles and essays. An editor of *The Varieties of British Political Thought, 1500–1800,* his current research focuses on Locke and religious liberty, natural law and "native peoples" in political theory.

LOIS G. SCHWOERER is the Elmer Louis Kayser Professor Emerita of history at the George Washington University. Author of numerous works, she has written *"No Standing Armies!" The Antistanding Army Ideology in Seventeenth-Century England, The Declaration of Rights,*

1689, and *Lady Rachel Russell: "One of the Best of Women."* She has produced prize-winning articles on the historiography of seventeenth-century women and the imagery of Mary II. A past president of the North American Conference on British Studies, she is currently on the steering committee of the Center for the History of British Political Thought, and editor of *Varieties of British Political Thought*.

MARY LYNDON (MOLLY) SHANLEY is professor of political science in the Margaret Stiles Halleck Chair at Vassar College. She is author of *Feminism, Marriage and the Law in Victorian England* (1989). She is co-editor with Carole Pateman of *Feminist Interpretations and Political Theory* (1990), and with Uma Narayan of *Reconstructing Political Theory: Feminist Essays* (forthcoming). In addition, her articles have appeared in *Victorian Studies, Political Theory, Western Political Quarterly, Signs, Hypatia,* and the *Columbia Law Review*. She is currently writing a book on ethical issues in contemporary family law.

HILDA L. SMITH is associate professor of history at the University of Cincinnati where she also served as director of Women's Studies from 1987 to 1993. The author of *Reason's Disciples: Seventeenth Century English Feminists* (1982) and co-compiler of the award-winning annotated bibliography, *Women and the Literature of the Seventeenth Century* (1990), she has recently completed the manuscript, "'All Men and Both Sexes': The False Universal in England, 1640–1832." In addition, she has published a range of articles in early modern women's history and the nature of women's history more broadly.

PATRICIA SPRINGBORG holds a chair in political theory in the Government Department of the University of Sydney. She has held visiting appointments at the universities of Pennsylvania and California at Berkeley, and the Woodrow Wilson Center and Brookings Institution in Washington, D.C. She has also been a recipient of a MacArthur Research and Writing Grant. The author of several books in political theory, she has just completed two editions of the High Church Tory pamphleteer and promoter of women, Mary Astell.

SUSAN STAVES is Paul Proswimmer Professor of the Humanities and chair of the Department of English at Brandeis University. She is the author of *Players' Scepters: Fictions of Authority in the Restoration* (1979) and *Married Women's Separate Property in England, 1660–1833* (1990). With John Brewer she has edited and contributed to *Early Modern Conceptions of Property* (1995) and with Cynthia Ricciardi she has edited *Elizabeth Griffith's Delicate Distress*. Currently she is writing a literary history of women's writing in Britain, 1660–1785.

BARBARA J. TODD is associate professor of history at the University of Toronto. Her previous articles have concentrated on early modern widowhood and have appeared in *Women and English Society, 1500–1800* (1985), *English Rural Society, 1500–1800* (1990), *Continuity and Change* (1994), *Women and History: Voices of Women in Early-Modern England* (1995), and *Widowhood in Medieval and Early Modern Europe* (forthcoming). This essay is part of her current research for a study of aspects of gender in the evolution of the common law.

MERRY WIESNER is professor of history and former director of Women's Studies at the University of Wisconsin-Milwaukee. She is author of *Working Women in Renaisssance Germany* (1986), *Women and Gender in Early Modern Europe* (1993), *Gender, Church and State in Early Modern Germany: Essays* (1997), and numerous articles on various aspects of women's lives and gender structures in early modern Europe. Past president of the Sixteenth Century Studies Conference and the Society for the Study of Early Modern Women, she currently holds a Guggenheim Fellowship.

JUDITH P. ZINSSER is associate professor of history at Miami University in Oxford, Ohio. She is the co-author with Bonnie S. Anderson of *A History of Their Own: Women in Europe from Prehistory to the Present* (2 vols., 1988). She also wrote *History and Feminism: A Glass Half Full* (1993) for the Twayne series, The Feminist Impact on the Arts and Sciences. She is currently working on an experimental biography of Mme. du Châtelet.

MELINDA ZOOK is assistant professor of history at Purdue University. She is author of "Early Whig Ideology, Ancient Constitutionalism, and the Reverend Samuel Johnson," *The Journal of British Studies* (1993) and "'The Bloody Assizes': Whig Martyrdom and Memory after the Glorious Revolution," *Albion* (1995), and she has a chapter in *Politics and the Political Imagination in Later Stuart Britain: Essays Presented to Lois Green Schwoerer* (forthcoming). She has recently completed a manuscript on the radical effect of the Exclusion Crisis on the revolution of 1689.

Preface

This collection emerged from a conference sponsored by the Center for the History of British Political Thought of the Folger Shakespeare Library on Political Women/Political Writings: Early Modern Britain in a European Context, held May 25–26, 1995. It is structured around the interdependent relationship between women's political writings and the intellectual and social institutions that determined their acceptance or dismissal. It focuses on the political ideas of a range of women authors who were more familiar to, but seldom fully accepted by, their contemporaries than they have become to those studying early modern politics and political thought. It is also comparative by design in order to focus on similar, but distinct, arguments offered in differing geographic settings both by women authors concerning women's political standing, and particular political values and customs that helped determined women's public role. It also seeks to move beyond a focus in which political realities and ideas are held constant, and the issue addressed is simply the integration of women into an accepted norm. The arguments of women writers, the political and intellectual institutions of place and period, regional differences, and evolving political and social norms are each considered problematic rather than normative; and the essays in this volume focus on the shifting interactions among them.

Acknowledgments

The conference on Political Writings/Political Women was held through the generous sponsorship of the Folger Institute, and I want to thank Lena Orlin, then Institute director, in particular, for her support. In addition, the entire staff of the Folger, but especially Kathleen Lynch, helped to make the conference a success. Members of the steering committee of the Center for the History of British Political Thought were invaluable in suggesting themes and participants for the conference, and for supporting a follow-up collection of essays, and I would also like to recognize their assistance. I would like to acknowledge the speed and skill with which the authors of this volume translated conference papers into published essays, and, I would especially like to thank Carole Pateman for her careful reading of the manuscript as a whole and the resulting integrative conclusion that assessed and analyzed with care each of the volume's chapters. I wish also to thank Cambridge University Press for its speedy and helpful assistance in bringing the collection to press, especially the support of William Davies and the efforts of the copy editor, Margaret Deith, to improve a lengthy and somewhat complicated collection. In addition, I want to express strong appreciation for the information and insights I have gained over the years through discussions with Berenice Carroll, Lois Schwoerer, and Barbara Todd on questions relating to women, politics, gender definitions, and political thought.

Anna Surangyi's work on the index was invaluable.

Introduction
Women, intellect, and politics: their intersection in seventeenth-century England

Hilda L. Smith

Relating women's intellectual history to British political thought in the early modern era leaves one in a perpetual state of schizophrenia. With rare exceptions, scholars working in these distinct areas do not pursue the same primary texts, or trust the judgments of the same set of contemporary scholars. Women's intellectual contribution to the era has been studied mostly through biography, or through a focus on individual authors, with a very few – Aphra Behn; Mary Astell; Margaret Cavendish, duchess of Newcastle; and Margaret Fell Fox – garnering the overwhelming attention. Otherwise, women have fallen within categories formed by broader alliances: sectarian women, Leveller women, sympathizers for royalist or revolutionary causes. Or, they have been tied to their genres, as writers of meditations, poets, tractarians, playwrights, and authors of domestic advice.[1]

---

[1] Treatments of women's writings during the seventeenth century, among more recent works, include my *Reason's Disciples: Seventeenth-Century English Feminists* (Urbana: University of Illinois Press, 1982), Sara Heller Mendelson's *The Mental World of Stuart Women: Three Studies* (Amherst: University of Massachusetts Press, 1987), and, among those studies treating women's religious works, Phyllis Mack's *Visionary Women: Ecstatic Prophecy in Seventeenth-Century England* (Berkeley: University of California Press, 1992), Patricia Crawford's *Women and Religion in England, 1500–1720* (London: Routledge, 1993), and Hilary Hinds's *God's Englishwomen: Seventeenth-Century Radical Sectarian Writing and Feminist Criticism* (Manchester: Manchester University Press, 1996). Recent studies and editions of an individual writer's publications include: Margaret Cavendish, *The Blazing World and Other Writings*, ed. Kate Lilley (London: Penguin Books, 1994) and *The Sociable Letters*, ed. James Fitzmaurice (New York: Garland Publishing, 1997); Mary Astell, *The First English Feminist: Reflections upon Marriage and Other Writings*, ed. Bridget Hill (New York: St. Martin's Press, 1986), and most recently, *Astell, Political Writings*, ed. Patricia Springborg (Cambridge: Cambridge University Press, 1996), as well as a biography by Ruth Perry, *The Celebrated Mary Astell* (Chicago: University of Chicago Press, 1986). Annotative bibliographies and commentaries on seventeenth-century women's writings include Elaine Hobby's *Virtue of Necessity: English Women's Writing, 1646–1688* (Ann Arbor: University of Michigan Press, 1988) and Hilda L. Smith and Susan Cardinale's *Women and the Literature of the Seventeenth Century: An Annotated Bibliography Based on Wing's Short-Title Catalogue* (Westport, Conn.: Greenwood Press,

There has been, and perhaps this is wise, little attempt to characterize women's writings generally, and virtually no attempt to do so for those of non-fiction authors whose primary interest was politics. In contemplating disparate approaches to seventeenth-century women's political writings, a number of questions arise in this volume based on traditional assumptions concerning women and politics. How can women write about what they cannot do? or about what is considered outside, and, by some, antithetical to their nature? or about which they have been kept essentially ignorant? All of these realities covertly and overtly confronted women when they wrote about political topics in the early modern period. How could they presume to give advice across such a large divide? And, when an individual woman did offer such advice, what was her inspiration, what empowered her to speak?

In other words, what did politics mean for the women included in this volume, and early modern women more broadly? To what extent and in what proportions was it composed of office holding (either by a female monarch or by lesser officials), of attendance at court, of involvement in parliamentary elections, of jury service, or of broadly defined duties and obligations of property holders and burghers in their locale? Certainly, as with others of their era, they would have thought more about obligations, less about privileges, and little about rights when discussing politics.

In offering analyses that begin to deal with these broader questions, while presenting a range of women authors not often known outside of feminist scholarly circles, this volume addresses a dual purpose. The first is to analyze and place in context the works of a range of women writing on politics from the fourteenth through the eighteenth century. The second is to provide an analysis of the political and intellectual structures in which these, and other, women operated. This volume will treat women's significant contributions to peace theory, to political

1990). For the eighteenth century, there are no broad studies of women's non-fiction writing, but there is a collection of women's writings compiled by Bridget Hill (London: Allen and Unwin, 1984) and studies, biographies, and editions of the work of individual writers including *The Republican Virago: The Life and Times of Catharine Macaulay, Historian* by Bridget Hill (Oxford: Clarendon Press, 1992), Virginia Sapiro's *A Vindication of Political Virtue: The Political Theory of Mary Wollstonecraft* (Chicago: University of Chicago Press, 1992), *The Works of Mary Wollstonecraft* in seven volumes, edited by Janet Todd and Marilyn Butler (London: Pickering, 1989) and Janet Todd's edition of *Mary Wollstonecraft: Political Writings* (Toronto: University of Toronto Press, 1993), as well as biographies of Wollstonecraft by Eleanor Flexner (New York: Coward, McCann and Geohegan, 1972), Jennifer Lorch (New York: Berg, 1990), and Claire Tomalin (London: Weidenfeld and Nicolson, 1974). The vast majority of scholarship on women's writings during the 1700s has been on their works of fiction, especially as early novelists.

thought, to revolutionary debates, to religious disputes, and to the operation of government more widely. But it will also discuss how their societies defined the political and where that definition intersected with views of women's nature and appropriate roles.

Women intellectuals faced a myriad of institutional and scholarly resistance to their writing and their ideas. Central to this resistance was the identification in the minds of their readers, and among later scholarly commentators, of learning with a few academic institutions and professional societies which excluded women. Intellectual histories for the period focus almost wholly on the writings of a few great male thinkers, and institutional histories focus overwhelmingly on Oxford, Cambridge, and the Royal Society in England, the University of Paris and the French Academy in France, and Lutheran theologians in the Imperial German states. Even with the great growth of popular political and legal publications by the mid-seventeenth century, there was still an acceptance of traditional institutions as offering not simply the atmosphere most conducive to scholarly creativity, but also its validation. The court was a competing institution for intellectual and cultural productivity in both France and England, and women fared better there than among more strictly academic institutions. Yet in both linguistic and visual imagery a scholar, an author, a learned or wise "person" was clearly situated within university and professional circles and embodied a male figure.

Reflecting their existence outside the boundaries of institutionalized learning, women were not expected to produce scholarly treatments on a range of topics. Rather, the types of writings expected from them were circumscribed. If they chose to write on religious subjects, most appropriate were works of private meditation or stories of personal faith, but not theological treatises or anything verging upon a sermon. Nor were they to critique ecclesiastical structure, as a number of Puritan and Quaker women did. And, if women wished to write works of advice, they should be directed to other women (or children if the authors were mothers). There was probably no category of acceptable political writings on the part of women, but, again, personal memoirs or pleading for the views or needs of male political allies was most apt to be tolerated. A female author was to avoid wide-ranging analyses and criticisms of the political system, or of a single political leader. And few women authors, at least during the seventeenth century, dealt with political topics unfiltered through a religious lens. During times of crises, Leveller and Quaker women used arguments that blended a need for immediate action or redress, biblical and historical injunctions to act, and the contention that they were as responsible for the well-being of society as their male colleagues. But they did not demand their own political rights – only, at points, a political voice.[2]

Why not? I should like to throw out a couple of suggestions: one, that these seventeenth-century women considered women's exclusion from all public and political roles less certain than we've come to believe today; thus they did not have to offer an explicit demand for such status when at least some women held it. And, women during the seventeenth century had at once a broader and more inclusive understanding of politics than we possess today. They considered local office holding, political obligations of families among the governing class, as well as voting and political rights, as constituting politics, while we would be more apt to equate the term only with the latter. Thus it was necessary for women writers to deal with broader issues of women's situation in seventeenth-century England, than simply a demand for political rights.

Margaret Cavendish, duchess of Newcastle's *Sociable Letters* (1664) offers one of the best examples of a seventeenth-century author grappling with the integrated realities that circumscribed women's political standing. Cavendish was both a royalist and a feminist who raised some of the most profound questions about the intersection of women's place in government, the common law, marriage, and motherhood during the 1600s. In her oft-quoted, evolving understanding of women's place in the state, she started with women's ignorance: "and, as for the matter of governments, we women understand them not." But Cavendish did not stop there. She next contended that women were almost not a part of government, then pointed out their not swearing either to loyalty or supremacy, and finally concluded with women's separation from the state: "If we be not citizens in the Commonwealth, I know no reason we should be subjects to the Commonwealth." It is not easy to decipher the duchess of Newcastle's intent, but I should like to stress her argument that women cannot be forced to serve two masters, a husband and the

---

[2] There has been a great deal of scholarship on the nature of women's writings. Perhaps most useful for an assessment of their religious and political views, and the prescriptions for such views for the period 1640–60, appears in *Pamphlet Wars: Prose in the English Revolution*, ed. James Holstun (London: Cass, 1992). The nature of women's religious writings and efforts is drawn most fully in Phyllis Mack's *Visionary Women*. Of the 637 works published by women from 1641 to 1700, 55 percent were on religious topics, and of these, 171 titles were from Quaker women (Smith and Cardinale, *Women and the Literature of the Seventeenth Century*, xii–xiii). A recent treatment of women Levellers by Ann Hughes, "Gender and Politics in Leveller Literature", appears in *Political Culture and Cultural Politics in Early Modern England*, eds. Susan Ammusen and Mark Kishlansky (Manchester: Manchester University Press, 1995). Greatest attention to women's personal censorship is presented in Elaine Hobby's *Virtue of Necessity*, and a recent and broad overview of the prescriptions for, and the nature of, women's writings (while tilted toward literary works) can be found in *Women and Literature in Britain, 1500–1700*, ed. Helen Wilcox (Cambridge: Cambridge University Press, 1996).

state. She was inclined to believe that women were not subjects at all, but, she concluded, if they were, "it is to our husbands." Ignoring the political standing of single women, Cavendish based her arguments on the married state.

Yet she was hardly alone in lumping all women under the disabilities of the wife. The most famous example was likely from the 1632 treatise, *Lawes Resolutions of Womens Rights* which noted that all women were understood "either as married or to be married." While women were not tied to the universalizing principles of individualism that were emerging for men during the century, they were defined by a particularist set of qualities denoting their essential and proper state as one of dependence, not individuality.[3]

For seventeenth-century women, it was likely more difficult than for men writing about politics, to ignore familial constraints while investing the state with power and authority, and the citizen with independence and judgment. Thomas Hobbes, for example, acknowledged little conflict between empowering women as mothers in the state of nature when he claimed in *De Cive* that "every woman that bears children, becomes both a *Mother*, and a *Lord*" and his definition of the family within civil society that not only empowered the father, but treated the mother as non existent. "A *Father*, with his *sonnes* and *servants* growne into a civill Person by vertue of his paternall jurisdiction is called a FAMILY."[4]

Women who wrote about politics, and did it from a consciously woman-centered perspective, embraced both the realities of some women's power and the need to define the state more broadly so that the family's reflection and engendering of political status would be recognized. But historians of political thought have, for the most part, ignored gender conflicts in earlier texts or in their own work. For them, politics have only occurred in a public arena, within established modes of governing, and among definable institutions. While feminist political

---

[3] Margaret Cavendish, *Sociable Letters*, 25–26; *The Lawes Resolutions of Womens Rights: Or, The Lawes Provision for Woemen* (London: Printed by the Assignes of John More, 1632), 7.

[4] Thomas Hobbes, *De Cive*, the English Version, ed. Howard Warrender (Oxford: Clarendon Press, 1983), 122–26. In addition to this assessment of women's authority within the state of nature, and their ultimate exclusion from the family in its relationship to the state, Hobbes similarly discussed women's standing in chapter 20 of *The Leviathan*, which includes the following:

> there be always two that are equally parents: the dominion therefore over the child, should belong equally to both; ... which is impossible; for no man can obey two masters. And whereas some have attributed the dominion to the man only, as being of the more excellent sex; they misreckon in it ... If there be no contract, the dominion is in the mother. (*Leviathan, Or the Matter, Forme and Power of a Commonwealth, Ecclesiastical and Civil*, ed. Michael Oakshott, Oxford: Blackwell, 1947, 130–31)

theorists, along with women's historians, have raised questions about the issues of women's exclusion from such a realm, they have done less to redefine the realm altogether. Questions have been raised in two areas: first, the feminist contention that the personal is political and thus what happens in the home, the school, the office, etc. is clearly based on power relationships, sets of strategies, and covert and overt agreements about the parameters of discourse and action. And, second, a myriad set of arguments contend that masculine and feminine qualities and spheres must be taken into account in defining the political, so that supposedly non-gendered terms such as public, reason, objective, and (on the negative side) less nurturing, empathetic, emotional, and sensitive are termed masculine, while the feminine is posited in opposition to positive male qualities and embodies those considered lacking in men.[5]

Such thinking is seen as anachronistic when applied to early modern political thought and political realities. And this criticism does not seem off the mark. As many social historians have contended, the distinction between private and public is to a great extent a product of the nineteenth century and the growth of bourgeois culture – but already under construction with the growing importance of sensibility during the eighteenth century. In the seventeenth century when the household functioned more clearly as a unit of the state in which the father established public order and enforced accepted moral and religious values for his various dependents, the distinctions between public and

[5] While works on traditional political thought and works in feminist political theory differ fundamentally in approach and subject matter, they are similar in one respect. Both consistently omit treatment of women's political writing. Two important collections which have recently appeared on early modern political thought, *Political Discourse in Early Modern Britain*, eds. Nicholas Phillipson and Quentin Skinner (Cambridge: Cambridge University Press, 1993) and *The Varieties of British Political Thought, 1500–1800*, ed. J. G. A. Pocock (Cambridge: Cambridge University Press, 1993) continue the pattern of omitting women authors – although there is a mention of one or two in the Pocock volume – and not treating women as political actors. Of feminist approaches to political thought, an older work such as Susan Okin's *Women in Western Political Thought* (Princeton: Princeton University Press, 1979) does offer historical grounding for conceptions of women by political theorists, but the work moves from Plato to Aristotle to Rousseau to Mill, and only mentions Mary Wollstonecraft once. More recent treatments, such as the collection *Feminists Theorize the Political*, eds. Judith Butler and Joan Scott (New York: Routledge, 1992), include mention of some women writers (here, George Sand and Hannah Arendt), but seldom placed within their intellectual context and rather studied as a lesson for current feminist theorizing. Other works such as Wendy Brown's *Manhood and Politics: A Feminist Reading in Political Theory* (Totowa, N.Y.: Rowman and Littlefield, 1988) and Christine di Stefano's *Configurations of Masculinity: A Feminist Perspective on Modern Political Theory* (Ithaca, N.Y.: Cornell University Press, 1991), conceptualize political theory and politics as a masculine arena; while offering useful critiques of the often unstated equation of male with political, still one effect of these works is to deny the existence of women's political writings, or to remove such writings from the intellectual and political debates they helped shape.

private, political and nonpolitical, were less clear. And, when dynastic politics and a court system meant socializing, plotting marriage and kinship strategies, and included a patronage system that used the standing and contacts of both male and female members of the governing class, then what was masculine and feminine, private and public, political and nonpolitical was blurred.[6]

Yet, the broadly gendered nature of early modern politics and citizenship has received little attention. Gender constructions are employed without their significance for actual men and women being clarified. Examples are numerous, but one example appears in John Guy's essay in *The Varieties of British Political Thought, 1500–1800*, where he delineated the importance of counsel to a prince in Tudor political thought. Generally a discussion of the role of gender is simply absent, but, when noted, it is usually as an unanalyzed aside such as in Guy's essay where he states: "In this mode *imperium* was represented as male and *consilium* as female: their relationship was conjugal. (A married woman shared in the administration of her husband's household and mitigated his *imperium* just as equity tempered the rigour of the common law.)"[7] Leaving this gendered terminology, he concludes that "good counsel" negotiates the difference between "order and chaos," and that advising rulers away from tyranny and toward "the ways of virtue and honesty" constituted "the touchstone of government." As with others, Guy does not mention women's absence as counselors or as authors of any of the classic humanist texts on the subject, nor assess what this gendered

---

[6] There are numerous treatments of the role of the family and gender in the construction of local communities and national politics in early modern England, as well as women's role at court. For discussion of these topics see Susan D. Amussen, *An Ordered Society: Gender and Class in Early Modern England, 1560–1720* (New York: Columbia University Press, 1988), Keith Wrightson, *English Society, 1580–1680* (London: Routledge, 1993), and an article by Barbara Harris on women's role in the Tudor court (*Historical Journal* 33(2) [1990]: 259–81), Linda Levy Peck's discussion of women's role in "Benefits, Brokers and Beneficiaries: The Culture of Exchange in Seventeenth-Century England," *Court, Country and Culture: Essays on Early Modern British History in Honor of Perez Zagorin* (Rochester: University of Rochester Press, 1992), 109–28, and on the importance of the duchess of Portsmouth in access to power and policy formation during the reign of Charles II in Nancy Klein Maguire, "The Duchess of Portsmouth: English Royal Consort and French Politician, 1670–85," *The Stuart Court and Europe: Essays in Politics and Political Culture* (Cambridge: Cambridge University Press, 1996), 247–73. For the best discussion of the developing ideology of sex differences that underlay the separate spheres ideology of the nineteenth century, see G. J. Barker-Benfield, *The Culture of Sensibility: Sex and Society in Eighteenth-Century Britain* (Chicago: University of Chicago Press, 1992).

[7] John Guy, "The Henrician Age," in Pocock, *The Varieties of British Political Thought*, 16; *Political Discourse in Early Modern Britain* includes a range of less prominent political writers, but still omits any women authors, or any analysis on the place of women or the role of gender in politics except in mentioning individual queens.

quality might mean for the men offering counsel and the men (and some women) who received it. Later in the same volume William Lamont, after presenting a long list of early and mid-seventeenth-century thinkers, without a single female voice, states that scholars are "not listen[ing] attentively enough to what the seventeenth-century source is saying"; and follows with, "if what he or she is saying seems actually contradictory" one must expand the set of contextual works. Although relevant writings by women clearly existed for Lamont's topic, the Puritan revolution, they appear only in this feminine pronoun.[8]

Also, two of the essays in *Varieties of British Political Thought* discuss Henry Parker's early arguments for parliamentary supremacy by undercutting Charles I's authority as built upon patriarchal authority within the family. Yet neither mentions Parker's clearly gendered argument about both the place of independent men in the state and the role of the wife in the household. The husband, he contends in *Observations upon some of his Majesties late Answers and Expresses* (1642), wields greater authority than the king because "the wife is inferior in nature, and was created for the assistance of man"; but, he continues, "it is otherwise in the State between man and man, for *that* civill difference which is for civill ends, and those ends are, that wrong and violence be repressed by one, for the good of all, not that servility and drudgery may be imposed upon all for the pompe of one." Yet, as is typical of other histories of political thought, such references to gender-based justifications in disputes over the legitimacy and sovereignty of a ruler are not explored.[9]

As we reassess the history of British political thought through the lens of gender, how would we come to see it differently? I think up to this point we do not have sufficient knowledge or a sufficiently integrated perspective to answer this question. Feminist scholars have contended the following: the writings of political theorists are masculine and thus have no relevance for women; or certain constructs such as the social contract were not intended for or do not work for women; or the canonical works of political thought are studied and thought of in a manner not afforded works by women; or such works, when in the rare instances they speak about women, do so outside their systematic analysis of the state; or, it is all pretty irrelevant for real women interested in politics because the canonical texts, and their later analyses, are mostly not about women, but about the supposedly "feminine," and its symbolic expressions. While each of these points of view may hold merit, it is difficult to bring them together to offer an integrated critique

[8] William Lamont, "The Puritan Revolution: A Historiographical Essay," in *The Varieties of British Political Thought*, ed. Pocock, 19.
[9] *The Varieties of British Political Thought*, 132–33, 152–56.

of political theory. We need, therefore, to think more clearly about how we apply gender when speaking of political writings and political actions in the past.

In considering early modern England, two propositions might prove useful: (1) that women had a clear, widespread, and real presence in political and economic structure and (2) that language was so constructed as to deny both the reality and the significance of their standing. Certainly the reality of women's standing is intertwined with how contemporaries and later scholars have defined it. In dealing first with the second point, it seems hard to grasp when language is meant to be gender inclusive or exclusive. Are there any principles or clues that can guide us here? One such pattern has struck me: that when an author wants to highlight the universal significance of a phenomenon or quality, he is most apt to ignore women, and the only sure, but not the only, indication of inclusion is a precise reference. For example, in Tudor politician Thomas Starkey's proposed council of fourteen to govern for parliament when not in session, his language was purposely inclusive, yet so framed that women were not directly represented. His council was "to represent the whole body of the people ... to see unto the liberty of the whole body of the rea[l]m, and to resist all tyranny which by any manner may grow upon the whole commonalty." Made up of clergy, judges and four "of the most wise citizens of London," its composition and representation surely did not incorporate women. But Thomas More, who was upset over anti-clerical sentiments being written in English, lamented that the work's author "would have the lay people both men and women look on them." Obviously "lay people" would have sufficed, but More wanted to emphasize that he meant to include women among those who could not normally read Latin. To what extent, then, are we to believe thinkers meant to include women only when they specifically referred to them?[10]

In studying the gendered nature of early modern English guilds, I was struck by the large amount of evidence, in statutes, in aldermanic records, and in apprenticeship rolls, to support the view that women were full members of guilds, that they wore livery, and that members of guilds were consistently called "brethern and sistern" or "freemen and freewomen," but that later historians utilized terms such as brothers, brotherhood, or members, that obscured the reality of women's standing. Earlier documents might use generic nouns such as members, but that term would be followed by a descriptor that noted it referred to

---

[10] Ibid., 19; Thomas More, *Selected Letters*, ed. Elizabeth Frances Rogers (New Haven: Yale University Press, 1961), 95–105.

both sexes. An example comes from Henry VIII's charter to establish a separate guild for London cloth workers in which he stated that the master and wardens should "make and have among the Citizens of the same City, being then Brethren and Sisters of the same Fraternity of Cloathworkers and the most sufficient thereunto, one livery or Robe." Later accounts, however, ignored the defining clause and employed only the inclusive noun, leading others to think that only men were intended. And many property-owning women shared with their male counterparts an amalgam of office holding, appointing others to office and voting. Perhaps what is needed is more serious attention to the underlying gender distinctions in terms, even when we assume that we know their meanings; and to wonder whether we are asking the right questions about women's political standing in the seventeenth century, or the early modern period more broadly.[11]

If we focus too narrowly on issues of rights, and voting, as constituting political standing, are we imposing a more recent understanding of politics than seventeenth-century authors would have employed? We need to ask more directly just what realities did early modern women take as a given about the standing of women from the governing classes; did they assume a greater role for women than we have seen or acknowledged based on our current-day lens and lack of a detailed or integrated picture of women's political actions on the local level, or even at court?[12]

Finally, it is important to give more attention to the gendered nature of male citizenship, and especially its tie to a system of male maturation in which men prepared to be independent adults, head families, own property, do politics, and be active economic actors. Much has been written on the growth of modern individualism, but less has been done about its gendered nature. Such investigations should lead to a revision of the accepted public/private divide. As men prepared for their independence in forms that ranged from apprenticeship to the Grand Tour, there evolved institutions both to support them and to provide ideological, professional, and emotional support. They included grammar schools and universities, guild structures, professional societies, local county societies, and even life at court. These institutions allowed men to take their private world with them into the public. Thus the nurturing, supportive function ascribed to the family which has enabled men to do productive work outside the home existed for them outside of

---

[11] The Charter of the Company of Clothworkers of London (London, 1648), 1–4; *The Ordinances of the Clothworkers' Company together with . . . fullers & Shearmen of the City of London,* transcribed from the Originals (London: Clothworkers Company, 1881), 13–22.

[12] The most comprehensive study of women's early political standing remains C. C. Stopes, *British Freewomen: Their Historical Privilege* (London: S. Sonnenschein, 1894).

the home as well. This support included payment in kind: high table and housing offered by universities; funeral arrangements, banquets, social honors by guilds; and recognition and camaraderie among a range of political, professional, and social groupings.

For example, when lawyers and judges were required to go on assize rounds, they could count upon the bar mess to provide them with all the comforts of home. In an account of the eighteenth-century bar, Daniel Duman (while failing to indicate its gender implications) notes that the bar mess was mostly involved with eating, entertainment, and drinking, but "in addition the messes acted as guardians of the professional conduct of the members and fostered a feeling of professional brother-hood and communal spirit among the barristers." Such ties between the socialization of adult males and their economic status blurred the distinction between personal and public life and created a system which taught and conferred a particular status and then reinscribed its nature and significance continually through the symbols and institutions that supported it. And there were so many institutions that continually aided men, inscribed their status, and supported their public and individual successes, that it is hard to argue that men embodied a distinctly public world, separate from the private world of the home. Surely this ability to integrate the support of the private into the world of the public was essential in distinguishing between men and women, even though individual women, usually single or widowed, did quite comparable things to their brothers.[13]

How can we, then, relate the reality of women's active political and economic roles to these institutions that validated and supported men's public standing? Women's public economic activities were broadly accepted, but when economic effort was used to buttress public standing or become the basis for citizenship, authorities resisted such a connec-tion for women. Yet guild membership and urban citizenship empowered men in their political efforts in England both during the Civil War and in the 1680s. While often performing the same functions as men, or similar ones, women seemed most excluded from the validation of public recognition and symbolic expressions of economic independence and the qualities of citizenship.[14]

Such confused realities are connected to women's failure to employ

[13] Daniel Duman, *The Judicial Bench in England, 1727–1875* (London: Royal Historical Society, 1982).

[14] See Natalie Davis's essay on the gendered nature of the crafts in sixteenth-century Lyon in her *Society and Culture in Early-Modern France* (Stanford, Calif.: Stanford University Press, 1975) and Merry E. Wiesner's discussion of women as skilled artisans in *Working Women in Renaissance Germany* (New Brunswick, N.J.: Rutgers University Press, 1986).

universalizing symbols, tying the public and political role of their group to discussions of what constituted political standing and national identity more broadly, as did men. For example, John Wildman, when defending in 1650 the free election of city officers by a cross-section of London freemen, unhampered by the dominant power of the mayor and council of aldermen, claimed that the privileges of London citizens, "in their elections of their chief officers," were tied to "those very foundations of Common Right which the parliament have declared to us." Such privileges were based on the principle "that the original of all just power under God proceeds from the People." In opposing aldermanic self-perpetuation, he does not include the interests of independent women, but does threaten the mayor and aldermen thus: "take some speedy course that the blood of the Fatherless and the Widow may not stick to these walls."[15]

In this rhetorical claim, as in so many others, women are characterized in a restricted way: as the whore of Babylon, as silly women open to the lure of competing religions, as the needy exemplified as widows, as the unlearned who are taken in by superficial arguments, or, on the positive side, as the naturally pious, or good, or caring, or peaceful. But it is difficult to imagine when women might say: "we as midwives, as rearers of children, as seamstresses, etc." represent that group tied to "those very foundations of Common Right which the parliament have declared to us." They may be included at some points, but it seems they can virtually never link their identity as a group of women, or women in a certain role, to the central qualities of the nation, or of humanity. To function effectively in politics, and as political thinkers, is it necessary for women to be able to incorporate such universal symbols of human nature and aspirations in their goals or vision of themselves? What is the power, then, of Wildman's call to the rights granted all the people, during an internal dispute with the mayor and aldermen of London? And how much has men's continual use of such imagery, and later scholars' failure to deconstruct such use on grounds of gender, contributed to the identification of men with the political realm? And, on the other side, how much has women's rare (and even more rarely successful) use of such universal symbols contributed to their absence (and supposed absence) from that realm?

To answer these questions, we need to complicate our understanding of gender values in early modern political thought. Not merely will we gain clues from listening to women who have been omitted from the

[15] *London's Liberties, Or a Learned Argument of Law & Reason, upon Saturday, December 14, 1650* (London: Printed by Ja. Cottrel for James Calver, 1651), preface, 4–5.

canon, but we will gain from seeing male theorists' views of the relationship of gender to the state in more complex terms. Both Hobbes and Locke held internally inconsistent, or at the least, evolving opinions about the nature of men and women, their relationship, their roles within the family, and their connection to the state. Hobbes shifts from his independent, powerful mother within the state of nature to a powerless/nonexistent wife under the state, and Locke shifts from equal honor due both parents in his *First Treatise* to a state formed by male property owners to protect their individual interests in the *Second*. Yet examining Hobbes's language in his discussion of the nature of dominion offers some clues as to conflicted views about sex difference and its relevance to the state.

He notes:

Among children the Males carry the preheminence, in the begining perhaps, because for the most part (although not alwayes) they are fitter for the administration of greater matters, but specially of wars; but afterwards, when it was grown a custome, because that custome was not contradicted; and therefore the will of the *Father*, unless some other custome or signe doe clearly repugne it, is to be interpreted in favour of them.[16]

One possible reading of this passage, and one that I lean toward, is that of a man hedging his bets and displaying discomfort with an easy acceptance of male superiority or male rule. Hobbes, for whom logic and reason were paramount, finally finds justification for any sexual difference in power and ability only on grounds of custom. Before he reaches the refuge of a customary explanation for male preeminence, he includes four phrases which question or limit the nature of male superiority: "in the beginning perhaps," "for the most part," "although not alwayes," and "specially of wars." And, even after reaching the point where male superiority "was grown a custome," he still does not seem home free and continues to write hesitantly in support of language concerning custom-bestowed ability and authority. The legitimacy of custom is acceptable only "because that custome was not contradicted," and remained subject to the following limitation: "unless some other custome or signe doe clearly repugne it." And his final positive phrase is hardly an outright acceptance of patriarchal authority "[it] is to be interpreted in favour of them."[17]

---

16 Hobbes, *De Cive*, 128.
17 For alternative interpretations of Hobbes's treatment of questions relating to gender and women's family and political status see Christine Di Stefano, "Masculinity as Ideology in Political Theory: Hobbesian Man Considered," *Women's Studies International Forum* 6 (1983): 633–44, Carole Pateman, "'God Hath Ordained to Man a Helper': Hobbes, Patriarchy and Conjugal Right," *British Journal of Political Science* 19

Analyzing such language more carefully can aid a reassessment of the operation of gender in early modern politics. We can clearly learn much both through reading the political writings of women and through analyzing the gender assumptions embedded within the intellectual and political structures of the period. This volume is intended as a step in that direction.

(1989): 445–64, and Gabriella Slomp, 'Hobbes and the Equality of Women," *Political Studies* 42 (1994): 441–52. Di Stefano emphasizes the masculinist quality of Hobbes's competitive vision of man; Pateman accepts his equal state for women in the state of nature while focusing on his empowering the husband within civil society in such a way that the wife loses political standing, and Slomp is more favorable to Hobbes's contention of sexual equality. However, she interprets the passage quoted here as restricting his acceptance of women's equality. In addition, Hobbes's emphasis on women's equal standing is often considered something found primarily in his early writings – it was presented most fully in the *De Cive* – but, he continued to insert gender into his writings quite late in life and in a manner that differed from his contemporaries. In defending himself against the charge of atheism, he includes the following passage in a work written in 1680, *Considerations upon the Reputation, Loyalty, Manners, & Religion, of Thomas Hobbes of Malmesbury*, where he states his opponents are offended by: "his Attributing to the Civil Soverign all Power Sacredotal. But this perhaps may seem hard, when the Sovereignty is in a Queen: But it is because you are not subtle enough to perceive, that though Man may be male and female, Authority is not" (*Considerations ... Written by himself*, By way of LETTER to a Learned Person. London: Printed for William Crooke, 1680, 40).

Part I

Women's political writings, 1400–1690

Introduction to Part I

Women's political expressions took disparate forms from the late medieval period through the seventeenth century, as these chapters make clear. In the early fifteenth century, Christine de Pizan, while today remembered primarily for her writings about women (especially *The City of Ladies*), wrote a range of political works for a largely aristocratic audience on statecraft, military strategy, the nature of war, and approaches to peace. Margaret Cavendish, duchess of Newcastle, while remembered for her scientific writings and works of fantasy (as well as her standing as an intellectual eccentric among the English aristocracy) in the middle of the seventeenth century also characterized the nature of the state in general and royal government in particular. Further, a range of genres (including prophecy, political tracts, and advice to political leaders) documents the growing political voice of women following 1640. Thus Aphra Behn's drama displayed not only her well-known Tory loyalties but her clear and purposeful use of past events (most often from the Exclusion Crisis of 1679–81) to illustrate the perfidy of the Whigs and the moral qualities of her Tory heroes.

Berenice Carroll's treatment of Christine de Pizan greatly expands our understanding of Christine's corpus. While there has been recent scholarship on her political thought, little of this scholarship has seeped into the broader academic assessment of her importance. She is much more apt to be taught in a medieval literature course, or a class focusing on women's writings, than incorporated into a discussion of medieval political thought, or a pedagogic or academic presentation on significant political acumen or influence. Other scholars have either dismissed her or minimized her innovative outlook, by claiming that she easily fell within the moral and Christian strictures of the best behavior for a monarch's pursuit. Yet Carroll notes that Henry VII commissioned a translation of her *Book of Feats of Arms and Chivalry* and that, according to William Caxton, the translator, the Tudor monarch urged that it should "come to the sight and knowledge of every gentle man and man of war." Obviously Henry understood the importance of force of arms in political maneuvering, and it was to Christine that he directed attention for guidance in the matter.

Carroll points especially to the differences between Christine and such theorists as John of Salisbury and Pierre DuBois, who promoted Christian and crusading models of governance and peace for Europe. She argues that Christine's attention to broader segments of the European population, particularly the middling and lower classes, removes her from the limited tradition of "the mirror for princes" genre so popular during the Middle Ages. Professor Carroll argues that Christine played a "pivotal role" in changes in political thought from the Christian universalism of the medieval period to the secular nation state of the modern period. This chapter thus offers us an insightful look into Christine's political writings and reassesses scholarly treatment of her that either overemphasizes her focus on women's place in society or reduces her work to repetition of moral and Christian homilies useful to a head of state.

Margaret Cavendish has also not been traditionally thought of as an individual or writer with serious political opinions. She has been characterized as a disorganized thinker, with little intellectual training, who allowed her wit to range over intellectual terrain with which she was little familiar. But here Anna Battigelli has placed her squarely within the Hobbesian camp, making it clear that Cavendish was familiar with his writings, and that the political order Hobbes envisioned underpinned the principles and questions Margaret Cavendish addressed in her work, especially in *The Blazing World* – a portrait of a fantastical island ruled by an empress. Yet, as Battigelli's title phrase "Hobbesian Dilemma" makes clear, Cavendish found it difficult to apply the ideas of sovereignty gleaned from Hobbes to the disputatious times in which she lived, or to the place of women in English society. According to Battigelli, she adopted Hobbesian views of a single, absolutist rule, but the power bestowed upon the monarch offered little space for women's political efforts and did not overcome threatening disputes. Battigelli claims this created tension between her political values and her career as an author: "Her prolific literary career is thus characterized by the tension between her compulsion to write herself into history and her anxiety regarding the power of the public word to spark controversies." Only in her mythical worlds could she adopt Hobbesian authority (although for ends which often sound closer to Plato's philosopher kings) for a female ruler who recognized the contributions from scholars and others of knowledge and wisdom. Only in creating fantasy could she partially overcome the political divisions and women's political exclusion embedded within both the English system and Hobbesian assumptions.

This chapter, then, offers us an analysis which focuses on the place of Cavendish within Hobbesian thought, but also clarifies the persistent fears Cavendish carried about political division.

Lois Schwoerer reaches beyond the witings and significance of a single author to assess the political nature of women's role in the popular press from 1640 to 1740. She contends that women's religious works, public advice, and political tracts constituted a form of political activity distinct from any offices or influence they might have held. As she states, "the currently popular idea of 'political culture' provides a useful conceptual framework for showing that political participation may take many forms." In addition to the production of popular treatises, other forms of political participation were "dispensing patronage, influencing decision makers and elections, petitioning, demonstrating, gift-giving, entertaining, haranguing, reporting seditious conduct," etc. Such a shift from traditional views as to what constituted "political" roles during the seventeenth century highlights the political activities of women in a setting that generally excluded them from politics.

Thus Schwoerer highlights the efforts of Elizabeth Poole, who advised the Army Council in 1648 against harming the king as the nation's patriarchal figure, and, from a similar perspective, the royalist Anne Halkett, who debated with an army officer in 1651 over the right to execute a monarch. Women took positions on a broad spectrum of political controversies, including Katherine Chidley's 1645 defense of religious toleration and Anne Docwra's arguments against the state's right to persecute Protestant dissenters. Other women pushed for particular social policies, with Mary (Rande) Cary supporting a postal tax to underwrite care for the poor, and the Quaker Hester (Esther) Biddle vividly portraying London poverty and urban indifference. Elinor James, an Anglican author of numerous tracts, not merely strongly supported the interests of the Church of England before parliament; she also offered suggestions to the House of Commons on reforming the press.

Following her discussion of individuals, Schwoerer raises the related issue as to whether one can decipher a feminine voice among these authors. While inclined to say no, she does point to their use of the imagery of childbirth and their tendency to self-deprecation. In addition, as one moves closer to 1700 and beyond, specific claims of men's oppression of women and calls for women to claim the rights of "freeborn Englishwomen" emerge. Most significant, Professor Schwoerer contends, is the medium of the popular press offering the means through which private women could use a public forum to offer varied and powerful political views.

Melinda Zook looks to Aphra Behn not primarily as the most prolific dramatist among late seventeenth-century women authors, but in terms of the specifically historical and political nature of her plays. In assessing current scholarship on Behn, Zook contends that "beyond the blanket assertion that Behn was a Tory propagandist, little analysis of her political vision exists." In addressing this lacuna, Zook mines Behn's plays produced during the 1680s for specific political arguments and historical references. She demonstrates that Behn exhibited a particular brand of Toryism that did not build upon the thought of Sir Robert Filmer, as did that of many of her Tory colleagues. Her chapter, in Zook's words, contends that "Behn's royalism ... revolved around an idealized aristocratic ethos that liberated the individual from the tyrannies of dull customs and traditions ... which shackled the noble mind and heart." This led Behn to defend Cavalier culture and satirize the Whigs and Dissenters, whose restrictive and unsophisticated values undercut the "best of men" as well as the "best" society. Such values were easily exemplified through the cavalier hero who recurs in her plays; his socially and sexually liberating ways were being increasingly threatened by the Whig hegemony of the 1680s. As the century progresses, and Behn's political vision becomes darker, the carefree, hopeful heroes of the earlier 1680s are replaced by more tragic heroes.

Unlike some scholars, Zook does not see women as central to Behn's plays or political perspective. Her dramas reflected the circumscribed roles for women in late Stuart society which left them little fitted for the heroic characteristics of their aristocratic fellows. The court offered both support and subjects for Behn's drama. In defending the court, she, along with so many of like view, worried that the Whigs were moving to repeat the mistakes of the 1640s. For the 1680s, threats came from the alliance of Whigs, Dissenters, and the "middling sorts" of London who Behn felt would lower both political and cultural standards, establishing a society in which no free-spirited and heroic man could survive.

In outlining her argument, for example in her discusion of Behn's *The Roundheads*, Professor Zook links the playwright's characterization (here of "a saucy dog of a Joyner") to actual historical figures such as, in this instance, "Stephen College, the so-called 'Protestant Joiner'" who took part in the politics of the Exclusion Crisis. This analysis of the historical and political grounding of Behn's plays offers a fresh interpretation of drama broadly familiar to students of late Stuart culture and clarifies the basis for Behn's politics, beyond the broad, familiar characterization of her as a Tory propagandist. Her political values sought to preserve the world of the "best people," ensuring that men of honor would not be overwhelmed by the *nouveaux riches* and others without good breeding associated with the Whig ascendancy. Sexual freedom and an end to restrictive social customs were paramount; she especially deplored the religion of narrowmindedness.

But Behn's attack on the duke of Monmouth led to her arrest and exclusion from the stage for four years; an attack against the king's illegitimate, but favorite son did not save even this uncompromising supporter of the royalist cause. Following Monmouth's rebellion, she displayed a more jaundiced view of royal rule and a sympathy toward this executed royal son. Such a transition reflected Behn's growing disillusion with the direction of James II's rule and demonstrates, again, the ties between historical reality and the political ideologies she portrayed in her plays. As Zook has clarified, Behn was not simply a one-dimensional propagandist for royal and Tory causes.

These chapters confirm the varied genres utilized by women to express their political thought and the impact they had on political leaders and events of their age. While there is no single generalization one can make about the nature of women's political views or writings, these chapters document women's strong political interests and under-cut any stereotype of their remaining isolated in private homes, ill informed, uninterested, and uninvolved in the political discourse sur-rounding them.

1   Christine de Pizan and the origins of peace theory

Berenice A. Carroll

> Nature willed that from my studies and experience there be born new works, and commanded: "Take up your tools and hammer out on the anvil the material I shall give you, as lasting as iron and impervious to fire and everything else, and forge objects of delight. When your children were in your womb, you experienced great pain bringing them into the world. Now it is my wish that new works be born from your memory in joy and delight, which will carry your name forever all over the world, and to future generations of princes."
>
> Christine de Pizan, *Lavision-Christine*, 1406 [1]

> Dans le monde immatériel de la pensée, rien ne meurt; la germination est continuelle.   Ernest Nys, *Etudes de droit internationale*, 1896[2]

.

"To discover by oneself some new and unknown thing"

Like much in Christine de Pizan's writings, the passage above is rich in complex images and meanings, forging links between nature and learning, work and childbirth, body and mind, the pain of labor and the joy and delight of creation. Significantly, Christine[3] attributed her intellectual creations to "Nature" rather than "God" and portrayed them as "objects of delight" rather than moral strictures. But the works Christine left us included major contributions in both moral philosophy and political theory.

Christine de Pizan is called "France's first woman of letters," "the

---

[1] Translation by Christine M. Reno, in *The Writings of Christine de Pizan*, ed. Charity C. Willard (New York: Persea Books, 1994), 17. Cf. *Lavision-Christine* (1405–1406), ed. Sister Mary Louis Towner, Ph.D. dissertation (Washington, D.C.: Catholic University of America, 1932), 163–64.

[2] Ernest Nys, *Etudes de droit internationale et de droit politique* (Brussels and Paris, 1896), 42.

[3] Consistent with medieval nomenclature, Christine may be cited as "Christine de Pizan" or by her first name alone (as in "Marsilius," for Marsilius of Padua). The spelling "de Pisan" appears here where used in cited works, but "de Pizan" is preferred today.

first feminist," and similar titles of precedence.[4] But Christine's life and accomplishments were set in a long history of learned and politically influential women.[5] Though excluded and overwhelmingly outnumbered by men in the dominant institutions of learning and politics, women were never entirely absent from the creation of theory, knowledge, and influential works in literary and political realms. Their theoretical contributions, however, have been made largely invisible by neglect and depreciation. The contemporary revival of an intense interest in Christine's works today is a marked exception, but attention has been focused mainly on her feminist or woman-centered ideas, and only recently extended to her other works on "the body politic."[6] Unfortunately, critical treatment of the latter tends to reproduce the classic ritual dismissals of women's political theory as "unoriginal" and "moralistic."[7]

This chapter suggests a different perspective on Christine's work. Christine was a pivotal figure not only in the arena of gender struggle

[4] Charity Cannon Willard, *Christine de Pizan: Her Life and Works, A Biography* (New York: Persea Books, 1984), 15; Régine Pernoud's *Christine de Pisan* (Paris: Calmann-Lévy, 1982), book jacket: "she is without doubt 'the first feminist' before the term"; but see Sheila Delaney, "History, Politics, and Christine Studies: A Polemical Reply," in *Politics, Gender, and Genre: The Political Thought of Christine de Pizan*, ed. Margaret Brabant (Boulder, Colo.: Westview Press, 1992), 202–203; and Sheila Delaney, "'Mothers to Think Back Through': Who Are They? The Ambiguous Example of Christine de Pizan," in her *Medieval Literary Politics: Shapes of Ideology* (Manchester: Manchester University Press, 1990), 89, 173, nn. 1, 2.

[5] For earlier "women of letters" in medieval Europe, see, in particular: Peter Dronke, *Women Writers of the Middle Ages* (Cambridge: Cambridge University Press, 1984); Patricia H. Labalme, ed., *Beyond Their Sex: Learned Women of the European Past* (New York: New York University Press, 1984); Elizabeth Alvilda Petroff, ed., *Medieval Women's Visionary Literature* (New York: Oxford University Press, 1986); Katharina M. Wilson, *Medieval Women Writers* (Athens: University of Georgia Press, 1984); and Mary Ellen Waithe, ed., *A History of Women Philosophers*, vol. II: *Medieval, Renaissance and Enlightenment Women Philosophers, A.D. 500–600* (Dordrecht: Kluwer Academic Publishers, 1989).

[6] For an overview of the literature on Christine, see Angus J. Kennedy, *Christine de Pizan: A Bibliographical Guide* (London: Grant and Cutler, 1984; 2nd ed., 1994); and Edith Yenal, *Christine de Pizan: A Bibliography of Writings by Her and about Her* (Metuchen, N.J.: Scarecrow Press, 1989). On Christine's politics, see especially: Brabant, *Politics, Gender, and Genre*; Maureen Quilligan, *The Allegory of Female Authority: Christine de Pizan's Cité des Dames* (Ithaca: Cornell University Press, 1991); and Karen Green, "Christine de Pisan and Thomas Hobbes," *Philosophical Quarterly* 44, 177 (October 1994): 456–75. See also Jacques Krynen, *Idéal du Prince et pouvoir royal en France à la fin du moyen âge (1380–1440)* (Paris: A. and J. Picard, 1981).

[7] See Berenice A. Carroll, "The Politics of 'Originality': Women and the Class System of the Intellect," *Journal of Women's History* 2, 2 (Fall 1990): 136–63. The French term "moraliste" suggests "moral philosopher" and is not a term of disdain (Eric Hicks, personal communication). But in the critical literature on women writers, the term "moralistic" is widely used to obscure or dismiss the political and theoretical significance of a writer or her works.

but also in changes in the theory of the state, secularization of political thought, codification of military practice, development of international law, and the origins of peace theory. Her work stood at a turning point in these arenas and contributed to significant changes in political thought.

This may seem too grandiose a role to attribute to this "little" woman, as she sometimes described herself, this "outsider" sitting alone in her study, churning out books filled with fantasy, borrowings, didactic lessons and exhortations, tailored primarily for aristocratic patrons. Though her writings were known and valued in upper-class circles in her time, and translated and printed in many editions in later centuries, she was often ridiculed or dismissed with contempt. Yet the very attacks upon her and the suppression of her authorship or attribution of her work to male authors (particularly her *Book of Feats of Arms and Chivalry*) also testify to her importance.[8]

Christine was born in Venice in 1364.[9] Her father, Thomas de Pizan, became court physician and astrologer to King Charles V of France, and in Christine's youth she led a comfortable and happy life at court. Her father encouraged her in learning and writing, as did her husband, Etienne du Castel, who was a secretary to Charles V. She bore three children, of whom two, Marie and Jean, survived. After the deaths of her father and husband, she lacked means to support herself and her family. She began writing poetry after her husband's death, and soon found it a source of livelihood. Her "creations" won the patronage of members of the royal family and nobility of France, England, and Italy, who provided her with handsome gifts in return for her books. Some of her works were spontaneous offerings, while others, such as her biography of Charles V, were specifically commissioned. Her success enabled her to pursue the studies that she loved and to produce over twenty-five volumes of poetry and prose. But Christine's tumultuous era drove her to withdraw from secular life into the cloister. She spent the last decade of her life in a convent, probably at Poissy, where her daughter was a nun. She died about the year 1430.

---

[8] See Willard, *Life and Works*, 186–87; and A. T. P. Byles, ed., "Introduction," 1932 edition of the middle English translation of Christine de Pisan, *The Book of Fayttes of Armes and of Chyvalrye* (New York: Kraus Reprint, 1971), xiv–xv, xxvi–xxvii. This work is cited below as *Fayttes*. There is no modern French or English translation, but an edition of the middle French appears in Christine Moneer Laennec, "Christine 'Antygrafe': Authorship and Self in the Prose Works of Christine de Pizan," Ph.D. dissertation, Yale University, 1988; Ann Arbor: University Microfilms, 1989.

[9] For biographical information, see especially: Willard, *Life and Works*; Willard, *Writings*; and Enid McLeod, *The Order of the Rose: The Life and Ideas of Christine de Pizan* (Totowa, N.J.: Rowman and Littlefield, 1976).

Christine was remarkably concerned with the question of "originality" in her work. In *The City of Ladies*, she asks Lady Reason to tell of women who "have themselves discovered any new arts and sciences which . . . had hitherto not been discovered or known. For it is not such a great feat of mastery to study and learn some field of knowledge already discovered by someone else as it is to discover by oneself some new and unknown thing."[10] This explicit concern was unusual in Christine's time, when it was the practice to borrow freely from others without acknowledgment.[11] In several of her works, Christine took pains to argue explicitly that, like an architect, she used the bricks, stone, mortar, and wood provided by others to construct a new edifice, a new creation.[12]

Christine, though conscious of her own daring in "creating new knowledge," took courage from the learning and literary achievements of women who went before her. She knew more of ancient and legendary examples than recent foremothers, but she wrote of some contemporaries in her *Book of the City of Ladies* and other works. She claimed to be following the inspiration of their wisdom, virtue, and talent, not to be blazing a wholly new path.

Nevertheless, there was much that was truly unique in Christine's life and works. After she was widowed, she earned her living as a writer at a time when (at least in northern Europe) there were no professional writers of either sex – writers were clerics, functionaries, or members of the aristocracy or the nascent bourgeoisie with other sources of income. The corpus of her writings was large, and among them were many that were brilliant, innovative, compelling, respected, and admired. She was learned far beyond most men as well as women, even among the upper classes of secular society in Europe in her time. A woman of no defined station other than widow, not a member of the nobility, she had unusual access to the French royal court, and to other members of the aristocracies of France, England, Italy, Belgium, and other countries. She posed extraordinary and sustained challenges to the misogyny of leading intellectuals of her time while retaining the support of powerful figures such as Jean Gerson, chancellor of the

---

[10] Christine de Pizan, *The Book of the City of Ladies* [1405], trans. Earl Jeffrey Richards (New York: Persea Books, 1982) 1.33.1, 70–71.
[11] See Ernest Nys, *Christine de Pisan et ses principales œuvres* (The Hague: Martinus Nijhoff, 1914), 20; G. W. Coopland, ed., Introduction, in Honoré Bonet, *The Tree of Battles* (Cambridge, Mass.: Harvard University Press, 1949), 24–25; Charity Cannon Willard, ed., Introduction, in *The "Livre de la paix" of Christine de Pisan* (The Hague: Mouton, 1958), 53–54 (cited below as "*Paix*").
[12] *Fayttes*, III.1, 189–90; *Paix*, 54.

University of Paris. Her works survive and continue to provoke debate six hundred years later.

"To the sight and knowledge of every gentleman and man of war"

In some respects, Christine's influence may have been most felt in England. A number of her important works were known there, perhaps as early as 1397, when she met the earl of Salisbury and he took her son, Jean de Castel, into his service.[13] Salisbury possessed a number of manuscripts of Christine's works, which were acquired by Henry IV – along with Christine's son – after Salisbury's execution in 1400. Henry invited Christine to come to his court, but she did not wish to go to England ("mal païs d'Angleterre, ou muable y sont la gent") and instead bought the return of her son with additional manuscripts.[14] As early as 1402, Thomas Hoccleve published an unacknowledged, modified translation of her *Letter of the God of Love*.[15] Anthony Woodville's translation of Christine's early moral poetry, published in 1478 as *The Morale Proverbes of Christyne*, was reprinted in 1480 and again in 1528. In 1521, Henry Pepwell published Bryan Anslay's translation into English of the *Livre de la cité des dames*, and by 1545, at least five of Christine's works had been translated and published in England.[16] Among these were several pertinent to the theory of war and peace.

In 1445, the earl of Shrewsbury presented to Margaret of Anjou and Henry VI, as a wedding gift, a manuscript collection including Christine's *Book of Feats of Arms and Chivalry*. It is possible to speculate on the work's unintended and ironic effects when Margaret ruled and directed armies on behalf of her mad husband and infant son.[17] In 1489,

---

[13] See J. C. Laidlaw, "Christine de Pizan, the Earl of Salisbury and Henry IV," *French Studies* 36, 2 (April 1982): 129–43; and Earl Jeffrey Richards, "The Medieval 'femme auteur' as a Provocation to Literary History: Eighteenth-Century Readers of Christine de Pizan," in *The Reception of Christine de Pizan from the Fifteenth through the Nineteenth Centuries: Visitors to the City*, ed. Glenda K. McLeod (Lewiston, N.Y.: Edwin Mellen, 1991), 101–26, esp. 118–21.

[14] Laidlaw, "Christine," 130, 135.

[15] See P. G. C. Campbell, "Christine de Pisan en Angleterre," *Revue de Littérature Comparée* 5 (1925): 659–70, esp. 661–63.

[16] See Enid McLeod, *Order of the Rose*, Appendix: "Christine and England," 162–67. The first English printing of *The Boke of the Cyte of Ladyes* featured only the name of the translator, Brian Anslay, but Christine's self-introduction and assertions of authorship were retained in the text. See John Rooks, "*The Boke of the Cyte of Ladyes* and its Sixteenth-Century Readership," in Glenda McLeod, *Reception*, 83–100, esp. 83–85; also Willard, *Life and Works*, 214–15.

[17] See Frances Teague, "Christine de Pizan's *Book of War*," in Glenda McLeod, *Reception*, 25–41, esp. 25–26, 37–38.

Henry VII commissioned an English translation of this work by William Caxton, published in 1490.[18] According to Caxton, Henry explicitly urged that it should "come to the sight and knowledge of every gentleman and man of war" and that "every gentleman born to arms and all men of war – captains, soldiers, victualers and all others should have knowledge how they ought to behave themselves in the feats of war and of battles."[19] An English translation of Christine's *Livre du corps de policie* was published by John Skot in 1521.[20] The *Livre de la paix*, it is true, was never translated or published in England.[21] But many of the ideas Christine put forward in that book, her last major work, had already been developed in the *Feats of Arms and Chivalry* and the *Book of the Body of Policy*, both in circulation in England from the early 1500s.

It is remarkable that Christine was the first female author in the series of Cambridge Texts in the History of Political Thought, where the first modern English translation of *The Book of the Body Politic* appeared in 1994.[22] Given this was the only work by a woman among the fifty-seven texts in the series until then, it might be seen as an ironic confirmation of Christine's claim, in the *Mutacion de Fortune* (1404), that she had been transformed by Fortune – or misfortune – from a woman into a man. Christine, however, said she preferred "To return as a woman and be heard."[23]

While this wish seems to have been granted today, especially in feminist scholarship, there are still many gaps. Among these, perhaps the most egregious is neglect of Christine's contributions to the study of war and peace.

Christine is best known today for her extraordinary *Book of the City of Ladies* (1405) and its sequel, the *Book of Three Virtues* or the *Treasury of the City of Ladies* (1405); and for her role in challenging Jean de Meun's *Romance of the Rose* (1401–1403). But Christine was widely known in her own time as well as later centuries for other writings of political significance. Her early works reflect the development of her ideas on government, war and peace, among these her long poetic allegories, *The*

---

[18] See Byles, "Introduction," *Fayttes*, xxix–xxx; and Caxton's epilogue, ibid., 291; also Teague, "Christine," 36–37.

[19] *Fayttes*, 291; Teague, "Christine," 36; Willard, *Life and Works*, 216.

[20] Diane Bornstein, ed., *The Middle English Translation of Christine de Pisan's LIVRE DU CORPS DE POLICIE* (Heidelberg: Carl Winter, 1977), 19–22.

[21] *Paix*, 7, 46–48. See also Kennedy, *[A] Bibliographical Guide*, 1984, 59, 99–100.

[22] Christine de Pizan, *The Book of the Body Politic*, trans. and ed. Kate Langdon Forhan (Cambridge: Cambridge University Press, 1994). In citing *Le livre du corps de policie* below, I use "*Body Politic*" for the Forhan translation and the concept this title emphasizes, and "Body of Policy" for other citations.

[23] Excerpts from *The Mutation of Fortune*, trans. Nadia Margolis, in Willard, *Writings*, 122, 126–27.

Letter of Othea to Hector (1401), *The Book of the Long Road of Learning* (1403), and *The Book of the Mutation of Fortune* (1404). Biography and autobiography were other vehicles for political commentary, particularly her biography of Charles V (1404) and the *Lavision-Christine* (1405–1406). Christine also wrote directly and at length on topics conventionally recognized in the canon of political theory: war and just war, arms and chivalry, the state and its classes, the nature and conditions of peace, the responsibilities of political authority, the horrors of civil war, and the causes and dangers of popular rebellion. Her works on these topics include: the *Letter to Queen Isabeau* (1405), *The Book of the Body of Policy* (1407), *The Book of Feats of Arms and Chivalry* (1409), the *Lamentation on the Woes of France* (1410), and *The Book of Peace* (1414).

The quest for "why there is no peace"

Christine first addressed her concern with the problems of war and peace in her early poetic allegory, *The Book of the Long Road of Learning*, where she lamented that "all the world is burdened with wars" and that "for lust of tribute and conquest of foreign lands, men destroy each other in mortal war." She tells herself that "God in heaven suffers such discord on earth for the benefit of mortal man, for when he sees such a world he must well desire Paradise," but she is not satisfied, and searches for an explanation: "As I thought of the ambitions, wars, afflictions, betrayals and ambushes of the world, and of the great evils committed that cause such great harm, I was perplexed by what could be the reason why there is no peace." Introducing a device she drew upon in later writings, Christine describes how she fell asleep amidst these troubling thoughts, and there appeared to her the Cumaean sibyl, Sebilla, who offered to guide her to "a more perfect world, where you will be able to learn much more than you can comprehend in this one," and promised to show her "the source of all the evils of the world."[24]

Christine did not, however, find a simple answer to her question in this allegory. She returned repeatedly in later years to studies that might cast light on the problem and point the way to a solution. This quest for a path to peace in Christine's work was identified half a century ago but has been little pursued by scholars since then.[25] It is true that the *Feats*

---

[24] Christine de Pisan, *Le Livre de chemin de long estude*, ed. Robert Pueschel (Berlin, 1887; Geneva: Slatkine Reprints, 1974), 15, 14, 19, 28 (lines 340–41, 352–54, 323–26, 329–30, 439–43, 650–51, 657–58); my translation.

[25] See Madeleine Fernande Rosier (Sister Marie, OSU), "Christine de Pisan as a Moralist," unpublished Ph.D. dissertation (University of Toronto, 1945), cited by Willard, *Paix*, 52–53. Another half-century earlier, Ernest Nys gave substantial attention to Christine's ideas on the laws of war in: *Les origines du droit internationale*

of Arms and Chivalry and the *Book of Peace* have never been translated
into modern English or French, making them relatively inaccessible to
those not specialists in medieval literature. Moreover, the form of her
main works pertinent to issues of war and peace, as advice to rulers and
notables rather than as abstract treatises, conceals their theoretical
contributions amidst practical lessons and examples. Thus these works
are seen as mere additions to a traditional moralistic "mirror of princes"
literature. But on closer examination, it becomes evident that Christine's
advice extends beyond the prince to other classes of society, and her
views embody many aspects of "modern" political perspectives.

In Christine's time, there was no systematic secular study of the
causes and conditions of war and peace nor any substantial body of
"anti-war" literature. The pacifism of early Christianity had been
abandoned by the Roman Church since the time of St. Augustine, and
by the fourteenth century was maintained only within some monastic
orders and sects such as the Cathars and Waldensians. Efforts of the
church to reduce the violence of warfare through the "Truce of God"
and other devices were undermined by its own endorsement of "just
war" and reluctance to declare any war "unjust."[26] Works by Dante
Alighieri, Pierre Dubois, Marsilius of Padua, and others who are often
cited in histories of peace theory, gave scant attention to either peace
itself or the control of warfare and argued rather for particular grand
schemes of universal governance in place of the Roman Church: Dante,
in *De Monarchia*, for restoration of the Roman Empire; Dubois, in *The*

(Brussels and Paris, 1894); "Honoré Bonet et Christine de Pisan," in *Etudes de droit
internationale*, 145–62 (n. 2 above); and *Christine ... et ses principales œuvres* (n. 11
above). Unfortunately, Nys's treatment was marred by the classic dismissals:

> Christine de Pisan was not at all a woman of genius; neither was she at all the
> author of original political theories; she made no innovations; but, laboriously
> [!], she reproduced in her books what she had learned in her readings and, in
> some emotional pages, she made herself the interpreter of those who wished, in
> her time and place, to cure the incalculable ills from which France suffered.
> (*Christine ... et ses principales œuvres*, 42, my translation; cf. Carroll, "Origin-
> ality," esp. 141)

Little wonder that contemporary scholars like James Turner Johnson have given
Christine only passing attention in the history of peace theory. See Johnson's *The Quest
for Peace: Three Moral Traditions in Western Cultural History* (Princeton: Princeton
University Press, 1987), 110–11, 130, 141. For revived interest in Christine's thought on
war and peace, see: Charity Cannon Willard, 'Christine de Pizan's Treatise on the Art
of Medieval Warfare," in *Essays in Honor of Louis Francis Solano*, eds. R. Cormier and
U. T. Holmes (Chapel Hill: University of North Carolina Press, 1970), 179–91;
Laennec, "Christine 'Antygrafe'," esp. 135–48; Margarete Zimmermann, "Vox Femina,
Vox Politica: The *Lamentacion sur les maux de la France*," in Brabant, *Politics, Gender,
and Genre*, 113–28; and other essays in the same volume.

[26] See Johnson, *Quest for Peace*, chaps. 1–3; Donald Wells, *The War Myth* (New York:
Pegasus, 1967), 32–24 and *passim*.

Recovery of the Holy Land, for subjugation of Europe to the domination of the French monarchy and mobilization of a united military force for a crusade against the Turks; Marsilius, in *Defensor Pacis*, for conciliar governance within the church and an abstract temporal "universal legislator" to supplant the dominance of the church.[27] On the other hand, the early rules of war developed by John of Legnano and Honoré Bonet were embedded in works expounding at length on the pervasiveness, necessity, and spiritual desirability of warfare on earth.[28]

In this setting, Christine broke new ground in the modern study of war and peace. In her *Letter to Queen Isabeau*, in the *Lamentation on the Woes of France*, and in *The Book of Peace* she offered impassioned condemnation of the evils committed in warfare, foreshadowing the rhetoric of Erasmus and later pacifists. In the *Feats of Arms and Chivalry*, she presented a study of the causes, methods, weapons, and laws of war shorn of the theological framing that dominated her sources. In *The Book of Peace* she offered the first attempt at a systematic analysis of the requirements of peace and the practical policies necessary to achieve it in the monarchical nation state. Throughout all, she defended her right as a woman to enter into these masculine realms of thought and policy.

Most of these ideas were brought together in *The Book of Peace*, her last major prose work. In Part I, Christine examines the sources of peace. Her presentation is couched in what appears to be a conventional discussion of "seven roots of virtue," but these, she makes clear, are a set of requirements based on reason, and the virtues in question have a very public character. Under the requirements of peace, in which "good order" figures (as it did, for example, in Marsilius's *Defensor Pacis*), Christine places enlarged emphasis upon the importance and requirements of justice, with explicit reference to the *rights* of different classes, including the bourgeoisie and "the people." This was not the modern concept of individual human rights, but it went well beyond a simplistic notion that a "virtuous prince" is all that is necessary for peace.

"The body of policy": class and state

Christine had already shown in *The Book of the Body of Policy* that she

---

[27] Dante Alighieri, *On World-Government (De Monarchia)* [1310?] (Indianapolis: Bobb-Merrill, 2nd edn, 1957); Pierre Dubois, *The Recovery of the Holy Land* [1302], trans. Walther I. Brandt (New York: Columbia University Press, 1956); Marsilius of Padua, *The Defender of Peace (Defensor Pacis)* [1324], trans. Alan Gewirth (New York: Harper and Row, 1967).

[28] Giovanni da Legnano, *Tractatus De Bello, De Represaliis et De Duello* [1360], ed. Thomas E. Holland (Washington, D.C.: Carnegie Institution, 1917), with an English translation by James L. Brierly; Bonet, *Tree of Battles*.

had a broader and more "modern" conception of the body politic than did her sources. She drew on an organic metaphor that was current in her day to present a systematic analysis of the emerging modern state.[29] What distinguishes Christine's "modern" conception of the body politic is, first, an expanded consciousness of emerging classes in society and attention to their needs and roles; and second, a reduction of the role and authority of the church and of theological explanation.

Thus Christine devoted the third part of *The Book of the Body of Policy* to "the universal people," including not only the bourgeoisie but also the laboring classes. As Kate Forhan notes, this is in marked distinction from John of Salisbury, who did not mention the middle classes and gave no sustained attention to the working classes.[30] Marsilius of Padua gave no more than passing mention to the agricultural and artisan classes, and none to the merchant class.[31] Egidio Colonna, who was acknowledged by Christine as the source of some sections of her book, addressed "the common people" in only one brief chapter of his *De Regimine Principum*.[32] It is noteworthy in this connection that Christine also devoted the third book of the *Treasury of the City of Ladies* to women of the middle and working classes.[33] And in the *Book of Peace* she addressed both how the prince should act to keep "the common people" at peace and the role of the middle classes.[34]

Christine opposed popular government. She was aware of examples of republican government that existed in Italy at the time, but explicitly rejected them.[35] Yet in both the *Book of the Body of Policy* and the *Book of*

---

[29] Kate Forhan asserts that the book "takes its name and organizing theme from John of Salisbury's twelfth-century work, *Policraticus*" (*Body Politic*, xx). But John did not use the metaphor for the title or the main organizing theme of his work. See John of Salisbury, *Policraticus* [1159] (New York: Cambridge University Press, 1990). As Charity Willard and Diane Bornstein have shown, there were other more likely sources than John for Christine's choice of the metaphor, and Christine had used it earlier in *The Long Road of Learning* [1403] (Willard, *Life and Works*, 177–78; Bornstein, *Middle English*, 15). Forhan herself shows that Christine's *Book of the Body Politic* follows a different scheme of organization and differs from John of Salisbury's views on the state in many significant ways ("Polycracy, Obligation, and Revolt: The Body Politic in John of Salisbury and Christine de Pizan," in Brabant, *Politics, Gender, and Genre*, 33–51).

[30] Forhan, "Polycracy," 38.

[31] Marsilius, *Defensor Pacis*, 15, 17.

[32] Egidio Colonna, *Li Livres du gouvernement des rois* (French translation of *De Regimine Principum*), ed. Samuel Paul Molenaer (New York: AMS Press, 1966).

[33] Christine de Pizan, *A Medieval Woman's Mirror of Honor: The Treasury of the City of Ladies*, trans. Charity Cannon Willard, ed. Madeleine Pelner Cosman (New York: Persea Books, 1989). Delaney, however, faults Christine for ignoring the independent bourgeois and laboring women of her time ("Mothers," 95, 96–97).

[34] See *Paix*, Part III; also Willard's summary, *Paix*, 37–39.

[35] *Body Politic*, III.2–3, 6; *Paix*, III.10–11. Concerning Christine's "conservatism" and attitudes toward the laboring classes, see Sheila Delaney, "Mothers" and "History, Politics, and Christine Studies"; Quilligan, *Allegory*, 253, 265; Christine M. Reno,

Peace she argued for assembling counselors from many classes to advise the king: "Given that what belongs to government of the empire, realm, or country comprises diverse or difficult things, it is appropriate that divers estates be represented among the counselors of the prince, and not taken all from one same estate."[36] Christine elaborated upon the duties and responsibilities of the upper classes and recognized a role of leadership and governance for the bourgeoisie going beyond her sources. While – like Hobbes – she was vitriolic against popular rebellion and civil war, she insisted a prince must treat the people with justice if rebellion was to be avoided. As a last resort, she recognized the right of subjects to overthrow a tyrant who ravages the land, citing the example of Judith and Holofernes.[37]

The essentially secular character of Christine's political works is somewhat obscured by many passages in which she cites scriptural authority and examples, and offers expressions of devotion and thanks to God. She urged the prince to "forbid on pain of severe punishment anyone swearing on or denying his Creator."[38] She exhorted princes to love God and seek divine guidance. Nonetheless, Christine gave little scope to the authority or guidance of the church as such in matters of secular governance.

As Kate Forhan notes, Christine included the clergy among "the universal people" in her *Book of the Body Politic*. In sharp contrast with John of Salisbury and others of her own time, Christine did not assign the clergy as a class a place in society superior to temporal lords and the knightly classes. Christine excised all explicit or metaphoric mention of the superiority of the pope and the church over secular rulers. John of Salisbury had placed the church (metaphorically the soul) above the secular ruler (metaphorically the head) in authority and primacy of place. But Christine gave the prince undisputed priority of place as head of the body and "Vicar of God on earth," implicitly contesting exclusive papal claims to this title.[39] Christine's use of the phrase has been overlooked, taken perhaps as an expression of her "moralistic" approach or as nothing new, a claim made by emperors and kings since at least Charlemagne. But considering the tensions between church and state in her time, this terminology aligns Christine sharply with the secular monarchy.

"Christine de Pizan: 'At Best a Contradictory Figure?'," in Brabant, *Politics, Gender, and Genre*, 171–92; and the introduction to the modern French translation of *La Cité des dames*, by Thérèse Moreau and Eric Hicks (Paris: Stock, 1986).

[36] *Paix*, I.10, 75.

[37] *Paix*, III.4–5, 119–23.

[38] *Body Politic*, 14–15.

[39] Ibid., 12. On the competing claims, see Walter Ullmann, *A History of Political Thought: The Middle Ages* (Harmondsworth: Penguin, 1965).

Christine had friends and allies in the church – foremost among them Jean Gerson – as well as detractors such as Jean de Montreuil, and was clearly not disposed to launch a frontal attack on its power and rights. But she had much more to say about the vices, corruption, and depredations of the clergy than about any positive services provided by the church to society. Moreover, she assigned to the prince the duty of reproving clergy for their greed and other "horrible faults": "because despite the fact that correction of people in the church is not his to undertake, nonetheless what prelate, priest or cleric is so great that he will dare withstand or complain about the prince who reproves him for his manifest vice or sin?"[40] Thus her exhortation that the good prince, "as vicar of God on earth, will care with all his heart for the welfare of the church, so that his Creator can be served as his reason demands" was hardly an expression of devotion to the church as much as a ground for the secular monarch to discipline the clergy.

"Ambitions, wars, afflictions, betrayals and ambushes"

Christine began the *Feats of Arms and Chivalry* with seven chapters in which, calling upon Minerva to defend her temerity in writing on such subjects, she discussed general questions concerning the lawfulness, the causes, and the responsibility for wars. The rest of Book I and the whole of Book II are devoted to details of military weapons, logistics, and strategy, drawn from ancient authorities and medieval military informants. Books III and IV deal with the laws of war, presented as a dialogue of questions and answers with "the Master," Honoré Bonet, author of *The Tree of Battles*.[41]

With respect to the causes and legitimacy of war, Christine formulated a position distinctly different from that of Bonet and other earlier writers on these questions. Bonet, like John of Legnano, viewed war as natural, inevitable, and commanded of God. As opposed to John Wycliffe and certain nonviolent sects such as the Waldensians, who rejected the legitimacy of war, Bonet believed that war was not only for

---

[40] *Body Politic*, 13–14; see also 10, 12–15, 19.
[41] On Bonet, see: Coopland, "Introduction," in Bonet, *Tree of Battles*; Byles, "Introduction," *Fayttes*; Nys, works cited above; Willard (who uses the current form "Bouvet"), *Life and Works*, 184–86, and *Writings*, 254–55, 260. In *Fayttes*, Christine explicitly defends her use of selected "fruits" and "branches" of Bonet's "tree," having him say that such borrowings give greater authority to his work and are common usage: "Did not master Jean de Meun help himself in his Book of the Rose from the sayings of Lorris, and similarly of others? It is then no rebuke, but it is laudable and praiseworthy when they be well and properly applied and set in order" (my translation from the middle English, *Fayttes*, III.1, 190–91). Christine makes explicit that she selects only those branches of Bonet's tree that are suitable to her creation.

the punishment of wrongdoing, but also for the expiation of sin and transgressions; and battle was the law of nature. Bonet even held that peace is not possible and that war is "good and virtuous."[42]

Christine presented a much more secular and less pessimistic view. Like Bonet, she accepted the legitimacy of some war, but had nothing to say about sin, transgression, and punishment from God. Rather, like later authorities on the laws of war, she was concerned about the legitimacy of war to render justice, and the limits of authority to make war and command others to engage in it.

In Christine's time, a critical aspect of the evolution of centralized monarchical power and claims of sovereignty was the assertion of an exclusive right to make war. John of Legnano argued that while in principle war could only be legitimately declared by the authority of a prince, in practice: "because there are peoples who do not recognize a superior in fact, the authority of a superior is not required, since they do not recognize one. Nay, every day wars are declared by one people against another, without asking leave of any one."[43] Both Bonet and Christine rejected any right to private war, insisting that only the sovereign is authorized to declare war. Bonet treated the matter very briefly, and Ernest Nys credits Christine with the full formulation and rationale for this position.[44] Her denial of authority to make war to any "baron whatever he may be nor to any other be he never so great, without license and permission of his sovereign lord" was an essential element in the claims of modern royal sovereignty. Whether it was also, in the long run, a step toward reducing the frequency and destructiveness of war may be questioned, but it undoubtedly appeared so, in Christine's time.

Nor did she look exclusively to "the ideal prince" to bring this about. Although the "mirror of princes" tradition plays a large part in her political works, Christine offered challenges, direct and indirect, to the theories of absolute monarchy that were developing in her time. The notion that "the will of the prince is law" is muted if not absent from her thought, and in various contexts she presents governance by mere will as dangerous or wrong. In her classification of the causes of war, she rejects wars for reasons "of will" (for vengeance and conquest) as unjust. And she argues in several places for decisions by council.

She insisted, indeed, that the prince is not free to decide on the matter

---

[42] See Nys, *Origines*, 47, 109; Bonet, *Tree of Battles*, 81, 118–19, 125.

[43] *Tractatus De Bello*, 234.

[44] *Fayttes*, I.3, 10–11; see also Nys, *Origines*, 91–92. Compare Bonet, *Tree of Battles*, Part IV, ch. iv, 128–29.

of going to war entirely on his own, nor even on the advice of selected councillors. Rather, the king or prince

must assemble a great council of wise men in his parliament, or in the council of his sovereign if he be subject; and he shall not only assemble them of his country, but so as to be free of any hint of favoritism, also of foreign countries that are known not to be adherents of any party, as well as senior nobles, jurists and others. In their presence, he will put forward or have put forward all the truth, without any disguise ... And in concluding shall say that he will report him and hold closely to the determination of right ...[45]

Christine's chapter on the causes of war in the *Feats of Arms and Chivalry* is a particularly interesting contribution. Analysis of the causes of war has been a central concern of peace studies. Christine broke new ground here in 1409, offering a classification of the main causes of war, outside the framework of theology. Her sources offered no such classification, and Christine signals her own contribution by saying '*it seems to me* that there are commonly five principal movements upon which wars are founded, of which three are of law and right, and two are of will.'[46]

Specifically, the causes for war "of law and right" are to overcome injustice, oppression, and usurpation, while both vengeance and conquest are rejected as legitimate grounds for war. Christine recognized a legal obligation of Christians to defend and protect the church, but she departed from the theological explanations or justifications elaborated by her predecessors, John of Legnano and Bonet, based on human sin, the will of God, or the dichotomous Augustinian worldview of *The City of God*.

"For lust of tribute and conquest of foreign lands"

Christine shifted political discourse away from the universalist struggles between papacy and Empire and issues of supremacy between church and monarchy, by choosing to omit many of the discussions by John of Legnano and Honoré Bonet on these topics. She also omitted their discussions of the legitimacy of war and acts of war against the "Saracens."[47] In so doing, she reflects a lack of enthusiasm – at this time of her life – for any form of crusading warfare in foreign lands.[48]

---

[45] *Fayttes*, I.4, 13; Nys, *Origines*, 111; my translation into modern English.
[46] *Fayttes*, 11.
[47] Nys credits Bonet with opposing unauthorized or gratuitous war against Saracens and Jews. But Bonet accepted the right of the Pope to grant indulgences and promote war to recover lands previously held by Christians, in particular the Holy Land itself. See Nys, *Origines*, 146–47; Bonet, *Tree of Battles*, 126–27.
[48] In her last poem, on Joan of Arc, Christine did espouse this crusading "Christian universalism." See Christine de Pisan, *Ditié de Jehanne d'Arc* (Oxford: Society for the

This is noteworthy in light of the recurrent calls for crusades to conquer or reconquer lands in the Middle East and North Africa. Although the era of the crusades directed to the "Holy Land" was waning, the idea was not yet dead in Christine's time, and soon the crusading spirit was to be revived, wedded to the search for new lands to conquer in the west.[49] Christine's choice in omitting this discussion contrasts sharply with some so-called "plans for peace" in late medieval times, which promoted the demonizing of other races and agitation for holy wars. The most prominent example is that of Pierre Dubois, described by Sylvester Hemleben as "the medieval herald of modern projects of world organization for peace."[50]

Dubois, a century before Christine, wrote a tract entitled *The Recovery of the Holy Land*. This embodied a plan for achieving peace within Christendom, coupled with a major new crusade to the east, under the leadership of the king of France, who was to establish world hegemony and "universal peace." Peace was to be made in Christian Europe by a process of conquest and ruthless subjugation of any who declined to accept submission to the domination of France, and thereafter by more pacific means such as internal arbitration and reform of education and the church, leading to the establishment of a united spiritual republic of Christendom. Warlike men would then be persuaded, "rather than remain idle in their lands" under conditions of peace, to embark on the crusade.[51]

Dubois prescribed a special role for women, who were to be educated for the purpose of being married to "the greater princes, clergy, and other wealthy easterners," in order to convert them and educate their husbands and children in Christianity.[52] Christine has been unfavorably

Study of Mediaeval Languages and Literature, 1977), 47; and Earl Jeffrey Richards, "French Cultural Nationalism and Christian Universalism in the Works of Christine de Pizan," in Brabant, *Politics, Gender, and Genre*, 75. But Richards finds that in earlier writings Christine's universalism is not jingoistic: "There is no national bias or partiality here" (83). See also Nadia Margolis, "Christine de Pizan and the Jews: Political and Poetic Implications," in Brabant, 53–73.

[49] See Joseph J. Fahey, "Columbus and the Catholic Crusades," *Peace Review* 4, 3 (Fall 1992): 36–40; David E. Stannard, *American Holocaust: The Conquest of the New World* (New York: Oxford University Press, 1992), 174–93.

[50] Sylvester Hemleben, *Plans for World Peace through Six Centuries* (Chicago: University of Chicago Press, 1943), 1 (reprinted New York: Garland Publishing, 1972).

[51] Dubois, *Recovery, passim*, especially Part II; Eileen Power, "Pierre Du Bois and the Domination of France," in *The Social and Political Ideas of Some Great Mediaeval Thinkers* [1923], ed. F. J. C. Hearnshaw (New York: Barnes and Noble, 1967), 139–66. See also W. S. M. Knight, "A Mediaeval Pacifist – Pierre Du Bois," *Proceedings of the Grotius Society*, vol. 9, Problems of Peace and War (London: Sweet and Maxwell, 1924), 1–16. Knight concluded: "Standing . . . upon such principles as these, it is not surprising to find that Du Bois has . . . very little to say about peace itself" (4).

[52] Dubois, *Recovery*, 59, 118–19, 139.

compared with Dubois as less "advanced" with respect to the "equal" education of women, but Dubois's purpose in educating women seems hardly feminist in character.[53]

Nor did the notion that peace in Christian Europe should be achieved through directing war against "others" in the Middle East die before Christine's time. Even a century later, such an ardent advocate of peace as Desiderius Erasmus could express a similar idea. Erasmus did not actively advocate a crusade. He preferred conversion "with honest doctrine and good example." Nonetheless, he wrote:

If, however, the disease of war is a malady of such a nature that it cannot possibly be extricated from men's minds, then let them expend their warlike efforts toward the extermination of the Turkish menace ... Would that there were some simpler means of solving disagreements among Christians. Certainly if mutual charity does not unite them, then some common enemy may perhaps do so.[54]

What distinguishes Christine's ideas on peace is precisely that she did not hold that "war is a malady of such a nature that it cannot possibly be extricated from men's minds." Though not a pacifist, she believed not only that limits should be set on the destructiveness of war, but also that peace could be achieved, through human efforts, in particular, efforts to secure justice, and efforts to educate the prince and the populace against the ravages of unlimited war.

It should be noted that passages of her work elaborating on the horrors of war are not merely impassioned outbursts, as they have been generally perceived, even when praised for their eloquence and strength. Christine made clear that her purpose in writing of these matters was an educational one. She argued explicitly that it is necessary to remember the evils and cruelty of war if it is to be avoided in future.[55] Not all peace educators today agree with this, but "anti-war" scholarship, literature, and films remain a mainstay in modern peace education.

---

[53] Dubois proposed education by a public foundation for both girls and boys, in separate schools and with different curricula, including surgery and medicine for girls. Sheila Delaney cites Dubois's plan to show that Christine was "in the rearguard of social thought" even in terms of feminism ("Mothers," 95, 97–98). The double standard in Delaney's critique of Christine is exemplified here by her euphemistic description of Dubois's plan for Christian colonialist marriage service under the world hegemony of a "superior" French race: "a scheme for sending a large corps of educated women into the Muslim East, to regain by propaganda and fraternisation [sic] what the Crusades had lost" (98) – ignoring Dubois's explicit plans for a new military crusade.

[54] John P. Dolan, trans. and ed., *The Essential Erasmus* (New York: New American Library, 1964), 196.

[55] *Paix*, II.3, 92.

"To return as a woman and be heard"

Christine stands in provocative and vital contrast to J. N. Figgis's judgment, in *Political Thought from Gerson to Grotius*, that the political literature of the period was "without charm or brilliancy or overmuch eloquence ... arid, scholastic ... dead beyond any language ever spoken."[56] Hugo Grotius, who wrote *Of the Law of War and Peace* in the early seventeenth century, is seen today as a monumental figure in the history of international law and peace theory. The distance between Gerson and Grotius was "the distance between the unitary society of the Middle Ages and the pluralistic, multinational society of modern times."[57] Christine, though allied with Gerson in the debate against Jean de Meun and in many of her political views, stood altogether outside his frame of reference as cleric and conciliarist. Insofar as "the unitary society of the Middle Ages" refers to the central political role of the Catholic Church, which Figgis saw as not merely "a state" but "the State," Gerson was still firmly situated in the theoretical and practical political struggles within the church and between the church and secular states. Christine, in contrast, was already firmly situated in "the pluralistic, multinational society of modern times." Unlike many of her medieval sources, such as Boccaccio, Christine rejected both a nostalgic image of a lost "golden age" and an Augustinian image of damned earthly carnality, in favor of the more "modern" conviction that reason, personified by female figures of both allegory and history, had marked the way to progress both past and future.[58]

Christine's politics and ideas were often not what a radical feminist – let alone a feminist pacifist – would like. In many ways she was closer to the thinking of Machiavelli and Hobbes than to the egalitarian and pacifist strains of contemporary radicalism – of her own time or ours. She was a theorist of royal power, monarchical hegemony, and "peace from above" rather than of democracy, revolution, and "peace from below." But she broke from the universalist, crusading, and dualist ideas that dominated medieval political thought to her time.

In the history of peace theory, Christine stands between the bizarre "peace project" of Pierre Dubois, who envisioned "peace" as the universalist subjugation of Europe and the world through French hegemony and Christian crusade, and the despairing irony of Desiderius

---

[56] J.N. Figgis, *Political Thought from Gerson to Grotius, 1414–1625* (New York: Harper and Bros., 1960), 2.

[57] Garrett Mattingly, Introduction, ibid., xv.

[58] See Rosalind Brown-Grant, "Décadence ou progrès? Christine de Pizan, Boccace et la question de 'l'Age d'Or'," *Revue des Langues Romanes*, 92, 2 (1988): 295–306.

Erasmus, who in the end also endorsed the idea of the crusade as the way to peace in Europe. In that context, we may see Christine's project as a fundamentally modern (certainly not "post-modern") argument that "peace is possible" in the real conditions of an emerging national state system. Some pacifists may think her wrong, arguing that the premises of that national state system are in contradiction with the requirements of real peace. Her vision, however, was both daring and important.

Christine wished intensely to be remembered, a wish astonishingly well fulfilled despite her detractors of varying persuasions and the gaps that are only being filled today. The heated debates that swirl around her reflect the complexity, magnitude, and evident inconsistencies of her works, and it is exhilarating to witness their intensity. Christine, who advocated valorous battle in many arenas, would surely delight in the fray. The survival and wide-ranging renown of her works six centuries later calls to mind Ernest Nys's remark: "In the immaterial world of thought, nothing dies; germination is continual."[59] Christine's works were not lost – they remained in archives and libraries in many countries. Though neglected, ignored, and like those of other women theorists "invisibilized," her ideas continued to spread their roots and germinate, in the subterranean common ground of social thought.

[59] Nys (n. 2, above), my translation.

2 Political thought/political action: Margaret Cavendish's Hobbesian dilemma

Anna Battigelli

An affiliation between Margaret Cavendish (1623–1673) and Thomas Hobbes (1588–1679) might on first consideration seem unlikely. Cavendish was by her own admission both unlearned and undisciplined; despite having attended a French queen as a maid of honor and having lived in exile for sixteen years first in Paris and then in Antwerp, she never became fluent in any language other than English.[1] Her reading, while substantially broader than has been acknowledged, was begun late and pursued haphazardly. Hobbes, on the other hand, though eager to demonstrate his independence from any religious or classical authority, was from his youth deeply steeped in the literate culture of Renaissance humanism, having translated Euripides' *Medea* before he left for Oxford.[2] Cavendish's rambling volumes appear to record the spontaneous stream of her thoughts with little or no system or method. Hobbes's work, despite its puzzling inconsistencies, is clearly the product of a system builder. He was widely admired for his witty conversation; she seems, for all the garrulity of her prose, to have been struck dumb in the company of others.

And yet unlikely as this pair might at first seem, they share similarities, beginning with their traditional reputations as isolated thinkers "without ancestry or posterity."[3] They traveled in the same circles. Both were considered mad by some and feared by others, in part because they insisted that the nature of God was unknowable and also

---

[1] From her first published work, *Poems and Fancies* (1653), she denied knowing French: "truly I understand no other Language; not French, although I was in France five yeares" (sig. A6r). In *The Philosophical and Physical Opinions* (1655), she repeated this claim in the course of defending herself from having plagiarized Descartes; while she met him frequently, she claims never to have "understood what he said, for he spake no English, and I understand no other language" (sig. B3v). In the same preface, she also defends herself from charges of having plagiarized Hobbes.

[2] Arnold A. Rogow, *Thomas Hobbes: Radical in the Service of Reaction* (New York: Norton, 1986), 36. For an excellent discussion of Hobbes's complex response to Renaissance humanism, see Quentin Skinner, *Reason and Rhetoric in the Philosophy of Hobbes* (Cambridge: Cambridge University Press, 1996).

[3] Hugh Trevor-Roper, *Historical Essays* (New York: Harper, 1966), 236.

because they shared a disturbingly pessimistic view of human nature. Both openly acknowledged their ambition to be widely read and to be taught in the universities, donating copies of their books in an effort to encourage this; both were in this respect disappointed. Both were protected by their reputations as eccentrics from closer scrutiny of and persecution for their unorthodox ideas. Perhaps most importantly, however, both had apprehensive, even fearful temperaments that shaped their political thought, particularly as they focused obsessively on the great problem that emerged in the wake of the English Civil Wars: the problem of maintaining political order.

Though Hobbes would no doubt have been displeased to know it, he was, of the many philosophers and scientists whom Cavendish met at her husband's extraordinary salon in Paris, the one who most profoundly influenced her political thought. That he may have been aware of Cavendish's interest in his work is suggested by the fact that he kept his disciple at a comfortable distance, refusing her invitation to dinner when they met by chance during her brief trip to London in 1651–52 and responding to her present of a volume of plays in 1662 with frosty civility.[4] His coolness did not, however, dissuade Cavendish from responding to his work. In fact, understanding Hobbes's influence on her political thought helps to make sense of one of the contradictions that most troubles modern readers of her work: while she articulates women's problematic political status more clearly than any of her contemporaries, she resists presenting any sort of unqualified reforming vision. As Hilda Smith has noted, "none of the [early] feminists considered sex roles more broadly than the duchess and none proved so reluctant to offer unambiguous conclusions."[5] This apparent paradox in Cavendish's political thought can be attributed, in large part, to Hobbes's complex influence.

I

As a new bride in Paris in 1645, Margaret Cavendish found herself at the center of a scientific salon at a moment of intense intellectual ferment, during which time Thomas Hobbes was one of its most eminent and valued members. It is worth remembering that, while Hobbes was viewed with suspicion in England, he "seems to have been widely

[4] For Cavendish's discussion of inviting Hobbes to dinner, see Margaret Cavendish, *Philosophical and Physical Opinions* (London, 1655), sig. B3v. See also Hobbes to Margaret Cavendish, marchioness of Newcastle, February 9, 1662, *The Correspondence of Thomas Hobbes*, 2 vols., ed. Noel Malcolm (Oxford: Clarendon Press, 1994), II, 524.
[5] Hilda Smith, *Reason's Disciples* (Urbana: University of Illinois Press, 1982), 76.

accepted abroad."[6] Cavendish thus met Hobbes in a context in which she might have felt freer to pursue his ideas than most English men or women back home. He was an intimate, though unofficial member of her household, having been for years a deeply valued friend of her husband, William Cavendish, then marquess of Newcastle, referred to hereafter as Newcastle. Five years older than Newcastle, Hobbes had been hired in 1608 to tutor Newcastle's cousin, another William Cavendish, later 2nd earl of Devonshire; except for a two-year period between 1628 and 1630, he remained part of the Devonshire household for the rest of his life.[7] From 1608 onward, then, Newcastle had had opportunities to meet Hobbes, and by 1630 they were discussing theories of light and optics.[8] By 1634 Hobbes was writing from London to apologize for not being able to locate a copy of Galileo's *Dialogue Concerning the Two Chief World Systems* for him because, so Hobbes explained, "it is not possible to get it for mony."[9] Newcastle invited Hobbes to join his household in 1636, an invitation Hobbes considered carefully and was inclined at one point to accept. He remained with the Devonshires, but his friendship with Newcastle and with Newcastle's brother, Charles Cavendish, intensified during the late 1630s.[10] In 1640, Hobbes dedicated the *Elements of Law* to Newcastle, and shortly after

6 Quentin Skinner, "Hobbes and His Disciples in France and England," *Comparative Studies in Society and History* 8 (1965–66): 153–67; see p. 163. See also Malcolm, *The Correspondence of Thomas Hobbes*, I, xxxiii.

7 Hobbes's biographer, Arnold Rogow, gives the difference in age between Newcastle and Thomas Hobbes as four years. Geoffrey Trease has suggested that Newcastle's christening date – 16 December 1593 – is evidence that he was born not in 1592 as has traditionally been thought but in 1593. Hobbes was born April 5, 1588, making their difference in age closer to five years. See Trease, *Portrait of a Cavalier: William Cavendish, First Duke of Newcastle* (New York: Taplinger, 1979), 18. It was probably at the Devonshire estates at Hardwick or Chatsworth that Hobbes first became acquainted with the William and Charles Cavendish with whom we are concerned. See Rogow, *Thomas Hobbes*, 110.

8 In dedicating "A Minute or first Draught of the Optiques" (1646) to Newcastle, Hobbes wrote that "that which I have writt of it, is grounded especially upon that which about 16 yeares since I affirmed to your Lordship at Welbeck, that light is a fancy in the minde, caused by motion in the braine" (fol. 3r). These dates place their discussion of light and optics in 1630. See Harley 3360, British Library.

9 Hobbes to William Cavendish, earl of Newcastle, January 26, 1634, *The Correspondence of Thomas Hobbes*, I, 19.

10 Rogow cites Newcastle's treatment by the court of Charles I as one reason for Hobbes's typically cautionary decision to stay with the Devonshire household in 1636. Newcastle had hoped to become governor to the Prince of Wales, but his appointment was not announced until March 1638. Rogow adds that the Devonshire household may have become more attractive as some of Hobbes's domestic duties were replaced with "less menial, more respectable chores" and as the third earl "turn[ed] his attention to the creation of a remarkable library." See Rogow, *Thomas Hobbes*, 12. A brief review of the acquaintance between Hobbes and Newcastle can also be found in Malcolm, *The Correspondence of Thomas Hobbes*, II, 812–15.

the meeting of the Long Parliament in November 1640, he fled into exile, in part because of his concern over potentially hostile reaction to *Elements of Law*, which was circulating widely in manuscript. In 1645, Hobbes joined the Newcastle salon in Paris. Largely through his membership in this salon, he was introduced to the circle of scientific figures both in England and in France that made possible his later boast of being "numbered among the philosophers" (26).[11] In 1646 he would dedicate *Of Liberty and Necessity* to Newcastle along with the manuscript of *A Minute or First Draught of the Optiques*.

We know from Margaret Cavendish's own account that her husband served as her tutor, "instruct[ing] me, reading several lectures thereof to me, and expounding the hard and obscure passages therein."[12] Charles Cavendish, Newcastle's less flamboyant and more intellectually rigorous brother, also served as Margaret Cavendish's tutor. He too hosted a scientific salon, although his was an epistolary salon through which he acquired, reviewed, and circulated new ideas, including those of Hobbes.[13] He was such an active and engaged correspondent that Miriam Reik appropriately calls him one of the seventeenth-century's "philosophical merchants."[14] In one letter alone, he asks his good friend John Pell for his reaction to Descartes's book on the soul (*Les Passions de L'Ame*, 1649), looks forward to reading Gassendi's book on Epicurean philosophy, asks about Hobbes, whose *Leviathan* he awaits, and reports that Sir William Davenant has "latelie sent my Brother a Preface to an intended Poem [*Gondibert*] of his not yet printed" with Hobbes's additions (87).[15] Surrounded by some of the world's most illustrious

---

[11] Benjamin Farrington, trans., "The Autobiography of Thomas Hobbes," *Rationalist Annual* (1958): 22–31.

[12] Margaret Cavendish, *The World's Olio* (London, 1655), 47. Cavendish revised her volumes frequently. Unless otherwise noted, I have used the earliest edition of each volume.

[13] A. R. Hall observes that the postal organizations of the early seventeenth century served to spread scientific news. "Problems could be exposed for general consideration: and criticism could be provoked and collated. In the mid-seventeenth century a number of men occupied a prominent position, less on account of their own intellectual capacities, than because of their indefatigability as correspondents" (191). See A. R. Hall, *The Scientific Revolution 1500–1800: The Formation of the Modern Scientific Attitude* (London: Longmans, 1954). Jean Jacquot similarly notes that men like Charles Cavendish "contributed to the advancement of learning mainly by providing an appreciative audience, by asking intelligent questions or formulating valuable objections, and by helping the circulation and exchange of scientific information" (13). See Jean Jacquot, "Sir Charles Cavendish and His Learned Friends," *Annals of Science* 8 (1952): 13–27.

[14] Miriam Reik, *The Golden Lands of Thomas Hobbes* (Detroit: Wayne State University Press, 1977), 208 n. 62.

[15] The letter is reprinted in Helen Hervey, "Hobbes and Descartes in the Light of some Unpublished Letters of the Correspondence between Sir Charles Cavendish and Dr. John Pell," *Osiris* 10 (1952): 67–90.

thinkers, equipped with translations and texts, and instructed by at least two indulgent tutors, both of whom were intensely engaged with Hobbes's thought, Margaret Cavendish could not have escaped being introduced to Hobbes's political ideas. When we add to this context the fact that she began her publishing career in 1653, in the wake of the publication of *Leviathan*, it becomes clear how strange it would be if she failed to reflect some awareness of his political thought.

At least at first, Cavendish was well positioned to experience Hobbes's thought as a powerfully enabling influence. In particular, his attacks on authority must have exercised a strong appeal: his gleeful and ruthlessly logical assaults on the universities, the schoolmen, Aristotle, parliaments, the pope, and Protestant archbishops and bishops must have pleased Cavendish, who all her life both envied and criticized the central institutions of power and learning. That Hobbes seems to have delighted in working his assaults on authority into everyday conversation is evident in John Aubrey's now famous record of Hobbes's boast that "if he had read as much as other men, he should have knowne no more than other men."[16] Coming from one of the most outstanding thinkers of the day, an offhand remark of this sort was bound to encourage, however unwittingly, Cavendish's confidence in her own enterprise. The corollary to Hobbes's assault on authority – his deductive method – also influenced Cavendish; like him, she not only rejected authority but also sought, as he put it, "to prove everything in my own way."[17] While Cavendish would take deductive reasoning to unsystematic extremes of which Hobbes no doubt disapproved, she found in Hobbes an eminent thinker whose method validated her participation in the life of the mind.

In the realm of speculative activity, then, Hobbes proved to be a powerfully liberating influence: his assault on authority, his deductive method, and his focus on the man-made nature of the polity equipped Cavendish with the tools of her own intellectual enterprise. His focus on the creative mental work behind the "artificial man" or "Leviathan" helps explain Cavendish's more extreme claims for the power of the imagination. Her claim, for instance, in *Nature's Pictures* that "fancy is not an imitation of nature, but a naturall Creation" reflects Hobbes's insistence on seeing the exclusively human design of the body politic.[18] Like Hobbes, she was keenly aware of the arbitrary nature of custom and tradition, and she explored the degree to which custom shaped and often confined women's lives, forcing women, in her words, to be

[16] Oliver Lawson Dick, ed., *Aubrey's Brief Lives* (Ann Arbor: University of Michigan Press, 1957), 154.
[17] Hobbes, "Autobiography," 24.
[18] Cavendish, *Nature's Pictures* (London, 1656), sig. C3v.

kept like birds in cages to hop up and down in our houses, not sufferd to fly abroad to see the several changes of fortune, and the various humors, ordained and created by nature ... thus by an opinion, which I hope is but an erronious one in men, we are shut out of all power, and Authority by reason we are never imployed either in civil nor marshall affaires.[19]

She explored all aspects of women's lives with an eye to the arbitrary constraints that prevented women from entering the world of politics.

Liberating as Hobbes proved to be in the realm of speculative activity, however, in the realm of political activity, he exerted a powerfully restraining influence. While his political theory had the effect of encouraging her to engage in political thought, even feminist political thought, his fear of factionalism imposed extreme limits on her faith in political action. She was drawn to Hobbes's political thought because it was motivated by anxieties she shared, and these counteracted for her, as they had for Hobbes, the more liberating elements of the assault on authority. His exaggerated sense of caution is well known: it is illustrated by his precipitous flight into France over his fear of the reaction to *Elements of Law*; more generally, it can be sensed governing his dark view of human nature. In this autobiography, he attributed his temperament to the rumors circulating at his birth regarding the possible invasion of the Spanish Armada: "Thus my mother was big with such fear that she brought twins to birth, myself and fear at the same time."[20] As Alan Ryan has noted, Hobbes treated fear or caution as "one of the primary political virtues." Fear, Ryan continues, helps to explain "the causes and character of the 'war of all against all' in the state of nature, in motivating persons in the state of nature to contract with one another to set up an authority to 'overawe them all' and make peace possible, and in persuading them to obey that authority once it has been established" (209).[21] Cavendish, too, was fearful by nature. Her repeated confessions to being bashful and unsure of herself in social situations are well known. More important, though less noted, is the fact that fear dominates her political thought: her work documents a lifelong anxiety regarding the disputatious nature of the human mind and the threat it posed to the body politic.

From her earliest volumes – *Poems and Fancies* (1653), *Philosophicall Fancies* (1653), and *The World's Olio* (published in 1655 but composed as early as 1650) – she warns of the instability posed to political institutions by the individual, or, as she put it, of the inevitability with which "self-

---

[19] Cavendish, *Philosophical and Physical Opinions*, sig. B2v.
[20] Farrington, "Autobiography of Hobbes," 24.
[21] Alan Ryan, "Hobbes's Political Philosophy," in *The Cambridge Companion to Hobbes*, ed. Tom Sorell (Cambridge: Cambridge University Press, 1996), 208–45.

love seeks and strives for Preheminency & Command, which all cannot have."[22] For her, the natural and political worlds are atomist units on the brink of imminent dissolution, evident in her reading a Hobbesian state of nature into the very fabric of the universe:

> Some factious Atomes will agree; combine,
> They strive some form'd Body to unjoyne.
> The Round beate out the Sharpe: the Long
> The Flat do fight withall, thus all go wrong.

Poems and Fancies 1653, 16

While she renounced atomism as a theory of matter in 1655, she retained it as a governing metaphor for political reality. She conceived of the body politic as a Hobbist–atomist system perpetually on the brink of war, in which mind confronts mind, and moral certainty, moral certainty. She marvels, for example, at the relative infrequency of war, writing, "It seems to me a thing above Nature, that Men are not alwaies in War one against the other, and that some Estates live in Peace, somtimes forty or an hundred years, nay some above a Thousand (as the Venetians) without Civil Warrs; for the old saying, 'So many Men so many Minds'."[23] Both her plays and her romances explore characters whose conflicting value systems pose irreconcilable differences. Similarly, her interest in natural philosophy returned obsessively to the problem of subjectivity.

At her more morbid moments – and morbidity punctuates her work – her fear of the inevitability of conflict seems to have caused her genuine despair. She claimed, for example, not to concern herself with her own grave because civil war was always imminent, and therefore no grave would remain unplundered for long:

I do not much Care, nor Trouble my Thoughts to think where I shall be Buried, when Dead, or into what part of the Earth I shall be Thrown; but if I could have my Wish, I Would my Dust might be Inurned, and mix'd with the Dust of those I Love Best, although I think they would not Remain Long together, for I did observe, that in this last War the Urns of the Dead were Digged up, their Dust Dispersed, and their Bones Thrown about, and I suppose that in all Civil or Home-wars such Inhuman Acts are Committed; wherefore it is but a Folly to be Troubled and Concerned, where they shall be Buried, or for their Graves, or to Bestow much Cost on their Tombes, since not only Time, but Wars will Ruin them. (*Sociable Letters*, 238–39)

She knew firsthand about the "Inhuman Acts" produced by civil war; in

---

[22] Cavendish, *The World's Olio*, 163. For Cavendish's discussion of the composition date of *The World's Olio*, see sig. A3v.
[23] Cavendish, *The World's Olio*, 162–63.

rapid succession she lost her brother, home, and country to civil war. After the siege of Colchester, the Lucas family vaults were plundered, and hair was cut from the recently buried bodies, which included Cavendish's mother, brother, sister, and niece, and worn profanely as "Hat-bands" and "Bracelets."[24] The civil wars had illustrated the inevitability of conflict between moral, political, or religious certainties and the ease with which such conflict could escalate into physical violence. The specter of atomistic individualism haunted Cavendish as it haunted Hobbes.

It is thus not entirely surprising that Hobbes's tragic sensibility, evident in his liberal allusions to the Book of Job, resonated with Cavendish.[25] Job's friends try inadequately to explain his suffering in human terms, but it is only when Job abandons that line of thought and realizes the limits of human understanding that he is spiritually transformed. Like Job, Hobbes was aware that concepts like "justice," for example, are human rather than divine concerns, that meaning is manmade, and that polities are, finally, mental constructs. Given these conditions, it was of the utmost importance to agree on certain definitions, such as "good" and "evil." Similarly, it was crucial to avoid controversy over unverifiable claims such as those purporting to depict the nature of God. And yet for Hobbes, men were likely neither to agree on definitions nor to avoid controversy over contested and unverifiable claims. He responded to this problem by embracing an Erastianism that deferred all definitions to an absolute sovereign.[26]

Cavendish shared Hobbes's concern regarding the problem of competing definitions. That she, like Hobbes, reached for Erastianism as a solution to this problem, at least at first, is evident in passages such as the following:

But it is Time and Occasion that makes most things Good or Bad: For example, it were a horrid thing, and against Nature, and all Civil Laws, for Children and Parents, Brethren and Neighbours, and Acquaintance[s], to kill one another, although their Offences to each other were very hainous; but when the King or chief Magistrate in a Commonwealth commands it, as they do to those that are of their side in a Civil War, then it is not onely Warrantable, but it is accounted

---

24 *The Loyall Sacrifice* ([London], 1648), 88.
25 In addition to naming two of his books *Leviathan* and *Behemoth*, both creatures mentioned in Job, Hobbes chose to inscribe the title page of *Leviathan* with a quotation from Job that constitutes a significant part of God's response to Job: "Non est potestas super terram quae comparetur ei." That response emphasizes the inadequacy of trying to explain cosmic order in human terms. See Job 41.
26 Samuel Mintz's note on the use of the term "Erastian" is worth repeating. Mintz uses the term "as it was commonly applied to Hobbes in the seventeenth century, and not as it was originally intended by Erastus." See Samuel Mintz, *The Hunting of Leviathan* (Cambridge: Cambridge University Press, 1962), 28 n. 3.

Sacred and Divine; because nothing pleaseth Divinity more than Obedience to Magistrates, and Nature loves Peace, although she hath made all things to War upon one another; so that Custome and the Law make the same thing Civil or Pious, Just or Unjust. (*The World's Olio* 1655, 81)

Similarly, she returns repeatedly to the time-worn image of the body politic, through which she depicts the ideal form of government as one in which the individual submits to an absolute authority. Such a commonwealth would be

governed by one Head or Governour, as a King, for one Head is sufficient for one Body: for several Heads breed several Opinions, and several Opinions breed Disputations, and Disputations Factions, and Factions breed Wars, and Wars bring Ruin and Desolation: for it is more safe to be governed, though by a Foolish Head, than a Factious Heart.[27]

She worried particularly about conflict over unverifiable beliefs such as those attempting to identify the nature of God. Like her husband, who had also absorbed from Hobbes an anxiety regarding the "dangers of the public word," she viewed religious certainty with suspicion.[28] While she herself did not promote the extreme political measures Newcastle put forward privately in his *Advice* to Charles II, she faithfully recorded them in her biography of him. She commended Newcastle's decision to regulate the content of sermons during the war, noting in particular his awareness that "Schism and Faction in Religion is the Mother of all or most Rebellions, Wars, and Disturbances in a State or Government."[29] Her fear of the destructive power of religious conflict can be seen in her comment that "it is better, to be an Atheist, then a superstitious man; for in Atheisme there is humanitie, and civility, towards man to man; but superstition regards no humanity, but begets cruelty to all things, even to themselves."[30] It is best, Cavendish suggests, to submit publicly

---

[27] Cavendish, *The World's Olio*, 205–206.

[28] Conal Condren, "Casuistry to Newcastle: 'The Prince' in the World of the Book," in *Political Discourse in Early Modern Britain*, eds. Nicholas Phillipson and Quentin Skinner (Cambridge: Cambridge University Press, 1993), 184. Condren makes a convincing case for the Machiavellian character of Newcastle's *Advice*, though he acknowledges that Newcastle may have absorbed from Hobbes a fear of the "dangers of the public word." Arnold Rogow and Thomas P. Slaughter argue that Newcastle's *Advice* is heavily indebted to Hobbes. See Rogow, *Thomas Hobbes*, 118; Thomas P. Slaughter, *Ideology and Politics on the Eve of the Restoration: Newcastle's Advice to Charles II* (Philadelphia: The American Philosophical Society, 1984), xiii. See also Gloria Italiano Anzilotti, *An English Prince: Newcastle's Machiavellian Political Guide to Charles II* (Pisa: Giardini, 1988). I would want to insist neither that Newcastle's *Advice* is purely Hobbesian nor that his wife was unfamiliar on some level with the political thought of Machiavelli; rather, I explore Cavendish's fear of the public word, a fear she shared with Hobbes.

[29] Margaret Cavendish, *The Life of . . . William Cavendish* (London, 1667), 14.

[30] Cavendish, *The World's Olio*, 46.

to the sovereign's definitions while holding silently to one's own beliefs; a monarchist by nature, she had seen firsthand what happened when subjects took it upon themselves to engage in disputes with their king.

Cavendish's Erastianism, though, led her to difficulties when she considered her own writing, which, she worried, might be misunderstood as inciting political antagonisms that threatened political stability. This anxiety increased after the Restoration when she began reading more broadly and responding in print to specific authors. She expresses concern, for example, that her husband, who otherwise always encouraged her to write, might be displeased with *Philosophical Letters*, which critiqued Hobbes, Descartes, Henry More, and van Helmont. In the preface, she worried that he might "be angry with me for Writing and Publishing this Book, by reason it is a Book of Controversies, of which I have heard your Lordship say, That Controversies and Disputations make Enemies of Friends."[31]

In *Orations* she goes so far as to suggest that writing itself poses a danger to the state, especially when it takes politics as its subject:

It is to be Observed, that much Writing of that [political] Nature makes much Trouble, wherein the Pen doth more mischief than the Sword, witness Controversies, that make Atheism; for the more Ignorant a people are, the more Devout and Obedient they are to God and his Deputies, which are Magistrates; Wherefore it were very Requisite, that all such Books should be Burnt, and all such Writers Silenced, or at least none should write of State-affairs, but those the State allows or Authorises.[32]

She was willing to allow subjects "Liberty of Conscience Conditionally, that they do not meddle with Civil Government or Governours" (69). Even eloquence worried her because of its power to "make Men like Gods or Devils, as having a Power beyond Nature, Custom and Force."[33] Her prolific literary career is thus characterized by the tension between her compulsion to write herself into history and her anxiety regarding the power of the public word to spark controversies.

II

Her anxiety regarding the power of the public word did not keep her from her compulsive writing, but it did determine the generic shape of her work. In the works she wrote after 1655, the problem of subjectivity emerged with a new anxiety attending it as she focused on the conflicts

[31] Margaret Cavendish, *Philosophical Letters* (London, 1664), sig. A1r.
[32] Margaret Cavendish, *Orations of Divers Sorts* (London, 1662), 63. In some copies of this volume, the imprint date has been altered in ink to 1663.
[33] Margaret Cavendish, *Sociable Letters* (London, 1664), 54.

that arose from multiple and discordant subjectivities. As a response to this concern, she deployed a rhetorical strategy that drew on her interest in atomism and on Hobbesian political theory. Repeatedly she constructed narrative frames that contained multiple and competing perspectives, no one of which can be easily identified with Cavendish's own perspective. Through these narrative frames, she was able to explore the disputatious nature of the human mind and its destructive consequences for political order. She had also found a way to explore heterodox ideas boldly without necessarily presenting them controversially.

Book I of *Nature's Pictures* (1656), for example, provides an example of the kind of narrative frame Cavendish liked to create. We are introduced to a group of storytellers, not unlike Chaucer's pilgrims, each of whom tells a story.

> In Winter cold, a Company was met
> Both Men and Women by the Fire set;
> At last they did agree to pass the time,
> That every one should tell a Tale in Rhime.   sig. B1r, ll. 13–16

What follows is a collection of tales in verse that become progressively disputatious. Each speaker's tale provides a moral that departs from or directly contradicts the previous speaker's moral. Thus a tale illustrating male inconstancy sparks a tale depicting female inconstancy, and so forth. Individually, each tale comments on the previous tale; taken as a whole, they illustrate the inevitability of disagreement over any number of issues pertaining to the internal world of the emotions or to the external codes of social behavior. The meta-narrative that results might be likened to a sort of troubled atomist system. Tale answers tale, not so as to reach a conclusion, but rather to highlight the inevitable problem of competing points of view and the tenaciousness with which men and women cling to them. Her aim is to highlight the problem of competing certainties and to illustrate the claim expressed repeatedly throughout her work that

different Opinions in Religion and Laws in a Commonwealth, cause Cruel Civil Wars ... whereof the late Wars in this Country are a woful Example, all being brought to Confusion with Preaching and Pleading, on the one side Preachers and Pleaders became Souldiers, on the other side, Souldiers became Preachers and Pleaders, so that the Word and the Sword made great Troubles, and grievous Calamities in these Nations, and though there hath been much Blood Shed, many lives Lost, Men Banish'd, and Families Ruined, yet there are Divisions still.[34]

---

[34] Cavendish, *Sociable Letters*, 84. The method of Book I seems to be reflected in the volume's frontispiece engraving by Abraham van Diepenbeeck. There, the Newcastle

She deployed a similar rhetorical strategy in *Orations of Divers Sorts* (1662). By 1662, of course, Cavendish and her husband had returned to their estate at Welbeck Abbey which had been partly destroyed during the English Civil Wars.[35] Surrounded by evidence of the ease with which the conflict of immaterial ideas escalated into material violence, she turned to another narrative frame in order to highlight conflict and its consequences. The volume itself is a catalog of competing points of view on key issues; its setting serves to highlight the destructive nature of the controversy it records. We are warned in the preface of *Orations* to expect controversy since "the Generality of the People [are] more apt to make Warr, than to keep Peace."[36] The wreckage of war is highlighted throughout the volume in passages such as the following:

In truth, there is Nothing so Miserable, Hatefull, Cruel, and Irreligious as Civil Warr, for it is an Enemy against Law, Nature, and God, it Pulls down the Seats of Justice, Throws down the Altars of Religion, Diggs up the Urns of their Parents, Disperses the Dust and Bones of their Dead Ancestors, Spills the Blood of their Fathers, Sons, Brethren, Friends, and Countrymen, and makes a Total Destruction and Dissolution. (264–65)

The orations within the volume help to account for this destruction by illustrating the inevitability of disagreement on key issues.

Later, she defended the *Orations* from charges that she was engaging in controversy by explaining that

As for my *Orations*, I have heard, that some do Censure me for speaking too Freely, and Patronizing Vice too much, but ... it is not out of Love to Vice that I Plead for it, but only to Exercise my Fancy, for surely the Wisest, and Eloquentest Orators, have not been Ashamed to Defend Vices upon such Accounts, and Why may not I do the like? for my Orations for the most part are Declamations, wherein I speak *Pro* and *Con*, and Determine nothing.[37]

According to this passage, we are to understand the various orations as mere exercises of fancy, exercises central to Renaissance theories of

family is portrayed sitting at a long rectangular table. Either because of the animation of the storytelling or because of the excessive fire in the fireplace, a steward is in the process of opening a window, a suggestion that the environment has become overheated. Whether the engraving is a joke played by the artist on his eccentric patron or whether he was instructed as to the method of Book I, there is an interesting match between the engraving and Book I's narrative frame. Both represent troubled atomist systems.

[35] For interesting discussions of the estates, see Richard W. Goulding, *Bolsover Castle* ([Oxford], 1917); A. S. Turberville, *A History of Welbeck Abbey and Its Owners*, 2 vols. (London: Faber and Faber, 1938–39); Mark Girouard, *Robert Smythson & the Elizabethan Country House* (New Haven: Yale University Press, 1983). Cavendish describes the ruined estates in *The Life of ... William Cavendish* (1667), 90–107.

[36] Cavendish, *Orations* (1662), sig. A3v.

[37] Cavendish, *Sociable Letters*, sig. C1v.

eloquence and designed more to sharpen one's skill at oratory than to arrive at truth.[38] And yet the persistent attention to the ravages of war throughout the volume suggests Cavendish's interest in revealing the morally destabilizing consequences of eloquence; like Hobbes, she seems to have been genuinely troubled by "the emphasis placed by the culture of humanism on the *ars rhetorica*, with its characteristic insistence that there will always be two sides to any question, and thus that in moral and political reasoning it will always be possible to construct a plausible argument *in utramque partem*, on either side of the case."[39] By placing her orations within the context of a war-torn setting, she suggests the dangers of the public word. Far from celebrating eloquence, then, *Orations* serves as a warning of its dangers.

If there is a truth to be arrived at in *Orations*, then, it is that conflict is inevitable. Some orations argue for war, others for peace; some argue for mutiny, others against mutiny; some for liberty of conscience, others against liberty of conscience. To illustrate the divisive nature of controversy, she even composes a series of misogynistic orations, which "so Angers" the women that "after the Mens Orations are ended, they Privately Assemble together, where three or four take the place of an Orator, and Speak to the rest."[40] Thus part XI of *Orations* is segregated from the rest of the text and titled *Femal Orations*. The first of these "female orations" calls on women to change their status by "unit[ng] in Prudent Counsels, to make our Selves as Free, Happy, and Famous as Men," adding, "the truth is, we live like Bats or Owls, Labour like Beasts, and Dye like Worms."[41] Even within this smaller group, however, the orators do not agree with one another. One orator urges women to imitate men; another argues that doing so would be unnatural. One orator complains that "our Words to men are as Empty Sounds, our Sighs as Puffs of Wind, and our Tears as Fruitless Showres"; another retorts that men "Dig to the Centre of the Earth for Gold for us; they Dive to the Bottom of the Sea for Jewels for us; they Build to the Skies Houses for us . . . Let us Love men, Praise men, and Pray for men" (226–28). Tempting as it might be to extract one of these statements and allow it to represent Cavendish's political thought, it is important to take seriously the context in which these statements appear; Cavendish's overriding concern is with the disputatious nature of the human mind. While she was certainly aware of women's problematical political status, she was more concerned with the inevitable conflict of opposing and

---

[38] For Quentin Skinner, it was precisely the tradition of disputation, so central to Renaissance theories of eloquence, that motivated Hobbes to create a science of politics. See Skinner, *Reason and Rhetoric*, 267–84.
[39] Ibid., 9.   [40] Cavendish, *Orations*, sig. A4r.   [41] Ibid., 225–26.

often unverifiable moral, political, and religious beliefs. Taken as a whole, *Orations* is thus less a feminist statement than it is a cautionary warning about the disputatious nature of the human mind.

III

If Hobbesian Erastianism was at times her solution to the problem of competing definitions, it was not, finally, satisfactory, perhaps because she seems to have held an even more pessimistic view of human nature than Hobbes. Partly as a result of having watched Henrietta Maria's disastrous attempts at imposing change on an unwilling country, Cavendish could never bring herself to put forward any sort of conclusive reforming vision, not even an Erastian vision. She directly questions Erastianism itself in *Blazing World* (1666), where she adopts in its stead political passivity. In *Blazing World*, Cavendish creates a fictional character who becomes an empress with "an absolute power to rule and govern all that World as she pleased" (13).[42] The problem, of course, is that having absolute power does not guarantee political stability. Not unlike Henrietta Maria in the 1630s, the empress finds her subjects' religion defective, and she sets about "convert[ing] them all to her own Religion, and to that end she resolved to build Churches, and make also up a Congregation of Women, whereof she intended to be the head her self, and to instruct them in the several points of her Religion" (60). By building two magnificent churches, the sheer beauty of which is designed to draw converts, the empress imitates Henrietta, whose magnificent chapel at Somerset House had been built in 1636 precisely for the purpose of attracting converts. One of the empress's churches is lined with diamonds. By the peculiar properties of firestone, which when wet flames fire, she achieved the necessary effects for sermons "of Terror to the wicked" (62). The other church is lined with star-stone, the cooler light of which is more appropriate for the "Sermons of Comfort" preached there (62). With these two magnificent churches, she converts the inhabitants of the Blazing World to her own religion.

While one might argue that Erastian politics are clearly at work in the empress's institutions of her own religion, the Erastianism is visibly complicated when the empress later confesses that

although this World was very well and wisely order'd and governed at first, when I came to be Empress thereof; yet the nature of Women being much delighted

---

[42] Margaret Cavendish, *Observations upon Experimental Philosophy: to which is added the Description of a New Blazing World* (London, 1668). *The Description of a New Blazing World*, hereafter referred to simply as *Blazing World*, first appeared in 1666, both separately and bound together with *Observations*.

with Change and Variety, after I had received an absolute Power from the Emperor, did somewhat alter the Form of Government from what I found it; but now perceiving that the World is not so quiet as it was at first, I am much troubled at it; especially there are such continual Contentions and Divisions ... that I fear they'l break out into an open Rebellion, and cause a great disorder, and the ruine of the Government; and therefore I desire your advice and assistance, how I may order it to the best advantage. (120)

The empress is advised by the duchess of Newcastle, who appears as a character in *Blazing World*, "to introduce the same form of Government again, which had been before" (121). The empress takes this advice and restores peace.

In *Blazing World* Cavendish illustrates the idea that, while making the sovereign the political arbiter of truth looked efficient in theory, it was hardly likely to work in practice. Her experience at the court of Henrietta Maria would certainly have reinforced such a conclusion. Yet *Blazing World* also reveals Cavendish's awareness that the urge to reform could not be entirely eradicated from the human spirit. The solution presented to the empress is quite simply to turn inward, to direct one's reforming energies to the fictional worlds of the mind, which can be controlled unproblematically with an efficient simplicity unattainable in the material world. The sages of *The Blazing World*, immaterial spirits, summarize the considerable benefits of turning inward, away from the material world:

For you can enjoy no more of a material world then a particular Creature is able to enjoy, which is but a small part, considering the compass of such a world; and you may plainly observe it by your friend the Empress here, which although she possesses a whole World, yet enjoys she but a part thereof; neither is she so much acquainted with it, that she knows all the places, Countries and Dominions she Governs. The truth is, a Sovereign Monarch has the general trouble; but the Subjects enjoy all the delights and pleasures in parts; for it is impossible, that a Kingdom, nay, a Country should be injoyed by one person at once ... Wherefore ... why should you desire to be Empress of a Material World, and be troubled with the cares that attend Government? when as by creating a World within yourself, you may enjoy all both in whole and in parts, without controle or opposition; and may make what World you please, and alter it when you please, and enjoy as much pleasure and delight as a World can afford you? (97)

Both the empress and the duchess in *Blazing World* turn to creating imaginary worlds, an emblem for the political passivity Cavendish seems finally to have adopted, not without apparent difficulty.

She puts this problem differently in *Philosophical Letters*, which contains an extended critique of Hobbes's mechanism. There she explains that no artificial system could govern subjects who do not already agree:

If men do not naturally agree, Art cannot make unity amongst them, or associate them into one Politick Body and so rule them ... The truth is, Man rules an artificial Government, and not Government Man, just like as a Watch-maker rules his Watch, and not the Watch the Watch-maker. (*Philosophical Letters*, 47–48)

For Cavendish, no machine, not even the monstrous artifice of Hobbes's *Leviathan*, could finally impose order on a disorderly body politic.

Here she turned Hobbes's own pessimism about the impulse to reform against Hobbes. Hobbes, of course, used the legend of Medea throughout the course of his career to warn that reform was dangerous and ultimately futile. In *Leviathan*, he explained that

they that go about by disobedience, to do no more than reform the commonwealth, shall find they do thereby destroy it; like the foolish daughters of Peleus, in the fable; which desiring to renew the youth of their decrepid father, did by the counsel of Medea, cut him in pieces, and boil him, together with strange herbs, but made not of him a new man.[43]

Yet while the danger attending the impulse to reform haunted both writers, Hobbes seems to have felt comfortable putting forward a solution to the problem of maintaining political stability with a confidence Cavendish resisted. Any political reform she envisioned was imposed on imaginary worlds or carefully placed within contexts that highlighted the dangers of trying to impose reform on the material world.

It is not, then, that Cavendish was unable to put forward a feminist reforming vision; rather, she seems to have been unwilling to do so. Her work documents her anxiety regarding the disputatious nature of the human mind, an anxiety she shared with Hobbes. While she finally disagreed with Hobbes's mechanistic view of human nature, she absorbed his political thought, taking it to its logical extreme. In the end, she was more of a Hobbesian than Hobbes. It is, finally, the problem of maintaining political order in the wake of the English Civil Wars that both governs her work and ultimately prevented her from presenting the kind of feminist reforming vision she was entirely capable of presenting had she cared to.

[43] *The English Works of Thomas Hobbes* (Aalen [Ger.]: Scientia, 1962), III, 326–27.

3   Women's public political voice in England: 1640–1740

Lois G. Schwoerer

It is the "usual work of women either to spin or knit, not to meddle with State Affairs," observed a commentator in mid-seventeenth-century England. Echoing the point later in the century a writer inquired of his readers: "Do you not think Learning and Politicks become a Woman as ill as riding astride?"[1] These two remarks, themselves typical of many others, express the prevailing view of women in politics in early modern England. This view (although sometimes contested)[2] held that women were not supposed to have a *public* voice, much less a public *political* voice. Nonetheless, starting in the 1640s and lasting to the mid-eighteenth century when their voices faded and their public role receded, a growing number of middle- and lower middle-class women in England (as distinct from aristocratic women, who had long exercised *private* political influence) did "meddle with State Affairs."[3] Their "meddling"

---

[1] Quoted in Patricia Higgins, "The Reactions of Women, with Special Reference to Women Petitioners," in *Politics, Religion and the English Civil War*, ed. Brian Manning (London: Edward Arnold, 1973), 212. [William Walsh], *A Dialogue Concerning Women, Being a Defence Of the Sex. Written to Eugenia* (1691), 32. The place of publication of contemporary tracts is London, unless noted otherwise.

[2] For the debate in England, see Katherine Usher Henderson and Barbara F. McManus, eds., *Half Humankind. Contexts and Texts of the Controversy about Women in England, 1540–1640* (Urbana and Chicago: University of Illinois Press, 1985); Suzanne W. Hull, *Chaste Silent & Obedient. English Books For Women 1475–1640* (San Marino: Huntington Library, 1982), 106–26; Robert H. Michel, "English Attitudes towards Women, 1640–1700," *Canadian Journal of History* 13 (1978): 35–60; and Jerome Nadelhaft, "The Englishwoman's Sexual Civil War: Feminist Attitudes towards Men, Women, and Marriage 1650–1740," *Journal of the History of Ideas* 43 (1982): 555–79. On the continent, see S. Davis, *The Idea of Woman in Renaissance Literature* (Lexington, Ky.: University Press of Kentucky, 1986), and Joan DeJean, *Tender Geographies: Women and the Origins of the Novel in France* (New York: Columbia University Press, 1991).

[3] Female politicization occurred earlier than sometimes assumed: see Dagmar Freist, "The King's Crown is the Whore of Babylon: Politics, Gender and Communication in Mid-Seventeenth-Century England," *Gender and History* 7 (1995): 458; Diane Willen, "The Politicization of Godly Women in Caroline England," unpub. paper. For aristocratic women: Barbara J. Harris, "Women and Politics in Early Tudor England," *The Historical Journal* 33 (1990): 259–81; Lois G. Schwoerer, *Lady Rachel Russell, "One of the Best of Women"* (Baltimore and London: Johns Hopkins University Press, 1988); Mark A. Kishlansky, *Parliamentary Selection: Social and Political Choice in Early Modern*

took various forms, none more important than that of printing their ideas on a variety of political, religious, administrative, social, and economic issues. For women the very act of using the printing press was of great significance. It was symbolic – a public defiance of traditional norms; in practical terms, it empowered women as nothing else had ever done, enabling them to make their ideas public, somewhat permanent, and available to a wider audience than would otherwise have been possible.[4] Further, in another fresh departure which cannot be explored in this chapter, women achieved a significant role in the printing industry as distributors (that is, mercuries, hawkers, and criers), publishers, printers, bookbinders, and booksellers. Thus females functioned at all the critical points in getting written material, much of it political, before the public for sale. The very existence of women in the industry and of their public political voice in print strikingly illustrates the distance that existed between prescription and reality even in that most masculine domain – politics.

It is, of course, true that if one applies to early modern England a conventional definition of politics – such as the competition for and exercise of political power – women played a minor role except at the highest level of monarch or, on the odd occasion, at the levels of sheriff or churchwarden. But today the conventional definition of politics seems rather quaint. Thirty years ago two scholars of modern America suggested a much broader definition which included even the act of following political events in a newspaper.[5] Ten years ago I applied to late seventeenth-century England some ideas for enlarging the concept of politics;[6] it seems to me now that the currently popular idea of "political culture"[7] provides a useful conceptual framework for showing that political participation may take many forms. Among those forms are dispensing patronage, influencing decision makers and elections, petitioning, demonstrating, gift-giving, entertaining, haranguing, reporting

England (Cambridge: Cambridge University Press, 1986). Women journalists appeared in France, but not in Germany, Italy, or the Netherlands: Nina Rattner Gelbart, "Female Journalists," in *A History of Women in the West*, eds. Natalie Zemon Davis and Arlette Farge (Cambridge, Mass., and London: Belknap Press of Harvard University Press, 1993), 420–21.

[4] Public preaching and/or prophesying also extended women's reach, but not so widely as the printing press.

[5] Gabriel Almond and Sidney Verba, *The Civic Culture: Political Attitudes and Democracy in Five Nations* (Princeton, N.J.: Princeton University Press, 1963), 53.

[6] Schwoerer, "Women and the Glorious Revolution," *Albion* (1986): 195–218.

[7] See Keith Baker, ed., *The French Revolution and the Creation of Modern Political Culture*, 2 vols. (Oxford: Pergamon Press, 1987–88); Lynn Hunt, *Politics, Culture, and Class in the French Revolution* (Berkeley: University of California Press, 1984); David Underdown, *Revel, Riot and Rebellion* (Oxford: Clarendon Press; New York: Oxford University Press, 1986).

seditious conduct, writing and disseminating ideas in printed form. This definition shifts the focus away from elite political structures (without denying their importance) and permits the inclusion of women from all classes (as well as more men).

Women's use of the printing press was of special importance because it positioned them in a "public space" that was outside of government and enabled them to comment on policies and actions of the government as well as those of religious institutions, whether the Anglican Church, the dissenting communities, or the Roman Catholic Church. Women's attitudes do not suggest a sharp dichotomy between, but rather the porosity of, private and public spheres. Interestingly, these developments invite modification of Jürgen Habermas's thesis.[8]

Although women writers in early modern England have received much scholarly attention during the past fifteen years, women's political writing and activity, except during the Civil Wars, have attracted less interest.[9] Several ideological and historiographical reasons no doubt explain why:[10] the feeling of some feminist historians that the study of politics should be abjured because it has traditionally excluded women; the stress on social history which no doubt deflected attention away from ideas; and the preoccupation with power relations *within* the family. But perhaps the most compelling reason was the difficulty of identifying and locating the scattered pertinent sources. Now, however, thanks to recent work, this last problem has receded.[11] At the present

[8] See Jürgen Habermas, *The Structural Transformation of the Public Sphere* (Cambridge, Mass.: MIT Press, 1988). Also Dena Godman, "Public Sphere and Private Life: Toward a Synthesis of Current Historiographical Approaches to the Old Regime," *History and Theory* 31 (1992): 1–20. And Retha Warnicke, "Private and Public: The Boundaries of Women's Lives in Early Stuart England," in *Privileging Gender in Early Modern England*, ed. J. R. Brink (Kirksville, Mo.: Sixteenth Century Journal Publishers, 1993), 123–40.

[9] Sectarian women during the 1640s and 1650s are an exception. See the early article by Ellen A. McArthur, "Women Petitioners and the Long Parliament," *English Historical Review* 24 (1909): 698–709. Interest was revived by Keith Thomas, "Women and the Civil War Sects," *Past and Present* 13 (1958): 42–62, and, in greater detail, by Higgins, "The Reactions of Women." Also, Phyllis Mack, *Visionary Women: Ecstatic Prophecy in Seventeenth-Century England* (Berkeley, Los Angeles, London: University of California Press, 1992). Marilyn L. Williamson, *Raising Their Voice: British Women Writers, 1650–1750* (Detroit, Mich.: Wayne State University Press, 1990), ch. 5. Rachel Weil, "The Politics of Legitimacy: Women and the Warming-pan Scandal," in *The Revolution of 1688–89: Changing Perspectives*, ed. Lois G. Schwoerer (Cambridge: Cambridge University Press, 1992), 65–82. Margaret J. M. Ezell, *Writing Women's Literary History* (Baltimore and London: Johns Hopkins University Press, 1993). Also references in n. 3 above.

[10] See Joan Scott, "Gender: A Useful Category of Historical Analysis," *American Historical Review* 91 (1986): 1053–75; Merry Wiesner, *Women and Gender in Early Modern Europe* (Cambridge: Cambridge University Press, 1993), 239–40.

[11] Patricia Crawford, "Women's Published Writings 1600–1700," *Women in English Society 1500–1800*, ed. Mary Prior (London and New York: Methuen, 1985), 211–82. Hilda L. Smith and Susan Cardinale, eds., *Women and the Literature of the Seventeenth*

time, then, the study of women's public political voice is feasible and opens up many related topics on which serious work is just beginning.

My concern in this chapter is with English women who, from about 1640 to about 1740, used the press to set out their ideas on many issues, both religious and secular in nature. The women I deal with are distinctive in that they come from the middle or lower middle ranks of society. Although only a few argued in theoretical terms, many applied political and religious ideologies to those issues, leaving no doubt that they understood the basic theoretical premises. An examination of the societal features that influenced these women to assume a public role, the rhetorical nature and substantive content of their publications, and the depth of their feminist self-consciousness and advocacy for change in women's status helps us to understand their significance for early modern England.

I

Many features of Stuart society (well-known to scholars) inhibited women from participating in public affairs and printing their views. In brief, religious injunction in homilies and sermons, courtesy books, prescriptive essays, custom, and patriarchal assumptions about family and state all promoted the idea that women were unsuited for political activity. For example, marriage manuals, among them R. Braithwaite's *The English Gentlewoman*, advised women to refrain from talking about "state matters" or "high points of divinity."[12] Patriarchical law and assumption held that every woman (except a widow) was subservient to a man – her father, her husband, or, in the absence of both, another male member of her family – and that her interest in public issues was to be subsumed in that of such persons. As traditionally defined, the family was inimical to a woman's assuming a public persona. Equally important, the education usually recommended for women gave them no training in political ideas, no rhetorical skills, and no expectation of public civic activity, but rather prepared them for household management, wifely duties, and child care.[13] As Hilda Smith has perceptively argued, early modern England defined the politically participating subject in masculine terms.[14]

Century: An Annotated Bibliography Based on Wing's Short-Title Catalogue (New York, Westport, Conn., and London: Greenwood Press, 1990). Also the RLIN/Eureka and the Early English Books microfilm projects.

[12] Quoted in Freist, "The King's Crown is the Whore of Babylon," 460.

[13] Writers like Richard Mulcaster and Juan Vives, although sometimes praised, really advocated a limited program of female education.

[14] Hilda Smith, "Masculinity as a Political Concept, 1600–1850," unpub. paper.

Further, a woman who violated the norm was liable to severe societal punishment, by the government, should her views be judged seditious, and/or by men who used the press to demean and humiliate her. Ironically, the press that enabled women to achieve a public forum was also the agent for circulating negative assessments of women. An activist woman was depicted as uninformed, unruly, disruptive of order, and, even more damaging, unchaste. For example, in the 1640s, critics of the very idea of public opinion used a derogatory image of a female to symbolize the popular press. They intimated that, like women who neglected their proper role, uninformed lower-class people who printed their views disrupted the state.[15] In 1650 a man excoriated his sister's "printing ... a Book" as an act "beyond the custom of your sex" that "doth rankly smell."[16] The attitude continued later in the century when a man condescendingly attributed a woman's interest in politics to a "Distemper." "Silence becomes your Sex," he counseled her, "especially in a matter so much above your Capacity and Reach."[17] Equally effective as deterrents were tracts that made women the butt of salacious jokes and stories. The notorious "Parliament of Women" tracts satirized women's imaginary election to a parliament, gave them comical names, like "Mrs. Whirligig" from Covent Garden, mocked their "political rights," and derided their complaints as centering on men's poor sexual service.[18] Deeply misogynist tracts had the same effect. Joseph Swetman's bawdy harangue stressed female lust and faithlessness,[19] while *A Discourse on Women Shewing Their Imperfections Alphabetically* started with avarice, and ran through the alphabet arguing that women excelled men in each undesirable quality.[20] Other examples abound, but the point is clear that there were powerful deterrents, all purveyed by the press, to women printing their views about public matters.

Yet some women overcame these obstacles. One hundred and twelve pamphlets by women appeared during the Civil War decade, compared

---

[15] Freist, "The King's Crown is the Whore of Babylon," 458–59, 462, 464.

[16] Quoted in Mack, *Visionary Women*, 118.

[17] *A Letter To A Gentlewoman Concerning Government* (1697) 2, 27.

[18] *A List of the Parliament of Women* (1679). Among many others: Henry Neville, *The Parliament of Ladies. Or divers remarkable passages of Ladies in Spring-Garden, in Parliament assembled [A Satire by H.N.]* (1647; 2 more editions, 1647; also 1768). See also *Now or Never: Or, A New Parliament of Women Assembled* (1656). *Great News from a Parliament of Women, Now Sitting in Rosemary-Lane* (1684).

[19] Joseph Swetman, *The Araignment Of Lewde, idle, froward, and unconstant women: Or the vanitie of them, choose you whether* (1615; reprinted 1660).

[20] The English translation of Jacques Olivier's *Alphabet de l'imperfection et malice des femmes* (1617) appeared in 1662. A popular piece, *Alphabet* had nine editions in England and France. See Felicity Nussbaum, *The Brink of All We Hate: English Satire on Women, 1660–1750* (Lexington, Ky.: University Press of Kentucky, 1984).

to only 42 tracts during the preceding *forty* years. From 1640 to 1700 there were approximately 700 tracts by women out of a total of approximately 53,350 tracts – about 1.2 per cent. The exact number of political and religious tracts by women is uncertain, but I would put it at about 300 written by about 30 women.[21] Whatever the precise figures, they are larger than might be expected. In contrast to French noble-women writing at the same time, most of these English women came from middle- or lower middle-class origins: thus, Katherine Chidley was the wife of a tailor, Anne Docwra the daughter of a justice of the peace, Elinor James the wife of a printer, and Elizabeth Poole a seamstress. They lived in or had some connection with London. As to religion, sectarian women were the majority, but many religious persuasions were represented: Chidley was an Independent, James an Anglican, Anna Trapnel a Fifth Monarchist, and the anonymous author of *An Answer to Pereat Papa: Or, A Reply by way of a Letter from a Gentlewoman to a Person of Quality* a Roman Catholic. For all these women, religious and political concerns were inextricably linked, but one should not under-value the secular nature of some of their interests. Despite their command of language, ideas, and especially the Bible and religious writings, they were neither learned nor (with few exceptions) formally educated.[22] Deeply committed, they were undeterred by the personal embarrassment, physical pain, and pecuniary costs of punishment. Finally, in contrast to earlier women who had *talked* and written *privately* about politics, they clearly recognized the popular press as important and the most effective agent available to women of their social standing.

How can one explain their violation of normative rules of conduct? Was there anything in this restrictive society that encouraged them? Surprisingly, perhaps, there was. First, the upheavals of the century from the Civil Wars on through the Revolution of 1688–89 created successive contexts favorable to unorthodox behavior. Tumultuous events turned the world "upside down,"[23] and women (like men, of course) were moved to speak out. Second, religion animated and empowered women, giving them confidence and a sense of responsibility for their church and society. Although not promoting the equality of

---

[21] My calculations include the Quaker Margaret Fell (Fox) and aristocratic women like Margaret Cavendish, Lady Newcastle, and Lady Eleanor Davies, but their writings figure little in this chapter. See Crawford, "Women's Published Writings 1600–1700," 212, 214, 265, 266, and 267 (Appendix 2); and Judith E. Gardner, "Women in the Book Trade, 1641–1700: A Preliminary Survey," *Gutenberg Jahrbuch* 53 (1978): 345.

[22] Elinor James confided that God "taught my Heart and my Heart taught me my Book" (*Mrs. James's Reasons* [1715], 4).

[23] Christopher Hill, *The World Turned Upside Down: Radical Ideas during the English Revolution* (London and New York: Viking Press, 1972) provides the classic statement.

women, radical sectarian groups (especially Quakers) allowed females more opportunities in the 1640s and 1650s than at any time earlier for the expression of religious and political views. But women of all religious persuasions saw themselves as fulfilling God's will in the public role they undertook. Third, pushing the boundaries of the traditionally defined family was possible for an energetic, highly motivated woman. The social origins and role in the family economy[24] of the women studied helped them escape the full weight of the restrictions mandated by ideal female behavior. These women expressed their independence in various ways: Chidley refused to be churched after childbirth, later traveled outside London with her son, Samuel (a Leveller treasurer), to spread the Independency message, and organized Leveller petitions.[25] Elinor James visited King James II in his bedchamber one night begging mercy for a doomed Dissenting minister.[26] She boldly suggested that she visit the Pope as James's emissary.[27] Undeterred by caring for her "many children . . . without any maid," she still found time, she said, "to come to Whitehall" on behalf of the public's interest.[28]

Fourth, the emergence of coffee houses benefited women. In their early days, coffee houses welcomed men and women of diverse classes, exposing them to and perhaps engaging them in political discourse and news.[29] Fifth, the example of female leadership at the highest reaches of the government also arguably encouraged the politically conscious woman. The memory of Queen Elizabeth I was kept alive, in part by the Whigs who exploited it for political purposes. The presence of Queen Mary II and Queen Anne provided concrete examples of female political capacity. The apologia for Mary as princess of Orange and as queen of England portrayed women in the most flattering terms.[30] Royal apologia reinforced the positive assessments of women's character that also appeared, as, for example, in 1670 in Henry Care's translation of Agrippa's *On the Excellence of Women*, or in 1677 in Poulaine de la Barre's *The woman as good as the man*, which maintained that women possessed the ability to perform any kind of political office. In addition,

---

[24] Susan Amussen, *An Ordered Society. Gender and Class in Early Modern England* (Oxford and New York: B. Blackwell's Press, 1988), esp. 119–20.

[25] Ian Gentles, "London Levellers in the English Revolution: The Chidleys and their Circle," *Journal of Ecclesiastical History* 29 (1978): 282, 285–86, 292.

[26] *Mrs. James Prayer for the Queen and Parliament, and Kingdom, to, that they may pray God to divert His Judgments from them* (1710).

[27] *Mrs. James's Reasons*, 4.

[28] Elinor James, *May It Please your most sacred Majesty* (n.p., 1685).

[29] Steve Pincus, "'Coffee Politicians Does Create': Coffeehouses and Restoration Political Culture," *Journal of Modern History* 67 (1995): 807–34.

[30] See Lois G. Schwoerer, "Images of Queen Mary II, 1689–95," *Renaissance Quarterly* 42 (1989): 717–48.

women themselves supported women's right to publish their writings and defended the female sex, as did Sarah Egerton in *Female Advocate*.[31] Such tracts helped to counterbalance the misogynist tracts mentioned above.

Still other developments of positive importance for women included the increase in female literacy in London.[32] A female audience was recognized and cultivated as early as the 1670s and was well established from the 1690s on. The fact that women achieved a wide role in the printing industry and that some, like Abigail[33] Baldwin, Jane Curtis, Joan Broome, Tace or Stacy Sowle, and Elizabeth Whitlock, became well known was arguably an inducement to venturing into print. Further, developments in the history of ideas at the end of the century indirectly advanced women's position. Cartesian ideas and methodology challenged the established intellectual canon and ways of reasoning, and Lockean ideas weakened the patriarchal order in family and state.[34] The published work of a group of intellectually inclined women now known as "Reason's Disciples" may have had the same effect.[35] Finally, scientific advancements encouraged a rational view of society and forced the retreat of Aristotelian derogatory notions about women.[36] In sum, these general features of Stuart society created a context within which individual women moved confidently enough to violate prescriptive rules.

[31] The full title is: *Or, An answer To A Late Satyr Against The Pride, Lust and Inconstancy, etc. of Woman. Written by a Lady in Vindication of her Sex* (1686).

[32] David Cressy, *Literacy and the Social Order: Reading and Writing in Tudor and Stuart England* (New York, 1980). Margaret Spufford, "First Steps in Literacy: The Reading and Writing Experiences of the Humblest Seventeenth-Century Autobiographers," *Social History* 4 (1979): 407–35. Margaret Spufford, *Small Books and Pleasant Histories: Popular Fiction and Its Readership in Seventeenth-Century England* (Athens, Ga.: University of Georgia Press, 1981). Keith Thomas, "The Meaning of Literacy in Early Modern England," in *The Written Word: Literacy in Transition*, ed. Gerd Baumann (Oxford: Clarendon Press; New York: Oxford University Press, 1986), 97–131. Jonathan Barry, "Literacy and Literature in Popular Culture," in *Popular Culture in England, c. 1500–1850*, ed. Tim Harris (New York: St. Martin's Press, 1995), 69–94.

[33] Not "Anne" as usually given: Michael Treadwell, "London Trade Publishers 1675–1750," *The Library*, 6th ser., 4 (1982): 110, n. 19.

[34] Gordon Schochet, *Patriarchalism in Political Thought: The Authoritarian Family and Political Speculation and Attitudes Especially in Seventeenth-Century England* (New York and Oxford: B. Blackwell's Press, 1975). Marjorie Nicholson, "The Early State of Cartesianism in England," *Studies in Philology* 25 (1929): 364–65; cf. Erica Harth, *Cartesian Women: Versions and Subversions of Rational Discourse in the Old Regime* (Ithaca, N.Y.: Cornell University Press, 1992).

[35] Hilda Smith, *Reason's Disciples: Seventeenth-Century English Feminists* (Urbana, Ill.: University of Illinois Press, 1982).

[36] Ian MacLean, *The Renaissance Notion of Woman: A Study in the Fortunes of Scholasticism and Medical Science in European Intellectual Life* (London and Cambridge: Cambridge University Press, 1980).

II

With some notable exceptions, for example Mary Astell, whose intellectual contributions are studied elsewhere in this collection, women's writings on religion and public issues neither rest on theoretical statements nor offer an original political theory. Rather, they are topical or responsive to events or circumstances of the time. None of the writings that I consider can compare in complexity, learning, or originality with the work of the great male political theorists of the period, like Hobbes, Harrington, or Locke. But, few other men equal those giants, and there are well-known reasons to explain why women failed to develop theoretical models.[37] That failure, however, does not mean that women were unable to grasp the tenets of political or legal theories. For example, Elizabeth Poole, in offering advice to the Army Council at its request[38] in December 1648, deployed one of the analogues of the theory of divine right kingship – that the king was the "father and husband" of the nation – to argue that the army must not harm the king. The army, as the king's wife, cannot raise a hand against him, for, just as a wife who "suffereth [her husband's] terror to her flesh," so the army, no matter the provocation, cannot harm the king. Applying another tenet of divine right theory, Poole maintained that only God, not the army, could punish the king.[39] Similarly, Elizabeth Lilburne rested her campaign in 1649 to obtain the release from jail of her husband John, the Leveller leader, on Leveller theory. Since the law is an "equal inheritance," the House of Commons must preserve the "Rights, Liberties and Freedomes of the People." Expounding on the jury rights of freeborn Englishmen, Lilburne insisted that her husband be tried by "men of his owne condition" in the House of Commons rather than in the House of Lords.[40]

A royalist, Anne Halkett, also showed an understanding of political ideas. In a rigorous conversation in 1651 with a Cromwellian army officer, she denied that success justified evil actions and, repudiating the right of resistance, insisted that no Scriptural authority existed for

---

[37] Berenice Carroll, "The Politics of Originality: Women and the Class System of the Intellect," *Journal of Women's History* 2 (1990): 136–63.

[38] Mack, *Visionary Women*, 78–79, 99–100. Richard L. Graves and Robert Zaller, eds., *Biographical Dictionary of British Radicals*, 3 vols. (Brighton, Sussex: Harvester Press, 1982), III, 49.

[39] Elizabeth Poole, *A Vision: Wherein is manifested the disease and cure of the Kingdome* (1649), 2, 3, 4, 5, 6.

[40] *To the Chosen and betrusted Knights, Citizens, and Burgesses, assembled in the High and Supreame Court of Parliament. The humble Petition of Elizabeth Lilburne, Wife to Lieut. Col. John Lilburne* (n.p., n.d.).

executing a king.[41] In 1659, Priscilla Cotton, influenced no doubt by Sir Thomas More's *Utopia*, painted a pointed fantasy (obviously in implicit criticism) of an ideal community in which state and church were separate, all faiths lived in harmony, no one attempted to suppress "heretics," and leaders provided hospitals, universal education for boys and girls, and workhouses for the poor.[42] In that same year, Sarah Jinner erected her criticism of Cromwell on a theory of government, writing that government "hath no other foundation than the humour of the people." Reflecting knowledge of a theory of rebellion, Jinner declared that people are not "bound to obey well, when governors do not govern well."[43] The Catholic author of *An Answer To Pereat Papa* built an argument on law and religious and civil history to prove that a Roman Catholic can *legally* inherit the English crown. Clearly, women of all political persuasions had the capacity to grasp and apply political theories to specific circumstances, an astonishing fact considering their lack of a classical education.

Religious conviction linked to a sense of social responsibility was central to these tracts, appearing in several forms. Bitterly anti-clerical, Sarah Blackborow condemned the "Ministers and Teachers Of The People Who Preach for hire, and persecute, and throw in prison ... the children of the Lord."[44] Grace Barwick and Mary (Rande) Cary called for the removal of tithes, described by Barwick as "the very crying oppression of our nation."[45] Some women championed religious toleration, none more powerfully than Katherine Chidley. Answering the Reverend Thomas Edwards in 1645 in three hard-hitting pamphlets, Chidley justified toleration on grounds of the sanctity of individual conscience and the principle of separatism. Using copious biblical references she insisted that humble people were capable of understanding religion and managing their own congregations and acidly criticized the Church of England.[46] Mary Howgill called Cromwell a

---

[41] Anne Halkett, *Memoirs*, 59–61, reprinted in *The Cultural Identity of Seventeenth-Century Woman: A Reader*, compiled and ed. by N. H. Keeble (London and New York: Routledge, 1994), 196–97.

[42] Priscilla Cotton, *A Briefe Description by way of supposition holding forth to the Parliament and such as have but common reason, wherein a true Commonwealth consisteth: as also the grand enemies of this Commonwealth plainly discovered* ([London], 1659).

[43] Sarah Jinner, *The Woman's Almanack: Or, Prognostication For ever, Shewing the nature of the Planets, with the Events that shall befall Women and children born under them. With several Predictions very useful for the Female Sex* (1659).

[44] Saraah [sic] Blackborow, *A Visit To The Spirit In Prison And An Invitation to all people to come to Christ the light of the World* (1658), 4–5. Also Judith Boulbie, *A Testimony for Truth against all Hireling-Priests and Deceivers* (1665).

[45] Grace Barwick, *To all present Rulers, whether Parliament or whomsoever of England* (1659).

[46] Chidley, *Justification of the Independent Churches of Christ Being an answer to Mr. Edwards his book* (1641), 27, 29, 42, 52, 55, 58, 61, 64, 67. Also Chidley, *A New-Years-Gift, or A*

"stinking dunghill" because he had acted cruelly toward "them who are in the fear of the Lord."[47] Anne Docwra, a well-educated Quaker woman, argued in *An Epistle of Love and Good Advice* (1683) that the state and the Church of England have no legal power to persecute Protestant dissenters. Charging "high-flown Churchmen" with making "a Trade of Religion," she insisted that "God alone" should "be King and Law-giver in mens Consciences."[48] In 1687 Docwra justified the king's use of the suspending power.[49] She provides an important and neglected example of a *woman* Dissenter supporting James II. Elinor James was also a proponent of liberty of conscience, but on different grounds. Spiritedly defending the Anglican Church, James described Dissenters as politically ambitious "Disturbers of Government"[50] and endorsed toleration on grounds that James II deserved obedience.[51] These women (and others) merit more credit than they have received for expressing the idea of religious toleration.

Women also commented and offered practical advice on issues of public policy, including administrative, social, and economic matters. Although without practical political experience, they somehow understood how government worked. For example, Cary suggested in 1653 that Cromwell appoint commissioners in the counties to dispatch business and hear complaints, thereby saving time and money by avoiding trips to London.[52] In 1681 Joan Philips confidently told the Duke of Monmouth how to conduct himself in the troubled politics of 1681.[53] Elinor James commented on London affairs, recommending a candidate for magistrate, urging a ban on squibs, and advising on the fate of the Old East India Company, favoring it over the New.[54]

Further, a strong social conscience accompanied by demands for

Brief Exhortation to Mr. Thomas Edwards (1645). See comment by Gentles, "London Levellers," 284–86.

[47] Mary Howgill, *A Remarkable Letter of Mary Howgill to Oliver Cromwell, called Protector* ([London], 1657), 1. Also, Judith Eedes, *A Warning to all the Inhabitants of the Earth* (1659).

[48] Anne Docwra, *An Epistle of Love and Good Advice To My Old Friends and Fellow Sufferers in the Late Times, The Old Royalists And their Posterity And to all others that have any sincere Desires towards God* (1683), 4, 5, 8, 9. Also *A Brief Discovery of the Work of the Enemy* (1683). For Docwra, see Mack, *Visionary Women*, 315–18.

[49] Anne Docwra, *Spiritual Community, Vindicated amongst people of different persuasions in some things* (1687).

[50] Elinor James, *Mrs. James's Defence of the Church of England* (1687), 3, 4.

[51] Elinor James, *Mrs. James's vindication of the Church of England in an Answer to a Pamphlet entituled a New Test of the Church of England's Loyalty* ([London], 1687), 7.

[52] Mary [Rande] Cary, *Twelve New Proposals to the Supreme Governours of the Three nations now assembled at Westminster concerning the Propagation of the Gospel, New modling of the Universities, Reformation of the Laws, supply of the necessities of the Poor* (1653), Proposal no. 8.

[53] [Joan Philips], *Advice to His Grace [Duke of Monmouth]* [1681].

[54] Elinor James, *Mrs. Jame's [sic] Apology because of Unbelievers* (1694); Also *Sir, My Lord*

reform characterized many of the tracts. For example, in 1653 Mary (Rande) Cary demanded that the government take care of the poor, declaring that it was a disgrace to see beggars going "up and down the land." Offering a specific and practical solution, she advised raising money by imposing a tax of three pence on all inland letters and a tax for sealing every contract and bargain.[55] On the eve of the Restoration, Hester (Esther) Biddle, a Quaker, painted a vivid picture of poverty in London, describing how well-to-do citizens of the city, in "gaudy apparel" with "outstretched neck" pass by the poor who, faint for lack of food, "lieth in [the] streets." Specifically fingering "all ye Kings and princes" as well as "Lords and Ladies," and "Priests and Jesuites," she warned that God would punish them so severely that they would "sit like a Widdow . . . bemoaning herself."[56] Elinor James also worried about the unfortunate, calling in 1683 upon London leaders and "Citizens" to think of those that starve and "not to hugg up your Money as if it were a God."[57] Later, James proposed to the Commons and the king that the government recover the former lands of the Roman Catholic Church which Henry VIII had "freely" given away and use the income for charitable purposes.[58] Although politically naive, the solution testifies to James's historical understanding and political imagination.

Joan Whitrow, describing herself as inflamed with love for mankind and especially for orphans,[59] wrote in passionate terms about the plight of the poor. Upbraiding King William III and Queen Mary II for lavishness and extravagance, she proposed that the Brewer's Tax (which hurt the poor) be levied on the "rich of all sorts," including "drunkards . . . whoremongers, the proud . . . playhouses and every one that goes to them."[60]

Showing great capacity for administrative organization, Elizabeth Cellier, a well-known Catholic midwife, in June 1687 addressed a paper to James II, asking him to support her "Scheme for the Foundation of a Royal Hospital." She envisioned a haven for foundlings and a college for midwives administered by women, with minimal involvement of

Major [sic] and the Aldermen, his Brethren [1690]; To the Honourable House of Commons (1699).

55 Cary, Twelve New Proposals, Proposals nos. 4, 6.

56 Hester (Esther) Biddle, A Warning From The Lord God of Life and Power, Unto Thee O City Of London, And To The Suburbs round about thee: To call thee and them to repentance & amendment of life, without which you cannot see God (1660), 11, 17.

57 Elinor James, To the Right Honourable, the Lord Mayor and Court of Aldermen, and all the rest of the Loyal Citizens (1683).

58 Elinor James, Most Dear Soveraign, I cannot but love (n.p., n.d.).

59 Joan Whitrow, Faithful Warnings (1697), 75.

60 Joan Whitrow, To Queen Mary: The Humble Salutation, and Faithful Greeting of the Widow Whitrow (1690), 12, 17, 18.

male professionals.[61] Although approved by the king, the proposal was assailed by critics and lost in the confusion of the Revolution of 1688–89.[62]

Another matter that animated Cary and Whitrow was the condition of the universities. Concerned about the nation's moral decay, Whitrow charged that the universities turn out young men lacking in moral integrity who as leaders of churches and schools set a poor example for young and socially inferior persons.[63] Cary recommended that scholarships be provided to fund the education of the poor and that universities be democratized. Her call for employing the "publick treasure for the publick benefit" was deeply radical, but she made no radical demand for the admission of women to universities.

Economic issues quite unrelated to domestic household economy also engaged the attention of women writers, an unexpected feature in view of their supposed confinement to the household. For example, in a printed petition of February 1641/42, London women identified as "wives of tradesmen and citizens" petitioned Queen Henrietta Maria not to leave the country because demand for goods they produced and sold would plummet.[64] The petition is a nice example of women showing self-serving interest in economic affairs. Similarly, Mary (Rande) Cary criticized employment standards in the Customs Office and other government offices. Castigating the patronage system, she recommended appointing godly men and, if none was available, men of the "most civil and blameless conversation." Agreeing that men of superior learning and talent should earn more than others, she insisted that no one should be enriched by service to the state.[65]

Elinor James had decided views on the printing industry. An experienced observer of "above forty years,"[66] in 1695, she boldly offered the House of Commons suggestions on how to reform the industry. Appealing to political interest, she predicted that if her advice were followed (basically to concentrate printing in the hands of a few London

---

[61] The title continued: "and Raising a Revenue of Five or Six Thousand Pounds a Year, by, and for the Maintenance of a Corporation of skilful Midwives and such Foundlings, or exposed Children, as shall be admitted therein." In *Harleian Miscellany*, 12 vols. (London: Printed for Robert Dutton [Harleian Miscellany], 1808–11), IX, 191–98.

[62] Elizabeth Cellier, *To Dr.——, An Answer to his Queries concerning the Colledg of Midwives* (1688). See Anne Barbeau Gardiner, "Elizabeth Cellier in 1688 on Envious Doctors and Heroic Midwives Ancient and Modern," *Eighteenth-Century Life* 14 (1990): 24–34.

[63] Whitrow, *Faithful Warnings*, 1–2.

[64] Quoted in Higgins, "The Reactions of Women," 188–89.

[65] Cary, *Twelve New Proposals*, Proposals nos. 10, 11.

[66] Elinor James, *Advice to all Printers in General* (n.p., n.d.), in John Nichols, *Literary Anecdotes of the Eighteenth Century; Comprising Memoirs of William Bowyer, F.S.A.*, 9 vols. (London, 1812), I, 307.

masters), "no one will go into holes and corners to Print Treason."[67] In another piece she advised press people on how to preserve harmony between masters and journeymen, train apprentices, and avoid competition among masters for promising apprentices.[68] Joan Whitrow was also interested in economic issues: her concern was to protect against false weight and measures, because they "rob the poor of their right."[69] Finally, an anonymous author identifying herself as "one of that sex" printed in 1678 *Advice to the women and maidens of London* to protect themselves against poverty. Recommending bookkeeping as an alternative employment, this author argued that accounting was no more difficult than needlework and illustrated the point by providing a sample ledger and inventory. The piece is remarkable for its prescience, the author's confidence in women's ability to master arithmetic and book-keepings skills, and her interest in job creation and training.

In sum, throughout the era, women raised their voices in print on both religious and secular questions that were remarkably broad considering the societal obstacles that they faced. They wrote about religion, politics, economic and social policy, and administrative matters in ways that revealed their knowledge of the workings of government. Several achieved notoriety, especially Elinor James. Narcissus Luttrell thought her newsworthy; Catholic clerics attempted to convert her; John Dryden, a lesser poet Elizabeth Rome, and others answered one of her tracts. James was credited with having "edified the Tripe-Women and Convinced the Porters" of her view of the Anglican Church. A contemporary dubbed her admiringly the "She-State-Politician."[70]

III

Was there a distinctive female political voice? What kinds of rhetorical devices were used? Defenses constructed? One woman insisted that when women used "equal Care ... [people] will no more be able to [discern] Man's stile from a Woman's, than they can tell whether this

---

[67] Mrs. *James's Application to the Honourable the Commons Assembled in Parliament, On the behalf of the Printers* (n.p., 1695[?]).

[68] Elinor James, *Advice to all Printers in General*, I, 307.

[69] Joan Whitrow, *To Queen Mary*, 18, 19.

[70] Narcissus Luttrell, *A Brief Historical Relation of State Affairs from September 1678 to April 1714*, 6 vols. (Oxford: Oxford University Press, 1857), I, 617. James, *Most Dear Sovereign.* John Dryden, *The Hind and the Panther, A Poem, in Three Parts* (London, 1687), preface, *The Works of John Dryden, now first collected in eighteen volumes,* (ed. Walter Scott [London: Printed for William Miller, 1808], x, 116–17). *An Address of Thanks, On Behalf of the Church of England, to Mris [sic] James, For Her Worthy Vindication of that Church* (1687). *Life and errors of John Dunton*, ed. J. B. Nichols, 2 vols. (London: Printed by and for J. Nichols, 1818), I, 334.

was written with a Goose's Quill or a Gander's."[71] In many instances women's writing is indeed indistinguishable from men's. Like men, women piled up examples, interlaced their text with copious quotations from the Bible, appealed to history, mentioned contemporary affairs, and sometimes cited learned authors. Whitrow especially displayed her knowledge of Socrates, ancient history, and languages. They dealt with the same subjects as men, offering no "feminist agenda." Like men, also, they were capable of sharp *ad hominem* attacks, as exemplified in Chidley's rude dismissal of Reverend Thomas Edwards (her opponent in the press) as "bloody minded," irrational, and silly, or in an anonymous Catholic woman's indignation over the stupidities of her correspondent. Like men, too, their announced audience was inclusive; they sought to reach members of lowly occupations that one author listed – "Taylors, Feltmakers, Buttonmakers, Shepherds, Ploughmen."[72] Sarah Cheevers saluted "All People Upon the face of the Earth" with her *Clear Manifestation Of The True Light*. A remarkable feature of these pamphlets, considering the boldness and self-confidence that the gesture suggests, is that many addressed persons at the highest reaches of government. For example, Mary (Rande) Cary aimed high in directing her *Twelve New Proposals* to *the Supreme Governours of the Three Nations now assembled at Westminster* (1653). Judith Boulbie expressed her indignation in *To all Justices of the Peace or other Magistrates to whom this may come* (1667). Elinor James, over many years, wrote to many leaders: James Stuart, as duke of York and king of England, William as prince of Orange and king of England, the Lord Mayor and aldermen of London, the 1689 Convention, the House of Commons, and the House of Lords. In sum, tracts by men and women had many features in common.

In some instances, however, there are clear marks that betray a woman's authorship beyond the fact that sometimes her name appears on the tract, as in the case of Hester Biddle, Katherine Evans, and Elinor James.[73] First, the imagery employed may suggest female authorship. Although it is not impossible for a man to draw upon the imagery of childbirth, passages that analogize London's suffering to a woman in

---

[71] [Judith Drake], *An Essay in Defence of the Female Sex. In Which are inserted characters of a pedant, a squire, a beau, a vertuoso, a poestaster, a city-critick, etc. in a Letter to a Lady* (1696), quoted in Smith and Cardinale, *Women and the Literature of the Seventeenth Century*, 53.

[72] Katherine Chidley, *The [J]ustification of the Independent Churches of Christ, Being an answer to Mr. Edwards his booke, which hee hath written against the government of Christs Church* (1641), 22–23.

[73] For example, [H]ester Biddle, *A Warning From The Lord God of Life and Power, Unto Thee O City Of London, And To The Suburbs round about thee* (1660). Katherine Evans, *A Brief Discovery Of God's Eternal Truth; And, A Way opened to the simple hearted* (1663). James's name appeared on many tracts.

childbirth (as in Biddle's tract) or a soul calling out to be delivered of sin to a "woman in travail crying to be delivered" (as in Judith Eedes's essay) seem to me to signal a woman's voice.[74] So, too, does the word picture of a people whom God punishes sitting "like a Widow ... bemoaning herself."[75] Moreover, it seems unlikely that a male would offer the idea (intrinsically Neoplatonic), as Blackborow did, that two seeds exist in humans: the "Seed of the Woman and the Seed of the Serpent." The one brings forth heavenly things and "begets to life"; the other "begets into the death."[76] Second, excessive self-deprecation seems to signal a female writer. Sectarian women devalued themselves, as no man would have done, insisting that they were unlearned and unfit for the task of writing. Thus, Chidley asserted that responding to the Reverend Edwards was "most befitting a woman" like herself, because if he won their debate, his victory would count for less because he had vanquished only a woman.[77] In a different way Quaker visionaries usually insisted that they were only the vessels of the Lord and that it was He speaking through them. For example, Sarah Blackborow declared that her witnessing came from God: "If I bore witness of myself, it were not true; but my witness stands in him."[78] For obvious reasons, these rhetorical strategies deflected criticism and provided protection. Yet, on the other hand, some women adopted a diametrically different strategy, insisting that they knew what they were talking about. For example, Mary Marsin emphatically denied that she read the Bible as she "fancied," saying that it was others who had made the Bible a "nose of Wax."[79] Mary Pope announced that it had taken her three years to write her *Treatise on Magistracy*; her confidence in the result was high enough for her to ask that her book be examined by "three or four godly men." Elinor James left no doubt and no apology that she was a woman. Underscoring her credentials, she reminded her readers that she had "moved in Government ... above 30 years."[80] and insisted that everything printed under her name she wrote herself without being "put on by any man."[81]

Did women authors protest women's status in society? According to a

---

[74] Biddle, *A Warning From The Lord God*. Eedes, *A Warning to all the Inhabitants of the Earth*.
[75] Biddle, *A Warning from the Lord God*, 17.
[76] Blackborow, *A Visit To The Spirit*, 12 [p. 14 recto].
[77] Chidley, *The [J]ustification of the Independent Churches of Christ*, 1, 80. Also *A New-Yeares Gift*, A2, 12, 22, 23.
[78] Blackborow, *A Visit To The Spirit*, 7 [p. 9 recto].
[79] Mary Marsin, *The Womans Advocate* (1697).
[80] Elinor James, *Mrs. James's Humble Letter to the House of Lords* (1699).
[81] James, *Mrs. Jame's [sic] Apology because of Unbelievers*.

recent assessment, they did not.[82] Although true that no woman asked directly for such change and some denied advocating it, others showed sharp impatience. Whatever the strategy of male Levellers,[83] the Leveller women's petition (1649) laid claim in print to "an equal interest" in "those liberties and securities" that protected men.[84] Sarah Jenner referred to men as "Caterpillers" who "would engrosse all knowledge" to themselves.[85] The most outspoken complaints in mid-century were those of Margaret Cavendish, duchess of Newcastle, who protested that "men from their first Creation usurped a Supremacy to themselves, although we were made equal by nature." This "tyrannical Government they have kept ever since ... They will not let us divide the world Equally with them, as to Govern and Command."[86]

Such harsh judgments multiplied during the Restoration. Describing men as "unjust invaders of [women's] native Rights," *Triumphs of Female Wit* (1683) charged that men were fearful of losing "their Empire" if women understood public affairs "as much as them."[87] Elinor James wrote (1687) wistfully but pointedly about the problems she faced: "Oh, that I were but a Man, I would study night and Day, and I do not doubt but I should be more than a Conqueror ... and so I hope to be nevertheless."[88] There was no such poignancy in Elizabeth Johnson's unsparing condemnation of men in 1697: "We [women] think with reason, that our fundamental constitutions are destroyed." "There are ... notorious violations on the liberties of freeborn English Women," she asserted, using the word "freeborn" with all its resonances.[89] Equally emphatic condemnations appeared in tracts in 1735 and 1749: the one asserted that the legal condition of English wives was worse than slavery, and, invoking Hobbes, claimed original dominion for women.[90]

---

[82] Williamson, *Raising Their Voices*, 259, 264.

[83] See Ann Hughes, "Gender and Politics in Leveller Literature," in *Political Culture and Cultural Politics in Early Modern England: Essays Presented to David Underdown*, eds. Susan D. Amussen and Mark A. Kishlansky (Manchester: Manchester University Press; New York: St. Martin's Press, 1995), 174–77.

[84] Quoted in Higgins, "The Reactions of Women," 217.

[85] Jinner, *The Woman's Almanack.*

[86] The Right Honorable, the Lady Margaret Newcastle, *The Worlds Olio* (1655), The Preface to the Reader. And *CCXI Sociable Letters* (1664), #16, p. 27, both quoted in Smith, *Reason's Disciples*, 79, 80.

[87] Anon., *Triumphs of Female Wit, In Some Pindarick Odes, or the Emulation ... an Answer to an Objector against Female Ingenuity and capacity of learning* (1683), 1, 4.

[88] Elinor James, *Mrs. James's vindication of the Church of England*, preface. Also *Mrs. James's Reasons Humbly Presented to the Lords Spiritual and Temporal* (1715), 4.

[89] Preface to Elizabeth Singer Rowe's *Poems on Several Occasions*, quoted in Smith, *Reason's Disciples*, 172–73. See also [Drake], *An Essay in Defence of the Female Sex*, Preface, 21, 23, 25.

[90] Anon., *The Hardships of the English Laws in Relation to Wives. With an explanation of the*

The other tract bitterly reproached men for their "spirit of violence, shameless injustice, and lawless oppression."[91] In sum, although no woman entered a specific claim, their words leave no doubt in my mind that they were desirous of changing the restraints on their public role and activities and their position at law.

IV

Custom, religion, prescription, patriarchal law, family structure, and ridicule were powerful deterrents to women exercising a public political role. Yet some women, animated by religious fervor and concerned about religion as well as secular issues, their numbers relatively small but still notable, did so anyway. Starting at the time of the Civil War, mostly middle- and lower-class women, although without practical political experience, printed their views on a broad range of issues, offering practical advice and showing their understanding of political and religious theories. Many focused on toleration for the dissenting communities. But women remained at the margins of public life and enjoyed no change in their status at law. By the mid-eighteenth century their polemical voice had faded, only to be revived stronger and more permanently by century's end.

Are we to conclude then that the women studied here were without significance? That their "meddl[ing] with State Affairs" was inconsequential? On the contrary, their activities provide a different perspective on the unfolding course of events, underlining the breakdown of society and showing how deeply held and widespread was anxiety over political, religious, social, and economic issues. These women illustrate (as underclass men did too) the steps that were available to persons outside the established political order, show the distance between prescription and reality, and suggest greater opportunities for women in Stuart England than previously accepted. They helped to create a new public space and change the nature of early modern English political and print culture. Their writings provided a backdrop for the emergence of a group of feminists in the eighteenth century. Moreover, women's activities were important enough to heighten awareness of the political role of women, moving contemporaries variously to response, ridicule,

---

original Curse of Subjection passed upon the Woman. In an Humble Address to the Legislature (1735), 46, 47, 49, 59, 63, 68.

[91] Sophia, *A Person of Quality, Woman not Inferior to Man: Or, A short and modest Vindication of the natural Right of the Fair-Sex to a perfect Equality of Power, Dignity, and Esteem with the Men*, quoted in Nadelhaft, "The Englishwoman's Sexual Civil War," 560, 573.

and disparagement, and the government to punishment. In sum, these females challenged patriarchal ideology, defying the stereotypic image of women as confined to the home and silent there with no interest in, knowledge of, or influence over public affairs. They have been too long ignored; their presence and activities require historians to readjust their understanding of both early modern English women and political culture.

Acknowledgments

I thank Michael J. Moore, editor, for permission to draw upon my article, "Women and the Glorious Revolution," *Albion* (1986): 195–218 and renew thanks to librarians named there. Laura Cofield, Acquisitions Librarian, secured microfilm of several tracts not at the Folger Shakespeare Library. Peter Blayney answered questions about the English press, while Catherine Lesko, Nancy Klein Maguire, Hilda Smith, and Elizabeth Sassi shared some findings with me. I learned from unpublished essays by Carolyn Edie, Hilda Smith, and Diane Willen. Barbara Taft and Michael Mendle commented on a draft of this chapter. Sara Fentress helped confirm some citations. I warmly thank them all and cheerfully acknowledge that errors that remain are my own.

4 Contextualizing Aphra Behn: plays, politics, and party, 1679–1689

Melinda Zook

The recent explosion of interest in the seventeenth-century English playwright, novelist, and poet, Aphra Behn, has led to numerous and diverse explorations of her life and work. Behn's colorful if often mysterious life has been the subject of five biographies and the stuff of at least two novels.[1] She has been celebrated as one of the most prolific and popular playwrights of the Restoration and an early practitioner of the novel.[2] Scholars have portrayed her as a thorough-going feminist, a libertine and an opponent of the domestic tyranny of patriarchy, and an abolitionist, writing one of the first anti-slavery novels in Western literature.[3]

Despite the recent avalanche of scholarship, little has been written

[1] George Woodstock, *The Incomparable Aphra* (London: Boardman, 1948); W. J. Cameron, *New Light on Aphra Behn* (Auckland: The University of Auckland Press, 1961); Maureen Duffy, *The Passionate Shepherdess: Aphra Behn, 1640–1689* (London: Jonathan Cape, 1977); Angeline Goreau, *Reconstructing Aphra* (New York: Dial Press, 1980); Sara Mendelson, *The Mental World of Stuart Women: Three Studies*, chap. 3, "Aphra Behn" (Amherst: University of Massachusetts Press, 1987), 116–84. I know of two novels about Behn: Emily Hahn, *Purple-Passage: A Novel about a Lady both Famous and Fantastic* (Garden City, New York: Doubleday, 1950); Ross Laidlaw, *Aphra Behn – Dispatch'd from Athole* (Nairn: Balnain Books, 1992).

[2] Behn wrote at least seventeen plays, fourteen prose fictions, several translations, and two volumes of original poetry. Judith Phillips Stanton has demonstrated that Behn was the second most successful female dramatist writing between the years 1660 and 1800. See her "'This New-Found Path Attempting': Women Dramatists in England, 1660–1800," *Curtain Calls: British and American Women and the Theater, 1660–1820*, eds. Mary Anne Schofield and Cecilia Macheski (Athens: Ohio University Press, 1991), 325–54. On Behn the novelist, see Paul Salzman, *English Prose Fiction, 1558–1700* (Oxford: Clarendon Press, 1985); Ros Ballaster, *Seductive Forms: Women's Amatory Fiction from 1684–1740* (Oxford: Clarendon Press, 1992).

[3] Warren Chernaik, *Sexual Freedom in Restoration Literature* (Cambridge: Cambridge University Press, 1995); Donald R. Wehrs, "Eros, Ethics, Identity: Royalist Feminism and the Politics of Desire in Aphra Behn's *Love Letters*," *Studies in English Literature* 32 (1992): 461–78; Cheri Davis Langdell, "Aphra Behn and Sexual Politics: A Dramatist's Discourse with her Audience," in *Drama, Sex and Politics*, ed. James Redmond (Cambridge: Cambridge University Press, 1985), 109–28; Laura Brown, *Ends of Empire: Women and Ideology in Early Eighteenth-Century English Literature* (Ithaca: Cornell University Press, 1993); Carl Plasa and Betty J. Ring, eds., *A Discourse of Slavery: Aphra Behn to Toni Morrison* (New York: Routledge, 1994).

about Behn as a political writer. This is a rather curious omission for several reasons. Scholars have long recognized the highly politicized nature of the theater in the 1680s.[4] Studies of the politics and ideology of male dramatists, particularly John Dryden, abound.[5] Behn, like her male competitors Dryden, Shadwell, Settle, Crown and others, also produced highly political stage plays, bursting with topical references, mired in the controversies of the time. Yet beyond the blanket assertion that Behn was a Tory propagandist, little analysis of her political vision exists.[6] This is particularly surprising for a rare female voice in the loud political cacophony of the 1680s. No other woman writer was as public, vocal, or prolific as Aphra Behn in the pre-Revolution era.

This chapter is an examination of the political content of Behn's work from 1678 to the year of her death, 1689. These years were some of the most traumatic in English history, beginning with the controversies over the Popish Plot and Exclusion Bill from 1678 to 1681; extending through the discovery of the Whig conspiracy known as the Rye House Plot in 1683 and Monmouth's Rebellion in 1685; and ending with the Glorious Revolution of 1688/89.

Behn was a full participant in this highly disputatious political culture. Her plays written in the 1680s, her poems on state occasions, and her first novel all reflect and comment upon the political milieu of London in the first age of party. Several of Behn's comedies were fierce political satires. Their humor revolved around ridiculing contemporary personalities, Whig slogans and idioms, popular fashions and literature. Behn's political vision was encoded in her satire. If we are to begin to discern her politics, let alone "get the joke," we must first understand the

---

[4] Allardyce Nicoll, "Political Plays of the Restoration," *Modern Language Review* 16 (1921): 224–42; George Whiting, "The Condition of the London Theaters, 1679–1683: A Reflection of the Political Situation," *Modern Philology* 25 (1927): 195–206. More recent work includes Douglas Canfield, "Royalism's Last Dramatic Stand: English Political Tragedy, 1679–89," *Studies in Philology* 82 (1985): 234–63; Susan Owen, "Interpreting the Politics of Restoration Drama," *The Seventeenth Century* 8 (1993): 67–97.

[5] Philip Harth, *Pen for a Party: Dryden's Tory Propaganda and Its Contexts* (Princeton: Princeton University Press, 1993); J. R. Moore, "Political Allusions in Dryden's Later Plays," *Proceedings of the Modern Language Association* 73 (1958): 36–42; Steve Pincus, "Shadwell's Dramatic Trimming," *Religion, Literature and Politics in Post-Reformation England,* eds. Donna Hamilton and Richard Strier (Cambridge: Cambridge University Press, 1995), 253–74; Richard E. Brown, "Nathaniel Lee's Political Dramas, 1679–1683," *Restoration* 10 (1986): 41–52.

[6] For example, A. E. Leja, "Aphra Behn – Tory," Ph.D. thesis, University of Texas, 1962; Mary Ann O'Donnell, "Aphra Behn: Tory Wit and Unconventional Woman," in *Women Writers in the Seventeenth Century,* eds. Katharina M. Wilson and Frank J. Warnke (Athens: Ohio University Press, 1989): 341–74.

political and religious debates, controversies, fears, and dilemmas facing Behn and her contemporaries.[7]

Scholars have asserted *ad nauseam* that Behn was Tory propagandist and Stuart apologist. I do not dispute either claim. But I think such broad characterizations are less then helpful. Historians of Restoration political thought are well aware of the varieties of early Whiggism.[8] Although Tory ideology in its genesis has received less scholarly attention, it is undoubtedly true that not all Tories thought alike, and this was as true for politicians and ideologues as it was for poets and playwrights.[9]

Unlike many royalists in the 1680s, Behn was not a follower of Sir Robert Filmer. Filmer's patriarchalism supplied much of the ideological stuffing for Tory propaganda in the 1680s. Tory propagandists popularized the principles of Filmer's *Patriarcha* and other works; royalist playwrights echoed Filmerian positions, Dryden notoriously so.[10] But Behn conspicuously did not. She asserted divine right tenets, but her devotion to monarchy did not rest on patriarchal theories.[11] Instead Behn's royalism, articulated time and again in her work, revolved around an idealized aristocratic ethos that liberated the individual from the tyrannies of dull customs and traditions, things acceptable for the common castes of society, but which shackled the noble mind and heart. In better times, Behn may well have concentrated solely on the need to break those traditional shackles which so confined a woman's life. But in the climactic atmosphere of pre-revolution London, Behn's focus re-

---

[7] As Robert Darnton reminds us, our "inability to get the joke is an indication of the distance that separates us" from the early modern world (*The Great Cat Massacre and Other Episodes in French Cultural History* [New York: Basic Books, 1984], 77–78).

[8] J. G. A. Pocock, "The Varieties of Whiggism from Exclusion to Reform," in *Virtue, Commerce and History: Essays on Political Thought and History* (Cambridge: Cambridge University Press, 1985), 215–310; Mark Goldie, "The Roots of True Whiggism, 1688–94," *History of Political Thought* 1 (1980): 195–236; Melinda Zook, "Early Whig Ideology, Ancient Constitutionalism and the Reverend Samuel Johnson," *Journal of British Studies* 32 (1993): 139–65.

[9] Work on individual Tory thinkers exists, but there is very little published work on Tory ideology as a whole. Two of the best recent studies in Tory politics are Harth, *Pen for a Party* and Tim Harris, "Tories and the Rule of Law in the Reign of Charles II," *The Seventeenth Century* 8 (1993): 9–27.

[10] Bruce King, "Dryden's Ark: The Influence of Filmer," *Studies in English Literature* 7 (1967): 403–14; Michael J. Conlon, "The Passage on Government in Dryden's *Absalom and Achitophel*," *Journal of English and Germanic Philology* 78 (1979): 17–32.

[11] Filmer's ideas rested on a Scriptural reading of history. Behn, however, asserted that Scripture had no instructional value insofar as "astronomy, geometry or chronology" were concerned. She believed Scripture was too often used "for mischief" when applied to secular concerns. See her preface to her translation of Fontenelle in *The Works of Aphra Behn*, ed. Janet Todd (Columbus: Ohio State University Press, 1992–95), 4 vols, IV: 79, 85.

volved around glorifying and defending the Cavalier culture of court and castigating its enemies, the Whigs and Dissenters.

Behn's political philosophy hence centered around a celebration of the young elite male, the cavalier, the epitome of individual freedom. She associated tradition and the rules of sexual behavior not only with Puritanism, resurrected she believed by the Whigs and Dissenters in the 1680s, but also with the middling and lower castes. True freedom was freedom from want, freedom from customary behavior, and freedom from religious fanaticism. In 1677, Behn located these qualities in the witty, genial, and womanizing cavalier Willmore in *The Rover*, whom she revived in a sequel, *The Second Part of The Rover* (January 1681). But as tensions in London swelled, Behn's hero became far more of a political animal, predatory and manipulative, yet retaining his wit, love for women, and royalism. This new cavalier, more rake than rover, reappears as the "Heroick" Loveless in *The Roundheads* (1681) and as the Tory, Tom Wilding, in *The City Heiress* (1682). By the late 1680s, Behn concentrated on the cavalier's more tragic and romantic dimensions, as seen in her portrayal of the "royal slave" in *Oroonoko* (1688) and in the warrior-hero, Nathaniel Bacon, in *The Widow Ranter* (1690).

The transformation of Behn's cavalier from merry rover to cunning rake to sacrificial martyr-hero reflected Behn's political anxieties in the 1680s. Tom Wilding and Loveless are savvy operators because the turbulent times demanded as much. They have all the characteristics of Behn's earlier rovers of the 1670s only, as their way of life is under siege, they are more calculating and less frivolous men. By the late 1680s, Behn placed the same attributes in her tragi-heroes, but her style and tone had changed. James II's revolutionary zeal in government and religion had begun to inspire more fear in old-time royalists like Behn than Whig demands had before him. By the time of the revolution, Behn's writing reflects a sense of resignation. Her cavaliers are already lost men, anachronisms. Nathaniel Bacon commits suicide; Oroonoko is crudely dismembered.

Women were participants in the cavalier's drama but were not themselves cavaliers. Behn might have come as close as any to a "she-rover" for a woman in the late seventeenth century; she was an extraordinary woman. But she realized that the cavalier's libertine lifestyle was ultimately unobtainable for most women. Behn's witty heroines may engage in clever banter; they may despise the drudgery of marriage; and they may even don male attire and draw their swords. Yet, most often, they must marry or be ruined. The narrow and circumscribed role in which "women of quality" could maneuver was demonstrated time and again in Behn's plays and novels. Behn raised disturbing questions about the treatment of women and the feminine identity. But ultimately her central concerns by the early 1680s surrounded her country's political future. Her work defended the world of those whom she admired, those who could obtain personal and public freedom, elite males.

In 1679, Aphra Behn wrote her first dedication, openly soliciting literary patronage for her plays for the first time. She had published her first nine plays, from 1670 to 1677, without dedications, an unusually long time to remain outside the patronage system.[12] But as the political climate changed in the late 1670s, and Behn's plays became ever more politicized, she may well have felt the need for publicly acclaimed alliances with powerful men and women. She dedicated her plays to those in and around the court, including those closest to the king himself. *The Feign'd Courtizans* (March 1679) was dedicated to Charles II's mistress, the actress, Nell Gwyn, who had played the prostitute, Angellica Bianca, in Behn's highly successful play *The Rover* (March 1677). In 1681, amid the fierce battle over the Exclusion Bill, Behn dedicated *The Second Part of The Rover* to the "popish successor" himself James, duke of York. She praised York for his "divine patience" as he withstood the insults of that "seemingly sanctifi'd Faction" (the Whigs) who wished to "Play the old Game ov'r again."[13]

The "old Game ov'r again" was, as Behn put it elsewhere, "the old beaten path of Forty-One."[14] The bloody civil wars of the 1640s played out again in the 1680s. The cry "forty-one all over again" was a common Tory propaganda ploy in the early 1680s. Behn used it repeatedly. Like all good propagandists, she belittled the grievances of the opposition, the Whigs and Dissenters. Her plays made the current crises look like the product of the personality flaws of a scheming, ambitious, and hypocritical few, whose intent it was to resurrect the Commonwealth by deluding the rabble through religion. But, in fact, the issues at hand could not have been more critical. The future of the polity and its confessional nature was being debated in Parliament and pamphlet.

Behn understood the significance of the political struggles which her

[12] Her first nine plays were *The Forced Marriage* (1670); *The Amorous Prince* (1671); *The Dutch Lover* (1673); *Abdelazer* (1676); *The Town Fop* (1676); *The Rover* (1677); *The Debauchee* (1677); *The Counterfeit Bridegroom* (1677); *Sir Patient Fancy* (1678).

[13] *The Second Part of the Rover* (1681), dedication. Throughout the 1680s, Behn continued to dedicate her works to powerful royalists and courtiers, including Henry FitzRoy, duke of Grafton, Charles II's illegitimate son by the duchess of Cleveland; and the Catholics James Cecil, earl of Salisbury, and Lord Richard Maitland, fourth earl of Lauderdale, both of whom became Jacobites after the revolution.

[14] *The City Heiress; Or, Sir Timothy Treat-all* (1682), Act III, i.

plays crudely satirized. Her constant references to events, personalities, and the political tropes of the times – along with the sharpness of her jabs at those she blamed for the public's discontent and the rabble's grumbling – reflected her anxiety over the current climate. At stake for Behn was not solely a matter of who governed or how or where one prayed, but an entire mentality and way of life which was imperiled by what she saw as the rancorous and selfish demands of the Whigs and Dissenters and their allies among London's mobile. The cavalier's sword, noble birth, and code of honor were in danger of becoming meaningless in a world run by the crude and ambitious middling sorts who knew no loyalty to the monarchy, deference to birth, or respect for a man's word. The exceptional individual, unbound by custom, law, or religion was lost in the din of the clamoring demands of the multitudes with their leveling politics and mercantile interests.

In the early 1680s, Behn wrote her most political comedies. In plays like *The Roundheads* (December 1681) the middling and lower ranks of society are portrayed as the political tools of the Whigs, seduced by their slogans and Puritan/Dissenting cant. *The Roundheads*, Behn's comic satire on the last days of the Commonwealth, begins with a street scene.[15] A group of soldiers confront two artisans, a joiner and a feltworker. The artisans are religious radicals, part of the "sanctify'd mobile" who speak the language of the godly and reiterate the tropes of the Good Old Cause. "Here's a saucy dog of a Joyner," says one of the soldiers, "Sirrah, get ye home and mind your trade and save the Hangman the labour." The Joiner retorts, "I fear no Hang-man in Christendom; for Conscience and Publick Good, for Liberty and Property, I dare as far as any Man" (Act I, i).

This opening scene was particularly meaningful to Behn's audience. They knew that the joiner (or carpenter) should have heeded the soldier's warning. Stephen College, the so-called "Protestant Joiner," meddled in the politics of Exclusion Crisis, authoring anti-papist, anti-duke of York ballads and satires. He was tried at the Old Bailey for seditious words and actions in July of 1681 but a Whig-packed jury came back, predictably, *ignoramus*.[16] He was not so fortunate a month later. At the Oxford assizes, College was tried for treason for his seditious

---

[15] *The Roundheads* was a loose adaptation from John Tatham's *The Rump* (1660). Behn added several characters, including all of the cavaliers, Lady Desbro, and the canting lay elder, Ananias Goggle. The opening street scene described below was also Behn's invention.

[16] Whig sheriffs empaneled London and Middlesex juries with those sympathetic to Whig defendants. A verdict of *ignoramus* meant that a jury considered the evidence against the defendant insufficient and they were freed from further prosecution.

behavior during the abortive Oxford Parliament. He was convicted, hanged, and quartered.

The allusion to the fate of Stephen College at the beginning of *The Roundheads* worked as a powerful warning not only about mobile meddling and its consequences, but also as a reminder to the audience of how similar times were then (the Interregnum) to their day. In the play, cavaliers are labeled "Heroicks" but also "Tories"; while the Roundheads are sometimes called "Whigs." Both the play's themes – political confusion, social leveling, irreverence to the monarchy, and religious hypocrisy – and Behn's numerous references to contemporary times reiterate the idea that "the Sins of Forty-One [were being] reviv'd again in Eighty-One."[17]

The Roundheads also echoes themes from Shakespeare's *Richard III*. In both plays, factionalism has resulted in political chaos and the crown is contested by bribery, deception, and the sword. Both recount the last days of disorder before a restoration of the rightful heir to the throne. Behn was particularly interested in Shakespeare's presentation of a hierarchy inverted, where "men are rul'd by women" and where the base-born are advanced over the noble. In *Richard III*, "the world is grown so bad/ That wrens make prey where eagles dare not perch;/ Since every Jack became a gentleman/ There's many a gentle person made a Jack."[18]

Women have clearly overstepped their bounds in *The Roundheads*, holding committee meetings, redressing petitions, advising men. Lady Lambert, the "she-Politician," rules her husband. Lord Lambert and the other Roundheads have usurped political power, noble titles, and estates through "Dissimulation, Equivocation, and mental Reservation." The "Heroick" Loveless, a cavalier, could once "have boasted Birth and Fortune ... Till these accursed Times, which Heaven confound,/ Razing our all Nobility, all Virtue,/ Has render'd me the rubbish of the world;/ Whilst new rais'd Rascals, Canters, Robbers, Rebels,/ Do lord it o'er the Free-born, Brave and Noble" (Act I, ii).

But true nobility is more than lands and titles; it is a style of behavior – "Wit, Softness, and Gallantry" – visible to all (Act II, i). Lady Lambert is dismayed when Loveless does not recognize her new position and power: "I thought I'd been so elevated above the Common Crowd, it had been visible to all Eyes who I was." Whereas Loveless's "Love, Wit

---

[17] The quote is from *The City Heiress* (Act III, i), which contains the same political messages.

[18] In *Richard III*, the base-born Elizabeth Woodville is thought to rule over her husband, the dying Edward IV (Act I, i). The Woodvilles and their relations are the "jacks" that have become "gentlemen" (Act I, iii).

and Beauty [are] revel'd in his Eyes" (Act I, i). The play ends with General Monk marching on London. The Roundheads scatter, and Lord Lambert is arrested. Her power lost, Lady Lambert sighs, "I'm a declining shade." But Loveless happily declares, "By heaven, you were never great till now." The social and political order is restored; Lady Lambert is no longer a meddling she-politician, but simply a woman in love (Act v, iii).

The cavalier's code of honor, wherein a man's word is his oath, a pledge of fidelity, trust, and loyalty, is another casualty of the topsy-turvy worlds portrayed in Behn's plays. In *The Roundheads* and in Behn's satire on contemporary Whig-governed London, *The City Heiress*, oaths are meaningless where guile, deception, and personal interest rule and loyalties alter with each shift of the political winds. "How cou'd I now advise you to be King," the cynical Lord Whitlock informs Lord Lambert, "if I had started at Oaths, or preferr'd Honesty or Divinity before Interest and the *Good Old Cause*?" (Act I, ii). Time and again, Behn equated Roundheads and Whigs with "Dissimulation and Hypocrisy," oath-breaking, and perjury and the "bare-fac'd" cavaliers and Tories with reverence for truth, loyalty, and the "code of the word."[19]

Behn's emphasis on oath-breaking in the early 1680s reflected a profound, yet common royalist concern over recent legal maneuvers taken by the Whig-dominated city government of London. Royalists like Behn were infuriated over the veracity given to the incredible popish plot tales of Titus Oates;[20] the perjured witnesses whose testimony led the Catholic lords to the scaffold; and the Whig-packed juries that refused to charge either Stephen College or the Whig leader, the earl of Shaftesbury, by returning *ignoramus* verdicts.[21] "The City's a grumbling, lying,

---

[19] *The Roundheads*, Act IV, i. See Douglas Canfield's discussion of the "code of the word" in "Royalism's Last Dramatic Stand," 234–38.

[20] There are several humorous references to the "Salamanca Doctor," Titus Oates, in Behn's plays. The joke is always a play on the absurdity of Oates's stories and those who believed him. In *The Lucky Chance*, the naive Bearjest asks Breadwell if he's heard of any miracles from St. Omers lately. Breadwell responds: "None, Sir since the wonderful Salamanca Doctor, who was both here and there at the same Instant of time."

BEARJEST: How, Sir? why, that's impossible.

BREADWELL: That was the Wonder, Sir, because 'twas impossible.

NOISEY: But 'twas a greater, Sir, that 'twas believed. (Act I, iii)

Also see *The City Heiress*, Act V, v.

[21] Like other Tory playwrights and propagandists, Behn ridiculed Shaftesbury. There are numerous references to him in *The Roundheads* as someone who switched political allegiance with each new government during the 1640s and 1650s. In *The City Heiress*, the absurd old Whig, Sir Timothy Treatall, is a Shaftesbury figure who is offered the crown of Poland. Shaftesbury was commonly lampooned in Tory propaganda as the "king of Poland," because it was thought that he wanted to set up an elective monarchy on the Polish model (K. H. D. Haley, *The First Earl of Shaftesbury* [Oxford: Clarendon, 1968], 689).

dissatify'd City, and no wise or Honest man regards what it says," exclaims the loyal country gentleman, Sir Anthony Merriwell in *The City Heiress* (Act I, i). Whig control of London made justice impossible. Perjury, bribery, and the packing of juries subverted the legal order. The "dissembling Whig," Sir Timothy Treatall in *The City Heiress*, knows that the Tories cannot touch him: "Let 'em accuse me if they please; alas, I come off handsmooth with *Ignoramus*" (Act III, i).

Behn's preoccupation with oaths and dissembling did not end with the Tory reaction that began in 1681 and led to their retaking of London. It was not simply city politics that concerned Behn, but a whole new modern age devoid of honor, loyalty, and trust. There is a deep sense of nostalgia, particularly in Behn's later work, for an older aristocratic code of values. The importance she placed on the oath, "the code of the word," took on darker shades in her novellas, particularly *Oroonoko*, first published in July 1688 on the eve of the revolution. The thoroughly Europeanized African prince Oroonoko, Behn's most tragic cavalier hero, is continually tricked by whites who give him their word. Lied to again after his failed slave rebellion, he concludes,

there was no faith in white men, or the gods they adored, who instructed them in principles so false honest men could not live amongst them . . . he knew what he had to do, when he dealt with men of honour, but with them a man ought to be eternally on his guard, and never to eat and drink with Christians without his weapon of defense in his hand, and, for his own security never credit one word they spoke.[22]

Men of honor understand, respect, and love one another in Behn's work. They are their own caste, a breed apart, freed from the dull customs, conventions, and taboos which order and circumscribe the lives of the rest of society. Marriage, in particular, stands out in Behn's work as a tiresome custom that kills free love. The assertion that "Love knows no ceremony," as Willmore declares in *The Second Part of The Rover*, was an oft-repeated motif in Behn's work. Not only were her cavaliers above the traditional rules of courtship, her she-rovers, such as Ariadne in *The Second Part of the Rover* and Sylvia in Behn's first novel, *Love Letters Between a Nobleman and His Sister*, were also advocates of love freed from marriage. Ariadne despises the courtly Beaumont to whom she is contracted and declares, "I'd have a Lover rough as Seas in Storms, upon occasion; I hate your dull temperate Lover, 'tis such a husbandly quality" (Act II, ii).[23]

---

[22] *Oroonoko, The Rover and Other Works*, ed. Janet Todd (London: Penguin Books, 1992), 130. Henceforth cited within the text as "Todd edition."

[23] Ariadne, however, marries Beaumont at the end of *The Second Part of the Rover*. Similarly, Sylvia is punished for her outlandish sexual behavior in *Love Letters* and must

The sexual activity of lovers outside the bounds of the "cold matrimonial embrace" is "scarce a sin." Only the arranged marriage is "flat
adultery."[24] Or as the Tory-cavalier, Tom Wilding states in *The City
Heiress*:

> According to the strictest Rules of Honour,
> Beauty should still be the Reward of Love,
> Not the vile Merchandize of Fortune,
> Or the cheap Drug of a Church-Ceremony.
> She's only infamous, who to her bed
> For Interest takes some nauseous Clown she hates:
> And though a Jointure or a Vow in publick
> Be her Price, that makes her but the dearer Whore.   Act VI, i

Behn's abhorrence of the "forced marriage" (the title of her first play)
was a constant and conspicuous theme. But Behn was not simply an
opponent of the prearranged marriage. Her cavaliers were above all
convention, the taboos against homosexuality and incest included. Even
"the law established" was made to hem in the little people, not men of
honor. *Love Letters Between a Nobleman and His Sister*, written between
1684 and 1687, was loosely based on real events and personalities.
Though Whig politics are chided (and punished) in the novel as sins
against "our good, our gracious monarch," transgressions against
custom by the novel's Whig-cavalier, Philander, are never condemned.

Philander eloquently convinces his sister-in-law, Sylvia, that they
should love freely and not be frightened by artificial conventions such as
marriage or that which calls their passion "incest." "What's a ceremony
imposed on man by custom," he exclaims:

Let us, (born for mightier joys) scorn the dull beaten road, but let us love like
the first race of men, nearest allied to God, promiscuously they loved, and
possessed, father and daughter, brother and sister met, and reaped the joys of
love without control, and counted it religious coupling, and 'twas encouraged
too by heaven itself; therefore start not (too nice and lovely maid) at shadows of
things that can but frighten fools. (Duffy edition, 4)

Sexual love between men and, particularly, men and boys was also a
condoned part of the cavalier's world despite the traditional regulations
and biases against sodomy. When Sylvia cross-dresses as a "youth" in
Love Letters, she "captivated the men no less than the women" (Duffy
edition, 119). In *The Second Part of the Rover*, Ariadne cross-dresses as a

---

live as a prostitute by the end of the novel. Behn's she-rovers must eventually conform
or suffer the consequences.

[24] *Love Letters Between a Nobleman and His Sister*, introduced by Maureen Duffy (New
York: Virago Classics, 1987), 8; henceforth cited within the text as "Duffy edition"; *The
Second Part of The Rover*, Act II, ii; *The False Count*, Act I, i.

boy and catches Willmore's attention. He decides to whisk a prostitute off to his bed instead, telling the "boy," "thou'rt a pretty Youth; but at this time I've more occasion for a thing in Petticoats – go home, and do not walk the streets so much; that tempting face of thine will debauch the grave men of business" (Act III, i). In *The Widow Ranter*, the heroic Captain Daring wants to make love with the rich widow while she wears male attire. "Take me that humour while thy breeches are on," he tells her, "for I never liked thee half so well in petticoats" (Act IV, iii).

In *The Widow Ranter* the protagonist, Nathaniel Bacon, is another "tragic masculine hero," who like Oroonoko believes in the "integrity of language: the oath and word of honour" and is thereby tricked by lesser, unscrupulous men.[25] The play was also a thorough attack on the formalized word, the law, when it binds "noble actions." Behn mocked Whig efforts to regulate the royal succession, the monarchy, and religion "by the law established." When Bacon defends the colonists against a raiding Indian tribe but without the colonial government's consent, the cowardly JPs threaten to hang him; exclaims one, "We'll teach you, sir, to serve your country against the law." Bacon replies, "I've not offended honour or religion . . . Should I stand by and see my country ruined, my King dishonoured and his subjects murdered?" (Act II, iii; Act II, iv). But Bacon has violated the law and is charged with treason. As one character sympathetic to Bacon puts it, "What pity 'tis there should be false maxims in the world, that noble actions, however great, must be criminal for want of a law to authorise them" (Act I, iii).

Behn blamed the legal and moral limitations placed on "noble actions" on the Whigs and Dissenters, whom she believed would gladly revive the prudish anti-pleasure principles of the Puritans. In the 1650s, "stage plays, horse-racing, cock-fighting, maypoles, and brothels had all been suppressed," and adultery was made punishable by death.[26] Despite these draconian measures, Behn's Puritans in *The Roundheads* "drink as deep and entertain themselves as well" as the royalists only they do so "with this silent way of lewd Debauchery." Puritans and Whigs entertain themselves as much with women and drink as the cavaliers but always for reasons of interest. Pleasure becomes debauchery; "harmless Wit and Mirth's a Sin, laughing scandalous, and a merry Glass an Abomination" (Act II, i).

In *The City Heiress*, the Tory, Tom Wilding, scolds his old Whig uncle, Sir Timothy Treatall, whose lavish public dinners are meant to convert all London to the Whig cause. "You keep open House to all the Party,"

[25] Janet Todd, *Gender, Art and Death* (New York: Continuum, 1993), 50–54.
[26] Lawrence Stone, *The Family, Sex and Marriage in England, 1500–1800*, abridged edition (New York: Harper and Row, 1979), 396.

exclaims Wilding, "not for mirth, Generosity or good nature, but for Roguery" and "in hopes of Debauching the King's Liege-people into Commonwealthsmen" (Act I, i). Behn's cavaliers, on the other hand, are barefaced and open-hearted, love wit, mirth, a hearty drink, and a pretty face. Moreover, they do their drinking and wenching openly. When Ariadne asks Willmore in *The Second Part of The Rover* if he can keep a secret, he replies, "Secrecy is a damn'd ungrateful Sin, Child, known only where Religion and Small-beer are current" (Act II, i).[27]

Not all religion, of course, was the "cozening, canting, sanctifying" kind. After attending an Anglican service, the royalist Sir Anthony in *The City Heiress* remarks, "I love good wholesome Doctrine, that teaches Obedience to the King and Superiors, without railing at Government, and quoting Scripture for Sedition, Mutiny, and Rebellion" (Act I, i). It was, of course, the Dissenters who, like the Puritans before them, were continually "quoting Scripture." In *The Roundheads*, Loveless exclaims that all Puritan women are "sanctify'd Jilts ... Make love to 'em, they answer in Scripture" (Act I, i).[28] This sanctifying religion was pure hypocrisy, a language used by "the Pulpit knaves" to "brew" treason among the ignorant.[29] "All the Rhetorick of the Learn'd or Honest" cannot move the "rascally Rabble" where "your seditious cant ... prevails" (Act III, ii). When the insipid Lord Fleetwood speaks in the language of the godly, Lady Lambert is infuriated. Whitlock patiently explains, "Madam, this is the Cant we must delude the nation with." Lady Lambert angrily replies, "Then let him use it there, my Lord, not amongst us, who so well understand one another" (Act I, ii). Godly cant was simply a means of deception.

The cavalier's world of honor and oaths, generosity and pleasure for pleasure's sake – where nothing is hidden and society's rules of social behavior simply don't apply – stood in stark contrast to a world of ambitious, dissembling upstarts. The clashing of these two worlds was a

---

[27] Small beer was less alcoholic. Temperance was a Puritan concern which Behn constantly lampooned, particularly in *The City Heiress*, which contains numerous references to Whigs drinking small beer. The loyal, hearty drinking Sir Charles Merriwell describes Sir Timothy Treatall's Whig friends as "Puritanical, Schismatical, Fanatical, Small-beer-Face[d]" (Act III, i).

[28] Behn was particularly harsh on Dissenting/Puritan women. In *The City Heiress*, Mrs. Clackett, "a City Baud and Puritan," is described as "A Saint in the Spirit, and Whore in Flesh;/ A Doer of the Devil's Work in God' Name" (Act IV, i). Mrs. Senure, Sir Timothy Treatall's maid, is caught in bed with her master, carrying a book of Richard Baxter's sermons (Act V, i).

[29] *The Roundheads*, prologue. Time and time again, Behn linked Dissent with sedition. Even as early as 1678, Behn's title character, a Dissenting Whig alderman in *Sir Patient Fancy*, is described as "vainly proud of his rebellious opinion, for his Religion means nothing but that" (Act II, i).

constant theme in Behn's work; it was her interpretation of the struggles she witnessed in London in the early 1680s; a struggle she believed the cavalier was losing to the "All-Powerful Whigs" and all they represented.[30]

In August 1682, Behn committed a political blunder. The consequences she suffered may have begun to transform her political vision. Her Tory politics went too far when she insulted the king's first and favorite bastard son, James Scott, duke of Monmouth. Tory attacks on Monmouth were nothing new. Monmouth, "the Protestant Duke," had become a popular Whig alternative to the much despised and feared "Popish successor," the duke of York. The duke of Monmouth, on the other hand, embodied the beautiful cavalier, adorned with the most tragic and romantic features of the Stuart dynasty. But Monmouth was seduced by ambition, Tory satirists asserted, bewitched by Whig promises of his father's throne despite his illegitimacy.

In 1682, Behn penned the *Epilogue to Romulus*, spoken on stage by the actress, Lady Slingsby. They were both arrested.[31] While the entire epilogue to *Romulus* satirized Monmouth, the lines which offended the court reflected his ambition for the throne: "Love! like Ambition, makes us Rebels too:/ And of all Treasons, mine was most accurst;/ Rebelling 'gainst a King and Father first/ A Sin, which Heaven nor man can ev'r forgive."[32] Monmouth may have been too much in Whig company, but he was still the king's son.[33] Behn's arrest must have felt a bit of a shock and a betrayal for someone who so "faithfully serv'd that royal cause."[34] Four years passed before Behn would again write for the stage. In the meantime, she wrote poems on state occasions, translations, and fiction. When she did return to the theater in April 1686, it was with *The Lucky Chance*, a comic satire on Whig aldermen meddling in London affairs. The play's politics were strangely anachronistic since the Whigs had lost control of London long ago and had been scattered in the wake of Monmouth's failed rebellion in 1685. James II was firmly in power; Whiggism appeared to be defeated.[35]

More successful than Behn's return to the theater was her epistolary

---

[30] *The False Count* (1681), prologue.

[31] The *Protestant Mercury* (August 12–16, 1682); The Newdigate Newsletters, L.C. 5/191, 100.

[32] *Prologue to Romulus* (1682). The *Epilogue* is printed on the reverse side.

[33] Dryden and Lee also felt the displeasure of the court for the same reason when they mocked Monmouth in *The Duke of Guise* (1683). As the author of the Newdigate Newsletters put it, though the king was angry at Monmouth, "yet he is not willing that others should abuse him out of a natural affection for him" (L.C. 5/144, 81).

[34] *The Lucky Chance* (1686), dedication.

[35] *The Lucky Chance* reflects the politics of Charles II's reign rather than James II's, including references to Titus Oates and the battle over London's city charter. It was

novel, *Love Letters Between a Nobleman and His Sister*, which was published in three parts between 1684 and 1687.[36] *Love Letters* was loosely based on a real social-sexual scandal, involving the prominent Whig noble, Lord Grey of Werk, an ally to the duke of Monmouth. In August 1682, Grey abducted his eighteen-year-old, unmarried sister-in-law, Henrietta Berkeley. He was charged with debauchery but was able to retain Henrietta by marrying her to his servant. The following spring, Grey and Monmouth were implicated in the Rye House Plot to assassinate the royal brothers. While Monmouth begged a pardon from his indulgent father, Grey and Henrietta escaped to Holland.

Love Letters charts a transformation in Behn's politics from a strident royalism to an increasingly tolerant view of the opposition. In 1684, when Part I was written, Behn was still propagating an orthodox royalist opinion. Her character, Sylvia (Henrietta), praises Charles II and preaches divine right tenets. "[He] was born your King," she reminds Philander (Grey) and "holds his crown by right of nature, by right of law, by right of heaven itself" (Duffy edition, Part I, 34–35). But three years later, when the third part of the novel was published in the reign of James II, Behn's outlook had changed.

This is most tellingly evident in her construction of Monmouth through the character, Cesario. Part III of *Love Letters* was written after Monmouth's futile rebellion. Monmouth and Lord Grey were both captured after the Battle of Sedgemoor and taken to London. Grey turned king's evidence and was pardoned, but Monmouth, whom James II detested, was not so fortunate. The gruesome beheading of this royal son made a powerful impression on the late Stuart consciousness. Behn was certainly free to attack Monmouth in 1687. But she saw him instead as a pathetically tragic figure. In Part III, the beautiful and romantic Cesario is betrayed and misled by those around him. He fights heroically at Sedgemoor, but after his capture he loses all courage and reason. He is a pitiful creature. Behn described his last moments on the scaffold and wrote, "so ended the race of this glorious youth, who was in his time the greatest man of a subject in the world, and the greatest favorite of his prince" (Part III, 460).

Behn's portrayal of Monmouth as a tragic figure in *Love Letters* is not the only evidence of a more indulgent view of the Whigs. The broadside poem, "Rebellions Antidote: Or A Dialogue Between Coffee and Tea,"

---

probably written around the same time as *The City Heiress* and *The False Count*, which it resembles.

[36] On the novel's popularity, see Judith Kegan Gardiner, "The First English Novel: Aphra Behn's *Love Letters*, the Canon, and Women's Tastes," *Tulsa Studies in Women's Literature* 7 (1988): 203.

recently attributed to Behn by Janet Todd and Virginia Crompton, also indicates a transformation in Behn's politics. Written in the spring of 1685, around the time of Argyle's and Monmouth's Rebellions, the poem clearly condemns such sedition. Yet while royalism is represented in the dialogue by "Tea," a more Whiggish perspective is voiced by "Coffee." The poem contains none of the shrill polemical venom so characteristic of Behn's prologues and epilogues of the early 1680s. Instead the tone of the poem alternates between optimism and anxiety. As Todd and Crompton put it, "If Tea is Behn, the poem offers a picture of an older professional woman who counters the political anxieties of Coffee with tolerant humour and compromise."[37]

The poems recorded in Behn's personal chapbook also suggest that she was more receptive to Whig concerns in the late 1680s. The political doggerel copied in "Astrea's Book of Songs and Satyrs" belongs to the period between 1685 and 1689. There are a few stridently Tory pieces, but there are also several Whig verses. The majority of the poems, however, strike the same note of caution and compromise as "Rebellion's Antidote." Some warn Whigs and Dissenters against supporting King James's Declaration of Indulgence (1687), which was seen by many as a first step toward the reintroduction of popery.[38] Others lament James II's treatment of the Seven Bishops. Still others see little difference between the extremism of the Whigs and Dissenters in the early 1680s and that of King James and his counsellors in the late 1680s.[39]

What seems to have transformed Behn's political vision was not only her personal humiliation in 1682 but an increasing concern over the direction of James II's administration. James's Romanizing policies and his heavy-handed use of kingly prerogative were the cause of much anxiety not only among the Whigs, but among the Tory elite as well. On the eve of the Revolution, James's appointing of papists and Dissenters in positions of power, his pardoning of Whig radicals and courting their

[37] Janet Todd and Virginia Crompton, "Rebellion's Antidote: A New Attribution to Aphra Behn," *Notes & Queries* 38 (June 1991): 175–77.
[38] See the last stanza of "The Story of the Pot and the Kettle," which Behn transcribed in her chapbook as:
> Learn hence (yee Whiggs) and act no more
> Nor trust their friendship who would make you tooles
> While empty praises and smooth flattery's
> Pay with feign'd thankes, what their feign'd smiles deserve
> But let not the alliance further pass
> For know that you are clay and they are brass.

("Astrea's Book of Songs and Satyrs," MS Firth c. 16, Bodleian Library, Oxford, fol. 263)
[39] See, for example, "The Confinement," about the Seven Bishops (MS Firth c. 16, fol. 288v); and "A Short Litany to the Tune of Cooke Lawrell," which equates the extremism of James with that of the Whigs (fol. 286v).

favor alienated Anglican clerics and the conservative elites who had been the bulwark of his brother's government.[40] Like numerous other Tories, Behn found herself a monarchist without a monarch she could trust. The political nation was as threatened by the zeal of James II's policies as it had once been by the Whigs' unruly demands under Charles II. Behn may well have perceived – as did others – that James was pushing Protestant England to the brink of revolution.[41]

Moreover, by 1688 Behn was also chronically ill and living in penury. Her own future was in doubt. Two of her final creations were the novel *Oroonoko* and the tragi-comedy *The Widow Ranter*. Both contain political commentary and tell us about the state of Behn's mind on the eve of the Glorious Revolution and her own death in April 1689. Behn stripped her cavalier down to his most noble and honorable features. But he was also a lost man; his time had come and gone.

Nathaniel Bacon, the tragi-hero of *The Widow Ranter*, epitomized Behn's lost cavalier. *The Widow Ranter* was based on the popular uprising, Bacon's Rebellion, which took place in Virginia in 1676. Much of the play was standard Behn fare: the social climbing, political meddling, base-born colonists and their Puritan minister are all dissembling upstarts, who insist on holding men of honor to "the law established." But the play also made several unsettling topical references. In Act IV, scene ii, the colony's JPs, all great cowards, have turned on each other amid the confusion of Bacon's Rebellion. Whimsey and Dullman decide to string up Whiff for running from the battlefield. Dullman declares, "one witness will stand good in law, in case of treason."

This line must have sent shivers through Behn's audience. It was an unhappy reminder of the notorious trial and execution of Colonel Algernon Sidney in 1683. Sidney was tried for high treason for his part in the Whig conspiracy known as the Rye House Plot, though there was only one witness against him, an infamous breach of tradition.[42]

---

[40] Laurence Eachard, *The History of England* (London: 1707–18), 3:78; J. R. Jones, "James II's Whig Collaborators," *Historical Journal* 3 (1960): 65–73.

[41] The diaries of Whigs and Dissenters record a sense of tremendous foreboding on the eve of the revolution; royalists and Anglican clerics as well felt uneasy and anxious, fearing James's ultimate goal was to restore Catholicism. For examples of both see *The Autobiography of William Stout of Lancaster, 1665–1752*, ed. J. D. Marshall (New York: Barnes and Noble, 1967), 91; Roger North, *The Lives of the Norths*, ed. Augustus Jessopp (London: George Bell and Sons, 1890), 3 vols., I: 358–61.

[42] Two witnesses were needed for a charge of high treason. Unable to find a second witness against Sidney, the government used Sidney's own republican manuscript, the "Discourses concerning Government," as evidence against him. See Craig Allen Houston, *Algernon Sidney and the Republican Heritage in England and America* (Princeton: Princeton University Press, 1991), 58–67.

Along with Lord Russell, who was also beheaded for the Rye House Plot, Sidney's Whig martyrdom had grown to legendary proportions by the time of the Revolution. Having a fool, Dullman, assert this extra-legal procedure, Behn not only reminded her audience of the means used by Charles II's government to execute the noble Sidney, she delegitimized it as well. Perhaps by 1688, the memory of aristocratic blood shed on the scaffold through the machinations of lawyers was more powerful to Behn than the image of a notorious Whig leader being punished.[43]

By the conclusion of *The Widow Ranter*, all its heroic characters are slain, destroyed by their own codes of honor. The central tragic hero, Bacon, is an ambiguous figure. He has many of the characteristics of Behn's earlier cavaliers. He is "by nature generous, brave, resolved and daring"; he is not bound by custom or law, but by his honor and his word. He even breaks racial boundaries by loving the Indian queen, Semernia. But he is also clearly motivated by ambition and becomes a popular hero. As the play progresses, he increasingly resembles the duke of Monmouth. The English gentleman, Friendly, informs the audience from the onset that Bacon, having studied "the lives of the Romans and great men that have raised themselves to the most elevated fortunes, fancies it easy for ambitious men to aim at any pitch of glory. I've heard him often say, 'Why cannot I conquer the universe as well as Alexander? or like another Romulus form a new Rome and myself adored?'" (Act I, i).

As crowds once shouted "A Monmouth, A Monmouth" in the early 1680s, so, in Act II, the rabble rescues Bacon from the clutches of the colonial magistrates hollering, "A Bacon, A Bacon." Bacon does not suffer the same gruesome fate as Monmouth. He will not allow himself to be made "a public spectacle upon the common theatre of death" and thereby falls upon his own sword. But his gasping last words remind us of Monmouth's failings: "never let ambition – love – or interest make you forget as I have done - your duty and allegiance" (Act IV, i). As a rebel, Bacon must die. His death is the victory of the cowardly and greedy upstarts of the colonial government. The chivalric, the romantic, the honorable – these men have no place in this new world, neither colonial America nor revolutionary England.

Unlike Bacon, Oroonoko's heroic status is unquestionable. He is Behn's ultimate aristocratic hero. Much has been written about

---

[43] Colonel Sidney's case may have been particularly poignant to Behn. She had some personal knowledge of Sidney as she had reported on his republican activities in Holland while she was there on a spying mission in the 1660s. See Cameron, *New Light on Aphra Behn*, 25–27, 47, 73, 79.

Oroonoko as a critique of both imperialism and slavery. But the central concerns of the narrative were not about colonialism or race. The racial "others" in the story are the native Indians, not "the royal slave," Oroonoko. What is important about Oroonoko is his class, his princely status. His treatment at the hands of the white colonists in Surinam is "an indignity to his class rather than his race."[44] After all, all three races represented in *Oroonoko* – the Europeans, the Africans, and the Indians – practice slavery. Moreover, in many ways, Oroonoko is more European than African. His physical features and his education are European. He had learned "morals, language and science" from his French tutor and, like Bacon, he admired the Romans. His politics were firmly royalist: "He had heard of the late Civil Wars in England, and the deplorable death of our great monarch, and would discourse of it with all the sense and abhorrence of the injustice imaginable." Oroonoko's long hair is even described as "cavalierish" (Todd edition, 80–81).

Oroonoko is not exotic because he is an African, but because he is a living anachronism plunged into a new world. He is the last honorable man, embodying "the Restoration heroic ideal: proud, honorable," a man of "wit and address" who follows chivalric notions of love and honor.[45] His aristocratic code is, nonetheless, his undoing as he is continually deceived by the "degenerate" whites. His own people fail him as well, and he declares that they are "by nature slaves" (Todd edition, 126, 130). Appropriately enough, Oroonoko's slave name is "Caesar" and like Caesar (to whom Bacon also compares himself) Oroonoko is betrayed and brutally sacrificed.

The dismemberment of Oroonoko is Behn's most grisly execution scene. Oroonoko is carved up piece by piece while he calmly smokes a pipe:

> the executioner came and first cut off his members and threw them in the fire. After that, with an ill-favored knife, they cut his ears, and his nose and burned them; he still smoked on, as if nothing had touched him. Then they hacked off one of his arms, and still he bore up, and held his pipe. But at the cutting of the other arm, his head sunk, and his pipe dropped, and he gave up the ghost without a groan or reproach. (140)

Behn's ultimate cavalier, flawless in every way, meets the most terrifying death.

Oroonoko has been analogized to Charles I and the duke of Monmouth, both of whom suffered spectacular executions, as well as to

---

[44] Ballaster, *Seductive Forms*, 81.
[45] Jane Spencer, *The Rise of the Woman Novelist* (New York: Basil Blackman, 1986), 48; Brown, *The Ends of Empire*, 37.

James II, on the eve of the Revolution that would overthrow him.[46] But there is no one-to-one political parallel in *Oroonoko*. Behn's Oroonoko would have been a roving cavalier in a happier time. But in the New World, he was both out of place and out of time – in much the same way as a sickly Behn must have felt in the spring of 1688 when *Oroonoko* was written and when the storm clouds of revolution loomed hauntingly.

The following spring, after the exile of James II and the coronation of William III and Mary II, Behn was asked by one of the great Whig architects of the revolution, Bishop Gilbert Burnet, to write some verses in celebration of the new king. She refused and wrote her last poem in response. In "A Pindarick Poem to the Reverend Doctor Burnet," Behn described herself as an "Excluded Prophet"; this "the Universal Turn" she wrote, "makes me Useless and Forlorn." Like her cavaliers, with whom she so much identified, the new age "leaves me unpity'd far behind."[47]

---

[46] Laura Brown equates Oroonoko with Charles I (*Ends of Empire*, 58); Janet Todd sees Monmouth as a possible inspiration (*Gender, Art and Death*, 33); and George Guffey identifies him with James II ("Aphra Behn's *Oroonoko*: Occasion and Accomplishment," in *Two English Novelists: Aphra Behn and Anthony Trollope* [Los Angeles, The William Andrews Clark Memorial Library, 1975], 3–41).

[47] "A Pindarick Poem to the Reverend Doctor Burnet, On the Honour he did me of Enquiring after me and my Muse," in *The Poems of Aphra Behn – A Selection*, ed. Janet Todd (London: William Pickering, 1994), 195–98.

Part II

Women's political and philosophical writings,
1690–1800

Introduction to Part II

Little attention has been given to women in the intellectual landscape of late seventeenth-century and eighteenth-century Britain and France. And the existing scholarship has focused overwhelmingly on feminist writings and on writings and efforts associated with the French Revolution, in Britain as well as France. This second part of *Women Writers and the Early Modern British Political Tradition* expands the reach to women writers and intellectuals beyond the radical and feminist debates of the late eighteenth century. Mary Astell and Lady Damaris Mascham are integrated into the philosophical discourse among Cambridge Platonists and Lockean epistemologists of the late seventeenth century, as active participants in the debate. The thought of Mary Wollstonecraft is placed in a broader and comparative context, linking her writings especially to those of her somewhat earlier contemporary, the historian Catharine Macaulay; and her response to Edmund Burke's *Reflections on the Revolution in France* is tied not alone to her views of women's place within the revolutionary debate, but to her radical theories of the nature of the state generally. Wollstonecraft's political views are also treated by integrating them into her portrayal of the family in eighteenth-century society. And finally, Emilie du Châtelet, the eighteenth-century French mathematician who produced the definitive translation of Newton's *Principia* so crucial for the evolution of Enlightenment thought, is studied to examine how genius remained a gendered concept among Enlightenment thinkers.

Patricia Springborg, building upon her earlier study of Astell's critique of Locke's *Second Treatise*, concentrates here on the role Astell and Locke's associate Damaris Masham played in the intellectual disputes of the late 1600s. Astell, a High-Church Anglican, was critical of Locke's overly rational Christianity and attacked it in a work, *The Christian Religion as Profess'd by a Daughter of the Church of England*, which Springborg notes Astell considered her *"magnum opus."* Masham, wishing to separate herself from any taint of having written either Astell's *Serious Proposal to the Ladies* (a plan for women's higher education) or the above attack on Locke's brand of Christianity, stated her own position in *Occasional Thoughts in Reference to a Virtuous or Christian Life*. While the wider backdrop for this work was the epistemological and contractual disputes among Filmer, Hobbes and Locke, Astell and Masham contributed to the debate based on their personal religious and intellectual loyalties and values.

Astell, in Springborg's analysis, supports the following Christian doctrine: "God is the only efficient cause of all our sensations and therefore the only worthy object of our love." This led her to reject Locke's "Ciceronian sociability" which focuses on love between men. Given the central love of God, Astell believed that love could not be directed toward humans and God "as bodies cannot have two Centers .. [nor] the Soul .. a twofold Desire." Such a view underlay her critique of both Hobbesian and Lockean contractual theory which she fought as subverting the importance of the deity. Greater attention in Springborg's chapter, though, is given to Masham, who has been less studied than Astell. Springborg points to the originality of *Occasional Thoughts*, showing how it revealed some continuing support of the Platonism of her father, Ralph Cudworth, along with clear agreement with Lockean Christianity. Masham did dispute the Platonist John Norris, whose ideas appeared in correspondence with Mary Astell in the *Letters Concerning the Love of God*, arguing that simply because God is the cause of our love does not mean all love must be directed towards him.

Accepting Locke's formulation that love is a "disposition toward that which pleases us," Masham rejected Norris's contention that we desire God but only experience "benevolent love" toward others. Platonists came close to mystical extravagances, in her view, and she directed her broad critique at Malebranch as well as Norris. Her analysis of the operation of cause and effect built upon Lockean epistemology, but she moved beyond Locke in arguing that focusing on God's love undercuts human purpose on earth and subverts God's stated purpose at creation.

Masham also directly took on, according to Springborg, Mary Astell's overly simple attachment to the deity. Using both Aristotelian appropriateness and Ciceronian sociability, she concentrated on the dual importance of human choice and experience, as well as qualities embedded in us by God. Masham distrusted any subversion of the social life, leading to an isolated existence, and she concluded that women might become the next generation of theorists, excluded from much of the *praxis* open to men in public settings. While Masham and Astell took opposite sides in the Platonic debates over the centrality of the love of God, they equally contributed to "establishing philosophy as a chosen realm of female endeavor." Astell's works went through numerous printings, and she was read and cited by leading male writers including Swift, Steele, and Berkeley; Masham was less cited, but her intellectual independence from both her father and Locke established her as a scholar pursuing her own claims to philosophical knowledge.

Wendy Gunther-Canada, in her comparative analysis of the reactions of Catharine Macaulay and Mary Wollstonecraft to Burke's views of the French Revolution, focuses on the dual values of sense and sensibility as central to eighteenth-century culture. Her analysis concentrates on Wollstonecraft's *The Vindication of the Rights of Men* and Macaulay's *Observations on the Reflections of the Right Honorable Edmund Burke*. It dissects the rhetorical style of each writer to highlight their differences. While Wollstonecraft's *Vindication of the Rights of Woman* is her most well-known work, it is her first *Vindication* that was the earliest critique of Burke's *Reflections*. Gunther-Canada notes that Wollstonecraft's use of sense and sensibility highlights binary opposites in late eighteenth-century thought, "reason and passion, masculine and feminine ... public and private." Utilizing recent studies of the growing importance of sensibility during the 1700s, which glorified female vulnerability, Gunther-Canada grapples with the conflict inherent in the positive use of "feminine" qualities in a society where public involvement is increasingly male. Thus, "to the extent that women aligned themselves with sensibility rather than sense, they were complicit in their own exclusion from wider participation in the public realm."

Burke's opposition to the revolution was tied to maintaining his view of proper class and gender hierarchies. He opposed the revolution not simply for its violence and lack of appreciation for custom; it also offended his sense of who should make decisions and who should act in a society. According to Gunther-Canada, this allowed Wollstonecraft and Macaulay to employ contemporary gender assumptions against him. Wollstonecraft viewed Burke's style as effeminate, reflecting the influence of sensibility in his passionate language, while Macaulay castigated Burke's "subtle sophistry" and believed that he had given up defense of liberty in support of faction. They each believed that sensibility subverted rational discourse, and understood its harm when applied to their own sex. But Wollstonecraft also turned to sensibility in the *Vindication*, and Macaulay only side-stepped the difficulty by ignoring any question of sexual inequality in her *Observations*. In the *Vindication*, Wollstonecraft sought to defeat Burke on his own rhetorical grounds; she claimed that Burke's "pampered sensibility" worked in his writing to "dispel the sober suggestions of reason" and led him to inflame rather than enlighten his readers. She was especially appalled at his non-rational assumptions concerning the women's march on Versailles and his defense of Marie

Antoinette. Rejecting Burke's reasoning, Wollstonecraft viewed him as resorting to emotionalism to defend his own indefensible advantages. Yet, Gunther-Canada contends, Wollstonecraft resorted herself to the values of sentimentality in her discussion of the Parisian poor.

Wollstonecraft hoped to end the negative impact of gender stereotypes on government through a "civic friendship" between men and women which would lead, in Gunther-Canada's words, to future good government "uncorrupted by the politics of sense and sensibility." Catharine Macaulay saw Burke's attack on "all the rights of man" sought in France as a new salvo in their earlier disputes. She represented uncompromising Whiggish principles during the 1770s, in her justification of revolutionary heroes of the 1640s and 1688 in her eight-volume *History of England*, and now in the *Observations on the Reflections of the Right Honorable Edmund Burke*. In these works she emphasized the need to grant fuller citizenship at home as well as to support revolutionary efforts abroad, both linked to the broad "enlightenment of the French people." Adopting Wollstonecraft's strategy of attacking Burke's style, she characterized the *Reflections* as a work of passion, not one characteristic of "reflecting men." Burke's corrupting ties to the English court denied him ability to view critically and objectively the problems at the French court. As a supporter of aristocratic self-interest, Burke, Macaulay claimed, ignored the people's actual role in selecting their own government and left them in a state of Hobbesian powerlessness where their natural rights were forfeited to an unaccountable monarch.

Finally, both Wollstonecraft and Macaulay adopted sense or reason as their political guide, severely criticizing the sensibility they associated with Burke's *Reflections*. Yet this tack, according to Gunther-Canada, may have solidified in the public's view the tie between sexual difference and the world of politics, thus further isolating women from a public role and "reifying a masculine model of political discourse." Still each author revealed that she had the confidence and authority to speak on topics and through venues not then proper for her sex, and, in her own writings, negated some of the public/private, male/female, rational/passionate splits.

Mary Lyndon Shanley integrates Wollstonecraft's critique of the operations of patriarchy in the home and in the state. In so doing, she assesses not merely Wollstonecraft's political writings, especially *The Vindication of the Rights of Woman*, but her works of fiction, in particular *The Wrongs of Woman, or Maria*. Shanley contends that Wollstonecraft's "understanding of 'sensibility' and of sexuality, as well as of 'rights' and legal equality'" was at the "center of her political thought." Yet Wollstonecraft makes maternity central to women's lives in her discourse of rights. Shanley contends that rights doctrine was not paramount for Wollstonecraft, and that her works are closer to "the examination of moral education of *Emile*" than to "the analyses of the legal foundations of citizenship in the treatises of Hobbes or Locke." Wollstonecraft, according to Shanley, in attacking Talleyrand's suggestions for a separate education for French women, ridiculed the socialization of both sexes that made them accept the subordination of the interests of one to the other. In her critique of sensibility in *The Vindication*, Wollstonecraft sought education for women as equal, rational creatures. Unlike Rousseau, she argued that women's duties as mothers did not exclude them from the state or deny them the need for serious education, but did mean that they, as mothers, had a special role in raising their children and assisting others, while their husbands were to be more active citizens.

Wollstonecraft's most important goal, as stated by Shanley, was to demonstrate "that difference need not inevitably lead to hierarchy and subjection." She sought a greater equality within marriage based on an understanding that the duties of both sexes were "human" duties. Education was essential both for mothers and for single women to maintain themselves. In *The Wrongs of Woman, or Maria*, Wollstonecraft carried forward this theme in a darker analysis of the control patriarchy placed on female sexuality, as well as the conservative politics she witnessed in England and during the Terror in France in the five years between the *Vindication* and *The Wrongs*. In the novel, set within a prison where lower- and middle-class women recount their abuses under patriarchy, Wollstonecraft outlines the seduction, rape, and abandonment that characterized the lives of so many of her British sisters, as well as her personal abandonment by Gilbert Imlay after giving birth to their child. While out-of-wedlock childbirth was devastating for women, according to Shanley, Wollstonecraft especially hated "marital slavery" because it was supported by the state and determined by women's negligible economic options. Thus women must base their life on a rational course – not reason separated from the demands of maternity – but one recognizing women's legal and martial powerlessness, providing them with income and independence to maintain themselves and their children. Such values led Wollstonecraft to urge social policies which would guarantee men's support of their children, provide adequate jobs for women, and give women a political and legal voice to defend themselves. It was necessary to have a legal and political system which recognized and respected the range of human responsibilities and which guaranteed women's equal recognition.

Judith Zinsser's study of Emilie du Châtelet seeks to bring this physicist and mathematician of early eighteenth-century France out of the shadows of her relationship with Voltaire, which has so dominated scholarly and popular accounts. Zinsser supports du Châtelet's placement within this collection on women's political writings by delineating the risks du Châtelet took to publish and her reception by the intellectual institutions, as well as the leading intellectuals of her day. The thrust of her thought carried with it its own political liabilities: "her explanations of English and German ideas of the universe disagreed with the prevailing Cartesian explanations of France's Royal Academy of Sciences and thus challenged the government's intellectual authority and political hegemony."

While du Châtelet lived a most unconventional life, living openly with Voltaire on her husband's estate, she performed the appropriate domestic duties for both households, and, according to Zinsser, raised her daughter "even more conventionally than she had been for the arranged marriage of an aristocratic woman's traditional life." She also deferred to Voltaire's needs, setting aside her own projects to offer diversion or to assist in his work. The households indulged in domestic theater, and she devoted time to entertaining guests. She did so in 1738 at a time, Zinsser points out, also marked by the following intellectual projects: "work in algebra and Euclidian geometry, Newton's optics, hypothesizing about the rational bases of French grammar, biblical exegesis, and Leibnizian metaphysics."

Du Châtelet doubted her own genius and thus she translated the works of others. She chose Mandeville's work because she considered it "the best book of morals that was ever written." Du Châtelet believed there were three varieties of genius: creative genius, a person with "natural ability," and those "pulling out the thorns" embedded in the paths of true genius. Clearly she identified with the latter category (while never formally claiming it), although Parisian scientists later made a higher claim for her work. Yet, while questioning her own talents, she still looked to women's limited education, which they "have a right to protest against," as the reason why no works of genius "left the hand of women." Sounding similar to Mary Astell and Mary Wollstonecraft, she criticized women being trained for fashion and dissipation. And she personally felt "all the weight of prejudice that excludes us so universally from the sciences." She experienced, according to Zinsser, exclusion from informal café gatherings of scientists and mathematicians as well as discussions of the Royal Academy of Sciences. Only through Voltaire's support was the cost of much of her scientific equipment and publication covered. She also experienced difficulty in securing tutorials with leading scientists, and her work on fire, published by the Royal

Academy, carried with it a dismissal of her as a "flighty woman" in the introduction. Many of her works remained in manuscript and were ultimately lost.

While accepting the circumscribed role of translator, companion, and student, the reality of du Châtelet's intellectual career was often quite different. As Zinsser notes, even in her translation of the *Fable of the Bees*, she altered the work to make it her own: "trimming the style, reframing examples for a French audience and adding her own reflections whenever the material suggested it." From 1736 until she died in 1749 she devoted attention to mastering the texts of natural philosophy and celestial mechanics. In 1735 she had left Paris for Cirey to be with Voltaire, who she wrote others she greatly loved, but later claimed it also allowed her to give up the frivolous life women faced at court. While praising isolation, she also took pride in the publication of her works, and their quality, even claiming that the "tyranny" of men might aid women's intellectual achievements by denying them the possibility of writing "bad books." Her serious commitment to science and philosophy paid off as her contemporaries gave her credit for making the theories of Newton accessible and for opening up Leibniz's ideas that others had not "yet dared to broach and which they regarded as almost indecipherable." While garnering intellectual praise for her work, she also took political risks in a nation where physics and metaphysics were still closely entwined, and any attacks on the beliefs of the Church were suspect. She protected herself through court contacts and by avoiding publication of her moral philosophy and biblical commentaries.

Du Châtelet's most important intellectual contribution, the translation of Newton's *Principia* (which remains the standard French translation today), was again more than simple translation. She clarified his meanings and included, as Zinsser notes, "the additions and corrections of Newton's work by French scientists." Du Châtelet worked to enhance women's intellectual respect; in her *Institutions de physique*, she remained anonymous but illustrated the title-page with a woman scientist instructing her sons, undercutting the chivalric and romantic images utilized by others, including Voltaire. She died during childbirth, pregnant by a French officer at age forty-two. Her complicated life revealed her as a leading scientific scholar, a wife, mother and companion, and a woman determined that her work be credited and respected. Working to fit an impossible schedule into a twenty-four-hour period, she, in so many ways, exemplified the realities and values that dedicated the intellectual world and its accomplishments to men. Yet, even in her relationship with one of France's most important intellectuals, she still could claim, by characterizing their libraries, different, and even superior, intellectual interests for herself; his, she claimed "was 'all anecdotes,' hers 'all philosophy.' "

The realities of these late seventeenth- and eighteenth-century women intellectuals and writers reveal both the restrictions on, and importance of, women writers in the political and intellectual circles of their day. They lacked the institutional affiliations that might bring recognition of their work, and even followers; but they possessed the abilities and sufficient contacts with leading male intellectuals for their works not to be ignored. The Platonist John Norris chose to publish his correspondence with Mary Astell, in part because of the acclaim she had received for *A Serious Proposal to the Ladies*, and Locke engaged in numerous debates with Damaris Masham because of both the quality of her mind and his connections to her family. Given women's exclusion from higher education in early modern Europe, it was these personal connections that brought attention to their work, but has ultimately led to their omission from the intellectual histories of their age. Mary Wollstonecraft and Catharine Macaulay have been less tied to the reputation of individual male thinkers, but Wollstonecraft has been consistently characterized by her personal relationships, either with Gilbert Imlay, or later with William Godwin, who controlled her literary estate and crafted the image he wanted left of her. Châtelet is forever bound to Voltaire, not simply because virtually all we know about her is embedded in his personal papers, but also because it is he, as a prominent *philosophe*, who has standing in our conception of eighteenth-century French thought. Thus our understanding of the nature of these women's writings, political and otherwise, remains complicated by the difficulty we face in viewing them as individuals and in reconstructing their full role in the intellectual and political disputes of their day.

5   Astell, Masham, and Locke: religion and politics

Patricia Springborg

Astell, Norris, and the Platonist critique of Hobbes and Locke

This chapter addresses a specific intervention in philosophy of mind debated at the turn of the seventeenth and eighteenth centuries between John Locke and Hobbesian materialists, on one side, and Cambridge Platonists, on the other, in which two women philosophers, Mary Astell (1666–1731) and Lady Damaris Masham (1658–1708), participated with as yet unacknowledged significance.[1] Astell, a northern English gentlewoman of little means, early established her philosophical credentials with *Letters Concerning the Love of God*,[2] published in 1695 at the instigation of her interlocutor, John Norris (1657–1711), Rector of Bemerton, a known Cambridge Platonist. Astell established her literary reputation, considerable in her day, as the author of a tract on women's education, *A Serious Proposal to the Ladies* (1694, 1697); for her *Reflections upon Marriage* (1700), in response to the scandalous divorce of Hortense Mazarine; and as a Cambridge Platonist and interlocutor with John Norris. On the strength of her philosophical credentials she was to enter political controversy in 1704 with three pamphlets on Occasional Conformity, the question whether occasional attendance at Anglican service sufficed as a test of state loyalty for civil servants and eligibility for office, on which religious toleration specifically turned.[3]

---

[1] For a general discussion of Astell's critique of Locke, see Patricia Springborg, "Mary Astell (1666–1731), Critic of Locke," *American Political Science Review* 89, 3 (September 1995): 621–33; and my introductions to *Mary Astell (1666–1731): Political Writings* (Cambridge: Cambridge University Press, 1996) and *Mary Astell, A Serious Proposal to the Ladies* (London: Pickering and Chatto, 1996).

[2] Mary Astell, *Letters Concerning the Love of God, between the Author of the Proposal to the Ladies and Mr. John Norris*, published by J. Norris, Rector of Bemerton nr. Sarum. London: Printed for Samuel Manship (Wing 1254) 1695.

[3] Astell's three Tory tracts of 1704, all probably commissioned by her High Church Tory printer, Ralph Wilkin, are in order of publication: *Moderation truly Stated: or a Review of a Late Pamphlet, Entitul'd Moderation a Virtue, or, The Occasional Conformist Justified from the Imputation of Hypocricy . . . With a Prefatory Discourse to Dr. D'Avenent, Concerning His Late Essays on Peace and War*, London: Printed by J.L. for Richard Wilkin, at the King's

Damaris Masham, wife of Sir Francis Masham, and famous as the companion of John Locke, who lived with the Masham family at Oates, was the daughter of the Cambridge Platonist Ralph Cudworth (1617–88). Lady Masham, whose work has received less recent attention than Astell's – and is for that reason addressed more fully here – showed philosophical acuity young as the dedicatee of an earlier work by Norris, *Reflections upon the Conduct of Human Life* (1690). When Astell's *Serious Proposal* was published anonymously in 1694, it was taken for the work of Masham and widely criticized for its Platonism and for smacking too much of an Anglican nunnery. Astell's *Letters Concerning the Love of God* of 1695, while naming Norris, referred to Astell herself anonymously as the author of *A Serious Proposal*, leaving it open for the public to conclude that these were the work of Masham as well. However, not only was this not the case, but to prove it Masham rushed into print with her impassioned rebuttal, *The Discourse Concerning the Love of God* of 1695, directed explicitly at Norris and at Astell by implication.

The three-cornered debate between Astell, Damaris Masham, and Locke which ensued represents an important episode in the discourse addressing the reception of Locke's *Reasonableness of Christianity* (1695), immediately perceived to be an inflammatory work.[4] Other important items in this debate, in which the foundations of modern philosophy of mind were disclosed, include: Locke's celebrated *Essay Concerning Understanding*,[5] his response to John Norris's critique of the *Essay*[6] and

Head, in St. Paul's Church-yard, 1704 (Folger Library, BX5202.A8.Cage); *A Fair Way with the Dissenters and their Patrons*, London, Printed for E.P. by R. Wilkin, at the Kings's Head in St. Paul's Church-yard, 1704 (Folger Library, BX5202.A7.Cage); and *An Impartial Enquiry into the Causes of Rebellion and Civil War in this Kingdom in an Examination of Dr. Kennett's Sermon, Jan. 31, 1703/4, and Vindication of the Royal Martyr*, London, Printed by E.P. by R. Wilkin, at the Kings's Head in St. Paul's Church-yard, 1704 (Folger Library, BV4253.K4.C75.Cage). They entered the Tory canon as specific responses to Whiggish works by James Owen, Daniel Defoe, and Bishop White Kennett, respectively. See James Owen, *Moderation a Vertue: Or, the Occasional Conformist Justify'd from the Imputation of Hypocrisy* (London, 1703); Daniel Defoe, *The Shortest Way with the Dissenters: Or Proposals for the Establishment of the Church* (London, 1702) and *More Short-Ways with the Dissenters* (London, 1703); and White Kennett's *A Compassionate Enquiry into the Causes of the Civil War: In a Sermon Preached in the Church of St. Botolph Aldgate, On January 31, 1704, the Day of the Fast or the Martyrdom of King Charles I* (London, 1704). The last two are published in *Mary Astell: Political Writings*, ed. Patricia Springborg.

4 John Locke, "The Reasonableness of Christianity, as Delivered in the Scriptures," in *The Works of John Locke* (London: Printed for Thomas Tegg, W. Sharpe and Son et al., [1695] 1823), VII, 1–158.
5 John Locke, *Essay Concerning Human Understanding*, in *The Works of John Locke*, I–IV.
6 John Locke, "Remarks upon some of Mr. Norris's Books, wherein he asserts P. Malebranche's Opinion of seeing all Things in God," in *The Works of John Locke*, X, 247–59.

his correspondence with Stillingfleet;[7] Masham's lesser known response to the Astell–Norris correspondence, the *Discourse Concerning the Love of God* (1696),[8] which Astell took to be the work of Locke; Astell's rebuttal, *The Christian Religion as Profess'd by a Daughter of the Church* (1705),[9] considered by her to be her *magnum opus*; and Masham's reply in turn, *Occasional Thoughts in Reference to a virtuous or Christian Life* (1705).

It is worth noting that Mary Astell, who challenged so many conventions of her age, challenges those of ours by turning back from explicitly political works to the field of religion and homily as her chosen stamping ground. Religion, after all, was the socially approved place for educated women, whose intervention in politics was not to be tolerated. But to consider religion in any way a private or non-political matter would be to adopt a division between the public and private spheres that, although endorsed by Hobbes and Locke, was vehemently rejected by Astell herself. The liberal contractarian view had been inserted into a much older organic theory to which Astell appealed, and which communitarian philosophers have attempted to restore along similar lines.[10] Astell believed that the richness and diversity of civil society and the state rely as much on the efforts of the lonely scholar or philosophical interlocutor as they do on the work of political delegates or representatives. For each citizen in undertaking her duty to work undertakes to represent every other. Astell was surely not wrong in judging that her contributions to philosophy, her true "calling" as she perceived it, were at least as important as her political works, already celebrated in her day. There she could feel at home in the company of René Descartes (1596–1650), Nicolas Malebranche (1638–1715), Antoine Arnauld (1612–94), Pierre Nicole (1625–95), and Locke himself, while abjuring the lampooning and acrimony that more overtly political works had brought down upon her head.

Astell's stance, so puzzling to commentators, trod a fine line between Filmerian royalist critique of the social contract theory of Hobbes, and subsequently Locke, and a trenchant anti-patriarchalism, as challenging to Filmer as that of Locke, but on entirely different grounds. For Astell

---

[7] Locke's first letter to Stillingfleet (Locke, *Works*, 1832 ed., IV, 1–96), is dated January 7, 1696/7; his second (*Works*, 1823 ed., IV, 97–184), is dated June 29, 1696; and his third (*Works*, 1823 ed., IV, 191–498), is dated May 4, 1698.

[8] Damaris Masham, *Discourse Concerning the Love of God*, London: Printed for Awnsham and John Churchill 1696.

[9] Mary Astell, *The Christian Religion as Profess'd by a Daughter of the Church of England in a Letter to the Right Honourable T.L., C.I.*, London: Printed by S.H. for R. Wilkin, at the King's Head in St. Paul's Churchyard, 1705 [Folger Library 216595].

[10] See especially Alasdair MacIntyre, *After Virtue* (Notre Dame, Ind.: University of Notre Dame Press, 1981); Michael Sandel, *Liberalism and the Limits of Justice* (Cambridge: Cambridge University Press, 1982), and the literatures these works have generated.

rejected appeals to Adamite patrilineal succession as grounds either for the subordination of women or the legitimization of kings. Indeed, in *Reflections upon Marriage* and *A Serious Proposal, Part II*, she rejected all customary authority except that of the church, arguing that precedent could not establish what reason would never admit: the categorial inequality of the sexes, or relations of domination and subordination more generally. The power of husbands over their wives, fathers over their children and kings over their subjects, had no philosophical justification as such. They were quite simply social and political expedients which the church tolerated in the name of social order in temporal society, a testing ground for the celestial Kingdom of God, in which souls would finally enjoy the deathless and sexless life of angels for which they were created. Astell both fundamentally challenged Hobbesian laws of natural reason, capable of creating from relations of equality between men and women, subjects and kings, a society founded on radical inequality. And she equally challenged the contractarianism of Locke and the Whigs, daring them to apply in the family the criteria by which they held kings to account: contractual relations between free and equal individuals.

Very rarely do commentators position the materialist epistemology of Hobbes and Locke in the political context to which it belongs: that of providing transparent foundations for a juridical-political solution by means of social contract to the dynastic instability of hereditary monarchy founded on patrilineality. The more acute dynastic volatility became, under the combined pressures of Stuart infecundity and the cross-pressures of Puritan and Filmerian patriarchalism, the more imperative a new and widely accepted juridical foundation for political obligation became. Hobbes had produced the original black box theory of mind in which sense data constitute inputs and ideas outputs. Incorporating the new science of optics and inspired by a desire to break the monopoly of scholastic theory in the universities,[11] Hobbes's epistemology, like that of Descartes, was designed to provide in philosophy scientific proofs as a substitute for truths wrapped up in sacred mysteries.[12] In this way he hoped with *Leviathan*, a work

---

[11] Note Hobbes's early insinuation to this effect in the closing lines of chapter 1 of *Leviathan*: "I say not this, as disapproving the use of Universities: but because I am to speak hereafter of their office in a Commonwealth, I must let you see on all occasions by the way, what things would be amended in them; amongst which the frequency of insignificant Speech is one" (Thomas Hobbes, *Leviathan* [1651 ed.], 4; ed. Richard Tuck [Cambridge: Cambridge University Press, 1991], 14).

[12] Note Astell's use of ecstatic Platonist language to characterize God, who "has folded up his own Nature, not in Darkness, but in an adorable and inaccessible Light" (*A Serious Proposal, Part II* [1697 ed., 74).

addressed to ordinary citizens and designed to be taught in the universities, to persuade Englishmen to apply to politics the self-confidence in their own counsel that as members of the Protestant community of believers they displayed in religion. Locke, although in different terms, displayed the same concern to provide grounds of obedience transparent and compelling to the common man. Locke, already further down the track, and perhaps less self-conscious than Hobbes about his project, not only subscribed to sensationalist psychology, but was equally zealous in defanging religion, source of civil conflict and war.

To anticipate charges of reductionism, let me point out that I assume their epistemologies corresponded to true beliefs unless proven otherwise. In Hobbes's case, certain antimonies suggest that this may have been a theory for others, however. In Locke's case, a man less bold than Hobbes, his epistemology, set out in the famous *Essay Concerning Human Understanding* of 1690, is less an exploration of human cognitive powers than of their limits. Locke expressed systematic doubt about the power of human understanding to determine causality and theorize universals from particulars, a Pyrrhonic scepticism for which Hume is so famous. In this respect Locke honestly followed the trail of Hobbesian sensationalism. For Hobbes subscribed to Stoic atomist metaphysics according to which matter in motion presented itself to cognition in cause–event sequences. But he could not furnish a metaphysics to make sure ontological facts knowable. As Hume was later to insist, apparent chains of causes can never on the basis of sense data be proven to be more than repeated coincidence. An infinity of repeated event sequences will not confirm causality at work in the absence of a causal mechanism, and this empiricism cannot supply.

Locke, whose epistemology is disarmingly humble, maintained that, as presented to cognition in the form of sense data, external entities exhibit primary and secondary qualities. Primary qualities are the grand dimensions of time, space, and extension. On these, the qualities of existence and substance, the mind has less purchase than on secondary qualities of color, texture, hot, cold, etc. Locke had endorsed Descartes's *cogito* as an observation even a child could make. But as easy as it was for a child to conclude from the reflexivity of thinking that he or she existed, was it impossible to go beyond the understanding of a child concerning what this "existence" constituted:[13] "when we talk of substances, we talk like children; who, being asked a question about somewhat which they knew not, readily give this satisfactory answer, that it is something."

---

[13] *Essay Concerning Human Understanding*, Bk. 2, chap. 23, §2, 1690 ed., 157–58.

Locke had the temerity to compare the mysteriousness of existence in the Christian mind with the "I-know-not-what" of Indian pantheism: "it is 'only an uncertain supposition of we know not what'. And therefore it is paralleled, more than once, with the Indian philosopher's 'He-knew-not-what'; what supported the tortoise, that supported the elephant, that supported the earth: so substance was found only to support accidents."

Such irreverence, equivalent to his passing remark that sensationalist psychology could not rule out the possibility that matter could think, was sufficient to galvanize Astell, who had reason enough to be critical of Locke.

The Astell–Norris exchange

It is noteworthy that Astell's strictly religious works both took epistolary form. It is a commonplace that eighteenth-century women were often confined to this mode, and Astell's *Letters Concerning the Love of God* are epistolary in this sense, the correspondence between a pious young woman and her preacher. Her *magnum opus*, *The Christian Religion as Profess'd by a Daughter of the Church of England*, is epistolary in a different mode, in imitation of the correspondence between the bishop of Worcester, Edward Stillingfleet, and John Locke; a philosophical debate over Locke's *Essay Concerning Human Understanding*, of which, among other things, it represents a continuation. Astell's career closes where it began on questions of the life of faith, the epistemology and metaphysics on which it is founded, the structures of church and government required to promote it, political machinations and the conspiracy of manners and mores designed to subvert it. Relative inattention to Astell's philosophical and theological works has meant that modern readers of her more ephemeral political pamphlets, and even the time-less *Reflections upon Marriage*, underestimate the degree to which they were embedded in these deeper philosophical issues.[14]

In the *Letters Concerning the Love of God Between the Author of the Proposal to the Ladies and Mr. John Norris*, published at Norris's instiga-tion, Astell discloses serious philosophical interests and already-formed opinions on political matters. We "put on our Religion as we do our

---

[14] No modern edition yet exists for what Astell herself considered to be her *magnum opus*, *The Christian Religion as Profess'd by a Daughter of the Church of England* (1705). The important preparatory work, Astell's *A Serious Proposal, part II*, an exposition of the philosophy of the Jensenist Port Royal School, so influential on Locke, and to which Astell holds him to account, is similarly neglected. See the Introduction to Patricia Springborg's edition of *A Serious Proposal to the Ladies*, Parts I and II (London: Pickering and Chatto, 1996).

Cloathes in Conformity to the Fashion," she says.[15] Early she complains against "the sottishness of those dull *Epicureans*, who make it their Business to hunt after Pleasures as vain and unsatisfactory as their admirers are Childish and Unwise."[16] Later she pillories those "pretenders to piety" whose language of utility, interest, advantage, and pleasure betrays their intentions.[17] In all these instances Locke would qualify. She also lets slip familiarity with the language of passive obedience and resistance in a remark designed to forestall debate over their relative merits:[18]

I cannot discern wherein the Virtue of a bare Submission consists, such a passive Obedience to GOD is like the new Notion some have got of passive Obedience to their Governors, a being content to suffer when we know not how to help it; but our Divine Amorist has an intire Complacency in whatever GOD allots, he in a manner goes forth to meet it, chuses, justifies, and rejoyces in it.

Moreover, she betrays some acquaintance with the demarcations made by Aristotle between the familial, political, and economic realms. Observing: "I cannot forbear to reckon it an irregular Affection, and an Effect of Vitious Self-love, to love any Person merely on account of his Relation to us,"[19] she concludes, "I should therefore chuse to derive the Reasons why we are in the first place to regard our Relations, rather from Justice, and the Rules of Oeconomy [Aristotle's household management], than from Love."[20]

---

[15] Letter IX, St. Philip and St. James, 1694; 1695 ed., 212.

[16] Letter VII, 1695 ed., 128.

[17] Letter XI, June 21, 1694; 1695 ed., 272–73:
> The vulgar and Men of carnal Appetites partly out of Ignorance, and partly to lighten as they fancy their own Crimes, being too prone to reflect that Dash of secular Interest, that time-serving or over-great Solicitude for the World, or perhaps their too great Opinion of themselves, or Censoriousness on others, which zealous Pretenders to piety are sometimes apt to slip into, even on that unblemished Beauty, whose Livery they wear, which I am sure gives no Allowance to such unsuitable Mixtures, however her Votaries happen to admit them.

[18] Letter XI, June 21, 1694; 1695 ed., 268–69.

[19] This remark has been widely read as Astell's confession of (lesbian) love of Lady Catherine Jones. Since it is a question on which we have no further evidence, I make no personal judgment.

[20] Letter XI, June 21, 1694; 1695 ed., 271. Aristotle in his distinctions in the *Politics*, between paternal, marital, despotic, and political power – as the powers of a father, husband, slave owner, and magistrate, respectively – had created a distinction between private and public spheres that Hobbes and Locke, for different reasons, were keen to revive. See Aristotle, *Politics*, Bk. I, para. 2, 1252a 9–15, Loeb Classical Library ed. (ed. H. Rackham, London: Heinemann, 1932), 3: "Those then who think that the natures of the statesman [*politikon*], the royal ruler [*basilikon*], the head of an estate [*oikonomikon*] and the master of a family [*despotikon*] are the same, are mistaken (they imagine that the difference between these various forms of authority is between greater and smaller numbers, not a difference in kind."

Astell already introduces a definite political dimension to her piety. At the same time she gives some hint of the strains placed upon her by the cross-pressures of an internal Anglican debate between the followers of Richard Hooker, who emphasized a classic formulation of tolerance for "things indifferent"; between Laudian Erastians, who pushed for greater conformity; and between supporters of Lockean rational Christianity who provided the basis for that conformity in religious toleration. Her thesis that God is the only efficient cause of all our sensations and therefore the only worthy object of our love, was pointed to emphasize its antithesis: that to love our neighbour as ourselves was therefore a species of benevolence and not of love. The passion behind the antithesis, and the language in which it is expressed, suggests that Astell takes strong exception to Ciceronian sociability as the basis for a civil society, on which the philosophy of Hobbes and Locke is founded. In the idiom of Platonism she disclaims: "He that has discovered the Fountain will not seek for troubled and failing Streams to quench his Thirst"; and again: "He can never be content to step aside to catch at the Shadow who is in Pursuit and View of the Substance."[21] Drawing on the metaphor of the love of God as a stream of affectivity whereby like attracts like, she declares: "The Soul that loves GOD has no occasion to love other things, because it needs nor expects Felicity from them whenever it moves towards the Creature it must necessarily forsake the Creator."[22] Wondering whether "this may be thought a skrewing up things to too great Height, a winding up our Nature to a Pitch it is not able to reach,"[23] she does not hesitate boldly to declaim:[24] "And therefore an ardent Lover of GOD will consider how incongruous it is to present him with a mean and narrow Soul, a Heart grovling on the Earth, cleaving to little dirty Creatures."

The passion of her antithesis, in which we see the faint outlines of a critique of Hobbes and Locke, is only matched by the extravagant transports of her thesis, earning her, not unjustly, the unwanted epithet of "enthusiasm". Addressing herself "to the World, to persons not sensible of their Obligations," she interrogates them:[25]

then let me ask them if they do not feel the Rays of his Goodness sweetly insinuating into every Part, clearing up the Darkness of their Understanding, warming their benummed Affections, regulating their oblique Motions, and melting down their obstinate, ingrateful, disingenuous Wills? Do they not feel these Cords of a Man as himself is pleased to call them, these silken Bands of

---

[21] Letter IX, St. Philip and St. James, 1694; 1695 ed., 203.   [22] Ibid.
[23] Letter IX, St. Philip and St. James, 1694; 1695 ed., 203–204.   [24] Ibid., 207.
[25] Letter XI, June 21, 1694; 1695 ed., 261–62.

Love, these odoriferous Perfumes drawing them after him, uniting them to him by the most potent Charms?

But behind the hyperbole a serious thesis lurked: "Love being the same to the Soul that Motion is to Bodies, as bodies cannot have two Centers, or different Terms of Motion, so neither can the Soul have a twofold Desire."[26] Astell uses the language of Hobbesian and Lockean mechanism, to convict their supporters of logical inconsistency.

Masham's response to the Astell–Norris correspondence

Damaris Masham's indictment of Norris, once held by her in regard, is extraordinary from the daughter of Ralph Cudworth, once a Cambridge Platonist herself. Commentators have speculated on likely causes for her animus. She may have been offended, as Hutton suggests, by his misinformation that her poor eyesight had already resulted in blindness, and by his subsequent advice to her that the pursuit of learning could only divert a mind which should be directed to spirituality. She might also have shared Locke's suspicion in 1692 that Norris had opened correspondence between Locke and his hostess at Oates.[27] Whatever the case, her well-reasoned response was devastating and by no means suggests a mere acolyte of Locke.

It is worth noting that in the more than 120 pages Damaris Masham devoted to refutation of Norris's *Practical Discourses*, she reproduced none of Locke's arguments verbatim, although in some important instances alluding to and developing his ideas, testimony to her independence of mind if such were needed. Masham is an important source for the influence of Malebranche and the Cambridge Platonists on Locke. From his correspondence of January 1682 we learn that Locke discussed with her John Smith's *Discourse Concerning the True Way or Method of Attaining Divine Knowledge*[28] and that Masham was not inclined to dismiss Smith's Platonist taxonomy of knowledge. She even conceded with him that there may be a "Higher Principle," named by Henry More "Divine Sagacitie": "a Degree of Perfection to be attain'd to in this Life to which the Powers of meere Unassisted Reason will never Conduct a Man," quickly reassuring Locke, "not that I think more meanly of Reason I beleeve then you do, much less would lay aside the use of it as many do."[29]

---

[26] Letter IX, St. Philip and St. James, 1694; 1695 ed., 201.
[27] See Locke, *Correspondence*, IV, #1546, #1564, #1575, #1606, cited by Sarah Hutton, in "Damaris Cudworth, Lady Masham: Between Platonism and Enlightenment," *British Journal for the History of Philosophy*, 1, 1 (1993), 35 n. 23.
[28] Smith, *Select Discourses*.
[29] Locke, *Correspondence*, 684, cited by Sarah Hutton, in "Damaris Cudworth, Lady Masham," 29–54, esp. 43. On Masham's influence on Locke's philosophy more

Locke, whose epistemological system does not easily admit differentiation of modes, had rejected Smith's specification of "four types of knowledge," preferring to call them "several degrees of the love of God and practise of vertue," which may assist knowledge but do not constitute different types of knowledge. Reason is a natural faculty, analysis cannot dissolve it into parts but, like eyesight, it can be assisted. Use of the eye metaphor, with which the *Essay* begins, suggests that, for Locke too, the image of "seeing all things in God" was powerful, if controversial: "The Understanding, like the Eye, whilst it makes us see, and perceive all other Things, takes no notice of it self: And it requires Art and Pains to set it at a distance and make it its own Object."[30]

The Locke *Correspondence* gives several instances of Masham's efforts to explain the Platonists to Locke – and one of her despair at being asked by him to explain further Smith's book, where she begs Locke:[31] "let me know what those things that you dislike in it, without applying your self (I beseech you) any more to mee to make you understand any thing which you did not before. What you Comprehend not I am not very likely to make you, and you may be still ignorant if the Author have not sufficiently expland himself." Hutton takes this statement by Masham to express an early lack of confidence, compared with her mature self-assurance as a follower of Locke.[32] But it may equally be interpreted as expressing the view that Locke is never going to commit himself on such matters because of epistemological doubts. Masham's letter of 1688 further suggests that she does not harbour Lockean skepticism on such matters just because the mechanical details of perception cannot be supplied:[33] "Besides, that being my self Cur'd of some sort of Scepticisme by arguments However Solid in themselves have beene to me effectual, I think that I may much more Advantageously employ my Houres in Pursuing the end of these Speculations then in indeavouring to Extricate those Difficulties that the Witts of Men have Intangled them with."

Published a year after the Astell–Norris exchange, *Letters Concerning the Love of God*, Masham's *Discourse* mentioned neither Astell nor Locke by name.[34] Masham's focus was different from that of Locke, empha-

---

generally, see Sheryl O'Donnell, "'My Idea in Your Mind': John Locke and Damaris Cudworth Masham," in *Mothering the Mind*, eds. Ruth Perry and Martine Brownley (New York: Holmes and Meier, 1984), 26–46.

[30] Locke, *Essay*, i.i.i, cited by Sarah Hutton, in "Damaris Cudworth, Lady Masham," 44, n. 62.

[31] Locke, *Correspondence*, #684, cited by Hutton, 48.   [32] Hutton, 48.

[33] Locke, *Correspondence*, #1040, cited by Hutton, 48.

[34] Hutton ("Damaris Cudworth," 34–35) states categorically: "The Book which occasioned the attack was a collection of letters by Norris and Mary Astell published as *Letters*

sizing the inherently solipsistic nature of the Malebranchiste theory of the love of God. She argued that Malebranche and Norris, as Platonists, denied inherent human sociability, which the second commandment to "love one's neighbour as oneself," vouchsafed. By making love of God the medium of perception in general, and by deeming love of creatures for their own sake idolatrous, Malebranche and Norris oriented individuals toward the otherworldly and away from society. Such otherworldiness made "it impossible to live in the daily Commerce and Conversation of the World, and love God as we ought to do."[35] Masham thus connected Norris's quietism to Astell's love of retirement in a devastating accusation of irrationality and enthusiasm:[36]

These Opinions of Mr. *N.* seem also to indanger the introducing, especially amongst those whose Imaginations are stronger than their Reason, a Devout way of talking; which having no sober, and intelligible sense under it, will either inevitably by degrees beget an Insensibility to Religion, in those themselves who use it, as well as others; By thus acustoming them to handle Holy things without Fear; or else will turn to as wild an Enthusiasm as any that has been yet seen; and which can End in nothing but Monasteries, and Hermitages; with all those sottish and Wicked Superstitions which have accompanied them where-ever they have been in use.

Masham accused Malebranche, Author of the *Christian Conversations*, of foreseeing this consequence and perhaps even intending it: "This in a Papist, and one of a Religious Order amongst them, cannot seem strange."[37] But in an Anglican divine it was much less excusable:[38]

But there can certainly be no greater Disparagement to Christian Religion, than to say; That it unfits Men for Society; That we must not only literally become Fools for Christ's sake; but also cease to be Men. Can any Rational Man, not bred up in the Bigottry of Popery, ever perswade himself that such a Religion can be from God?

Masham's refutation of Malebranchiste occasionalism

Masham began her critique of the *Letters Concerning the Love of God* by observing that from Norris's central proposition "1. *That god is the only Cause of our Love*," his conclusion, "2. *That he is also the proper object of*

Concerning the Love of God (London, 1695)," referring to "other works of Norris's to which Masham refers" as if he referred to this. But I can find no direct reference to the Astell–Norris correspondence unless the nonspecific reference to "his Discourse" in the following sentence (Masham, *Discourse*, 1696, 120–21) is taken to refer to it: "But however that were, he concludes his Discourse of our being obliged to have no Love for any Creature, with a sincere Acknowledgment that if this be true (which he has concluded it is) it is then absolutely necessary to renounce the World and betake our selves to Woods and Desarts."

[35] Masham, *Discourse*, 1696, 121.   [36] Ibid., 120.   [37] Ibid., 122.   [38] Ibid.

it" does not follow.[39] His proof for the first proposition rests on "what (plainly express'd) cannot be contested; *viz.* That we receive the Power which we have of Desiring, from God." Proof of the second, "That God is the only proper Object of our Love, as being the only Cause of all our pleasing Sensations," is lacking. Instead Norris offers "his Opinion, that God (who doubtless made all things for himself) because his own Glory was his primary End in creating all things, had not therefore Secondary, and intermediate Ends for which he made the Creatures to operate one upon another: Which is but a tacit Way to beg the Question."[40] "*Upon this Hinge* (says he) *the whole Weight of the Theory turns*, viz. That God is the only proper Object of our Love as being the only Cause of all our pleasing Sensations."[41] It is interesting that Masham does not accept the necessary revision which Astell pointed out:[42] that if God is the only cause of our pleasure he is equally the only cause of our pain. This would be to introduce a Manichean principle forcing Norris to conclude that, if God is therefore the only object of our love, he is equally the object of our fear. Astell had a way out of the theodicy problem, which makes God the author of good and evil: if not only pleasure but also pain can be said to contribute to our Good, then God as the only author of our Good is the only worthy object of our love.

It is a solution to which Masham only later alluded, addressing instead the corollary of Norris's argument, Malebranchiste occasionalism, to the refutation of which her work is devoted. Masham defines occasionalism as the principle of God's "Creatures have no Efficiency at all to operate upon us; they begin only occasional Causes of those Sentiments which God produces in us"; and further that "every Act that carries our Desires towards the Creature is sinful." Masham immediately declares: "Which Opinion if receiv'd and follow'd, must necessarily bring in the like unintelligible Way of Practical Reason, which the Bishop of *Worcester* has justly censured in the Church of *Rome*."[43] Her remark is prescient: the bishop of Worcester, Edward Stillingfleet, was to be Locke's respondent in an important epistolary debate, from 1697 to 1699, over the doctrinal implications of Locke's epistemology.

If other creatures are occasional causes of our sensations, only God can be the object of desire, Norris had argued, taking desire clearly to be a motivational force consistent with Epicurean attraction to pleasure and resistance to pain. Masham rejects the corollary, that we "desire God," but experience only "benevolent love" for our fellows.[44] She

---

[39] Ibid., 8.
[40] Ibid., 9.   [41] Ibid.
[42] Astell, *Letters Concerning the Love of God*, 1695, 4–7.
[43] Masham, *Discourse*, 1696, 9.   [44] Ibid., 12–13.

follows Locke in declaring love to be a disposition toward that which pleases us, denying Norris's differentiation of love into modes, which she attributes to a confusion between love and its consequences determined by its different, and equally legitimate, objects.[45] Masham insists that love is a simple, focused act of mind.[46] That we receive all good from God does not entail that God is the author of our pleasing sensations, a precarious hypothesis that pays no tribute to God[47] – and here Masham may indeed be addressing Astell's revision. For she dismisses as paying equally scant honor to God, "Pompous Rhapsodies of the soul debasing herself, when she descends to set the least part of her Affections upon any thing but her Creator, [which] (however well they may possibly be intended) are plainly but a complementing God with the contempt of his Works, by which we are the most effectually led to Know, Love and Adore him."[48]

Masham dealt a cruel blow to the Platonists, of whose "Extravagance" "perhaps some of the Mystical Divines are an Example," claiming that their revolt against the passions has led them "to dress out in an intire System intelligible only by Sentiment, not to Reason."[49] Norris had in her eyes abandoned any claim to credibility as a professional philosopher, by breaking the rule that, "whenever any one pretends to prescribe Measures of Duty, not suited to a Popular Audience, but such as shall challenge the strictest Attention and Scrutiny of Reason, he ought to exclude all Metaphor and Hyperbole."[50] The outcome was devastating for his own theory. For "Notions .. which are usher'd in, or attended with Flights, not only out of the reach of common Sense, but which oppose the Experience of Mankind,"[51] cannot advance us "one jot further in the Knowledge of our Ideas, and Perceptions; which is the thing it was Primarily pretended to be design'd for."[52] "They who advance this Notion, do only fetch a Circuit,"[53] at the same time rendering the Malebranchiste formulation of efficient and occasional causes irrelevant.

Masham demonstrates considerable philosophical agility in her technical discussion, employing a Lockean conception of strict entailment to demolish Malebranche's and Norris's distinction between "efficient" and "occasional" causes:[54]

---

[45] Ibid., 18–19:

> Love being only a Name given to that Disposition, or Act of the Mind we find in our selves towards any thing we are pleas'd with; And so far as it is simply Love consists barely in That; and cannot be distinguish'd into different Acts of wishing well, and desiring; which are other different Acts of the Mind consequential to Love, according to the difference of the Object.

[46] Ibid., 24–25.   [47] Ibid., 26.   [48] Ibid., 27.   [49] Ibid., 28.
[50] Ibid., 29.   [51] Ibid.   [52] Ibid., 30.   [53] Ibid.   [54] Ibid., 31.

The Creatures they say are occasional Causes of our pleasing Sensations. Then, however, they are Causes of them. They deny not also, That they are such Causes as are always accompanied with the Effect, and without which the Effect is not produced. And are they not then consider'd as Goods to us, just the same as if they were efficient Causes?

Masham's employment of Locke's notions of cause, as "that which produces any simple or complex idea," and of effect, as "that which is produced,"[55] earned her work its reputation as a work by Locke. Her demonstration of the argument against Malebranche and Norris is strikingly Lockean. Taking the example of a flower, reminiscent of Locke's image of the "marygold," Masham, using Lockean language of powers, argues that we cannot know how color, one of Locke's secondary qualities, mediates between God's intention and the excitation of enjoyable sensations:[56]

Or must we think a beautiful Flower has not the same Appearance, whether it be believ'd that God has lodg'd a power in the Flower to excite the Idea of its Colour in us, or that he himself exhibits the Idea of its Colour at the presence of that Object? If the Flower is either way equally pleasing (as certainly it is) then it is also equally desireable.

Masham's attack on Platonist "enthusiasm" and "anti-socialism"

Masham delivered her master-stroke when she pointed out that Malebranchiste distinctions are not only irrelevant but also irreverent. Here she uses an argument straight from Locke's refutation of Norris,[57] to accuse him of rendering God's creations pointless and superfluous:[58]

But the Wisdom of God cannot herein be equally admired, because it is not equally conspicuous. For if God immediately exhibits to me all my Idea's [*sic*], and that I do not truly see with my Eyes and hear with my Ears; then all that wonderful Exactness and curious Workmanship in framing the Organs of Sense, seems superfluous and vain; Which is no small reflection upon infinite Wisdom.

It is an argument that Masham extends into territory into which Locke in his response to Norris does not venture. Just as "seeing all things in God" renders perceptual apparatus of sensation irrelevant, "occasionalism" renders the instrumentalities God has chosen "wilfully" perverse. If creatures cannot excite pleasure (love), due only to God, then God has wilfully obscured our purposes here on earth.[59] Masham develops a powerful argument about the presumptuousness of Norris's

---

[55] Locke, *Essay*, Bk. 2, chap. 26, §1.   [56] Masham, *Discourse*, 1696, 31–32.
[57] Locke, "Remarks," in *Works*, 1823 ed., X, 249.
[58] Masham, *Discourse*, 1696, 32.   [59] Ibid., 33.

theory, by pointing out that by accepting it we posit the period up to enlightenment provided by "Heads cast in *Metaphysical Moulds,*" like Norris's, as millennia-long dark ages of ignorance concerning God's purposes.[60] But Norris's thesis is patently false, the result of misapplied "Logick and Grammar" to Scripture, the understanding of which is accommodated to ordinary language, and not "the Opinion of Divines."[61] Masham discusses at length the second commandment to Moses, "Love thy neighbour," citing in defense a jingle by Henry More, "no Religious Rant" but a principle made good by experience.[62] God "has laid no traps and snares, to render us Miserable,"[63] from which she draws some surprising conclusions. Far from our senses misleading us, they affirm divine purposes in the construction of Nature.

Developing ideas that were the mainstay of Stoic and Epicurean thought in the injunction to lead "a life according to Nature" (*kata phusin*), Masham goes on to discuss "Wants of Nature" compared with "Wants of our own making."[64] These are ideas that in early modern thought awaited full discussion until Rousseau in his *First* and *Second Discourses*, indebted, as he acknowledges, to Locke. Masham's discussion, noting the legacy of Chrysippus,[65] may be evidence of familiarity with the arguments of Jensenists Nicole and Abbadie, who broached the topic in terms of a distinction between *amour de soi* and *amour propre*.[66]

---

[60] Ibid., 33–34:

> We are moreover told, That the whole of our Duty, and Happiness, consists in making God the sole Object of our Desires; *The least spark of which sacred Fire cannot light upon the Creatures, without so far defrauding him*: And that the Reason of this Duty is, because *the Creatures are not the efficient Causes of our Sensations.* If this be so, this seems also to lay an Imputation upon the Wisdom of the Goodness of God, who has laid the foundation of our Duty in a Reason which he has concealed from us. For this great Cause why we should love him alone, (*viz. because the Creatures are not the efficient Causes of our Sensations*) is so hidden from us by all the Art, and Contrivance, observable in Nature, that if it were purposely design'd to be conceal'd, and we purposely intended to be misled, it could not be more so. For in Effect till this last Age, it has not been discover'd; Or at least very sparingly; And even still (as it seems) only Heads cast in *Metaphysical Moulds* are capable of it.

[61] Ibid., 38–39.   [62] Ibid., 55–56.   [63] Ibid., 57.

[64] Ibid., 57–58.   [65] Ibid., 58.

[66] Pierre Nicole (1625–95), like Antoine Arnauld (1612–94), was very influential on Astell and much cited in *A Serious Proposal, Part II*. Nicole's *Essais de Morales*, the first four volumes of which reached an English audience from 1677 to 1680, were translated by a Gentleman of Quality who was very likely Locke. Locke is believed to have undertaken the translation at the instruction of his patron, Anthony Ashley Cooper (1621–83), first earl of Shaftesbury, although it is claimed by Harry M. Bracken in the *Encyclopedia of Philosophy* (London: Macmillan Co., 1967, v, 502) that Locke's translations were not published until the nineteenth century. However, the Folger Shakespeare Library holds translations of the 1680s by "A Gentleman of Quality," the pseudonym used elsewhere by Locke and/or Shaftesbury, which bears his stamp. For the wider influence of Nicole

Whatever the case, the proposition that "the gratification of Appetites which are not properly Natural, but which we have receiv'd from Custom, and Education, is not always sinful," and the admission that "Custom .. is oftentimes as strong as Nature in us,"[67] are in stark contrast to Norris's claim that no creature can be loved without idolatry and that we may desire only God. Even more challenging is Masham's argument that "God is an invisible Being" and "the Loveliness of his Works" is what causes us to love him, and specifically the loveliness of his creatures.[68]

Aware that she has in fact reversed the thesis of Norris (this time accepting Astell's revision), Masham notes the Malebranchistes would counterclaim "That we have Pleasing Sensations ('tis true) as soon as Perception; But that we have them not from the Beings which surround us, but from God."[69] To this she responds with observations from the behavior of infants that knowledge of God does not accompany the first "cry for the Fire, or the Sucking-Bottle," but "is a Proposition containing many complex Ideas in it; and which we are not capable of framing, till we have been long acquainted with pleasing Sensations."[70] It is an idea certainly beyond the capacity of the child in the cradle to frame, who in the meantime necessarily learns to love that which appears to be the cause of its pleasure.[71]

This passage in Masham reads as a direct refutation of Letter IX of Mary Astell's correspondence with Norris, in which she expresses the Malebranchiste notion that "we suck in false Principles and Tendencies betimes, and are taught, not to thirst after GOD as our only good," apparently from an early age:

'tis our Misfortune that we live an animal before we live a rational Life; the good we enjoy is mostly transmitted to us through Bodily Mediums, and contracts such a Tincture of the Conveyance through which it passes, that forgetting the true Cause and Sourse of all our good, we take up with those occasional goods that are more visible, and present to our animal Nature.

and Abbadie see Patricia Springborg, *The Problem of Human Needs and the Critique of Civilization* (London: Allen and Unwin, 1981), 36ff.

[67] Masham, *Discourse*, 1696, 60.   [68] Ibid., 62, 64.   [69] Ibid., 65.

[70] Ibid., 65–66. The passage, an important one, reads in full:

> Let it be true, that the Creatures have receiv'd no efficiency from God to excite pleasing Sensations in us, and are but the occasional Causes of those we feel: Yet does a Child in the Cradle know this? Or is this apparent so soon as it is that the Fire pleases us when we are Cold? or meat when we are Hungry? No, nor is it at any time a self-evident Truth. We must know many other Truths before we come to know this; which is a Proposition containing many complex Ideas in it; and which we are not capable of framing, till we have been long acquainted with pleasing Sensations. In the mean while, it is certain, that till we can make this Discovery, we shall necessarily Love that which appears to us to be the Cause of our Pleasure.

[71] Ibid.

This is a tendency reinforced by education, Astell maintains, in a surprising concession to the principles of Lockean sensationalist psychology.[72]

This is an argument Masham simply denies. Distinguishing between reality and appearances, she argues that while the passions and appearances move us first, we learn to sift appearances through the filter of ideas:[73]

So soon as we do begin to leave off judging by appearances, and are Capable of being convinc'd that the Diameter of the Sun exceeds that of a Bushel; We are capable also of understanding that there is a Superior Invisible Being, the Author of those things which afford us pleasing Sensations, who is therefore supreamly to be loved.

Her example of the appearance of the sun probably draws on the moon-illusion discussed by Malebranche, whose *Conversations Chrestiennes* she quotes on concupiscence at length in French, along with Norris's translation in the *Unintelligible way of Practical Religion*.[74] She refutes as ridiculous Malebranche's notion of the transmission of ideas – a revision of the Platonist theory of innate ideas – that the baby in the mother's womb feels like her and thinks like her, has bodily desires, and is born a sinner.[75] She expends considerable effort in refuting Malebranche's belief that love of creatures, based on an error of deduction, is a punishment of the Fall, as a proposition not only false, but pernicious to piety and morals.[76] And she simply rejects as "utterly false" Norris's claim that love of God and love of creatures are mutually exclusive, because *"our Capacities are too narrow and scanty to be employ'd upon two such vastly different Objects."*[77] Experience tells us, she insists, that there is no more reason "That Love of the Creature should exclude the Love of God; any more than that the Love of Cherries should exclude the love of our Friend that gives them us."[78]

Norris had entered the dangerous waters of distinguishing between "our good" and "our true good," where Masham easily catches him: "But certainly whatever is a Good to us, is a *True Good*, since whatever pleases us, pleases us":[79] "the word *True* (otherwise very impertinent here) is Subtilty to insinuate that which should be prov'd, viz. *That the Creatures are not the Efficient Causes* of our Pleasing Sensations."[80] She notes the incongruousness of the Malebranchiste position which cannot admit creatures as the proper object of our love and sees them only as a derogation from the duty to love God, and yet can admit God as the author of sinful as well as innocent feelings of pleasure:[81]

[72] Astell, Letter IX, St. Philip and St. James, 1694, 209–10.
[73] Masham, *Discourse*, 1969, 68.   [74] Ibid., 72–76.   [75] Ibid., 74–75.
[76] Ibid., 76–77.   [77] Ibid., 87.   [78] Ibid., 88.   [79] Ibid., 89.
[80] Ibid., 90–91.   [81] Ibid., 102.

But the Author of this Hypothesis tells us, That this is that indeed which makes Sin to be so exceeding sinful, *viz.* That we oblige God in Virtue of that first immutable Law or Order, which he has establish'd (that is, of exciting sentiments of Pleasure in us upon some operation of Bodies upon us) to Reward our Transgressions against him with Pleasure, and Delight. It is strange that we cannot seem sinful enough, without having a Power of forcing God to be a Partner in our Wickedness!

This is a formidable argument for rejecting Malebranche and Norris's position. But without doubt Masham considers yet more telling the argument to which she returns. It is the Aristotelian argument of appropriateness, matched to the Ciceronian argument for natural sociability. The Malebranchiste thesis does no justice to man's nature as a social and worldly creature. It is no more appropriate to wish for men the nature of "Angels, and Arch-Angels .. (at least whilst upon Earth) then it would be for the Fishes (if they were capable of it) to propose, or pray to God, that they might fly in the Air like Birds; or Ride Post-Horses as Men do." She points to the hubris of those "who will venture to ask God for their sakes, to change the Order of Nature, which he has establish'd." Furthermore, "It is certain, that if we had no Desires but after God, the several Societies of Mankind could not long hold together, nor the very Species be continued."[82] It is an argument, after a curious discussion of the possibility of other worlds, to which Masham finally returns,[83] insisting that the greatest condemnation of the Malebranchiste thesis is its injuriousness to social life, making it "absolutely necessary to renounce the World, and betake ourselves to Woods and Desarts," and "impossible to live in the daily Commerce and Conversation of the World, and love God as we ought to do."[84] Masham comes perilously close to the Deists and anti-clerical Arminians in her Ciceronian eulogy to human sociability:[85]

There is nothing more evident than that Mankind is design'd for a Sociable Life. To say that Religion unfits us for it, is to reproach the Wisdom of God as highly as is possible; And to represent Religion as the most mischievous thing in the World, dissolving Societies. And there could not be a greater Artifice of the Devil, or Wicked Men to bring Christianity into contempt than this.

Masham's paean to the possibility of other worlds is curious. Is it a concession to Locke on "thinking matter"? Or is it a venture into the New Science, for which Astell herself was to claim women as reflective persons were exceptionally suited?[86]

And since it is allow'd on all hands, that the Mens Business is without Doors,

---

[82] Ibid., 82–83.   [83] Ibid.   [84] Ibid., 120–21.
[85] Ibid., 123.   [86] Astell, *The Christian Religion* (1705 ed.), 296.

and theirs is an Active Life; Women who ought to be Retir'd, are for this reason design'd by Providence for Speculation: Providence, which allots every one an Employment, and never intended that any one shou'd give themselves up to Idleness and Unprofitable Amusements. And I make no question but great Improvements might be made in the Sciences, were not Women enviously excluded from this their proper Business.

Masham presents beautifully an image that Astell had already presaged: women, whom men cast in the role of observers, were the true practitioners of *theoria*: observation as the basis of philosophy and science. If in the fragment of Heracleitus three types of people came to the Olympic games, some to compete (*praxis*), those to observe (*theoria*) and those to make money (production), it fell to women to be the theorists of the new age:[87]

Yet were our Views larger than to comprehend only the compass of our little Globe, they would probably afford us still further Matter for our admiration. For 'tis a thought too limitted [*sic*] and narrow for Women and Children now to be kept in, that this Spot of ours is all the Habitable part of the Creation. But without understanding the System of the World, or considering what Mathematicians and Naturalists offer to convince us, that so many Regions fit for Inhabitants are not empty Desarts, and such numberless Orbs of Light more insignificant than so many Farthing Candles; We read, in the Scripture, of other Ranks of Intelligent Beings besides our selves; Of whom, tho' it would be Presumption to affirm any thing beyond what is reveal'd, yet we know not what Relation may possibly be between them and us.

Although apparently on different sides of the particular debates this paper addresses, Astell and Masham contributed equally in establishing philosophy as a chosen realm of female endeavor. Moreover, theirs was a contribution which eighteenth-century readers, paradoxically, were far more willing to credit than those of subsequent centuries up to and including our own. Astell, and to a lesser extent Masham, were celebrated in their day, their works, in Astell's case regularly running to multiple editions, only recently having dropped out of the canon. Not only did Dean Swift, Richard Steele, Daniel Defoe, Bishop George Berkeley, and Samuel Richardson pay deference to Astell's views, whether by imitating, plagiarizing, or lampooning them, but her public persona lived on in various disguises until the nineteenth century. Thus Valeria, "that little She-Philosopher" of Susanna Centlivre's *Basset Table* (1706), founder of "a College for the Study of Philosophy where none but Women should be admitted,"[88] and Madonella, founder of an

---

[87] Masham, *Discourse* (1696), 110.
[88] *The Works of the Celebrated Mrs. Centlivre*, 3 vols., London, 1761, I, 210, 218, cited in Hill, "A Refuge from Men: The Idea of a Protestant Nunnery," *Past and Present* 117 (1987): 107–30 (esp. 120). Susanna Centlivre, a gentlewoman whose family fled to

academy of "superannuated virgins" of Steele's satire in *Tatler* numbers 32 and 63,[89] had more benign counterparts in Defoe's *Essay upon Projects*[90] and Richardson's *Clarissa*.[91] In the nineteenth century Astell provided the model for Tennyson's Lilia of *The Princess* (1847), who dreams of a women's college cut off from male society, over whose gates the inscription would read, "Let no man enter on pain of death" – a work later translated for comic opera by Gilbert and Sullivan as *Princess Ida*.[92] Damaris Masham, who can boast neither such fame nor such notoriety, still enters history in the shadow of her male associates – her father, Ralph Cudworth, and her companion, Locke. But since she abandoned the views of the former, and proved herself no mere acolyte of the latter, she, like Astell, deserves better – a more discerning modern audience, which it is the purpose of this chapter to promote.

Acknowledgments

I would like to thank Bridget Hill, Mark Goldie, John Pocock, Quentin Skinner, Lois Schwoerer, Johann and Margaret Sommerville; my editor, Hilda Smith, and participants in the Folger Conference on Political Writings, Political Women: Early Modern Britain in a European Context (Washington, D.C., May, 1995), for their comments on an earlier

---

Ireland at the Restoration, may have disliked Astell's politics, *Basset Table* having been written after the publication of Astell's royalist political pamphlets of 1704.

89 See Astell's Foreword to the second edition of *Bart'lemy Fair*, 1722 (A2a), on how Swift put Steele up to the satire of her *A Serious Proposal*, 1694 in *Tatler*, no. 32, from White's Chocolate-house, June 22, 1709, "a little after the Enquiry [*Bart'lemy Fair*] appear'd."

90 Daniel Defoe (1661?–1731), although expressing admiration for Astell's proposal, argued against it on account of women's incorrigible levity, substituting his own proposal for an "Academy of Women" (1697) which differed in no significant aspects from hers. See Defoe, *An Essay upon Projects* (1697) in *The Earlier Life and Chief Earlier Works of Daniel Defoe*, 154–46, cited in Hill, "A Refuge from Men," 118.

91 Lady Mary Wortley Montagu (1689–1762), to whose famous *Letters from the East* (published only in 1763) Astell was later to supply a preface, remarked of Richardson's *Sir Charles Grandison* that its only redeeming feature was his proposal to found Protestant nunneries, "in which single women, of small or no fortunes might live with all manner of freedom," in every English county, after the manner of Astell's *A Serious Proposal*. See *The Works of Samuel Richardson*, 19 vols. (London, 1811), XVI, 155–56, cited Hill, "A Refuge from Men," 121. See also the authoritative modern edition of Richardson's *History of Sir Charles Grandison*, 3 vols., ed. Jocelyn Harris (Oxford: Oxford University Press, 1972), II, 255–56 and notes. But this was a plagiarism on no comparable scale to the some 147 pages of ch. 3, sections 1–5 of the 1697 edition of *A Serious Proposal, Part II*, which were excerpted without acknowledgment in *The Ladies Library* of 1714 by Bishop Berkeley. Published by Richard Steele, *The Ladies' Library* was a work widely circulated in eight impressions up to 1772 as well as being translated into French and Dutch.

92 *The Works of Alfred, Lord Tennyson* (London, 1905), 167, 176, cited by Hill, "A Refuge from Men," 107.

version of this piece. Sincere thanks to the Australian Research Council, the Folger Shakespeare Library, the Woodrow Wilson International Center for Scholars, and the John D. and Catherine T. MacArthur Foundation, under whose joint auspices it was written.

6 The politics of sense and sensibility:
Mary Wollstonecraft and Catharine Macaulay Graham on Edmund Burke's *Reflections on the Revolution in France*

Wendy Gunther-Canada

> When this Right Honorable Author first threw down the gauntlet, and entering the ground from whence Sir Robert Filmer was forced so shamefully to retire, stood forth the champion of hereditary right, he undoubtedly expected to be opposed by all those men, who in a liberal and enlightened age, had ranged themselves on the side of liberty; but how deeply must it wound the feelings of a chivalrous knight, who owes the fealty of "proud submission and dignified obedience" to the fair sex, to perceive that two of the boldest of his adversaries are women!
> *Analytical Review,* 1791

At the end of the eighteenth century Mary Wollstonecraft and Catharine Macaulay were considered by their contemporaries to be among Edmund Burke's "boldest adversaries." Wollstonecraft's *A Vindication of the Rights of Men* was the first published reply to the *Reflections on the Revolution in France* as well as the pioneering feminist's earliest argument for equal rights and democratic government. Macaulay's *Observations on the Reflections of the Right Honorable Edmund Burke, on the Revolution in France* represented the last volley in a war of words between the celebrated republican historian and the famed parliamentarian. In this chapter I argue that by using the notions of sense and sensibility we are better able to understand how Wollstonecraft and Macaulay challenged the gender and class hierarchy of the *Reflections*. These terms played a central part in each woman's rhetorical strategy and made it possible for both to invert the gender logic of the *Reflections*. This rhetorical device allows me to demonstrate how Wollstonecraft and Macaulay used their replies to Burke to advance reformist political agendas of their own. More importantly, by focusing on a discursive dynamic that I term the politics of sense and sensibility, I am able to highlight significant differences between the *Vindication* and the *Observations*. The chapter concludes by suggesting that these different approaches to sense and sensibility have had far-reaching consequences for women's political writing and the political rights of women.

What do I mean by the politics of sense and sensibility? I use this phrase to foreground the gender politics of late eighteenth-century rights discourse in England and to emphasize how the binary oppositions of reason and passion, masculine and feminine, both justified and reinforced the emerging division of the political world into dichotomous public and private spheres. An examination of how Wollstonecraft and Macaulay developed the tensions between sense and sensibility in their replies to Burke complicates the traditional opposition of public man and private woman as well as our understanding of the sexual politics of the rights debates of the 1790s. As a number of contemporary studies have shown throughout the second half of the eighteenth century, English society was becoming increasingly heterosocial, with members of both sexes adhering to the literary forms and behavioral norms dictated by what G. J. Barker-Benfield has called the "culture of sensibility."[1] Yet sensibility, identified with the female virtues of sympathetic feeling and empathetic behavior, posed a significant political and moral dilemma for women. Sensibility highlighted the physical vulnerability and emotional delicacy of females at a crucial time when some women were gaining access to new public spaces as well as claiming authority to enter previously forbidden discursive domains. Sensibility held special dangers for women. To the extent that women aligned themselves with sensibility rather than sense, they were complicit in their own exclusion from wider participation in the public realm.

Perhaps no event within the long eighteenth century so challenged notions of women's place and public space as the French Revolution. More than any other book of the 1790s, Burke's *Reflections on the Revolution in France* set the tone for the conservative reaction to the social and political changes just across the Channel. Here Burke attacked the false universalism of the philosophy of the rights of men, noting that the radically inclusive logic of rights theory could be applied to all human beings, rich or poor, male or female. Tom Furniss,

[1] Historian G. J. Barker-Benfield identifies the culture of sensibility with a feminization of English society that accompanied the rise of commercial trading and consumerism during the long eighteenth century. "This culture was brought into existence in decisive part by the pubic 'awakening' of a critical mass of Englishwomen." But, as the Barker-Benfield study demonstrates, over the course of the century the radical potential of sensibility to transform the relationship of the sexes was never realized, in part because women, such as Wollstonecraft, mistrusted sensibility (*The Culture of Sensibility* [Chicago: University of Chicago Press, 1992], xviii). See also Syndy Conger, *Mary Wollstonecraft and the Language of Sensibility* (Rutherford, N.J.: Fairleigh Dickinson University Press, 1994); Claudia Johnson, *Equivocal Beings* (Chicago: University of Chicago Press, 1995).

interpreting the *Reflections* in light of his reading of Burke's earlier essay, *A Philosophical Enquiry into the Origin of Our Ideas of the Sublime and Beautiful*, has argued that the "way Burke organizes his thought on a range of issues into gendered binary oppositions . . . is characteristic of the discourse of the period."[2] Furniss claims that Burke attempted to naturalize the opposition of masculine and feminine in the *Reflections* in order to stabilize gender categories threatened by revolutionary excess. For Burke, the art of politics was the sublime activity of men of hereditary rank and courtly privilege. These activities were closely tied to the dual codes of chivalry and religion that he believed to be the foundation of the golden age of European civilization. His rhetorical strategy in the *Reflections* centered on a powerful representation of this world turned upside down, a world in which the boundaries of court culture were in danger of being transgressed by the political ambitions of swinish men and brutish women. The democratic rebellion in France signified a class warfare that Burke equated with the loss of patriarchal control and the revolting specter of gender uncertainty.[3]

It was just this gender trouble that made the replies of Wollstonecraft and Macaulay to Burke so bold. Both women turned the tables on Burke by employing a dual strategy of battling his interpretation of the rights of man and belittling the effeminate style of his rhetoric. Wollstonecraft asserted that Burke's effeminate "parade of sensibility" in the *Reflections* only masked the weakness of his arguments for hereditary right and political patrimony.[4] She argued that Burke's passionate

---

[2] Tom Furniss, *Edmund Burke's Aesthetic Ideology* (New York: Cambridge University Press, 1993), 5.

[3] Most contemporary readings of the *Reflections* tend to ignore the centrality of gender to Burke's analysis of the events in France. There have been a number of notable exceptions to this trend that have led to exciting new work on Burke. Along with Tom Furniss, there is the recent work of feminist theorist Linda Zerilli, who argued that Burke's conservative classic portrays the revolt in France as a sexual revolution. In *Signifying Woman*, Zerilli claims that woman acts as both sign and signifier of the boundaries of political discourse and the gendered borders of the public sphere. Zerilli's elegant argument is persuasive but her critical treatment does not examine if or how actual historical women contested Burke's representation of the revolution in France. In fact, while Zerilli's gender criticism seems to be at odds with more established interpretations of the *Reflections*, it has much in common with the rhetorical analyses of two earlier critics of Burke: Mary Wollstonecraft and Catharine Macaulay. See *Signifying Woman: Culture and Chaos in Rousseau, Burke, and Mill* (Ithaca: Cornell University Press, 1994). Wollstonecraft scholar Virginia Sapiro also provides a feminist reading of the *Reflections* in her study of Wollstonecraft's political theory, *A Vindication of Political Virtue*. My own interpretation of Wollstonecraft's reply to Burke in the next section highlights the differences between our understanding of the role that gender plays in *A Vindication of the Rights of Men*.

[4] Mary Wollstonecraft, *A Vindication of the Rights of Men*, in *The Works of Mary Wollstonecraft*, vol. v, eds. Janet Todd and Marilyn Butler (New York: New York University Press, 1989), 18.

language accounted for the popularity of the *Reflections*, noting that "Sensibility is the *manie* of the day." The lady novelist, turned manly polemicist, chided the famed parliamentarian that "[e]ven the Ladies, Sir, may repeat your sprightly sallies, and retail in the theatrical attitudes of many of your sentimental exclamations."[5] Catharine Macaulay, too, found fault with the stylized language of Burke's text. "[W]hat, indeed, but the *delusive* power of a subtle sophistry, can produce an apparent *concord* between propositions the most *opposite of nature*? and what but an appeal to the passions of the reader, can prevent his assent to the *most obvious truths*?"[6] For her, the only reasonable answer to this question was that Burke, who had once held the bright torch of liberty, now sought to fan the flames of faction. Macaulay echoed Wollstonecraft's contention that in the *Reflections* sensibility clouded common sense, and that in Burke's argument wit was opposed to judgment.

The publication of the *Vindication of the Rights of Men* and the *Observations on the Reflections of Edmund Burke* marked the intellectual convergence of the ideas of two of eighteenth-century England's most important female political writers. Recently Bridget Hill has uncovered evidence that the younger Wollstonecraft sent a copy of her pamphlet to Macaulay with a note of admiration, remarking that the famed historian was "the only female writer who I coincide in opinion with respecting the rank our sex ought to endeavour to attain in this world."[7] Macaulay responded with a copy of her pamphlet and extended an invitation for a meeting.[8] Sadly, there is nothing to suggest that this meeting ever took place as Macaulay died the following year. Yet in their replies to Burke we have a meeting of the minds as each woman reflected on the meaning of revolution in France and reform in England. Moreover, these pamphlets highlight the fact that both Wollstonecraft and Macaulay believed the language of sensibility was incompatible with rational discourse and

[5] Ibid., 8.
[6] Catharine Macaulay, *Observations on the Reflections of the Right Honorable Edmund Burke, on the Revolution in France, In a Letter to the Right Honorable Earl of Stanhope* (London: Edward and Charles Dilly, 1790), 42.
[7] Even in her praise of Macaulay, Wollstonecraft distinguished sense from sensibility. "I respect Mrs. Macaulay Graham because she contends for laurels whilst most of her sex only seek for flowers" (Bridget Hill, "The Links between Mary Wollstonecraft and Catharine Macaulay: New Evidence," *Women's History Review* 4, 2 [1995]: 177).
[8] Macaulay's response is interesting in that it indicates that she was surprised to find the author of the *Vindication* to be a woman.

> I was pleased at the attention of the public to your animated observations, pleased with the flattering compliment you paid me in a second rememberance, and still more highly pleased that this publication which I have so greatly admired from its pathos and sentiment should have been written by a woman and thus to see my opinion of the powers and talents of the sex in your pen so early verified. (Ibid., 178)

that each personally understood the political perils of sensibility for their sex. However, their recognition of the dangers of sensibility did not mean that either woman was able to avoid the conflict entirely. Indeed, Wollstonecraft's *Vindication* provides an intriguing example of a woman being silenced by sensibility, whereas Macaulay avoided sensibility by absenting any formal discussion of sexual inequality from her *Observations*. Ultimately, the replies of Mary Wollstonecraft and Catharine Macaulay to Edmund Burke demonstrated that women could forcefully defend the rights of man. More importantly, these pamphlets underscored the fact that before women could claim political rights for themselves, they needed to confront the politics of sense and sensibility.

★ ★ ★

> Judgment is sublime, wit beautiful; and, according to your own theory, they cannot exist together without impairing each other's power. The predominance of the latter, in your endless *Reflections*, should lead hasty readers to suspect that it may, in a great degree, exclude the former.
>
> Mary Wollstonecraft, 1790

A Vindication of the Rights of Men was the first published reply to Burke, released just twenty-eight days after the *Reflections*. This anonymous pamphlet proved to be an instant success.[9] So much so that, only a month after its initial release, a second edition was issued, where the author was revealed to be the little-known novelist and educational writer, Mary Wollstonecraft.[10] The response to the second edition indicated that a number of the journals which reviewed the first edition for their readers had assumed that the anonymous defender of the rights of men was a man himself. The *Gentleman's Magazine* in reviewing the second edition, attributed to a "Mrs. Wolstonecraft" [*sic*], confronted with the reality of its female author, still proceeded to doubt that this tract which attacked the "demon of property" was written by "a real,

---

[9] William Godwin recounts in his memoir of Wollstonecraft that the

> applause which attended her *Reply to Burke*, elevated the tone of her mind. She had always felt much confidence in her powers; but it cannot be doubted, that the actual perception of a similar feeling respecting us in a multitude of others, must increase our confidence, and stimulate the adventure of any human being. Mary accordingly proceeded, in a short time after, to the composition of her most celebrated production, the *Vindication of the Rights of Woman*. (*Memoirs of the Author of "The Rights of Woman"*, ed. Richard Holmes [New York: Penguin Books, 1987], 230)

[10] Ralph Wardle, who wrote the first critical scholarly biography of Wollstonecraft in the twentieth century, asserted that *A Vindication of the Rights of Men* was the product of overheard conversations and quick scribbling. He considered the success of the tract to be a fluke as he wrote: "What could Mary Wollstonecraft have known about the rights of men?" (*Mary Wollstonecraft: A Critical Biography* [Lawrence, Kans.: University of Kansas Press, 1951], 117–18).

and not a fictitious lady."[11] Likewise, the editors of the *Critical Review* noted that their reviewer had assumed the author was male, and had the true sex of the author been known, the review would have been less critical.[12]

What made *A Vindication of the Rights of Men* a remarkable tract was that its author sought to meet Burke on his own rhetorical terms and better him.[13] Virginia Sapiro has noted in her ground-breaking study of Wollstonecraft's political thought that the *Vindication* "responded both to *what* Burke wrote and *how* he wrote it."[14] Yet while Sapiro's

---

[11] Anonymous, "A Vindication of the Rights of Men; in a Letter to the Right Honorable Edmund Burke, occasioned by his *Reflections on the Revolution in France*, by Mary Wolstonecraft [*sic.*]" (*The Gentleman's Magazine* (61 [February 1791], 154).

[12] The anonymous reviewer for the *Critical Review* wrote,
> It has been observed in an old play, that minds have no sex; and in truth we did not discover this Defender of the Rights of Man to be a Woman. The second edition, however, which often reveals secrets, has attributed this pamphlet to Mrs. Woolstonecraft [*sic*], and if she assumes the disguise of a man, she must not be surprised that she is not treated with the civility and respect that she would have received in her own person. As this article was written before we saw this second edition, we have preferred an acknowledgement of this kind to the necessary alterations. It would not have been sufficient to have corrected merely verbal errors: a lady should have been addressed with more respect. ("A Vindication of the Rights of Men; in a Letter to the Right Honorable Edmund Burke, Occasioned by his *Reflections on the Revolution in France*," 70 [1790], 694)

[13] The spirited nature of Wollstonecraft's reply to Burke appealed to many of her eighteenth-century readers and reviewers. Early in this century historian George Stead Veitch wrote that he found it "strange" that "the only reply to Burke which is adequate on the emotional side should have lapsed into obscurity, for Burke's strength was due as much to the intensity of his feelings as to the power of his mind, and the antagonist who was sufficiently sympathetic to meet him on his own ground had manifest advantages over the other controversialists" (*The Genesis of Parliamentary Reform* [Hamden, Conn.: Archon Books, 1913/1965], 167).

[14] Virginia Sapiro, *A Vindication of Political Virtue* (Chicago: University of Chicago Press, 1992), 201. I agree with Professor Sapiro that any discussion of Wollstonecraft's reply to Burke demands a critical examination of the language politics of the late eighteenth century. However, my own interpretation of the *Vindication* represents a fundamental departure from Sapiro's work in that I seek to understand the role of gender in Wollstonecraft's argument as well as in the reception of her pamphlet. Sapiro discounts the influence of gender on the style and substance of the *Vindication*. She states, "Whether there is strong evidence that gender accounts for differences in Wollstone-craft's and Burke's displays of emotion (I would be very surprised if there were), it is probably easier for reader's eyes to see natural and explicable emotion in a woman's than a man's text" (ibid., 206). Surprise aside, my point is that the evidence suggests that, while Burke's display of emotion made him widely popular with readers, including "the Ladies," Wollstonecraft's own emotional reply to Burke was dismissed as unfair and sensational because she was a woman. While I certainly do not claim that Wollstonecraft had a fully developed theory of gender at the time she wrote her defense of the rights of man, I do believe that her personal and political experience as a woman writing in response to Burke led her to vindicate, in a subsequent text, the rights of her sex.

treatment focuses on the language politics of the *Vindication*, she does not sufficiently explore the gender dynamics that authorized Wollstonecraft's defense of the rights of man. The lady novelist confounded gender categories and crossed genre boundaries in order to respond to Burke and in the process reinvented herself as an author. Her rhetorical strategy was based on an elaborate ruse that subverted the conventions of political discourse. An anonymous Mary Wollstonecraft, masquerading as a man, promised her readers that she would "show Burke to himself."[15]

In the first pages of her reply, Wollstonecraft proclaimed that she intended to undermine the very foundation of Burke's theory rather than counter each aspect of his argument in the *Reflections*. "I shall not attempt to follow you through 'horse-way and foot-path;' but, attacking the foundation of your opinions, I shall leave the superstructure to find a center of gravity on which it may lean till some strong blast puffs it into the air."[16] She argued that the true "foundation" of his opinions was his "pampered sensibility," which acted to "dispel the sober suggestions of reason."[17] This sensibility, reflected in the seductive language of his text, jeopardized the very basis of his assault on the rights of man because sensibility was incompatible with reason.[18] It seemed to Wollstonecraft that Burke attempted to enflame the passions of his readers rather than enlighten their minds. "It is impossible to read half a dozen pages of your book without admiring your ingenuity, or indignantly spurning your sophisms. Words are heaped on words, till the understanding is confused by endeavoring to disentangle the sense, and the memory of tracing contradictions."[19] Repeatedly, the anonymous advocate of the rights of men exhorted Burke to be manly and to do the difficult work of critical thinking. "Quitting the flowers of rhetoric, let us, Sir, reason together."[20] The author, rejecting all effeminate language, challenged Burke to emerge from the text in his

---

[15]   But it was not my intention, when I began this letter, to descend to the minutiae of your conduct, or to weight your infirmities in a balance; it is only some of your pernicious opinions that I wish to hunt out of their lurking holes; and to shew you to yourself, stripped of the gorgeous drapery in which you have enwrapped your tyrannic principles. (Wollstonecraft, *A Vindication of the Rights of Men*, 37)

[16]   She continues, "[o]r your teeming fancy, which the ripening judgment of sixty years has not tamed, produces another Chinese erection, to stare, at every turn, the plain country people in the face, who bluntly call such an airy edifice – a folly" (ibid., 9).

[17]   "It is not in this view surprising, that when you should argue you become impassioned, and that reflection inflames your imagination, instead of enlightening your understanding" (ibid., 9).

[18]   "I perceive, from the whole tenor of your *Reflections*, that you have a moral antipathy to reason" (ibid., 10).

[19]   Ibid., 50.   [20]   Ibid., 9.

nakedness and address his fellow men without the garlands of rank and luxury.

Indeed, Wollstonecraft believed that naked self-interest accounted for Burke's defense of monarchy and aristocracy in the *Reflections*. Stripped to the flesh, Burke appeared to her as a mere apologist for a corrupt aristocratic order whose time was past. To make her case, Wollstonecraft repeatedly contrasted the diseased anatomy of the aristocracy to the healthy physique of the middle classes. At the center of her analysis was an attack on the twin evils of female degeneracy and male effeminacy, both of which she associated with the gender politics of court culture.[21] Her portrayal of the servile nature of the aristocracy underscored her belief that kings and courtiers, emasculated by a hereditary effeminacy, were unable to exercise legitimate power in an age of democratic revolution. Turning to Burke, Wollstonecraft argued that the display of effeminate sensibility in the *Reflections* proved he was incapable of the manly efforts demanded by philosophical endeavor. "If I were not afraid to derange your nervous system by the bare mention of a metaphysical enquiry, I should observe, Sir, that self-preservation is, literally speaking, the first law of nature; and that the care necessary to support and guard the body is the first step to unfold the mind, and inspire a manly spirit of independence."[22] To Mary Wollstonecraft, her own female body garbed in the cloak of manly reason, Edmund Burke appeared in his nakedness to have been unmanned by sensibility.

Certainly, Wollstonecraft's writing reversed the roles of rank and sex, overturning the moral order encoded in Burke's notions of the sublime and the beautiful. Nowhere was this reversal of order more evident than in each author's representation of October 6, 1789. While Burke used the image of the hungry women of the October Days as an example of the brutish nature of democracy, Wollstonecraft represented these same women as the suffering subjects of a tyrannical government. She dismissed his representation of the "furies of hell, in the abused shape of the vilest women" as just another "empty rhetorical flourish." Wollstonecraft directly challenged Burke to redefine the feminine with reference to rank and education in order to see these poor women as human beings. "Probably you mean women who gained a livelihood by selling vegetables or fish, who never had had any advantages of

---

[21] Tom Furniss writes that Wollstonecraft's "central strategy is to identify the feminine with the *ancien régime* and the masculine with bourgeois radicalism. She thus challenges conventional assumptions about the relation between gender characteristics and sexual anatomy by insisting that the 'manly' and the 'feminine' are, at best, unnatural exaggerations of physiological differences between the sexes" (*Edmund Burke's Aesthetic Ideology* [New York: Cambridge University Press, 1993], 191).

[22] Wollstonecraft, *A Vindication of the Rights of Men*, 16.

education; or their vices might have lost a part of their grossness." Wollstonecraft asserted that the condition of womanhood itself provided the human bond that could unite the bread marchers with their queen.[23] "The Queen of France – the great and small vulgar, claim our pity; as they have almost insurmountable obstacles to surmount in their progress toward true dignity of character; still I have such a downright understanding that I do not like to make a distinction without a difference."[24] Sexual difference was an obstacle to political equality for all women regardless of rank. It was these distinctions without difference that highlighted the sexual politics of the rights debate in England and France. Wollstonecraft charged that Burke was blinded by false distinctions in the *Reflections*. How else could one explain his nightmarish depiction of the bread marchers or his celestial description of the young Marie Antoinette, a description which Wollstonecraft singled out as bearing the telltale marks of sensibility not the *"regal* stamp of reason."[25]

For Wollstonecraft the real horror of Edmund Burke's representation of October 6 was his feigned chivalry in supporting the queen of France when just a few years earlier he had been among the loudest voices in Parliament supporting the Regency Bill. (George III was pronounced mad by court doctors in November of 1788, at which time the Prince of Wales rallied his friends in Parliament to declare him Regent.) Wollstonecraft questioned why Burke had not displayed the same sympathy for the sufferings of his own monarch, Queen Charlotte, during the Regency Crisis that he now extended to Marie Antoinette.

---

[23] Virginia Sapiro has noted of this passage that Wollstonecraft "[c]ontrasted his nightmare women with his dream woman: the queen, whom he envisioned as immaculate beauty and domesticity ... Where Burke, in effect, employed the classic Eve and Mary ideals to illustrate different sectors of the moral world, Wollstonecraft drew them together in a common portrait of human life" (*A Vindication of Political Virtue: The Political Theory of Mary Wollstonecraft*, 203).

[24] Wollstonecraft, *A Vindication of the Rights of Men*, 30.

[25] Burke recounts his famous vision thus:

> It is now sixteen or seventeen years since I saw the queen of France, then the dauphiness, at Versailles, and surely never lighted on this orb, which she hardly seemed to touch, a more delightful vision. I saw her just above the horizon, decorating and cheering the elevated sphere she just began to move in – glittering like the morning star full of life and splendor and joy. (*Reflections*, ed. J. G. A. Pocock [Indianapolis: Hackett Publishing, 1987], 66)

In the *Vindication*, Wollstonecraft contrasted Burke's vision of Marie Antoinette to Dr. Price's view of the promise of democratic revolution.

> Tottering on the verge of the grave, that worthy man in his whole life never dreamt of struggling for power or riches; and, if a glimpse of the glad dawn of liberty rekindled the fire of youth in his veins, you, who could never stand the fascinating glance of a *great* Lady's eyes, when neither virtue or sense beamed in them, might have pardoned his unseemly transport, – if such it must be deemed. (Ibid., 18)

She denounced the parliamentarian: "When you descanted on the horrors of the 6th of October, and gave a glowing, and, in some instances, a most exaggerated description of that infernal night, without having troubled yourself to clean your palette, you might have returned home and indulged us with a sketch of the misery you personally aggravated."[26] Burke's inconsistent treatment of his own queen had left a bad taste in Wollstonecraft's mouth, but she was aware that the flavor of his remarks would be savored by many of the powerful. "The rich and weak, a numerous train, will certainly applaud your system, and loudly celebrate your pious reverence for authority and establishments – they find it pleasanter to enjoy than think; to justify oppression than correct abuses. – *The rights of men* are grating sounds that set their teeth on edge; the impertinent enquiry of philosophic meddling innovation."[27] Wollstonecraft surmised that Burke's attack on the National Assembly and his defense of the French monarchy were meant to appeal to a different brand of political Epicurean.

But political tastes are subject to change. While in Paris women marched for bread, in London much of the hunger for liberty which Burke had once fed with his support for the colonial cause had been sated by the revolution in America. Wollstonecraft claimed that Burke had been "the Cicero of one side of the house for years," but with time he had been surpassed by other students in the "school of eloquence." In his slow withdrawal from the public eye he had witnessed the fade of his own "blooming honors." It was this vision, not the revolt in France, which "produce[d] the impassioned *Reflections* which have been a glorious revivification of your fame." Wollstonecraft claimed that in his desire to be a "great man" he had "deserted his post" as the herald of liberty and freedom.[28] Burke had switched sides and become a traitor to the rights of men. She asserted that another man was revealed in his text:

There appears to be such a mixture of real sensibility and fondly cherished romance in your composition, that the present crisis carries you out of yourself; and since you could not be one of the grand movers, the next *best* thing that dazzled your imagination was to be a conspicuous opposer. Full of yourself, you make as much noise to convince the world that you despise the revolution, as Rousseau did to persuade his contemporaries to let him live in obscurity.[29]

Undoubtedly, Wollstonecraft's likening of the pragmatic parliamentarian Edmund Burke to the romantic theorist of the *Social Contract*,

---

[26] Ibid., 26. Ida Macalpine and Richard Hunter provide a fascinating study of madness and eighteenth-century medicine in *George III and the Mad-Business* (London: Pimlico, 1993).
[27] Ibid., 52.   [28] Ibid., 43.   [29] Ibid., 44.

Jean Jacques Rousseau, would have seemed absurd to many of her contemporary readers. Rather than revealing the true nature of Burke's motivations in writing the *Reflections,* this statement may reflect Wollstonecraft's own ambitions. The publication of her first *Vindication* was an exercise in political polemic aimed not so much at cutting a great man down to size but at increasing the stature of a little-known novelist.

Given the discursive context of the early 1790s, Wollstonecraft's rhetorical strategy enabled her not only to enter the debate about the rights of man but to engender larger theoretical issues about sexual politics.[30] However, this elaborate subterfuge ultimately backfired in the last pages of the *Vindication.* Contrasting the misery of the masses in London with the hungry women of the bread march, Wollstonecraft asked Burke, "What were the outrages of a day to these continual miseries?" For her it was the wretched conditions in which the majority of men and women lived out their days, not the fate of French monarchs, that constituted the "present crisis" in politics. Wollstone-craft, too, was "carried away from herself" by the contemplation of this crisis. Indeed, she was overcome by the very sensibility she had tried to pin to Burke. "Man preys on man; and you mourn the idle tapestry that decorated a gothic pile, and the dronish bell that summoned the fat priest to prayer." Full of her own feeling, she chided Burke:

Did the pangs you felt for insulted nobility, the anguish that rent your heart when the gorgeous robes were torn off the idol human weakness had set up, deserve to be compared with the long-drawn sigh of melancholy reflection, when misery and vice are thus seen to haunt our steps, and swim on the top of every cheering prospect?

In an enlightened age, "Hell stalks abroad; – the lash resounds on the slave's naked sides; and the sick wretch, who can no longer earn the sour bread of unremitting labor, steals to a ditch to bid the world a long good night."

We can only speculate whether Mary Wollstonecraft as a woman writer with her own bread to earn may have tasted the sour flavor of unremitting labor on her tongue before she lashed out at the pensioned Burke:

---

[30] In the discursive context of the late twentieth century Wollstonecraft's rhetorical ploy raises critical questions about democratic thought and feminist theory. A number of contemporary feminist scholars have argued that Wollstonecraft's appropriation of the language of the rights debates suggests a fear of women's abuse of language. See Cora Kaplan, *Sea Changes: Essays on Culture and Feminism* (London: Verso Press, 1986); John Landes, *Women in the Public Sphere in the Age of the French Revolution* (Ithaca: Cornell University Press, 1988). Both of these studies focus on Wollstonecraft's later treatise *A Vindication of the Rights of Woman* and do not explore the lessons she may have learned about authority and audience from the publication of her reply to Burke.

"Such misery demands more than tears – I pause to recollect myself; and smother the contempt I feel rising for your rhetorical flourishes and infantine sensibility.

◆ – – – – – – – – – – –

◆ – – – – – – – – – – –"

Losing control of herself, Wollstonecraft was reduced to responding to Burke with two lines of dashes, rather than her own words, leaving an empty space on the printed page. She quickly attempted to return to character but instead found herself too shaken to continue. "Taking a retrospective view of my hasty answer, and casting a cursory glance over your *Reflections*, I perceive that I have not alluded to several reprehensible passages, in your elaborate work; which I marked for censure when I first perused it with a steady eye." Knocked off balance by her own recollection of self, Wollstonecraft admitted that she was at a loss. "And now I find it almost impossible to candidly refute your sophisms, without quoting your own words, and putting the numerous contradictions I observed in opposition with each other." Contemporary readers are left to ponder whether this gap represents an "embarrassing silence" as Sapiro asserts or the first self-conscious moments of *A Vindication of the Rights of Woman.*[31] Her own naked humanity revealed by her tears on the page, Mary Wollstonecraft, at least momentarily, was silenced by sensibility.

A Vindication of the Rights of Men concluded with Wollstonecraft's own scheme for political reform. Instead of the corruption of a court culture which promoted its own gender crisis, she offered men and women civic friendship as the foundation of political virtue. Wollstonecraft argued that this virtue could not be inherited; it could only be acquired by hard work. Real progress in Europe would not occur until there was an end to the patriarchal succession of hereditary honors. "Whether the glory of Europe is set, I shall not now enquire; but probably the spirit of romance and chivalry is in the wane; and reason will gain by its extinction."[32] Only a truly democratic nation would be able to achieve the humanistic goals of the Enlightenment. In looking to the future, Wollstonecraft vindicated the members of the National Assembly. "Time may shew, that this obscure throng knew more of the human heart and of legislation than the profligates of rank, emasculated by hereditary effeminacy."[33] The future good of government and the

---

[31] "Perhaps with an implicit reference to the difference in their power, she acknowledged that even if she wrote more, she would in effect be silenced anyway" (Sapiro, *A Vindication of Political Virtue*, 205).

[32] Wollstonecraft, *A Vindication of the Rights of Men*, 29.

[33] Ibid., 40.

people required a new breed of men and women uncorrupted by the
politics of sense and sensibility.

★ ★ ★

> It cannot be denied that Mr. Burke has made a display of very
> *uncommon* abilities in his attack on the French Revolution; but why
> has he deigned to make use of the *mean arts* of abuse as an *auxiliary*
> in the contest? Why has he, by the most *invidious* comparisons, and
> *groundless* accusations, endeavored to rouse all nations and all
> descriptions of men against them, and thus to *crush in their ruin all the
> rights of man?*
>
> Catharine Macaulay, 1790

A later response to Edmund Burke came from an old adversary, the
historian and republican polemicist, Catharine Macaulay. Macaulay's
*Observations on the Reflections of the Right Honorable Edmund Burke, on
the Revolution in France* appeared before the end of 1790. However, this
was not her first reply to the theoretical arguments of Burke. Two
decades before she had engaged him in a debate about Whig policy in
his manifesto of the Rockingham Party, *Thoughts on the Cause of the
Present Discontents*. Barbara Brandon Schnorrenberg has recently argued
that "Edmund Burke was Macaulay's chief opponent in the pamphlet
wars of the later eighteenth century."[34] Indeed, Burke himself acknowledged the power of her pen by labeling her the "republican Virago."
Still, Macaulay's real claim to the republic of fame was her eight-volume
*History of England, from the Accession of James I to that of the Brunswick
Line* produced between 1763 and 1783. This collection revived the
republican heroes of seventeenth-century England and provided a Whig
interpretation of the Glorious Revolution. Macaulay's own reputation
grew with the publication of each quarto volume. The *History* was
widely read in England, America, and France, where she traveled as a
celebrated friend of liberty and was a first-hand witness to the historic
struggles for democratic government.[35]

Macaulay's personal experience of early republican America and of
ancien régime France informed her political understanding of the
meaning of revolution. These experiences, combined with her knowledge of history, empowered her to challenge forcefully Burke's
arguments in the *Reflections*. In the *Observations*, the historian disputed
both the parliamentarian's reading of history as well as his rendering of
current events in London and Paris. Macaulay took a long view of the
first year of the French Revolution. From her vantage point, the events

---

[34] Barbara Brandon Schnorrenberg, "An Opportunity Missed: Catharine Macaulay and
the Revolution of 1688," *Studies in Eighteenth-Century Culture*, 20 (1990): 231.
[35] Carla Hay, "Catharine Macaulay and the American Revolution," *The Historian* 56, 2
(Winter 1994): 301–16.

of 1789 in France brought to mind parallels with the English Civil War and the Glorious Revolution of 1688. However, she cautioned against interpreting the revolution in France through the lens of 1688. As Schnorrenberg suggests, in the *History* Macaulay had portrayed the Glorious Revolution as an "opportunity missed," for the people of England to secure their freedom from tyrannical government.[36] A century later the French Revolution offered mankind another opportunity to assert the native dignity of humanity and to claim the God-given right to rule themselves. Given this perspective, the politics of seventeenth-century England could not provide an adequate template for the political analysis of eighteenth-century France. "We can gain no light from history; for history furnishes no *example* of any government in a large empire, which, in the strictest sense of the word, has secured to the citizen the *full* enjoyment of his rights."[37]

What social process could illuminate this historic shift in power from a king to the third estate? Throughout the pamphlet, Macaulay argued that the real difference between 1688 in England and 1789 in France was the enlightenment of the French people. The revolution in France "appeared as a *sudden spread of an enlightened spirit*, which promised to act as an effectual and permanent barrier to the inlet of those usurpations which the *crafty* have imposed on *ignorance*."[38] She evoked the force of this spirit and the magnitude of this moment of chance and change in the first pages of her *Observations*. "It is not surprising that an event, the most *important* to the dearest interests of mankind, and most *singular* in its nature, and the most *astonishing* in its means, should not only have attracted the curiosity of all civilized nations, but that it should have engaged the passions of all *reflecting* men."[39] Indeed, from the beginning of her response to Burke, she repeatedly returned to the tensions between reflection and passion revealed within this statement. In this manner, Macaulay's rhetorical strategy was to distance herself from Burke by taking up her position among the other "reflecting men" in both countries who supported the rights of man.

Yet as my previous discussion of the *Vindication* demonstrates, one of

[36] Schnorrenberg, "An Opportunity Missed," 233.
[37] Macaulay, *Observations*, 87–88: "Some attempts indeed have been made of this kind; but they have hitherto failed, through the *treachery* of leaders, or the *rash folly* of the multitude."
[38] Ibid., 22. She would reiterate this theme throughout the *Observations*. Later she recounted an address of the National Assembly to Louis XVI in which the representatives of the people stated that it was not the "ill conduct of his Majesty that had provoked the people to emancipate themselves from his power," rather their "liberty was the *necessary* consequence of their *enlightened* spirit" (ibid., 56).
[39] Ibid., 6.

the more astonishing aspects of the French Revolution was that it drew reflecting women to the defense of rational self-government. Macaulay's response to Burke had much in common with that of Mary Wollstonecraft. Both challenged Burke's objectivity by claiming that his emotional description of the events in France revealed a sensibility at odds with common sense. However, there were significant differences in substance and style between the two pamphlets. Whereas Wollstonecraft linked Burke's sensibility to his effeminate aristocratic nature, Macaulay contended that his passionate arguments were grounded in his partisanship. Ironically, one of the biggest criticisms of Wollstonecraft's reply to Burke was that, while she derided his style, she nevertheless engaged with him in the sensationalist rhetoric of revolution.[40] Macaulay observed that on reading Burke with a philosophical eye, "We find him then obliged to substitute a warm and passionate declamation to a cool investigation and to address the passions instead of the reason of mankind."[41] Thus, in the *Observations*, she attempted to escape the theoretical trap of impassioned prose by crafting her response to Burke from virtues she derived from a careful study of republican history.

Taking her cue from republican heroes of the past, a rational and disinterested Catharine Macaulay argued that her old adversary Edmund Burke had aligned himself too closely with the court interests in England and that therefore he was incapable of critically investigating the intrigues that reigned over France. For her, the very enthusiasm of Burke's language revealed a party politics opposed to the true interests of liberty and fraternity. In the *Observations*, she tried to awaken her readers from Burke's nightmarish representation of the revolution by portraying the same events as heralding the dawn of freedom. Yet Macaulay observed that this daybreak in France had brought to light old controversies in England. "Two parties are already formed in this country, who behold the French Revolution with a very opposite temper: to the one, it inspires the sentiments of *exultation* and *rapture*;

---

[40] Philip Anthony Brown argued of Wollstonecraft's reply to Burke, "It is unfair and disordered. But it is charged with emotion; and she has divined the characteristics of Burke's attitude." Brown concluded that other "more deliberate writers" like Paine and Mackintosh treated many of her themes with greater sophistication (*The French Revolution in English History* [London: Frank Cass and Company, 1965], 44–45).

[41] "Is there a rational observation, or argument, in moral existence, which this gentleman (so highly favored by nature and circumstances for public debate) could possibly have passed over, on a subject which he has taken a full leisure to consider?" These remarks raise provocative questions about Macaulay's understanding of her own position within the debates of her age. The ironic tone of the passage indicates that she was well aware that nature and circumstance favored few women with the leisure to engage in political discourse (Macaulay, *Observations*, 7).

and to the other, *indignation* and *scorn.*"[42] Tellingly, she categorized these two parties as the "Democratists" and "Aristocratists."[43] She insisted that only self-interest and class bias could explain the exaggeration of circumstance and the hostility toward reform found among the aristocrats in England who opposed the revolution in France.

With the publication of the *Reflections*, Burke had become the leader of the opposition aristocratic party in England. Macaulay asserted that his behavior as the mouthpiece of this faction was unbecoming to him. She suggested that she would "have expected *a more sympathizing* indulgence towards the *friends* and *promoters* of liberty," from an Englishman.[44] Indeed, Burke's attack on the National Assembly seemed beneath the stature of the famed parliamentarian.

I must own that I was somewhat surprised to find a gentleman of polished manners, who has spent the best part of his life in the company of those who *affect* the nicest conformity to the rules of a refined civility, addressing the august representatives of the most *gallant* and *respectable* of European nations, in terms which I should not use to a set of chimney-sweepers, though acting most ridiculously out of their sphere.[45]

Undoubtedly, Macaulay's political opponents may have considered her address to Burke as evidence that she had ventured "ridiculously out of her sphere."[46] But in taking the side of the rights of man, Catharine Macaulay proved that she was no political outsider. Her defense of the French Revolution provided a masterful critique of parliamentary politics in England that implicitly called into question the class divisions and gender boundaries of public life.[47]

In the *Observations*, Macaulay asserted that members of the National Assembly should not be constrained by their own history or attempt

---

[42] She remarked that the French Revolution had brought to the forefront of English politics longstanding rivalries. "I shall not take upon me to consider what are the secret passions which have given birth to these last sentiments; and shall content myself with observing that Mr. Burke has undertaken to be the oracle of the last party" (ibid., 6).

[43] Ibid., 25.   [44] Ibid., 24.   [45] Ibid., 31.

[46] A number of scurrilous tracts appeared following Catharine Macaulay's second marriage to William Graham in November of 1778. See Anonymous, *A Remarkable Moving Letter!* (London: Shakespeare Press, 1779); Anonymous, *The Female Patriot* (London: J. Bew, 1779). How could the woman who had been celebrated for her masculine mind succumb to the desires of the female flesh?

[47] Curiously, Bridget Hill wrote five chapters of her carefully researched life of Catharine Macaulay before discussing at length the implications of gender on Macaulay's experience as a historian. Hill's sixth chapter, entitled "A Woman in a Man's World," does not develop a convincing answer to the question of how gender influenced her interpretation of republican history (*The Republican Virago*, Oxford: Clarendon Press, 1992). For a much more provocative treatment of Macaulay's feminist leanings see Susan Staves, "'The Liberty of a She-Subject of England': Rights Rhetoric and the Female Thucydides," *Cardoza Studies in Law and Literature* 20 (1990): 161–83.

to follow Burke's advice of modeling their new constitution and institutions on British examples. She challenged the parliamentarian's assessment of the English past as well as his prescription for the future of France. Taking aim at Burke's use of English history, she systematically countered his arguments about the origin of the rights of the English people. Paradoxically, the historian suggested that one need not be an antiquarian to reclaim the rights of Englishmen. To Macaulay the deposition of James II and the succession of William and Mary to the throne provided a clear example of the people exercising the right to form their own government. "The facts may warrant a plain thinking man in the opinion that the family owes its monarchy to the people."[48] It was certainly plain to her that one did not need to follow Burke back in time to make a case for the people's right to choose their king.

To Macaulay, Burke's analysis of history in the *Reflections* suggested a return to the unenlightened politics of the "fanatic atheist Hobbes: *For he supposes an original right in the people to choose their governors*; but, in exerting this right, the citizen and his posterity forever lose their native privileges, and become bound through a series of generations to the service of a master's will."[49] She ridiculed his claim that all succeeding generations must live according to the political agreements of their fathers, bound for eternity by the permanent chains of unalterable law. For her the deposition of James II decisively demonstrated the people's right to cashier their rulers for misconduct. Yet she tempered this observation with the qualification that "it is a right that ought *never* to be exercised by a people who are satisfied with their form of government, and have spirit enough to correct its abuses."[50] But even with her stated preference for reformation over revolution, Macaulay asserted that in the case of the French, the abuse of arbitrary power by Louis XVI and his ministers demanded his removal from the throne. Thus she argued that the single lesson that France could gain from looking back to the England of 1688 was that the active consent of the people was the only legitimate justification for government. Then, as now, the power of the people rested in the natural rights of man. Unfortunately, in 1688 the members of Parliament obscured this fact "in as great a mist of words as possible" in order to appease the new king and advance their

---

[48] Macaulay, *Observations*, 11.
[49] Ibid., 14.
[50] "As to the right of *cashiering* or *deposing* monarchs for misgovernment, I cannot possibly agree with Mr. Burke, that in England it only existed in that Convention of the Two Houses in 1688, which exercised this power over King James and his legal successors" (ibid., 18).

own political careers.[51] Macaulay asserted that if there had been a declaration of the rights of men at the time of the Glorious Revolution, then perhaps the continual conflicts between the Tories and the Whigs would have come to an end. Finally, she criticized members of parliaments, past and present, for engaging in partisan politics instead of securing the liberty of the people.

In the *Observations*, the charge of partisanship was tantamount to an accusation of corruption. Burke's rhetorical style in the *Reflections* made him an easy target for reproach. Macaulay proposed that in good government obedience and flattery were no substitute for the solid and dignified support of popular choice. Burke employed the method of all "enslaved" people in his paeans to monarchy. She claimed that his arguments would be offensive to a wise monarch, who would prefer that his rule be grounded in the rights of men, "as the noblest and safest title."[52] Macaulay rebuked Burke for relying upon passive obedience instead of the active consent of the people as the foundation of good government. "Mr. Burke seems to adopt *prejudice*, opinion and the powers of the imagination, as the *safest* grounds on which *wise* and *good* statesmen can establish and continue the happiness of societies." Indeed, prejudice, opinion, and imagination "have always been imputed by philosophers as causes which have produced all that is *vicious* and *foolish* in man."[53] It was Edmund Burke, not the philosophers of the rights of men, who had conjured up the recipe for political revolt.

Macaulay followed Wollstonecraft in turning her reader's eye from the sensational scenes of the *Reflections*.[54] It is clear from the *Observations*

---

[51] Here Macaulay underscored her belief that at the time of the Glorious Revolution, the English people, "poisoned" by church and party, were not enlightened enough to secure their rights fully.

> However strongly the warm friends of freedom might wish that this abstract right of the people, to choose their own magistrates, and deposing them for ill conduct, had been laid open to the public by a formal declaration of such a right in the acts of succession, this certainly was not a period of time for carrying these wishes into execution. The whole body of the people had swallowed deeply the *poison* of church policy; *passive obedience*, by their means, had so entirely supplanted the *abstract notion* of the *rights of men*. (Ibid., 12)

[52] Ibid., 15.

[53] "These have always been imputed by philosophers (a tribe of men whom indeed Mr. Burke affects much to despise) as causes which have produced all that is *vicious* and *foolish* in man, and consequently have been the fruitful source of human *misery*" (ibid., 16).

[54] Macaulay claimed Burke had let his imagination run wild in his accounts of October 6, 1789. "Mr. Burke is now come to a scene which is calculated to draw forth *all* the energies of his imagination, and which consequently he describes with the *highest possible coloring*. This is no other than the 6th of October 1789, when the king and queen were led in triumph to Paris." What was to Burke a death march was to Macaulay a triumphant procession. Unlike Wollstonecraft, she made no mention of the sex of the

that she viewed the French Revolution as an event of millennial significance.[55] She directed Burke to read Newton's *On the Prophesies*, which
suggested that in the last days "the iron scepter of arbitrary sway shall be
broken."[56] Indeed, the revolution could be interpreted in messianic
terms as a true sign of the enlightenment of the French people.

> The French Revolution was attended with something so *new* in the history of
> human affairs; there was something so *singular*, so *unique*, in that *perfect*
> unanimity in the people; in that *firm* spirit which baffled *every hope* in the
> *interested*, that they could possibly divide them into parties, and render them the
> instruments of a re-subjection of their old bondage: that it naturally excited the
> *surprise* and the *admiration* of an *enlightened spirit*, which promised to act as an
> effectual and permanent barrier to the inlet of those usurpations which from the
> very beginning of social life the *crafty* have imposed on *ignorance*.[57]

The revolution was not just an Enlightenment project but a measure of
Christian faith. Macaulay mocked Burke's rhetorical defense of institutionalized religion as a hymn to property not piety. A true believer would
welcome the revolution in France as an attempt to secure the "*present
and future happiness of twenty-four millions of their people, with their
posterity.*"[58] She argued that Burke was "interested" in the outcome of

marchers or of women's participation in the capture of the royal family. She focused her
attention on the behavior of Louis XVI rather than on Marie Antoinette. Indeed, Marie
Antoinette only makes one appearance in the *Observations*. "In the personal mortifica-
tions of the Queen of France, Mr. Burke finds great reason to lament that the age of
chivalry is no more; for, had the same spirit existed in this, that existed in past ages, 'ten
thousand swords might have leaped from their scabbards, to *avenge even a look* that
threatened her with insult.'" Macaulay argued that Burke had used "those scenes of
royal distress" to "captivate the imagination of the greater number of his readers, in a
degree equal to the effects produced on the author by the *charms* of the Queen of
France." Yet these scenes of virtue in distress had a different effect on the renowned
female patriot; she directed her reader's inner eye to rational contemplation of the
public good. "But *delusions* of fancy are apt to subside in men of cool minds, when any
great object of public concern is held up to their view, to the prejudice of even beauty
and dignity, all those external objects, adapted rather to *enslave* our affections, than to
lead our judgment" (ibid., 56).

55   The *events* of a human life, when *properly* considered, are but a series of
benevolent *providences*: many of them, though very important in their consequences, are too much confounded with the common transactions of men, to
be observed; but whenever the believer thinks he perceives the *omnipotent will*
move immediately declaring itself in favor of the future *perfection* and *happiness*
of the moral world, he is naturally led into the same ecstasies of *hope* and
gratitude, with which Simeon was transported by the view of the infant Messiah.
Has Mr. B. never heard of any millennium, but that fanciful one which is
supposed to exist in the kingdom of the Saints? (Ibid., 20–21)

Lynne Withey has argued, "The doctrine of post-millennialism was central to
Macaulay's religious beliefs. She believed that gradual improvement in human nature
and society would lead to a period of perfection on earth, prior to the second coming of
Christ" ("Catharine Macaulay and the Uses of History: Ancient Rights, Perfectionism,
and Propaganda," *The Journal of British Studies* 16, 1 (1976), 63).

56   Ibid., 21.   57   Ibid., 22.   58   Ibid., 20.

the democratic revolution in France. As the author of the *Reflections*, he, too, was guilty of attempting to hold the ignorant in bondage.

Macaulay's *Observations on the Reflections of the Right Honorable Edmund Burke, on the Revolution in France* challenged Burke's interpretation of British history. She summarized his argument by saying: "The opinion which Mr. Burke endeavors to establish in his elaborate Reflections on the Revolution in France, is the *incompatibility* of a truly popular government with the human constitution."[59] Thus Burke became the symbol of the anti-enlightenment establishment which in seeking to subjugate the common people only succeeded in increasing the misery of men and women of all ranks in society. Macaulay's story of the founding of political societies suggested that where in the past conquest and brutality had been the basis of political authority, the future of government required the consent of an enlightened citizenry to save princes and paupers from the rise of anarchy. While Burke had reservations about the progress of the revolution toward liberty and equality, Macaulay was ready at this early stage in the rebellion to give the revolution in France her full support. In the autumn of 1790, Edmund Burke looked back to a golden age which was lost. Catharine Macaulay, the republican historian, looked to the future for human happiness.

★ ★ ★

> The rights of men asserted by a fair lady! The age of chivalry cannot be over, or the sexes have changed their ground ... We should be sorry to raise a horse-laugh against a fair lady; but we were always taught to suppose that the rights of women were the proper theme of the female sex; and that, while the Romans governed the world, the women governed the Romans.
> *Gentleman's Magazine*, 1791

The replies of Mary Wollstonecraft and Catharine Macaulay to Edmund Burke's *Reflections on the Revolution in France* highlighted the fact that the discourse on the rights and duties of citizenship as well as substantive claims to these civil rights had been "confined to the male line from Adam downwards."[60] Yet these bold female, if not feminist, interjections to the historical debate proved that women could forcefully defend republican political principles, and, in the case of Wollstonecraft, led directly to the articulation of a theory of the rights of woman.[61] Thus, just as the *Reflections* was not simply a rebuttal of the ideas of

---

[59] Ibid., 86–87.

[60] Wollstonecraft, *A Vindication of the Rights of Woman*, in *The Works of Mary Wollstonecraft*, eds. Janet Todd and Marilyn Butler (New York: New York University Press, 1989), 157.

[61] I have argued elsewhere that Wollstonecraft might never have written *A Vindication of the Rights of Woman*, if she had not first authored her reply to Burke. See "Mary Wollstonecraft's 'Wild Wish': Confounding Sex in the Discourse on Political Rights,"

Dr. Richard Price, the *Vindications* and the *Observations* were much more than mere replies to the Right Honorable Edmund Burke. A critical examination of these works offers us a richer interpretation of the *Reflections*, and, more significantly, engenders larger issues about the sexual politics of rights discourse at the end of a century of Enlightenment.

Certainly, Wollstonecraft's *Vindication* and Macaulay's *Observations* had a significant impact on the other advocates of the rights of men. Wollstonecraft's response has been credited with influencing the writings of both Thomas Paine and James Mackintosh. Macaulay's reply, coming at the end of a life devoted to shaping republican history, endorsed a millennialist future of equality and liberty. Yet while many of their ideas about class distinctions and party politics were echoed by their male counterparts in the rights struggle, the questions their writings raised about sexual difference were largely ignored.

Why? I believe that the politics of sense and sensibility offer us a partial explanation of why sexual difference proved to be so problematic for advocates of political equality. Wollstonecraft and Macaulay responded to Burke in a manner that underscored the late eighteenth-century premise that before a woman could articulate a theory of political rights she must first denounce the poetic language of sensibility and embrace rational discourse. What was evident from their arguments was that each woman believed that only sense, defined as reason, offered the possibility of democratic politics. Indeed, their arguments suggest that sensibility, so often associated with women, but in the case of the *Vindication* and the *Observations*, identified with Burke, represented a form of anti-democratic politics that preserved a monarchical and patriarchal social and moral order. Burke's "parade of sensibility" in the *Reflections* aimed at restoring the status quo ante, a world in which gender and class differences were stable and understood.

However, Wollstonecraft and Macaulay recognized that sense and sensibility were gender constructs in conflict. Rather than providing social symmetry and sexual harmony, the political consequence of defining difference in terms that identified masculinity with sense and femininity with sensibility was the continued subjugation of women. Wollstonecraft and Macaulay aligned themselves with reason to refute Burke, positioning themselves within the rights debate as rational subjects capable of comprehending the meaning and moment of the revolution in France. This self-positioning required the repudiation of

in *Feminist Interpretations of Mary Wollstonecraft*, ed. Maria Falco (University Park, Pa.: Penn State University Press, 1996), 61–84.

sensibility, and at least in the case of Wollstonecraft, implied a denial of self.[62] Both women appropriated masculine sense in order more effectively to denounce the effeminate display of sensibility in the *Reflections*. Accordingly, by attacking as effeminate the substance and style of Burke's tract, Wollstonecraft and Macaulay convincingly demonstrated that these gender categories were inherently artificial and unstable. The politics of sense and sensibility could be used against men as well as women in the battle of the sexes.

However, there were significant pitfalls inherent in this rhetorical strategy, not the least of which was that Wollstonecraft's manly masquerade and Macaulay's dispassionate delivery stressed the incompatibility of sexual difference with political equality. Thus, it is possible to read the *Vindication* and the *Observations* as reifying a masculine model of political discourse. We must ask in the end whether these pamphlets play against, or play into, the gender assumptions of the late eighteenth century. I believe that to answer this question we must again return to the writings and to the lives of the women themselves. In *A Vindication of the Rights of Men* Wollstonecraft began to connect her analysis of property rights and primogeniture to a larger critique of patriarchal politics. Two years later, in *A Vindication of the Rights of Woman*, she would deny sexual difference, claiming that both men and women derived their rational capabilities from God. Moreover, Wollstonecraft argued that virtue in either sex required that the mind be guided by the heart; the exercise of sense must be united with the empathy of sensibility. As for Macaulay, the *Observations on the Reflections of the Right Honorable Edmund Burke, on the Revolution in France* represented the culmination of a lifelong investigation of republican theory and democratic practice. She summarized in this pamphlet many of the themes which she had examined within her eight-volume *History of England*. While none of Macaulay's writings, with the exception of her late *Letters on Education*, can be said to be explicitly feminist in its aims, the corpus of her work provided an immanent critique of the idea of the masculine mind embodied in a female frame. In the final analysis the radical assertion of the rights of man by the little-known lady novelist Mary Wollstonecraft and the celebrated female historian Catharine Macaulay paved the way for the even more revolutionary declaration of the rights of woman.

---

[62] Indeed, a number of recent studies that look at Wollstonecraft's later works suggest that her political aims were always in danger of succumbing to the perils of sensibility. See Mary Poovey, *The Proper Lady and the Woman Writer* (Chicago: University of Chicago Press, 1984); Barker-Benfield, *Culture of Sensibility*; and Conger, *Mary Wollstonecraft and the Language of Sensibility*.

7   Mary Wollstonecraft on sensibility, women's rights, and patriarchal power

Mary Lyndon Shanley

One of the results of the resurgence in feminist scholarship over the past twenty-five years has been the inclusion of Mary Wollstonecraft in the ranks of early modern political theorists. The "rediscovery" of Wollstonecraft focused attention on both her life and her writings. It was not surprising that feminists interested in politics and political theory found Wollstonecraft's life a source of inspiration. In an age when female writers were rare and a challenge to "the traditional male monopoly of literacy, learning, and publication,"[1] Wollstonecraft was one of the few women of her day who supported herself by her writing. She was a versatile writer, author not only of her famous *A Vindication of the Rights of Men* (1790) and *A Vindication of the Rights of Woman* (1792), but also of a book on female education, *Thoughts on the Education of Daughters* (1787); the novels *Mary* (1788) and *The Wrongs of Woman, or Maria* (1798); *An Historical and Moral View of the Origin and Progress of the French Revolution* (1794); and a book of observations on nature and culture, *Letters Written During a Short Residence in Sweden, Norway, and Denmark* (1796). She supported the French Revolution, and then traveled to France to witness its aftermath for herself. While in France she had an unhappy love affair and bore a child out of wedlock. In 1796 she became pregnant by the English philosopher and anarchist William Godwin, whom she then married. She died eleven days after giving birth in August 1797.[2]

Although she deeply engaged the political issues of her day, Wollstonecraft's ideas concerning women and political life have defied ready

---

[1] G. J. Barker-Benfield, *The Culture of Sensibility: Sex and Society in Eighteenth-Century Britain* (Chicago: University of Chicago Press, 1992), 310.

[2] On Mary Wollstonecraft's life see Eleanor Flexner, *Mary Wollstonecraft* (New York: Coward, McCann and Geoghegan, 1972); Emily Sunstein, *A Different Face: The Life of Mary Wollstonecraft* (New York: Harper and Row, 1975); Moira Ferguson and Janet Todd, *Mary Wollstonecraft* (Boston: Twayne-G. K. Hall, 1984); Jennifer Lorch, *Mary Wollstonecraft: The Making of a Radical Feminist* (New York: St. Martin's Press, 1990); and Janet Todd, "The Biographies of Mary Wollstonecraft," *Signs: Journal of Women in Culture and Society* 1 (1976): 721–34.

categorization. This chapter analyzes one aspect of Wollstonecraft's political thought, her biting condemnation of both domestic and political patriarchy. Her discussion of patriarchy – what it is, how it affects both men and women, and how it is sustained by both social practice and public law – is one of the most thorough and unrelenting in modern European political theory.[3] Wollstonecraft developed her analysis of the relationship between women's subjection in the household and in the state first in *A Vindication of the Rights of Woman* (1792) and then in *The Wrongs of Woman: or, Maria* (1798). In the preface to *A Vindication of the Rights of Woman*, a critique of contemporary social mores, Wollstonecraft promised that the book would be followed by another specifically about the laws pertaining to women's rights. That sequel was never written, but in many ways *The Wrongs of Woman: or, Maria* takes up in novelistic form the issues of women's legal status that Wollstonecraft had promised to consider. This chapter will argue that, taken together, *A Vindication of the Rights of Woman* and *The Wrongs of Woman: or, Maria* made clear Wollstonecraft's understanding of the integral relationship between social practices and political power, between a society's view of personal virtue and its political culture.

This reading of Wollstonecraft's work places her understanding of "sensibility" and of sexuality, as well as of "rights" and legal equality, at the center of her political thought. The titles of *A Vindication of the Rights of Men* and the *A Vindication of the Rights of Woman* can be somewhat misleading in this respect; as Virginia Sapiro has observed, "the apparently widespread view that Wollstonecraft should be known exclusively for her advocacy of 'women's rights' is inappropriate. Most of what she wrote was not on rights, or not on rights as most people understand the term."[4] Moreover, while Wollstonecraft seemed to want to extend "the natural and imprescriptible rights of man ... liberty, property, security, and resistance of oppression"[5] to women, she accepted the notion that one of women's primary roles and social contributions (and one not shared by men) was nurturing and raising

---

[3] The themes of J. S. Mill's *The Subjection of Women* bear a close resemblance to many of Wollstonecraft's arguments. Virginia Sapiro says no one who played a key role in the feminist movement except Lucretia Mott appears to have read Wollstonecraft prior to the late nineteenth century (Virginia Sapiro, *A Vindication of Political Virtue: The Political Theory of Mary Wollstonecraft* [Chicago: University of Chicago Press, 1992], 227), and no entry to "Wollstonecraft" appears in the Index to the *Collected Works of John Stuart Mill*. But Mill may have known Wollstonecraft's work through William Thompson's *Appeal of One Half of the Human Race, Women, Against the Pretensions of the Other Half, Men, to Retain Them in Political and Thence in Civil and Domestic Slavery* (1825).

[4] Sapiro, *A Vindication of Political Virtue*, xxv.

[5] Mary Wollstonecraft, *An Historical and Moral View of the Origin and Progress of the French Revolution* (1974), 162, quoted in Sapiro, *A Vindication of Political Virtue*, 90.

children.[6] Squaring Wollstonecraft's seeming acceptance of some aspects of the sexual division of labor with her espousal of universal human rights as the foundation of women's citizenship has proven a daunting task. The sexual division of labor with respect to childrearing did not mean, however, that women (or men) should accept certain damaging popular cultural notions of female "sensibility." Exaggerated notions of female sensibility corrupted both women and men, and worked against the extension of fundamental rights of citizenship to women. In their engagement with social mores and cultural practices, both *A Vindication of the Rights of Woman* and *The Wrongs of Woman: or, Maria* were much closer in their concerns to the examination of moral education of Jean Jacques Rousseau's novels *Emile* and *La Nouvelle Héloïse* than to the analyses of the legal foundations of citizenship in the treatises of Thomas Hobbes or John Locke.

Wollstonecraft's argument that political freedom required not only the overthrow of hereditary aristocracy but the overthrow of sexual aristocracy – an argument developed in the context of democratic revolutions on both sides of the Atlantic – was repeatedly ridiculed for well over a century.[7] It was nonetheless correct. While her critique drew upon laws and practices of late eighteenth-century England, the argument that private relationships and public power are interdependent and have historically given men power over women in both family and state is not only descriptive of her society but is still relevant today. So, too, is her insistence that the workings of patriarchy depend on both the enforcement of socially constructed gender roles and formal legal and economic structures. Two centuries after her death, Wollstonecraft's legacy of personal courage and intellectual insight into the dynamics of tyranny and subjection continue to inspire and instruct those interested in both women's liberation and the meaning of equal rights for men and women in a liberal state.

---

[6] Zillah Eisenstein, *The Radical Future of Liberal Feminism* (New York: Longman, 1981); Jean Grimshaw, "Mary Wollstonecraft and the Tensions in Feminist Philosophy," *Radical Philosophy* 59 (Summer): 11–17; Moira Gatens, "'The Oppressed of My Sex': Wollstonecraft on Reason, Feeling and Equality," in *Feminist Interpretations and Political Theory*, eds. Mary Lyndon Shanley and Carole Pateman (Cambridge: Polity Press and University Park: Penn State University Press, 1991), 112–28; Sapiro, *A Vindication of Political Virtue*.

[7] The reception of Wollstonecraft's work was mixed. On favorable reactions see R. M. Janes, "On the Reception of Mary Wollstonecraft's *A Vindication of the Rights of Woman*," in *A Vindication of the Rights of Woman*, 2nd ed., ed. Carol Poston (New York: W. W. Norton, 1988), 297–307; on the ridicule heaped on Wollstonecraft see Sapiro, *A Vindication of the Political Virtue*, 28–30 and 274–77.

Patriarchy and the gendering of sensibility: *A Vindication of the Rights of Woman*

A Vindication of the Rights of Woman analyzed the ways in which patriarchy was rooted in what Wollstonecraft called "sensibility" and social mores; its goal was the reformation of manners in order to reeducate the passions and undermine the habits that sustained patriarchy. In her "Dedication" to M. Talleyrand-Perigord, former French bishop and member of France's revolutionary legislature, Wollstonecraft set forth her disagreement with this defender of men's rights on issues of women's education and citizenship. In September, 1791, Talleyrand submitted a *Rapport sur l'instruction publique* to the National Assembly. In it he argued that both sexes should be educated, but he advocated different instruction for women than for men, since women would not perform the same public duties as men.

It seems incontestable to us that the common happiness, especially that of women, requires that they do not aspire to exercise rights and political functions ... [L]et us teach them the real measure of their duties and rights. That they will find, not insubstantial hopes, but real advantages under the empire of liberty; that the less they participate in the making of the law, the more they will receive from it protection and strength; and that especially when they renounce all political rights, they will acquire the certainty of seeing their civil rights substantiated and even expanded.[8]

In response, Wollstonecraft asked whether it was not inconsistent for Talleyrand to insist that free men "be allowed to judge for themselves respecting their own happiness," while allowing such men to "subjugate women, even though you firmly believe that you are acting in the manner best calculated to promote [women's] happiness?" One of the properties of free men, this suggested, was their ability, supported by social custom and law alike, to subjugate women. If all human beings shared in reason, then to "*force* all women, by denying them civil and political rights, to remain immured in their families groping in the dark" was a kind of tyranny. Under such tyrannical rule, women became "convenient slaves," but slavery would have a "constant effect, degrading [to] the master and the abject dependent" alike.[9]

---

[8] Charles-Maurice de Talleyrand-Périgord, *Rapport sur l'instruction publique fait au nom du Comité de constitution, à l'Assemblée nationale, les 10, 11, et 19 de septembre 1791* (Paris, 1791), quoted in Karen Offen, "Was Mary Wollstonecraft a Feminist? A Contextual Re-reading of *A Vindication of the Rights of Woman*, 1792–1992," in *Quilting a New Canon: Stitching Women's Words*, ed. Uma Parameswaran (Toronto: Sister Vision, 1996), 3–25, p. 7.

[9] Wollstonecraft, *A Vindication of the Rights of Woman*, in *The Works of Mary Wollstonecraft*, v, eds. Janet Todd and Marilyn Butler (New York: New York University Press, 1989), 67–68.

The belief that men and women would (and, further, should) occupy separate spheres and perform wholly different tasks resulted in their receiving quite distinct educations, and led to the corruption that Wollstonecraft deplored. Many of the characteristics of both sexes had been instilled in them through highly damaging socialization. *A Vindication of the Rights of Woman* was at its core about what was wrong with the social construction of the sexes in her society, how this might be changed, and why such change was imperative.

A Vindication of the Rights of Woman attempted to show that men deliberately encouraged certain characteristics in women (and discouraged others) which kept women subordinate to them. As Sapiro noted, "Men, the more powerful agents in society, had rigged the system to make strength an asset for them (but not for women) and weakness more valuable to women. Self-degradation and weakness therefore become women's illusory rational choice because they are more likely to lead to 'success' as defined by the participants in the system."[10] In response to Rousseau's claim that women exercised power over men through sexual attraction combined with physical weakness, Wollstonecraft insisted, "I do not wish them [women] to have power over men, but over themselves."[11] By being regarded above all as objects of male sexual desire, women had become not the rulers but the "slaves" of men.[12] Male lust and the desire to possess women corrupted both men and women; male domination of women had become a source of sexual attraction for both sexes. Wollstonecraft described women who had become "the slaves of casual lust"; they were like "standing dishes to which every glutton may have access."[13] And since bodily weakness was regarded as sexually attractive in women, "genteel women ... are slaves to their bodies and glory in their subjection."[14] The desensualization or desexualization of women in men's eyes would de-eroticize female helplessness and languor. *A Vindication of the Rights of Woman* was, as Barbara Taylor has remarked, "an exposé ... of the degeneracy of modern womankind which has as its central target women's sexuality."[15]

[10] Sapiro, *A Vindication of the Rights of Woman*, 124 (reference omitted).

[11] Wollstonecraft, *A Vindication of the Rights of Woman* 131.

[12] For Rousseau's views, which Wollstonecraft clearly had in mind, see Jean Jacques Rousseau, *Emile*, trans. Barbara Foxley (New York: Dutton, Everyman's Library, 1966), Book v, 321–444. *A Vindication of the Rights of Woman* was in many respects a response to *Emile*. Wollstonecraft agreed with and admired much of what Rousseau had to say about moral education, but disagreed sharply with his understanding of women's proper education and role in civil society.

[13] Wollstonecraft, *A Vindication of the Rights of Woman*, 208.

[14] Ibid., 112.

[15] Barbara Taylor, "Introduction," in Mary Wollstonecraft, *A Vindication of the Rights of Woman* (New York: Everyman's Library, Knopf, 1992), xviii.

Wollstonecraft's condemnation of corrupted sensuality and distorted "sensibility" was related to the eighteenth-century criticisms of aristocracy as well as of romantic fiction. Women's participation in the deliberate construction of pallor, softness, frailty, ornament, and finery as marks of sexual desirability necessitated a certain amount of leisure and luxury. Karen Offen links Wollstonecraft's criticism of women's use of sexuality as a way to gain power and influence with contemporary criticism of "courtly society, aristocratic manners, 'learned women' ... and encroaching commercialism."[16] She points out that at the time Wollstonecraft wrote, the French queen, Marie Antoinette, "was under sharp attack by certain revolutionaries as the very epitome of politically irresponsible seductiveness and sensuality – the very embodiment of all that was wrong with the old regime."[17]

While it was clear that Wollstonecraft abhorred the sharp division between men and women that underlay popular notions of female sensuality and male rationality, the question of whether she advocated equal rights and similar social roles on the one hand or saw men and women as fulfilling different roles on the other cannot be answered unequivocally. In her letter dedicating *A Vindication of the Rights of Woman* to Talleyrand, Wollstonecraft emphasized the universality of reason and the equal natural rights of all humans: "if women are to be excluded ... from a participation of the natural rights of mankind, prove first, to ward off the charge of injustice and inconsistency, that they want reason."[18] Wollstonecraft believed that women must be educated for the independence of judgment suitable to all rational creatures: "The grand end of their exertions should be to unfold their own faculties and to acquire the dignity of conscious virtue."[19] Women's "first duty is to themselves as rational creatures."[20] Wollstonecraft also insisted that all women should be able to lead an independent existence. In order for women's "private virtue [to become] a public benefit, they must have a civil existence in the state, married or single."[21] Wollstonecraft asserted that no woman, including married women, should "want, individually, the protection of civil laws."[22] She repeatedly wrote that women had a right to earn their own living, and urged that the professions be opened to women.[23] Acknowledging that she would be ridiculed, she confessed that she thought that "women ought to have representatives, instead of being arbitrarily governed, without having any direct share allowed them in the deliberations of government."[24]

[16] Offen, "Was Mary Wollstonecraft a Feminist?", 10.   [17] Ibid., 10.
[18] Wollstonecraft, *A Vindication of the Rights of Woman*, 68.   [19] Ibid., 95.
[20] Ibid., 157.   [21] Ibid., 219.   [22] Ibid., 216.
[23] Ibid., 218–20.   [24] Ibid., 217.

Wollstonecraft, however, also assumed that some duties of men and women would be different, and saw these duties as rooted in nature, not simply in social convention. The care of infants was "one of the grand duties annexed to the female character by nature."[25] Like Rousseau, Wollstonecraft regarded the practical and moral education of children as of the utmost importance, and as a task belonging particularly to mothers. Unlike Rousseau, however, Wollstonecraft did not think that maternal duties made civic participation unnecessary or unwise for women.[26] Women's "first duty" was to themselves, as rational creatures, and "the next, in order of importance, as citizens, is that, which includes so many, of a mother."[27]

Because of their duty to care for young children, women (or at least mothers) would take a somewhat different role in civic life than men. In *A Vindication of the Rights of Woman* Wollstonecraft asserted that the civic duties of men and women were not identical: while men were to engage in politics, it was the part of a woman to "superintend her family and suckle her children, in order to fulfil her part of the social compact."[28] In *A Vindication of the Rights of Woman*, Wollstonecraft envisioned a state of society in which "a man must necessarily fulfill the duties of a citizen, or be despised, and that while he was employed in any of the departments of civil life, his wife, also an active citizen, should be equally intent to manage her family, educate her children, and assist her neighbors."[29] In a letter, she remarked that "Considering the care and anxiety a woman must have about a child before it comes into the world, it seems to me, by a natural right, to belong to her."[30]

Wollstonecraft tried to show, however, that difference need not inevitably lead to hierarchy and subjugation. It is true, Wollstonecraft admitted, that women and men "may have different duties to fulfil," but these "are *human* duties, and the principles that should regulate the discharge of them, I sturdily maintain, must be the same."[31] Wollstonecraft held out hope that with new social practices as well as legal reforms, the human species could develop to new levels of refinement and appropriate sensibility. She believed that "as sound politics diffuse

---

[25] Ibid., 222. One of a mother's duties was that she should nurse her children (in this Wollstonecraft fully agreed with Rousseau): "Her parental affection, indeed, scarcely deserves the name, when it does not lead her to suckle her children ... What sympathy does a mother exercise who sends her babe to nurse, and only takes it from a nurse to send it to school?" (223).

[26] Rousseau expressed his views about motherhood and citizenship in *Emile*, Book v.

[27] Wollstonecraft, *A Vindication of the Rights of Woman*, 216.

[28] Wollstonecraft, *A Vindication of the Rights of Men*, 24.

[29] Wollstonecraft, *A Vindication of the Rights of Woman*, 216.

[30] Letter, 1794: 242, quoted in Sapiro, *A Vindication of Political Virtue*, 157.

[31] Wollstonecraft, *A Vindication of the Rights of Woman*, 120.

liberty, mankind, including woman, will become more wise and virtuous."[32] The development of the species held out the possibility of "a new kind of marriage" and "a reformed family, generating the social bond of sympathy as well as individualism."[33] Wollstonecraft put great hope in all that women might accomplish for society if they properly performed their functions as mothers. "[T]he affectionate family and, at its heart, mothering ... generated traits (the happy energy of social affections) that society needed."[34] One strong argument for improving women's education was that it would enable them to be better mothers: a mother's duty to care for her child "would afford many forcible arguments for strengthening the female understanding, if it were properly considered."[35] Education was also important for women who did not marry; it would enable them to support themselves and prepare them for the independence that Wollstonecraft saw as "the grand blessing of life, the basis of every virtue."[36] This independence would be enjoyed by men and women, married and unmarried alike, who might hope to be true companions and friends in a reformed society.

Improper social mores and corrupted sensibility would condemn women, men, and society alike to stagnation or degeneration. A reformed society would require not only a new education in rational thought and moral sensibility, but also legal reform and the extension of certain rights of citizenship to women. While women's sensibility was the main topic of *A Vindication of the Rights of Woman*, in *The Wrongs of Women: or, Maria*, Wollstonecraft examined the evils wrought by contemporary laws affecting women.

Patriarchy and the legal subjection of women: *The Wrongs of Woman: or, Maria*

The Wrongs of Woman: or, Maria was a much darker and more pessimistic work than *A Vindication of the Rights of Woman*, due perhaps both to events in Wollstonecraft's life that made her feel the power of patriarchy with particular force, and to the way in which attention to law made her see the relationships between legal and social change as thoroughly intertwined. Too often in analyses of Wollstonecraft's ideas, as Janet Todd has noted, "the life, which is remembered because of the

---

[32] Ibid., quoted in Barker-Benfield, *The Culture of Sensibility*, xxxi.
[33] Anne K. Mellor, "Introduction," Mary Wollstonecraft, *Maria or the Wrongs of Woman* (New York: W. W. Norton, 1994), xvi; Barker-Benfield, *The Culture of Sensibility*, 286.
[34] Barker-Benfield, *The Culture of Sensibility*, 276.
[35] Wollstonecraft, *A Vindication of the Rights of Woman*, 222.
[36] Ibid., 65.

works, tends to overshadow those works" and biography takes the place of critical analysis.[37] Yet Anne Mellor has argued persuasively that both "Wollstonecraft's own sexual experiences and the repressive, anti-revolutionary acts of the conservative British government dominated by William Pitt and Edmund Burke" illuminate the greater sense of danger and pessimism that infuses *The Wrongs of Woman: or, Maria* when compared to *A Vindication of the Rights of Woman*.[38]

In the five years between the publication of *A Vindication of the Rights of Woman* (1792) and Wollstonecraft's writing of *The Wrongs of Woman: or, Maria* (left unfinished at her death in 1797), Wollstonecraft had toured revolutionary France, witnessed the Terror there and seen the conservative reaction in England to the French Revolution. She had also entered into a passionate love affair with Gilbert Imlay, borne their child, and discovered Imlay's infidelity. She tried to commit suicide with an overdose of laudanum, after which Imlay sent her, with their daughter, Fanny, to Scandinavia to try to recover a shipment of goods he had lost. When Wollstonecraft returned to London, she found that Imlay was now living openly with his new mistress. Leaving Fanny with a nursemaid, Wollstonecraft again unsuccessfully attempted suicide by jumping off the Putney Bridge. In April 1796 she met the philosopher William Godwin; within three months they were lovers, although they continued to live in separate households. Wollstonecraft became pregnant, and she and Godwin married; their daughter, Mary, was born on August 30, 1797.[39] Wollstonecraft died from complications arising from the birth. She had worked on *The Wrongs of Woman: or, Maria* during 1797, and left it unfinished at her death. Godwin published it with other posthumous works in 1798.

The Wrongs of Woman: or, Maria, a novel, was intended for a broader pubic than *A Vindication of the Rights of Woman* and tells a number of intertwined stories. The main one is that of Maria Venables, an upper middle-class woman, perfectly sound of mind, committed to an insane asylum by her husband who, in exercising his right to consign Maria to the asylum, separated her from her infant daughter. Also confined in the asylum is Mr. Darnford, a middle-class man whose relatives have had him kidnapped and locked up, apparently to get control of the property to which he is heir. Darnford tells the history of his failed venture to settle

---

[37] Janet Todd, "The Biographies of Mary Wollstonecraft," *Signs* 1 (1976): 721–34, esp. 721.

[38] Mellor, "Introduction" to *Maria or the Wrongs of Woman*, vii.

[39] Their daughter, Mary Wollstonecraft Godwin, married Percy Bysshe Shelley and wrote the novel *Frankenstein*. For her biography see Emily W. Sunstein, *Mary Wollstonecraft Shelley: Romance and Reality* (Boston: Little, Brown, 1989).

in America to Maria and her keeper, Jemima, and Maria falls in love with him. Jemima, in turn, recounts the story of her life to Maria and Darnford. Jemima is at the lowest rung of the social scale, born out of wedlock to a mother who was abandoned after Jemima was born and who died shortly thereafter. Jemima herself was seduced and abandoned, and struggled to support herself throughout her life. Within these narratives are other tales, most strikingly that of Peggy, sister of Maria's childhood nurse, now the lower middle-class wife of a sailor who was impressed into the British navy and died while in service, leaving Peggy penniless.

The multiplicity of women's life stories, and the fact that they reflected the experiences of women from the poorest to the middle class, reinforced Wollstonecraft's assertion in the Author's Preface that Maria's plight was not unique; the ills that beset her were representative of the "wrongs" that plagued all British women. One such wrong was the tremendous vulnerability facing any woman who did not marry; another was the same vulnerability, along with the obliteration of her separate legal status, faced by every married woman.

In *The Wrongs of Woman: or, Maria* Wollstonecraft depicts woman after woman seduced or raped, "ruined" and reduced to penury. For poor unmarried women the effects of men's desire to possess women's bodies were particularly devastating. As Virginia Sapiro remarked, "These are not delicate reservations about tarnished reputations or lost innocence. The question for women was rape, dangerous and unwanted pregnancy, and the possibility of literally being cast out to the streets, with all that implied."[40] Jemima was motherless because her father seduced her mother, whom he never married, and who died nine days after Jemima's birth. Jemima herself was raped by her employer and thrown out of doors. She later formed a liaison with a tradesman whose mistress she barred from the house, only to find that the woman subsequently drowned herself because she could not support herself. Mr. Venables seduced and abandoned a servant who later died; the child of that seduction was near starvation when Maria began giving money to the woman to whose care the mother entrusted the child.

While the devastating consequences of bearing a child out of wedlock for poor women might involve starvation and death, middle- and upper-class women could also be "ruined" by pregnancy before marriage. Part of their vulnerability stemmed from the moral code that declared that no woman could be regarded as "virtuous" who had sexual relations outside of marriage.[41] Even without such moral condemnation,

---

[40] Sapiro, *A Vindication of Political Virtue*, 129.
[41] Wollstonecraft, *A Vindication of the Right of Woman*, 140.

however, an unmarried mother would have suffered economic ruin. Women could not keep their freedom by deciding not to marry; there were few ways except marriage by which women could earn their living. As John Stuart Mill remarked nearly a century later, men had made marriage a "Hobson's choice" for women, "that or none," by closing all other remunerative occupations to them.[42]

Marital enslavement was particularly odious because it was sanctioned and supported by the power of the state.[43] Not only were there few remunerative occupations open to women, but if a woman did have any moveable property, it became her husband's when they married. A husband might be both intemperate and profligate, but "over their mutual fortune she has no power, it must all pass through his hand."[44] Any money she might subsequently earn or inherit also became his, and she could not enter into contracts or sue or be sued in her own name. Indeed, Maria exclaimed, a wife "has nothing she can call her own. [Her husband] may use any means to get at what the law considers as his, the moment his wife is in possession of it, even to the forcing of a lock" on her writing desk.[45]

A married woman's inability to own property in her own name reflected the fact that in many ways "the prejudices of mankind" had "made women the property of their husbands."[46] A wife was "as much a man's property as his horse, or his ass."[47] The notion that a wife's person as well as her possessions belonged to her husband underlay the legal action for "criminal conversation," whereby a husband could sue another man for "damages" for having sexual relations with his wife, despite the fact that the husband "never appeared to value his wife's society, till he found that there was a chance of his being indemnified for the loss of it."[48] No such action was available to a wife, regardless of the severity of a husband's offense. In one of the most chilling scenes in the novel, when Venables offers sex with Maria to his friend for a loan of five hundred pounds, both men regard the action as a plausible extension of Venables's prerogative as a husband.[49]

Not only was a woman the property of her husband, but their child was also his. When Venables committed Maria to the asylum, he separated her from her daughter, and Maria's struggle to free herself from her imprisonment was simultaneously a struggle to rejoin her

---

[42] John Stuart Mill, *The Subjection of Women* [1869], in *Essays on Sex Equality*, ed. Alice Rossi (Chicago: University of Chicago Press, 1970), 156.

[43] On the legal status of married women see Mary Lyndon Shanley, *Feminism, Marriage and the Law in Victorian England* (Princeton, N.J.: Princeton University Press, 1989).

[44] Wollstonecraft, *The Wrongs of Woman*, 145.

[45] Ibid., 149.   [46] Ibid., 139.   [47] Ibid., 149.

[48] Ibid., 146.   [49] Ibid., 151–52.

child. Wollstonecraft repeatedly depicted mothers torn from their children by a combination of male irresponsibility and the law. A female inmate who sings "the pathetic ballad of old Robin Gray" lost her mind and was separated from her child "during the first lying-in."[50] Peggy, sister of Maria's nurse and wife of the sailor, Daniel, found she could not support herself and her children on what she could earn after Daniel died despite the fact that she labored grueling hours; she feared the state would remove the children and send them to Daniel's distant parish.[51] The woman who took in Maria after she left Venables was beaten by her husband "though she had a child at the breast," and she was without recourse to stop the beatings or protect the child.[52]

A woman, once married, could not regain her freedom or her claim to her child, no matter what the offenses her husband committed. When Maria appeared before the judge at Darnford's trial for "criminal conversation" (that is, for seduction and adultery), she declaimed, "I exclaim against the laws which throw the whole weight of the yoke on the weaker shoulders, and force women, when they claim protectorship as mothers, to sign a contract, which renders them dependent on the caprice of the tyrant, whom choice or necessity has appointed to reign over them."[53] In order not to be a slave, a woman had to be able to separate from her husband, and to retain custody of her child when she did so. But even as Maria announced, "I claim then a divorce," she, the judge and the reader all knew that the legal bond of marriage was not severed by such a pronouncement, and not even by offenses as heinous as Venables's acts. The legal rules governing marriage "forge adamantine fetters" between those who do not love one another and were even "more inhuman" than those that "commanded even the most atrocious criminals to be chained to dead bodies."[54]

The core of Wollstonecraft's feminist vision was her belief in the desirability and moral necessity of women's independence. "Independence I have long considered as the grand blessing of life, the basis of every virtue," she wrote in her dedicatory epistle to Talleyrand in *A Vindication of the Rights of Woman*, "and independence I will ever secure by contracting my wants, though I were to live on a barren heath."[55] In order to live independently, women had to have the possibility of supporting themselves. As Jemima lamented, "How often have I heard in conversation, and read in books, that every person willing to work may find employment? It is the vague assertion, I believe, of insensible indolence, when it relates to men; but, with respect to women, I am sure

[50] Ibid., 95.   [51] Ibid., 128.   [52] Ibid., 158.   [53] Ibid., 179.
[54] Ibid., 154.   [55] Wollstonecraft, *A Vindication of the Rights of Woman*, 65.

of its fallacy."[56] Almost no jobs save those of "milliners and mantua-makers" were open to women, and all too often "an attempt to earn their own subsistence, a most laudable one!" sunk women "almost to the level of those poor abandoned creatures who live by prostitution."[57]

The possibility of maintaining oneself was crucial not only to those who did not marry, but also to the moral reformation of marriage itself. Unless women could earn their own living, they would be forced to marry, leading to the kinds of loveless and corrupt unions that Wollstonecraft depicted so bitterly. If decent jobs were open to women, "women would not then marry for a support," which turned marriage into a kind of "legal prostitution."[58] Moreover, husbands and wives could not experience the kind of equality that Wollstonecraft saw as a prerequisite for "friendship" within marriage unless women had the opportunity to earn their living (although Wollstonecraft did not contend that married women *should* work beyond the household, and clearly expected mothers would make the care of their children their first priority). Unless a woman knew that she could work, she would find it impossible even to contemplate leaving a marriage, for she would have no way of maintaining herself. And women's inability to leave could not but affect the quality of any marriage, even an otherwise healthy one.[59] Wollstonecraft wanted to keep women from this vulnerability by making certain that they would be able to earn their keep when necessary.

Guaranteeing women's independence, in Wollstonecraft's eyes, meant guaranteeing women the ability to support not only themselves but any children they might have. While she by no means thought that every woman would be or should be a mother, she did regard women as the proper and rightful custodians of children, and therefore any policy to provide for women of necessity had also to provide for their children.

Part of the reason to place children in women's custody was that men were often indifferent fathers. *The Wrongs of Woman: or, Maria* was full of depictions of men who seduced or raped and then abandoned the woman and child. Venables took no responsibility for his nonmarital child. When her mother died nine days after giving birth, Jemima was left with only "a Christian name."[60] Later she laments, "I had no one to love me ... I was an egg dropped on the sand; a pauper by nature,

[56] Wollstonecraft, *The Wrongs of Woman*, 115.
[57] Wollstonecraft, *A Vindication of the Rights of Woman*, 218.
[58] Ibid., 218.
[59] Susan Okin has analyzed the effect of the inequality of men's and women's economic resources and employment opportunities on present-day marriage and divorce, in Susan Moller Okin, *Justice, Gender, and the Family* (New York: Basic Books, 1989), 134–69.
[60] Wollstonecraft, *The Wrongs of Woman*, 88.

hunted from family to family, who belonged to nobody – and nobody cared for me . . . I was, in fact, born a slave."[61] She was a "slave" because she was penniless and no one had responsibility to maintain her; without any resources, she could not hope to become a self-determining and self-possessing individual (a citizen rather than a slave). But she was neither a pauper nor a slave by "nature"; no infants have property by nature, but only through the laws establishing affiliation and rights of inheritance. Similarly, Jemima had a biological father, that is, one by "nature," but none in the eyes of the law. When she reached puberty, Jemima herself was raped by her employer and abandoned when she became pregnant. Venables seduced and abandoned his servant girl and their child, and Maria judged the abandonment more severely than the seduction: I "could excuse the birth, [but] not the desertion of this unfortunate babe."[62]

Wollstonecraft's sole portrait of a man able and willing to discharge the responsibilities of fatherhood was Maria's bachelor uncle. It is he who provided her with constant love and support and who extended his protection to her sisters and her child as well. He was, Maria said, "the dear parent of my mind."[63] His paternal solicitude extended to Maria's daughter, whom he offered to adopt.[64] His willingness to act as father to Maria's daughter, perhaps, made her exclaim when he died that she was "widowed by the death of my uncle";[65] his care of her daughter was like that a husband might have provided. In *The Wrongs of Woman: or, Maria* Wollstonecraft gave the title of "father" to a man who was neither a biological father nor the spouse or sexual partner of the mother. In her eyes, it would seem, the rights of fatherhood derived neither from nature nor from marriage; they had to be established through concrete acts of care and responsibility.

Maria was "imprisoned" long before Venables committed her to the asylum; as she put it, "Marriage had bastilled me for life."[66] She had little choice but to get married. When she married, she lost legal control of both her possessions and her body; she could neither control her earnings nor refuse her husband sexual access. When she had a child, her husband could remove the child from her care and custody. When Wollstonecraft addressed what needed to be done to right the legal underpinnings of "the wrongs of woman," she began with what she regarded as the two most serious of those wrongs, the impossibility of a woman – married or single – to earn enough to support herself and her children, and the denial of maternal custody rights.

---

[61] Ibid., 110.   [62] Ibid., 179.   [63] Ibid., 163.
[64] Ibid., 165.   [65] Ibid., 166.   [66] Ibid., 146.

While Maria's suffering stemmed mainly from male perfidy and the workings of the law, Wollstonecraft also suggested that some of her difficulties were exacerbated by occasional flights of fancy unchecked by reason, the exaggeration of sensibility that Wollstonecraft had analyzed in *A Vindication of the Rights of Woman*.[67] Maria was both a reader and a writer: she borrowed books from Darnford even before she met him, and she composed her memoirs so that her daughter would have a reflective account of Maria's life. Maria valued rationality and self-awareness, and a mind eager for improvement. But her emotions at times overwhelmed her reason. The anguish she felt at her separation from her daughter "rendered [her] incapable of sober reflection."[68] Reading Dryden's romance of Guiscard and Sigismunda and Rousseau's *Julie, ou la nouvelle Héloïse* that Darnford lent her "alternately soothed and inflamed her 'intoxicated sensibility.' "[69]

Maria's understanding of the abusive power of her husband and of its roots both in his personality and in law and economic structures was astute. As Anne Mellor noted, however, Maria committed a great error, one attributable to excessive sensibility, in turning Darnford into a romantic hero:

> as she reads Darnford's jottings in a book he lends her, her "treacherous fancy" immediately begins to "sketch a character, congenial with her own, from these shadowy outlines." A glimpse of his back, the sound of his voice, afford "coloring for the picture she was delineating on her heart," and mere "animation of countenance" is sufficient to persuade this "enthusiast" that Darnford is not only sane but the very embodiment of that "ideal lover" and "demi-god," Rousseau's St. Preux.[70]

While both were confined in the asylum, Darnford expressed his wish that she " 'put it out of the power of fate to separate them,' " and "[a]s her husband she now received him, and he pledged himself as her protector – and eternal friend."[71] Maria's confidence was misplaced. In Wollstonecraft's notes for the conclusion of the novel, Darnford was away from Maria on business and his return was delayed; "his delaying to return seemed extraordinary" but love "to excess, excludes fear or suspicion."[72] Suspicion would have been wise, for in one of the several plot sketches "Her lover [proved] unfaithful."[73]

---

[67] This paragraph draws on insights found in Mellor, "Introduction" to *Maria or the Wrongs of Woman*.

[68] Wollstonecraft, *The Wrongs of Woman*, 86.

[69] Mellor, "Introduction" to *Maria or the Wrongs of Woman*, xiii (page references omitted).

[70] Ibid., xiv (page references omitted).

[71] Wollstonecraft, *The Wrongs of Woman*, 173.

[72] Ibid., 182.   [73] Ibid., 183.

In Wollstonecraft's view, true sensibility, "the sensibility which is the auxiliary of virtue, and the soul of genius," was, as Maria wrote in her memoir to her daughter, "so occupied with the feelings of others, as scarcely to regard its own sensations."[74] Maria, nonetheless, was sometimes swept away by sensation fostered by her own imagination. Right sensibility, by contrast, was always allied with reason. The lesson of *A Vindication of the Rights of Woman* and of *The Wrongs of Woman: or, Maria*, read together, was that sensibility would remain mired in sensuality unless women's public roles and rights expanded, while rights unaccompanied by proper sensibility would not produce the changes in character necessary for enduring social reform.

Sexual inequality and women's citizenship: the legacy of Wollstonecraft's dilemma

When Wollstonecraft spoke of the "slavery" of women in eighteenth-century England, she clearly described circumstances vastly different from those of chattel slavery. Yet like many British and American abolitionists, she found women's inability to earn money, married women's legal incapacity to hold property in their own names, and mothers' inability to have custody of their children sure marks of their slavery.[75] To establish a just regime, social practice and law would have

---

[74] Quoted in Mellor, "Introduction" to *Maria or the Wrongs of Woman*, xv.

[75] It is interesting to compare this aspect of Wollstonecraft's thought to that of two nineteenth-century works that also discussed women, slavery, and citizenship. In 1869 John Stuart Mill's *The Subjection of Women* compared the situation of married women to that of slaves; in 1861 Harriet Jacobs's *Incidents in the Life of a Slave Girl* recounted the story of her life as a slave in North Carolina. Mill's analysis of women's subordination in the family and in civil society, and his insistence that married women's position amounted to a form of "slavery," paralleled Wollstonecraft's very closely. Like Wollstonecraft, Mill showed how married women's lack of rights and legal equality with their husbands not only subjected them to male domination in the household, but made their equal participation in civil society impossible. Mill's solution to the problem of women's subjection, however, was to equalize the rights of women and men. In *The Subjection of Women* he wrote that nothing more was needed for women to achieve equality than that "the present duties and protective bounties in favour of men should be recalled" (Mill, *The Subjection of Women*, 154). With respect to child custody, mothers and fathers would have equal claims, and if they disagreed they would have to advance their claims through litigation. As Christine di Stefano has said, in advocating equal treatment for women and men, Mill allowed women to become citizens if they would become like men (Christine di Stefano, *Configurations of Masculinity* [Ithaca: Cornell University Press, 1991], 185–86). This assimilation of women into a gendered model for the citizen resulted from the fact that Mill paid little attention to women's bodies or sexuality.

Jacobs's account of her struggle for freedom contained her reflections on both citizenship and maternity. While from one perspective the situation of all slaves was similar, a state of radical lack of freedom, Jacobs repeatedly insisted that the experience

to guarantee women the possibility of being autonomous, of supporting themselves and their children. This would require a number of measures. First, men had to be made to support their children, whether born in or out of wedlock, and the state had to guarantee women's rights to custody, so that children did not become pawns by which men bound women to them. Second, jobs would have to be open to women, and would have to pay enough for women to be self-supporting; without such jobs, women could neither support children born out of wedlock nor leave abusive marriages. Wollstonecraft's outrage was directed not only at the closing of professional positions to women, but at the low wages of working-class women. Jemima could find no work other than prostitution, assisting in the Poor House, or working at the asylum. Peggy, who worked back-breaking hours as a laundress to feed her children, was utterly ruined when vagabonds stole sheets she had hung out to dry.

Given her understanding of the psychological, cultural, and legal reach of patriarchy, it is neither surprising that Wollstonecraft suggested that women needed political representation, nor that she did not give it more than the passing mention she did in *A Vindication of the Rights of Woman*. The workings of patriarchy infused everything from the legal rules governing marital property to the dynamics of sexual attraction. The vote would be a means by which women might acquire a sense of themselves as independent creatures, and by which they might affect their ability to acquire the material preconditions of independence by influencing public policy and legislation.

Wollstonecraft was acutely aware of the part that sexual difference played in women's subordination: biology assigned women and men different roles in human gestation and lactation, and these became the rationale for different social roles. The ensuing social differentiation between men and women then became the basis of disparity of political

---

of slavery was different for males and females. In slavery men were deprived of the ownership of their bodies and of their labor. Women suffered these injustices, but were also the objects and instruments of their masters' sexual appetites, and had no custodial claim to their children. The appropriation of women's procreative as well as their productive labor, and the denial of the claims of maternity were, for Jacobs, the particular evils of slavery for women. Her understanding of what freedom would mean was also inextricably linked to women's role as mothers. On several occasions she said that, were she free, she would be able to marry and have her maternal rights recognized as wife and mother. But since her children were in fact conceived and born out of wedlock (their father was a prominent white man in Jacobs's home town), she focused her attention on her need and her right to keep her children with her, to be able to support them, and to provide them with a home (Harriet Jacobs, *Incidents in the Life of a Slave Girl*, ed. Jean Fagan Yellin [Cambridge, Mass.: Harvard University Press, 1987]).

and economic resources. Socially created hierarchy thus took on the appearance of natural distinction, and male domination became eroticized for both men and women, and a part of heterosexual attraction. For women to participate in civil society as independent citizens, the inequality that underlay the eroticization of domination had to be eliminated or at least greatly diminished. *A Vindication of the Rights of Woman* condemned the culture of sensibility that sustained the erotic dynamic of inequality, while *The Wrongs of Woman: or, Maria* explored the impact of law on creating and perpetuating sexual inequality. Together they constituted an extraordinary analysis of both the public and interpersonal workings of patriarchal power.

Wollstonecraft's depiction of sexual and marital relationships in *A Vindication of the Rights of Woman* and in *The Wrongs of Woman: or, Maria* indicated that she had come to believe that, while women's role as childbearer was given by nature, the social consequences of that role were constructed by notions of proper sensibility as well as by law, and were thus under human control. From Wollstonecraft's day to our own, feminists have debated how best to construct law and social policy to take account of the different biological functions of men and women in human procreation and their different social roles in childrearing. For some feminists of the nineteenth and twentieth centuries, legal equality promised the end to male domination.[76] Others, however, remained skeptical about whether laws that made no distinction between the rights and responsibilities of mothers and fathers could procure justice for women.[77] Wollstonecraft believed that the law allowed men to "possess" both women and their children, and her work suggested that she would have given both married and unmarried mothers custodial rights to their offspring.[78]

---

[76] Mill, *The Subjection of Women*; see the discussion of various theorists, including Mill, in Eisenstein, *The Radical Future of Liberal Feminism*.

[77] See, for example, Carole Pateman, *The Sexual Contract* (Stanford: Stanford University Press, 1988); Martha Albertson Fineman, *The Neutered Mother, the Sexual Family, and Other Twentieth Century Tragedies* (New York: Routledge, 1995).

[78] In her concern to break the hegemony of male power and control over women and children, Wollstonecraft anticipated the perspective of that branch of feminist legal theory of our own day that contends that only if law abandons the notion of the gender-neutral citizen will women receive justice in matters like rape, sexual harassment, and domestic violence; see Susan Estrich, *Real Rape* (Cambridge, Mass.: Harvard University Press, 1987); Catharine MacKinnon, *Toward a Feminist Theory of the State* (Cambridge, Mass.: Harvard University Press, 1989); Christine Littleton, "Reconstructing Sexual Equality," *California Law Review* 75 (1987): 1279–1337. The argument of *The Wrongs of Woman* bears a striking resemblance, for example, to that of Martha Fineman's *The Neutered Mother*, which condemns the trend of the past twenty-five years of giving fathers and mothers equal rights with respect to such matters as child custody. Both Wollstonecraft and Fineman espouse what Fineman calls the "threatening"

Wollstonecraft knew that to attempt to alter the social construction of gender would be an extremely difficult and risky endeavor that would not only require great political effort but also place severe strain on intimate heterosexual relationships. Although she died before she finished her novel, *The Wrongs of Woman: or, Maria*, she sketched a number of endings which provide clues to her thinking. One of the concluding fragments ends with Maria suffering a miscarriage and then dying herself.[79] Another reunites Maria with the daughter she thought had died, and causes Maria to exclaim, "I will live for my child!" Even this "happy" ending, however, would have followed upon a life in which Maria had been imprisoned in marriage, and then in an asylum. The laws that "enslaved" Maria might also trap others; they had not been altered at the novel's end. Even if Maria were to raise her daughter, she would do so outside of marriage with the companionship of the social outcast, Jemima.

In her insightful "Introduction" to *The Wrongs of Woman: or, Maria*, Anne Mellor notes that it would be "nearly a century before the reform of the marriage laws removed the legal basis for the oppressive conditions that Maria depicts so unsparingly."[80] But despite extensive changes in the law, patriarchy in law and social practice is not yet a thing of the past. Carole Pateman has characterized those who struggle to achieve equal civil and political rights for women as well as some kind of public acknowledgment and accommodation of the distinct demands of motherhood as "impaled on the horns of ... Wollstonecraft's dilemma." Whether to give men and women identical social roles and legal rights, or whether to recognize certain social effects of sexual difference and create "equality within difference" is still widely debated among feminist political and legal theorists. The dilemma is that under "existing patriarchal conceptions of citizenship, the choice always has to be made between equality and difference, or between equality and womanhood."[81]

The challenge for theorist and activist alike is what to do with our knowledge that equality under the law may lead not to equality of

---

proposal that law support "unmediated motherhood – motherhood outside of patriarchal controls" (Fineman, *The Neutered Mother*, 233).

[79] Wollstonecraft, *The Wrongs of Woman*, 182–84.
[80] Mellor, "Introduction" to *Maria or the Wrongs of Woman*, xviii.
[81] Carole Pateman, "Equality, Difference, and Subordination: the Politics of Motherhood and Women's Citizenship," in *Beyond Equality and Difference*, eds. Gisela Bock and Susan James (London and New York: Routledge, 1992), 20.

For a good account of the debates on equality and difference, see Deborah L. Rhode, *Justice and Gender: Sex Discrimination and the Law* (Cambridge, Mass.: Harvard University Press, 1989).

circumstances and opportunities but to continued subjection. While differential rights offer a way to obtain women's freedom from patriarchal control in both family and civil society, they may purchase that present freedom at a serious cost for the future. Differential rights run the danger of reinscribing sex-based roles (women as childrearers), offer little incentive to men to take responsibility for the private realm (particularly the care of children), and may treat unfairly some men who do in fact assume that responsibility. Unless deeply rooted notions about sexuality and rationality, masculinity and femininity change, legal reform alone will not bring about the transformation to the new society which Wollstonecraft hoped to usher into being. "Wollstonecraft's dilemma" is a dilemma for those living between an oppressive past of sexual inequality, and a hoped-for future of sexual equality whose institutions and social practices can only at present be imagined. What the laws in such a future should be requires theoretical argument informed by difficult judgments about the dynamics of social life, and what forms of life and social practices are likely to lead to greater lived equality in the future. In debating these matters, contemporary feminists are greatly enriched by Wollstonecraft's rich depictions of the relationships between mothers and fathers, parents and children, and her passionate commitment to free women from the bonds of patriarchy in social custom and law alike.

Acknowledgments

I thank participants in the conference "Vindicating Wollstonecraft," sponsored by the Center for the Study of Women at the University of California at Los Angeles, May 5–6, 1995; participants in the conference "Political Writings, Political Women: Early Modern Britain in a European Context," held at the Folger Shakespeare Library, May 26–27, 1995; and Ellen Feder and Hilda Smith for helpful comments on an earlier draft of this chapter.

8   Emilie du Châtelet: genius, gender, and intellectual authority

Judith P. Zinsser

As Sarah Hanley's essay on Christine de Pizan and the Salic law demonstrates (chapter 13), France has a long tradition of women writing and writing on political subjects. In England the Civil War and Glorious Revolution increased the numbers and status of writers on many kinds of topics; Louis XIV's reordering and consolidation of monarchical authority had the opposite effect in France. In the seventeenth and eighteenth centuries the French government gained more control over publications on all subjects whether by women or men. Every book required the "Approbation," a testimony to the value of the work, and the "Privilège du roi," royal permission granted to the printer to undertake publication. Permission was refused to any book deemed critical of the government, the established church, or offensive to the royal definition of "morality."[1]

It was in this context that Emilie du Châtelet became the principal woman "physicien [physicist]," and "géomètre [mathematician]" of the first half of the eighteenth century. Ironically, of all the known European women writers of this era, she is the only one whose separate reputation has been lost. Although she has been remembered in traditional historical narratives, it is her liaison with Voltaire, not her own accomplishments as an interpreter of Newton's natural philosophy and Leibnitz's metaphysics that has justified her inclusion. Even scholars of eighteenth-century French history know du Châtelet from Nancy Mitford's *Voltaire in Love*, not from her own work, the *Institutions de physique*, and her translation of Sir Isaac Newton's *Principia*.

Du Châtelet belongs in this collection on the political history of the intellect, not only because of her role in the dissemination of Newton's

---

[1] There is an extensive history of printing in France and of the clandestine trade that developed as a result of the government's strict censorship. For an introduction to the subject see Roger Chartier, *The Culture of Print in Early Modern France*, trans. Lydia G. Cochrane (Princeton, N.J.: Princeton University Press, 1987) and Robert Darnton, *The Forbidden Best-Sellers of Pre-Revolutionary France* and the companion volume of quantitative analyses, *The Corpus of Clandestine Literature in France, 1769–1789* (New York: W. W. Norton and Co., 1995).

approach to knowledge, but also because of the risks she took.[2] She was an aristocrat, a woman educated for the entertainments and intrigues of the court, but an aristocratic woman who chose to write for publication. Instead of novels or fairy tales, acceptable enterprises for women writers, she studied and wrote about natural philosophy.[3] This at a time when any serious study of the workings of the universe led inevitably to metaphysical questions about God's powers and thus to potential conflicts with Catholic dogma. Perhaps more serious, her explanations of English and German ideas of the universe disagreed with the prevailing Cartesian explanations of France's Royal Academy of Science and thus challenged the government's intellectual authority and political hegemony.

Why did du Châtelet choose such unorthodox behavior and activities? What role did gender play in her decisions and in the reactions of her contemporaries? What can she tell historians about intellectual authority in the first decades of the French Enlightenment?

Though only thirty-two, by December of 1738 Emilie du Châtelet had already established an unorthodox life for herself. Since the summer of 1735 she and Voltaire had lived nearly continuously at her husband's modest estate in Champagne. The marquis du Châtelet had long since been reconciled and become accustomed to the arrangement. Mme. du Châtelet had dutifully borne him three children, two sons and a daughter, in the first years of their marriage, and it was then assumed that they would both have sexual liaisons.[4] Even so, Voltaire's move to and renovation of the marquis's château at Cirey bordered on the inappropriate even for such a permissive society. In the early months of their affair Mme. du Châtelet had enlisted a mutual friend and former lover, Louis François Armand Du Plessis, duc de Richelieu, to smooth the way when it became obvious that her husband would be on leave from his military duties for an extended period of time. She believed that, with Richelieu's intervention and explanation, her husband would not be jealous "of a wife with whom one is content, that one esteems and who conducts herself well."[5]

[2] For an excellent analysis of the significance of Newton's work and its broad consequences see I. Bernard Cohen, *The Newtonian Revolution* (New York: Cambridge University Press, 1980).

[3] For studies of French women writers in the eighteenth century see: Elizabeth C. Goldsmith and Dena Goodman, *Going Public: Women and Publishing in Early Modern France* (Ithaca: Cornell University Press, 1995).

[4] Gabrielle-Emilie de Breteuil married Florent-Claude du Châtelet [Chastellet] in June of 1725. Her daughter, Gabrielle Pauline, was born in June 1726, her son, Florent Louis-Marie, in November 1727 and Victor Esprit in April 1734 (died, August of 1734).

[5] "[L]a paix détruirait toutes nos espérances"; "d'une femme dont on est content, qu'on

She was right, but she took care to look after the marquis's basic comforts on the occasions when he joined them at the château in between King Louis XV's numerous wars. He was an uncomplicated man who preferred to dine early with the children, but otherwise joined in his wife's and her lover's numerous activities. He became a loyal friend to Voltaire and was content to choose sexual partners from the young women of the surrounding villages.

Although du Châtelet might refer to the "duties and useless detail when you have a house and a family," she never questioned the practical nature of her betrothal and marriage or her responsibilities for the numerous households – at Cirey, in Paris, and, on the occasions when she and Voltaire traveled together to Belgium, in rented accommodation.[6] She raised her daughter even more conventionally than she had been for the arranged marriage of an aristocratic woman's traditional life.

In addition to fulfilling her obligations as a wife and mother, du Châtelet took very good care of Voltaire. She often abandoned her own projects to divert him or to assist in his work. When he was ill with one of his many complaints, du Châtelet sat by his bedside and read to him. Mme. de Graffigny, one of their many visitors, described a Thursday morning early in December, 1738. Du Châtelet read aloud to them on the way to calculate the height of the inhabitants of Jupiter and the other planets. Aside from commenting on du Châtelet's ability to translate from Latin and to puzzle out the mathematical calculations at sight, de Graffigny explained: "we were very entertained by it."[7] Desmarest, Mme. de Graffigny's lover, joined them in February, 1739. A small theater with a painted outdoor scene for a backdrop had been built in the attic of the château. In the course of the weekend Desmarest participated in "44 actes en 48 heures," with Mme. du Châtelet playing

---

estime, et qui se conduit bien" (#37, May 22, 1735, *Lettres de la marquise du Châtelet*, ed. Theodore Besterman [Geneva: Institut et Musée de Voltaire, 1958], I, 67, 69).

[6] Du Châtelet to Maupertuis, #148, October 24, 1738, *Du Châtelet Correspondence*, I, 267. For descriptions of her activities in Belgium see Esther Ehrman, *Mme. du Châtelet: Scientist, Philosopher and Feminist of the Enlightenment* (Dover, N.H.: Berg, 1986), 33. This is the best short biography and contains excellent summaries of all of du Châtelet's writings. See also on du Châtelet's activities from 1739 to 1745, Linda Gardiner [Janik], "Women in Science," in *French Women in the Age of Enlightenment*, ed. Samia I. Spencer (Bloomington: Indiana University Press, 1984), 188. See the account of the Paris household in 1746 by Voltaire's valet, J.-A. Havard, ed., *Voltaire et Mme du Châtelet: révélations d'un serviteur attaché à leurs personnes* (Paris, 1863).

[7] "[D]es habitans des autres planettes"; "nous en sommes fort divertie" (Graffigny to Devaux, #62, December 11, 1738, *Correspondence of Mme. de Graffigny*, ed. J. A. Dinard [Oxford: The Voltaire Foundation], I, 211.

the title role, her son, her husband, a neighbor and the visitors the others.[8]

In addition to these diversions and varied social responsibilities, Mme. du Châtelet had many unorthodox projects that winter of 1738. Her letters and papers indicate work in algebra and Euclidian geometry, Newton's optics, hypothesizing about the rational bases of French grammar, biblical exegesis, and Leibnizian metaphysics. A woman of seemingly unlimited energy, du Châtelet also decided to translate Bernard Mandeville's work, *Fable of the Bees*, because, as she explained in her preface, she feared that she was neglecting "my spirit and my understanding."[9] Neglected, ideas are lost. "It is a fire that dies if one doesn't continually give it the wood that serves to sustain it."[10]

Du Châtelet told her perspective readers that she had chosen the Mandeville because of its general appeal and because "it is, I believe, the best book of morals that was ever written."[11] She also explained why she had chosen translation rather than the composition of her own moral treatise.[12] It represented a compromise. As she later wrote to Pierre Robert le Cornier Cideville, one of Voltaire's closest friends with whom she also corresponded: "God has refused me any kind of genius, and I spend my time unraveling truths that others have discovered."[13] Translation was one means of doing this; it gave knowledge and pleasure. Even if such an enterprise brought less glory to the author, certainly it held "the first rank in the empire of the fine arts."[14]

To us it is perhaps difficult to imagine why this exceptional woman so readily dismissed her claims to the title of "genius," an honor later accorded her by those in the vanguard of Parisian science.[15] In 1738, the term "genius," like so many other aspects of intellectual authority in

---

[8] Desmarest and Graffigny to Devaux, #90, February 12, 1739, *Graff. Corr.*, I, 137.

[9] "[M]on esprit et mon entendement." The word "esprit" in French seems almost untranslatable. It means everything from "spirit" to "wit," from "intellect" to "soul." To du Châtelet and her contemporaries it signified all that the mind could sense, know, and do. Sometimes it was synonymous with the term "genius."

[10] "Cest un feu qui meurt, si on n'y iette pas continuellement le bois qui sert a l'entretenir" (*Fable of the Bees*, in Ira O. Wade, *Studies on Voltaire with Some Unpublished Papers of Mme. du Châtelet* [Princeton: Princeton University Press, 1947], 131). All quotations from this work are given as they appear in Wade's edition.

[11] "C'est ie crois le meilleur livre de morale, qui ait iamais esté fait" (*Bees*, 137).

[12] She would write such an essay in the 1740s (scholars are still trying to decide on a date), *Réflexions sur le bonheur*, Bibliothèque Nationale, Mélanges, fol. #13084, pp. 1–37. The published edition is *Discours sur le bonheur*, ed. Robert Mauzi (Paris: Les Belles-lettres, 1961).

[13] Du Châtelet to Cideville, #198, March 15, 1739, *Du Chât. Corr.*, I, 346.

[14] "[L]e premier rang dans l'empire des baux arts" (*Bees*, 133).

[15] Erica Harth considers this the standard women writer's trope of self-deprecation. A letter seems an unlikely place for such conventions and du Châtelet makes no such equivocations in her published works. See Erica Harth, *Cartesian Women: Versions and*

early Enlightenment France, was in flux. Even in the 1750s when *L'Encyclopédie* appeared, the editors offered two definitions of "Génie, Philos. Litt." by two different authors. They made no effort to reconcile them and instead printed one after the other without comment.[16]

In contrast, in her preface to Mandeville du Châtelet showed no such confusion about the term. She described three kinds of genius, of which our idea of "creative genius" is the first.[17] This she imagined as "The perfection of a soul with more than [simple] facility." Voltaire was her example: "grand metaphysicien, grand historien, grand philosophe, etc." The second kind of genius was taken from the literal French translation of the Latin *ingenium*, a person with natural ability, "a decided talent where one only has to abandon oneself to the force of their [*sic*] genius." Asked for an example, she would probably have named Newton.

Most interesting is du Châtelet's third category, a genius that she admits is not as grand as the other two "génies sublimes," but none the less, worthy of mention. "It happens sometimes that work and study force genius to declare itself like those fruits that art makes develop in a terrain for which nature did not [intend] them, but these efforts of art

---

Subversions of Rational Discourse in the Old Regime (Ithaca: Cornell University Press, 1992), 207.

[16] The *Encyclopédie* offers six different kinds of "genius," of which the "Génie, Philos. Litt." is the second. The first part of that entry, the one written by Saint-Lambert, sounds very much like du Châtelet's. It begins: "L'étendue de l'esprit, la force de l'imagination, & l'activité de l'âme, voilà le *génie*." The "genius" is definitely male, a person of energy, breadth of interests, and most especially imagination. The editor, not Saint-Lambert, inserted Voltaire's name at the end as the example of this kind of genius. The second part, written by Marmontal, is quite different, closer to our twentieth-century notion of the term. It focuses on the difference between "genius" and "talent" and emphasizes "originality" as a characteristic (*Encyclopédie ou Dictionaire Raisonné des Sciences des Arts et des Metiers* [Lausanne: Chez les Sociétés Typographiques, 1779]).

[17] The concept of "genius" has a long history. Classical writers thought of it as the ability to describe and represent the natural world. It was in the eighteenth century that the "genius" became a special, superior individual who had made "original," "creative," and "lasting contributions." The uncritical acceptance of these definitions led nineteenth- and twentieth-century psychologists to seek a genetic explanation for the phenomenon of "exceptional achievement," or "greatness." The most famous of these, *Genetic Studies of Genius* by L. M. Terman and M. H. Oden (1925–59) filled five volumes. Historians and literary critics have also sought to explain "genius". Dean Keith Simonton tried to quantify the lives of "great men" in *Genius, Creativity, and Leadership: Historiometric Inquiries* (Cambridge, Mass.: Harvard University Press, 1984). Only in the 1970s, with studies like Robert K. Merton's *The Sociology of Science* (Chicago: University of Chicago Press, 1973), did social science and humanities scholars begin, like Thomas Kuhn, to see "genius" as the product of social and cultural perceptions. Christine Battersby's *Gender and Genius: Towards a Feminist Aesthetics* (London: Women's Press, 1989) gives a feminist critique of the term and the exclusion of women by definition.

are almost as rare as natural genius." As the definition continues, she explains that these are the people who "occupy [themselves] with pulling out the thorns that delay the true geniuses in their courses," those who "[create] so many dictionaries, and works of this sort."[18] It is as if knowingly, or perhaps unconsciously, du Châtelet imagined a role and a kind of genius to which she, and others without formal education or professional training, could aspire, a way for women in particular to claim intellectual authority in the world of rational inquiry, a world usually closed to them by definition.[19]

However suggestive this third definition of "genius" might be to historians, du Châtelet made no claim to it nor to unusual natural gifts or talents. Instead she cautioned the readers of her preface to value "the little that one has received in the division [of benefits] and not to fall into despair because one has only two arpents [one arpent is approximately one acre] to cultivate when there are others who have ten leagues."[20] Such sentiments suggest that the parceling out of resources was random. Du Châtelet believed, however, that she suffered from more calculated disadvantages as a female. In the Mandeville preface she asked the familiar question posed by those seeking approbation from traditional institutional authorities according to traditional criteria: why, over all these centuries, given their similarity in understanding to men, "has a good tragedy, a good poem, a respected history, a beautiful painting, a good book of physics, never left the hand of women?" She accepted that "naturalistes" may find a physiological explanation. In the meantime, "women have a right to protest against their education." She offered what sounds like the feminist manifesto of the 1960s, reclaiming

---

[18] "[L]a perfection d'un seul avec plus de facilité"; "un talent bien decidé, n'on qu'a se laisser aller à l'impulsion de leur genie"; "Il arrive quelques fois que le travail et l'etude, forcent le genie a se declarer, comme ces fruits que l'art fait eclore dans un terrain pour lequel, la nature ne les avoit pas faits, mais ces efforts de l'art sont presque aussi rares, que le genie naturel"; "s'occupent a arracher les épines qui retarderoient les vrais genies dans leur course"; "procure tant de dictionaires, et d'ouvrages de cette espece" (*Bees*, 131–32).

[19] Genevieve Lloyd's *The Man of Reason: "Male" & "Female" in Western Philosophy*, 2nd ed. (Minneapolis: University of Minnesota Press, 1993) gives an excellent introduction to philosophical ideas about women's intellectual capacity in Western culture. For the arguments about women's capacity to reason according to the precepts of Descartes, see also Harth's *Cartesian Women*. She also considers whether or not women could take the title "philosophe." Londa Schiebinger in *The Mind Has No Sex? Women in the Origins of Modern Science* (Cambridge, Mass.: Harvard University Press, 1988) explores the "gendering" of science in the eighteenth century and thus the exclusion of women as recognized practitioners.

[20] "[L]e peu qu'on a receu en partage et ne pas entrer en desespoir, parce qu'on n'a que deux arpents a cultiver et quil y a des gens qui ont dix lieues de pays" (*Bees*, 132).

for "half of human kind" participation in all the rights of humanity, "and above all those of the spirit."[21]

Like Wollstonecraft at the end of the eighteenth century, du Châtelet focused on the education women received as the cause of their apparent lack of achievement. A "vice," in her words, rather than a virtue, their education only gave them knowledge of "le monde, la dissipation." As a result, women were ignorant of their talents, raised without any idea of how to think, buried by prejudice and "loss of spiritual courage [faute de courage dans l'esprit]." It seems that the marquise, despite her father's obvious enjoyment of her remarkable intellectual skills as a little girl and the encouragement of the "gens des lettres" who came to the Hôtel du Breteuil, had only a "glimpse" of herself as "a thinking creature." Now in 1738, as a woman of thirty-two with a particular interest in physics and astronomy, she felt "all the weight of prejudice that excludes us so universally from the sciences."[22]

Over the last two decades of European women's history certain truisms have emerged about such "prejudice," about the ways in which intellectual pursuits have been denied to women: the difficulties encountered in gaining access to specialized education, to knowledge of current methods and research, to books and equipment; the problems of completing projects and then finding a publisher (buyer, or patron in the case of artists), the devaluation and/or appropriation of work; the conflicting demands in terms of time and energies from traditional roles and activities within the family.[23] Each constraint challenged women's ingenuity and stamina.

Whether or not du Châtelet would have created a similar list, she certainly experienced all of the difficulties identified by women's histor-

---

[21] "[J]amais une bonne tragedie, un bon poëme, une histoire estimée, un beau tableau, un bon livre de physique, n'est sorti de la main des femmes?"; "[L]es femmes seront en droit de reclamer contre leur education"; "la moitie du genre human"; "et surtout a ceux de l'esprit" (*Bees*, 135, 136). Madame de Graffigny heard part or all of the preface when she visited Cirey in the winter of 1738–39. She found the translation "admirable," "une chose surprenente." So impressed was she (perhaps with the sentiments expressed as well) that she suggested to her friend Devaux: "Notre sexe devroit lui élever des autels [Our sex should erect altars to her]." Granting du Châtelet these accolades, she queries: "Mais combien de siècles faut-il pour faire une femme comme celle-la? [But how many centuries must there be to create a woman such as this one?]" (Graffigny to Devaux, #67, December 25, 1738, *Graff. Corr.*, I, 245).

[22] "[U]ne creature pensante"; "tout le poids du prejugé qui nous exclude si universelle-ment des sciences" (*Bees*, 135). For the description of her education see René Vaillot, *Madame du Châtelet* (Paris: Albin Michel, 1978), 31, 34.

[23] See Germaine Greer, *The Obstacle Race: The Fortunes of Women Painters and Their Work* (New York: Farrar, Straus and Giroux, 1979), for an early version of this list; see Gardiner, "Woman in Science," for the problems of an eighteenth-century woman scientist (182–83, 193).

ians in the twentieth century. A few examples should suffice. She herself chafed against her exclusion solely on the basis of her sex from the informal and formal discussions of scientists and mathematicians at the Café Gradot and the regular Wednesday meetings of the Royal Academy of Sciences in the King's Library at the Louvre.[24]

French customary law gave her no separate financial resources of her own, nor rights over her 150,000 livres dowry.[25] Every expenditure required permission from her husband, even the hiring of a tutor for their son. She and Voltaire filled the front hall of the château with scientific equipment. But Voltaire's money paid for it. In 1737 a telescope alone cost 2,000 livres, the "cabinet de physique" with its vacuum machine, selection of lenses and pendulums, another 9–10,000 francs.[26]

[24] The standard history of the French Academy is by Roger Hahn, *The Anatomy of a Scientific Institution: The Paris Academy of Sciences, 1666–1803* (Berkeley: University of California Press, 1971). Perhaps more useful in gaining an image of this as a formative era is Charles B. Paul's *Science and Immortality: the Eloges of the Paris Academy of Sciences (1699–1791)* (Berkeley: University of California Press, 1980), which includes a quantitative analysis of Academy members. He demonstrates how similar du Châtelet's training was to that of other mathematicians, including Clairaut. Most of the twenty-two members in this category who died between 1699 and 1791 had spent only a brief time at a college, and had learned on their own or from a mentor (see pp. 75–77 and Table 3, p. 76). Fontenelle, the first permanent secretary and creator of the image of the academy "scientist" through his eulogies for deceased members, had written plays, poems, and a popular book about Descartes before being appointed to his post. With Fontenelle as the model, it is not surprising that Voltaire, with an even more impressive list of similar publications, aspired to the secretaryship. Paul's study also underlines the significance of gender and of du Châtelet's exclusion despite her scientific writings. On Fontenelle, see Robert Niklaus, "Fontenelle and the Vulgarisation of Ideas," *Voltaire and His World: Studies Presented to W. H. Barber*, eds. R. J. Howells, A. Mason, H. T. Mason, and D. Williams (Oxford: Voltaire Foundation, 1985). See also Harth, chap. 3, on the gendering of the Academy. For a clear discussion of the role of gender in the development of French science, see Mary Terrall's two key articles: "Gendered Spaces, Gendered Audiences: Inside and Outside the Paris Academy of Sciences," *Configuration* 2 (1994): 207–32 and "Emile du Châtelet and the Gendering of Science," *History of Science* 33 (1995): 283–310, Jane Flax, "Post-Modernism and Gender Relations in Feminist Theory," *Signs* 12, 4 (Summer 1987): 622–43; and Kathleen Canning, "Feminist History after the Linguistic Turn: Historicizing Discourse and Experience," *Signs* 19, 2 (Winter 1994): 368–404, describe gender as an exclusionary category, particularly in terms of the establishment of intellectual authority in the Enlightenment and afterwards.

[25] Vaillot, *Madame du Châtelet*, 38.

[26] On the fitting out of the château ses *Lettres autographes* (to Maupertuis), BN fols. 12268, #38, 66v; Geoffrey V. Sutton, *Science for a Polite Society: Gender, Culture, and the Demonstration of Enlightenment* (Boulder, Colo.: Westview Press, 1996), 227–28.

Although Barbara Maria Stafford takes the perspective of a historian of visual culture, in *Artful Science: Enlightenment Entertainment and the Eclipse of Visual Education* (Cambridge, Mass.: The MIT Press, 1994), she describes many of the instruments and experiments made accessible to elite society in the eighteenth century. See also the "liste de divers machines" made and sold by Pierre van Musschenbroek at the end of volume II of his *Essai de physique*, trans. Pierre Massuet (Leyden: chez Samuel Luchtmans, 1739), separately paginated, 3–8. This edition also has excellent engravings of the equipment du Châtelet would have used.

Voltaire also assumed some of the costs of publishing her books.[27]

Du Châtelet suffered all the humiliations of the eager student in need of a mentor. Voltaire boasted that she learned geometry and calculus on her own. She did study assiduously if sporadically from 1733 on, but in an era when only a few men could fathom the new calculus she counted on Pierre-Louis Moreau de Maupertuis and Alexis-Claude Clairaut (two of the preeminent mathematicians and physicists of her day) to instruct her and to verify the explanations and calculations in her scientific writings. Her letters to Maupertuis often refer to "indifference," and to apparently unanswered requests for opinions of work she had sent to him and to Clairaut.[28] Both men had their own projects and careers that took precedence over sojourns at Cirey or an evening tutorial at her house in Paris.[29]

Samuel Koenig, the young tutor whom she hired in 1739, made précis for her of Christian von Wolff's commentaries on Leibniz that influenced the final draft of her *Institutions de physique*. On the basis of these summaries, he claimed credit for the work when it was within months of publication.[30] Jean-Baptiste Dortous de Mairan, the Cartesian loyalist and permanent secretary of the Academy of Sciences, accepted her authorship of the *Institutions* but took offense at her criticism of one of his scientific *mémoires*. In response, he ridiculed her as a flighty woman of the aristocracy and her text as foolish misquotations of his findings.[31]

[27] On publication costs, see Vaillot, *Madame du Châtelet*, 194–95.

[28] See, for example, du Châtelet to Maupertuis, #43, October 3, 1735, *Du Chât. Corr.*, I, 84.

[29] Maupertuis led the French Academy expedition to Lapland to establish the shape of the earth, and Clairaut became embroiled in the race to find the mathematical solution to the irregularities in the moon's apogee. Clairaut is supposed to have written his *Elémens d'Algebre* for her, though there is no mention of du Châtelet in the book.

[30] Samuel Koenig joined Parisian scientific circles under the sponsorship of Maupertuis and Clairaut. He returned to Berlin and later instituted a similar controversy. In addition to giving a very complete explication of du Châtelet's metaphysics, Linda Gardiner Janik, by her careful reconstruction of the fragmented manuscript of the *Institutions*, proves when and how Wolff's ideas affected its composition. See Gardiner Janik's "Searching for the Metaphysics of Science: The Structure and Composition of Madame du Châtelet's *Institutions de physique*, 1737–1740," *Studies on Voltaire and the Eighteenth Century* 201 (1982): 85–113. It is likely that du Châtelet studied and wrote much like Voltaire, taking paragraphs from one authority, sentences from another, mixing them together in her own order and to prove her own point.

[31] On Mairan's support for Descartes's "tourbillons [swirling vortices of particles which move planetary bodies]" over "universal attraction" while still accepting other aspects of Newtonian celestial mechanics, see Ellen McNiven Hine, "Dortous de Mairan, the 'Cartonian,'" *Studies on Voltaire and the Eighteenth Century* 266 (1989): 163–79. Hine praises Mairan for his "impartiality" throughout his time as secretary. The attack on du Châtelet is not mentioned. See du Châtelet, *Institutions de physique* (Paris: Prault fils, 1740), 429–37, for du Châtelet's paraphrase of part of his 1728 *mémoire* and of his

Voltaire acknowledged her guidance and collaboration in the writing of his *Eléments de la philosophie de Newton* (1738 edition), but contemporaries could dismiss the lavish homage of his dedicatory epistle as the extravagant praise of a lover:

> You call me to you, great and powerful genius,
> Minerva of France, immortal Emilie.
> Disciple of Newton and truth,
> You penetrate my senses with the fires of your bright clarity.[32]

His readers might look instead to his preface, which ended with a more credible, less effusive acknowledgment of what he had learned in England from Samuel Clarke and his own reading of Newton.

Like that of other exceptional women authors, much of du Châtelet's writing remained unpublished. The *Examen de la Genèse* (and of the New Testament), her commentary on the Bible from the perspective of a Newtonian universe, only circulated in manuscript. In the twentieth century the *Examen* was, in fact, attributed to others.[33] Much has been lost or destroyed. When she died suddenly as a result of complications after childbirth in September 1749, Voltaire returned to Cirey to arrange their papers and "to put everything in order."[34] Some unpublished fragments, like the Mandeville, were among Voltaire's papers sold to Catherine the Great by Mme. Denis, his niece and du Châtelet's successor as his companion. Unfortunately, the bulk of their letters to each other and the printer's manuscript of her translation of and commentary on Newton's *Principia* have disappeared.

In the 1738 preface to Mandeville, du Châtelet implied her acceptance of these traditional women's disadvantages by describing a limited role for herself. She asserted that nature had refused her "the creative genius that found new truths." She had reconciled herself, she explained, to an apparently secondary role, "to convey those [truths] of others with lucidity," one of the "entrepreneurs [négocians] of the republic of letters."[35] In fact, however, she never managed to restrict herself to so

---

"mauvais raisonnement." In an earlier section she had praised his 1735 *mémoire* on pendulums (see 378–79).

[32] "Tu m'appelles a toi, vaste et puissant genie,/ Minerve de la France, immortelle Emilie,/ Disciple de Neuton, et de la verite,/ tu penetres mes sens des feux de ta clarte" (Voltaire, *Eléments de la philosophie de Newton*, eds. Robert L. Walters and W. H. Barber in *The Complete Works of Voltaire* [Oxford: The Voltaire Foundation, 1992], xv).

[33] Until a copy was discovered at Troyes clearly attributed to her, the Paris Academy of Sciences library listed the author as anonymous. Historians have speculated that it might have been written by Voltaire.

[34] Voltaire to Mme. Denis, #146, September 23, 1749, *Lettres d'amour de Voltaire à sa nièce*, ed. Theodore Besterman (Paris: Librairie Plon, 1957), 195.

[35] *Bees*, 136–37, 133.

simple a function. Even as the translator of Mandeville, she chose to omit the actual verse fable and instead gave her energies to trimming the style, reframing examples for a French audience, and adding her own reflections whenever the material suggested it.[36]

Increasingly, from 1736 until her death in 1749, she focused her efforts on mastering and interpreting the principal texts of natural philosophy and the monographic literature on celestial mechanics printed under the auspices of the Academy of Sciences. Newton's *Opticks* (1718 edn), the *Principia* (1726 edn), and his *System of the World* (1731 Latin edn) formed the core of her studies. The following is only a partial list of the other authorities she cited in her letters or her published writings: John Keill's *Introduction to the true astronomy [Introductio ad veram physicam]* (1700), Hartsoeker's *Principes de physiques* (1696), Christian van Huygens's *The celestial worlds discover'd; or, Conjectures concerning the inhabitants, plants and productions of the world in the planets* (1698), Wilhelm 'sGravesande's two-volume *Mathematical Elements of Natural Philosophy confirmed by Experiments* (1721 English translation), the Leibniz–Clarke correspondence (1717 English edn, 1720 French edn), Le Monnier's collection of astronomical observations [*Histoire céleste ou recueil de toutes les observations astronomiques faites par ordre du roy*] (1741), Henry Pemberton's *A View of Sir Isaac Newton's Philosophy* (1728) and J. T. Desaguliers's *A Course of Experimental Philosophy* (1734).

It is these contradictions that differentiate du Châtelet from other elite, intellectual women of the early Enlightenment. There was the apparent acceptance of disadvantages, the definition of a "lesser" place in the eighteenth-century French hierarchy of letters; and then the disadvantages were ignored, more prestigious ranks were aspired to, the highest cultural and political authorities challenged. Beginning in 1734 with the move from Paris to Cirey, du Châtelet lived in a whirlwind of tensions and excitements that bore little relationship to the quiet, studious translator she presented in her preface to Mandeville's *Fable of the Bees*.

Initially, she went to the country retreat because she was so enamored of Voltaire. Both described her arrival in Champagne in the same extravagant phrases. She wrote to the duc de Richelieu: "I love him enough, I confess it to you, to sacrifice without worry all that I could find of pleasure and amusement in Paris for the happiness of living with him."[37] This grand gesture, however, also appealed to du Châtelet's

---

[36] See for example, *Bees*, 137–38.
[37] "Je l'aime assez, je vous l'avoue, pour sacrifier au bonheur de vivre avec lui sans alarmes ... tout ce que je pourrais trouver de plaisir et d'agrément à Paris" (#37, May

sense of drama; for "love changes all the thorns to flowers as it makes the mountains of Cirey paradise on earth."[38]

Three years later in 1738 she offered a second reason for her move to the Champagne countryside. Away from Paris and the court she had renounced the life of most women, one dedicated "aux choses frivoles [to frivolous things]" for one of study, the ultimate "consolation for all of the exclusions and dependencies to which [women] find themselves condemned by their status [état]."[39] She now explained that the opportunity to lead a different life had come just in time. At thirty-two she could gratefully acknowledge that she had been born in an age "where there is still time to become reasonable." In words that would be echoed in Voltaire's *Candide*, she wrote of the happiness that came with the decision to develop a taste for study, a happiness dependent only on one's own efforts, protected from ambition, "and above all" with the knowledge of "what we want to be." Then "we [can] decide on the route we want to take for our life and try to [cultivate] the flowers."[40]

The fruits of her study brought a new determination and insight "about what one wants to be and do," that she believed differentiated her from "almost all men."[41] In reality this difference set her apart from most men and from all the women of her circle.[42] Almost by definition her excitement with calculus, optics, mechanics, and the search for unifying scientific principles for the whole "system of the world" led her away from "la semer de fleurs" into the public world of physics and mathematics. Du Châtelet might admit her misgivings as she embarked on such inappropriate activities for a woman of her class, but she also had her own brand of ambition. She might lament its dependence on the views of others, and submit her works anonymously, but still she bragged to Cideville about the Academy of Sciences' plans to publish her essay on fire in 1738, and to Maupertuis about her victory over

30, 1735, *Du Chât. Corr.*, I, 69); see also Voltaire: "qui a quitté pour moi Paris, tous les amis et tous les agréments de sa vie" (#D1221, December 9, 1736, *Volt. Corr.*, IV, 149).

[38] "[L]'amour change toutes les épines en fleurs, comme il fera des montagnes de Cirey le paradis terreste." The quotations on love are from *Bonheur*, 25.

[39] Ibid., 19. See also Mauzi edition of the treatise with its extensive explanatory introduction.

[40] "[O]u il est encor tems de devenir raisonable"; "et surtout sachons bien ce que nous voulons être, decidons nous sur la route que nous voulons prendre pour passer notre vie, et tachons de la semer de fleurs" (see ibid., 14, 36).

[41] "[A] ce qu'on veut être et a ce qu'on veut faire"; "presque tous les hommes" (see ibid., 14).

[42] Harth describes the royal and aristocratic women of the seventeenth century who became learned in Cartesian physics. Gardiner wrote the chapter on "Women in Science" in Spencer, *French Women in the Age of Enlightenment*, and mentions du Châtelet's contemporaries, principally secondary collaborators with astronomer or chemist fathers and husbands.

Mairan's effort to humiliate her three years later. In her preface to Mandeville she suggested that men's "tyranny" over women could become a "happy necessity." Excluded, women who hoped to succeed had an advantage, they could not afford to write "bad books."[43]

To write only good books meant taking risks as an intellectual. And it was her studies that enabled her to believe that she had overcome the most constraining aspect of her life, the simple fact of her sex. Instead she turned it to advantage. Barred from Paris's official scientific circles, as the chatelaine of a country estate and Voltaire's companion, she established her own "Academy" at Cirey.[44] She and Voltaire created a unique intellectual environment. In January, 1736, he was writing his history of Louis XIV and "moi je neutonise tant bien que mal."[45] Younger men like Maupertuis, Clairaut, David Bernoulli (the Swiss mathematician), and Francesco Algarotti (the Italian popularizer of Newton) wanted to meet Voltaire. Du Châtelet invited them "to spend the winter quietly philosophizing with us" and described Cirey as "mon colonie." She learned Italian in preparation for Algarotti's visit and, perhaps to entice him, described her library and Voltaire's. His was "all anecdotes," hers "all philosophy."[46] Older, established scholars like Father François Jacquier, holder of the chair of experimental physics at the College of Rome and editor of the 1739 Latin edition of the *Principia*,

---

43 On ambition, *Bonheur*, 18; Du Châtelet to Cideville, #198, March 15, 1739, *Du Chât. Corr.*, I, 346; and to Maupertuis, #129, June 21, 1738, 235–36 and #272, May 29, 1741, II, 56; *Bees*, 138.
44 Du Châtelet never wanted to have a "salon" in the sense of those she attended in Paris in the 1730s and 1740s, and she would have been equally uncomfortable in those of the later decades of the Enlightenment. She had no skill for facilitating others' conversation, she had too much to say herself. There are two now classic studies of the seventeenth-century origins of the salon, Carolyn C. Lougee, *Le paradis des femmes: Women, Salons and Social Stratification in Seventeenth-Century France* (Princeton: Princeton University Press, 1976), and Dorothy Anne Liot Backer, *Precious Women: A Feminist Phenomenon in the Age of Louis XIV* (New York: Basic Books, Inc., 1974). Chapters 2 and 3 of Dena Goodman's *The Republic of Letters: A Cultural History of the French Enlightenment* (Ithaca: Cornell University Press, 1994) give a clear description of the mediating, facilitating role of the famous eighteenth-century *salonnières* like Mme. Geoffrin, Julie de Lespinasse, and Suzanne Necker.
45 Du Châtelet to ?, #52, January 3, 1736, *Du Chât. Corr.*, I, 95. See Ira O. Wade, *Voltaire and Mme. du Châtelet: An Essay on the Intellectual Activity at Cirey* (Princeton: Princeton University Press, 1941) and *The Intellectual Development of Voltaire* (Princeton: Princeton University Press, 1969), and the commentaries on many of his works from 1736 to 1749 in *Complete Works* for extensive discussions at what Wade calls the "highly charged intellectual atmosphere" at Cirey, the nature of their collaboration, and particularly the influence of du Châtelet's thoughts on the *Eléments de la philosophie de Newton*, *Treatise on Metaphysics*, *Mondain*, *Ingénu*.
46 Du Châtelet to Algarotti, #44, vers October 10, 1735, *Du Chât. Corr.*, I, 85. See also her letter to Richelieu, #45, vers October 15, 1735, I, 86.

also spent time with them and became du Châtelet's correspondent and supporter.[47]

It was sheer determination that won her this respect and mention in the 1750 *Encyclopédie* entry on "newtonianisme" along with Pemberton, 'sGravesand and Jacquier as one of six authors "who attempted to make Newtonian philosophy easier to understand."[48] She was among the select few, as she described it to Frederick II of Prussia, not "frightened by words like lemmas, theorems [and] proofs when they are used outside of geometry."[49] Popularizers like Abbé Nollet (author of *Leçons de physique*, 1743) and experts like Deschamps (*Cours abrégé de philosophie wolffienne*, 1743) recommended her *Institutions* for information on Leibniz's theories. Deschamps was delighted that she of all the French nation had "open[ed] the door to a philosophy which none of them had yet dared to broach and which they regarded as almost indecipherable."[50]

Contemporaries accepted her mathematical and scientific expertise.[51] She became "l'illustre Marquise" in the "advertissement" for the posthumous edition of her translation of ˙˙ *Principia*. Admirers praised the eloquence and clarity of her writing, and her ability to reason, "like a man," they implied. The *Institutions de physique* was published in Italy and the German states;[52] her *Principia* remains the authoritative French translation of Newton's work.

In many ways these projects represented a political risk. The period before 1760 in France was a time of police surveillance and active

[47] In 1746 Jacquier successfully nominated her for the Bologna Academy of Science on the basis of her *Institutions de physique*.

[48] *Encyclopédie* (1779 edn), XXII, 414.

[49] [August 11, 1740] Quoted in Ehrman, *Mme. du Châtelet*, 47.

[50] See Sutton, *Science for a Polite Society*, p. 263; as quoted in Ehrman, *Mme. du Châtelet*, 55.

[51] See Sutton, *Science for a Polite Society*, ch. 7, and his conclusion, on the significance of her acceptance by the French Newtonians. Twentieth-century historians of science usually gloss over her contributions or ignore them altogether. See, for example, Pierre Brunet, *L'Introduction des théories de Newton en France au XVIIIe siècle avant 1738* (Paris: Librairie Scientifique Albert Blanchard, 1931), who makes no mention of her at all. More recently, Derek Gjertsen, *The Newton Handbook* (New York: Routledge and Kegan Paul, 1986) gives Clairaut credit for her translation of the *Principia* and does not even list her *Institutions* among the commentaries on Newton.

[52] This translation of her work and her election to the Bologna Academy of Science are perhaps related to the north Italian tradition of honoring learned women. Bologna awarded two doctorates to women in the eighteenth century. With the support of Cardinal Lambertini, archbishop of Bologna, Laura Bassi taught at the university and spread Newton's ideas among her students. For a description of her career and the differences in social context see Gabrielli Berti Logan, "The Desire to Contribute: An Eighteenth-Century Italian Woman of Science," *American Historical Review* 99, 3 (June 1994): 785–812. On the Italian Enlightenment see the collection of articles by Franco Venturi, *Italy and the Enlightenment: Studies in a Cosmopolitan Century*, ed. Stuart Woolf and trans. Susan Corsi (New York: New York University Press, 1972).

government intervention. "Science," or "natural philosophy" as it was called in the early decades of the eighteenth century, had not yet been separated from "metaphysics." Therefore, anything involved with the "study of nature" could be considered political, for it inevitably led to questions about the Divine. Newton and du Châtelet hoped to discover "a system of the world" that would explain the connections between an omniscient, omnipresent God and the mathematical demonstrations of the laws of the universe.[53] Such efforts could be interpreted by royal censors as a threat to the established faith and an effort "to weaken in people's spirits the principles of religion and of subordination to the Powers, established by God."[54]

Out of fear of such royal persecution, du Châtelet hid under locked key some of Voltaire's writings while they lived together,[55] but she was an astute courtier as well. She maintained her friendships with the leading court functionaries and government ministers. She delighted in her dresses and jewels, in assisting at the king and queen's table when they stopped at Choisy en route between Fontainebleau and Versailles, and in Paris, meeting at the salons and playing pharon or cavagnole at the gaming tables with her friends.

Du Châtelet took pride in acquiring the perquisites of her rank (a tabouret at court after she had managed to marry her daughter to a Neapolitan duke) and the royal favors that advanced the careers of her military husband and son. In 1747 negotiating the office of farmer general for a wealthy bourgeois meant that she could pay off some of her debts.[56] In addition, du Châtelet negotiated on Voltaire's behalf in

[53] On Newton's metaphysics, see Betty Jo Teeter, *The Janus Face of Genius: The Role of Alchemy in Newton's Thoughts* (New York: Cambridge University Press, 1991), or the briefer *Newton and the Culture of Newtonianism* (with Margaret C. Jacob) (Atlantic Highlands, N.Y.: Humanities Press, 1995). Harth gives the neatest description of du Châtelet's melding of metaphysics and natural philosophy: "she replaces the Cartesian idea of God as first causal principle by Leibnizian sufficient reason, while in physics she replaces Descartes by Newtonian mechanical principles and Leibnizian dynamics" (see 197).

[54] On the assumptions made by the authorities, see Margaret C. Jacobs, *Living the Enlightenment: Freemasonry and Politics in Eighteenth-Century Europe* (New York: Oxford University Press, 1991), police code, 6; see also Ira O. Wade on *The Clandestine Organization and Diffusion of Philosophic Ideas in France from 1700–1750* (Princeton: Princeton University Press, 1969). On the more or less automatic connection between philosophical questions about the nature of the universe and religion see the extensive discussion in Peter Gay, *The Enlightenment: The Rise of Modern Paganism* (New York: Vintage and W. W. Norton and Co., 1966) and the more recent analyses by Sutton (*Science for a Polite Society*), who connects not only Newton, Locke, and constitutional monarchy but also Fontenelle, Descartes, and absolutism (251).

[55] The *Traité de métaphysique* and *La Pucelle* (see Theodore Besterman, *Voltaire* [New York: Harcourt, Brace and World, 1969], 374).

[56] Vaillot, *Madame du Châtelet*, 272–73.

audiences with Cardinal Fleury, with the king (for example, an "official authorization to harbor" Voltaire granted in June 1735), and used her connections to angle for the admission to the Academie Française that he wanted so badly.

On the other hand, du Châtelet was careful about overt political risks for herself. She seems never to have sought publication for her writings in moral philosophy, or her scientific commentaries on the Bible. The manuscript revisions to the *Institutions de physique* show that she took out sections that might have been politically offensive – for example, a series of paragraphs on "les causes finales" and their relation to physics in Chapter II on the existence of God.[57]

Nonetheless, as Linda Gardiner has pointed out, du Châtelet sought to answer controversial, potentially dangerous questions: on "the nature and basic constituents of the universe," on "the relation of God to the world," on "the possibility of human freedom." When Voltaire's *Eléments* failed to be the "comprehensive treatise on physics" that she believed was needed, she undertook it herself. In the resulting book, the *Institutions de physique*, she not only challenged those in France loyal to Descartes, but also the French Newtonians who derided causal explanations of universal attraction that relied on divine intervention. Even her work on the nature of fire involved speculating beyond the elementary chemistry of the day.

Contemporaries acknowledged that her *Principia* was more than a simple translation. The unidentified editor, describing the additions and transposition of ideas, says: "as a result one will often find Newton more intelligible in this translation than in the original and more even than the English version."[58] Her commentary included mathematical and prose

---

[57] The different versions of the opening of chapter II can be found in BN fol. #12265, 59–60. Many paragraphs are excised and replaced with the promise to give a précis of the proofs of the existence of God, "par lequel vous pourrez juger par vous-même de son Evidence."

[58] "En consequence on trouvera souvent Newton plus intelligible dans cette traduction que dans l'original; & même que dans la traduction Angloise." For the editor's comments, see the Avertissement, *Principes mathématiques*, I, i. A number of historians have analyzed du Châtelet's scientific contributions and the risks she took. I am particularly indebted to Gardiner Janik, "Searching for the Metaphysics of Science"; Carolyn Merchant Iltis's "Madame du Châtelet's Metaphysics and Mechanics," *Studies in the History and Philosophy of Science* 8, 1 (1977): 28–48; W. H. Barber's "Mme du Châtelet and Leibnizianism: The Genesis of the *Institutions de Physique*," in *The Age of Enlightenment: Studies Presented to Theodore Besterman*, eds. W. H. Barber et al. (Edinburgh: Oliver and Boyd, 1967); Harth, *Cartesian Women*; Ehrman, *Mme. du Châtelet*. Janik and I disagree about du Châtelet's limiting of herself. I would argue that it was politic, she that it was lack of confidence, the result of prejudice and disadvantage (see p. 187). On the need for a "treatise" see du Châtelet's review in *Journal des savants*, September 1738 in Voltaire's *Works*, xv, 84.

sections explaining the additions and corrections of Newton's work by French scientists: Maupertuis on attraction (1732), Daniel Bernoulli on the tides (1738), Clairaut on refraction (1739) and on the shape of the earth (1740).

Perhaps the risk for du Châtelet was not political, not as a natural philosopher and metaphysician who excited government opposition. Instead, the challenge arose out of circumstances unique to women – traditional social and cultural attitudes that denied intellectual authority to the female sex. For du Châtelet the challenge became how to ensure that she received credit and acceptance of her writings on the same terms as a man, how to avoid having her work summarily dismissed for the simple reason that it was written by a woman. As she explained in her preface to Mandeville, "I believe myself especially obligated to give [this project] all of my care because only success can justify me."[59] In the world of Voltaire, failure meant "ridicule," especially for a woman doing science. One of the first books read by anyone interested in the study of the universe was Bernard le Bouvier de Fontenelle's *Conversations on the Plurality of Worlds* (*Entretiens sur la pluralité des mondes*, 1686 and numerous subsequent editions). His explanation of Descartes's universe took the form of dialogues between a lovely young marquise and a learned gentleman, while strolling in her gardens each evening after dinner. Fontenelle explained that he had chosen this fiction to encourage women to follow his "plot" and by implication to ensure that the ideas would be intelligible to anyone.[60]

In the next century, one of du Châtelet's visitors to Cirey, Francesco Algaretti, used the same device in his *Il Newtonianismo per le Dame [Newton for the Ladies]* (1736). Although the frontispiece was omitted from the Paris edition, contemporaries knew of the engraving: obviously a portrait of du Châtelet, the "Marquise" of his dialogues, standing beside her tutor, the elegant, more delicately boned, male companion, Algarotti, "the swan" as Voltaire called him. This fictional marquise called his descriptions of the nature of color "a labyrinthe for me" and insisted on her need of his guidance. She is such an enthusiast in one dialogue that she cannot sleep, then petulant and childish when asked to consider space as a void in another conversation. Rash one minute, penitent the next, pledging to learn the "truth" but unable to compre-

---

[59] "Je me crois d'autant plus obligee d'y donner tous mes soins que le succes seul peut me justifier" (*Bees*, 138).

[60] See the Preface and opening letter to "Monsieur L * * *" in Bernard le Bouvier de Fontenelle, *Conversations on the Plurality of Worlds*, trans. H. A. Hargreaves (Berkeley: University of California Press, 1990), 3–8. Harth also discusses Descartes's use of the vernacular so that "even women" could "understand something" (Descartes as quoted on 64).

hend mathematics, she is told at the end that she will be criticized for having acquired so much knowledge. It is a sly caricature of the woman the French elite would see extravagantly portrayed also in 1738 by Voltaire. The frontispiece of Voltaire's *Eléments* showed her as inspiration to his genius, the "Minerva" of France in matters Newtonian, dressed in a flowing robe, one breast bare, held aloft by numerous putti.[61]

Algarotti's book is supposed to have spurred Voltaire on to do a scientific explanation of Newton. Du Châtelet was guarded in her response to the book, but it must have steeled her determination to distance herself from both men's portraits, Algarotti's flirtatious marquise or Voltaire's Minerva, and to prove her greater mastery of the material, greater than the fictional pupil and more serious than either male author.

Du Châtelet was canny in her initial forays into publication. It was no accident that the title page of the first edition of the *Institutions* indicated no author and the text identified her as a parent writing for a son without specifying that she was not, as her readers would have assumed, the father.[62] The Paris edition also had a frontispiece, the image of that same allegorical female figure, this time fully clad, ascending into the clouds toward a nude figure of "Nature." Thus, she offered her readers a counter-image to those of Algarotti and Voltaire – a learned woman instructing a son, in language so clear that anyone, even a male child, could understand.[63] Neither Koenig's accusations of plagiarism nor

[61] See, for example, M. Algarotti, *Le Newtonianisme pour les Dames ou entretiens sur la lumiere, sur les Couleurs et sur l'attractions* trans. M. Duperron de Castera (Montpellier: chez Montalant, 1738), two volumes in one; 68, 100 in I; 32, 183, 286ff., 308–309 in II. For Harth's interpretation, see 201–203.

This and other engravings were for the Dutch edition of Voltaire's *Eléments* [*Elémens de la Philosophie de Neuton* ... (Amsterdam: chez Jacques Desbordes, 1738)]. The frontispiece shows Voltaire, the intent writer, sitting at his desk dressed in classical garb complete with a laurel wreath. A woman whom contemporaries might imagine to be the "immortal Emilie" posed as an allegorical figure looks admiringly at Newton seated above her in the clouds and beams the light of the great Englishman's reason to Voltaire with a large mirror held in her arms. The same allegorical figure – perhaps Science or Truth, if the artists were following Cesare Ripa's *Iconologia* – appears in the vignettes at the beginning of many of the chapters, sometimes in a study, sometimes outside, always in partial disarray, one breast bared, a lock of hair falling characteristically onto one shoulder, and always surrounded by symbols of mathematics and physics. Voltaire supervised these engravings, and contemporaries might have viewed them as yet another tribute to his mistress. See Robert L. Walters, "The Allegorical Engravings in the Ledet–Desbordes Edition of the *Elémens de la philosophie de Newton*," in Howells et al.

[62] On the ways in which du Châtelet pictures herself in the *Institutions*, see Julie C. Hayes, "Emilie du Châtelet: Physics, Fiction, and the Strategies of the Self," unpublished, presented at ASECS Convention, Charleston, March 13, 1994.

[63] Harth, Gardiner, and Terrall interpret the frontispiece and her portrayal of herself as a significant statement by du Châtelet about learned women.

Mairan's mockery of her references to his work now could prevent acceptance by France's elite scientific circles of the image she hoped to portray: a learned "physicien" and "philosophe," author of a serious work of natural philosophy.

Her essay on the nature of fire submitted to the Academy of Sciences prize competition in 1737 shows the lengths to which she would go to avoid premature censure or ridicule. Voltaire had already written and submitted his entry. As du Châtelet confided to Maupertuis, the material was new to her, and she had just a month to complete her experiments. She wrote at night after the household had retired in order to keep it secret from everyone but her husband, and especially Voltaire. As she explained, she risked embarrassment by presenting Voltaire with a project that would displease him. She admitted that she disagreed with almost all of his ideas. Subsequently, when the Academy planned to print both of their entries though neither had won, she was very open about her views and her authorship. She made enough of a fuss to have an addition to the errata showing that she now also disagreed with Maupertuis and the Newtonians. She thus publicly declared her support for Leibniz, whose ideas on the nature of force were anathema to her circle.[64]

Her letters in 1740 indicated her satisfaction in silencing Koenig, in being challenged by a man of Mairan's standing and then in besting him in what she described as superficial pleasantries and veiled sarcasm. To his patronizing suggestion that she "read .. and reread" his *mémoire* so that she would see the error of her criticisms, she replied, "I can assure you that the more I read and reread, the more convinced I am that your supposition" will never be right.[65] However brilliant her retorts, no one in her circle of correspondents and visitors to Cirey wrote on her behalf. Clairaut proposed Koenig for foreign membership in the Academy of Sciences in the midst of the controversy over her authorship. Even Voltaire, still eager to ingratiate himself to gain membership or even the secretaryship, chose to speak to the Academy of Sciences in opposition to the views she expressed in her argument with Mairan. Perhaps Mairan's attack and the silence of the other "physiciens" and "géomètres" influenced her decision to translate Newton's *Principia* and to turn the

[64] See letters to Maupertuis, #129, June 21, 1738, 236; and #148, October 24, 1738, *Du Chât. Corr.*, I, 267. See Barber, "Mme du Châtelet," 207.

[65] Her letter to Maupertuis, #272, May 29, 1741, speaks of "le ridicule de la lettre du secretaire" and her response (*Du Chât. Corr.*, II, 56–57). The specific interchange on "reading and rereading" is in *Lettre de m. De Mairan Sur la Question des Forces Vives, en réponse aux Objections qu'elle lui a fait sur ce sujet dans ses Institutions de physique* (9) and in her response (5–6). Bound together with her *Dissertation sur la Nature et la Propagation du Feu*, Huntington Library, San Marino, Calif., #RB479741.

projected second volume of her *Institutions* into her own commentary on Newton's universe and his celestial mechanics.

In the *Principia* commentary, she also relied on a number of other devices to assure that she would be taken seriously as a scientist. She no longer presented herself as the "entrepreneur" of the Mandeville translation. In the preface to the *Institutions* she claimed a different function. There she described "la Physique" as "an immense building, greater than the powers of a single man; some place one stone while others build whole aisles." She was among those "who read the plan of the building," and by implication revealed its majesty.[66] Thus, in her Commentary she often spoke as the conduit for male authorities. She did not plagiarize; she authoritatively summarized their findings, cited sources, and gave page numbers. She concluded her section on light with a tribute to Clairaut, who has "encapsulated all of the theory of refraction in a single problem in such a way that I don't believe anyone could improve on it in the elegance and clarity of his demonstration, I will be content to give it here."[67]

Considering the nature of the social and intellectual environment in which du Châtelet worked, we should marvel that she accomplished as much as she did. To contemporaries it must have seemed as if she lived two days in one. Letters speak of no time to consult "big quarto volumes" or the most recent books, of requests to tutors like Koenig "to make abstracts for me of the chapters I required."[68] Her manuscripts reflect the rushed concentration, calculations, and explanations done amidst many other activities and multiple demands on her time and attention. Du Châtelet scribbles, runs words together, and lets the lines curve down the right-hand side of the *cahiers*. She draws the charts in free hand, is so intent on her thoughts or on saving paper that she cramps the writing at the bottom of the page. She often crosses out in bold strokes, and smudges the ink. The paper is sometimes of different sizes, corrections added on scraps of her own pale, green-bordered stationery, or the back of a letter she received. Such additions she

---

[66] "La Physique est un Bâtiment immense, qui surpasse les forces d'un seul homme; les uns y mettent une pierre, tandis que d'autres batissent les ailes entieres ... il y en a d'autres qui levent le Plan du Bâtiment, & je suis du nombre de ces derniers" (*Institutions*, 12).

[67] "[R]enfermé toute la théorie de la réfraction dans un seul Problème comme je ne crois pas qu'on puisse n'en ajouter à l'élégance & à la clarté de sa démonstration, je me contenterai de la donne ici." For refraction, see Commentary, *Principes mathématiques de la philosophie naturelle par M. Newton*, trans. Mme. la marquise du Châtelet (Paris: Desaint and Saillant, 1759), II, 189. Also in manuscript, Bibliothèque nationale, fols. #12266–68.

[68] Du Châtelet to Maupertuis, #241, June 30, 1740, *Du Chât. Corr.*, II, 18; #148, October 24, 1738, I, 267.

attached to the text with sealing wax. Almost every page has evidence of rewriting, sometimes in marginal notes to herself, "there [are] errors in some of the calculus entries of propositions 22 and 23. Redo and Correct them."[69]

The descriptions of her days and nights when she was working intensively on projects sound like college students cramming during exam week. Mme. de Graffigny reported how she had completed the essay on fire: eight consecutive nights in which she slept only one hour and kept herself awake by putting her hands in ice and then walking up and down beating her arms.[70] Du Châtelet wrote her own description of how she managed to finish her work on the Newton translation in June of 1749. The letter was to Jean-François, marquis de Saint-Lambert, the young army officer by whom she had become pregnant while she and Voltaire (long since platonic companions) were in attendance at the duc de Lorraine's court at Lunéville.[71] The hectic tone and running commentary are typical and demonstrate the many facets of her life and the diversity of her emotional responses: "I get up at 9:00, sometimes at 8, I work until 3, I take my coffee at 3:00, I resume work at 4, I leave it at 10 to eat a bit alone, I chat until midnight with m. de V., who is with me during my supper and I take up work [again] at midnight until 5:00." In the other parts of the letter she wrote of her need for quiet, for absolute separation, that she was ready to "risk all for all," and to do nothing but work on her book and consult with Clairaut. Then she went on to tell Saint-Lambert of her fears of death because of the pregnancy, to describe her love for him and her hope that he would recognize her despite having lost her "figure." In the midst of all these thoughts, she paused to report: "my child moves a lot and I hope is in as good health as I am."[72]

Both du Châtelet and Voltaire found her pregnancy at forty-two an embarrassment. Together with Saint-Lambert they arranged for two seductive weeks with the marquis to prevent a possible scandal. That du

---

[69] "[I]l y a erreur dans quelques entraits des CalCuls des prop. 22 et 23. Les Refaire et Coriger." The manuscripts are those at the BN, fols. #12266–68 and #12265.

[70] Graffigny to Devaux, #67, December 25, 1738, *Graff. Corr.*, I, 245.

[71] Sometime early in the 1740s Voltaire seems to have lost interest in du Châtelet sexually. He had a brief affair with a Spanish noblewoman in 1736 and in the summer of 1745 began his relationship with his niece, Mme. Louise Denis. The infatuation with Saint-Lambert appears to have been du Châtelet's only affair while living with Voltaire. See Vaillot for the sequence of liaisons, and Besterman's edition of Voltaire letters to Denis.

[72] "Je me lève à 9 heures, quelquefois à 8, je travaille jusqu'à 3, je prends mon cafe à 3 heures, je reprends le travaille à 4, je le quitte à 10 pour manger un morceau seule, je cause jusqu'à minuit avec m. de V., qui assiste a mon souper et je reprends le travail à minuit jusqu'à 5 heures"; "mon enfant remue beaucoup, et se port à ce que j'espère aussi bien que moi" (#476, *c.* June 15, 1749, *Du Chât. Corr.*, II, 294).

Châtelet died as a result of the child's birth presented a similar irony to contemporaries. Du Châtelet had lived in two worlds, the courts and households of a privileged woman courtier and in the company of Paris's elite, learned men. She tried to avoid the contradictions and constraints implicit in these relationships. She wrote disparagingly of the one and idealized the other, but never rejected the possibility that she might be a full participant in both. As she wrote to d'Argental at the height of her controversy with Mairan, she appreciated that she was not "secretary of the Academy," and therefore at a disadvantage, but "I have reason, and that is worth all the titles."[73]

The reality was quite different. For although Voltaire and Cideville in their correspondence would refer to her as "génie," the eighteenth-century version of the term had already acquired a masculine, exclusionary cast. Voltaire's early descriptions of her intellectual activities did compare her to men, but attributed male, not neutered, qualities to her: "a woman unique for her class who read Ovid and Euclid and has the imagination of the one and the justice of the other." And he was well aware of the contradictions in such "cross overs." As he explained to Cideville, whose friendship and sensitivity he was extolling: "You are Emilie as a man and she is Cideville as a woman."[74]

Voltaire did not publish her most challenging project, the translation of Newton's *Principia*, until 1759, ten years after her death.[75] He took care to control how contemporaries would remember her. In prefatory materials he included the laudatory epistle from his *Eléments*, and the equally lavish eulogy he wrote and had published in 1752.[76] For him du Châtelet was unique, remarkable, memorable, "a very rare spirit," and allowed to participate in his elite circle specifically because she was not aspiring to be a man. By willingly retaining her womanliness she proved,

---

[73] Du Châtelet to d'Argental, #269, May 2, 1741, *Du Chât. Corr.*, II, 51.

[74] Cideville to Voltaire, #D644, August 11, 1733: "une femme unique dans son espèce qui lit Ovide et Euclide, et qui a l'imagination de l'un et la justisse de l'autre" (Voltaire to Thieriot, #D899, *c.* August 15, 1735); "Vous êtes Emilie en homme, et elle est Cideville en femme" (Voltaire to Cideville, #D645, August 14, 1733; *Volt. Corr.*, II, 374, 378; III, 181).

[75] A 1756 edition was incomplete and had a very limited printing. See, on the 1756 edition, Bernard I. Cohen, "The French Translation of Isaac Newton's Philosophiae naturalis principia mathematica," *Archives internationales d'histoire des Sciences* 21 (1969): 261–90; and on the role of Clairaut in the writing and perhaps delay in the printing of the text, see René Taton, "Mme. du Châtelet, traductrice de Newton," *Archives internationales d'histoire des Sciences* 22 (July–December 1969): 185–209.

[76] The text which Voltaire reprinted in du Châtelet's translation of the *Principia* is somewhat different than the version in the *Eléments*. For example, it begins: "Tu m'appelles à toi, vast & puissant génie,/ Minerve de la France, immortelle Emilie,/ Je m'éveille à ta voix, je marche à ta clarté,/ Sur les pas des vertus & de la vérité" (*Principes mathématiques*, prefatory material, unpaginated).

according to Voltaire, that one of her sex could make use of her intelligence, give much honor to science and still not neglect any of women's obligations to "la vie civile."[77]

Maupertuis summed up why she was acceptable even to members of the Academy of Sciences. He described her as a "noble and pleasant figure of a woman who .. having great wit .. never put it to bad use." "How marvelous," he continued, and what a "surprising feat," "to have been able to ally the pleasing qualities of her sex with that sublime science which we believe to be meant only for us."[78] In this way du Châtelet continued an honored women's tradition that left the prevailing assumptions about gender and intellectual authority intact. She was, in the words of Voltaire's preface to her *Principia*, the most learned woman ever, but for all that, a "prodigy," an anomaly, the self-proclaimed exception, that proved the old rule.[79]

Acknowledgments

Research for this chapter was made possible by a Faculty Research Grant to Paris from Miami University (Ohio) and by a Mayers Fellowship at the Huntington Library. Hilda L. Smith, Mary Frederickson, Michael O'Brien, Carl Pletsch, and Murray D. List have raised many important questions in the course of its formulation. I am grateful to them for their expertise and encouragement.

---

[77] From Voltaire's Dedicatory Epistle to *Eléments*, see *Compl. Works*, xv, 192. For this ability to do both kinds of activities see also Voltaire's Preface Historique in her *Principes mathématiques*, I, xii.

[78] Maupertuis quoted in Ehrman, p. 43. Other Academicians saw her in the same way. A preface to the Academy edition of her and Voltaire's essays on fire suggested that "the names of the authors alone are capable of engaging the curiosity of the public ... one by a woman of the highest rank ... and [the other] by one of our best poets" (as quoted in Vaillot, *Madame du Châtelet*, 151).

[79] See Preface Historique, *Principes mathématiques*, I, x, v.

Part III

The intellectual context and economic setting for early modern women

Introduction to Part III

Women as intellectuals, political writers, and simply inhabitants, of early modern Britain lived their lives through frameworks that defined their natures and their interests as distinct from (and inferior to) their male counterparts. This part of the book, while focusing on the writings of individuals including Hobbes, Filmer, Locke, and Catharine Macaulay, treats in greater depth the intellectual and economic structures that restricted, but did not prevent, women's acceptance as public actors and authors. It highlights the power of intellectual values and circles as controlling forces which operated similarly to economic, political, and legal restraints in restricting women's public place and public voice in English society. The questions and assumptions of early modern political thought are assessed not simply for its content but for its force, through inclusion and exclusion of appropriate topics and individuals, in framing the treatment of women politically and as political authors. The authors of this part do not all agree on the nature of such a canon and its influence on women's intellectual and political standing, but they each treat the topic in provocative ways.

Jane Jaquette analyzes the operation of gender assumptions in Hobbes's discussion of the social contract in *The Leviathan*. In so doing, she offers a more positive interpretation of the use women could make of contract theory than does Carole Pateman in her monograph, *The Sexual Contract*. (Professor Pateman will respond to these differences in her concluding chapter in this work.) In her chapter on Hobbes, Jaquette rejuvenates the reputation of "Enlightenment liberalism," arguing its use by women to support their enhanced moral and domestic standing in the seventeenth and eighteenth centuries. She sees contract theory as both central and positive to such enhancement because it "is normative in favor of equality, not asymmetry." Reliance on a contract underlay goals for "justice," according to Jaquette, within both the home and the state.

Hobbes is central to this debate because he makes explicit in his discussion of both the state of nature and the origins of the state distinct gender roles. Hobbes's acceptance of women's natural equality evolves with state formation into civil disability because, as he states, "for the most part, Common-wealths have been erected by the Fathers, not the Mothers, of families." He thus opens up a debate that has dominated much of feminist discussion over women's nature, and its relevance to their standing in the state.

Jaquette contends that Hobbes saw the hierarchical power relations within a family as a male affair, with age and class divisions predominant, not gender. Jaquette thus seeks the reasons both men and women entered the contract of marriage. She finds gains for women from the operation of contract and insists they entered marriage for their own interests, not simply as weak apolitical beings under the power of men. Women, like most men in civil society, lose authority to those heads of households who form the state, though not as women but as individuals with limited power. And, according to Jaquette, women gain in two ways from this arrangement: they gain protection when they are weakened through childbearing and, as the seventeenth century progresses, they increasingly possess enhanced moral authority within the family. Contracts, for Hobbes, gave sufficient security to all so that they could act justly, and it aided women as much as men in this regard. Thus he, in Jaquette's view, saw women as "in no way naturally or morally disqualified for citizenship." Women were not simply Pateman's "passive victims," but under Hobbes's "stern gender egalitarianism" and its implementation through liberal contract theory, there formed an agreement "foundationally critical to women's subsequent claims to equal rights." While thus placing Hobbes within the influential framework of a canon of political thought offered earlier in this introduction, still Jaquette sees both his arguments and contract theory as offering as many opportunities as restrictions for women's standing within English society.

Gordon Schochet is less favorable to Robert Filmer and, to a lesser extent, John Locke, in discussing their essential omission of women from political constructs. Filmer thoroughly dismisses women in his works, even though his "patriarchal conception of familial authority" would seem to require his including their status. Filmer's discussion of patriarchal authority emerging from the Garden of Eden includes children and servants, but not women. Schochet places this analysis within a broader assessment of the influence of political theory on women's political standing, and the power of accepted social norms, both embedded in Filmer's writings. John Locke, according to Schochet, also ignored women in his conception of the nature and origin of the state and perpetuated its negative impact on women's ability to gain political standing. For Locke, women had a role within the household, but none within the state. Yet Locke, according to Schochet, "through a shift in the focus of politics from the patriarchal *father* to the rational, rights-bearing *individual* . . created the theoretical possibility of full political membership for women."

Again this demonstrates the power of political theorists to frame the debate over the nature of the state, and any role gender might have played in it. "I am especially concerned," Schochet contends, "to argue that there are important connections among abstract political theory, lower-level and perhaps even unarticulated and unappreciated ideology, and the arrangements and practices that characterize a society." Political theory provides the "ideological and intellectual" force behind the state's imposition of its will.

In supporting this contention, Schochet analyses the power of "Lockean voluntarism" to open up the "concept 'person,'" ultimately enabling women's "political membership." He integrates the political realities and assumptions of Stuart England with the more philosophical disputes of political theorists, to grapple with those forces that defined women's political (or non-political) standing. Moving beyond political thought as abstract discourse alone, Schochet offers an intellectual and historical framework that situates both the limits of Locke's thought and its potential use by later feminists. And, by grounding his analysis in the historically possible, as well as the theoretically constructed view of the state, Schochet adds to our understanding of the influence of political theory and the manner in which that influence is limited by its historical context. While in disagreement with some of Jaquette's arguments, Schochet contributes in a similar fashion to our understanding of the integrated reality of the historical context, the intellectual influences on political theorists, and the theory that emerged from this integration. Finally, Schochet's chapter is tied to Jaquette's treatment of Hobbes, in seeing positive aspects in contract theory for women. Viewing women as individuals, he claims, is the central demand of modern feminists and gained from Locke's evolution of contract theory even though Locke, grounded in the customs and structures of Stuart England, never made that claim.

J. G. A. Pocock's discussion of Catharine Macaulay as historian offers a different perspective on Macaulay from the earlier chapter by Wendy Gunther-Canada (chapter 6) which compared Macaulay's and Wollstonecraft's critique of Edmund Burke's *Reflections on the Revolution in France*. Pocock is concerned, though, with understanding her as a writer of history. It was the genre she chose, as much as her views, that both framed and limited her account of the British state, and women's relationship to it. He is specifically concerned with her eight-volume *History of England from the Accession of James I to that of the Brunswick Line*, and the radical Whiggism she expressed there. One must look therefore to her multi-volume work, rather than her scarce political tracts, to discover her intellectual contribution to the eighteenth century. Such a focus allows us to pursue two goals: understanding the nature of historical scholarship and writing following 1750 and recognizing her unique intellectual role: "she was primarily a woman who crashed her way into the writing of history, normally defined as a specifically masculine activity."

One can best understand Catharine Macaulay, then, as a practitioner of "the writing of history, as a branch of political argument in eighteenth-century Britain." As a radical Whig historian she used the past to document how the current Whig aristocracy, according to Pocock, had deserted its principles and to illustrate the expression and embodiment of those principles in the past. Yet as a woman, her role as interpreter of the past was suspect. To understand her history, we need to recognize her as a "patriot historian," one who loved her country more than its regime. As such she identified with those opposing the king in the king's name in the 1640s and those who sought to preserve the constitution in 1689. Catharine Macaulay, as "both a 'patriot' and a 'republican,'" while still suspicious of hereditary monarchy, believed the virtue of the people could make it an effective form of government. In the need to construct an ideological and historical context for her historical assessments, she turned to the republic as a "community of virtue" and built upon Greco-Roman ideals of public virtue. In Pocock's view, Macaulay utilized history as "moral exhortation," and it proved "the best possible way for a woman to practice public virtue."

It was her historical scholarship that led her to admire ancient formulations of civic virtue and to separate from the values of her urban, bourgeois family. While the progressive, commercial interests of the late 1700s paved the way for later feminist claims, it did not appeal to Macaulay the patriot historian. With little sympathy for "the unlettered multitude," she looked to the virtuous individual, or "morally free and politically self-determining agents" as her historical and political actors. In characterizing Macaulay, Pocock terms her "an eighteenth-century Hannah Arendt, a woman wholly committed to the ancient ideal of active citizenship." Yet it was the construction of her history that drove her political characterization of women, leading her to harsh assessment of queens and praise for individuals such as Lady Rachel Russell as a Whig heroine. While analyzing her as a woman writer, Pocock focuses

Milk   Tofu
Onion   Pasta
Tomato   Sesame Oil
Bagel   Cake
Salad leaves
Yogurt(?)

Paper Tower
Apple Cider Vinegar

Milk.   Eggs
Onion   Sesa
Tomato
Bagel   Cake/9C
Tofu   Pasta
1 Veggie   Leafs.

not primarily on the nature of Macaulay's thought, but links her political views to the requirements of her historical analysis, and reminds readers that to understand her we must continually remember that she was Catharine Macaulay, Whig historian.

Susan Staves, in an analysis of the public role of women in the chartered national companies of the first half of the eighteenth century, offers both a political and an economic context for women's inclusion in, as well as exclusion from, the political realm. Up to this point, the authors in Part III have devoted more attention to the intellectual constraints on, and parameters of, women's public space. But Staves, while contending that her study situates women's writings (or lack thereof) on economic experience as well as their actual role as investors, still moves us to a closer analysis of the tie between economic and political power in England from 1700 to 1750, and its impact on women's public and literary lives. While reviewing a range of literary works, the chapter looks specifically at what women could and could not do as shareholders of the increasingly important companies involved in trade, in both London and national politics. Her analysis leads us to understand that women were allowed participation in this new arena, but only in ways that continued to circumscribe independent efforts and to deny them roles as full political and economic actors.

Staves treats the intersection of these companies and Parliament. As she states, that "these companies were chartered by statute in return for payment to the state [meant] that the companies were dependent upon politicians" to introduce bills in their favor. Thus company decisions were in many ways also political decisions. Yet these joint-stock companies did admit women "as voters on the same terms as men." And women controlled significant amounts of a company's stock; for instance, in 1783 16.2 percent of shareholder accounts in the East India Company were held by women. Thus companies had reason to court women's favor and to seek their support for particular policies. But we know little of women's relationships to the companies or commercial London generally because they wrote few of the texts emerging from disputes about either company or government policy. And, except for Susanna Centlivre, they authored little of the satire generated about the unholy alliance between jobbers and politicians.

Centlivre, whom Staves characterizes as "a woman of the world, a successful writer of comedies, and a would-be political writer for the Whigs," fits within an eighteenth-century journalistic career and advancement path where political authors supported a cause for personal preferment. In her case, through a poem, *A Woman's Case: In an Epistle to Charles Joye, Esq; Deputy-Governor of the South Sea* (1720), she seeks reward in stocks for her support of Whigs, as she could not gain the offices pursued by Swift, Addison, or Steele. The humor she expressed in plays and poetry still point, in Staves's view, to the "gender asymmetry of the new political world" in which women could be political writers, but still closed to "places and preferments" open to their male counterparts.

Staves, in exploring these realities, again identifies the links between intellectual and political assumptions and controls. Disputes, such as those between companies and the government, were outside the private sphere and women were discouraged from writing political or economic treatises, or from offering accounts of their involvement in these realms. Those who had done well in this market, such as the duchess of Marlborough, could take little public credit for her insights; and someone like Mary Barwell, who assisted her brother (an employee and later director of the East India Company) with his London efforts while he remained in India, was seen not as a shrewd political operator, but one serving her family's interests. Yet those discussing the market, such as Thomas Mortimer in his *Every Man his own Broker; or, a Guide to Exchange Alley*, do make space for both satirical as well as prescriptive references to the female investor. Women both invested their own funds and lobbied and bribed various government ministers to gain economic rewards for themselves and others. But such efforts did not lead to public recognition of their competence, or for any company official openly to embrace their public role, either economically or politically. And, Staves claims, it was more important to eighteenth-century society to maintain the myth of women's domestic isolation and innocence than to recognize their significant role in the London market.

In each of these four chapters, the authors sought to understand how the intellectual and political assumptions of the age influenced how women were assessed as purveyors of political views and as political actors. Jaquette and Schochet look to classic political theory to discern intellectual values and assumptions that sometimes aided women, such as their possible use of contract, but most often defined them as non-political and outside the legitimate scope of political writings. Pocock and Staves both discuss the writings of women in the early and mid-eighteenth century, Catherine Macaulay the historian and Susanna Centlivre, playwright and poet. Each see intellectual and political values influencing what women wrote, but Pocock sees a greater opportunity for Macaulay as a writer of history than does Staves for Centlivre to be heard concerning London political and economic society. Yet, while differing on a number of points, each of these writers perceives intellectual genre and opinion, embedded in social and political realities, as strongly influencing what women wrote about politically and why they were seldom political actors in the seventeenth and eighteenth centuries.

9   Contract and coercion: power and gender in *Leviathan*

Jane S. Jaquette

> Sexual difference is political difference; sexual difference is the difference between freedom and subjection.   Carole Pateman[1]

> Although the ideology of liberalism has always proclaimed the values of freedom and equality, liberal societies have always been underpinned by a sexual contract in which these ideals have been systematically violated.   Quentin Skinner[2]

Contemporary feminism has attacked the male biases of liberalism, labeling as convenient fictions notions that "citizen" is a gender-neutral concept, or that distributive justice is possible when "universal" laws fail to take the female body into account. When combined with a long tradition of anti-capitalist thought, these critiques add up to an indictment of Enlightenment liberalism, which is then portrayed as a barrier to solving contemporary problems rather than as a basis on which to build.[3]

Among feminist critiques, Carole Pateman's *The Sexual Contract* is powerfully argued and provocative, and has become a classic of feminist theory. Pateman attacks liberalism at its origin in the theories of social contract, beginning with Hobbes's *Leviathan* but relying heavily as well on the theories of Locke and Rousseau.[4] My argument is not with her

[1] *The Sexual Contract* (Stanford, Calif.: Stanford University Press, 1988), 6. Hereinafter, *The Sexual Contract*.
[2] Quentin Skinner, "Modernity and Disenchantment: Some Historical Reflections," in *Philosophy in an Age of Pluralism; The Philosophy of Charles Taylor in Question*, ed. James Tully (Cambridge: Cambridge University Press, 1994), 42.
[3] For a review of anti-liberal thought from the right, and the left, see Stephen Holmes, *The Anatomy of Antiliberalism* (Cambridge, Mass.: Harvard University Press, 1993).
[4] Pateman examines Locke and Rousseau as well as Hobbes, and many of her criticisms are directed at Locke or Rousseau rather than Hobbes, whom she sees as a more consistent thinker, and more consistently gender-egalitarian. Her case against Hobbes is made specifically in "God Hath Ordained to Man a Helper" in *Feminist Interpretations of Political Theory*, eds. M. L. Shanley and C. Pateman (University Park, Pa.: Pennsylvania State University Press, 1991), 53–73, hereinafter "God Hath." The quotations from Hobbes, unless otherwise noted, are from Thomas Hobbes, *Leviathan*, edited and introduced by C. B. Macpherson (London: Penguin, 1985).

views of Locke and Rousseau, but stems from my concern that her critique of Hobbes, which is central to her case that the subjection of women is foundational in liberal contract theory, is wrong about Hobbes and has the effect of alienating feminist theory from contract theory, with potentially harmful consequences for feminist political practice.

Pateman charges that Hobbes's social contract conceals a prior "sexual contract" that men impose on women, whom they conquer in the state of nature. Far from rejecting patriarchalism, Pateman argues, Hobbes modernizes patriarchy, making the state the coercive guarantor of male domination. And women, by accepting the social contract and agreeing to the marriage contract, fall for the liberal myth that contract signifies consent, and accede to their own subjugation.

These are serious charges. Liberalism claims to be founded on consent because it is founded on contract, but if, as Pateman argues, "contract and coercion are the same," it is in fact founded on force. "A free social order cannot be a contractual order," she maintains, and "the sexual contract and the social contract, the 'individual' and the state, stand and fall together." "Taken to a conclusion, contract undermines the conditions of its own existence." Contract implies freedom but delivers control: "Hobbes showed long ago that contract ... requires absolutism and the sword to keep [the war of all against all] at bay."[5]

To buttress her argument, Pateman "retrieves the story" of the "sexual" contract, filling in a significant ellipsis in Hobbes's account with a logical but compelling speculation: if men and women are declared equal by Hobbes in the state of nature, why is it that fathers (as heads of families) make the social contract? Pateman surmises that the social contract myth hides a missing story: men must have subjected women, forcing them to enter families, so that by the time they enter the social contract, it is only men who remain free individuals.

This chapter argues that Pateman's speculation is not the only credible one, and that reading the social contract as excluding women categorically is not consistent with Hobbes's position. It further suggests that Pateman's assertion that Hobbes elides contract and coercion cannot be sustained: if coercion could produce authority (i.e. the unquestioned assertion of power) unproblematically, there would be no problem of political dissent, no Civil War in England – and no need for a social contract theory or indeed any other theory of authority.

I conclude that Pateman's critique of contract is not adequate against contract in the abstract, but depends on the conditions of relative power

---

[5] *The Sexual Contract*, 232.

under which contracts are negotiated, about which contract theory is normative in favor of equality, not asymmetry. Contract theory demands attention to the power relations within which contracts are made if contract is to align with consent and provide the conditions for justice within families as well as within states.

Although faith in contractarianism can mislead the weak into assuming equality between the parties to any contract – as Pateman argues, the notion that women who were denied political and legal rights could make marriage "contracts" is a profound contradiction in liberal practice – I would argue that the fact that women's claims to contract-equality were the most effective platform from which to attack women's political and legal marginalization. Even in today's very complex feminist debates, notions of contract-equality inform the most contemporary critiques of male dominance in the private as well as the public sphere.

Finally, I offer the speculation that the overall context in which women "contracted" – as wives but also in the wide range of roles in which women must relate to and negotiate with men – was in a process of rapid transformation by the mid-seventeenth century. Changes in women's roles as wives and mothers, the invention and domestication of the "private" sphere, and the rapidly changing meanings of the public and the political carried with them new possibilities for women's agency as well as new opportunities for their political and economic oppression.

The case

In his historical account of the creation of states, Hobbes writes that, "[f]or the most part, Common-wealths have been erected by the Fathers, not the Mothers, of families."[6] Pateman argues that this inconsistency is revealing, and that Hobbes's narrative can be reconstructed to show that the social contract not only hides but legitimizes the prior defeat of women and their subjugation in families. Although women may feel that the marriage contract makes them an equal consenting party with men, they are misled. Women are merely allowed to become "citizens for a day" to acknowledge that they accept their servitude.

The social contract itself further ensures women's subjugation by turning raw male power into legitimate political right and by backing the marriage contract – as it does all contracts – with the "publique Sword." The social contract exemplifies what is wrong with contract itself, which

[6] *Leviathan*, 253.

is that it provides a veneer of consent to relations determined by force. Women cannot have consented because "[w]omen are not party to the original contract through which men transform their natural freedom into the security of civil freedom." Instead, "[w]omen are the subject of the contract" which is made by men.[7]

The social contract also legitimizes the division between the public and the private in liberal theory: "The private, womanly (natural) and the public masculine sphere (civil) are opposed but gain their meaning from each other ... What it means to be an 'individual', a maker of contracts and civilly free, is revealed by the subjection of women in the private sphere."[8] Further, Pateman argues, at every stage of this process, Hobbes conflates consent and coercion; the fiction of contract hides the reality of coercive power beneath all contracts, just as the social contract hides the coercive gender relations that make it possible.

Patriarchal power as conjugal right

Pateman begins her reconstruction of the missing narrative by trying to show that Hobbes is a covert patriarchalist. She observes that the patriarchalists' argument that political authority is derived from God's grant of fatherly authority to Adam ignores the fact that "Adam's political title must be granted *before* he becomes a father" because "[i]f he is to be a father, Eve has to become a mother." Therefore, "sex-right or conjugal right must necessarily precede the right of fatherhood."[9]

Hobbes's opposition to patriarchalist arguments for kingly authority do not vitiate his support for the authority of fathers as citizens and within the family itself. This is not immediately obvious. Hobbes asserts, against Renaissance opinion, that women share the "generative" reproductive role with men, that "God hath ordained to man a helper," and "there be always two that are equally Parents,"[10] and he undermines the patriarchalists' reliance on the notion of inheritance through the father by observing that, although a woman's status as the mother is always secure, the father must rely on the mother's word ("birth follows the belly"). He finds that in the state of nature the child is born totally dependent on the mother, and that "[E]very woman who bears children becomes both a *mother* and a *lord*."[11]

But, as Pateman rightly points out, the issue is far from settled there. Although Hobbes finds marriage laws conventional, not natural, he does refer to "wives" in the state of nature, implying that there is male

---

[7] *The Sexual Contract*, 6.   [8] Ibid., 11.   [9] Ibid., 53.   [10] *Leviathan*, 253.
[11] Hobbes, *Philosophical Rudiments* 116, quoted in "God Hath," 61.

political authority over women prior to the social contract. In addition, he traces the evolution of states to their origin in families. His rational actor account of why an individual would subject his freedom to the authority of another begins with the observation that "[t]here is no man who can hope by his own strength, or wit, to defend himself from destruction without the help of confederates," which implies that individuals join consensually into confederations for their mutual defense, but he then observes that historically most such "confederations" were based on conquest. Combining the historical and rational actor analyses, he then appears to find the origin of the state in the coercive power relations between masters and servants: "conquered and conquerer then constitute a little body politic, which consists of two persons, the one sovereign, which is called the *master*, or the lord, the other subject, which is called the *servant*."[12] Hobbes explicitly compares states formed by conquest to families, "as when a man maketh his children to submit themselves and their children to his government."[13]

Pateman then builds her case by trying to show that "masters" and "servants" are really husbands and wives. She finds Hobbes's recognition of the legitimacy of male subjection of women reinforced by his failure to distinguish "servants" from "slaves," because servants, like slaves, become virtually the property of the master: "The master of a servant is a master of all he hath ... that is to say, of his goods, of his labor, of his servants, and of his children, as often as he shall think fit,"[14] just as, under the rules of coverture in the late seventeenth and eighteenth centuries, a woman's property, the fruits of her labor, and even her legal identity belonged to her husband.

But why would a woman "contract of her own free will to enter into a long-term sexual relationship" and become a "wife" – that is "to become the servant (slave) of a man?"[15] Filling in Hobbes's origin story, Pateman conjectures:

> At first women, who are as strong and capable as men, are able to ensure that sexual relations are consensual. When a woman becomes a mother and decides to become a lord and raise her child, her position changes; she is put at slight disadvantage against men, since now she has her infant to defend too. Conversely [the man] is able to defeat the woman he had initially to treat with as an equal.

In this way, "[e]ach man can obtain a 'family' of a woman servant and her child."[16] Thus "mother-right is overturned" and the state of nature

---

[12] Quoted in "God Hath," 64.
[13] Hobbes, *Leviathan*, quoted in ibid., 64.
[14] Ibid. See n. 30.   [15] Ibid., 64.
[16] Ibid., 65. Note that Hobbes never asserts directly that wives are subject to their husbands, as Nancy Hirschmann claims, but then she argues that women's subjection

becomes filled with patriarchal families. And, by the time the social contract is entered into, "all the women in the natural condition have been conquered by men and become servants."[17]

Families without women?

Pateman's conjecture seems convincing because it resonates with contemporary critiques of the family and because it seems to explain the "anomaly" of women's exclusion from the liberal polity. However, there are some very serious problems with it. Even if we assume that Hobbes equates families with (proto-)states, nevertheless his "families," "little bodies politic," and "confederations" are not male/female dyads, but are usually described as hierarchical relations *among men*. In *Leviathan*, to take one of many examples, a family is "a man and his children, or a man and his servants, or a man and his children, and his servants together, wherein the father or master is the sovereign."[18]

Thus a different feminist question might be to ask why women disappear. We could, for example, begin as Hobbes does by making men and women more or less equal in the state of nature, and agree that individuals form confederations for protection, and that those confederations are often created by conquest. However, it is far from the case that the "little bodies politic" Hobbes is thinking of are "families" in our sense of the term. Rather, I would argue, they are more like clans, held together by elite men and their male retainers. More importantly, in such confederations, all the benefits men gain from enslaving women in marriage (which in Pateman's account gives men the *desire to oppress*

is part of the "deep structure" of social contract theory. See Nancy J. Hirschmann, *Rethinking Obligation: A Feminist Method for Political Theory* (Ithaca, N.Y.: Cornell University Press, 1982).

17 Ibid. Hobbes uses both a "historical" analysis of state evolution (following Aristotle and Machiavelli) that states evolved from families and a "rational actor" or what Leo Strauss calls a "mechanistic" analysis to show why individuals might have chosen to submit themselves to the authority that most, if not all, groupings of more than one person imply. See Jean Hampton, *Hobbes and the Social Contract Tradition* (Cambridge: Cambridge University Press, 1986) and Gregory Kavka, *Hobbesian Moral and Political Theory* (Princeton, N.J.: Princeton University Press, 1986) for examples of recent work following the rational actor approach. See Leo Strauss, *The Political Philosophy of Hobbes: Its Basis and Genesis* (Chicago, Ill.: University of Chicago Press, 1936), for the argument that the two halves of Hobbes's theory are inconsistent. Hampton's view that the state is necessary for any society, combined with Hobbes's view that matrimonial laws are conventional, implies that authority in the state *precedes* the father's authority (as opposed to "meer lust") in the family.

18 *Leviathan*, 191. Pateman's point is not only that families are formed but that they are stabilized prior to civil society; but see note 17. If authority relations are always some mixture of coercion (or anticipated punishment) and consent, the issue is where on the spectrum does marriage – or do particular forms of marriage – fall?

women, namely control over sexual and domestic service, and the guarantee of heirs) can be gained without conquering women. Assuming (as the notion of "sex-right" does not) that women also desire sex, men could have fleeting sex with "free" women, then capture their children (who are, in Pateman's account, a burden to women in any case). With servants – male confederates, coerced or voluntary – and children, a master does not need to turn women's "help" with reproduction into permanent domestic servitude, as her service would be redundant.

This alternative narrative jibes more closely with Hobbes's repeated descriptions of families as groups primarily of men and of the master/ servant relation as a relation between males. It also fits Hobbes's view (despite his declaration that women in the state of nature are roughly equal to men in "strength" and "prudence") that men are "naturally fitter than women in actions of labor and danger,"[19] and the latter is significant, as defense is the primary purpose of the confederation as Hobbes defines it.

In this alternative account, gender domination in the state of nature is not a prerequisite to family formation: families exist not only without male domination, *but without women.* Hobbes does describe men as desiring power, which he defines in terms of service and respect from others, but the relevant "others" are men. If this narrative can be sustained, then the patriarchal assumption of sex-right is not foundational in Hobbes's social contract.[20]

Does conquest create authority?

Jean Hampton's account of sovereignty provides yet another way to sketch in Hobbes's troubling ellipsis. Hampton argues that the formation

---

[19] *Leviathan,* 250.

[20] I would argue that Hobbes is simply reflecting as natural the hierarchical patron–client world in which he lived, which was not yet a world in which reciprocal personal relations had been replaced by the "cash nexus." This also explains Hobbes's concern to maintain good manners and proper behavior between the "naturally" more authoritative (fathers, those with property or reputation) and those with less social weight, who are enjoined against being "sawcie" to their betters. Of course, Hobbes's positing of equality as an initial state responds to and disarms the egalitarian theories of the sectarians, whom he opposed. But see Christopher Hill, *The World Turned Upside Down: Radical Ideas during the English Revolution* (London: Penguin, 1972), for a discussion of the egalitarian ideas of the Puritans and sectarians and for an interesting comparison of Hobbes and the radical, Gerrard Winstanley, in "Hobbes and Winstanley: Reason and Politics," Appendix 1, 387–94. For Hobbes's anti-aristocratic bias against heroic virtue and the criticism that he is too "democratic" in his writing, see Strauss, *The Political Philosophy of Hobbes,* chapters 4 and 7; for a defense that Hobbes is thoroughly monarchist, see Quentin Skinner, *Reason and Rhetoric in the Philosophy of Hobbes* (Cambridge: Cambridge University Press, 1996).

of confederations (creating the "mature" state of nature) is a crucial step toward creating sovereignty, or legitimate political authority. In her account, Hampton also begins with Hobbes's egalitarian axiom of rough equality among all individuals. But this rough equality does not contradict the proposition that "differences in strength and intelligence enable some of them to do better in the state of war than others."[21] This is not a simple matter of coercion. Instead, Hampton describes the bargaining situation between the "less successful" inhabitants of the state of nature and the "more successful" one, whom Hampton calls the "sovereign-entrepreneur":

> This entrepreneur says, "Look, you're getting noplace on your own. But, if you join forces with me *and do my bidding* (so that I am your sovereign), then you will have more security than you now have." If the [weaker individual] does not accept the rather attractive looking positive incentive, he might also be "offered" the following negative incentive ... "Do my bidding or I will harm you!" And this threat would be real.[22]

At this early stage, as in Hobbes's notorious example of the "contract" between mother and child (the child accepts the care and protection of the mother, and therefore has tacitly assented to her authority), the power relations between the sovereign-entrepreneur and the potential member of the family/confederation are highly unequal, and any agreement on the part of the servant would most certainly be on the coercive rather than the consensual end of the spectrum.

However, this is not the final state of the negotiation between sovereigns and subjects in Hampton's view. As with the mothers and children, the relations between the sovereigns and subjects alter over time. Just as the mother must anticipate that the child will grow up and contend with her for power unless she makes an ally of him, so the ruler begins with a high degree of dominance over his subjects, yet, over time, their power relation shifts. Fearing he will lose the support of his subjects who could exit to another confederation or combine against him (contracts being unenforceable in the state of nature), the sovereign must add some positive incentives to his offer of protection in order to maintain his subjects' obedience. In Hampton's view, "the problem with an attempt to legitimate a regime via a coerced contract between sovereign and subject is that such an attempt will mistakenly *reverse* the power relationship between the people and the Ruler. Although a ruler may be able to dominate each individual physically ... for a while ... he can never physically dominate all of them."[23]

[21] Hampton, *Hobbes and the Social Contract Tradition*, 167.
[22] Ibid., 31.   [23] Ibid., 32.

The unexpected result is that "the sovereign gets power from the people."[24]

For our purposes, two important conclusions can be drawn from Hampton's account. First, *most individuals* – both women *and men* – become servants as the state of nature matures, so that, if anything can be said to be hidden behind the original myth of the social contract, it is *class*, not gender, oppression. The "heads of families" whose covenant establishes the social contract are the few (usually "but not alwayes" male) rulers ("masters"; "heads of families") who are left after the competition in the state of nature has made subjects ("servants") of most women – and men. Heads of families make the social contract because the mature state of nature is a condition of anarchic competition among confederations or ("families"), not individuals.

Second, Hobbes recognizes that master/servant relations are not natural but inherently unstable: "Master and Servant were not introduced by the consent of men," or by differences of Wit, as Aristotle had argued, but by force. The degree of conflict likely to exist between masters and servants depends in Hampton on the terms of exchange between them – with the ruler having to provide positive benefits to his subjects if he wishes to maintain his rulership. For Hobbes, this does not mean simply that all individuals are agents, but also that the self-assessment of subjects conditions the means by which they can be ruled: "[T]here are few so foolish, that had not rather governe themselves, than be governed by others ... If Nature have made men equall, that equalitie is to be acknowledged: or if Nature have made men unequall; yet because men that think themselves equall, will not enter into conditions of Peace, but upon Equall termes, such equalitie must be admitted."[25]

There are no "natural" justifications for one individual's rule over another, and relations established by conquest do not settle into permanent or even stable forms of obligation – at least among individuals who *think themselves equal*. If such individuals do not feel "equally treated," they "will not enter into conditions of Peace," and continually having to impose one's rulership by force is costly. In the state of nature, at least, the possibility of "exit"[26] also moderates the

---

[24] Ibid., 33. This is even more plausible if power can create benefits for confederates to share, rather than having authority be perceived simply as the institutionalization of dominance relations.

[25] *Leviathan.*

[26] For a discussion of exit and consent, see Albert O. Hirchmann, *Exit, Voice and Loyalty: Responses to Decline in Firms, Organizations and States* (Cambridge, Mass.: Harvard University Press, 1970).

behavior of rulers, and subjects, voluntary or conquered, are not totally powerless.

Thus a woman who was outwitted and overcome by a man because she was weakened by having to defend an infant would be under no obligation to stay under his rule. Once she had recovered her strength, the outcome (as between men) would again be decided by a contest of bodies and wills, that is (as Hobbes puts it), by "Battell." At one point she might win, becoming a sovereign herself and making the man a servant, a possibility Hobbes allows when he finds that heads of families have by and large "but not alwayes" been men, and when he argues that men may be subject to women, as husbands of queens are subject to the authority of their wives.

Or a woman could ally with her child in a confederation against the father, an outcome that is not implausible given Hobbes's understanding that the mother is the child's "lord." Or a woman could simply flee into the wild, where she would likely be importuned to join another confederation – perhaps a confederation of women. Hobbes entertains this possibility when he discusses the Amazons who "Contracted with the Men of the neighboring Countries, to whom they had recourse for issue, that the issue Male should be sent back, but the Female remain with themselves; so that the dominion of the Females was in the Mother."[27]

Pateman dismisses these possibilities on the grounds that "[I]n Hobbes's theory we do know who wins, and thus there is only one story to be told."[28] Yet, Pateman's story, as I have argued, is not Hobbes's and, as Hobbes did not write a history of families but a history of states, we can only speculate how it has "ended." In Hobbes's state of nature, "families" are (usually male-led) confederations for protection and benefits; the master/servant relation is not male/female but male/male; and there is no basis to argue, at least in the state of nature, that women, once conquered, are obliged to obey.

It was Hobbes's insight that all relations of authority (unchallenged power) have some element of consent. But he did not argue that conquest creates obligation. It is true that Hobbes says that "Convenants entered into by fear, in the condition of meer nature, are obligatory,"[29] implying that coerced "consent" can be obligatory. This is logically required by his argument that the social contract, which is agreed to

---

[27] *Leviathan*, 254. On the increasingly critical use of the term "Amazon" during the course of the eighteenth century, see G. J. Barker-Benfield, *The Culture of Sensibility* (Chicago, Ill.: University of Chicago Press, 1992), chap. 7. Of course, there is no "wild" in Hobbes's state of nature, only anarchy.
[28] "God Hath," 66. [29] Quoted in *The Social Contract*, 198.

because the contractors fear one another (not the sovereign), is binding in civil society. If contracts entered into in fear were never obligatory, the social contract itself would not be binding.

But this logical requirement does not mean that, in all cases, individuals must obey when they agree to perform from fear or harm. Hobbes also writes that, although an individual is obliged to honor a contract made under threat – for example, to give a thief what one has promised him at gunpoint – such obligations do not hold in civil society (that is, under law) unless the law so stipulates. And although all law is "positive" in Hobbes, so that the law of the sovereign cannot be questioned by calling on a higher standard of religious or natural law, there is nothing in Hobbes to suggest that positive law would be arbitrary or unjust, or that it would uphold the claims of highway robbers. Positive law in Hobbes's ideal civil society – a society in which sovereignty is absolutely internalized in every citizen – will conform to the principles of natural law.

In fact, Hobbes states explicitly that conquest alone cannot produce obligation: "No one is obliged because Conquered; that is to say, beaten, and taken, or put to flight; but because he commeth in, and submitteth to the victor."[30] Historically states have been formed by conquest and by agreement, but in both cases political authority does not exist until there is some form of consent.

Contracting and agency

It is important to remember that Hobbes's account of the social contract (as opposed to his conventional discussion of the evolution of states) is not historical but analytical, setting out the steps each individual would follow – if she thought about it consciously – to be able to obligate herself to the sovereign.[31] In Hobbes, people do not live and have never lived in the state of nature. They have historically always lived under some form of political authority. The problem Hobbes was addressing was that one of the most important historical supports to political

---

[30] *Leviathan*, 256. R. E. Ewin observes of Hobbes that "His insistence that not even subjects by conquest are slaves and his retention of the natural right to self-preservation suggest that we should, if possible, avoid reading him as making subjects into slaves. He has a proper distinction to make between conscience and private conscience" (*Virtues and Rights: The Moral Philosophy of Thomas Hobbes* [Boulder, Colo.: Westview Press, 1991], 48).

[31] Much of this argument is taken from Ewin, who argues that "Hobbes in fact employs a *reductio* argument about authority: He argues that authority . . . is necessary to human life, and he argues this by showing that authority is what distinguishes the radical form of man's natural condition from life in civil society and by showing that the radical form of man's natural condition is an impossibility" (*Virtues and Rights*, 101).

obligation – religious consensus – had broken down, and Hobbes was seeking a firmer, "rational" basis on which political order could be securely built. At the same time, individuals are also always subject to some forms of anarchy, as states are in anarchic relations with one another, and as travelers can be attacked by highway robbers where the law is not effectively enforced.[32]

It is Hobbes's view that if individuals better understood the nature of their choices, they would create more effective forms of political authority, as a mathematician understanding the principles of geometry can draw a better circle.[33] The point of effective political authority is not to create subjects who live in fear of the absolute sovereign but to create conditions of trust sufficient to allow individuals to act justly, that is to keep their promises to others without fear that they will be taken advantage of.

In imagining the social contract as that solution, and in making the keeping of contracts the highest good, Hobbes was not sufficiently concerned with the problem of unequal contracts. Perhaps he took for granted the social rules of the hierarchical society in which he lived, a world in which contracts had long been accepted as valid and even just, even when there were substantial differences in status and power between the contracting parties. Hobbes's egalitarian principle was not drawn from "life" but from geometry; as an element of Hobbes's rationalist understanding of the world it could not be contradicted by the "facts" of everyday life. It represented Hobbes's view that individuals are all, equally, "reckoning" or rational agents, despite their differing circumstances and experiences.

For Hobbes, the problem of authority comes first, not to ensure that some can dominate others, but because it makes all forms of society possible. The more secure, the more rational, understood, and accepted are the foundations of political authority, the more justice can be expected, both in the way sovereigns relate to subjects and individuals to one another. Under civil society properly constructed, natural laws (the

[32] In Ewin's formulation,

> It is not that there was a state of nature that we have somehow left, with all the traditional problems about how we might have left it; there still is a state of nature in which we live as well as a civil society in which we live. The state of nature is not simply a condition of the world; it is a sort of relationship, and a relationship in which the terms can change. (Ibid., 103)

[33] Much depends on understanding Hobbes's method which, Ewin argues, is rationalist, not empiricist, based on the principles of geometry. The contract is not the empirical cause of the state – states have historically been formed in many ways just as circles can be drawn and are created in nature in a myriad of ways. But the contract is the model of authority, just as geometry can tell what a circle is – and also how to draw one. See *Virtues and Rights*, 1–3 and *passim*.

norms by which individuals act toward each other, and which Hobbes puts forth in some detail in Chapters 14 and 15 of *Leviathan*) bind "in foro externo" as well as "in foro interno,"[34] that is, in behavior as well as in conscience.

Hobbes can be criticized, as Leo Strauss does, for so narrowing his concept of citizenship that it becomes practically meaningless.[35] But Strauss's argument is anti-democratic and anti-egalitarian, and thus should not be employed without due care in any feminist critique of Hobbes. I would argue instead that Hobbes be viewed in the light of recent revisionist scholarship as attempting to create a version of politics based on individual human agency and yet capable of peace – a difficult challenge in a world that could no longer rely on faith and custom as the accepted bases of political authority.[36] For Hobbes to exclude women from citizenship would have required him to exclude women from human agency, and this he emphatically does not do.

Contracts and agency

Pateman's critique of contract focuses on the events prior to the social contract – women's defeat in the state of nature – but is directed at contracting itself. The fact that political authority is established *by contract* makes the idea of a social contract itself suspect. Conquest is declared consent, but by men alone (who make the social contact) and not by the women who are not present at the creation.

However, women are not foundationally excluded from the social contract in Hobbes. His version leaves out most women (and most men) contingently, but not categorically: *"for the most part,"* fathers not mothers established historical Common-wealths, implying that some-times women do "make" commonwealths and women have been and can be rulers. Because women are not categorically excluded, they are no different from most men, who historically have not been "heads of

---

[34] *Leviathan*, 215.

[35] Strauss, *The Political Philosophy of Hobbes*.

[36] See, for example, revisionist work by Ewin, *Virtues and Rights*; Deborah Baumgold, *Hobbes's Political Theory* (Cambridge: Cambridge University Press, 1988); S. A. Lloyd, *Ideals as Interests in Hobbes's Leviathan* (Cambridge: Cambridge University Press, 1992); Mary G. Dietz, "Hobbes's Subject as Citizen," in *Thomas Hobbes and Political Theory*, ed. Dietz (Lawrence, Kans.: University Press of Kansas, 1990); David Johnston, *The Rhetoric of Leviathan: Thomas Hobbes and the Politics of Cultural Transformation* (Princeton, N.J.: Princeton University Press, 1987); David Boonin-Vail, *Thomas Hobbes and the Science of Moral Virtue* (Cambridge: Cambridge University Press, 1994); and Quentin Skinner, *Reason and Rhetoric*. For a feminist critique that is more sympathetic to Hobbes, see Kathleen B. Jones, *Compassionate Authority: Democracy and the Representation of Women* (New York: Routledge, 1993).

families" (as Hobbes describes those who make the social contract). No less than the majority of men, who are also servants, women have standing and can make contracts; they are equally "individuals" in Hobbes's sense. The social contract does not make men "public" and women "private."

On the contrary, Hobbes directly challenges the arguments that were traditionally used to bar women from citizenship and public life. By finding women equal to men in "strength and prudence," Hobbes denies both classical opinion and the views of his contemporaries who argued that women cannot be citizens because they lack reason, because they are too passionate or variable. Unlike Descartes, Hobbes is a consistent materialist; he finds the passions necessary to reason and does not separate the mind from the body. Using Hobbes, feminists can argue that women are in no way naturally or morally disqualified from citizenship. As important, in my view, Hobbes's materialism rejected witchcraft as a natural phenomenon, and he does not find that women have magical or feminine powers that should be feared and therefore controlled.[37]

Yet, contracts can mask power asymmetries, and the case might be made that Hobbes's individualist assumptions conflict with his own recognition that actual relations among individuals are often hierarchical. The marriage contract is thus only the most egregious example of asymmetrical power legitimized by "consent." It can also be argued, however, that by positing equality Hobbes's contract theory creates a new norm: equality between the contracting parties becomes the ideal against which practice must be measured.

Some have found contract theory problematic because it is a form of "rights" theory. They argue that contractual understandings of social relations deny important values such as familial love, altruism, or connectedness. This is what John Hardwig maintains when he says that the category of rights is not an appropriate ethical category for healthy personal relationships and why Carol Gilligan succeeded in opening up a new discussion of political possibilities when she opposed the Western "ethic of rights" to a feminist "ethic of care."[38]

But Hobbes does not suggest reducing all personal relations to contract, and I do not see this as the point of Pateman's critique. Rather,

---

[37] The case that military service should be considered in addition to property as a qualification for citizenship is argued, for example, in the Putney debates of Cromwell's New Model Army; *Leviathan*, Chapter XIV.

[38] John Hardwig, "Should Women Think in Terms of Rights?" in *Feminism and Political Theory*, ed. Cass Sunstein (Chicago, Ill.: University of Chicago Press, 1990), 55. For an insightful effort to apply this reasoning to politics, see Joan C. Tronto, *Moral Boundaries: A Political Argument for an Ethic of Care* (New York: Routledge, 1993).

like Nancy Hartsock in her critique of exchange,[39] I think Pateman's quarry is *capitalist* social relations and contract connects capitalism and liberal theory.

In *The Sexual Contract*, Pateman quotes William Thompson, a nineteenth-century critic, who satirized the "moral miracle" of marriage, which "reduce[s] the two identities [of husband and wife] to one." Thompson wrote that the marriage contract was an "audacious falsehood":

> A contract! where are any of the attributes of contracts, of equal and just contracts, to be found in this transaction? A contract implies the voluntary assent of both the contracting parties. Can even both the parties, man and woman, by agreement alter the terms, as to *indissolubility* and *inequality*, of this pretended contract? No. Can any individual man divest himself, were he so inclined, of his power of despotic control? He cannot. Have women been consulted as to the terms of this pretended contract?[40]

Commenting, Pateman says that Thompson's book "laid the foundation for subsequent feminist criticism of marriage" and that Thompson placed little weight on a proper contract as the solution to the problems of conjugal relations:

> In this respect, his argument differs ... from John Stuart Mill's much better known *The Subjection of Women*. According to Thompson, political rights for women and an end to the economic system of individual competition (capitalism) are the crucially important changes that are needed. Only political rights can bring an end to the "*secrecy* of domestic wrongs," and free relations between the sexes will be possible only within a social order based on "labour by mutual co-operation" or co-operative socialism.[41]

But following Thompson's argument could produce the opposite conclusion. In the paragraph Pateman quotes, Thompson can be seen as defending the *ideal* of contract and as criticizing the marriage contract for its failure to live up to its promises. Contracts reflect power relations, but contract theory does not justify dominance. Hobbes aligns his theory of contract to a theory of individualism that is radically egalitarian,

---

[39] Nancy Hartsock, *Money, Sex and Power: Towards a Feminist Materialism* (Boston: Northeastern University Press, 1984). The argument that Hobbes is the theorist of capitalist social relations is made most forcefully by C. B. Macpherson in *The Political Theory of Possessive Individualism* (London: Oxford University Press, 1962). For a historical critique of both Macpherson's and Strauss's characterization of Hobbes as "bourgeois," see Keith Thomas, "The Social Origins of Hobbes's Political Thought," in *Hobbes Studies*, ed. K. C. Brown (Cambridge, Mass.: Harvard University Press, 1965). 185–236. See also Alan Ryan, "Hobbes and Individualism," in *Perspectives on Thomas Hobbes*, eds. G. A. J. Rogers and Alan Ryan (Oxford: Clarendon Press, 1988), 81–106.

[40] William Thompson, quoted in *The Sexual Contract*, 157.

[41] *The Sexual Contract*, 156.

challenging all claims of "natural" dominance. Thus the hypocrisy of actual contracts, as the quote from Thompson shows, only serves to make the ideal of contract that much more compelling.

If that is so, however, why have contracts, and particularly the marriage contract, done such disservice to women? Hampton's account of the negotiation between the sovereign/entrepreneur and the subject suggests some possible answers, forcing us to look beyond the "conjuring trick" of contract to the history of the ongoing negotiations of gender relations in different cultural and historical contexts. It is not contract, one can argue, but such factors as custom, anti-egalitarian social norms, kinship obligations, the availability of social alternatives to marriage for women, and even the belief that women should not be able to contract – that must be brought to bear to understand the power relations of gender.[42]

The conditions of consent depend in no small part on the views held by women themselves. As Hobbes argues, to take away self-government from those who think of themselves as equal invites resistance and is a "threat to peace." Consent to authority, even *de facto* authority, is not maintained because the ruler uses force on a daily basis, but because subjects have developed habits of obedience; or because their obedience is reinforced by ideological or religious faith – or because they do not believe themselves to be equal. Hobbes does take women as "equal," that is, as rational agents. A critique of contract alone is inadequate to explain women's subjection in families or in states.

In the state of nature, and in Pateman's account, women are "born free." But the question of why women would choose marriage over freedom is not relevant to women's real world choices; the important issue is how they negotiate their interests within the cultural context of "marriage."

The seventeenth century: changing the context changes the contract

Historians appear to agree that the origins of the modern family, of capitalist economic organization, and of liberal theory can be traced to the seventeenth and early eighteenth centuries, and that these changes had immense consequences for women. The irony is that, as men gained greater political and economic freedoms, wives were increasingly bound more tightly to their husbands, legally and economically, and to an

[42] For an extended discussion of the range of marriage "contracts" in the Third World today, for example, see Maila Kabeer, *Reversed Realities: Gender Hierarchies in Development Thought* (London: Verso, 1994), chap. 5.

emerging ideological concept of the middle-class family. This increased their power in the expanding "private" sphere, while making them more dependent on their husbands and increasingly isolating them from both the public sphere economy as well as from political life.[43]

Rather than argue that the Enlightenment, like the Renaissance, represents a further step backward for women,[44] I would like to suggest that, despite the increasing patriarchalism of family life, the changes taking place in the seventeenth century altered gender relations significantly in ways that eventually made it possible for women to argue for their equal rights. Further, women were far from passive in bringing about these changes. For most women (in England at this time, though the middle-class family eventually becomes a widely accepted ideal), the emerging form of "companionate" marriage, emphasizing the nuclear family and giving women increasing moral and management power in the domestic sphere, represented an improvement, not a loss, over earlier marriage forms, and one that also responded to new economic imperatives.[45]

One of the most remarkable changes that began in the seventeenth century was the moral repositioning of women, the beginning of the transformation of women from morally dangerous "others": temptresses, viragos or witches, to the nineteenth-century "angel of the house." As noted, the mid-seventeenth-century family was patriarchal, with men at its moral center, but the change was that the family itself was a critical space in which citizens were molded, and over time women moved into the central moral role as the family became increasingly characterized by ties of affection.[46] The seventeenth century

---

[43] See, for example, Gordon J. Schochet, *Patriarchalism in Political Thought* (New York: Basic Books, 1975) and Levin L. Schucking, *The Puritan Family* (London: Routledge, 1969).

[44] Hill, *The World Turned Upside Down*. The reference to women and the Renaissance is from Joan Kelly's essay in *Women, History, and Theory* (Chicago: University of Chicago Press, 1984), 19–50. See also Pamela Joseph Benson, *The Invention of the Renaissance Woman: The Challenge of Female Independence in the Literature and Thought of Italy and England* (University Park: Pennsylvania State University Press, 1992); Constance Jordan, *Renaissance Feminism* (Ithaca, N.Y.: Cornell University Press, 1991); and Ian MacLean, *The Renaissance Notion of Woman* (Cambridge: Cambridge University Press, 1980).

[45] Amy Louise Erickson, *Women and Property in Early Modern England* (London: Routledge, 1995). For the view that the seventeenth century represents a sea change in women's status and roles, see Shari L. Thurer, *The Myths of Motherhood: How Culture Reinvents the Good Mother* (London: Penguin, 1994).

[46] Although she does not subscribe to the view that there was a "progressive evolution in family emotion," referring to the thesis most prominently argued by Lawrence Stone in *The Family, Sex and Marriage in England, 1500–1800* (London: Weidenfeld and Nicolson, 1977), Erickson does argue that women continued to manage property and to defend their interests through marriage contracts and concludes that legal changes

also marks the beginning of "civility" as a norm of public and private life.[47]

Nancy Armstrong and Catherine Belsey suggest some of the consequences of the shift to what became the "middle-class" and ultimately universalized model of the family. As Armstrong shows, the new "domestic woman" of the late seventeenth- and eighteenth-century conduct books was the harbinger of the new middle-class ideal. This domestic ideal "succeeded where Defoe's island kingdom had failed. It established a private economy apart from the forms of rivalry and dependency that organized the world of men."[48]

Further, the "new language of the household acquired a power akin to that of natural law."[49] Conduct books also offered "self-transformation" and, with it, upward mobility. The key to this change was women as decision-makers, as agents, but within a world that valued self-mastery, frugality, and self-control. In Armstrong's analysis, self regulation became the measure of moral action, and women set the standard: "the domestic woman executes her role in the household by regulating her own desire."[50]

Armstrong's narrative suggests that women in the household were far from marginalized as economic actors. Yet this transformation had its costs. "Women as subjects f[ound] a place – in the home, in the bosom of the family," but at the cost of "their exclusion from the political," as Catherine Belsey observes.[51] After 1660, the family became "a privileged realm of retreat from the public world increasingly perceived as hostile and alien." The "depoliticization of the family" excluded power relations in the family from political analysis. Yet "to have a place in discourse, even a domestic one, to have a subject-position from which to speak, however inadequate, is to be able to protest."[52]

G. J. Barker-Benfield makes a parallel case, recounting the rise of "sentiments" (by the eighteenth century) as a measure of moral virtue,

may not be an adequate representation of women's status, as legal reforms over the last two centuries have not changed women's wages, the proportion of women who are poor, "and the same majority of single parents as women in early modern England, living in a radically different ideological world" (236).

[47] For an extended discussion, see Barker-Benfield, *The Culture of Sensibility.*

[48] Nancy Armstrong, "The Rise of the Domestic Woman," in *The Ideology of Conduct: Essays in Literature and the History of Sexuality,* eds. Nancy Armstrong and Leonard Tennenhouse (New York: Methuen, 1987), 96. See also Peter Stallybrass and Alison White, *The Politics and Poetics of Transgression* (Ithaca, N.Y.: Cornell University Press, 1986).

[49] Armstrong, "Rise of the Domestic Woman," 113.

[50] Ibid., 120.

[51] Catherine Belsey, *The Subject of Tragedy: Identity and Difference in Renaissance Drama* (London: Routledge, 1985), 192.

[52] Ibid., 193.

and documenting the "reformation of male manners" away from the public executions, bear baiting, swearing and "voiding" in public, and wife-beating at home. The domestication of men and the feminization of public life would change the content of public and private, but at a cost, as the seventeenth-century model of gender equality, the mind as a "tabula rasa," gave way to a belief in innate sexual differences. Women came to be seen as more moral, but more "delicate" than men; more capable of sentiment and feeling, but less "rational" and thus less suited for the harsh realities of economic and political life.[53] Whatever the costs and benefits, however, my point is that the context changes, and with it the meaning of marriage and the sexual contract. It was not the social contract, but the "cult of sentimentality" and women's power in the home that legitimized the division between public and private in the ways we now lament, even as we remain compelled by Rousseau's construction of gender difference. Belsey, Armstrong, and Barker-Benfield help us understand the mystery of why women might choose to become (Rousseauian) "wives." They suggest why women were the subjects as well as objects of marriage contracts, not passive victims or misled by a liberal theory of contract that promised them agency but made them slaves.

Conclusion

I have tried to show that key elements of Pateman's theory that women are foundationally excluded from the social contract can be questioned, at least as her theory is applied to Hobbes. I also argue that contracts do not exist outside the "web of social relations" but within historical, political, and economic contexts. What contract provides indispensably is a strong commitment to individual agency and a clear indication of what justice in a dynamic society requires: equality, choice, negotiation. Contract theory does not deny community but calls on members actively to create it. With Jean Hampton I would argue that love (or altruism) and contracts are not oppositions. Understanding the role of contract in emotional commitments makes it possible to maintain them and develop trust.[54]

It is Hobbes's stern gender egalitarianism, not Locke's soft patriarch-

---

[53] Barker-Benfield, *The Culture of Sensibility*, xviii and *passim*.

[54] See Martha Nussbaum's review of Jean Hampton's essay in Louise M. Antony and Charlotte Winn, *A Mind of One's Own: Essays on Reason and Objectivity* in the *New York Review of Books*, October 20, 1994, 59–63. See also Susan Okin's commentary on Roberto Unger's critique of contract as incompatible with family life in Susan Moller Okin, *Justice, Gender and the Family* (New York: Basic Books, 1989), 117–24.

alism or Rousseau's romanticized version of sex difference, that has proven foundationally critical to women's subsequent claims to equal rights in all spheres, not least in the broadened and deepened political arena that Locke's and Rousseau's criticisms of Hobbes helped to create. Far from being foundationally established, women's oppression is recreated daily and must be challenged daily by women, who must "think themselves equal" – even when they choose to use their power to pursue agendas based on difference.

Acknowledgments

This chapter is part of a larger project on theories of power in the work of Machiavelli and Hobbes. My deep thanks to Hilda Smith for her detailed comments on the manuscript and to those who attended the conference for their contributions to the discussion. I take full responsibility for the errors that remain.

10 The significant sounds of silence: the absence of women from the political thought of Sir Robert Filmer and John Locke (or, "Why can't a woman be more like a man?")

Gordon Schochet

The subjection of women and their exclusion from civic membership and social significance played important, but largely implicit, roles in the patriarchal political theory of Sir Robert Filmer, the mid-seventeenth-century apologist for Stuart absolutism. His theory rested upon an extremely oppressive, patriarchal conception of familial authority, and, accordingly, there is something puzzling about the fact that Filmer said little explicitly about the status of women. He argued from a divinely ordained inferiority of women manifested in their natural status as wives and the equally natural and divine subjection of children and servants to their natural, male superiors – husbands, fathers, and masters – to the divinely natural and patriarchal character of politics. Kings, he insisted, and others in authority, rule by a natural, patriarchal entitlement instituted by God before the expulsion of Adam and Eve from Paradise. Although children and servants appear frequently in his reasoning, Sir Robert's theory was constructed with hardly any mention of women.

Filmer's relative indifference toward women invites two related inferences, which, together, diminish the puzzlement: first, that – however unwittingly – Filmer accepted the practices and beliefs of his society and tacitly built his theory upon these conventions, and second, that the exclusion by silence effectively rendered women invisible in his scheme. The family, of course – pun and all – is inconceivable without women, so the result of Filmer's silence is a powerful paradox in which the central and foundational figures are effectively ignored. Women are not even off-stage characters; they are altogether missing.

John Locke, the latter-day respondent to Filmer's patriarchalism, had rather more to say about women. His comments enhanced their status within the household: he granted them considerable authority over servants, at least gave them a share of the power over children, and defended their right to divorce. But like Filmer, Locke did not call for the inclusion of women in the political community (which, for the most part, he termed "civil society," thereby sowing the seeds of interpretative confusion among later generations); also like Filmer, he was relatively silent about their general social status. He left women pretty much as he had found them in Stuart society, but through a shift in the focus of politics from the patriarchal *father* to the rational, rights-bearing *individual* – who remained an adult male – Locke created the theoretical possibility of full political membership for women. That move, to be sure, was not to be made until many years after the publication of the *Two Treatises*, and Locke's having prepared the way for it was preceded by an astoundingly radical assertion by Thomas Hobbes about female status that ascribed male dominance to convention rather than to God or nature but, at the same time, embraced the patriarchal structure championed by Filmer.[1]

In the end, it was the anti-Filmerian perspective of Locke that prevailed, not the conventional absolutism of Hobbes. Certainly, Locke's substitution of a political voluntarism rooted in individual rights for Filmer's irresistible and divinely ordained state was a crucial step toward the development of modern understandings of justice and politics. Without Locke – or at least without that particular shift – late twentieth-century discussions of authority, rights, and the status of women would be very different from what they are today.

I shall discuss the differences between Filmer and Locke on the question of the social and civil status of women as well as some aspects of the contemporary continuation of that debate. The extension of effective, participating membership in society to classes of people who have traditionally been excluded – most prominently for present purposes, women – is among the urgent concerns of the modern world. In Anglo-American societies, the derogated status of women is a lingering manifestation of the perspectives championed by Sir Robert Filmer. So considered, the historical question of Locke's attack on patriarchalism is no more significant than the implications of that attack for the twentieth century. Traditional patriarchalism, grounded as it is in

---

[1] I have discussed this aspect of Hobbes in a number of previous publications: "Thomas Hobbes on the Family and the State of Nature," *Political Science Quarterly* 82 (1967): 427–45; *Patriarchalism in Political Thought* (Oxford: Blackwell, 1975; 2nd ed.: New Brunswick: Transaction Books, 1988), chaps. 9 and 12; "Intending (Political) Obligation: Hobbes on the Voluntary Basis of Society," in *Thomas Hobbes and Political Theory*, ed. Mary Dietz (Lawrence, Kans.: University Press of Kansas, 1990); and "De l'idée de sujétion naturelle à l'indifférenciation par convention," in *Encyclopédia politique et historique des femmes: Europe, Amérique du nord*, ed. Christine Fauré (Paris: University Press of France, 1997).

Filmer and seventeenth-century patriarchal political thought, is among the progenitors of the world we are seeking to overthrow.[2]

In addition, this chapter addresses the history of political thought and the ways it should be approached, analyzed, and *used*. I am especially concerned to argue that there are important connections among abstract political theory, lower-level and perhaps even unarticulated and unappreciated ideology, and the arrangements and practices that characterize a society.[3] Political theory has always been about the standards to which political practice is to be held accountable. Politics involves domination and the imposition of will, and political theory is the ideological and intellectual criticism and justification of that domination.

I

All discussions of the place of women in early modern political thought must now be indebted to Carole Pateman, who, in *The Sexual Contract* and other, related publications, has made the subject very much her own.[4] This chapter is often constructed as a dialogue with Pateman, not so much with her analyses of Locke and Filmer as with her conclusion about the apparently irreducibly patriarchal nature of contractual thinking. Pateman contends that there are two steps presupposed by social contract theorizing: the founding of society by the conquest and the permanent subjugation of women and, next, an agreement among fathers of families to form civil or political society (the state).

The very idea of social contract, according to Pateman, irremediably

---

[2] In a fascinating new study, *Founding Mothers and Fathers: Gendered Power and the Forming of American Society* (New York: Knopf, 1996), Mary Beth Norton uses Filmerian and Lockean categories as tropes to contrast what she sees as the familial-based culture of seventeenth-century New England with the contractual society of the Chesapeake.

[3] While I do not want here to defend a *strong* version of this claim, I think that it can be argued that political theory is generally an ideational reaction to and sometimes even a reflection of – with varying degrees of accuracy – the institutional and structural politics of the world it inhabits. It is also true that political theory sometimes *leads* those structures and institutions and is ultimately responsible for their being preserved or changed. The relationship between "theory and practice," as it were, is notoriously complex, and it would be foolhardy to attempt to deal with it any further in this context.

[4] Carole Pateman, *The Sexual Contract* (Stanford, Calif.: Stanford University Press, 1988). See also some of the essays collected in her *The Disorder of Women: Democracy, Feminism, and Political Theory* (Cambridge: Polity Press, 1989); the "Afterword" to the 2nd edition of her *The Problem of Political Obligation: A Critique of Liberal Theory* (Berkeley, Calif.: University of California Press, 1985); Pateman, "Introduction: the Theoretical Subversiveness of Feminism," in *Feminist Challenges: Social and Political Theory*, eds. Pateman and Elizabeth Gross (Boston: Northeastern University Press, 1989); and Pateman, "'God Hath Ordained to Man a Helper': Hobbes, Patriarchy and Conjugal Right," reprinted in *Feminist Interpretations and Political Theory*, eds. Mary Lyndon Shanley and Pateman (University Park, Pa.: Pennsylvania State University Press, 1991).

rests upon the exclusion of women; Henry Sumner Maine's classic account of a movement "from status to contract" – from conditions into which we are born to situations in which we determine those conditions – describes the emancipation of men, who are (still) the only members of civil society. Early modern appeals to contractual thinking, then, covered patriarchalism with a patina of voluntarism that disguised the conceptual impossibilities of extending full civil status to women.

While I agree with much of Pateman's analysis, I do not accept the impossibility of women's being comprehended by the voluntarism of modern, so-called "liberal" political theory. Quite the contrary: my concluding argument is that it is precisely that Lockean voluntarism in a radically different, modernized context opens up the concept "person" and makes possible political membership and significance beyond the narrow realm of white males.

Filmer's theories stand as a significant measure of how far we have come since the seventeenth century. Even though he had little directly to say about women, female inferiority was thoroughly embedded in his political outlook. With Filmer as an ideological point of departure, we can begin to comprehend the steps that were necessary before women could emerge from their subordination in the traditional, western European household.

The status of women in the political thought of seventeenth-century England is here treated from the perspective of ideological analysis in two senses: as lower-level, non-theoretical, and often unwitting prejudice and as thought or doctrine that is related to political, economic, legal, and other forms of social structure. My intention is to suggest parallels between intellectual and social history without derogating either by "reducing" one to the other, for the historical study of social and political thought ought to bear a direct relationship to social history. But that relationship has been difficult to establish, given conflicts between the perspectives and concerns of social and intellectual historians. Those differences all too frequently become debates about the extent to which ideas "reflect" and/or are "caused" by "underlying" social forms. This is not simply a dispute between Marxists and their critics so much as it is a continuing consequence of the ambiguous status of the study of ideas and ideology within historical, literary, and social studies.

We know that the social roles of and statuses occupied by women have changed since the seventeenth century and that attitudes toward women have undergone drastic alterations as well. At the same time – even as historians, social scientists, and political theorists – we do not know very much about the ways in which these changes occurred or what they have (or had) to do with the political theories of Filmer and Locke. This is that very troublesome area in which the histories of political theory and what we loosely call ideology meet; changes in and persistence among "discursive structures" – so popular now among historians of political thought, who often call their new study "the history of political discourse" – will not, by themselves, reveal the full story.[5]

Histories of discourse must understand the process of ideational change; otherwise, they are nothing more than highly abstract and narrowly antiquarian accounts of reconstructed thought. But moving beyond this self-justifying historicism requires that histories of ideas be informed by social structural history and joined to judgments about the kinds of societal changes to which ideological alterations are related. Ideas, and especially political ideas, are not free-floating speculations; nor do they merely address other (sets of) ideas. All ideas are artifacts in important and irreducible senses; social and political ideas are precisely about preserving or changing political, social, and legal arrangements and systems. They are action-implicated even when they are shaped as analyses and criticisms of other ideas. To appreciate the actions contemplated by political ideas, it is necessary to understand the political arrangements to which those ideas are (or were) addressed and to know what is (or was) at stake in the debates to which they are (or were) contributions.

Placing the doctrines of Filmer and Locke against the background of Stuart society allows us to appreciate what little they actually did say about women as well as to grasp the significance of those very large silences. We may presume where they said nothing, either that they were content tacitly to endorse prevailing practices or that they were oblivious to the presuppositions from which they argued.

My analysis is largely theoretical, gives preeminence to Filmer, and argues that his conceptualization defines the ideological context against which Locke's treatment of women is most readily understood. Pateman has made the case that Locke failed to address the strictures imposed on women by Filmer; she further argues that their conclusions about women come to much the same thing. I am rather more forgiving of

---

[5] For the purposes of this chapter, I am assuming a compatibility – asserted but not here examined – among the historical studies of what are called "political thought," "political ideas," and "political discourse." I realize that for some, each of these terms suggests a different kind of emphasis and conceptual orientation and, further, that the growing popularity of "discourse" – where it is not bare imitation of literary analysis – is intended to underscore the linguistic and "conversational" nature of the subject. Nonetheless, all three share a core subject matter. More important, however, is my stylistic goal of varying the words I use; my usage should not be construed as conceptual bluff or prestidigitation.

Locke's failure and see greater contrasts between their positions than she does.

The difference between Filmer and Locke is rendered even sharper when it is recalled that Hobbes generally reached the same conclusions about the ordering of society as Filmer but from a thoroughly conventional understanding of the social and political worlds. This move would later, somewhat ironically, open the door to the inclusion of women in the polity.[6] Locke accepted the political part of Hobbes's conventionalism. His view of familial relationships, on the other hand, was based on a mixture of conventionalism and divine institution, which shifted the discussion away from the *power* of rulers (parents, fathers in particular) to the *entitlements* and needs of subjects (children), for whose benefit God instituted familial authority. Yet, he ignored the larger issue of women's civic identity outside the household.

II

While he was not particularly profound or complex, Filmer was virtually alone in his understanding of the fact that the foundations of English society and social structure were being challenged. As Peter Laslett shrewdly observed, "Filmer, for all his brash naivety and his obviously amateur outlook, was that extremely rare phenomenon – the codifier of conscious and unconscious prejudice."[7] And he seems to have grasped this situation before anyone else did, but his was precisely the sort of defense that raises foundations to the level of consciousness and therefore opens them to debate. Filmer made this move at a time of the expanding dissemination of ideas through print media[8] and thus contributed to the magnification of the speed and intensity with which the public debate took place. Once something is in print and available for

---

[6] This is the part of my argument that stands in sharpest contrast to Pateman, who claims that conventionalist – or, in the terminology that she prefers, contractual – thinking is built upon the exclusion of women, which it retains, perpetuates, and even intensifies precisely because, in the third case, it adds the protective covering of voluntarism.

[7] Peter Laslett, Introduction to Sir Robert Filmer, *Patriarcha and Other Political Works*, ed. Laslett, Blackwell's Political Texts (Oxford: Blackwell, 1949), 41. All references to Filmer, unless otherwise indicated, will be to this edition, cited only by the name of the individual work itself.

[8] On the important issue of the social consequences of what is increasingly called "print culture," the pioneering work of Elizabeth Eisenstein, *The Printing Press as an Agent of Change: Communications and Cultural Transformations in Early Modern Europe*, 2 vols. (Cambridge: Cambridge University Press, 1979), remains the starting point. For mid- to late seventeenth-century England, see Lois G. Schwoerer, "Liberty of the Press and Public Opinion, 1660–1695," in *Liberty Secured? Britain before and after 1688*, ed. J. R. Jones, The Making of Modern Freedom (Stanford: Stanford University Press, 1992). There is no comprehensive study for the Civil War and Interregnum periods.

discussion, its components become more sharply defined, debated, and challenged. In a sense, then, Filmer unintentionally gave rise to the discussion that would ultimately subvert the traditional patriarchal household that he set out to defend.

We cannot establish a direct relationship either between Filmer and the social structural beliefs of Stuart England or between those beliefs and Filmer's assumptions. The most we can say is that the ideas and the structure supported one another. When we reach the ineradicably ideological component of Filmer's political thought, it is difficult to determine precisely what he believed, and we must resort to inference. Thus, unless there is a reason to the contrary, we must be permitted to *presume* that he accepted the standards and practices of his society.[9] In that society, widows and daughters were allowed to inherit[10] but were considered "*to bee one person*" with their husbands,[11] who represented them to the outside world, a relationship that William Blackstone, more than 100 years later, would call "coverture."[12] Although women were not in Parliament, the law provided for queens regnant, and England had twice been ruled by a queen in the sixteenth century.

Filmer never commented on this apparent anomaly and referred to Elizabeth's and Mary's gender only once, noting that they, "by reason of

---

[9] However, in two works that have been omitted from the Filmerian canon since the seventeenth century – *An Advertisement to the Jurymen of England, Touching Witches; Together with a Difference Between a Hebrew and an English Witch* (London, 1652) and *Quaestio Quodlibiteca: or, A Discourse Whether It May Be Lawful to Take Use for Money* (London, 1653) – Sir Robert did challenge prevailing doctrines. In the first – rather uncharacteristically if his political writings are the standard – he substituted reason for biblical superstition and denied that the accused witches of his day satisfied the requirements of the Hebrew Bible; in the second, he defended the charging of interest for loans.

[10] See *The Lawes Resolutions of Womens Rights: or, The Laws Provision for Women* (London, 1632), 9–10. This work is generally but erroneously attributed to one "T.E.," who signed the Preface in which he (presumably) said, "By whom this following Discourse was Composed I certainly know not" (sig. Ar). For a general discussion of *The Lawes Resolutions*, see W. R. Prest, "Law and Women's Rights in Early Modern England," *The Seventeenth Century*, 6, 2 (Autumn 1991): 169–87. Authorship and the identity of "T.E." are discussed on pp. 172–75.

[11] *The Lawes Resolutions*, 116; see also 119.

[12] By marriage, the husband and wife are one person in law: that is, the very being or legal existence of the woman is suspended during the marriage, or at least is incorporated and consolidated into that of the husband: under whose wing, protection, and *cover*, she performs every thing; and is therefore called in our law-french a *feme-covert*; is said to be *covert-baron*, or under the protection and influence of her husband, her *baron*, or lord; and her condition during her marriage is called her *coverture*. (William Blackstone, *Commentaries on the Laws of England* [1765–1769], I, 15, §III; text from the facsimile ed. by Stanley N. Katz, 4 vols. [Chicago: University of Chicago Press, 1979], I, 430)
(A portion of this same, well-known passage is quoted by Pateman, *Sexual Contract*, 91.)

their sex, being not fit for public assemblies," stopped the practice of formally meeting with Parliament.[13] Elizabeth was often mentioned, but Mary hardly at all, perhaps because she was Roman Catholic. Thus, Filmer was not nearly so extreme as the Presbyterian reformer John Knox who, in 1558, had railed against what he called "the Monstrous Regiment of Women." "To promote a woman to bear rule, superiority, dominion or empire above any realm, nation or city is repugnant to nature," Knox declared, "contumely to God, a thing most contrarious to His revealed will and approved ordinance, and finally it is the subversion of good order, of all equity and justice."[14] These words could easily have been written by Filmer, but he avoided the entire matter, apparently content simply to presume that women were like children and servants in their lack of civil status. The only roles for women that Filmer's argument appears to allow are wife and mother, and it is the latter that makes fatherhood possible. Thus, it is not unreasonable – especially from the perspective of the twentieth century – to conclude with Carole Pateman that, despite his explicit silence on that matter, "The genesis of political power [for Filmer] lies in Adam's sex-right or conjugal-right, not in his fatherhood. Adam's political title is granted *before* he becomes a father."[15]

Filmer's world was patriarchally structured and presumed the inherent, natural inferiority of women.[16] But the derogation or suppression of women was not an overt, intentional part of Filmer's design.[17] Rather, it

[13] Filmer, *The Freeholder's Grand Inquest, Touching Our Soveraigne Lord the King and His Parliament* (1648), 154. Cf. pp. 163 and 178, where Filmer specifically referred to the "duty ... to obey the Queen" and to Elizabeth's warning to Parliament "not to meddle with the Queen's Person."

[14] John Knox, *The First Blast of the Trumpet against the Monstrous Regiment of Women* (1558), as reprinted in Knox, *On Rebellion*, ed. Roger Mason, Cambridge Texts in the History of Political Thought (Cambridge: Cambridge University Press, 1994), 8. Although his book was directed at the two Marys, it was Knox's misfortune to have published it the same year that the Protestant Elizabeth succeeded to the throne of England, for his general arguments applied to her with equal force. The *First Blast* provoked a considerable literature, for which see my *Patriarchalism*, chap. 3.

[15] Pateman, *Sexual Contract*, 87.

[16] In this, I agree with Anthony Fletcher's analysis of what he calls "the God-given naturalness of the patriarchal order" and its presumption that "women were inferior" ("The Protestant Idea of Marriage in Early Modern England," in *Religion, Culture, and Society in Early Modern Britain: Essays in Honor of Patrick Collinson*, eds. Anthony Fletcher and Peter Roberts [Cambridge: Cambridge University Press, 1994], 161–81, quotations from 175). Cf. Susan Dwyer Amussen, *An Ordered Society: Gender and Class in Early Modern England* (Oxford: Blackwell, 1988), for an interpretation that sees the society as somewhat less repressive of women.

Fletcher's argument has been incorporated into his *Gender, Sex, and Subordination in England, 1500–1800* (New Haven: Yale University Press, 1995), which did not reach me in time to be used in the preparation of this chapter.

[17] See Margaret J. M. Ezell, *The Patriarch's Wife: Literary Evidence and the History of the Family* (Chapel Hill: University of North Carolina Press, 1987), 129–44 and 169–90.

was part of the ideology on which his society's view of the world was built. On the other hand, numbers of his contemporaries do seem to have been overtly and self-consciously antagonistic to the granting of full civil status to women. Institutional sexism operated somewhere beneath the level of consciousness, where it was important in maintaining social order and could be called upon when that social order was threatened.[18] And that is precisely what Filmer did despite the fact that he showed little explicit concern for the restrictions against women.

In the final analysis, what was at issue in the mid-seventeenth-century political debates to which Filmer contributed was the possession and control of the state. The English had been able to avoid such fundamental questions at least since Henry VIII's Reformation had succeeded in making the religious establishment an arm of the polity. Thanks to the myth of "king-in-parliament," a tacit if uneasy constitutional accommodation had permitted the question of "fundamental law" to be sidestepped until 1642. Like all deep, conceptual conflicts that are not abandoned, this one had to be settled by force rather than principle.[19]

Among the important sub-disputes were the questions of whether politics and the state were natural or the results of human artifice and whether political origins were to be found in familial, patriarchal organization or in a so-called state of nature. If the latter, what made people sufficiently free to establish civil society? The patriarchal response was much the easier alternative, and Filmer attacked the notions of "natural freedom" and individual "rights" that the state of nature and contract theories presupposed as "a New, Plausible and Dangerous Opinion."[20] The effect of his remark for women is that only a radical

---

[18] For accounts and explanations of that invocation, see Amussen, *An Ordered Society*, chaps. 2 and 5, and Lena Cowen Orlin, *Private Matters and Public Culture in Post-Reformation England* (Ithaca: Cornell University Press, 1994), esp. chap. 2.

[19] See my "The English Revolution in the History of Political Thought," in *Country and Court: Essays in Honor of Perez Zagorin*, eds. Bonnie Kunze and Dwight Brautigam (Rochester: University of Rochester Press, 1992), and J. G. A. Pocock and Gordon Schochet, "Interregnum and Restoration," in *The Varieties of British Political Thought, 1500–1800*, eds. Pocock, Schochet, and Lois G. Schwoerer (Cambridge: Cambridge University Press, 1994). For the constitutional background, see Margaret A. Judson, *The Crisis of the Constitution: An Essay in Constitutional and Political Thought in England, 1603–1645* (originally published 1949), reprinted with a forward by J. H. Hexter (New Brunswick: Rutgers University Press, 1988). The same period is covered with rather different emphases by J. P. Sommerville, *Politics and Ideology in England, 1603–1640* (London: Longman, 1986), and Glenn Burgess, *The Political of the Ancient Constitution: An Introduction to English Political Thought, 1603–1642* (University Park, Pa.: Pennsylvania State University Press, 1993).

[20] Filmer, *Patriarcha: A Defence of the Natural Authority of Kings Against the Unnatural Liberty of the People* (written *c.* 1630–40; first published, 1680), 53. The claim of novelty, of course, was part of Filmer's rhetorical ploy. Versions of many of these arguments could be traced back as far as St. Thomas Aquinas. See James Tully, "Locke on

transformation of social and political conceptualizations could alter their status.

III

Locke's response to all this was somewhat ambiguous. Like Hobbes, he built his arguments upon rights and *political* conventions, but his conception of civil society retained considerably more of nature than Hobbes had permitted. Women were still denied a civil identity, but because of his detailed criticism of Filmer, Locke ultimately recognized somewhat limited entitlements for women within the household.

He insisted that power over children was not due to fatherhood but was a consequence of the law of nature. All parents since Adam and Eve had been placed *"under an obligation to preserve, nourish, and educate the Children* they had begotten, not as their own Workmanship, but as the Workmanship of their own Maker, the Almighty, to whom they were to be accountable for them."[21] It followed that "The *Power*, then *that Parents have* over their Children, arises from that Duty which is incumbent upon them, to take care of their Off-spring during the imperfect state of Childhood." "It [i.e., parental power] is but a help to the weakness and imperfection of their Nonage, a Discipline necessary to their education" (II, ¶¶ 58 and 65). Accordingly, the child was bound to obey whoever maintained and cared for it whether that person was the natural parent or not (I, ¶ 100, and II, ¶ 65).

Familial authority belonged to both parents, Locke asserted, and he chided Filmer for ignoring the fact that the Fifth Commandment named both parents, not just the father (II, ¶¶ 6, 11, 60–66).[22] Thus, even if parental power did come from generation, "This would give the *Father* but a joynt Dominion with the Mother over them [the children]. For no body can deny but that the Woman hath an equal share, if not the greater, as nourishing the Child a long time in her own Body out of her own Substance" (I, ¶ 55). It followed, according to Locke, that paternal power ought "more properly [to be] called *Parental Power*. For whatever

---

Liberty," in *Conceptions of Liberty in Political Philosophy*, eds. Zbigniew Pelczynski and John Gray (London: Athlone Press, 1984), esp. 59–64, reprinted in Tully, *An Approach to Political Philosophy: Locke in Contexts* (Cambridge: Cambridge University Press, 1993), chap. 9, 284–91.

[21] John Locke, *Two Treatises of Government* (1690), II, ¶ 56; see also II, ¶ 60. Quotation from the edition by Peter Laslett (Cambridge: Cambridge University Press, 1960), the text of which is identical to the Cambridge Texts in the History of Political Thought edition (Cambridge: Cambridge University Press, 1988). All citations will be identified by book and paragraph number, and all quotations will be from the Laslett edition.

[22] See also II, ¶¶ 52–53.

obligation Nature and the right of Generation lays on Children, it must certainly bind them equal to both concurrent Causes of it" (II, ¶ 52). But Locke violated his own injunction almost immediately, reverting to the phrase "*Paternal Power*" (II, ¶ 69), and subsequently suggested that the terms could be interchanged (II, ¶¶ 170 and 173).

In general, Locke treated the husband as the superior mate, but left a realm of freedom to the wife:

But the Husband and Wife, though they have but one common Concern, yet having different understandings, will unavoidably sometimes have different wills too; it therefore being necessary that the last Determination, *i.e.* the Rule, should be placed somewhere; it naturally falls to the Man's share, as the abler and the stronger. But this reaching but to the things of their common Interest and Property, leaves the Wife in the full and free possession of what by Contract is her peculiar Right, and gives the Husband no more power over her Life than she has over his. (II, ¶ 82)

What was more, this marital power did not provide the basis for civil government. If God's command to Eve that "thy Desire shall be to thy Husband, and he shall rule over thee" (Genesis 3.16)

must needs be understood as a Law to bind her and all other Women to subjection, it can be no other Subjection than what every Wife owes her Husband, and then if this be the *Original Grant of Government and the Foundation of Monarchical Power*, there will be as many Monarchs as there are Husbands. If therefore these words give any Power to *Adam*, it can be only a Conjugal Power, not Political, the Power that every Husband hath to order the things of private Concernment in his Family, as Proprietor of the Goods and Land there, and to have his Will take place before that of his wife in all things of their common Concernment; but not a Political Power of Life and Death over her, much less over any body else. (I, ¶ 48)

Quite simply, the complex society of the household, with its conjugal, parental, and master–servant relations "wherein the Master or Mistress of it had some sort of Rule proper to a Family . . . came short of *Political Society*" (II, ¶ 77).[23] But the basic structure of the family remained essentially patriarchal, and the members of civil society were men who were heads of households or otherwise enjoyed an economic and social independence. In this, Locke did not depart from the Filmerian understanding of the world. The important departure was the movement out of the pre-political and supra-human world of nature and into the realm of artifact and convention. Locke's state was a constitutional, limited

---

[23] I have discussed this latter passage and its significance in greater detail in *Patriarchalism*, chap. 13, in my essay on Locke in *Classics of Modern Political Thought*, ed. Steven Kahn (Oxford: Oxford University Press, 1997), and in a forthcoming essay, "From Nature to Politics and Back Again: John Locke on Civil Society and the State of Nature."

polity instituted to protect and maximize the rights and liberties of its members.

IV

The derivation of politics from a conception of rights and liberty, while certainly not original to Locke, was the theoretical target of Filmer's patriarchalism and a denial of his providential political naturalism. Filmer used the term "rights" throughout his writings, but he generally intended a kind of entitlement that came from and was attached to superior status.[24] Rarely did he mean the natural or personal rights that belonged equally to each individual.

The early modern appeal to individual rights suggested voluntarism and conventionality, a world in which each rights-bearing person had the capacity to make and be responsible for his – and ultimately *her* – own place. These notions are altogether absent from Filmer, whose theory could be described as a kind of divine-right naturalism; he looked to nature and the structures created by God for standards. But he appreciated the *logic* of the rights argument and saw that it would have to extend much further than its advocates intended.

Hugo Grotius, Filmer contended, had departed from the natural and original equality and common ownership of the state of nature and had endorsed the existence of private property and status in civil society. In a pointed criticism of Grotius that is applicable to all natural law theories, Filmer said:

> dominion ... was brought in by the will of man, whom by this doctrine Grotius makes to be able to change that law which God himself cannot change, as he saith. He gives a double ability to man; first to make that no law of nature which God made to be the law of nature: and next to make that a law of nature which God made not; for now that dominion is brought in, he maintains, it is against the law of nature to take that which is in another man's dominion.[25]

His arguments against the fictitious contract of government that ended the state of nature were even more telling and recognized that the exclusion of women would violate the law of nature. The majority cannot bind any but itself, he said; all who dissented from the pact would have to retain their original liberty. Anything short of this would violate the putative natural right of liberty. Second, he found it incon-

---

[24] See, e.g., Filmer, *Patriarcha*, 59–61.

[25] Filmer, *Observations Concerning the Originall of Government* (1652), 266. Although Locke never cited this criticism, the attempt to meet it is probably the source of his doctrine of property and his refinement of the Grotian argument by the implicit use of a scholastic conception of *potentia*.

ceivable that a multitude of people freely living without the constraints of society should come together to make such an agreement.[26] Not only that, but "infants and others under the age of discretion; not to speak of *women, especially virgins, who by birth have as much natural freedom as any other, and therefore ought not to lose their liberty without their own consent.*"[27] Locke certainly knew of this argument but did not refer to it. However, his friend James Tyrrell inserted the following "Advertisement" to the first of the thirteen dialogues that comprised his *Bibliotheca Politica* (1691–94):

I Desire always to be understood, that when I make use of the word People, I do not mean the vulgar or mixt multitude, but in the state of Nature the whole Body of Freemen and women, especially the Fathers and Masters of Families; and in a Civil State, all degrees of men, as well the Nobility and Clergy, as the Common People.[28]

If Tyrrell was aware of the problem, Locke should have seen it as well. At some level, he should have accounted for the relative absence of women from his conception of civil society and explained why women apparently did not have rights. Locke seems to have ignored the question altogether, which his conventional theory of political society should have prevented. As we shall see below, there is a way of accounting for Locke's silence here, and that has to do with his understanding of the differences between "society" and politics.

---

[26] Filmer, *The Anarchy of a Limited Mixed Monarchy* (1648), 286.

[27] Ibid., 287; emphasis added. Filmer carried this argument even further, saying that consistency would require that "children and servants [who] are a far greater number than parents or masters" be permitted to participate, which would lead to a "most unnatural" conclusion by giving "the children the government over their parents" (ibid.).

[28] [James Tyrrell], *Bibliotheca Politica: or, An Enquiry into the Ancient Constitution of the English Government ... in Thirteen Dialogues* (London, 1691–94), sig. A4v. Italics in original. The dialogues were originally published separately but with continuous pagination. *A General Alphabetical Index* was published in 1694; it was bound with all thirteen dialogues, and the collection was published as a single book, also in 1694, with a "second edition" in 1701. A fourteenth dialogue was published in 1702, and new editions of the enlarged work were published in 1717 and 1727.

Tyrrell was a competent if undistinguished Whig historian and controversialist. He was a friend of Locke's during their undergraduate days at Oxford, and the ups and downs of their association, which continued throughout Locke's life, can be traced in their surviving correspondence, published in *The Correspondence of John Locke*, ed. E. S. de Beer, 8 vols. (Oxford: Oxford University Press, 1976–89). Although there are references to him in works on the political thought and ideology of the 1680s and 1690s, Tyrrell is relatively obscure. His best-known work is an attack on Filmer, *Patriarcha non Monarcha*, written at about the same time that Locke was composing the *Two Treatises* and published anonymously in 1683. For further discussion, see J. W. Gough, "James Tyrrell, Whig Historian and Friend of John Locke," *Historical Journal* 19 (1976): 581–610, and my "James Tyrrell and the Post Revolutionary Debate on the English Constitution," forthcoming in a memorial volume for John Wallace, eds. Derek Hirst and Richard Strier.

Ultimately, of course, he accorded women no more civil being than had Filmer. In Filmer's case there were at least the excuses that his naturalistic conception of politics did not leave space for women and the fact that, in the final analysis, no one but the sovereign was a civil person. Even the patriarchal heads of households did not enjoy civil status under the absolute monarchy Filmer envisioned.

In Filmer's view, the world was coherent, systematic, and orderly; it was structurally and naturally uncomplicated. To see this clearly is to appreciate the larger social and theoretical structures that supported the devaluation of women. According to Filmer, everything proceeds from God's will. Therefore, one must find where that will was most clearly expressed and subsequently manifested. Filmer argued from the Bible; human beings are obligated to obey God's will as it is expressed in the Scriptures, which "have given us the true grounds and principles of government."[29] The problem with an argument from Providence is that it necessarily leads to the conclusion that "whatever is is right." It is impossible both to maintain a reliance upon Providence and to argue for standards or principles on which humans should base their conduct, for the latter implies a degree of freedom and volition.

The model for political authority was Adam, whose sovereignty had been established by God in Paradise and was passed on unaltered to his lineal heirs:

Most of the civilest nations of the world labour to fetch their original from some one of the sons or nephews of Noah, which were scattered abroad after the confusion of Babel. In this dispersion we must certainly find the establishment of regal power throughout the kingdoms of the world.

It is a common opinion that at the confusion of tongues there were seventy-two distinct nations erected. All which were not confused multitudes without heads or governors, and at liberty to chose what governors or government they pleased, but they were distinct families, which had Fathers for rulers over them, whereby it appears that even in the confusion God was careful to preserve the fatherly authority by distributing the languages according to the diversity of families.[30]

The larger, polemical point of all this was to undermine the increasingly popular political doctrine of natural human liberty and equality as the basis on which society was voluntarily established.[31] "This tenet was first hatched in the Schools for good Divinity," he wrote, and has been adopted "by succeeding Papists," the "Divines of the Reformed

---

[29] Filmer, *Anarchy*, Preface, 278.
[30] Filmer, *Patriarcha*, 58. See also *Anarchy*, 83 and 290.
[31] See, e.g., *Patriarcha*, 79. Filmer had in mind here the arguments of Bellarmine, Suarez, and Grotius.

Churches," and "the common people everywhere," none of whom remembers "that the desire of liberty was the cause of the fall of Adam." This notion, which lay at the heart of the challenges to Charles I, contradicted "the doctrine and history of the Holy Scriptures, the constant practice of all ancient monarchies, and the very principles of the law of nature. It is hard to say whether it be more erroneous in divinity or dangerous in policy."[32]

To his providentialism Filmer added a Bodinian conception of sovereignty. One of his tracts, *The Necessity of the Absolute Power of All Kings* (1648), was a string of excerpts from the 1606 English translation of Bodin's *République*.[33] He joined divine-right absolutism and the doctrine of sovereignty by means of the simple assertion that since the "Kingly power is by the law of God, so it hath no inferior law to limit it."[34] It was axiomatic that "There can be no laws without a supreme power to command or make them," from which it followed that "in a monarchy the King must of necessity be above the laws. There can be no sovereign majesty in him that is under them."[35] Thus, the true question of politics

is not, whether there shall be an arbitrary power; but the only point is, who shall have that arbitrary power, whether one man or many? There never was, nor ever can be any people governed without a power of making laws, and every power of making laws must be arbitrary: for to make a law according to law, is *contradictio in adjecto*.[36]

Yet another important ingredient in the structure of Filmer's patriarchal political theory is the *way* that the household was used to prefigure politics. Filmer's conception was not an analogical or metaphorical claim that the family *suggests* or *implies* things about the state, which can be seen as somehow *like* the household. Rather his theory was based

[32] Filmer, *Patriarcha*, 53.
[33] Reprinted in *Political Works*, 315–26. The tract was reissued in 1680 as *The Power of Kings: And in Particular the King of England*. The author was identified on the title page as "John Bodin A Protestant according to the Church of Geneva."
[34] Filmer, *Patriarcha*, 96.
[35] Ibid., 105.
[36] Filmer, *Anarchy*, Preface, 277. At the end of a commentary on Aristotle's *Politics*, Filmer set forth a number of propositions that he said was "the plain mind of Aristotle":

> 1. That there is no form of government, but monarchy only. 2. That there is no monarchy, but paternal. 3. That there is no paternal monarchy, but absolute, or arbitrary. 4. That there is no such thing as an aristocracy or democracy. 5. That there is no such form of government as a tyranny. 6. That the people are not born free by nature. (*Observations upon Aristotles Politiques Touching Forms of Government* [1652], 229)

In *Patriarcha* (79), Filmer went so far as to say of Aristotle, "In the first of his *Politics*, he agrees exactly with Scriptures."

upon *identity*, not *similarity*. Thus, the family *was* a polity, and the polity *was* a household, and the patriarchal, biblical family was not a prototype but was the very wellspring of politics. Theoretically, one could either accept such an argument, as Hobbes did, and then go on to claim that both institutions are conventional, or simply deny the identity altogether. Locke took the latter course and insisted that civil society was conventional and that the family was theoretically irrelevant to it, thereby avoiding even the question of the extent to which they were related.

These two moves were capable of providing the opening that was necessary for the long-term emergence of women as politically visible. Both loosened the stranglehold that patriarchal naturalism had on the politics of early modern Europe and replaced divine-right absolutism with a political conventionalism derived from personal and natural rights. That Locke himself did not carry his argument to the necessary next step and fully incorporate women into his political doctrine is altogether separate from the implications of that argument. Locke accepted a significant part of the patriarchal structuring of Stuart society, to be sure; he endorsed its exclusion of women from the political process but at the same time prepared the way for the eventual admission of women to the category of citizen.

V

The weakest part of Filmer's argument was his attempt to demonstrate that each successive sovereign had the same entitlements as every one of his[37] predecessors; he was thus forced to ignore the impact of history. According to Sir Robert's logic, nothing on earth other than the sovereign's own will could bind him. And even then, should the ruler give his word, there was no earthly power that could legitimately hold him to it. It followed, according to Filmer, that the king could not be bound by the laws of his predecessors. Certainly, wisdom, prudence, self-interest, even a concern for the welfare of his subjects[38] all dictated moderation, and Filmer was well aware of the classical conception of a tyrant as one who ruled in pursuit of his own interests rather than those of his subjects.[39]

Nevertheless, in terms of the *entitlements* and powers of monarchy, only God could discipline a king, and subjects should patiently suffer

---

[37] For the sake of clarity and in order to remain faithful to Filmer's own practice and the gendered basis of his doctrine, I have used the masculine pronoun rather than the more cumbersome and textually less accurate "he or she," "him or her," etc.

[38] Filmer, *Patriarcha*, 63.   [39] See *Patriarcha*, 92–94.

whatever their rulers imposed while awaiting providential deliverance. Filmer had logic and the definition of kingship of his side, but for all its ruthless consistency, his hard-headed positivism failed to acknowledge that societies are continuous over time and that each successive generation makes its own contributions to the process of maintaining social practices and institutions. In England, this was an exceptional difficulty, for it effectively eliminated the common law,[40] the society's central political institution.

Political practice is simply not logical and coherent in the ways that Filmer's patriarchal absolutism – or any architectonic theory – requires. Rather, it is a continuing series of adjustments and accommodations that cannot be *fully* captured by theory. This is even more problematic for a providential theory that also has a political agenda. Filmer probably knew all this, for at the end of his life, with his beloved King Charles executed, the monarchy overthrown and a republic – of sorts – established in its place, he halfheartedly defended taking the Engagement to support Cromwell's government on the ground that:

in usurpation, the title of the usurper is before, and better than any other than of him that had a former right: for he hath a possession by the permissive will of God ... Every man is ... so far to obey a usurper as may tend not only to the preservation of his King and Father, but sometimes even to the preservation of the usurper himself, when probably he may thereby be reserved to the correction or mercy of his true superior.[41]

As he had remarked in a tract published in 1648 when Charles's fortunes had yet to be determined:

many times by the act either of a usurper himself, or those that set him up, the true heir of a crown is dispossessed, God using the ministry of the wickedest men for the removing and setting up of Kings: in such cases, the subjects'

---

[40] For instances of Filmer's obtuseness on the subject of the common law, see, e.g. *Patriarcha*, 110, and *Freeholder*, 172.

[41] Filmer, *Directions for Obedience to Governours in Dangerous and Doubtful Times* (1652), 232. The *Directions* was published with the *Observations upon Aristotle*. Filmer discussed the Engagement more extensively in a holograph manuscript now entitled "Two Treatises against Rebellion" (written *c*. 1651–52), Bodleian Library, MS. Tanner 233 (title from Bodleian Library Catalogue). Another version of this manuscript was subsequently published anonymously as *A Discourse Concerning Supreme Power and Common Right* (London, 1680); it has long been attributed to Sir John Monson. For Filmer's authorship and the relation of the manuscript to the printed book, see Schochet, "Sir Robert Filmer: Some New Bibliographic Discoveries," *The Library* 26 (1971): 135–60. This attribution has been challenged on textual grounds by James Daly, *Sir Robert Filmer and English Political Thought* (Toronto: University of Toronto Press, 1979), 194–98. Daly seems indifferent to the textual inconsistencies that run through works for which he is willing to accept Filmer's authorship and does not account for fact that the Bodleian manuscript is written and *corrected* in what is unmistakably Filmer's hand.

obedience to the fatherly power must go along and wait upon God's providence, who only hath right to give and take away kingdoms, and thereby to adopt subjects into the obedience of another fatherly power.[42]

It was a peculiar argument, but it was probably the best that could be made of the providentialist injunction to obey the powers that be because they are ordained of God.[43] To this Filmer added the more overtly prudential principle that "protection and subjection are reciprocal, so that when the first fails, the latter ceaseth."[44] Thus, it seems to follow that the subject's duties to Charles I had ended when he lost the Second Civil War – even before the Regicide – and were immediately transferred to the Parliamentary forces that had defeated and replaced him because they had shown themselves to be the *effective* civil government.

Admitting that it was "true [that] all Kings be not the natural parents of their subjects," Filmer nevertheless insisted that "they all are, or *are to be reputed*, as the next heirs of those progenitors who were at first the natural parents of the whole people, and in their right succeed to the exercise of supreme jurisdiction."[45] Accordingly, "It skills not which way Kings come by their power, whether by election, donation, succession or by any other means, for it is still the manner of the government by supreme power that makes them properly Kings, not the means of obtaining their crowns."[46] Finally, to clinch the point, "all Kings that now are, or ever were, are, or were either Fathers of their people, or the heirs of such Fathers, or *usurpers* of the right of such Fathers."[47] It was a neat, compact theory, but, as all of Filmer's critics pointed out, it had the effect of altogether undermining patriarchalism and lineal succession.[48]

VI

A large part of what is involved in all this is Filmer's rather anxious attack on *convention* and the resultant reconfiguration of the world that

---

[42] Filmer, *Anarchy*, 289.
[43] The doctrine of Romans 13.1: "Let every soul be subject unto the higher powers. For there is no power but of God: the powers that be are ordained of God." This passage was one of the primary sources of divine-right theory in the early modern period.
[44] Filmer, *Directions*, 234. This was precisely the formula Hobbes had employed: the principal "design" of the *Leviathan*, he asserted at the end of his book, was "to set before mens eyes the mutuall relation between protection and obedience" (Thomas Hobbes, *Leviathan: or, The Matter, Forme, and Power of a Commonwealth Ecclesiastical and Civil* [1651], Review and Conclusion, text from the edition by Edwin Curley [Indianapolis: Hackett Publishing Co., 1994], 497). For further discussion, see Schochet, "Intending (Political) Obligation," *passim*.
[45] Filmer, *Patriarcha*, 60–61. Emphasis added.
[46] Ibid., 106.   [47] Filmer, *Anarchy*, 288. Emphasis added.
[48] See Schochet, *Patriarchalism*, 171–75 and 196–99 for details.

we have come to describe as "modernity."[49] It is probably the case, however, that Filmer did not so much understand modernity as defend the stable but declining traditional, natural order against the challenges of precarious institutions and practices that were subject to human will. It is in the nature of architectonic theories to reject uncertainty and instability, and here, as elsewhere, Filmer provides illuminating examples of the kinds of ideological and structural changes in the larger ideational and social worlds that would be necessary before ideologies could develop that would facilitate the emergence of women into civil personhood.

Filmer stood for a conception of society in which whatever identities women were afforded were effectively derived from the males on whom they were dependent. Their status as wives and daughters rendered them radically different from men; they could never attain the familial headship that had been a prerequisite to functioning membership in civil society at least since the time of Aristotle. Women in early modern society needed a kind of *individualism* that would give them identities that were not *inherently* distinct from those of men. The transition to this modern outlook was already underway when Filmer was writing, but it was to be a protracted process of change, and Filmer stood somewhere near its beginnings.

Implicitly, Filmer rejected the modern conceit that authority is socially and culturally constructed and therefore controllable. One consequence of this view is the assertion that the roles assigned to women are no less conventional and artificial than politics itself. More so perhaps than anyone else in the early modern period, Hobbes represents that view. He is one of the most thoroughgoing social constructivists in the history of Western thought.[50] In the end, however, Hobbesian conventionalism did not emancipate women.

Locke stood somewhere between Filmer and Hobbes on this issue.

---

[49] I have discussed some of this, but without extensive references to Filmer, in "Patriarchalism, Naturalism, and the Rise of then 'Conventional State,'" in *Categorie del reale e storiografia: aspetti di continuità e trasformazione nell'Europa moderna*, eds. F. Fagiani and G. Valera (Calabria, Italy: Franco Angeli, 1986) (also published in *Materiali per una storia della cultura Guiridica* 14 [1984]). See also Schochet, "Constitutionalism, Liberalism, and the Study of Politics," in *NOMOS XX: Constitutionalism* (1979), as well as *Patriarchalism*, chap. 14.

[50] See, e.g., Thomas Hobbes, *Philosophical Rudiments Concerning Government and Society* (1651), an English translation of *De Cive* (1642), Preface, paragraph 3:

> for as in a watch, or some such small engine, the matter, figure, and motion of its wheels, cannot well be known, except it be taken in sunder, and viewed in parts; so to make a more curious search into the rights of States, and duties of Subjects, it is necessary . . . they be so considered, as if they were dissolved. (Text from Hobbes, *De Cive: The English Version*, ed. Howard Warrender [Oxford: Oxford University Press, 1983], 32 [italics in original])

He embraced that part of the conventionalist argument that applied to politics, but he was silent about the status of the family. What he did accomplish was the separation of politics from society, thereby making any attempt to infer the nature of the state from the household futile. The fact that the powers of a father and a civil ruler were sometimes resident in the same person was purely contingent, Locke insisted, in an effort to undermine Filmer's contention that as subjects of their parents, individuals can never be the authors of their own political obligations. The granting of Locke's point sets the stage for rendering all political relations indeterminate. His long-run contribution to political philosophy is the liberty that is required for humans to control their own destinies, and it is precisely that liberty that Filmer resisted.

Conclusion

It has been the genius of modern feminism to insist upon a place and identity for women independent of their membership in households or families. For political as well as conceptual reasons, it has been a long and arduous struggle, but for what might be the first time in recorded history, we are able to talk of women apart from their traditional roles as wives, mothers, and daughters. This change is related to the growing dissatisfaction – itself part of the twentieth century's distrust of metaphysical speculation – with "essentialist" formulations in general. And all this, in turn, is related to the malaise that is sometimes said to accompany the contemporary world's readjustment of long-standing identities and relationships. While it is far too early to determine precise causal connections, it is certainly clear that feminism has played an important role in generating and perpetuating this entire series of complaints.

The stakes are very high, for the members of modern society are being asked to reconsider some of their most fundamental self-understandings and to alter the relationships and social structures that have sustained the distribution of power and social advantage at least since the Reformation. Metaphysics, the irreducible conceptions of the self to which it gives rise, and the role-assignments that result function like "totalizing" institutions – society-wide, conceptual prisons that contain and restrain the inmates as well as the guards, both of whom appear to have some interest in maintaining the system.

It is often painful and usually costly to alter the characterisic ways societies describe themselves; resistance to this sort of change is generally grounded in attempts to retain status and power, but even those who might benefit can find reformation too unsettling. The entire process rarely occurs at this level of consciousness, but desires to retain status and anxieties about potential dislocations help explain the mixed and often implicit motives peoples may have for preserving social order without in any way denying that they might be perfectly sincere.

In many respects, modern feminism has been unusually successful, for one of the most conspicuous consequences of the contemporary debate is that the meaning of "woman" (and of "man" too, for that matter) is no longer stable. What is more, our understanding of the family has been altered, partially in response to feminist criticisms and partially because the institution itself has changed. Because many people still resist the changes, these alterations continue to reverberate throughout society rather like an earthquake and its after-shocks.

There is something fascinating about the entire business, for, in the adult lifetimes of many of us, a set of linguistic conventions that have held sway for more than 500 years has been successfully modified through the conscious efforts of feminist political reformers. It is a major accomplishment when apprehended from that perspective. This success would have been altogether lost on Sir Robert Filmer, for it represents the ultimate victory of his posthumous adversary, John Locke.

I should leave no room for misinterpretation of what is being claimed here, both *about* Locke and *for* modernity. Locke's conception of the polity is certainly not one of non-gendered participation. He was not an egalitarian on any grounds, not least among them the sexual. Nonetheless, his theory considerably widened the category of the political person even though it restricted that status to males. Pateman is correct in her implicit protestation that the very important separation of the social from the political that Locke made[51] allowed him to endorse (or potentially blinded his readers to) the continued oppression of women and their exclusion from politics.

This criticism can be carried much further. Locke's civil society was built on top of a set of not merely non- but determinedly *pre*-political arrangements that are sustained by and themselves sustain the resulting polity. In these terms, the deep danger of so-called "liberal" political neutrality in which the state evinces no interest in the outcome of the conflicts it mediates is that it becomes officially blind to *social* injustice and virtually prides itself on that fact by insisting upon this state/society (or public/private) separation. At the same time, it is precisely the questioning of the legitimacy of the differential distribution of benefits and burdens from the perspective of social-justice-denied that alerts us to presumptive injustices and ultimately undergirds their removal.

---

[51] I have discussed this in *Patriarchalism*, chap. 13, and in the forthcoming essay "From Nature to Civil Society and Back Again."

Locke's accomplishment in these terms was his recognition that women had a level of *interest* that permitted them to engage in the contractual relationship of marriage. Historically and conceptually, this move opened doors to a wider and more overtly political participation founded upon social visibility and voice. While insufficient in itself, Locke's shift is part of the historical story that must be told to account for the movement from Filmer, through Blackstone, to the twentieth century within an unbroken line of political development. What is not clear is whether the limitations on women that Locke retained and which have been passed on to subsequent ages *necessarily* sustain a sexual oppression that cannot be overcome – as Pateman seems to think they do – or today provide negative standards to be overthrown and which reveal the failings of our own social and political practices. Pateman's argument rests on an unspecified and unwarrentedly essentialist conception of historical development that makes it impossible to alter institutions and practices without first rooting out their historical foundations.

On the other hand, my response to Henry Higgins's question that I made into my parenthetic subtitle is that in all relevant respects, men and women are already indistinguishable and that once we understand that fact, it is up to us to remove the obstacles to the actual achievement of that equality. More importantly – and this is an argument that must be made in another place[52] – this achievement is most likely to occur through the realization of the conception of rights that is the central part of Locke's response to Filmer and of the Lockean legacy that frames much of our politics.

Acknowledgments

The final form of this chapter owes much to the suggestions of Jonathan McFall. I am also indebted to Ed Angelina, Paul Babbitt, Gregory Finnson, Kiki Jamieson, and Pat Moloney – along with McFall, all friends, students, and critics – who, over the past few years, have listened to and helped me to clarify some of the theoretical arguments.

My principal inspiration has been the friendship, the writing, and the teaching of Peter Laslett, who supervised my earliest work on Filmer more than thirty years ago and who first awakened in me a sense that the *history* of political thought had to be written in conjunction with what he termed "the history of population and social structure." This chapter is

---

[52] See my *Rights in Contexts: The Historical and Political Construction of Moral and Legal Entitlements* (Lawrence, Kans.: University Press of Kansas, 1998).

in part a small repeat of his calls – relatively unheeded – for such histories in *The World We Have Lost* (London: Methuen, 1963, etc.) and "The Wrong Way through the Telescope: A Note on Literary Evidence in Sociology and Historical Sociology," *British Journal of Sociology*, 26 (1976): 319–42. See also my "Patriarchalism, Politics, and Mass Attitudes in Stuart England," *Historical Journal*, 13 (1969): 413–41.

11   Catharine Macaulay: patriot historian

J. G. A. Pocock

Let us begin by recalling the best-known facts about Catharine Macaulay.[1] She wrote a number of works, of which by far the most prominent is a *History of England from the Accession of James I to that of the Brunswick Line* (i.e., that of George I), which appeared in eight volumes between 1763 and 1771 and, after an interval of ten years, 1781. During that interval she began a separate history of England from the revolution of 1688 to her own time in a series of letters to a friend; but she fell out with the friend (on account of her second marriage) and only one volume of this appeared, in 1778. She wrote several political pamphlets, one attacking Edmund Burke for not being radical enough in his criticism of the policies of George III in the 1760s, another for being too conservative in his *Reflections on the Revolution in France*; there is one essay in straight political theory, in the shape of some reflections on Thomas Hobbes, and some reflections on education which show she had been reading Rousseau. This last may be considered feminist in the limited sense that it is concerned with the education of women, but is of course one of many works written on the same subject, by both women and men, of which some are not to be considered feminist at all and several consider history, her chosen subject, as a branch of literature which women should read. Macaulay is not much interested in this question, but she devoted her life to writing history and did this so well that the historians of her time – nearly all male – were obliged to take her very seriously. She was primarily a woman who crashed her way into the writing of history, normally defined as a specifically masculine activity, and made other readers and writers respect her; not, I submit, because her writing of history has anything specifically female about it but because it is politically most outspoken in ways that caught attention, and still more because she was, quite simply, very good at it.

[1] Bridget Hill, *The Republican Virago: The Life and Times of Catharine Macaulay, Historian* (Oxford: Clarendon Press, 1992).

She died aged sixty in 1791, and would certainly not have enjoyed the next ten years if she had lived to see them. There is a growing literature about her,[2] and a prize has been named after her, but the only detailed study of her historical writings I know is the work of an Italian historian.[3]

To understand her correctly there is one thing we must constantly bear in mind: she was primarily a historian rather than a social or political theorist; not that she had not political principles of the most articulate kind, or that she could not express them in theoretical form when she wanted to, but that they were in themselves of a kind best articulated in the writing of history. In formal terms, she was a humanist and rhetorician, not a philosopher, theologian, or lawyer. She would have been most eloquent in denying that she was either of the latter two. We must attend to the proposition that the writing of history, as a branch of political argument in eighteenth-century Britain, is the historical context which has to be reconstructed as a field of study if we want to understand Catharine Macaulay's utterance and reception – her discourse in her time.

Catharine Sawbridge Macaulay Graham bore three surnames at different times in her life, one derived from a father and two from husbands. Her contemporaries referred to her as "Mrs. Macaulay," and certainly no one thought she was, except in law, included in or subject to her husband of that name. We can learn most about her politics by attending to the first of her surnames, the patrilineal name of Sawbridge. The Sawbridges were a London aldermanic family of considerable means, active in City of London politics in ways normally opposed to the ministry in office, whatever it was. They attacked the alliance between high politics and high finance, which usually dominated both London and national politics through the structure of public credit that kept governments solvent and the government's creditors powerful. These governments were usually Whig, conducted by the great families of the Whig aristocracy, and when we call the politics of the Sawbridges and those like them "radical Whig," we are implicitly appealing to

---

[2] Barbara Brandon-Schnorrenburg, "The Brood Hen of Faction: Mrs. Macaulay and Radical Politics, 1767–75," *Albion* 11, 1 (1979): 33–45; "*Observations on the Reflections*: Macaulay Graham v. Burke, Round Three," in *The Consortium on Revolutionary Europe, 1750–1850: Proceedings, 1987*, eds. Warren Spencer and Ellen Evans (Athens, Ga.: University of Georgia Press, 1988), 215–25; "An Opportunity Missed: Catharine Macaulay on the Revolution of 1688," *Studies in Eighteenth Century Culture* 20 (1990): 231–40; Natalie Zemon Davis, "History's Two Bodies," *American Historical Review* 93 (1988): 231–40.

[3] Rolando Minuti, "Il problema storico della liberta inglese nella cultura radicale dell'età di Giorgio III: Catharine Macaulay e la rivoluzione puritana," *Rivista Storica Italiana* 98, 3 (1986): 793–860.

usages of the term like "Old Whig," "True Whig," "Real Whig," "Honest Whig," which indicated that there was a faction of purists according to whom the Whig aristocracy had deserted the principles of their ancestors. What these principles had been, and how this desertion had happened, was perhaps the main question which Catherine Sawbridge Macaulay wrote her *History* to answer; but the problem is complicated for us, and for her, by the facts that opposition to Whig ministries was regularly termed Tory, many of the principles of radical-Whig criticism of the regime had been adopted by Tories, and not a few of the authors on whom she relied in writing parts of her history were Tory authors – Davenant, Swift, and Bolingbroke. At the same time, of course, she regarded the Tories as the party of Charles I and James II, the High Church-and-King supporters of non-resistance, hereditary monarchy, and the Church of England ascendancy which excluded dissenters from public life. Her attitudes toward both Tories and Whigs are therefore deeply ambivalent, and she was a good enough historian to know this and to write her *History* to find out why. We have to understand and in our own way share the ambivalence to understand her; and it needs to be said that she was in no way alone in perceiving that English party history had followed this tangled and contradictory course. The Huguenot historian Paul Rapin Thoyras knew it;[4] her great antithesis, the sceptically conservative Scot David Hume knew it;[5] her fellow radical, the London Scottish novelist and historian Tobias Smollett, knew it.[6] She was sharing a discourse, and a problematic, with others, but the names I have just given indicate that she was, through sheer ability, the only English historian of her generation capable of dealing with the problems. This is why one writer of the day remarks that, "though one of the more delicate part of the creation," she is one of the only two English historians currently doing serious work – the other was Lord Lyttleton, who had written a life of King Henry II – and that it was her militant adherence to the principles of liberty which had made her one of them.[7] Edward Gibbon and his friends, about the same time,

---

[4] His *Histoire d'Angleterre* appeared in English translation in 1725–31; his *Dissertation on the Whigs and Tories* in 1721. See Rolando Minuti, "Il problema costituzionale nell'*Histoire d'Angleterre* di Rapin Thoyras," *Studi Settecenteschi* 5 (1984): 49–107.

[5] His *History of Great Britain* in six volumes appeared between 1754 and 1762. See Nicholas Phillipson, *Hume* (Historians on Historians Series; London: Weidenfeld and Nicolson, 1989).

[6] His *History of England from the Revolution of 1688 to the Death of George II*, intended as a continuation of Hume, appeared in 1763. I know no specialized study of Smollett as a historian.

[7] James Parsons, *Remains of Japhet, being historical enquiries into the affinity and origin of the European languages* (London, 1767), xxi–xxii.

preferred to advance the names of David Hume and William Robertson, both of whom were Scots.[8]

Aside from her marriages to Scotsmen resident in London, Catharine Macaulay is thoroughly an English figure; is this part of what I have meant by styling her a patriot historian? Not really, because though her sense of nationality is certainly strong, the meaning of the word "patriot" has changed a great deal since she used it of others and it could be used of her. In more than one European language of the eighteenth century, "patriot" had a measurably subversive significance. It meant in the first instance one who loved his or her country more than its ruling family or even its institutions, and might be found rebelling against the king in the king's name, as had happened in the English Civil Wars, or against the monarchy in the name of the nation or the people. As late as 1820, in Byron's *Vision of Judgment*, the ghost of Junius sums it all up, when confronted with the ghost of George III, by crying to the heavenly hosts: "I loved my country and I hated him." It is not certain that she hated George III, but she was not far distant from those who did. Richard Price, whom she did know and admire, provoked Burke to write *Reflections on the Revolution in France* by publishing a *Sermon on the Love of our Country*, in which he presented this love as a duty and made it clear that it might entail strong support for the French National Assembly and the March to Versailles. The patriot, then, was one who loved his country according to definitions of his own and demanded that others should share the definitions as well as the love. Since Bolingbroke, writing in the 1730s, if not earlier, the term had denoted one opposed on principle to the actions of the king's ministers; this was what moved Dr. Johnson to define patriotism as the last refuge of a scoundrel. The patriot was one whose *patria* was a common possession, easily identified with those who possessed it; the commonweal or commonwealth, the *res publica* or republic; and this is the sense in which Catharine Macaulay could be and was described as both a "patriot" and a "republican." She was what Caroline Robbins taught us to recognize as *The Eighteenth-Century Commonwealthman*, a term for which no feminine equivalent has been found.

To call her a "republican" does not mean that she desired a kingless form of government, though she admired these when she saw them. She strongly supported the trial and execution of Charles I, and she adopted an interpretation of the revolution of 1688 which affirmed that James II had been deposed by his people and that, in both 1688 and 1714, new

---

[8] [Edward Gibbon and Georges Deyverdun], *Mémoires Littéraires de la Grande Bretagne pour l'an 1767* (London, 1768), 29. For Macaulay see p. 27.

kings had been chosen and elected by them. But she had no objection to lodging the executive power in a single person accountable to the law and people, and not much to making that office hereditary instead of elective at every vacancy. It is true that she mistrusted hereditary monarchy as likely to produce dynastic loyalties and court politics, but she thought these defects remediable by the virtue of the people if that could be maintained. To discover in what sense she was a "patriot" and a "republican" we have to look elsewhere, and we can do this by turning to the introduction to her *History*'s first volume.[9] Here it will appear that she defines the *res publica*, or political community, as a community of virtue; that the *raison d'être* of a republic or a democracy is to maintain the level of public virtue; that histories are written in order to praise the memory and hold up the examples of those who have it; that this must be done because any republic contains many – normally including the ignorant vulgar or multitude – who cannot be trusted to maintain virtue, as well as the morally weak who will probably, and the wicked who will certainly, betray it. It will further appear that liberty, which is the liberty to practice virtue, is as much threatened in the England of 1763 as at any other time; and that the historian's function is exemplary and exhortatory, to remind her readers what virtue is and to oblige them to maintain it.

I suspect that it was this character of moral exhortation which made her see the writing of history as the best possible way for a woman to practice public virtue. She did not expect to see women as actors in public affairs, but since at latest the turn of the century they had increasingly been readers of history, histories were by now normally written with women readers in mind; and what they read might teach them to speak, and keep up the flow of exhortations and examples on which the practice of virtue depended. The enterprise was that of involving women in the communication of morally important information which humanist literature had aimed at since the Renaissance; the word was supplementary to the deed, and this was crucial to the gender-relations involved. If women could not act, they could speak and write; and "parole femminili, atti maschi" is a motto of the State of Maryland to this day[10] (the public command of Italian not having got around to challenging it). Macaulay's history, therefore, is strictly and purely humanist, and so are her politics. The end of history is to teach examples of public virtue; the end of politics and liberty is to act on those examples and supply them. The study of character is very

[9] *History of England*, I, xii–xxviii.
[10] It was previously the motto of the Calvert family.

important, and so is the study of action; not just because these are the keys to history, but because politics exists to generate people whose virtue is fulfilled in action.

But there are still some unanswered questions. What was a Sawbridge, and what was a woman, doing adopting so unreservedly an ideology based wholly on ancient civic virtue, on a reading of the Greek and Roman classics which she tells us formed her second religion (she does not go into details about her first)? The Sawbridge males were aldermen, Londoners, merchants, and investors; their political radicalism ought therefore – at least if you follow Professor Isaac Kramnick[11] – to have been bourgeois and progressive, based on the virtues of thrift and industry and on contempt for the leisured class which employed itself in politics. Catharine ought therefore to have written as a modern, a despiser of slaveholding and unproductive antiquity, and to have dismissed admiration of ancient citizenship as the nostalgia of an under-capitalized provincial aristocracy and gentry, hungering for a lost world of patriarchalism, deference, and hierarchy. Now there were value systems abroad in eighteenth-century Britain which were modern in precisely these senses, and though these were mainly deployed on the side of the Whig aristocracy and its new world of commerce and empire, it is possible to find critics of their regime who expounded modern values and wanted to put the ancient world behind them. Had she made her home not in London, but in Birmingham or the Potteries – the homeland of those provincial dissenting industrialists of whom Kramnick writes – she might have written very differently. But she was a Londoner and a republican; she considered civic virtue to be the end of political life and the end of writing history, and it was a consequence that she was both a strong democrat and a strong elitist. She wanted the people to be free of monarchical, aristocratic, and clerical control, in order that they might practice an active civic virtue; but she did not expect them to produce more than a limited number of patriot leaders to set examples to the others. She wanted England to be a republic in order that these patriots might come to the head of affairs, and she wrote history in order to celebrate the patriots of Charles I's reign, the Long and Rump Parliament, and the opposition to Charles II. She was quite clear that the mob, the vulgar, the unlettered multitude, had no virtue of its own and could not be trusted to support the patriotic elite; and in both London and Birmingham, Church-and-King mobs, shouting for constituted authority and burning down dissenting chapels, were phenomena which appeared from time to time. She believed in liberty, but not in equality in

---

[11] *Republicanism and Bourgeois Radicalism* (Ithaca: Cornell University Press, 1990).

our sense of the term, and as for fraternity nobody in England appears to have heard of it before 1789. This is not because she was this or that kind of snob, but because her notion of politics was exclusively centered on the moral personality. She wanted people to be free, not because of what they were but of what they might become: morally free and politically self-determining agents. In a free society, there would be an elite of such citizens; it existed to produce them.

If we enquire from what rank or class in society the patriot elite are to be drawn, we shall probably receive the Aristotelian answer that they will be of the middling sort; neither the aristocracy, great enough to be corrupted by the pursuit of power over others, nor the dependent poor, indigent enough to be corrupted by the power of others over them. Some democrats of the period wanted to extend the franchise in order to bring in more free and independent electors, others wanted to restrict it in order to keep out more who were neither free nor independent; we may wonder which way Macaulay would have leaned. Now this is the eighteenth century, and there are sentences here and there which indicate that the middling rank capable of citizenship will be drawn from those who have created their own wealth by thrift, industry, and the other virtues of capital accumulation. One may of course seize on these sentences to insist that she was a bourgeois radical in an increasingly capitalist society; but perhaps we should wait until we know what she had to say about the gentry, yeomanry, and freeholders of the country, whose liberty and virtue might be grounded on the independence of their tenures and estates. But if we choose to apply the overworked term "bourgeois" to Catharine Macaulay, we will have to admit that it is wholly compatible with a total commitment to a value-scheme of the austerest civic virtue and active citizenship. The strategy of opposing these values to those of urban radicals, and presenting them as the regressive nostalgia of a pre-capitalist landed class, was indeed invented in the eighteenth century itself; but in the twentieth, it has been a historiographical mistake. Catharine Macaulay furnishes an excellent warning against committing it.

But the problem of gender remains. Why should a woman admire the Greco-Roman ideal of citizenship? It was male-centered; it was warrior; it was slaveholding – many London merchants owned West Indian plantations, but I dare say Macaulay disapproved of slavery. It was above all patriarchal, and assumed a rigid separation between the public and private spheres, which (at least in Athens) left the woman confined within the household while the male went out into the assembly to practice citizenship. We might bear in mind that Macaulay read more Roman than Greek history, and that the position of Roman ruling-class women was rather different; but the values were at bottom the same. There of course exists a modern feminist strategy which consists in denying the separation of private from public and – what is not quite the same thing – decentering the primacy of the political on which so much in Western values and philosophy has been founded. Not just the interactions between citizens and decision-takers at the level of public power, but the interactions between humans at all levels of social existence, are shown to have had their political dimension, and the notion of politics as taking place at the public level is exposed to deconstruction as having been a male preserve – which it has been – and as having been invented as a form of male domination[12] – which is not quite as certain.

None of this can be imagined as appealing in the least to Catharine Macaulay. If she had heard of it – which was probably not possible in her time – she would have suspected something sinister behind it. There is no sign that she knew of Mary Astell, but Astell's High Church Toryism would have come under her strongest disapproval, and since she was a militant anti-clerical I can imagine her regarding Astell's feminism as a product of that power of priests, confessors, and spiritual directors over female weakness which she could denounce as readily as any anti-clerical and misogynist male. But the decentering of the political was going on in her time, for reasons not immediately connected with gender (though the connections can be found). It was implicit in the debate over commerce and virtue, which carried with it the suggestions that in a world increasingly commercial, all manner of transactions and interactions between human beings were becoming as important as the classically political and were developing politics of their own. New conceptions of liberty were needed, and the individual might find his or her freedom in the ability to move in this new, sociable, and polite world, developing new cultural and productive capacities under the protection of a stable government which extended over wide areas.[13] It cannot be too much emphasized that the great writers who expounded this new primacy of social over political – Defoe, Addison, Hume, on the whole Adam Smith – were all supporters of the Whig financial aristocracy which Macaulay incessantly denounced, or that they leant visibly toward the view that women were better placed in modern than

---

[12] Gerda Lerner, *The Creation of Patriarchy* (Oxford: Oxford University Press, 1986); Patricia Springborg, *Western Republicanism and the Oriental Prince* (Cambridge: Polity Press, 1991).

[13] J. G. A. Pocock, *The Machiavellian Moment* (Princeton: Princeton University Press, 1975); *Virtue, Commerce and History* (Cambridge: Cambridge University Press, 1985); Albert Hirschman, *The Passions and the Interests* (Princeton: Princeton University Press, 1976).

in ancient civilized life. David Hume, for example, writes somewhere that modern conversation is superior to ancient, for the reason that women are admitted to it instead of being excluded. I suggest that this is one reason why he could write quite amiably, and not very patronizingly, to Macaulay about their profound differences over English history, remarking in his letter that her notion of liberty was very different from his.[14] That indeed was the point. The decentering of politics had begun, not as a feminist but as a Whig strategy, and was seen as having a relevance to women which Macaulay altogether rejected. There is a question where that leaves her.

I am arguing that she was a patriot, committed to the ancient primacy of civic virtue among the defining human values. Modern feminism on the other hand, in so far as it bases itself on a decentering and redistribution of politics, might seem to derive more from the other side of the great eighteenth-century debate, that which asserted the primacy of commerce over virtue and the social over the political.[15] The advocates of women's education and women's rights might claim a place among the radical bourgeois intellectuals, if you think that term of much use in historical analysis, but Catharine Macaulay will not fit in there. She begins to look like an eighteenth-century Hannah Arendt, a woman wholly committed to the ancient ideal of active citizenship and wholly undeterred by its hyper-intense masculinity. I am tempted to suggest that women political thinkers have faced a hard choice since her time: whether to claim and conquer citizenship, or to deconstruct it; and it is a choice more philosophical than tactical.

The ideology of commerce in her active years was still working on the side of Whig commercial aristocracy, which was supposed to be a major force replacing ancient with modern values. When there first came to be a democratic or feminist radicalism basing itself on the modern and the suppression of the ancient is a complicated question; Mary Wollstone-craft knew Macaulay's works, and greatly admired her. The lines along which we organize the history of eighteenth-century thinking, and of these women as part of it, may seem more important to us than they did to them.

What has Macaulay's *History of England* to say about women in general or the women who appear in it? The majority of these allusions condemn rather than praise the individuals concerned. This can be largely explained, of course, by noting that most of the women she needs

---

[14] R. Klibansky and E. Mossner, eds., *New Letters of David Hume* (Oxford: Oxford University Press, 1954), 81–82.
[15] Minuti ("Il problema storico," 820, n. 91) quotes a passage in which her judgment on the moral and historical effects of commerce inclines to the negative side.

to mention were princesses and queens – Elizabeth I,[16] Henrietta Maria, Mary of Orange, Anne – and therefore involved in upholding that Tudor regime in church and state of which Macaulay heartily disapproved, both because it was monarchical and absolutist and because it was Anglican and ecclesiastical. But she can be equally scathing about women of less than royal rank who intervene in politics or political writing on what she considers the wrong side. There is such an allusion to Margaret duchess of Newcastle,[17] and another to a 1643 riot of London women against the war, which are altogether contemptuous, though counter-balanced by the one woman praised at length – predictably Lady Rachel Russell,[18] wife of the Whig martyr of 1683. It is these cases which make me confident that I know what Macaulay will have thought about Astell if she knew of her; party mattered to her a good deal more than gender. But we find also several disapproving remarks about women in general; there are observations about female weaknesses which strike me as integral and not just conventional in her rhetoric. What I think we have here is that common enough phenomenon, the woman of great character and intelligence who can hold her own anywhere and rather despises the generality of women because they can't, or don't if they can. In Macaulay's case, it is of the same order as her democratic elitism, which made her worship liberty and despise the mob. She believed in the equality of human capacities, and felt contempt for the inequality of human performances. She knew what human virtue was and never altered her definition of it; either you had it, therefore, or you had not. This is more a patriot than a liberal attitude, and large questions open up from that point; a cultural pluralist she certainly was not.

I want now to turn to a rather different historical framework, and examine Macaulay in the context of the literary activity in which she was chiefly engaged, that of English historical and political writing between the accession of George III and the end of the American War. We can look at her in the context of the history of historiography, the craft of historical writing, and here it jumps to the eye that she was a very able practitioner indeed. The rules of historiography in her time were different from what they later became – one worked from printed authorities far more than from manuscript archives – and here she

---

[16] "The vices of this princess were such as could not exist with a good heart, nor her weaknesses with a good head: but to the unaccountable caprice of party-zeal she owes the reputation of qualities that would do honour to a masculine mind" (*History*, I, 2).

[17] *History*, IV, 120–21 (footnote).

[18] *History*, VII, 444–46. Lois G. Schwoerer, *Lady Rachel Russell: One of the Best of Women* (Baltimore: Johns Hopkins University Press, 1989).

covered the ground; there were very few printed narratives or collections of documents she did not use, and she was one of the first to work in what became the British Museum and Library, and may have had some access to the great Thomason Collection of Civil War and Interregnum pamphlets. As a result, her account of the Army's revolution between 1647 and 1649 is very likely to prove the best written in the eighteenth century and perhaps well into the nineteenth. There are gaps in her knowledge; she does not seem to know that *The Ready and Easy Way to Establish a Free Commonwealth* – which she cites – is by John Milton, a hero of hers; but by the standards of 1771 this is to judge her by an exacting set of criteria. She began to publish her *History* in 1763, the year after David Hume published the final collected version of his *History of England* – which is the greatest work of its kind in the century – and engages Hume in vigorous and sometimes acid debate. It is clear that Hume took her seriously and that others did. No historian tried pronouncing on her the kind of judgment which John Adams passed on Mercy Otis Warren,[19] that history was no pursuit for a lady; but the point there is that Warren was trying to write history of the most classical kind there was, the narrative of the acts and decisions of statesmen still living, and that Adams, objecting quite justly to her account of his own motivation, was telling her that, as a woman, she hadn't been there and didn't know what it had been like. This kind of history was supposed to be written by a statesman, out of experience. Macaulay, basing on documents and narratives a history of events a century before, was not open to that criticism, and there was nothing about the writing of documented history that she did not know as well as anybody knew it then.

Her *History of England*, covering a century and published over nearly twenty years, is perhaps the only full-length history of the Stuart period to the Hanoverian accession written from the patriot or Old Whig standpoint; its only competitor from that standpoint is Tobias Smollett's attempt to carry the narrative from 1688, where Hume left off, past her stopping-point into 1714, down to 1760 or later. Macaulay's history has to be compared with Hume's, to which it is antagonistic, and here it must appear less innovative. Hume does employ very complex and sophisticated models of social and mental change in his attempt to account for the seventeenth-century crisis, and Macaulay does not. The reason is that her historiography is still rhetorical and humanist, whereas his is philosophical; she celebrates the triumphs of civic virtue in

---

[19] Author of *A History of the Rise, Progress and Termination of the American Revolution* (Boston, 1805); correspondent and friend of Catharine Macaulay.

England and analyzes its corruption, where Hume is seeking the historical causes which established a modern world in which civic virtue is (he believes) no longer possible nor desirable.[20] The effect is that the more conservative ideologue is the more innovative historian.

This is not to say that there is anything merely conventional about her volumes; they are very independent indeed. Especially in her history of the Commonwealth period, she is attempting something not undertaken by Hume and not attempted again until William Godwin:[21] a history of the English republic written by one in sympathy with republican principles. The difficulty here, most of us would say, is to find anyone in regicide England who had a clear set of republican principles, but she boldly asserts that between the execution of the king and Cromwell's dissolution of the Rump Parliament, there was a shining moment in which it would have been possible to erect an English republic and reform the nature of the English people so that they became capable of sustaining one, as in the fallen world of reality they never have been.[22] Macaulay does not identify the virtuous patriots, the potential philosopher-legislators of this window of opportunity, but I suspect that we are looking at a Miltonic moment, and that they are the individuals later celebrated by Wordsworth as

> the elder Sidney, Marvell, Harrington,
> Young Vane and others who called Milton friend,

to whom she would have added the names Marchmont Nedham and Edmund Ludlow. These are the so-called "Commonwealth canon," brought together about 1700 by John Toland, who wrote Milton's biography, edited the works of Harrington and Sidney, and rewrote Ludlow's memoirs;[23] there is probably a continuity between their religious heterodoxy, Toland's, and the radical unitarianism to which Macaulay may have subscribed. But she describes the closing of the window by the essentially reactionary dictatorship of Oliver Cromwell, which was bound to lead to a restoration of the monarchy sooner or later. Macaulay had no insight into Cromwell's character or motivation, but she was not so far wrong about the ultimate effects of his actions.

If Oliver Cromwell is the first lost leader or grand betrayer of

---

20 Phillipson, *Hume,* and Duncan Forbes, *Hume's Philosophical Politics* (Cambridge: Cambridge University Press, 1976).

21 *A History of the Commonwealth of England,* 4 vols. (London, 1824–28). See John Morrow, "Coleridge and the English Revolution," *Political Studies* 40, 1 (1988): 128–41.

22 The closest study of her treatment of this theme is in Minuti's article, "Il problema storico."

23 Macaulay's Ludlow is certainly Toland's. See Blair Worden, ed. and intro., *A Voyce from the Watchtower* (London: Royal Historical Commission, 1978).

Macaulay's radical history, the second is William III. She belonged to a current of thinking that has been traced back very close to 1688 itself,[24] according to which the Revolution of that year had disastrously failed to seize the opportunity of reforming politics and renegotiating the powers of the crown. In some hands, such as Smollett's but not hers, this came close to a nostalgic Jacobitism; perhaps it would have been better to keep James II as king and impose limitations upon him, rather than letting William enlarge the crown's authority in an entirely new direction by transforming Britain into a powerful military monarchy perpetually engaged in European wars, which is what republicans like Andrew Fletcher, Tories like Jonathan Swift, and Jacobites like Thomas Carte all came to believe had happened. Macaulay held that the danger of a Stuart despotism by absolute prerogative rule had given way to the much greater, more subtle, and more subversive danger of the corruption of parliamentary virtue by the influence of the crown, exercising the awesome patronage which it derived from a civil list, the maintenance of a professional army, and a system of public credit which kept the nation forever in debt. These were the themes of eighteenth-century political argument, and there were few – even David Hume himself – who did not accept this thesis to some extent.

Like others, Macaulay is not saying simply that an opportunity of limiting the crown's powers was lost in 1688–89; she is saying that a major historical change occurred then, with the result that these powers greatly increased. This change was in part the result of William of Orange's dynastic ambitions; you may find in her subtext the hint that the aim of putting a stop to the dangers presented by James II did not have to be attained by making William a king, least of all on his terms. This unites the Tory and Jacobite contention that James might have been kept on the throne with the ultra-Whig contention that the monarchy might have been made more truly conditional and elective than it had been. She further holds that this vast increase in the crown's patronage and influence was made possible by England's and Scotland's involvement in the great European war conducted by William against Louis XIV, an involvement which – as she rightly sees – it was William's objective to bring about when he landed in England with his army. Here she is carrying on what is known as the blue-water rhetoric which various Tory oppositions had kept up throughout the reigns of Anne and the first two Georges, insisting that Britain ought not to fight great wars in Europe, which corrupted the state and increased the public debt, but

---

[24] Mark Goldie, "The Roots of True Whiggism," *History of Political Thought*, 1, 12 (1980): 195–236.

should grow great at sea and by commerce instead. As far back as 1620, speaking of the war which James I failed to fight for the liberation of Protestant Germany, she says it was the only continental war in which England should ever have been engaged.[25] This rhetoric upheld the republican dream of keeping the commonwealth virtuous and free from corruption, as well as the widespread perception that professional armies and systems of public credit were great new historical forces which were transforming and perhaps corrupting the political life of Britain and Europe. Macaulay perceived 1688 as beginning a process through which parliaments down to her own time had grown increasingly subject to the corrupting influence of an over-militarized and over-financed executive branch, but the rhetoric she is using was historically Tory rhetoric, though structurally unconnected with that of divine right and hereditary succession, and had been used by Tories since the reign of William III. Most of the authors she cites in tracing the growth of corruption are Tory, and she cannot quite admit how many of her republican doctrines have passed through a Tory filter before reaching her.

I am emphasizing all this because it is the way to placing Macaulay in the history of British political rhetoric and ideology. The Sawbridge connection were London commonwealth radicals who had long maintained political positions, shot through with republican Old Whig language, which were Tory in the sense that they were persistently hostile to the Whig parliamentary regime. They had been ardent supporters of the elder William Pitt,[26] whom they had seen as winning great victories in America for the patriot and blue-water cause, but had watched him being isolated, defeated, and bought off by George III and his new ministers. The last pages of Macaulay's *History* give an account of his corruption.[27] They identified the king with a sinister Scottish faction led by the earl of Bute, who were supposed to be restoring Stuart absolutism by means of Hanoverian corruption; this accounts for Macaulay's evident animus – in spite of her married surname – against the Scottish nation, and her insistence that the process of corruption has reached its climax as she is writing, and that virtue is making its last stand against the faction's plans to bring back despotism. In the United States thirty years earlier, the enemies of Alexander Hamilton would be talking in precisely the same way.[28] She was as hostile as ever to the

---

[25] *History*, I, 148.
[26] Marie C. Peters, *Pitt and Popularity: The Patriot Minister and London Opinion during the Seven Years War* (Oxford: Clarendon Press, 1980).
[27] *History*, VIII, 335.
[28] Lance Banning, *The Jeffersonian Persuasion* (Ithaca: Cornell University Press, 1978).

Whig aristocracy now partly alienated from the crown, and her anger against Edmund Burke stems from her perfectly accurate perception that he was trying to mobilize opposition to George III in support of that group among the great Whig families who had been excluded from office; she saw all that as part of the system.

The Sawbridge connection and many others like them – David Hume called them "those insolent rascals in London and Middlesex,"[29] but they were important in Yorkshire and the provinces generally – emerged as a radical opposition in the years before and during the American crisis, the years in which the *History of England* was written and published. Their language was sometimes extremely violent, and a latent anti-Hanoverian traceable to their Tory antecedents merged with their insistence that England – they did not address the Scots except to detest them – was an elective monarchy and potentially a republic. There was no longer either a Jacobite or a republican alternative, and yet one feels that the throne of George III was not fully secure. In a valuable book called *Disaffected Patriots*[30] John Salisbury has traced how the London aldermanic opposition tried to unify their discontents with those of the American colonists, and how utterly destructive to their cause the Declaration of Independence turned out to be. Just what they were trying to achieve the student of Catharine Macaulay would have to decide – it may have more to do with the religious infrastructure to her thinking than I have found time to indicate – but whatever it was, they were defeated and there is a sense in which her *History of England* is part of the last hurrah of mid-Georgian radical opposition. The political nation rallied to George III; Hume had feared that the London democrats would provoke the absolutist response they were always talking about, but what happened was that by 1784 the king had recovered the leadership of Parliament and kept it for the rest of his life. Patriotism, in the sense in which one uses the term of Macaulay, was a lost cause. It did not disappear; it persisted as part of the rhetoric of the next fifty years; but the ideological climate of British politics was already changing by the time of the French Revolution, and after that – remember that she died in 1791 – new kinds of radicalism and conservatism began to be born. The mental world of Mary Wollstonecraft is already very different from that of Catharine Macaulay – less classical, less rhetorical, less theatrical. One does not feel that Wollstonecraft wanted to be a Roman matron or a Goddess of Liberty, but Macaulay of course dressed the part; and in Wollstonecraft one finds an

[29] J. Y. T. Greig, ed., *The Letters of David Hume* (Oxford: Clarendon Press, 1932), II, 303.
[30] *Disaffected Patriots: London Radicals and Revolutionary America* (Kingston and Montreal: Queen's-McGill University Press, 1987).

authentic feminism, born of Rousseau and her own revolt against Rousseau, which belongs to another world than Macaulay's. The heirs of the latter were the friends of Mr. Fox and the guardians of his flame, not Godwin's.

12 Investments, votes, and "bribes": women as shareholders in the chartered national companies

Susan Staves

To understand the extent of women's political participation in the early modern period we need to exercise historical imagination to see beyond courts and legislatures to the myriad other institutions in which significant sorts of political power have been exercised. Although the histories of companies are usually thought of as proper subjects for business or economic history, I want to consider here two companies that ought also to be considered subjects of political history: the South Sea Company and the East India Company.[1] Both companies were joint state/private ventures, chartered by the state and given monopoly trading privileges in their respective areas of the world.[2] Both were involved in underwriting the national debt, a fact which produced company leverage on government officials. Government officials were also significantly involved in the affairs of each company. Parliament passed, in addition to the statutes granting and renewing the charters, a series of regulatory statutes concerning each company.

---

[1] The classic treatment of both companies is William Robert Scott, *The Constitution and Finance of English, Scottish and Irish Joint-Stock Companies to 1720*, 3 vols. (1910–12; reprint ed., Bristol: Thoemmes Press, 1993). Most of the literature on the South Sea Company focuses on the crash of 1720, though the company continued to exist and its shares to trade long after. The standard work is now John Carswell, *The South Sea Bubble* (Stanford, Calif.: Stanford University Press, 1960). John Keay, *The Honourable Company: A History of the English East India Company* (New York: Macmillan, 1991), offers an overview of the India Company's long history from 1600 to 1820, emphasizing its activities in India. Lucy S. Sutherland's *The East India Company in Eighteenth-Century Politics* (Oxford: Clarendon Press, 1952) remains invaluable on internal company politics and on the relations between the company and the English government. More recent excellent work has been done by Huw V. Bowen in *Revenue and Reform: The Indian Problem in British Politics, 1757–1773* (Cambridge: Cambridge University Press, 1991) and a number of articles.

[2] On the general idea of joint state/private ventures and the construction of national identity in this period, see Susan Staves, "English Chattel Property Rules and the Construction of Personal and National Identity," *Law and History Review* 12 (1994): 123–53.

A corollary of the fact that these companies were chartered by statute in return for payments to the state was that the companies were dependent upon politicians to introduce bills they wanted, to muster parliamentary support for their passage, to organize the defeat of unwanted bills, and, in general, to see to it that negotiations between the state and company produced results advantageous to the company. Or, as we might put it today, the companies depended on lobbying to produce a "favorable regulatory climate." Moreover, the companies' foreign trade was vulnerable to conditions determined by the state's foreign policy. Not only did this give the companies an interest in influencing foreign policy, but both government officials and company officers and servants made substantial personal financial gain by trading on inside information.

Unlike other eighteenth-century political institutions, joint-stock companies had constitutions that admitted women as voters on the same terms as men. Women acquired shares of the South Sea and East India companies, attended stockholder meetings, and voted on questions put to shareholders. As early as 1691, fifty-six women were shareholders in the East India Company, twice as many as in 1675.[3] In 1783, 16.2 percent of shareholder accounts in East India stock were women's; this amounted to 12.5 percent of all India stock, with an average holding of £911 per woman.[4] As the questions voted on by shareholders included matters involved in state financing and issues of foreign policy such as the terms of Clive's or Hastings's service in India, women's participation as shareholders was, potentially, a site of women's political power. Moreover, since one reason why upper-class people not normally associated with the City became shareholders was to participate in their distribution of various kinds of patronage (for example, company jobs or access to initial public offerings of stock), access to the control of that kind of patronage was another familiar kind of political power. English women did not have the parliamentary franchise, but, as we shall see, it was soon enough realized that some women might be appropriate targets of company or ministerial lobbying and at least one woman became a lobbyist on behalf of her family's India interests.

---

[3] K. G. Davies, "Joint Stock Investment in the Later Seventeenth Century," *Economic History Review*, 2nd ser., 4 (1952): 300.

[4] H. V. Bowen, "Investment and Empire in the Later Eighteenth Century: East India Stockholding, 1756–1796," *Economic History Review*, 2nd ser., 42 (1989): 201. A printed *List of the Names of All the Proprietors of East India Stock; Distinguishing the Principal Stock Each Proprietor Now Holds, and the Time when such Proprietor became Possessed thereof* (London, 1771) was used by some contemporaries to help organize their interests and has been used by a number of modern economic historians. The list gives the size of each person's holdings and the marital status of each woman holder.

Our study of women's political writing in the early modern period would gain from consideration of the reasons for the relative paucity of such writing. Although debates over the South Sea Company and the East India Company produced huge numbers of contemporary texts, almost none of them were written by women. Just as we need to consider histories of institutions in order to understand the nature of women's political participation, so we also need to consider relations between institutions and the histories of discourses in order to understand women's participation, or lack of participation, in political writing. To take an obvious example, in eighteenth-century England women had no occasion to write parliamentary speeches. Rarely, an eighteenth-century woman might, as a sort of thought experiment, attempt to write in a genre from which women were institutionally excluded; for example, Miss R. Roberts published Church of England *Sermons Written by a Lady* (1770), despite the fact that women were excluded from the pulpit. But such experiments were, unsurprisingly, rare. Lois Schwoerer, in chapter 3, has argued that in the early modern period the popular press gave women a new discursive sphere in which to be politically active despite their exclusion from political institutions. This is certainly true, and yet, for reasons I want to try to tease out later, it did not lead to significant participation by women writers or women stockholders in the pamphlet wars over the joint-stock companies.

Although the South Sea Company was politically and economically less important than the East India Company, it was there that the phenomenon of the woman stockholder first gained widespread notice during the rise in the price of South Sea stock in the second decade of the century. Certain patterns of company, ministerial, and shareholder behavior emerged which were repeated and developed later in the century in East India Company affairs. Contemporaries noticed that some women were buying shares for themselves, either directly on Exchange Alley (where the presence of ladies created a sensation) or by using brokers as intermediaries.

The duchess of Marlborough demonstrated notable political and financial sagacity in handling her own South Sea stock. By 1715 her own fortune, more than £100,000, was mostly invested in South Sea stock and government funds. She correctly guessed that the Pretender's invasion was not a serious enough threat to justify selling her holdings. By 1717 she had over £30,000 of her own fortune in South Sea stock. Yet she believed that the dramatic rise in share prices was a speculative bubble and that the actual "purpose of the scheme was to 'put power into such hands, that nobody doubts considers their private interest more then paying debts or publick good.'" Consequently, she sold out shortly before the peak, and persuaded the duke to sell his holdings also, making them a profit of £100,000.[5]

Contemporary satirists were drawn to this novelty of women share-holders, and worked to frighten and cajole women out of a new field of economic and political activity for which women had no evident physical disability. Considerable cultural work was required to construct the buying and selling of stock as an activity suitable for patriotic and prudent gentlemen, but dreadfully ill-advised and dangerous for ladies. A major assault came at the time of the South Sea Bubble when, in many satires, women's participation in the stock market was represented as unsexing them and threatening their chastity. A typical satire, *A Poem Occasion'd by the Rise and Fall of South-Sea Stock* . . ., by "J.B., Gent.," laments that all sectors of genteel society have been caught up in speculative fever, but devotes particular attention to trying to develop an antithesis between desirability to men and an interest in finance.[6]

One of the more unusual South Sea pamphlets inadvertently gives a glimpse of a less sexist, more modern way of thinking about women as investors, one that reveals the potential of investing for developing women's knowledge. *Letter to the Patriots of Change-Alley. Offering some Considerations to prove Stockjobbing to be a great Security and Advantage both to Church and State* offers an insight into the effect of speculation and investing on women. The purported author is "Elizaphan She-majah, A Converted Jew," clearly, I would say, a pseudonym for an anti-Semite. He offers an ironic panegyric, praising stock-jobbing for having diverted people from their hysteria about the church's endangerment and from their obsession with masquerades. Ladies who formerly idled away their time perfecting costumes and appropriate masquerade banter now prattle on "the new Discovery of gaining *Cent.* per *Cent.*":

This Intentness of Thought and unusual Application in our *British* Dames, seems a promising Omen that they will soon out rival the Red-herring ladies in the Mannage of the Counting-house; and that the growing Beauties of our Isle will no longer submit to the Pedantick Education of Receipts to make a Pudding, but shoot out into the more becoming studies of *Arithmetick* and *Algebra*.[7]

---

[5] Francis Harris, *A Passion for Government; The Life of Sarah, Duchess of Marlborough* (Oxford: Clarendon Press, 1991), 210, 227–28.

[6] J.B., Gent., *A Poem Occasion'd by the Rise and Fall of South-Sea Stock. Humbly Dedicated to the Merchant-Adventurers trading in the South Sea* (London, 1720); Goldsmith-Kress 5898.64. For another perspective on the satires, see Catherine Ingrassia, "The Pleasure of Business and the Business of Pleasure: Gender, Credit, and the South Sea Bubble," *Studies in Eighteenth-Century Culture* 24 (1995): 191–210.

[7] "Elizaphan Shemajah, A Converted Jew," *Letter to the Patriots of Change-Alley. Offering some Considerations to prove Stockjobbing to be a great Security and Advantage both to Church and State* (London, 1720), 12–13.

"Intentness of Thought" and "Arithmetick" here figure as unbecoming and undesirable for ladies, but this author has at least noticed that the prospect of profit from stock investing provides incentives to acquire knowledge, indeed, knowledge women might easily acquire were there not strong cultural taboos against it, taboos this sort of satire contributed to constructing.

In some cases, particular women's large holdings of South Sea or East India stock was a sign that they already possessed political power. Some of the stock (or stock options) held by great ladies was acquired, according to the unsympathetic, as "bribes" intended to procure influence-peddling, or, more sympathetically, as "doceurs" suitable for great ladies in the normal patronage system. Company directors wanted politically powerful and fashionable people to be known to hold shares for a variety of reasons. First, it was in the interest of those City folk not accustomed to having power at court or in Parliament to create some identity of interest between themselves and the great ones of the land. Second, in a marketing logic not unlike that of writers who sought the names of the mighty and the fashionable for their subscription lists, the directors justifiably believed that the known participation of the great as shareholders would prompt more ordinary gentlepeople, otherwise unfamiliar with and nervous about financial assets, to become stock-holders too. (Here, of course, the directors encountered some resistance, as upper-class people, embarrassed to be known to be holders of stock, never as respectable an asset as land, tried to conceal the fact of their ownership through devices like maintaining stock accounts through straws.) Third, company management early on got the idea of using gifts to the great of stock (or options) to influence government officials on matters like charter renewals or threatened regulatory legislation.

Certain new issues of South Sea or East India stock had features of modern initial public offerings or "IPOs." In both cases, more people want to get in on the offering than the number of shares available, and the first owners expect to profit by a rapid run-up in price once broad trading begins. Only those who are especially favored by company directors or others with some control over the initial offering (as now, major clients of the brokerage firm shepherding the issue to market) are allowed to "get in on the ground floor." For example, Carswell points out that in the third Money Subscription for the South Sea four-fifths of the offering was allotted by directors and government ministers, with only one million left for the general public.[8] The subscription list for

---

[8] Carswell, *South Sea Bubble*, 160.

this offering featured the names of half the members of the House of Lords and over half the members of Parliament, as well as all the directors of the East India Company. Among the great ladies sharing in this subscription were the Princess of Wales; her daughters; the countess of Portland, their governess; and their sub-governess. Distressed contemporaries felt that speculation in South Sea stock caused the social world to turn upside down. As the marquis of Reading rightly observed, court was now paid not to aristocratic ministers but to company directors of low social origin like Blount and Knight, as even "Ladies young and old flocked to Blount's levee to beg for admittance to the subscriptions."[9]

Several very great ladies, who no doubt found it unnecessary to cool their heels at a director's levee, were thought by the directors to be powerful enough to be worth special favors: Sophia Charlotte, George I's illegitimate half-sister (later countess of Darlington); Countess Platten, Sophia Charlotte's sister-in-law, believed by many to be George I's mistress but probably not; and, most importantly, the duchess of Kendall, George I's German mistress. Ragnhild Hatton, in a sympathetic biography of George I, acknowledges that these ladies received secret "doceurs" from the company. Sophia Charlotte and the duchess of Kendall each received stock options valued at £15,000: "in the expectation that 'George I's ladies' would speak in the company's favour with the king and demonstrate their confidence in its future to the public, thus encouraging other investors."[10] The ladies paid in no cash but were given book entry holdings that they could sell later if and when the share price appreciated. Stock options distributed among "George's ladies" in hopes that they would become effective lobbyists for the company became particularly controversial, in part because the ladies were German, not English, and in part because the duchess of Kendall played a role in hampering the parliamentary investigation unleashed after the collapse of the Bubble. After the Secret Committee report on the Bubble had been read to the House, a motion was made to print the report, which would have meant printing the names of Countess Platten and the duchess of Kendall, as well as several ministers.

Sir Robert Walpole persuaded Parliament that a printed list would be unwise, but the House did try directors and ministers and passed a number of resolutions, one of which attempted to articulate the evil of conflict of interest:

---

[9] Viscount Erleigh [Gerald Rufus Isaacs, 2nd marquis of Reading], *The South Sea Bubble* (1933; reprint ed., Westport, Conn.: Greenwood Press, 1978), 101–102.

[10] Ragnhild Hatton, *George I: Elector and King* (Cambridge, Mass.: Harvard University Press, 1978), 152.

The taking in, or holding of stock, by the South Sea Company for the benefit of any member of either house of parliament or persons concerned in the Administration (during the time that the Company's Proposals or the Bill relating thereto were depending in parliament) without giving valuable consideration paid ... were corrupt, infamous, and dangerous practices, highly reflecting on the Honour and Justice of Parliaments, and destructive of the Interest of His Majesty's Government.[11]

While the 1720 and 1721 parliamentary investigations and proceedings against South Sea directors and ministers who had accepted stock, stock options, or loans from the company and who were involved in conflicts of interest made some impact on later company directors and ministers, they certainly did not extinguish such behavior.[12]

As I have observed, few women published contributions to the large literature of South Sea and the East India company controversy.[13] The work of one woman who did, Susanna Centlivre, sheds light on why most women stayed away from these subjects and from writing about contemporary politics more generally. Centlivre was a woman of the world, a successful writer of comedies, and a would-be political writer for the Whigs. She actually proposed that her political writing deserved to be rewarded with a present of South Sea stock.

Centlivre's writing career extended from 1700 to her death in 1714, a period in which the development of political parties and the rise of journalism significantly affected how writers imagined their careers. An important eighteenth-century paradigm began to emerge in which young writers early displayed their abilities in conventional genres, including panegyric, then experimented with periodical journalism that had an identifiable political slant, trying to attract the notice and favor of some great man who could advance them through posts ranging from humble private secretaryships to important public offices. They later hoped for assistance in getting into Parliament, and ultimately independence. Centlivre's contemporaries included Addison, Steele, and Swift, all of whom made efforts to progress along this career trajectory (although Swift wanted a bishopric rather than a seat in the Commons). Addison and Steele both got into Parliament and Addison rose to be Secretary of State. Later in the century, the poet James Macpherson,

---

[11] Carswell, *South Sea Bubble*, 241.

[12] On officials trading in India stock, see Huw V. Bowen, "'Dipped in the Traffic': East India Stockholders in the House of Commons 1768–1774," *Parliamentary History* 5 (1986): 44.

[13] In addition to Centlivre cited below, I have found a broadside by Elinor James, dated Feb. 3, 1714/15, addressed "Gentlemen of the *South-Sea* Company," supporting the company. Anne Finch, countess of Winchilsea, also published a South-Sea poem beginning "Ombre and Basset laid aside" that appeared as an anonymous broadside entitled "The Stock-Jobbing Ladies."

early known as the "editor" who produced *Fingal* (1762) as the supposed work of Ossian, later wrote in support of Lord North, held office in India, worked for the nabob of Arcot, and finally became a member of Parliament. The supreme realization of the dream of passing from impecunious writer to great statesman by attracting suitable patronage was achieved later in the century by another student of India affairs, Edmund Burke.

In the eighteenth century, a very large percentage of all "political writing" was produced by people attempting to progress from writing to wealth and office along this career trajectory. Much political writing was published as by ministers or other officials in defense of themselves or their policies, but, as contemporaries knew, often these speeches or pamphlets had been composed by secretaries or other assistants. Most political writing was produced in expectation of some return, not merely an increase in the writer's reputation if published with his name (which it often was not), but frequently of some present from the great person whose interests it advanced. Presents might come in the form of money, or help with gaining office, or in the newer forms of stock or access to initial public offerings.

In the early eighteenth century, at the beginning of party and print journalism, it was not immediately obvious that women could not be political writers. Delarivière Manley wrote extensively about politicians and collaborated with Swift on the Tory periodical, *The Examiner*.[14] Particularly after 1712, Centlivre identified herself as a Whig in various poems and dedications. Against the advice of Steele, she dedicated her play, *The Wonder: A Woman Keeps a Secret* (1714), to the duke of Cambridge, soon to be George I. According to John Mottley, her dedication appeared while George was still at Hanover,

just at the Time when a Writ had been demanded, but refused, to call him to his Seat in the House of Peers in *England*. Mrs. *Centlivre* did this, to shew her Attachment to the House of *Hanover*, and was rewarded for it when the present Royal Family came to the Throne, who bespoke this Play, which they honoured with their Presence and made the Author an handsome Present.[15]

She celebrated George's accession to the throne with a six-page poem, signed, praising him as the champion of Protestantism and liberty, and as a rescuer of England from discord and faction.[16]

In a signed poem published in 1720, *A Woman's Case: In an Epistle to*

---

[14] The classic article is Gwendolyn B. Needham, "Mary de la Rivière Manley, Tory Defender," *Huntington Library Quarterly* 12 (1948–49): 253–88.

[15] Quoted in John Wilson Bowyer, *The Celebrated Mrs. Centlivre* (1952; reprint ed., New York: Greenwood Press, 1968), 152–53.

[16] Quoted in ibid., 156.

Charles Joye, Esq; Deputy-Governor of the South Sea, Centlivre boasts of
her faithfulness to the Whig cause in difficult times, notes that the Tories
have rewarded their writers, even their "Female Wits," and boldly, if
amusingly, demands that she be rewarded too, preferably with South
Sea stock. The poem is framed by a conventional apostrophe to its
recipient (accompanied by an unusually candid admission that the poet
does not know him personally) and a final promise that, if her request is
fulfilled, she will sing his fame:

> JOYE shall resound from every Tongue,
> And *South-Sea* be like Tagus sung.[17]

That early modern poets normally celebrated the subjects of their
panegyrics and dedications in expectation of tangible reward was, of
course, well known. Centlivre's realistic comic eye makes this expectation explicit, thus moving the relationship out of a mystified gift
economy into an open commercial market transaction, words of praise
in exchange for stock. She points to her "frequent Rhimes" against the
"Misleaders" of Queen Anne, which proved, "I durst be good in Worst
of Times," but laments:

> *Anna* Resign'd, and *Brunswick* Came,
> And yet my Lot is still the same.[18]

Even with George on the throne, she complains, the Tories keep their
"Herd" of writers "in constant Pay," while the Whigs allow loyal
Centlivre herself to be derided and unprovided for.

The best comedy of Centlivre's poem arises from the dialogue she
reports between her and her husband, dialogue that precipitates her
demand for stock. Joseph Centlivre, whom she had married in 1701,
actually did have a place at court, albeit a humble non-sinecure as
Yeoman of the Mouth (cook) under William, then Anne, then George.
In the poem, Joseph worries that his wife's political writing will lose him
his place. During the heyday of the Tories, Centlivre says, she has
consoled him with promises of advancement once the Whigs got in; yet,
now, he daily quarrels with her about the profitlessness of her writing,
which has still failed to yield either cash for her or promotion for him. It
is Joseph who suggests she ought to buy a South Sea "*Subscription*":

> Your Brother Bards, you see, have don't;
> Mayn't JOYE as generous be as *Blount*?[19]

One cannot be sure exactly which "Brother Bards" he had in mind, but

---

[17] Susanna Centlivre, *A Woman's Case: In an Epistle to Charles Joye, Esq; Deputy-Governor
of the South Sea* (London, 1720), 13.
[18] Ibid., 4.   [19] Ibid., 9.

we do know Pope, and, more surprisingly, the poorer and more frugal Swift (despite his public opposition to the scheme) had purchased shares; most spectacularly, Gay had received £2,000 of South Sea stock as a gift from James Craggs, the younger, Secretary of State.[20] Centlivre's poem uses the same eye for topical detail and novel social forms that make her stage comedies appealing.

The open brazenness of Centlivre's request for stock, no doubt, made it less likely to succeed than the more usual panegyric or dedication that at least pretends to be part of a gift economy in which all presents come unsought. Yet, although Centlivre exploits the comic novelty of an exchange of words of praise for stock, she insists that such exchanges are a feature of modern life.

Problems women confronted in imagining themselves as political writers are suggested by Centlivre's farce, *A Gotham Election* (1715). Given the pattern of writers looking to exchange their work for preferment to office, there were very few offices women could seek. Centlivre creates comedy by imagining "places" women might solicit in exchange for helping candidates. Lady Worthy, campaigning for her husband, promises Goody Gabble a place nursing children if she will influence her husband's vote.[21] After Mr. Mallet goes through a long list of places he wants from Tickup for his male relatives, a list partly drawn from a printed list of "all the great Places ... in the present State of *Gotham*," he finally thinks to ask for a place for his wife Joan. Yet he cannot think what the name of such a place would be. Racking his brain, Tickup invents the post of "Oyster-Cracker to the Court."[22] Presumably this was designed to get a laugh of recognition from an audience who knew the playwright was married to the Yeoman of the Mouth. Yet it also hints that far too many "places" were archaic sinecures.

Centlivre's joke also underlines the gender asymmetry of the new political world in which women may write about party politics, as Manley and Centlivre did, and may campaign for candidates, as in *A Gotham Election*, but in which important rewards for political activity, places, and preferments, are in short supply for women. Such conditions might drive a woman to ask for stock – or to write more directly for money from the booksellers by producing translations from the French,

---

[20] Virginia Cowles, *The Great Swindle: The Story of the South Sea Bubble* (New York: Harper and Bros., 1960), 132, 148. On Gay see David Nokes, *John Gay: A Profession of Friendship* (Oxford: Oxford University Press, 1995), 288–93, 310–12.

[21] *The Gotham Election*, in *The Works of the Celebrated Mrs. Centlivre*, 3 vols. (London, 1872), III, 169. The Lord Chamberlain refused to license this play for performance, so Centlivre was forced to see it appear in print only; she dedicated it to Secretary Craggs.

[22] Ibid., 169.

books of advice to women, plays, or novels, as most women writers in the generations immediately following Manley and Centlivre did.

Literary sources give the misleading impression that women investors were a fleeting South Sea Bubble phenomenon. Carswell, for example, remarks: "For a brief moment fashion and the existence of a market in which women could deal legally ... gave great married women prominence and wealth in their own right ... Like other signs of the emancipation of manners which are characteristic of the period leading up to the Bubble, such demonstrations of female independence did not survive it."[23] It is true that literary and visual sources in the later eighteenth century tend to ignore women shareholders, yet women did hold India shares. While a gendered division of competence with respect to stock investing was constructed, the external and internal politics of the East India Company make the situation more complicated than might appear.

The dominant construction of stock investing as an activity suitable for patriotic and prudent gentlemen, but ill-advised and dangerous for women, is evident in Thomas Mortimer's *Every Man his own Broker: or, A Guide to Exchange Alley.* Describing himself as having lost "a genteel fortune, by being the innocent dupe of 'Change-Alley,'" Mortimer first published his popular book in 1761. Many of the thirteen subsequent editions published before 1807 were revised to keep up with new developments in stock investing. Mortimer was enthusiastic about investing in stock, especially stock in the public funds and in the great national companies whose share prices were regularly listed in the newspapers – the Bank of England, the South Sea Company, and the East India Company – but he abhorred stockbrokers, whom he describes as parasitic middlemen preying on the genteel public and encouraging destructive speculation. He, therefore, offers nuts-and-bolts instructions to ordinary gentlemen about how to purchase and sell shares directly, without using a broker.

Mortimer constructs active management of one's own portfolio as a patriotic and manly activity. Writing the first edition during the Seven Years' War, he tells his reader that buying government securities is mutually advantageous to his country and to himself.[24] Men who might shrink from direct contact with the hurly-burly of low characters on Exchange Alley are urged "boldly and manfully" to transact their own

---

[23] Carswell, *South Sea Bubble*, 144.

[24] Philantropos [Thomas Mortimer], *Every Man his own Broker: or, A Guide to Exchange-Alley* (London, 1761), 4. Later editions were published with Mortimer's name on the title page.

business directly "to rescue the best of governments from a slavish dependence on these sons of rapine . . . in time of war."[25]

Mortimer blames the rise of stockjobbers on the ladies' alleged need for intermediaries and urges gentlemen to buy and sell for their female relations. Gentlemen can become chivalric rescuers of "the fair sex" from all connection "with that medley of Barbers, Bakers, Shoe-makers, Plaisterers and Taylors, whom the mammon of unrighteousness has transformed into Stock-Brokers"; in so doing, they will destroy a pernicious set of men, one of whose "principal emoluments arises from the management of the fortunes of women."[26] In the first edition of 1761, his chief anxiety about the ladies seems to be that they be protected from contact with the low men who are brokers. By 1784 he has added comments about women's incapacity for investing arising from their "ignorance, joined to a propensity for gaming."[27]

Mortimer's detailed instructions would enable any literate person with sufficient cash, male or female, to trade in stock. He explains exactly where to go, what to say, and what written transfer forms to use. Knowing how arithmetically challenged the eighteenth-century gentleman was likely to be, he even explains how to calculate share prices that involve fractions. All this information might be used by a lady as well as by a gentleman. Encouraging gentlemen to be bold and manful in venturing into Exchange Alley, to brave the "wild uproar, and confused noise that will first strike your astonished senses," he points out that "many of you have supported more for your amusement, on the first night of a new play" – but then so had many ladies, since plays, pleasure gardens, or masquerades hardly restricted their audiences to the male sex.

Mortimer's reasonable belief that understanding the accuracy and significance of political news was crucial to managing one's portfolio of government and company securities is implicit in his construction of women as financially incapable.[28] He worries that, like unscrupulous native stockjobbers, foreigners too often plant false news in the British press to manipulate the market. Manly men can develop the capacity to disregard such rumors, while ladies and other feeble persons are apt to

---

25 Ibid., 103–104.   26 Ibid., xi–xiii, xix.
27 Mortimer, *Every man his own Broker*, 1785, xix.
28 For modern considerations of the eighteenth-century stock market, see S. R. Cope, "The Stock Exchange Revisited: A New Look at the Market in Securities in the Eighteenth Century," *Economica* 45 (1978): 1–21; Philip Miroski ("The Rise [and Retreat] of a Market: English Joint Stock Shares in the Eighteenth Century," *Journal of Economic History* 41 [1981]: 559–77) contains a useful table of annual prices for South Sea and East India shares; Huw V. Bowen, "Lord Clive and Speculation in East India Company Stock, 1759," *Historical Journal* 30 (1987): 905–20.

be stampeded into premature buying and selling, which only profits the brokers and manipulators: "the antiquated maiden, who subsists on the annual income of her property in the funds; and the miser, who always hated paper money, tremble for their property, and reason thus with themselves: 'STOCKS are fallen on the news 3 per *Cent*. Perhaps to-morrow it may be worse, and the following day worse still; better sell before all is lost.'"[29] Market prices, especially of foreign trading companies, did indeed rise and fall on news, true and false, and there was a relationship between understanding contemporary politics and foreign affairs and an ability to be a successful investor. The duchess of Marlborough's political understanding, for example, was surely one reason she profited so dramatically from her South Sea investment.

Reading Mortimer or other texts more narrowly addressed to East India Company shareholders, one might erroneously suppose that the significant number of women stockholders in the East India Company in the later eighteenth century represented only family decisions to use East India stock in trusts for female relations. *The East India Examiner* (a periodical for shareholders) and all the pamphlets I have read attempting to sway votes in the Court of Proprietors assume their readers are gentlemen. Certainly some India stock was held in trusts for women, although India bonds were preferred by many for such purposes.[30]

Yet an important value of East India stock was the franchise it gave in Court of Proprietors' meetings, and the constitution of the company did not permit trustees to vote stock held in trusts. There is evidence that many (I think most) women who held East India stock held it in their own names (not as trust beneficiaries); that most such holders were single women, spinsters, or widows, rather than wives; that at least some of the women shareholders attended meetings to vote in person, and more voted by ballot; and that some actively participated in the "share splitting" procedures developed to create voting blocks in the Court of Proprietors. My evidence on these questions is admittedly limited, yet I think it is at least enough to question the conventional view of women's lack of participation. Women shareholders certainly did not coalesce into a "women's lobby" representing "women's interests," but some did play active roles in company politics, and, by extension, in national politics. Beginning in the 1760s the Court of Proprietors of the East India Company was the locus of heated contests between the directors of the company and government ministers as well as between both of

---

[29] Mortimer, *Every Man his own Broker*, 4.
[30] Even as early as 1685, when women held "no more than 2–4% of India stock, they held nearly 60% of the bonds" (Davies, "Joint Stock Investment," 300).

these and company employees or servants working or having worked in India.[31]

One way in which women became involved in the politics of the Court of Proprietors arose from the tactic of stocksplitting. Unlike twentieth-century companies in which one share yields one vote and one thousand shares yield one thousand votes, in the early eighteenth century in the Court of Proprietors holders of less than £500 had no votes and holders of £500 had one vote. The Regulating Act of 1773 altered this to disenfranchise the £500 holders, making the minimum required for voting £1,000; by a sliding scale, owners of £10,000 had four votes, the maximum allotted to any holder. Thus, as far as voting power went, holdings in excess of £10,000 were useless. Blocks of excess shares were, consequently, split off to be transferred to supporters to create more votes.

Splitting first became important in the company election of directors in 1763, hotly contested between Laurence Sulivan, a merchant and a former company director, and Robert Clive, the hero of the Battle of Plassey and a company servant. Issues included not only the appropriate level of dividends after the company's new territorial acquisitions in India and the extent to which company servants should individually profit from their activities, but also the terms of the Treaty of Paris affecting the company. Using a banker as agent, the anti-Sulivan forces bought up enough stock to create 83 votes and in addition could use perhaps £100,000 of Clive's personal funds, also for splitting. As Dame Lucy Sutherland explained, this tactic was progressively refined and successfully used by both company and government interests. In this company election, Sutherland found,

For the first time the great Whigs now in opposition, the Marquess of Rockingham, the Duke of Portland, Lord Midleton, Lord John Cavendish, and others, took up voting qualifications in the Company and went down to India House to cast their votes for a party in the Company. For the first time the Paymaster-General, Henry Fox, put the accumulated funds of his department through its own officials at the service of the rival party to procure them votes.[32]

In this contest and later ones, managers tried to get current shareholders to vote with them, and also to create new "owners" of split stock who would do the same – "owners" who could be trusted to return the stock to its original owner when the election was over.

---

[31] In addition to Sutherland, see Huw V. Bowen, "The 'Little Parliament': the General Court of the East India Company, 1750–1784," *Historical Journal* 34 (1991): 857–72. For a detailed treatment of one of the early contests, see Bruce Lenman and Philip Lawson, "Robert Clive, the 'black jagir,' and British Politics," *The Historical Journal* 29 (1993): 901–29.

[32] Sutherland, *The East India Company*, 103–104. On contested elections, see also Bowen, "'Little Parliament.'"

Managers could not afford to overlook women shareholders in these contests. Sulivan wrote to Lord Shelburne in February of 1767: "Your Lordship told me you had secured Lady Betty Germain's 25,000£ stock which makes fifty votes. Since I had the honour to see you here a friend acquainted me that through Lord Vere he could obtain her stock. If therefore your Lordship has met with difficulties, I beg to know directly ... Marchioness Montandres [has] 12,000£."[33] Neither the Regulating Act nor an act to prevent the collusive transfer of shares fundamentally changed the use of stock splitting in company elections.

At least one woman worked behind the scenes as her family's financial and political agent: Mary Barwell. William Barwell was a company servant and later director who had ten children, Mary, the first-born, in 1733, and several sons who became company servants, most notably Richard, born in 1741.[34] Richard rose through the ranks on the civil side of the company in India, beginning in 1756. He was appointed a member of the four-man Council created by the Regulating Act to serve with Warren Hastings, the Governor-General of India. Finally, after an unusually long period of service in India, he returned to England in 1780 and became an MP in 1781.[35] An extraordinary series of letters from Richard in India to his sister Mary in London survives. These demonstrate that she was authorized by him to act as the manager of his money and as his political agent.

Like a number of other company servants in India, Richard decided that he needed a London agent to represent his interests, and, given the year-long turn-around time for communications from India to London, that the agent needed considerable discretion to adjust instructions according to ever-changing political circumstances at India House and in Parliament. He reiterates his trust in his sister's judgment and his understanding that she must be guided by local facts known to her but not to him. In 1769 when Mary seems first to have begun asking what she could do in London to advance his interests, he replies: "How can I point out the mode, which must depend entirely on the circumstances and the disposition of those it might be necessary to address?," then stipulates the money he would be willing to have her spend (in presents or bribes) to attain various high company posts.[36]

[33] Quoted in Sutherland, *The East India Company*, 104.
[34] "The Barwell Family," *Bengal Past and Present: Journal of the Calcutta Historical Society* 26 (1923): 184–87.
[35] James M. Holzman, *The Nabobs in England. A Study of the Returned Anglo-Indian, 1760–1785* (New York: no pub., 1926), 131–32.
[36] "The Letters of Mr. Richard Barwell," published in eleven installments in *Bengal Past and Present: Journal of the Calcutta Historical Society*, vols. 8–13, 1914–16. I will give letter nos. and dates in citations. No. 132, Jan. 20, 1769.

Events in 1773 made Richard place more dependence on Mary. After a brother died in 1773, Richard gave Mary power of attorney to act for him in settling their brother's estate. Even before this he had declared, "my purse is in a great measure put into your hands and confided to your discretion."[37] When their father also died in 1773, Richard wrote another brother, "I want to throw money into my sister's hands to strengthen those particular interests which must make way for our family pursuits in the East."[38] From this point on he writes more substantive long accounts of financial and political matters. He gives her what amounts to a course on topics an agent would need to understand, including interest and exchange rates, foreign bills of exchange, and the salt and opium monopolies.

Despite apparent grumbling from surviving brothers, Richard persisted in his choice of Mary as the family manager. He believed that she was more trustworthy than any man friend because he thought it was only human nature for such friends to fall away and pursue their own interests if opportunity offered. In this sibling collaboration, he insisted that his decision to throw "the whole of [his] fortune into [her] hands" was "the only safe and certain mode ... of giving [to her] personal powers that additional influence proceeding from a command of money."[39]

Richard proposed to advance their joint fortunes not only by sending Mary money, bills of exchange, and jewels, but also by feeding her information on which she could trade in India stock. He expected her to accumulate substantial positions and to manage them effectively in Court of Proprietors' contests. Learning that his brothers had been frightened by recent news and were tempted to sell stock, he wrote to her: "I desire ... that no India Stock may be sold out at a loss, but that I may answer for such stock by repaying the first purchases; ... as I ... can do without the interest which is necessary to subsist a man in England, I can very well wait the rise of the stock to sell ..."[40] Knowing that the market in India stock was subject to manipulation by rumor or merely erroneous news, Richard urged his sister to take full advantage of his privileged access to good information by never selling on news unless he confirmed it. Confident about the fundamental state of the Indian revenues in August of 1775 he wrote to assure her that the stock would only fall as a consequence of manipulation by speculators and, therefore, if it did fall, she ought to be a buyer.

Increased government control of the company through the Regulating

---

[37] Ibid., no. 180, Sept. 10, 1773.   [38] Ibid., no. 206, Oct. 20, 1773.
[39] Ibid., no. 287, no date.   [40] Ibid., no. 207, Oct. 20, 1773.

Act increased the politicization of the Court of Directors and the Court of Proprietors. Responding to a friend's letter in November of 1773, Richard declared that the servants abroad must *"interfere with the election of Directors . . .* indispensably so because it is the only step that promises to secure them that countenance from which alone they are enabled to derive a support to their just pretensions and to protect them from that superior weight of influence which men by resigning the Company's service and repairing to England, too often acquire."[41] Barwell's sense that a man needed advocates on the spot in London can only have been intensified by the arrival of the truly poisonous Philip Francis (formerly, unbeknownst to almost all contemporaries, "Junius"), who was sent out to serve with Barwell on the Council as a government representative and who then began the long campaign against Hastings (and secondarily Barwell) that ultimately culminated in Hastings's impeachment.

Richard urged Mary to pursue English officials on financial matters related to official business. For example, he suggested she seek an Admiralty official amenable to helping him with a partial solution he invented for the problem of transferring his Indian fortune back to England. Repatriating assets was a serious problem for servants who made significant sums in India;[42] Richard, whose final fortune contemporaries estimated at £400,000, had more to remit than most.[43] Servants could lend their personal money in rupees in India to the company for bills of exchange payable in London, but large sums so remitted aroused opposition from the directors, and the government had also set limits on the amounts of bills of exchange the company could issue. Thus, Richard asked Mary to help him transfer some of his funds by using Admiralty officials to make an end-run around the company. The government's local expenses in maintaining the India fleet created bills for these expenses, bills Richard knew were paid at no fixed rate of exchange. It occurred to him that Mary might induce someone at the Admiralty to order that Indian money be taken up from Richard at a fixed rate, then, after certification of payment, paid to Mary in London. Discussing the parameters of the exchange rate she should try to negotiate, he tells her, "If you can make it two shillings and two pence the current rupee, I could then afford to allow for a gratuitous fee [or bribe] to any member of the Admiralty one thousand pounds to expedite and secure the remittance of five lacks [of rupees]."[44]

[41] Ibid., no. 212, Nov. 5, 1773.
[42] The best discussion of this problem I have found is P. J. Marshall, *East Indian Fortunes: The British in Bengal in the Eighteenth Century* (Oxford: Clarendon Press, 1976), chap. 9, "A Settling of Accounts."
[43] Ibid., 244.   [44] Barwell, "Letters," no. 287, no date.

Richard relied on Mary to circulate among directors, proprietors, and relevant politicians to offer his versions of the many disputes that touched his or Hastings's reputations, including his handling of the salt revenues, the indictment of Nuncomar for conspiracy and forgery, and the Rohilla war. She was to circulate copies of his letters and make personal visits in which her arguments and testimony would serve to supplement written presentations. Commenting about her contacts with Sulivan, he adds, "This being intimated by you will have more weight than all the letters I write for the intimacy of friendship in which we have lived, may naturally be supposed to have given you the most perfect knowledge of my character and disposition."[45] Transmitting to her his "public minute and letters to Sulivan" on his conduct of the opium monopoly, he adds, "your ingenuity may suggest other [arguments] more forcible and conclusive."[46] On occasion his letters to her enclose letters for Lord North or the earl of Sandwich, which he expected her to deliver in person. By May 1775 Richard is suggesting that she might obtain the services of a Mr. Kelly, an able controversial writer, in support of his causes. Should his actions be misrepresented in the press or elsewhere, "you will use his pen, cultivate his acquaintance and reward his labours in the genteelest and most unexceptionable manner."[47] Whether she did this or not, I do not know, but we do know that Hastings's agent, Major John Scott, laid out the small sums that were needed to hire political writers and to place articles in the press.

Richard expected Mary to amass significant positions in India stock, to see that it was voted in accord with his interests, and, once he had decided that loyalty to the ministry was in his best interest, in accord with ministerial directives. He offered to begin a correspondence with John Robinson, Lord North's secretary and India specialist, volunteering useful local information, and also introducing Mary as his "confidential agent ... to be wholly directed by you in all matters that shall be agitated in the Proprietors' Court."[48] He urged Mary to promote "all matters which the Minister shall chose to pass through the medium of the Company ... and engag[e] all the friends you can influence to carry them through the Proprietary Courts."[49] Eschewing any desire to dictate the detailed management of the sums he remitted to her, he repeated: "Your discretion must influence you solely in the disposal, but ... I conceive your supporting a large proprietary interest in the stock of the India Company to be essential. The Minister will

---

[45] Ibid., no. 377, Nov. 30, 1774.
[47] Ibid., no. 443, May 19, 1775.
[49] Ibid., no. 393, Dec. 1, 1774.

[46] Ibid., no. 448, p. 87, Aug. 5, 1775.
[48] Ibid., no. 398, Nov. 30, 1774.

naturally expect such an influence should be preserved and at his command."[50]

In addition to lobbying and organizing that a male agent might also have done, Mary Barwell attended to a more female side of connection-building: work with women of families the Barwells wished to cultivate. She distributed Indian muslins and other presents her brother sent back; she also took pains to promote suitable marriages. Major Scott, writing from London to Mrs. Hastings in India, reports that Mary Barwell has called on him repeatedly " '& begs I will recommend ... to your serious Consideration' that Miss Williams in Bengal has not yet found a husband."[51] (And Miss Williams did in due course marry a gentleman follower of Hastings.)

In this chapter I have tried to suggest the significance of women's stockholding, a topic that deserves more investigation. Representations of women as having abandoned stock or as entirely passive holders in the period after the South Sea Bubble are not supported by company records. I will confess that, knowing that the constitutions of the South Sea Company and the East India Company permitted women's full participation in debates and votes where state interests were at stake, I hoped to find at least one woman taking advantage of this legal situation to make a substantive speech on some momentous political question, perhaps Clive's jagir or Hastings's conduct. I continued to seek such a voice even though I knew from Bowen's work that, in the intensely politicized debates of 1772–73, "Five of the seven most frequent speakers at the court between 1766 and 1773 were M.P.s and because of this the voice of the ordinary non-political investor was seldom heard."[52] The publicity accorded to these debates as well as extensive news coverage of India issues more generally certainly helped some women at least to have opinions on matters like Hastings's impeachment. There may yet be evidence of women's speaking. I have certainly not exhausted the copious available materials, and my own experience in looking for evidence of the realities of women's lives in the eighteenth century has on occasion led me to discover evidence sages assured me was not to be found. So far, though, the records suggest that, once again, the socialization of women not to act was more powerful than a legal regime entitling them to full participation.

Instead of the hard-hitting, historically informed speech one might imagine Catharine Macaulay could give in a Court of Proprietors meeting, I found evidence of women (except for Centlivre) behaving

[50] Ibid., no. 448, Aug. 5, 1775.
[51] Quoted from Scott manuscript in Holzman, *Nabobs in England*, 65.
[52] Bowen, " 'Little Parliament,' " 865.

rather like Namierite men, uninterested in ideology, collecting and distributing presents (or bribes), and developing connections for their family interests. Mary Barwell's work for her family looks rather like the work building connections other historians have documented business-men's wives doing in the eighteenth century, except that the degree of government involvement in the great national companies required contact with government officials and additional kinds of political work. And we do have to remember, in this age when politics can appear to be entirely a matter of television commercials, that the labor of organizing interests one person at a time, one favor at a time, as the old ward-healers used to say, is political work.

The new joint-stock companies threatened the position of upper-class men as the legitimate political rulers of the land. The social dread elicited by the South Sea moment when the wealth of low traders made aristocrats court them was later followed by hysteria over returning nabobs like Richard Barwell, who demonstrated that money could buy them seats in Parliament.[53] These signs that, as Barwell put it to his sister, "a command of money" produces influence and political power challenged assumptions about the naturalness and inevitability of upper-class rule. Moreover, the very idea that only upper-class men were capable of possessing that wide and realistic knowledge of the world that entitled them to a monopoly on governance was directly tested in battles between speculators in the stock market. City men, as the most successful speculators in East India stock, thereby seemed to demonstrate that they could understand and evaluate world news better than the "natural rulers" of the land. Yet, as long as women did not have direct experience of office either in the companies or in government, they lacked some of the "intelligence" so useful both for profit and for political power.

---

[53] Philip Lawson and Jim Phillips, "'Our Execrable Banditti': Perceptions of Nabobs in Mid-Eighteenth-Century Britain," *Albion* 16 (1984): 25–41.

Early modern legal and political prescriptions for women

Introduction to Part IV

The last part of this collection of essays concentrates on the political/ legal values and structures of fifteenth- and sixteenth-century France, sixteenth- and seventeenth-century imperial Germany, and seventeenth- and eighteenth-century Britain. More than the other sections of this work, it provides a comparative framework through which to view the intersection between how women viewed the state and their relation to it. It clarifies the need to move beyond any single form of government, scenario of political change or specific historiography if we are to understand the role gender plays in state formation and political values. While women in each case almost invariably lacked the political standing of men, and wrote less on explicitly political topics than did their male counterparts, still their political selves (and their conception of public space and exchange) were strongly affected by the power realities of their time and place.

These four chapters explore the distinct cultural and material parameters that dictated both the language and acceptable evidence for use by both women and men in framing arguments concerning women's political standing. Chapter 13 reassesses the construction and use of Salic law in late medieval and early modern France to document how jurists and clerics fabricate its origin and authenticity. Chapter 14 turns to imperial Germany and moves beyond the assumptions embedded in the vast majority of scholarship on women's early modern political nature and writings. Here was a society that lacked the liberal debates and evolution of seventeenth-century England or the revolutionary cauldron of eighteenth-century France. Thus the reform versus revolution dichotomy which so dominates early modern political discourse, and later scholarship, simply does not apply to the German states, nor can one simply insert gender into that accepted debate.

Chapter 15 focuses on the political and intellectual values inherent in legal treatises and precedents, their gender implications, and how discussions of women's political nature were fundamentally tied to a legal system that resisted seeing women as individuals. This chapter analyzes a presumably obscure and unimportant legal case from 1739, *Olive v. Ingram,* in which it was debated in King's Bench whether women could vote for and could hold the office of sexton in a London parish. Both the disputes during the case's hearing, as well as its subsequent influence on women's suffrage debates in the nineteenth century, highlighted the importance of "false universals" in which the disputants seemed to be using inclusive terms such as inhabitants, office holders, scot and lot voters, etc., but in reality these were gender-exclusive terms. The last chapter focuses on the political and intellectual values inherent in legal treatises, especially *The Hardships of the English Laws in Relation to Wives ... in an Humble address to the Legislature,* written by an anonymous woman in 1735, demonstrating how women's political nature was fundamentally tied to a legal system that resisted seeing them as individuals. Taken as a whole, these essays provide a useful context for debates over women's intellectual productivity, and their political standing and political thinking.

Sarah Hanley, in her study of the nature and influence of the "Salic law" on women's political status in late medieval and early modern France, highlights the use of historical texts – in this case misinterpreted and forged early legal documents – in both denying women office and dismissing their political writings. She treats the debate between Christine de Pizan and Jean de Montreuil over the authenticity of the Salic law and its application to women's rule, its continued use by early modern French jurists, and the long-term misogynist tradition into which these disputes were situated. Originally drawn from the law of the Salian Franks, the Salic law, according to Hanley, was reproduced first in 507–11 under the Merovingians, and later in a Carolingian version of 802–803. In dispute, for purposes of her study, was the transference of a supposed exclusion of women from land inheritance to royal rule. The dispute from 1400 to 1429 between Christine and Montreuil was over the validity, interpretation, and application of the Salic law. Hanley's analysis highlights the scramble of French writers, especially Montreuil, to exclude the female line in the period following the claim made by Edward III through his mother to the French throne.

Professor Hanley shows that such a case was made without offering any original legal text, or with forged documents, or with the correct text but a commentary appended claiming that Salic law had indeed excluded women when in fact it had not. All that could be claimed, according to the documents, was a custom that favored male over female inheritance. Montreuil, to win his dispute with Christine, had altered the original document. In Hanley's words: "This experienced politician and humanist writer deliberately chose to privilege forgery over philological

integrity, his own legal opinion against the text of the Salic Ordinance."
His effort fit within what she has termed a "defamation litany," which
underlay "'male mastery' of women (their bodies, knowledge, words)
aimed at removing women from learned disputation." Women were
subsumed under the fiction "woman," an entity which displayed an
"incapacity for governance either of self or of policy," Hanley concluded.
Thus this forgery of an early legal text was situated within a much older,
and continuing litany of views surrounding female inferiority; and it is
not possible, Hanley contends, to grasp the exclusion of women from the
French state or the opposition to Christine's political views without
understanding how these two realities are bound together. And Christine
took on this litany directly, recognizing its import, and defending female
rule in principle and example.

Thus Christine de Pizan represents that female political writer who
not simply conceptualized the state, but did so within the context of the
real exclusion of women from its reach. Hanley, in agreement with the
views of Berenice Carroll expressed in Part I of this volume, believes
that Christine has been slighted as a "critical political thinker" partially
because of the negative reaction her work received from contemporary
opponents.

Merry Wiesner, in her study of women in the Holy Roman Empire,
contends that many of the generalizations offered about women and
politics in early modern Europe do not hold for the German states
under the Holy Roman Empire. An amalgam of states "stretching
across central Europe," the Empire does not fit the "absolutist nor
constitutionalist" models familiar to those studying western Europe.
But the scarcity of works relating to the *querelle de femmes* in the Empire
has encouraged scholars to generalize about gender and the state from
"developments largely within centralizing nation states." In trying to
overcome such an anomaly, Wiesner focuses on the political implications of religious writings and actions by early modern German
women. Most importantly she makes clear that our analyses about
gender and the early modern state assume an undifferentiated model of
the state and have led to models that do not apply to all women during
this period. The Empire has much to tell us about the nature of urban
citizenship, something characterizing German women more than their
Western counterparts.

Both the writings of early modern German women, and the conceptualization of their political status, reflected their particular standing
within towns and resulted from political and religious disputes emerging
from the Reformation. Even though German women's religious works
had clear political import, they have seldom been interpreted as such.

The writings of Argula von Grumbach, Katherine Zell, and Anna Hoyer, according to Wiesner, offer clear examples of female religious figures integrating their religious and political goals. In addition, to document the tie between women's political writings and their political standing, Wiesner turns to a seldom-studied group, Catholic and Protestant abbesses in Lutheran territories, as well as to women rulers who governed very small states. In this study, Wiesner documents that Catholic nuns converted to Lutheranism to be able to maintain their convents and continue with their traditional activities of founding "schools, orphanages, and other similar institutions." The abbess of a free convent "was the penultimate legal authority in her area; her only overlord was the emperor." Her office did not simply incorporate religious and charitable functions but she appointed officials and sent representatives to the Reichstag, as well as holding legal courts. In Protestant areas, three options were possible: convents remained Catholic while coming under Protestant rule; their members converted to Protestantism and the abbess became a force to further Lutheran policies; or, some houses had both Catholic and Protestant nuns under one roof. Such realities document the greater desire for independence and autonomy on the part of these women, providing them with both political and economic standing. Thus, Wiesner makes us rethink the degree to which women's religious loyalties were always paramount, and the extent to which we can predict their political loyalties from such affiliation.

Issues of independence and authority operated among religious women in Germany along with spiritual influences; yet scholars have given little attention to this reality. Yet, according to Wiesner, until 1807 "ambivalence in gender and religious ideology . . . allow[ed] abbesses a wide range of powers." Another contrast between central and western Europe was the distinct role women played in central European towns from the fourteenth through the sixteenth centuries. Historians, concentrating on the national monarchies of the West, have underplayed the importance of urban citizenship. Even though the criteria for citizenship in these towns came under the headings, notes Wiesner, of "war, work, and wealth", all of which would have presumably excluded women, they, in fact, did not. Women were citizens and "the bases for accepting them as such . . . were explicitly the same three as for men." Thus, up through the late medieval period, women were considered "burghers" in a range of German cities, "and were obligated to swear an oath and provide soldiers and arms." But by the mid-sixteenth century, women were being isolated from citizenship, based on a range of causes: expanded humanist training in classical law and political theory, the growing importance of bourgeois families, which undercut the greater independence of aristocratic women; increased public swearing of allegiance restricted to male citizens as symbolizing "membership in the political community." All of these factors presented by Wiesner offer us valuable historical variables through which we can judge what religious principles, level of government, and economic structures aided or discouraged women's participation as citizens.

Returning to early eighteenth-century Britain, Hilda L. Smith looks at a legal claim for the amount of five shillings brought before the Court of King's Bench over a dispute as to whether a woman was duly elected as sexton of the London parish, St. Botolphs without Bishopsgate, and whether the female voters whose votes gave her the victory were legitimate electors. The case, *Olive v. Ingram* of 1739, remains an extraordinary one for a number of reasons. First, King's Bench met for three sessions, with both the Attorney-General and Solicitor-General in attendance, over a dispute involving little money and a minor office. Second, the Chief Justice and at least one other member of the court began with at least an open mind toward, and likely an acceptance of, women having held widespread offices in English history, and, as single householders, returning members of Parliament. And, finally, it was cited as a precedent as late as 1868 in the suffrage case, *Chorlton v. Lings*, as being the strongest precedent for women's early political standing and office holding, and is generally cited as the most important precedent used to grant women local suffrage during the late nineteenth century.

In analyzing the case, Smith reviews prior cases used by those arguing on each side, as well as by those cited by members of King's Bench. And she places the case within a broader context of false universals, where terms which would appear prima facie to include women, such as people, scot and lot voters, inhabitants, etc., were construed to exclude women as a group even though some or all women clearly fell under their rubric. In so doing, Smith sees a shift from the more open views of the Chief Justice William Lee, presumably under government pressure given the strong opposition of the Solicitor-General to women's voting or office holding, from the first session during Hilary term to the following two sessions later in 1739. Lee, in referring to the case of *Catherine v. Surrey*, states, "a *feme sole*, if she has a freehold, may vote for members of Parliament" and thus, it seems, "there was no disability." In opposition, the Solicitor-General, John Strange, contends "that usage is the only evidence of right at common law," and thus if women do not vote they can be designated "*non user* [which] shall be evidence of a waiver of their right, if ever they had any." He continues that women, as regards elections, "are put in the same class with infants," and concludes with a practical reservation, "elections being already too popular" they could not accommodate large numbers of women.

During the second and third sessions of the trial, Lee shifts from his earlier view that the case "may be a very extensive determination" if linked to women's general political standing, to a conclusion that as this is a private and not a public office "it cannot be drawn into precedent." Yet, even though the Chief Justice offers this observation early in the case's second hearing, each side continues to argue principles and precedents far beyond the reach of a minor parish post. The ultimate decision was in favor of the defendant, Sarah Bly, and the court determined that she indeed had the right to hold the post and that the female members of the parish had the right to vote for her. In deliberations over these issues, those in favor of Bly offered a range of precedents for women holding previous offices, including governess of a house of correction, governor of a workhouse, and, finally, voters "in the great companies." The dispute hinged on the rather dubious distinction of a public versus private trust, with the former open to women in the opinion of the majority of the court. Yet not all were willing to abandon women's broader political rights, as in the case of Justice Page, who states: "I see no disability on a woman from voting for a Parliament-man."

Thus, as Smith notes, while the case ultimately was decided in favor of the woman based on its nature as a private, minor office, still the court's proceedings witnessed one of the more important debates over women's political standing in the first half of the eighteenth century. And it was picked up and abstracted in Charles Viner's *A General Abridgment of Law and Equity* (1793). Later, in 1868, the justices of the Court of Common Pleas considered it a strong precedent which required a response, in their denial that women should be included as voters under the Second Reform Bill. They rejected its precedence as follows: "in the course of the discussion of *Olive v. Ingram*, Lee, CJ, appears to have at last satisfied himself that women could not vote for members of parliament." And, finally, in placing the case within the operations of falsely universal terms (within both legal language and political thought) the 1868 court turned the normal view of an inclusive generic "man" on its head. "No doubt, the word 'man,'" the jurists argued, "in a scientific treatise on zoology or fossil organic remains, would include men, women and children . . . But, in almost every other connection, the word 'man' is used in contradistinction to 'woman.'" Thus, as Smith concludes, this eighteenth-century case about a minor church office not merely granted women standing and served as an important precedent for later decisions, but also demonstrated the important debates over "universal" terms that were sometimes construed to include women and sometimes not, with important implications for their political standing.

Barbara Todd, in her effort to account for the legal shifts that underlay women's declining status beginning in the late seventeenth century turns to *The Hardships of the English Laws in Relation to Wives . . . in an Humble address to the Legislature* from 1735. The work, written by an anonymous woman, falls within that genre normally termed Christian feminism. According to Todd, the author treats the legal disability of married women and the inadequate education of women "based on moral philosophy, political and constitutional theory, scripture and theology." This work condemns the "despotic" powers now granted to English husbands and seeks relief from women's inferior legal status. In analyzing the viewpoint of this eighteenth-century commentator, Todd reveals that her justification for writing is grounded upon the traditional claim for a right to petition granted the English people, and the immediate impetus was some especially grievous decisions against wives. Later in the work, she accepted husbandly rule as a directive from God, but still believed in women's important moral and maternal role. Women, like all members of the community, have "a degree of liberty and property correspondent to the constitution."

Todd, to aid us in understanding this author's perspective and to present an analysis of the legal decisions which framed both *The Hardships* arguments and the realities of women's legal standing, explores cases from the late seventeenth century considering the nature of the wife's position. Building upon the work of Susan Staves for a portion of her argument, she looks at those cases which recognized the "wife's legal individuality," but also "her right to benefit from her relational identity as spouse." These cases dealt with the wife's ability to make a contract, to indebt herself or her husband, in essence to have an independent identity. While earlier cases had denied such independence, by 1770, Todd notes, decisions for a few years favored wives' "full membership in civil society." While these cases focused on members of the middle and upper classes, another set of cases considered "the separate legal identity of poor married women." They emerged from the efforts of poor married women to claim poor relief. Issues here revolved around whether a woman was to be taken as an independent "person" for purposes of settlement and assistance, or defined by family status. Beginning with the 1730s, a conservative trend emerged in which the wife's settlement was tied to the husband, and legitimate children, irrespective of the custody, received their father's settlement.

Yet complications arose as the century continued, as women with legal settlements (claim upon a place of origin) as single women married male vagabonds who had none. In such cases, patriarchal standing was limited and suspect, and private separations allowed. Yet independence, according to Todd, was not necessarily beneficial to most women, and thus feminist claims for such independence could harm these women in need. These settlement cases reveal the complexities of determining women's best interests, depending upon class, maternity, and other relevant factors. The years 1750–70 witnessed reversals over the issue of settlements, with some decisions favoring maintaining the family at all costs, and others supporting independent settlement for women. There were real stakes here, and overseers of the poor continued to try to avoid having to support wives and children of "unsettled men." Such disputes had wide-ranging reverberations, affecting cases well into the twentieth century that considered women's domicile and nationality. Todd concludes that these decisions continually circled back to the issues posed by the author of *The Hardships*, and that the problems of providing for the needs of women and children often conflicted with the independent legal standing of the wife.

Each of these chapters treats the wider context of women's political standing and the possibilities for their political voice. Hanley reveals that scholars and political figures were willing to alter original texts to create an intellectual justification for denying women's right to rule, and that that justification had a significant impact because it was framed as part of an ongoing misogynist litany. Wiesner shows that women's political standing might have required particular circumstances such as those of Protestant abbesses who put their office and independence before their confessional loyalties. Smith reveals that debates over the meaning and inclusiveness of such common terms as "people" often were tied to legal debates over women's citizenship and their membership within the nation. And Todd demonstrates that attitudes can drive court cases concerning the legal standing of married women, but that such views or legal decisions can hardly be easily characterized, for they shift over time, given both the values of the age and the interests of those debating the issue. Finally, all of these chapters emphasize the need for us to understand the political and legal context which framed the questions available to women in their political writings and determined their political standing in early modern Europe.

13 The politics of identity and monarchic governance in France: the debate over female exclusion

Sarah Hanley

In the public realm of France, amidst growing national consciousness, 1200s–1400s, through the period of nascent state building and centralization, 1500s–1700s, two juridical frameworks shaped political identity. The first, a resurrected *French Salic law* (Salic Law Code, 500s–800s), briefly mentioned in 1358, was alleged in the 1400s to be a public law excluding women (and their sons) from rule in a *body politic* represented, by some, as *The king's one body*. The second, a *French Law Canon* (civil law and public law) rooted in natural law, was formulated from the 1550s to the 1650s, establishing a monarchic state that privileged the male right to rule in state (king) and household (husband) through a parallel system of *marital regime* governance.[1] Reflection upon the history of those law partners reveals the contested processes through which political identity was culturally configured in late medieval and early modern France, first as a neutral *body politic*, then as a political body incorporated in *The king's one body*. The odyssey of the Salic law offers an interesting trajectory, given its failure to attract attention (1358–1400), debated validity (1400s–1480s), tempered success (1480s–1530s), and awkward collapse (mid-1500s) under the accumulated weight of forgery and fraud requiring juridical revision.

In the 1400s some writers insisted that an ancient Salic ordinance juridically established the exclusion of women from rule in the kingdom of France.[2] Yet the Franco-Germanic Salic Law Code, rendered in a Merovingian redaction (*c.* 507–11), then an expanded Carolingian one

---

[1] The complete study, Sarah Hanley, *State Building in Early Modern France: Law, Litigation, and Local Knowledge* (forthcoming); "The Monarchic State: Marital Regime Government and Male Right," in *Politics, Ideology, and the Law in Early Modern Europe*, ed. Adrianna E. Bakos (Rochester, N.Y.: Rochester University Press, 1994), chap. 7; and "Engendering the State: Family Formation and State Building in Early Modern France," *French Historical Studies* 16, 1 (1989): 4–27. All italics are mine.

[2] Hanley, "La loi salique," in *Encyclopédie politique et historique des femmes*, ed. Christine Fauré (Paris: Presses Universitaires de France, 1997), I, 11–30; and "Mapping Rulership

(802–803),[3] did not contain an ordinance regulating succession to realm and rule. And when a Salic Ordinance (Title *De allodio*, art. 6) supposedly denying female rule was resurrected in the 1400s, the text proved unyielding on that point. A Carolingian redaction reads as follows: "Indeed concerning Salic land no part of the inheritance may pass to a woman, but all the inheritance of land goes to the virile sex."[4] Standing alone, that civil ordinance is perplexing; in context, less so. An integral part of a section titled *De allodio* ("On allodial [lands]"), the ordinance (art. 6) was mediated, even contradicted, by others in that title and in other titles. Taken as a whole, Salic laws permitted women to inherit allodial lands (essentially family farms), sometimes favored transmission through female lines, and also allowed other lands held in grant from rulers to pass (in the absence of males) to females.[5] That said, around 1000 when Salic laws and Roman laws had meshed through concurrent usage, the Salic Code disappeared.

In northern France, 1100s–1300s, a fusion of laws – Salic, Roman, feudal – produced regional customary laws (*coutumiers*), written laws collected by jurists and treated as "French common laws" applied in a kingdom deemed a public realm regulated by public law.[6] Official compilations were ordered by kings in 1454, 1494, and 1509, then redacted in the *Coutume de Paris* (1510, revised 1580).[7] In accordance

---

in the French Body Politic: Political Identity, Public Law, and *The King's One Body*," *Historical Reflections* 23, 2 (1997): 1–21.

3 For Latin, Karl August Eckhardt, ed., *Monumenta Germaniae Historica, Leges Nationum Germanicarum* (Hanover: Historisches Institut des Werralandes, Göttingen, 1962, 1969), IV, pt. 1 (1962): *Pactus Legis Salicae* [Merovingian]; and IV, pt. 2 (1969): *Lex Salica* [Carolingian]. See the study of Katherine Drew, *The Laws of the Salian Franks* (Philadelphia, Pa.: University of Pennsylvania Press, 1991) for analysis of ordinances.

4 Eckhardt, *Monumenta*, IV, pt. 2, 214: "De terra vero Salica nulla portio hereditatis mulieri veniat, sed ad virilem sexum tota terre hereditas perveniat" (*Lex Salica*, Tit. 34, art. 6); and Drew, *Salian Franks*, 198 (*Lex Salica*, Tit. 34, art. 6 [Systematic Version]; this is Tit. 62, art. 6 [Standard Version]); my translation retains "virile sex," as in the original (rather than substituting "male sex," as does Drew).

5 Salic ordinances made no distinction between "allodial land" (i.e. family farms) and "Salic land"; and even if "Salic land" were taken to refer to lands held by special grant from the king, women (in the absence of male heirs) could also inherit lands held by grant; see Drew, *Salian Franks*, 39–45, 149; examples, Suzanne Fonay Wemple, *Women in Frankish Society: Marriage and the Cloister, 500–900* (Philadelphia, Pa.: University of Pennsylvania Press, 1981); and Emile Chénon, *Histoire générale du droit français public et privé des origines à 1815* (Paris, 1926), I, no. 178, "the exclusion of women was only relative and not absolute," "they were not incapable of inheriting paternal land."

6 François Olivier-Martin, *Histoire de la coutume de la prévôté et vicomté de Paris* (Paris, 1922), I, 86–88, 99–101; Pierre Petot, "Le Droit Commun selon les coutumiers," *Nouvelle revue historique du droit français et étranger* 28 (1960): 412–29; and Chénon, *Histoire*, I, nos. 194–95, inalienability of a public realm.

7 François André Isambert et al., eds., *Recueil général des anciennes lois françaises depuis l'an 420 jusqu'à la revolution de 1789* (Paris: Belin-le-Prieur, 1821–33): Charles VII (IX, 252,

with French customary law, women succeeded to lands, including duchies, fiefs, and apanages, and rendered homage for them; and some women who did not inherit directly passed inheritance rights to successors, as practiced in the Paris region.[8] Contrary to false allegations made in the 1400s, those practices prevailed right into the early 1500s.[9] As a result, the attempt to transform the Salic Ordinance from a civil law of the Salian Franks (regulating inheritance of allodial lands) into a public law of the French kingdom (regulating succession to monarchic rule) met with contextual and textual obstacles that triggered a protracted debate over political identity and the exclusion of women from rule (1400s–1530s).[10] The analysis presented here recounts the opening phase of that political debate, 1400–1429, when Jean de Montreuil responded to the challenge launched by Christine de Pizan validating rule by women in the French *body politic*.

The contested precept of male rule–female exclusion was mired in a troubled political past. In 1317 an Assembly of Notables approved the exclusion in 1316 of a young Capetian royal daughter, Jeanne of France (sole surviving issue of Louis X [son of Phillip IV]), who was pressed into renouncing her succession rights and bypassed by uncles, Phillip V and Charles IV (both deceased without male issue). On the death of Charles IV in 1328, another Assembly of Notables approved exclusion of his sister, Isabelle of France, queen in England since 1308 (now sole surviving issue of Phillip IV) and also her young son, Edward III (king in England 1327). Therewith a Capetian first cousin, the Valois Phillip VI, was crowned. At the time, however, the Notables offered no grounds in law, or even in reason, for such momentous decisions and did not allege a Salic law in either case.[11] And later on, the grounds alleged for

---

art. 125); Charles VIII and Louis XII (XI, 292 and 457–61); redactions, Olivier-Martin, *Histoire de la coutume*, I, chap. 2, pts. 1–3, and chap. 2, pt. 4.

[8] Charles T. Wood, *The French Apanages and the Capetian Monarchy, 1224–1328* (Cambridge, Mass.: Harvard University Press, 1966), chaps. 1–5, noting the regent Phillip's scheme, as early as 1314, to set Jeanne aside.

[9] In error, Alain Chartier (secretary to Charles VI and Charles VII) said (as did Baldus) that feudal law prevented women (and sons) from succession to noble fiefs; a mistake corrected later by Charles Dumoulin (*Commentaire*, chap. 14, no. 20) citing cases where women (in the absence of men) transmitted succession rights to sons; see Antoine Loisel, *Institutes coutumières*, ed. André Dupin (Paris: Durand, 1846), II, no. 325. Removal of the ritual kiss from homage acts (due to the participation of women) is traced in J. Russell Major, "Bastard Feudalism and the Kiss: Changing Social Mores in Late Medieval and Early Modern France," *Journal of Interdisciplinary History* 17 (1987): 509–35.

[10] Hanley, "Loi salique."

[11] The case made for the absence of Salic law in official circles (1300s) still holds: Paul Viollet, "Comment les femmes ont été exclues en France de la succession à la couronne," *Mémoires de l'Académie des Inscriptions et Belles-Lettres* 34, 2 (1895): 125–78; John M. Potter, "The Development and Significance of the Salic Law of the French,"

justifying female exclusion were supplied not from law but from political necessity.

The cleric and historiographer Richard Lescot (1329, fl. 1358), who held a royal commission to investigate the succession claim of Charles II (son of Jeanne), apparently found a Carolingian redaction of Salic law in the archives of his abbey of Saint-Denis. In a Latin tract, *Genealogy of the Kings of France* (1358),[12] Lescot referred to "Salic law" by name (for the first time) and attached his comment about its Merovingian and Carolingian origins to his genealogy of French kings. But he provided no text for perusal.[13] The resulting subterfuge implied that the custom of male rule (observed in the royal genealogy) was prescribed by an ancient Salic law (founding the kingdom).[14] Still, Lescot's alleged Salic law was ignored at the time, or even rejected, in official circles.[15] Perhaps settlement of Charles II's claim in 1359 was a factor. Or perhaps the Salic law text, if shown to jurists in the Parlement of Paris, was judged inapplicable to royal succession. Whatever the case, French ordinances took no notice either. In both the Parlement of Paris and the Royal Council, Charles V and Charles VI held *Royal Seances*,[16] where

---

The English Historical Review 52 (1937): 235–53; Ralph E. Giesey, "The Juristic Basis of Dynastic Right to the French Throne," *Transactions of the American Philosophical Society* (Philadelphia, Pa.: American Philosophical Society, 1961, new ser., vol. 5, pt. 5), 3–42; and Kathleen Daly and Ralph E. Giesey, "Noël de Fribois et la loi salique," *Bibliothèque de l'Ecole des Chartes* 151 (1993): 5–36; and Hanley, "Mapping Rulership in the French Body Politic."

[12] Richard Lescot, *Genealogia aliquorum regum Francie per quam apparet quantum attinere potest regi Francie rex Navarre* (1358), in *Chronique de Richard Lescot, religieux de Saint-Denis (1328–1344)*, ed. Jean Lemoine (Paris: Librairie Renovard, Société de l'Histoire de France, 1896), 173–78.

[13] Lescot, *Genealogia*, 178: "Legem vero salicam" linked with Clovis, Childebert, Clothaire; "Item legis salice, id est francisce" with Charlemagne and Louis; a Carolingian copy of Salic law (see n. 4 above) was in the archives of the abbey of Saint-Denis (BN ms. Latin 4628A), and his investigation resulted from a royal commission tendered by a councillor in the Parlement of Paris (Lemoine, *Chronique*, vi, xiii, and 173).

[14] In 1410 Lescot was accused by monks of Notre Dame of earlier forgeries and interpolations (Lemoine, *Chronique*, vi–viii).

[15] The Anonymous manuscript (*c.* 1390–99, Bibl. Royale, Brussels, 10306) does not claim a Salic law–public law connection. But the author (who may have been Montreuil) refers to [Lescot's] discovery of a "loy salica," claims to have read the law in this "exact form," and gives a fragment with an interpolation, *in the realm* (not found in the original, see n. 4): "Indeed, no part *in the realm* may pass to a woman" (Mulier vero nullam *in regno* habeat portionem) (Lemoine, *Chronique*, xiv–xv, and n. 3 on Montreuil's repetition of this interpolated passage; see n. 22 below).

[16] Hanley, *The Lit de Justice of the Kings of France: Constitutional Ideology in Legend, Ritual, and Discourse* (Princeton, N.J.: Princeton University Press, 1983; French ed., Paris: Aubier, 1991), chap. 1, on *Royal Seances* of 1375, 1392, 1407; Table 1 distinguishes between medieval *Royal Seances* (which were held in both Royal Councils and Parlement), and the later innovative *Lit de Justice* assemblies, first convened in 1527

they promulgated ordinances (1375, 1392, 1403, 1407) regulating succession to rule: father-king to son-dauphin regardless of age.[17] Two of them (1403, 1407) referred to that system of male preference obliquely as a "right of nature," but none established strict female exclusion or cited a Salic law prohibiting succession of royal daughters (and their sons) should no royal sons survive. Aside from a few stray rumors about a missing law,[18] therefore, the only grounds sanctioning strict female exclusion in the 1300s and up to 1409 were sporadic and vague references to a custom.[19] The compelling silence in juridical and royal quarters confirms that Salic law was unknown, or, if known, had no standing in official circles; and that succession of royal daughters (or sons through them) was possible in the absence of royal sons. And the lack of resolution bred apprehension in other quarters.

The prelate, politician, and diplomat, Jean de Montreuil (c. 1361–1418), secretary for Charles V, *prévôt* of Lille and humanist literary figure in the reign of Charles VI, was uneasy with silence. Determined to remove a vague precept on exclusion from the risky arena of custom (subject to change through usage), he sought juridical confines in a fixed Salic law (founding the kingdom). In his works Montreuil fastened on a popular theme invented by French propagandists: the illusion of English designs on the French crown (supposedly stemming from 1328).[20] But his noteworthy introduction of a Salic law text actually was provoked by events in French circles, especially Pizan's case made in 1405 for a custom of female inclusion. In his treatise, *To All the Knighthood* (1409–13),[21] written in French for a wide

(but given fictive medieval origins in the 1300s), defined as constitutional assemblies, and convoked only in Parlement thenceforth.

[17] *Ordonnances des roys de France de la troisième race* (Paris, 1723–1849), eds. Eusèbe de Laurière et al.: VI, 26–32, 45–49 (1374, revised 1375); VIII, 518 (1375); VII, 530–38 (1392); VIII, 581–83 (1403, Royal Council); IX, 267–69 (1407).

[18] Colette Beaune, *The Birth of an Ideology: Myths and Symbols of Nation in Late-Medieval France*, trans. Susan Ross Huston (Berkeley, Calif.: University of California Press, 1991), 249–52 (mistaken pagination on Lescot) attempts to accord Salic law recognized status in the 1300s based only on several rumors about a custom, or a law, and on Lescot's allegation. However, rumors about a law (neither identified nor textually cited) suggest wishful thinking, or political aim; and Lescot, who named Salic law but provided no text, was ignored in political circles, including those where French ordinances were written (n. 17 above).

[19] Potter, "Development and Significance of the Salic Law," 235–53, Pope Benedict XII (1340), Baldus de Ubaldis (1377) on custom; Viollet, "Comment les femmes ont été exclues," 139–41, on the absence of Salic law (despite Lescot's naming the Ordinance).

[20] Peter S. Lewis, "War Propaganda and Historiography in Fifteenth-Century France and England," *Transactions of the Royal Historical Society*, ser. 5, 15 (1965): 7–13; the weak and sporadic English claims were aimed at securing other French lands, not the crown.

[21] Jean de Montreuil, *A Toute la chevalerie* (c. 1409–13, in French, no. 220, 89–149), *Opera: L'Œuvre historique et polémique*, II, eds. Ezio Ornato, Nicole Grévy and Gilbert

audience, Montreuil claims he has read a Latin copy of the "Salic Law," pronounces it a founding "constitution and ordinance" that sanctioned the exclusion of women in 1328, and holds that Charlemagne excluded their sons as well. What he offers, however, is a Latin fragment that he wrote in 1406, taken, it would appear, from a manuscript of the 1390s. That alleged Salic law fragment, moreover, contains a misleading interpolation, the phrase *in the realm*, not found in the Salic Ordinance. "Indeed no part *in the realm* may pass to a woman."[22] In *Knighthood*, therefore, Montreuil's interpolated passage and commentary accomplished the work of a forgery, albeit one swiftly repaired.

Right away in all three versions of his *Treatise Against the English* (1413, 1415, 1416),[23] Montreuil replaced the forged fragment with a fuller correct Latin passage (the first clause, "Indeed concerning Salic land," still missing). In the *Treatise* (1413) written in French to ensure a wider audience, he cites the ordinance: "No part of the inheritance may pass to a woman but all the inheritance of land goes to the virile sex."[24] Then he attempts to cover the textual loss (*in the realm*) and other lacunae with commentary. Accordingly Montreuil attaches to the end of the Salic law text his own opinion stating that this law absolutely "excludes and prevents women from any and all ability to succeed to the crown of France." And he repeats his addendum excluding their sons.[25] In the *Treatise*, therefore, he maintained the substance of the forgery just corrected in *Knighthood*. He also chose his audience carefully. In his *Treatise* (1415), written in Latin and destined for the entourage of Queen Isabelle of Bavaria, regent for the incapacitated Charles VI, Montreuil

Ouy (Turin: G. Giappichelli, 1975). Note the lines 1284–1489 on Salic law date to 1406 (ibid., intro., 10–12; *Knighthood*, 131a). Parts of *Knighthood* (written after the Latin, *Regali ex progenie*, c. 1408, without Salic law) are repeated in *Treatise* (1413); *Opera*, intro., 12, n. 4, and 21–22.

22 Montreuil, *Knighthood*, 131–32, "loy Salica," "loy salique." But his source is not the Salic Ordinance (in n. 4 above): it is the Anonymous manuscript (1390–99, see nn. 15, 21 above) from which he produces a long passage, including the interpolated fragment, "Mulier vero *in regno* nullum habeat portionem," insinuating that he (Montreuil) has read the Salic law in this "exact form."

23 Montreuil, *Traité contre les Anglais*, in *Opera*: II, written in three stages: (1) *c.* 1413 in French, no. 222, pp. 159–218; (2) *c.* 1415 in Latin, no. 223, pp. 219–61; (3) 1416 in French, no. 224, pp. 262–313.

24 Montreuil, *Treatise* (1413), 168: "Nulla portio hereditatis mulieri veniat sed ad virilem sexum tota terra perveniat" (n. 4 above); *Opera*, pref., xiv, notes Montreuil made the correction but does not analyze his ensuing fabrication.

25 Ibid., 168: "qui exclut et forclot femmes de tout en tout de pouoir succeder a la couronne de France, comme icelle loy et decret die absolument que femme n'ait quelconque portion ou royaume (c'est a entendre a la couronne de France)"; and 209, sons. He transposes *[allodial] land* into the *kingdom of France* (the public domain) and *inheritance* (in families) into *succession* to the *crown of France*.

removed his spurious opinion forbidding rule to women.[26] Finally, in his *Treatise* (1416), also written in French for a larger audience, Montreuil again attached to Salic law the same opinion definitively excluding women from rule in France.[27] Yet once the correct text appeared in 1413, manipulated or not, it was clear that Salic law did not prohibit women from monarchic rule in any realm and certainly not in the kingdom of France.

This experienced politician and humanist writer deliberately chose to privilege forgery over philological integrity, his own legal opinion against the text of the Salic Ordinance. Those who followed him did the same. Textual evidence to the contrary, what sustained their unequivocal stance that women were legally excluded from rule in the French realm? The exclusionists, it may be argued, grounded arguments primarily in the weighty moral injunctions of the ubiquitous *defamation litany* which always supported their case;[28] not in the weak text of a Salic law which constantly fell short. Stamped with the imprimatur of Greek and Roman writings, the late medieval *defamation litany*, cited and recited over centuries, constituted a body of knowledge in itself, and subscription to it proved exclusion. Genre and trope in form, misogynist dicta designated women as generic *woman*, removing from each the human essence of individuality.[29] Readings of Aristotelian and Ovidian works informed a model of "male mastery" of women (their bodies, knowledge, words) aimed at removing women from learned disputation.[30] Important here, lessons from the *defamation litany*, inflated and politicized in the 1400s, supported a model of male command of the *body politic* aimed at excluding women from succession to rule.

The *defamation litany* attained a political thrust in two ways. Interpretations of *nature* and *woman* took on public dimensions moving from person to polity; and the "right of nature," which only signaled male preference in succession (ordinances 1403, 1407), was aligned with an

---

[26] Montreuil, *Treatise* (1415), 226–27, presented to the dauphin [Charles VII]. Charles VI (king 1380–1422) suffered crippling bouts of dementia from 1389; Isabelle (queen 1385) acted as regent intermittently and was officially appointed in 1408.

[27] Montreuil, *Treatise* (1416), 274: "qui exclut et forclot femmes de tout en tout de pouoir succeder a la couronne de France."

[28] My term, inspired by Pizan, denotes a body of politicized defamatory injunctions that through rote repetition and rare intervention assumed moral stature used to define political command. Helen Solterer, *The Master and Minerva: Disputing Women in French Medieval Culture* (Berkeley, Calif.: University of California Press, 1995), recounts the defamation dilemma: women (slandered) were warned against critical response by subtle threats to charge them as defamers if they disputed authors.

[29] R. Howard Bloch, *Medieval Misogyny and the Invention of Western Romantic Love* (Chicago, Ill.: University of Chicago Press, 1991), 197.

[30] Solterer, *Master and Minerva*, chap. 1, on that model and the Aristotelian shift discussing *woman* as a "thing."

alleged Salic law, which instead dictated strict female exclusion. A few litanized examples suffice. Ovidian literary lessons, rooted in nature, reduced *woman* to mindless animal prey driven by wanton lust and stalked and captured by men.[31] Reshaped, those lessons linked female deficiency, body and mind, with incapacity for governance either of self or of polity. Above all, Aristotelian biological lessons, dictates of nature, posited defective *woman* imperfectly reproduced, deficient in body and mind, and passive in propagation (lacking the seminal force of formative male seed).[32] Reshaped, those lessons linked female deficiency in generation and propagation with incapacity for rule in a *body politic*. Finally, Salic law, a product of combined forces – defamation that induced moral certainty, and legal evidence fabricated to conform with moral certainty – was drawn into the *litany* in the early 1400s. A presumptive body of knowledge, the *defamation litany* shaped political identity in an era when French political thinkers, contrary to English cohorts,[33] postulated metaphysical notions of the French kingdom as an immortal *body politic* perpetuated by incorporation in *The king's one body*; that is, in a series of related kings biogenetically regenerated over time.[34] Germane to Pizan and Montreuil are several propagators of defamation whose serial reach in the chain of male mastery colored notions of governance.

The cleric and teacher at the University of Paris, Jean de Meun, an author of *The Romance of the Rose* and much indebted to Ovid, had pronounced the body of *woman*, root of female inconstancy, the implacable enemy of mind in his famous dialogue between Genius and Nature. A popular work praised by writers, including Matheolus, Jean Le Fèvre, and Jean de Montreuil, some later copies also contained miniatures illustrating defamatory invectives.[35] The cleric and lawyer, Matheolus,

31 Ovid, *The Art of Love* (Cambridge, Mass.: Harvard University Press, 1985), trans. J. H. Mozley, Bk. I, lines 22–51, 89–159, 257–87, prey, and 318–50, lust and crimes against famous men; Bk. III, lines 118–75, 772–806, female cunning, secrets, stealth, deception, adultery, seduction.

32 Aristotle, *The Generation of Animals*, trans. A. L. Peck (Cambridge, Mass.: Harvard University Press, 1943), Bk. IV, pt. 3 on biology; and pt. 6 on woman as a deformity.

33 Ernst H. Kantorowicz, *The King's Two Bodies: A Study in Mediaeval Political Theology* (Princeton, N.J.: Princeton University Press, 1957), 332–33, notes that the *two-bodies* concept (delineating the mortal prince and the immortal office, or *body politic*) was well developed in England but was absent from France. But he does not treat French alternatives in train, or Salic law. For English notions and female succession in the 1500s, see Marie Axton, *The Queen's Two Bodies* (London: Royal Historical Society, 1977).

34 For the way French writers molded an Aristotelian-oriented *one-body* concept based on male generative capacity (male replication in propagation) likewise reflected in the *body politic* (male replication in succession), see Hanley, "Loi Salique," "Mapping Rulership in France," and "The Monarchic State."

35 Jean de Meun, *Le Roman de la Rose* in *Histoire de la littérature française* (Paris: A. Colin, 1959), wrote the second part (*c.* 1275–80); see lines 16293–16676.

author of *The Book of the Lamentations of Matheolus*,[36] borrowed from
Aristotle, Ovid, Theophrastus, and Meun's *Romance*. Matheolus warns
notable men active in public life, including the chancellor and councillors in the Parlement of Paris, against the carnal appetites of women that
ensnare men, the frightful woes of marriage, and his own bouts of
impotence. Those warnings were capped with evident disgust for the
female body, which he graphically described in salacious and sordid
terms.[37] A cleric and lawyer in the Parlement of Paris, Jean Le Fèvre,
translated Ovid and praised Meun's *Romance*, borrowing excerpts from
Genius and Nature. Openly admiring Matheolus, Le Fèvre translated
the *Lamentations* into French; and at least one copy contained miniatures depicting the female body as a gross monstrosity.[38] Finally, Jean de
Montreuil praised and defended the great teacher at the University of
Paris, Jean de Meun, and his *Romance of the Rose*, ornament of poetic
genius, focus of humanist adulation. Yet by the 1400s there was more at
stake. Poetics served politics in that a priori literary injunctions on
female incapacity upheld political exclusion far better than vague
memories of an alleged custom, or readings of a Salic law text that
collapsed under historical and philological scrutiny. That Pizan divined.

The prolific writer, Christine de Pizan (*c*. 1364–*c*. 1431), was the
daughter of an officer in the court of Charles V, spouse (and widow) of a
notary-secretary for Charles VI, and mother of a son also notary-
secretary for that king and a daughter in a convent. An active author
from 1390 to 1429, Pizan was the commissioned biographer of Charles
V, wrote political missives to Queen Regent Isabelle of Bavaria, and
composed her last work early in the reign of Charles VII. At home in
political circles and law courts, archives and libraries, she understood
the moral intent of female defamation and its negative political ramifica-
tions. Pizan wrote in French (and illustrated) a treatise, *The Book of the
City of Ladies* (1405),[39] which recorded and validated rule by women in
the world over time. Recognizing no custom or law excluding women
from governance, the *City of Ladies* pointedly addressed current efforts
to link precepts of female defamation and exclusion from rule.

[36] Matheolus (or Mathieu), *Liber Lamentationum* (*c*. 1298), trans. *c*. 1371–72, Jehan Le
Fèvre, de Resson, *Les Lamentations de Matheolus et Le Livre de Leësce*, ed. A. G. van
Hamel (Paris: E. Bouillon, 1892), I, *Lamentations*; II, *Leësce*.
[37] Ibid.: van Hamel's analysis of *Lamentations*, a work unknown before Le Fèvre's trans., is
in II, lxviii–cvii; notes on Matheolus (defrocked for marrying), cvii–clxxiv, and some of
the worst defamation of his wife.
[38] Ibid.: notes on Le Fèvre, II, clxxv–ccix.
[39] Christine de Pizan, *Le Livre de la Cité des Dames* (December 1404–April 1405); *The
Book of the City of Ladies*, ed. and trans. Earl Jeffrey Richards (New York: Persea Books,
1982), Bks. I–III.

Pizan denounced the defamatory impulse calibrated by ancient and medieval writers and defended women's capacity for intellectual pursuits and talent for governance. She exposes the array of misogynist injunctions repeated over the ages – the malicious slander of women as *woman*, the trumpeting of female inferiority – as unworthy of learned men. "Like a gushing fountain, a series of authorities" who appear to "speak from one and the same mouth" demean women, whose perfections are legion.[40] She charges defamers with fabricating lies about *nature* and *woman* for personal reasons, not learned ones. Some of the worst attacks, she says, are fueled by sex-based jealousy actually born of male imperfections, as exemplified in Aristotle, whose ugly body seeded his malice toward women, and in Ovid, whose castration spurred his anger toward them.[41] If the learned writer Jean de Meun, purveyor of "badly colored lies," the mediocre writer Matheolus, "an impotent old man filled with desire," and a contemporary writer (Jean de Montreuil) who "*mis*-takes the situation" in praising Meun's work, sought truth, they would employ their own critical faculties, distinguish fact from fiction, and commend the admirable "natural behavior and character of women." Instead they maliciously turn *woman*, the "entire feminine sex," into "monstrosities in nature."[42] In the *City of Ladies*, she unmasked by name and association a lineage of public defamers – Aristotle, Ovid, Meun, Matheolus, and Montreuil. She also reversed the thrust of misogynist dicta by recasting defamers as writers who lacked critical faculties, men whose self-proclaimed expertise issued not from universal strength of mind but from individual sexual weakness of body, hence mind. And she demanded an end to the *defamation litany*, attacks on women: "Let all of them be silent ... from now on let them keep their mouths shut."[43] This condemnation set the groundwork for a discussion of good governance, self, and polity.

Pizan took a historical stance for her discussion of governance by women. She refuses the reduction of individual women to generic *woman* and offers historical proofs of women active in politics, past and

---

[40] Pizan, *City of Ladies*, quotes I.I.I, I.2.2.

[41] Ibid., Aristotle I.14.1–3, I.9.2, I.14.1–3, and III; Ovid I.9.2, II.54.1, III.19.6; passages covertly related, I.8.4–5, I.8.7–9, I.14.1, linking Aristotle, Ovid, Matheolus (and Meun).

[42] Ibid., lies I.I.I, II.68.2; Meun and Matheolus, fact and fiction, I.I.I, I.2.2; Matheolus II.19.I, impotence I.8.5. She names Meun and the *Romance*, II.25.I, and covertly refers to her own criticism of Montreuil for defending it [1401–1404] in the remark on men "naturally given to slander" who "*mis*-take the situation – as I well know!" (I.8.9–10); cites her poem against slander, *Letter by the God of Love* [May 1399], and covertly refers to her earlier writings castigating Ovid and Meun and by association Montreuil, II.54.1 (see n. 54).

[43] Ibid., quotes I.38.4–5; her call for men to "keep their mouths shut" mimics and defies Montreuil's earlier abusive *Letter*, no. 154 (see n. 55).

present, named and placed in legend and life. Denying the body–mind distinctions applied to learning, judging, and governing, she declares that "a woman's mind is fit for all tasks" when properly educated. She objects to the definition of public officeholding, judicial and military, as male exercises in judgment and prowess requisite for rule. Admitting that men presently are taught such skills and exercise those offices, she insists that women at any time may be taught and readied for office should they be called and invested with authority. As she points out, woman have demonstrated a "natural sense for politics and government" abroad and at home.[44] Women rulers such as Semiramis, queen of the Assyrians, and Dido, founder of Carthage, have built, ruled, and defended empires and cities with political astuteness, military might, and spiritual merit.[45] Queens in France, including Fredegund, Clotilda, Jeanne, Blanche, and Isabelle of Bavaria who is "reigning now" have served well as consorts, rulers, and regents in the kingdom.[46] Noblewomen in France, wives and widows, such as the late duchess of Anjou, who quelled a revolt in Provence; and presently Anne of Bourbon, a "most great landowner" and a "good and wise ruler," have demonstrated capacity for governance over vast principalities.[47] Pizan drew a striking conclusion: women are capable of learning the rudiments of good governance, have ruled, do rule, and in the future may rule in empires, cities, kingdoms, and subaltern principalities.[48] Moving on, she addressed spiritual matters that were no less political.

In the *City of Ladies*,[49] Pizan actually amended a current tenet of political thought that seriously threatened her case. Familiar with the way the polity, in England and France, was represented as a *body politic* (head and members),[50] she would have known the *body politic–body mystic* analogy on rulership as well. Rendered in a popular medieval marriage metaphor, that analogy likened the political marriage of prince

---

[44] Ibid., on mind 1.13.8; political sense 1.11.1.

[45] Ibid., Semiramis 1.15.1–2; Dido 1.46.1–3; 11.54.1; both Pizan and Montreuil use legend and history.

[46] Ibid., queen regents in France: Fredegund [for Clotaire II] 1.13.1, 1.23.1; Clotilda [saint, wife of Clovis I] 11.35.1; Blanche [of Castile, for Louis IX, saint] 1.13.2, 1.13.7, 11.65.1; Jeanne [of Evreux, third wife of Charles IV], Blanche [of Navarre, second wife of Phillip VI], Blanche of France [daughter of Charles IV, wife of Phillip d'Orléans], Isabelle of Bavaria [for Charles VI] 11.68.1.

[47] Ibid., noblewomen 1.13.1–8: the duchess of Anjou [daughter of Saint Charles of Blois, duke of Brittany, and widow of a brother of Charles V] 1.13.6; Anne of Bourbon 1.13.7, 11.68.10; and others "well-informed in government" 11.68.1–10.

[48] Ibid., 1.11.1, 1.13.8.

[49] Ibid., Bk. III, which many readers have found difficult to connect with Bks. I and II.

[50] Pizan, *The Book of the Body Politic* (*Le Livre du corps de policie* [c. late 1404–1407]), ed. Kate Langdon Forhan (Cambridge: Cambridge University Press, 1994); see I.1, III.1.

and realm (a *body politic*) to the spiritual marriage of prelate and church (a *body mystic*).[51] And the ritual tie common to both was the sacred anointment (holy oil) of French kings in the coronation ceremony (like bishops in ecclesiastical ordination). Pizan created an alternative for that male route to coronation. For that purpose, she introduced a range of holy women whose spiritual roles benefit humanity and the polity, whose spiritual merits match those of men.[52] That spiritual body, an alternative female *body mystic*, is governed by God's specially crowned and anointed ruler, Mary, queen of heaven and *head of the feminine sex*, who could have been called (as any woman) to terrestrial rule, coronation and anointment, and is called by Reason, Rectitude, Justice, and Nature to rule the *City of Ladies*.[53] The superior edge given that female *body mystic* headed by Queen Mary (notably anointed and crowned by God) compared with the male one headed by bishops (merely anointed and mitred by other men) opened a route for the anointment of a queen called to coronation. And Pizan's accommodation of queens in the French *body politic* launched the debate over political identity. The *City of Ladies* with its bold interpretations of history, political thought, and realignment of a French *body politic* open to rule by women appeared just after Pizan's serious dispute with Montreuil over the practice of defamation.

From 1399 to 1404 Pizan indicted and judged the deceased Jean de Meun a public defamer, his *Romance of the Rose*, "a doctrine full of lies," a charge applied also to Jean de Montreuil (Meun's defender) and repeated in the *City of Ladies*.[54] During an epistolary quarrel, 1401–1404, Montreuil denounced "that woman Christine," purportedly incapable (as *woman*) of comprehending the *Romance*; and likened her to a courtesan for criticizing the great teacher Meun and especially for "taking her writings to the public."[55] Undeterred by defama-

---

[51] Lucas de Penna (1320–*c*. 1390), *Commentaria in Tres Libros Codicis*: "Just as there is contracted a spiritual and divine marriage between a church and its prelate, so there is contracted a temporal and terrestrial marriage between the prince and the realm" (cited in Kantorowicz, *King's Two Bodies*, 221–23); see Hanley, "Monarchic State," for its redefinition as a marital maxim in the 1500s.

[52] Pizan, *City of Ladies*, III, the list of women (married, single, secular, religious), III.12.1, III.13.1, includes two monks (women disguised as men) lauded for (male) constancy by other (unsuspecting) monks, III.1.1.–3.

[53] Ibid., Mary III.2.1.

[54] *Le Débat sur Le Roman de la Rose*, ed. Eric Hicks (Paris: H. Champion, 1977), for letters and analysis. Pizan calls *Romance* a "gross" work that "accuses, blames, and defames women" and indicts Meun (and Montreuil by association) a "public defamer" who "dares to defame and blame one entire sex without exception" (sec. V, 11–22); and see n. 42 above.

[55] *Le Débat*, Montreuil's *Letter*, no. 54, disparages *woman*, invokes the Greek courtesan Leuntion who criticized Theophrastus [student of Aristotle], and complains it is

tion,[56] Pizan around 1403 rhetorically situated herself in the office of a judge capable of rendering ethical and political opinions infused with civic import.[57] In tandem, she moved the issue of defamation, a charge akin to the crime of libel,[58] from literary quarters to political ones, including councillors in the Parlement of Paris, the provost of Paris, and the circle of Queen Regent Isabelle of Bavaria. By 1404, however, Montreuil lost that quarrel in an embarrassing denouement witnessed in learned and political groups.[59] At this point, Pizan composed the *City of Ladies*, 1404–1405, unmasking the union of female defamation and political exclusion and circulated it in prime political circles, 1405–15;[60] while Montreuil from 1406 held a problematic fragment of Salic law in the wings. Neither kings nor queens had ever acknowledged the strict exclusion of women from rule, and Pizan capitalized on that profound political silence witnessed in recent French ordinances. The groundbreaking *City of Ladies*, unprecedented in tone and topic, launched a full-scale public challenge to writers currently maneuvering to exclude women from political rule by resort to defamation. The twin charge struck home.

In this milieu of legal doubt and moral certainty, the actions of Montreuil are instructive. During anxious years shadowed by Charles VI's incapacity and Isabelle's regental rule, Montreuil took up the political cause of exclusion. As the *City of Ladies* circulated, 1405–15, Montreuil at some point, probably between 1406 and 1409, decided to refute some of its principal arguments. That he did in the *Treatise* (1413, 1416), where he addressed claims set forth in the *City of Ladies* but did not name the work or its author, thereby sidestepping both its repute and its challenge of male mastery. His refutation route, in any case, is traceable. First, Pizan lauded Queen Semiramis and also French queens, queen regents, and noblewomen involved in governance, including Queen Regent Isabelle. To the contrary, Montreuil dismisses the exploits of Semiramis, alleging the widowed queen sometimes donned "the clothing of a man and pretended to be the king's son," so

---

impossible "to close the mouths of those who say unjust things" about great works. A cohort, Col, pronounces Pizan (as *woman*) lacking reason, crazy, and demands she retract erroneous charges (sec. VI, 23–24).

[56] Ibid., disdaining defamation aimed at her as *woman* denied the "faculty" of "reason" and censuring letters "reproaching my feminine sex which you say is passionate by nature and led by craziness and presumption" (sec. VII, 24–26).

[57] Solterer, *Master and Minerva*, chap. 6, treating *L'Epistre au Dieu d'Amours*, the epistolary quarrel and especially *Le Livre du chemin de long estude* (1402–1403).

[58] Hicks, *Le Débat*; like Pizan, Jean Gerson complains some defamers add to "defamatory libels" indecent pictures in "miniatures" (63, 72, 209).

[59] Ibid., he pleads for supporters, who ignore him (*Letters*, 27–45).

[60] Richards, *City*, xliv–xlv.

no one can know whether a man or a woman accomplished the deeds. For him in any case the example is merely a "particular [local] case which established neither law nor custom" there or anywhere.[61] While he mentions some French noblewomen, including daughters of kings, he denies them the status of rulers in principalities "great and small." One moment he reverses himself and admits (correctly) that women have held lands (some in benefice) in the French kingdom. The next moment he insists that women cannot exercise authority over others, so they cannot succeed to the crown of France.[62] Mired in confusion, Montreuil turned to defamation.

Second, Pizan denounced the *defamation litany* and its corollary, exclusion of women from rule, and focused on the natural courage and capacity demonstrated by women rulers already charged with governance. To the contrary, Montreuil identifies governing authority as a male prerogative and draws on defamation for proofs. He charges that women, who by nature suffer ungovernable carnal passions, often marry men of lower status, an act of derogation most unworthy in a queen. Worse, rule by a queen, who by nature lacks "virility" (that is, generative male seed) would (in propagation) undermine exalted royal lineage "descending from male to male" and always observed in France.[63] Those politicized proofs drawn from the *defamation litany* sustained Montreuil's view that a queen cannot govern herself, let alone a polity; that a queen in office would disembody a *body politic* incorporated in *The king's one body* regenerated over time.

Third, Pizan denied male definitions of public office, judicial and military, prerequisites for rule, and stressed the ability of women, when taught and readied, to exercise offices. To the contrary, Montreuil adamantly prohibits women from holding judicial, military, or royal office by resorting to defamatory moral injunctions. Due to the innate "instability" of *woman*, body and mind, and the consequent inability of women to separate mundane personal passions from public political interests, they are incapable of rule and cannot be designated.[64] Officeholding in both polity and church, Montreuil held, adheres to the male principle.

Fourth, Pizan realigned the male *body politic–body mystic* analogy by positing a worthy female *body mystic*, which enabled sacred anointment of a queen called to rule and coronation. To the contrary, Montreuil focuses on the dearth and minor status of church offices open to women, reminds readers that women cannot be anointed, cannot hold

---

[61] Montreuil, *Treatise* (1413), 173–74.   [62] Ibid., 169–17, 173.
[63] Ibid., 167, 172.   [64] Ibid., 171–73.

either papal office (head of the church) or bishoprics (head of sees), and cannot take part (as prelates in church councils) in the appointment of popes. Conflating coronation (king) and ordination (bishop) as unique male exercises marked by sacred anointment,[65] he holds to the male correspondance between a *body politic* and a *body mystic* and repudiates any female surrogate.

Fifth, Pizan did not deny that male preference in rule was observed in France, but she staunchly held that circumstances might call a woman to rule (as queen or as regent) and recognized no custom, or law, prohibiting assumption of office. To the contrary, around 1409 Montreuil introduced his trump card, a Salic law held in the wings (since 1406). First, he gave a forged rendition of the Salic Ordinance in *Knighthood*, then a correct text in *Treatise* suitably fabricated to exclude women (and their sons) from rule in France. Montreuil's fraudulent French Salic law represented his last hope for defeating Pizan's influential argument, which validated rule of a *body politic* by women in the *City of Ladies*, and his best hope for restoring his own reputation, which was stung by the earlier conflict with her over defamation now recorded in that treatise. This opening phase in the debate over political identity ended in 1418 with the Burgundian attack on Paris, when Pizan took up residence in a convent and Montreuil was killed in the fray. Pizan composed the final footnote, her poem, *The Story of Joan of Arc* (1429),[66] which instanced her stand in a living example: the patriotic and valiant Joan called by God and king (Charles VII) to serve the polity, a woman whose political purpose and military prowess saved France.

There is no doubt that Christine de Pizan, whose *City of Ladies* in 1405 instigated a long debate over political identity and the right to rule, earned the status of political author, then and now. Modern scholars who have excluded the treatise from the present canon of political writings – judging it anti-humanist, or moralist, or prudish – should reassess such views still held in thrall to the judgments of medieval writers Pizan opposed.[67] In this debate over political identity and

---

[65] Ibid., 173.

[66] Pizan, *Le Dittié de Jehanne d'Arc* (July 31, 1429), the only French work honoring Joan before her death; Pizan died (c. 1430) before Joan was executed (1431). For the next stage of this debate, 1420s–1460s, see Hanley, "Mapping Rulership in the French Body Politic."

[67] See André Vachet, *L'Idéologie liberale* (Paris: Editions Anthropos, 1970), 44, judging hers a moralistic critique of the humanists; Richards, *City*, xxxi–xxxii, repeating that moral concerns prompted her attack on Meun's *Romance of the Rose*, an opinion shared with Pierre-Yves Badel, *Le Roman de la Rose au XIVe siècle, étude de la reception de l'œuvre* (Geneva: Librairie Droz, 1980); and Hicks, *Le Débat sur* Le Roman de la Rose, xii–xiii, xxix, judging her stance a moral and prudish one compared to the robust

governance of a *body politic*, Pizan was the critical political thinker, Montreuil and humanist cohorts the moralists. Then and later in the 1430s and 1460s when a French Salic law dictating female political exclusion was put to the test and failed again, subscription to defamatory moral injunctions kept the false juridical claim afloat in forgery. Reciting Jean de Montreuil, disputing Christine de Pizan, other exclusionists reaped some rewards when that Salic law, albeit still contested, achieved popularity through extended forgery set in the medium of print, 1480s–1530s. Still, the time for reckoning arrived in the mid-1500s when Salic law collapsed and jurists scrambled to extricate the French monarchy from the grip of forgery and fraud.[68] That they did by abandoning the fraudulent Salic law (now deemed a custom) and introducing a *French Law Canon*, which juridically designed the early modern monarchic state as a *marital regime* system of governance privileging male right in parallel realms, household and state, a system contested in turn.[69]

Acknowledgments

My appreciation to the Camargo Foundation, Cassis, France, and the Guggenheim Foundation for generous support of the project, and to Marilyn Hanley for pressing questions that drove the analysis.

humanism of Meun's work. Hicks repeated that view in "The Political Significance of Christine de Pizan," in *Politics, Gender, and Genre: The Political Thought of Christine de Pizan*, ed. Margaret Brabant (Boulder, Colo.: Westview Press, 1992), chap. 2. Acknowledging the modern tendency to ignore Pizan as a political author (from Jules Michelet, *Histoire de France* [Paris, s.d.], to *Nouvelle histoire des idées politiques*, ed. Pascal Ory [Paris: Hachette, 1987]), Hicks agrees with that exclusionary stance. He highlights moral (rather than political) dimensions of Pizan's writings (during the epistolary exchange with Montreuil) on the grounds that she was not "heard"; yet he allots political dimensions to works of Jean Gerson (defending her position), because they were "heard" (in his sermons) and thus constituted "political acts." The distinction is false on a number of grounds: historically, political acts have not been disconnected from reading; from 1399, Pizan understood how female defamation and exclusion were linked; moreover, her writings *vis-à-vis* Montreuil, 1402–1404, were read in political quarters and swiftly integrated in 1404 into the *City of Ladies*, which sparked a century-long political debate.

68 Hanley, "Loi salique," "Mapping Rulership in the French Body Politic," and "Monarchic State."

69 Hanley, "Social Sites of Political Practice in France: Lawsuits, Civil Rights, and the Separation of Powers in Domestic and State Government, 1500–1800," *American Historical Review* 102, 1 (1997): 27–52.

14 The Holy Roman Empire: women and politics beyond liberalism, individual rights, and revolutionary theory

Merry Wiesner

The vast majority of studies exploring aspects of gender and power in early modern Europe have focused on England, France, and Italy, with developments in Germany – in the Holy Roman Empire – investigated only rarely. There are several reasons for this. Some of these come from its politics: the Empire, that loose amalgam of secular and religious states stretching across central Europe, does not fit into the way early modern political history is often taught – it is neither absolutist nor constitutionalist – so it is easier simply to leave it out. Its political history is, in comparison with England in the seventeenth century and France in the eighteenth, rather boring, seemingly backward, and tediously complex.

Descriptions of its politics – boring, backward, and tedious – have also been applied to its few well-known early modern women writers, who, like their male counterparts, were busier founding learned literary societies than thinking about the human condition. Where is the Empire's Mary Wollstonecraft? Its Mary Astell? Even its Margaret Cavendish? Why did the *Querelle des femmes,* that springboard for so much thought and writing about women, leave so few traces in the Empire? Or is it just that we don't know about German women's political writings, that they are waiting to be rediscovered, translated and edited in the way that Christine de Pizan's *City of Ladies* was two decades ago?

This neglect or avoidance of issues of gender and power in the Empire has led to two kinds of distortions. First, early modern German political events and political writing have not been analyzed in gendered terms in ways that are familiar to historians of England or France. Second, assertions about gender and power in early modern "Europe" rely on developments largely within centralizing nation states.

This article will address both of these distortions by focusing on two areas in some detail: religious writings and actions by early modern

German women that have political implications, and German ideas about or practices regarding gender and citizenship that resonate with those in western Europe. It will thus range very broadly, and include consideration of what historians of England may view as odd or marginal figures and issues. The article will argue that they are not so marginal, and that the Empire was indeed part of Europe. Though the Holy Roman Empire was beyond liberalism, individual rights, and revolutionary theory, it was a source for other perhaps equally important political notions, and developments within it will deepen our understanding of the relationship between gender and political power in the early modern period.

The political implications of women's religious writings and actions

The writings of women in support of or opposition to the Protestant Reformation are only beginning to receive scholarly attention, and because of this the interpretation of these writings is still in its early stages.[1] Only rarely have these writings been viewed as political, which seems odd given the political nature of almost all polemical religious writing of the sixteenth century, as well as the recognition in contemporary feminist scholarship that *any* published writing by a woman contradicted the injunction to silence and so was viewed as a threat to the social order.

The writings of Argula von Grumbach were not only political in content, but also in their consequences. She was a Bavarian noblewoman who in 1523 wrote both to the faculty of the University of Ingolstadt and the duke of Bavaria, her overlord, protesting the university's treatment of a young teacher accused of Lutheran leanings. Her letter was published, leading to her husband's being deposed from his position and consequently treating von Grumbach badly; several other letters, however, led to an invitation to speak to the imperial diet which met in Nuremberg in 1523. Reports about her appearance there remind one of those describing the duchess of Newcastle's visit to the Royal

---

[1] The only book-length study which includes discussion of several women's writings is Paul Russell, *Lay Theology in the Reformation: Popular Pamphleteers in Southwest Germany* (Cambridge: Cambridge University Press, 1986). Argula von Grumbach has been the subject of several recent studies, including Peter Matheson, *Argula von Grumbach: A Woman's Voice in the Reformation* (Edinburgh: T. and T. Clark, 1995) and Silke Halbach, *Argula von Grumbach als Verfasserin reformatorischer Flugschriften.* Europäische Hochschulschriften, Reihe 23, Theologie; Bd. 468 (Frankfurt: Peter Lang, 1992). Elsie Anne McKee is currently working on a biography of Katharina Zell and a critical edition of her writings, to be published by E. J. Brill in 1998.

Society; she was a curiosity whose words were not taken seriously.[2] After this appearance, she disappears from the records, but shows up again forty years later, imprisoned by the then duke of Bavaria for circulating Protestant books, conducting funerals, and holding private conventicles in her house.

In her words as well as her actions, von Grumbach makes political points, using very lively language and creatively interpreting biblical texts. For example, when explaining her reasons for speaking out even though she was a woman, she cites the words of Isaiah 3.12, "I will send you children to be your princes and women to be your rulers."[3] Taken in context, the words describe God's punishment for Judah's turning away from him and are certainly not a positive assessment of female rule or women's public role; this is a passage that John Knox repeats and refers to constantly in *The First Blast*. Von Grumbach uses this passage as a justification for her speaking out, however, commenting that the university authorities were neglecting God's word in the same way the leaders of Judah had, thus forcing her to speak. Elsewhere she notes that according to Matthew 10.11-14, cities, towns, and households are all held equally responsible for their "worthiness" before God, which she interprets to mean that women who are in charge of households have the same duty to speak out on religious matters as men who are in charge of city governments do. This is a good example of the way in which the notion of the household as the smallest public institution can be used in ways that are supportive of women's wider public role, instead of its more common use as a reason for strengthening the position of the male head of household.[4]

This sentiment – that a woman's duty as a member of a Christian household extended well into the public realm – comes out even more strongly in the actions and writings of Katherine Zell. She wrote several polemics in the form of letters which she published, one of which was addressed specifically to a group of women. The men of Kenzingen, a small town near Strasbourg, were forced into exile by Archduke Ferdinand in 1524 because of their Protestant sympathies. Zell wrote *To the Suffering Women of Kenzingen Parish* as a consolation for the women

[2] Th. Kolde, "Arsacius Seehofer und Argula von Grumbach," *Beiträge zur bayerische Kirchengeschichte* 11 (1905): 49–77, 97–124, 148–88.
[3] "Wie ain Christliche Fraw des Adels ... Sendtbrieffe/die Hohenschul zu Ingolstadt" (1523), reprinted in Ludwig Rabus, *Historien der heyligen Ausserwolten Gottes Zeugen, Bekennern und Martyrern* (n.p., 1557), fol. 42.
[4] Luise Schorn-Schütte takes this idea even further, particularly in reference to pastors' wives, in "'Gefährtin' und 'Mitregentin': Zur Sozialgeschichte der evangelischen Pfarrfrau in der frühen Neuzeit," in *Wandel der Geschlechterbeziehung zu Beginn der Neuzeit*, eds. Heide Wunder and Christina Vanja (Frankfurt: Suhrkamp, 1991), 201–27.

left behind, urging them to hold firm: "When you fall into trouble, have the faith to suffer all sorts of trials, slander and pain; even if they put neck rings on you, exile you, or kill your husbands, you must remain faithful to Christ."[5] Later that year she wrote one of the few polemical pieces written by a woman in the Reformation which was not couched in the form of a letter, a defense of clerical marriage published several months after she had married Matthias Zell, who had been a priest. Its non-traditional form and explosive subject matter led to her being criticized not only by Catholics but also by fellow Protestants; the Strasbourg city council was so horrified that they ordered Matthias to forbid his wife to publish anything further – a request which she honored, as she did not write anything again until after Matthias had died. (Though she didn't wait long; after the formal eulogy at Matthias Zell's grave by Martin Bucer, Katherine added a long comment which was later printed.)

Toward the end of her life, Zell wrote her most complex piece, the "Letter to the whole citizenry of Strasbourg ... concerning Ludwig Rabus."[6] Rabus was a Lutheran pastor, now living in Ulm, who was a harsh critic of toleration and advocate of very rigid Lutheran confessionalism. In the "Letter," Zell reminds the citizens of Strasbourg of their earlier toleration, and develops a theological justification for this as well as for other points on which she disagrees with Rabus. She also adds a spiritual autobiography, and it is here that we can best see her awareness of the political implications of her actions. She comments: "I haven't stood in the pulpit because I didn't need to to carry out my duties, so I have followed the rule that St. Paul set for believing women of his time" (G, ii), but also that "I have done more work with my life and mouth than any chaplain of the church" (G, iii). She knows she has been and will be criticized for this, asking "Is this the sin of disorder, that I have served the ill and dying, visited prisoners, comforted them and talked to them about God?" (G, ii) and further asking that the citizens of Strasbourg judge her "not according to the standards of a woman, but according to the standards of what God through his Spirit has given to me" (A, ii).

Neither of Zell's requests to the citizens of Strasbourg were granted. The city adopted a rigid Lutheranism and attempted to forget that other

---

[5] Russell, *Lay Pamphleteers*, 207.
[6] *Ein Brieff an die genze Burgerschafft der Statt Strassburg ... / Betreffend Herr Ludwig Rabus* (n.p., 1557). All citations in the text refer to this copy, now in the Herzog August Bibliothek in Wolfenbüttel; all translations are my own. I have discussed this work more fully in "Katherina Zell's 'Letter to the whole citizenry of Strasbourg' as Theology and Autobiography," *Colloquia Germanica* 28 (1995): 245–54.

Protestant views had ever been accepted; Calvinist services were banned in 1577. Zell's work was judged, not as that of a lay Christian, but as that of a woman, and was never read. Its publication provoked one pseudonymous reply, which may have been written by Rabus, but which pointedly specified that the author had only bothered to read her preface and not the whole piece.[7] Her work was not used by other lay writers championing their rights *vis-à-vis* the clergy, nor was it mentioned by later advocates of toleration. None of this affected Zell's own views, however, for several months before her death she led funeral services for a woman accused of heretical leanings after the Strasbourg clergy refused to do so. Thus in her actions as well as her writings, Zell advocates a clear public role for women, based on her vow to follow "Christ's words to Peter, that he would make him a fisher of men" (A, iii).

The writings of female reformers, like those of lay male reformers, are concentrated in the first years of the Reformation; Katherine Zell is the only one known to have published anything after the 1520s. The long period of confessionalization in the Empire, which lasted from the 1550s until the outbreak of the Thirty Years War, was a time of the hardening of religious lines and the cementing of church and state in most parts of Germany. A new class of officials, the *Beamtentum*, developed, whose male members filled church, government, and university positions; particularly in Lutheran areas, clerical positions became more or less hereditary. In the same way that women had published works opposing the Roman Church in the first years of the Reformation, a few women also wrote against these developments; the disorder of the Thirty Years War allowed their works to be published.

Most prominent among these was Anna Hoyer, who had been driven from her native Holstein by the Thirty Years War, a war which she blamed on the "devil priests." She attacked the Lutheran clergy in a number of works for laxness, greed, pride, and trust in worldly learning. In her "Spiritual Conversation between a Mother and Child About True Christianity," the mother first asks, "What did you learn about salvation and the Bible in church today?" "Nothing." "About the prophets and Revelation?" "Nothing." The mother then launches into a harsh critique of the clergy:

> I know both women and men
> Who I could name if I had to
> In whom one could find

---

[7] Robert Kolb, *For All the Saints: Changing Perceptions of Martyrdom and Sainthood in the Lutheran Reformation* (Macon, Ga.: Mercer University Press, 1987), 43.

Much more clarity in the understanding of
Jesus Christ (God be Praised!)
Than in those who are supposed to teach.
But even if the others have better understanding
They are supposed to be silent
And just listen in the congregation
For the pastor alone has the word
As if it belonged only to him.
He never wants anyone to interrupt
Much less to correct him.
No one may question him.
He alone says what he wants
And all others have to be quiet.
No one is allowed to contradict him
Even if he says that crooked is straight
And black is white. He must be right.
He flatters himself because the peasants
Who only look to their pastor
Never understand much about the crooked and straight.
Isn't that a shame!
Was there anything like this at the time of the Apostles?
Did Paul teach like this?[8]

In this poem, Hoyer uses a conventional literary form, and one felt especially appropriate for women – the conversation between mother and child – but alters it to make a political statement in a way that was probably startling to her contemporaries. The Lutheran pastors she criticizes here are state officials, and the church itself is a state church; it is not only in the sixteenth century that religion and politics are so closely interwoven in the Empire.

Along with lay Protestant women criticizing Catholic and Lutheran clergy, another group of women within the Empire needs to be placed within a political context – female rulers. Imperial law and tradition did not exclude women from ruling territories in their own right, and in addition many spent years as the actual rulers during the minority of their sons. These women are slowly are emerging from the obscurity of local dynastic histories, and their roles as political and religious leaders are receiving greater attention.[9] A major new study by Heide Wunder, Helga Zöttlein, and Barbara Hoffman, for example, will explore the relations between political actions and religious ideology in the women

---

8 "Gespräch/Eines Kindes mit seiner Mutter/ Von dem Wege zur wahrer Gottseligkeit" (1628), reprinted in Gottfried Arnold, *Fortsetzung und Erläuterung Oder Dritter und Vierdter Theil der unpartheyischen Kirchen und Ketzer-Historie* (Frankfurt: Fritsch, 1729), 106. My translation.
9 See e.g. Heide Wunder, *" 'Er ist die Sonn', sie ist der Mond": Frauen in der Frühen Neuzeit* (Munich: C. H. Beck, 1992), 208–16.

who ruled very small states, where women's rule was viewed as quite normal.[10] Many of these women had pietist leanings, and this, combined with their sense of office, led them to found schools, orphanages, and other similar institutions. This process has been described as part of a long-running move toward "social discipline," but rarely have women's distinctive activities in this been assessed (they have more often been viewed as its victims). This new study will also investigate the ways in which women rulers in these small states created a new understanding of the proper role of a ruler. Louis XIV was not the only one who viewed himself as embodying the state; but what difference did this make when that body was female?

Along with secular rulers which parallel those in western Europe, the Empire also had a type of female ruler unknown in western Europe – abbesses of free imperial convents. The writings and the actions of these abbesses challenged both political theory and political realities in early modern Germany, and also challenge some current assumptions about women's rule throughout Europe.

The abbess in a free imperial convent, like the city council of a free imperial city, was the penultimate legal authority in her area; her only overlord was the emperor. She appointed secular and church officials, sent a representative to the Reichstag, heard legal cases, built and supported hospitals, orphanages, and occasionally schools. Though the usual story told is that all convents were closed in Protestant areas after the Reformation, in fact this did not happen; many abbesses retained their powers and independence after the Reformation, even in Protestant territories, with their convents either remaining Catholic or transforming themselves into Protestant convents. Of twenty-two female convents in the bishoprics of Magdeburg and Halberstadt, eleven were still in existence and still Catholic in 1648, though the bishops had turned Protestant in the 1520s.[11] Convents in Augsburg, Nuremberg, and Strasbourg put up increasingly well-known fights to remain Catholic, as did those in the duchies of Brunswick and Lüneberg.[12]

---

[10] This project is titled "Konfession, Religiosität und politisches Handeln von Frauen vom ausgehenden 16. bis zum Beginn des 18. Jahrhunderts." My thanks to Heide Wunder for sharing the proposal with me.

[11] Franz Schrader, *Ringen, Untergang und Überleben der Katholischen Klöster in den Hochstiften Magdeburg und Halberstadt von der Reformation bis zum Westfälischen Frieden,* Katholisches Leben und Kirchenreform im Zeitalter der Glaubensspaltung, 37 (Münster: Aschendorff, 1977), 43.

[12] Georg Deichstetter, ed., *Caritas Pirckheimer. Ordensfrau und Humanistin – Vorbild für die Ökumene* (Cologne, 1982); Lyndal Roper, *The Holy Household: Women and Morals in Reformation Augsburg* (Oxford: Oxford University Press, 1989), 206–51; Thomas A. Brady, Jr., "'You Hate Us Priests': Anticlericalism, Communalism, and the Control of Women at Strasbourg in the Age of the Reformation," in *Anticlericalism in Late Medieval*

The ability of these convents to survive was the result of a combination of factors, some of which were clearly political.[13] Abbesses and nuns were able to take advantage of confessional differences between local nobles and the emperor, or local nobles themselves, differences which of course were not simply matters of theology in early modern Germany, but were shaped by and in turn shaped political life. Abbeys were enmeshed in networks of patronage, and used their connections with the emperor, noble families and their religious orders to put pressure on local secular rulers.[14] Practical politics also led some abbesses to put independence and spiritual practices above mere theology, and they agreed to accept Lutheran doctrines as long as their lives were not radically changed. Indeed, it is often difficult to tell exactly what religion a convent was at any particular point, as Catholic and Protestant women lived together and their observances and rules were a mixture of both.

Along with abbesses who became Protestant for practical political reasons, there were also some who accepted the new theology and energetically introduced it into their territories. They took to heart Luther's early teachings about the possibilities of a truly Christian convent life, and seemed to ignore his later opinions and those of more radical reformers such as Andreas Karlstadt and Thomas Müntzer. Abbess Elisabeth von Weida of Gernrode sent a representative to the Diet of Worms in 1521 to get a first-hand report about what Luther was saying. She began to name Protestant pastors to all the churches under her control in 1525, expecting the new teaching to bring a further deepening of the spiritual life in her convent and the territory she controlled.[15] Anna von Stolberg, who was the abbess of Quedlinburg from 1515 to 1574, controlled nine churches, a hospital, and two male monasteries. She accepted the Protestant Reformation in the 1540s, started a consistory, made all priests swear to the Augsburg confession,

---

and Early Modern Europe, eds. Peter A. Dykema and Heiko A. Oberman (Leiden: E. J. Brill, 1993), 167–227.

[13] For a broader discussion of the convents' survival, see Merry E. Wiesner, "Ideology Meets the Empire: Reformed Convents and the Reformation," in *Germania Illustrata: Essays in Honor of Gerald Strauss*, eds. Andrew Fix and Susan Karant-Nunn (Kirksville, Mo.: Sixteenth Century Journal Publishers, 1992), 181–96. For translations of the writings of both Protestant and Catholic nuns, see Merry Wiesner and Joan Skocir, *Convents Confront the Reformation: Catholic and Protestant Nuns in Early Modern Germany* (Milwaukee: Marquette University Press, 1996).

[14] Adolph Wrede, *Die Einführung der Reformation im Lünebergische durch Herzog Ernst der Bekenner* (Göttingen: Dietrich, 1887), 131, 224.

[15] August Franke, "Elisabeth von Weide und Wildenfels: Aebtissin des freien weltlichen Stiftes Gernrode 1504–1532," *Mitteilungen des Vereins für Anhaltische Geschichte und Altertumskunde* 8 (1899): 328; Hans K. Schulze, *Das Stift Gernrode* (Cologne: Böhlau, 1965), 51.

and set the salaries for church and school officials. In 1680 her successor the abbess Anna Sophia issued a new baptism ordinance, and in 1700 the abbess Anna Dorothea an "edict against the separatists," that is, those who wished to leave the Lutheran state church.[16]

Abbesses clearly recognized their special social and political status, and reflected it in their writings as well as actions. Anna Sophia of Quedlinburg, for example, published a book of meditations entitled *Der treue Seelenfreund Christus Jesus*, which includes a long introduction and afterword discussing the special duties of virgins, the most important of which was praising God.[17] Her work was criticized and regarded as theologically suspect by some Lutheran theologians, who thought she stressed the ubiquity of Christ's presence too strongly in her comments that women could feel this presence equally with men.[18]

Though continuation of convents was rarely challenged in practice after the mid-sixteenth century, there were still doubts about the appropriateness of this peculiarly German form of female rule. In 1564, Stephan Molliter, a Lutheran pastor who had in fact received his initial appointment from the first Lutheran abbess of Gernrode, used the funeral of one of her followers as the occasion to rail against female rulership. He chose as his text the passage from Ecclesiastes, "Woe to you, O land, when your king is a child" (10.16) to criticize the young age of the new abbess (who was in the audience) and the childlike nature of all women.[19] Even those Lutheran commentators who chose to praise the abbesses felt it necessary to justify and explain their power. Friedrich Kettner, who wrote a long history of Quedlinburg published in 1710, includes a lengthy discussion about why the titles "abbess," "prioress," and "canoness" could legitimately be maintained, using examples from the New Testament and early church to show that these were not later popish inventions. Just like Argula von Grumbach and John Knox, he feels compelled to discuss Isaiah 3.12 ("I will give you children to be your oppressors and women to be your rulers . . .") and agrees with John Aylmer that Isaiah was not talking about the female sex here, but those of the feminine temperament (*weibliche Gemuth*). As in the English defenses of gynecocracy, Kettner includes a long list of ancient and contemporary female rulers who do *not* have such a "weibliche Gemuth."[20]

In the long run (or at least until the secularization of church property

---

[16] Friedrich Ernst Kettner, *Kirchen und Reformations Historie des Kaysel. Freyen Weltlichen Stiffts Quedlinburg* (Quedlinburg: Theodore Schwan, 1710), 127–32.
[17] Published in Jena by Georg Sengenwald in 1658.
[18] Kettner, *Kirchen*, 164.   [19] Franke, "Elisabeth," 328.
[20] Kettner, *Kirchen*, 130.

in 1807) doubts and debates did not matter. Patronage networks combined with ambivalence in gender and religious ideology to allow abbesses a wide range of powers. They, along with their noble secular sisters (and abbesses were often the actual, rather than simply metaphorical, sisters of secular female rulers) demonstrated that at this social level, class was more important than either gender or religion, able to overcome both sexism and confessionalism. We might regard this, in comparison with seventeenth-century England or eighteenth-century France, as a sign of the "backward" nature of the Holy Roman Empire, of its clinging to "medieval" notions of social orders (*Stände*), but it also might be viewed slightly differently. Heinz Schilling has recently rightfully stressed the political and cultural triumph of the nobility in the Empire after the Thirty Years War.[21] We can thus view the abbesses of the sixteenth and early seventeenth centuries as harbingers rather than throwbacks. For these women, as for the upper-class English women Hilda Smith has investigated in *Reason's Disciples*, the lessening of the privileges of rank would not have been beneficial. For much of German scholarship from Max Weber through the present, the resurgence of the nobility after the Thirty Years War was an embarrassment, and the period of urban flourishing and village communalism which preceded it took on – and still does take on – the aura of a golden age. When we shift the focus from the political rights of men to those of women, however, the assessment may look slightly different.

Urban and rural communalism

In the same way that we can find parallels to west European female monarchs in the German rulers of small states and imperial abbesses, we can also find interesting parallels between the German cities and villages and the west European nation states in many issues involving female citizenship and political rights. To do this, we must look at the "golden age," at the free imperial cities and the south German villages of the Holy Roman Empire during the period of their growth and strength, roughly the fourteenth through the sixteenth centuries.

As noted above, recent scholarship on the development of citizenship in early modern Europe has taken for granted that "citizenship" means *state* citizenship and so focuses on the emergence of centralized states. There is, of course, another type of citizenship, one which historians of the Empire have written a great deal about – urban citizenship. Beginning with Max Weber's massive *Wirtschaft und Gesellschaft*, published in

---

[21] Schilling, *Aufbruch und Krise: Deutschland 1517–1648* (Frankfurt: Siedler, 1988).

the 1920s, theorists of urban development have argued that a new and distinctive type of city began in the medieval West.[22] The key factor distinguishing this city from those of other periods and places was the notion of citizenship (*Bürgertum*), for it was citizenship which created the urban "community." Interest in urban citizenship among German scholars has not been limited to the medieval period, however, for notions of urban community based on citizenship have also been a key part of research on the urban Reformation since Bernd Moeller's *Imperial Cities and the Reformation*, and a recent study of German towns between the Thirty Years War and Bismarck asserts: "Any town's citizenship policy and citizenship grants are usually the best place to read its history."[23]

This scholarship on the urban community has been joined over the last fifteen years by scholarship focusing on the rural community, particularly the Swiss and German village communes between 1400 and 1600.[24] Like cities, villages were also oath-bound confederations (*Gemeinde*) and by the sixteenth century these confederations had, in turn, formed themselves into larger federations of villages. Though their primary decisions were economic ones relating to regulation of agricultural production, by the early sixteenth century they were also concerned with religious issues, in particular demanding that "we ought to have the authority and power for the whole community to elect and appoint its own pastor."[25]

Who made up these urban and rural communities? In the cities – though there are some differences from town to town – citizenship was generally based on three factors: military obligations and an oath of allegiance formalizing these (a swearing of *Treue und Gehorsam*); prop-

---

[22] Max Weber, *Wirtschaft und Gesellschaft*, selectively edited and translated by Don Martindale and Gertrud Neuwirth and published as *The City* (New York: Free Press, 1958); see also Hans Planitz, *Die deutsche Stadt im Mittelalter* (Graz: Böhlau, 1965); Edith Ennen, *Die europäische Stadt des Mittelalters* (Göttingen: Vandenhoeck and Ruprecht, 1972).

[23] Bernd Moeller, *Imperial Cities and the Reformation* (Philadelphia: Fortress, 1972), first published as *Reichsstadt und Reformation* (Gutersloh, 1962). For a survey of studies of the urban Reformation since Moeller, see Kaspar von Greyerz, "Stadt und Reformation: Stand und Aufgaben der Forschung," *Archiv für Reformationsgeschichte* 76 (1985): 6–63. The quote in the second half of the sentence is from Mack Walker, *German Home Towns: Community, State and General Estate, 1648–1871* (Ithaca: Cornell University Press, 1971), 139.

[24] See the work of Peter Blickle, most recently *Communal Reformation: The Quest for Salvation in Sixteenth-Century Germany*, trans. Thomas A. Brady, Jr. and H. C. Erik Midelfort (Atlantic Highlands, N.J.: Humanities Press, 1992), and Heide Wunder, *Die Bäuerliche Gemeinde in Deutschland* (Göttingen: Vandenhoeck and Ruprecht, 1986).

[25] Twelve articles of the peasants (1525), quoted in Blickle, *Communal Reformation*, 21.

erty ownership (*Eigentum*); honorable means of support (*Bürgerliche Nahrung*) – what we can in shorthand term war, work, and wealth. These three bases also seem to be applicable to village communes, though in these the issue of property ownership was more complicated.

At first glance, any of these three factors might have been used as a reason for limiting citizenship to men, which could explain why most studies of urban citizenship in the Empire or the development of the village commune have focused on the meaning of these for men. Women did not perform military duties in medieval cities or villages; they could lose their right to control property on marriage; the types of work available to them independently were as likely to be dishonorable as honorable or to provide less than an adequate means of support. The problem with this is that it didn't happen. Not only were women citizens, but the bases for accepting them as such – at least in cities where this is spelled out – were explicitly the same three as for men in the medieval period. When referring to citizens, many medieval sources are explicitly gender-inclusive – they use the phrase "Bürger und Bürgerin" when referring to all the citizens of a town, or "alle Bürgern, Mann und Frau" or "Bürgern, es sey mannisname oder wybisname."[26] Women were listed on new citizens' rolls in Nuremberg, Frankfurt, Munich, Nördlingen, Memmingen, Strasbourg, Augsburg, and many other south German towns, and were obligated to swear an oath and provide soldiers and arms for the city's defense.[27] Until the late sixteenth or early seventeenth century, women were able to pass citizenship rights on to non-citizen men they had married, in the same way that foreign women who married male citizens also became citizens.

Thus in terms of the bases of urban citizenship, and to a large degree the responsibilities and rights it entailed, there was less distinction based on gender in most south German cities before 1500 than one might have assumed. This rather off-hand acceptance of women as citizens began to change in the sixteenth century, however. In Nuremberg, for example, women made up 13 percent of the new citizens in the 1460s, a share which declined to 4.6 percent by the 1500s and to less than 1 percent by

---

[26] See e.g. Frankfurt, Stadtarchiv, Verordnungen und Gerichtssachen; Nuremberg, Staatsarchiv, Ratsbücher, Rep. 60b (henceforth RB); Memmingen, Stadtarchiv, Bürgerbücher (BB); Munich, Stadtarchiv, Ratsitzungsprotokolle (RSP).

[27] Nuremburg, Staatsarchiv, Amts- und Standbücher, Rep 52b, nos. 299–300, 305–306 – Neubürgerlisten (NBL); Memmingen, BB; Augsburg, Stadtarchiv, Nr. 269 – Bürgerbücher (BB); Frankfurt, Stadtarchiv, Bürgermeisterbücher (BMB), 1495, fol. 26a; 1505, fol. 15b; Beata Brodmeier, *Die Frau im Handwerk* (Münster: Handwerkswissenschaftliches Institut, 1963), 14–20; Erika Uitz, *The Legacy of Good Women: Medieval Women in Towns and Cities*, trans. Sheila Marnie (Mount Kisko, New York: Mayer, Bell, Ltd., 1990), 55–62.

the 1550s.[28] Beginning in the mid-sixteenth or early seventeenth century, the widows and daughters of male citizens were prohibited from marrying foreigners unless they got the approval of the city council.[29] In 1631 in Lutheran Strasbourg, a distinction was made between male and female citizens who married Calvinists; a woman was to lose her citizenship "because she would let herself easily be led into error in religion by her husband and be led astray," while a man would not, "because he can probably draw his spouse away from her false religion and bring her on to the correct path."[30]

What might account for these developments? Two factors are often noted: first, many towns went through a period of economic decline in the sixteenth century, when they increased the standard fees for citizenship to bring in more money and prevent poor people from immigrating, and granted citizenship free of charge less often.[31] Because women were generally poorer than men, this meant that fewer of them were able to afford citizenship. Second, Martha Howell has concluded, based on studies of cities in north Germany and the Low Countries, that when citizenship brought political rights rather than simply economic ones, women were excluded. She notes: "female registration fell off exactly when citizenship was redefined so as to make it directly or indirectly equivalent to access to rule."[32] Both of these are undoubtedly important but cannot explain the change everywhere, as not all cities experienced decline and in not all cities did citizenship bring access to political rights.

Might explanations for women's exclusion from citizenship which have been developed for other parts of Europe also be applicable to the Empire? Studies of state citizenship in western Europe and of Italian city republics have concluded that once the individual became more

---

[28] Nuremberg NBL.
[29] Strasbourg, Archives municipales, Statuten, vol. 18, no. 3, fol. 74 (1557) and reissued in 1594, 1627, 1687. Memmingen, Stadtarchiv, Ratsprotokollbücher (RPB), June 21, 1602; March 13, 1616; Augsburg BB, 1580 and elsewhere.
[30] Strasbourg, Archives municipales, Akten der XXI (XXI), 1631, fol. 40.
[31] Werner Schultheiss, "Das Bürgerrecht der Königs- und Reichstadt Nürnberg," in Festschrift für Hermann Heimpel, II (Göttingen: Vandenhoeck and Ruprecht, 1972); Gerard Dilcher, "Zum Bürgerbegriff im späteren Mittelalter: Versuch einer Typologie am Beispiel von Frankfurt am Main," in Ueber Bürger, Stadt, und städtischen Literatur im Spätmittelalter, eds. Joseph Fleckenstein and Karl Stackmann (Göttingen: Vandenhoeck and Ruprecht, 1980); Franz Gschwind, Bevölkerungsentwicklung und Wirtschaftsstruktur der Landschaft Basel im 18. Jahrhundert (Liestal: Kantonale Druchsachen, 1970); Hans R. Guggisberg, Basel in the Sixteenth Century: Aspects of the City Republic before, during and after the Reformation (St. Louis: Center for Reformation Research, 1982), 39; Roper, Holy Household, 55.
[32] Martha C. Howell, "Citizenship and Gender: Women's Political Status in Northern Medieval Cities," in Women and Power in the Middle Ages, eds. Mary Erler and Maryanne Kowaleski (Athens, Ga.: University of Georgia Press, 1988), 47.

important politically than the kin or corporate group, women were excluded.[33] The problem with applying this analysis to the Empire is that, rather than declining, familial and corporate values remained strong or, as studies of ideas about the family and community during the century of the Reformation have argued, became even more important than they had been earlier.[34] In these cities, the central political unit remained the household in both theory and practice, a household of which women were part and which they very often headed.[35]

To get a full explanation for the decline in the significance of female citizenship, then, we must explore why, in the sixteenth century, corporatist and family values in south Germany became more masculine, and then see what effects this had on female citizenship. This is an area in which research is only beginning, but four factors appear to be important.

First, both Greek philosophy and Roman law put greater emphasis on the mental weakness of women, rather than their inability to bear arms, as the reason for their exclusion from politics and secondary legal status. Thus city leaders educated as humanists and jurists trained in Roman law were able to justify making distinctions between male and female citizens by using a new standard rather than reinterpreting war, work, and wealth in gender-specific ways.

Second, though urban values remained corporatist and family-centered they were middle class rather than noble, so that families in which women held independent power were regarded as disruptive and disorderly.[36] Adult women were to have authority over dependent members of their households, but this authority was derivative, coming from their status as wife or widow of the male household head. The derivative nature of women's acceptable authority is made clear by referring to a woman as "wife" rather than "mother" even in legal documents describing her relations with her

---

[33] The literature on this is vast. See especially Joan Landes, *Women and the Public Sphere in the Age of the French Revolution* (Ithaca: Cornell University Press, 1988).

[34] Dilcher, "Bürgerbegriff," 82; Heinrich Schmidt, *Die deutschen Städtechroniken als Spiegel des bürgerlichen Selbstverstandnisses in Spätmittelalter* (Göttingen: Vandenhoeck and Ruprecht, 1958); Steven Ozment, *When Fathers Ruled: Family Life in Reformation Europe* (Cambridge, Mass.: Harvard University Press, 1983).

[35] Heide Wunder, "'L'espace privé' and the Domestication of Women in the Sixteenth and Seventeenth Centuries," unpublished paper. For statistics on female heads of household see Merry E. Wiesner, *Working Women in Renaissance Germany* (New Brunswick, N.J.: Rutgers University Press, 1986), 4–5.

[36] This has been argued most fully for Italy in Diane Owen Hughes, "Invisible Madonnas? The Italian Historiographical Tradition and the Women of Medieval Italy," in *Women in Medieval History and Historiography*, ed. Susan Stuard (Philadelphia: University of Pennsylvania Press, 1987), 25–34, and for France in Landes, *Women and the Public Sphere*.

children.[37] The suspicion of women with independent power was not based solely on theories of sexual difference, but also on urban and village communities' actual experiences with noblewomen who held power. By the sixteenth century, this was generally during wartime, when the noblewomen led military forces acting against city or village interests, such as Bianca Maria Sforza and Elisabeth, the daughter of Duke George of Bavaria-Landshut and widow of Count Palatine Ruprecht, who both directed action against the Swabian League.[38]

Third, as the urban and village community was sacralized in the sixteenth century, a development traced in many studies of the communal Reformation, greater distinctions were made between male and female citizens because the former regularly swore oaths to uphold the city's religion while the latter did not.[39] Thus not only did the difference between male and female citizens acquire religious connotations, but there was also a new distinction between male and female Christians; for the former, faith was also a ritualized civic matter while for the latter it was not. This led to uncertainty about how to handle the citizenship status of certain women. In Protestant cities, one of the key political effects of the Reformation was the integration of the male clergy into the citizenry, ending the distinction between clerical and lay status. In most cases, these priests also married, but this was not a requirement for obtaining citizenship. For nuns, however, it was. The only way they could become citizens was to marry, which meant, of course, they were no longer nuns. A priest could be both a citizen *and* a priest, but a nun could not be a citizen and a nun. In some cities there was debate about whether even marrying was enough to make certain women citizens. In Nördlingen, for example, though priests were required to become citizens, there was great debate about whether the women who married them should be considered as such, for they were tainted with the "dishonorable" status of priests' concubines.[40]

[37] Roper, *Holy Household*, 59.

[38] These incidents are described in Thomas Brady, *Turning Swiss: Cities and Empire, 1450–1550* (Cambridge: Cambridge University Press, 1985), 63–64 and 79. The fact that using arms to gain freedom from noble domination was seen as the "Swiss way" has particular irony when those nobles are female, for even in the early modern period Swiss cantons were more restrictive of women's legal and economic rights than their south German neighbors. Given the history of women's political rights in Switzerland since the early modern period, it is probably fortunate that the south German towns Brady investigates were foiled in their attempt to "turn Swiss."

[39] See Moeller, *Imperial Cities*; Ebel, "Bürgereid," 39; Richard Stauffer, "Das Basler Bekenntnis von 1534," in *Ecclesia semper reformanda: Vorträge zum Basler Reformationsjubilaum*, eds. Hans R. Guggisberg and Peter Rotach (Basel: Friedrich Reinhardt Verlag, 1980), 28–49.

[40] Hans-Christoph Rublack, *Eine bürgerliche Reformation: Nördlingen* (Gütersloh: Gütersloher Verlagshaus Mohn, 1982), 174–75.

Fourth, and somewhat in contradiction to the previous factors, urban and village corporatist values had always been somewhat male-defined, so that sixteenth-century developments were not a complete break with tradition. Though women swore oaths of loyalty on first becoming citizens and were otherwise obligated to perform most of the duties of citizenship, they did not participate in the annual oath-swearing, affirming their loyalty, which took place in most German towns and villages until well into the early modern period. That annual oath-swearing was not limited to male citizens, however, but was also expected of adolescent boys before they became citizens.[41] More clearly than citizenship, this oath-swearing (*Schwörtag*) determined membership in the political community.[42]

What were the consequences of defining the urban community in increasingly male-specific terms? Though women were never categorically excluded from citizenship in German towns and villages, notions of women's proper place within the family and community increasingly made the only type of female citizenship which was acceptable a derivative one. Fewer women were accepted for citizenship independently or allowed to pass it on to non-citizen husbands.[43] At first it was new intellectual and religious criteria which were used to make distinctions between female and male citizens, but gradually the traditional bases of urban citizenship – war, work, and wealth – also came to be interpreted in gender-specific ways. German Neo-Aristotelians in the seventeenth century added women's inability to bear arms and economic dependence on their husbands to their mental and moral weakness as reasons for excluding them from all aspects of public life; in the eighteenth century, women in Prussia were ruled ineligible for one of the benefits of citizenship, a pension, because their labor was not judged to be "work," even though it was exactly the same as that of men; women who had, by virtue of property ownership, participated in citizens' assemblies in Glarus were excluded in the mid-seventeenth century (and would not be readmitted until 1972.)[44] Thus by the time

---

41 Dilcher, "Bürgerbegriff"; Schultheiss, "Bürgerrecht" (though he reports that by the seventeenth century the oath-swearing was held only every seven years in Nuremberg); Lyndal Roper, "'The Common Man', 'the Common Good', 'Common Women': Gender and Meaning in the German Reformation Commune," *Social History* 12 (1987): 10–12. The participation of citizens' adolescent sons is similar to the custom in English towns of boys being sworn into a tithing.

42 Though they approach it from vastly different perspectives, this is the conclusion of both Ebel, "Bürgereid," and Roper, "'Common Man'."

43 For other consequences see Roper, "'Common Man'"; Kristin Zapalac, *"In His Image and Likeness": Political Iconography and Religious Change in Regensburg, 1500–1600* (Ithaca: Cornell University Press, 1990), 135–66.

44 MacLean, *Renaissance Notion*, 52–55; Jean Quataert, "The Shaping of Women's Work

state citizenship became an issue in Germany, war, work, and wealth appeared to be natural and long-standing reasons for excluding women, as the writings of the nineteenth-century jurist Carl Welcker make clear.[45]

Conclusions

One of the standard explanations for the exclusion of women from early modern political life is the way in which during this period civic virtues were increasingly viewed as male; women could not be "free born Englishmen," nor be part of an ideal of *fraternité*. Women's virtues, it is argued, remained within a private moral and religious sphere, which was increasingly viewed as secondary to a public, secular one. Mary Maples Dunn put this succinctly in her addition to Jean Bodin's comment that "to be a good man is to be a good citizen," by noting that "but to be a good woman was to be a good Christian."[46]

Several very recent studies of English and Anglo-American political theory, however, have emphasized the continued connection rather than disjuncture between religion and politics through the eighteenth century. These studies point out links between sixteenth-century Swiss, German, and Dutch notions of liberty or the covenant and later English or American ones; they also stress the continued importance of corporate and collective elements in early modern political revolutions.[47] What these studies leave out – often bizarrely – is any mention of the

in Manufacturing: Guilds, Households and the State in Central Europe, 1648–1870," *American Historical Review* 90 (1985): 1124; Louis Carlen, *Die landsgemeinde in der Schweiz: Schule der Demokratie* (Sigmaringen: Jan Thorbecke, 1976).

[45] Heide Wunder, "Von der frumkeit zur Frömmigkeit: Ein Beitrag zur Genese bürgerlicher Weiblichkeit (15.–17. Jahrhundert)," in *Weiblichkeit in geschichtlicher Perspektive*, eds. Ursula A. J. Becher and Jorn Rusen (Frankfurt: Suhrkamp, 1988), 175. By the late eighteenth century, women as well viewed bearing arms as essential to citizenship. Olwen Hufton points out that club women during the early stages of the French Revolution demanded the right to bear arms, and that debates about wearing the cockade revolved around whether only those citizens who bore arms (i.e., men) should be required to wear it, or whether women should as well (Olwen H. Hufton, *Women and the Limits of Citizenship in the French Revolution* [Toronto: University of Toronto Press, 1992], 23–24, 36–37). This point is also made in Claudia Opitz, "Der Bürger wird Soldat – Und die Bürgerin? Die Revolution, der Krieg und die Stellung der Frauen nach 1789," in *Sklavin oder Bürgerin: Französische Revolution und neue Weiblichkeit 1760–1830*, ed. Viktoria Schmidt-Linsenhoff (Frankfurt: Joan Verlag, 1989), 38–54.

[46] Mary Maples Dunn in J. James, ed., *Women in American Religion* (Philadelphia: University of Pennsylvania Press, 1980), 39. Bodin's comment is from the *Six Books of the Commonwealth*.

[47] See Charles S. McCoy and J. Wayne Baker, *Fountainhead of Federalism: Heinrich Bullinger and the Covenantal Tradition* (Louisville: Westminster/John Knox Press, 1991) and J. C. D. Clark, *The Language of Liberty 1660–1832: Political Discourse and Social*

gendered nature of these notions in their continental, English, and later American variations.[48]

Like these recent studies, this chapter has demonstrated that state policies toward citizenship were not created *ex nihilo*, but were an outgrowth of earlier developments within smaller political communities, and that religion and politics were more closely linked than is often asserted. In contrast to these studies, it has also argued that gender distinctions are at the heart of both religious and political understandings of community. Dunn's addition to Bodin is correct in the way that it reads, but not correct if it is stood on its head: to be a good citizen was of course to be a man, but to be a good Christian was also to be a man. In the milieu of village, city, and later national communalism, to be a good Christian – that is, one who could vote for a pastor in a Swiss village or publish Congregational tracts defending New England's liberties – one had to be male.

Thus as we increasingly highlight the religious nature of early modern political discourse, we must also highlight what we might term the politicization and masculinization of religion. The first elections in Europe which involved common "people" rather than nobles were in villages and towns of south Germany and Switzerland, where, beginning in the late Middle Ages, the men of the parish elected their priest.[49] Thus in the church as well as the state, republicanism and democracy marked a division between women and men that had not existed when priests were appointed. The abbesses Elisabeth von Weida or Anna von

Dynamics in the Anglo-American World (Cambridge: Cambridge University Press, 1994).

[48] The omission does not appear to be limited to the two works cited in note 47. Other than one study of Anne Hutchinson, McCoy and Baker's 20-page bibliography on federal theology and political philosophy contains no works specifically about women or gender issues. The extensive notes in Clark include not a single study which focuses on these, other than one reference to Gordon Schochet's *Patriarchialism in Political Thought* (Oxford: Oxford University Press, 1970). (Clark's own use of the term "patriarchy," e.g., pp. 14–15 and 158–59, is in a completely male context.) This is not to say that such studies do not exist – recent feminist analyses of seventeenth-century England and the American Revolution certainly belie this – but simply to indicate that there are large numbers of works which share their blind spot.

[49] Dietrich Kurze, *Pfarrerwahlen im Mittelalter. Ein Beitrag zur Geschichte der Gemeinde und des Niederkirchenwesens*, Forschungen zur kirchlichen Rechtsgeschichte, vol. 6 (Cologne and Graz: Böhlau, 1966). It is important to note that the election of pastors predates the Reformation by at least a century in some areas. There has been a great deal of scholarship pointing out how well Protestant theology fit with various existing aspects of urban and village life, which helps explain the speed and pattern of the Reformation's acceptance. This is only beginning to be noted in terms of ideas about women and the family, as it becomes clear that what are generally seen as "Protestant" ideas – such things as companionate marriage – result *from* rather than *in* urban bourgeois views of the place of women.

Stolberg might choose the pastors for the villages under their control, but no woman could vote for one. The community of Christians was as male as the free individual.

In the conclusion to his study of the communal Reformation, Peter Blickle comments, "communalism as a way of life shows a marked affinity to republicanism as a form of government."[50] Though he nowhere acknowledges that this affinity includes the exclusion of women from the community and the republic, we must be sure that the newest scholarship exploring this affinity is held to task when it does not. Jonathan Edwards based his claims to authority on his rights as a Christian, terming these "the liberty of a minister of Christ." Though Katherine Zell also called herself a "minister of Christ," that title brought her – and the women who came after her – no liberties.

[50] Blickle, *Communal Reformation*, 193.

15   Women as sextons and electors: King's Bench and precedents for women's citizenship

Hilda L. Smith

In January, 1738/9, the Court of King's Bench took up a case, *Olive v. Ingram*, that seemed legally and politically insignificant. It involved a dispute between two claimants for the post of sexton in the London parish of St. Botolphs without Bishopsgate, and the amount in dispute was just five shillings. Yet the court continued the case for five months and held three separate sessions concerning its resolution. The facts of the case involved a woman who had been elected sexton through the support of women members of the congregation; five of their votes were necessary for her victory. King's Bench thus confronted two separate but related issues: could a woman occupy this minor church office, and could other women vote for her to do so?[1]

The office of sexton had been held by Robert Bly, and upon his death, his widow Sarah Bly and a male rival, John Olive, competed for the post. A popular abridgement of English law describes the contest thus:

Two candidates offered themselves to be elected ... viz. the widow of the sexton deceased, and the plaintiff: that upon casting up the books the plaintiff appeared to have a majority of male votes, but that afterwards, the widow polled 40 women, and then she had the majority; that the widow, and all the female voters were house-keepers paying scot and lot, and to all parish rates and assessments.[2]

---

[1] *Olive v. Ingram*, Hilary term, 12 George 2, 7 Mod. 263, *English Reports*, vol. 87 (Edinburgh, 1932), 1230–37. St. Botolphs without Bishopsgate was a large parish immediately outside the city walls to the northeast. In a work on the seventeenth century, it is described as an area with "a large number of tenements," a generally poor parish, but one in which "a group of well-to-do tradesmen ... were able to maintain its parochical stability. It also had a consistent and well-managed poor relief system" (Tai Liu, *Puritan London: A Study of Religion and Society in the City Parishes* [Newark, Del.: University of Delaware Press, 1986], 42–43). It should be noted that Strange, in his brief account of the case, states the parish as St. Botolph without Aldersgate, 2 Strange 1114 *English Reports*, 1067–68. Court personnel included Sir William Lee, Chief Justice; Sir Francis Page, Sir Edmund Probyn, and Sir William Chapple, justices; Dudley Ryder, Attorney-General and John Strange, Solicitor-General; and Thomas [?] Bootle, William Wynne, and Abel Kettleby for the defendant, and [ ] Marsh and Thomas Dennison for the plaintiff.

[2] *A General Abridgement of Law and Equity*, XIII, ed. Charles Viner, Esq. (London: Lincolns

The election was held in the room of Sarah Bly's deceased husband. The victor (presumably Olive) was a man who gained the office through support from men and a minority of women parishioners. But then the widow, Sarah Bly, polled forty additional women and was declared the winner. Logically the case could have been decided by simply claiming that Bly's extra effort was irregular, and that the original election result should stand. However, King's Bench chose not to do so, and, at first, the justices suggested it was a case of broad implications, even linking the holding of this office to the parliamentary franchise. Why, one might ask, did the court not take the easy way out and decide against the plaintiff on procedural grounds?

While the court ultimately determined that women could both vote for and hold the office of sexton, it reached such a decision based upon the insignificance of the office, and its standing as a private rather than a public trust. Yet during the course of the court's deliberations, the Attorney-General and the Solicitor-General, justices of the court, and lawyers representing each side foraged widely in precedents concerning women's past political, legal, and social standing.[3]

The case opens promisingly for scholars interested in issues relating to women's citizenship in early modern Britain.[4] The reporter's summa-

Inn, 1793) includes a section on "feme," the first part entitled "Capable of What." Here *Olive v. Ingram* gains the greatest attention among other precedents for women holding offices such as mower of a manor, bailee (one chargeable for goods), hospital sisters choosing a master equally with brothers, and, finally, women holding custody of a castle and being the governess of a workhouse.

[3] There is a range of unresolved questions concerning identities and facts surrounding this case. One of the most perplexing is the identity of the defendant Ingram. While it is possible that it is a subsequent married name of Sarah Bly, she still continues to be termed Bly in Viner's 1793 discussion of the case as well as in reference works mentioning the case. It may have been a parish official who counted the votes or certified the election, but such information is not confirmed, or finally, someone acting in her behalf to establish the legal fiction on which the assumpsit is raised. How the case reached King's Bench is also unclear although, in a report of the case by Strange (who was Solicitor-General during the hearing) in 2 Strange. 1114, it appears it was on *nisi prius* rather than appeal.

[4] Discussions of women's legal and political status in the early modern period appear in Carole Pateman's *The Sexual Contract* (Stanford: Stanford University Press, 1988) and her recent essay entitled "The Rights of Man and Early Feminism," in *Frauen und Politik/Femmes et politiques*, Schweizerisches Jahrbuch für Politische Wissenschaft, no. 34 (1994), 19–31; Gordon Schochet's *Patriarchalism in Political Thought* (New York: Basic Books, 1975); Mary Lyndon Shanley on "Marriage Contract and Social Contract in Seventeenth-Century English Political Thought," *Western Political Quarterly* 32 (1979): 79–91; and Lois Schwoerer in "Women and the Glorious Revolution," *Albion* 17 (1986): 195–218. Among works on law are Susan Staves's *Married Women's Separate Property in England, 1660–1833* (Cambridge, Mass.: Harvard University Press, 1990); *Women, Crime and the Courts in Early Modern England*, eds. Jennifer Kermode and Garthine Walker (Chapel Hill: University of North Carolina Press, 1995); Amy L. Erickson's *Women and Property in Early-Modern England* (London: Routledge, 1993); Cynthia Herrup's *The*

tion of arguments offered on behalf of the plaintiff presented a broadly outlined synopsis of the issues at hand:

It was objected against the competency of the sex on these occasions, that they are under a legal incapacity of bearing public offices of trust; that they cannot either act personally, or make a deputy; that a woman is not bound even to take an oath of allegiance, nor can she vote for a member of Parliament.[5]

But those taking the side of the defendant Bly argued to the contrary that:

There was no judgment or experience necessary for performing this office; and as to their [women's] voting, there was no legal restraint, but they are not compellable; and the reason why they did not vote for members of Parliament was, because they were not contributory to the expences, the heir coming in the place of the ancestor, and not from any legal restraint.[6]

Following these summary introductory statements, a hodgepodge of legal and linguistic precedents was listed to support the one side, then the other. Chief Justice William Lee next posed the issues and precedents he considered crucial to the case's unfolding. He first noted the likelihood that the resolution of this case "may be a very extensive determination" if tied to women's voting as scot and lot voters. If primogeniture was key (as the defendant's side argued), with the cost of elections borne by local families, women could not inherit or bear costs, and therefore their property holding and rate paying would not qualify them for the vote. Yet such an argument would seem prima facie invalid since men voted without such restriction.

Lee posed the wider definition of access to the suffrage when he stated: "The question here is whether a woman is to be taken within the general words of 'all persons paying scot and lot'?" If so, local rate paying and parish assessments could qualify one to vote in parliamentary

---

Common Peace: Participation and the Criminal Law in Seventeenth-Century England (Cambridge and New York: Cambridge University Press, 1987); and W. R. Prest's "Law and Women's Rights in Early Modern England," *The Seventeenth Century* 5 (1991): 169–87. For the continent, see Sarah Hanley's "Engendering the State: Family Formation and State Building in Early Modern France," *French Historical Studies* 16 (1989) and Merry Wiesner's essay on women's defense of their public role in *Women in the Middle Ages and the Renaissance: Literary and Historical Perspectives*, ed. Mary Beth Rose (Syracuse, N.Y.: Syracuse University Press, 1986). Feminist scholars have also raised fundamental questions about the field of history through the lens of gender. While each of these works has provided guidance in rethinking the role of gender in early modern Britain, for this specific project, the most useful work remains Charlotte Carmichael Stopes's *British Freewomen* (London: S. Sonnenschein and Co., 1894), which continues to offer the greatest documentation of women's early citizenship and to suggest the political shifts of the seventeenth century as key to understanding women's lost political standing.

[5] *Olive v. Ingram*, 1230.   [6] Ibid.

elections. He then offered three separate precedents: Lady Packington's case where she "returned two members to Parliament to serve in her name," *Coates [Holt] v. Lisle* [14 James I], and, finally, *Catherine v. Surry*, in which "a feme sole, if she has a freehold, may vote for members of Parliament." He concluded from these precedents that "it seems as if there was no disability." Yet, he concluded, "the nature of the office to be executed may determine the question."[7]

I want to analyze *Olive v. Ingram* from three distinct but integrated perspectives: the facts, deliberations, and resolutions; the legal and linguistic precedents used by those on either side of the dispute; and, finally, the case's legal and historical significance for women's later political standing. In pursuing these analyses, one is drawn into a series of textual ambiguities and through a set of inferences rather than sureties. First, there is general and justified complaint about the quality of the case's account, as compiled by Thomas Leach in the *Modern Reports*, which listed precedents without dates or references, offered lists of cases without designating their connection to individual arguments, and failed to identify the principals involved.[8] Further, it is clear that many of the arguments, and the court's application of precedents, were based upon unspoken assumptions about gender relationships in early

---

[7] *Olive v. Ingram*, 1230. Mark Kishlansky in *Parliamentary Selection: Society and Political Choice in Early Modern England* (Cambridge and New York: Cambridge University Press, 1986) verifies the voting precedents of Lady Dorothy Packington and Elizabeth Copley (for a discussion of the Copley case see p. 337 of this chapter), 42–43; and J. K. Gruenfelder, *Influence in Early Stuart Elections, 1604–1640* (Columbus: Ohio State University Press, 1981) includes five women in his list of those whose influence was crucial to parliamentary elections during the early seventeenth century (Elizabeth Cavendish, countess of Devonshire; Susan Fielding, countess of Denbigh; Margaret Howard, countess of Nottinghamshire; Elizabeth Stanley, countess of Derby and Elizabeth Wriothesley, countess of Southampton, Appendix 7).

[8] While it is not totally clear who was either the reporter or compiler of the case which appeared in 7 *Modern Reports*, it was most likely Thomas Leach who compiled a series of volumes of *Modern Reports*, including proceedings of King's Bench which included the period of *Olive v. Ingram*. John William Wallace in *The Reporters Arranged and Characterized with Incidental Remarks* offers the following information: "Leach. K.B. (Crown Side.) 3 Geo. II–55 Geo. III. (1730–1815). (There are editions in 1789, 1792, 1800 ...; the best and most complete is in 2 vols. 1815)" (Edinburgh: Carswell and Co., 1882), 430. As reprinted in *English Reports*, it appears in "King's Bench Division XVI" in vol. 87, containing "Modern, 3 to 7" with no reporter or compiler identified; but it is not included in the list of "Anonymous, 7 Mod." in the relevant Table of Cases. A shorter account appears in 2 Strange, 1114; John Strange participated as Solicitor General during the case, as well as later writing this brief report. There are general concerns as to the quality of the *Modern Reports*, and concern over the *Modern Reports* version of the case was offered during deliberations in *Chorlton v. Lings* (1868) as follows: "There is a case of *Olive v. Ingram* in 7 Modern Reports, which, though that volume of reports is not of high authority, is supported by the judgment given in 2 Strange" (*Chorlton v. Lings, Law Reports, Court of Common Pleas*, vol. 4, London: William Clowes and Sons, 1876–80), 379.

modern Britain. Thus one is continually trying to understand the nature of a precedent, grapple with its relevance to an argument (especially when it often seems to support the opposition), and read between the lines as to why members of the court chose to bring up certain issues and not others. Also, citations include references to dictionaries and other guides to the law as much as to earlier cases, suggesting that the justices believed that the issues at hand were tied to questions of definition. Simply put, it is difficult to find out the facts, to discover the political and personal reasons influencing the principals in the case as well as the court personnel, and to ascertain how widely this case was known or discussed during its hearing and afterward. While such ambiguities are not unusual, this case offers special difficulties.[9]

---

[9] William Lee, in Lord Campbell's *Lives of the Chief Justices*, is described as not a leading jurist, but knowledgeable, and likely the best qualified for appointment to Chief Justice in 1737. His brother Sir George Lee served simultaneously as Dean of the Arches and Judge of the Prerogative Court of Canterbury. William was known as rather dull, but well versed in cases of special pleading. He was first supported by C. J. Raymond as a member of King's Bench because of this expertise where he was more "eminent . . . than any other man in the profession," and was appointed by Chancellor Hardwicke on June 15, 1730. He was then appointed Chief Justice in June, 1737. In assessing Lee, Campbell focuses strongly on *Olive v. Ingram* and states: "His fame may have increased from his having had the good word of the fair sex; he certainly stood up for the rights of woman more strenuously than any English judge before or since his time." And, of *Olive v. Ingram*, Campbell notes: "I do not find any other cases which came before him in King's Bench so fully reported" (*The Lives of the Chief Justices of England*, III [New York: Cockcroft and Co., 1878], 101–20). Even so, and while there are limited numbers of cases while Lee was Chief Justice, still *Olive v. Ingram* is not included in *Cases Argued and Adjuged in The Court of King's Bench . . . in the Reign of His late Majesty, King George the Second; during . . . Lord Chief Justice Harwicke [and] Some Determinations of the Late Lord Chief Justice Lee* (London: R. Pheney and S. Sweet, 1815). While my search has hardly been exhaustive, I have not discovered mention of the case in any source relating to court, Parliament, or London politics. It occurs too early for, and is not mentioned in, Horace Walpole's *Memoirs of King George II*, the first volume of which begins with 1751 (Horace Walpole, *Memoirs of King George II*, 3 vols., ed. John Brooke [New Haven, Conn.: Yale University Press, 1985]); nor was the case mentioned in Walpole's *Letters*, which do cover the period; however, he was still a young man (aged twenty-two) and spent 1739 traveling abroad in Reims and Paris (*The Letters of Horace Walpole, Fourth Earl of Orford*, vol. I: *1732–1743*, ed. Paget Toynbee, Oxford: Clarendon Press, 1903). There was no daily recording of discussions in the House of Commons, but it does not appear in *The Parliamentary History of England*, vol. x: *A.D. 1737–1739* (London: T. C. Hansard, 1812), nor does it appear in either E. R. Turner's *The Cabinet Council*, volume 1 which covers the years 1622–1784 (Baltimore, Md.: Johns Hopkins University Press, 1930) or the *House of Lords Sessional Papers*, ed. F. W. Torrington (Dobbs Ferry, N.Y.: Oceana Publications, 1978). While one could easily expect that such an obscure case would not gain wider attention, I did not find it mentioned for 1739 in either *The Gentleman's Magazine*, *The London Gazette*, or *The Historical Register*, and it is too early for the *Annual Register*. Individuals connected with the case did gain prominence: Dudley Ryder (the Attorney General) later became Chief Justice of the Court of King's Bench; Sir John Strange (Solicitor General and Reporter) remained royal counsel and represented the crown in treason cases following the uprising of 1745; Thomas Dennison (for the plaintiff) was made justice of King's Bench from 1741 to 1765, bypassing

Yet these difficulties in many ways make the case more complex and puzzling in an interesting way, and demonstrate its significance both during its hearing and later during debates over women's suffrage. In 1738/39 and later, those involved in defining women's political standing apparently could not (or chose not to) resist inserting *Olive v. Ingram* into a dispute much larger than who would hold a minor church office in a single London parish. It seems significant that Charles Viner in his *General Abridgement of Law and Equity* printed in 1793 gave the greatest attention to *Olive v. Ingram* among precedents concerning women's legal and political capacity. The case was used widely by suffragists (as in *Chorlton v. Lings* [1868]), who scoured the law for precedents of women's earlier enfranchisement. Also telling was the King's Bench decision in 1738/39 to hear the case and ultimately decide in the defendant's behalf.

In understanding the values and decisions of those involved, it helps, I believe, to place the case within a broader theoretical framework of a "false universal" as the organizing principle for gender values dominating the early modern period. Such a universal underlay women's exclusion from the state or civil society and any supposed masculine or feminine qualities attached to men and women or male and female roles. It helps us understand discussions of, first, categories of status such as citizenship, adulthood, independence, and, second, the qualities attached to them such as judgment, reason, maturity.[10]

This false universal led contemporaries, and later scholars, to use words such as people, person, citizen, England, etc. in ways that excluded women without explicitly saying so. This has made it difficult to penetrate the assumptions and realities reflective of such falsely universal usage whether in a legal report or a historical account. During *Olive v. Ingram*, members of the court seldom considered political and legal discourse as it related to gender inclusion or exclusion. Terms that

intermediate offices; Thomas Bootle (for the defendant) was dominant in the bar by the 1720s, lead counsel for the South Sea Company and later MP for Midhurst; also for the defendant were Abel Ketelby "an eminent Tory barrister . . . never distinguished by office" and William Wynne, a sergeant-at-law who defended Bishop Atterbury in 1723 and was "the trusted advisor of some of the leaders of the church" and continued to be involved in ecclesiastical cases. (Source for the above biographical information is David Lemmings, *Gentlemen and Barristers: The Inns of Court and the English Bar, 1680–1730* [Oxford: Clarendon Press; New York: Oxford University Press, 1989], 96, 116, 137–38, 173–76, 195.)

[10] I am developing this analysis in a monograph I am currently completing, *"All Men and Both Sexes": The False Universal in England, 1640–1832*, which outlines the economic, political, and social values that cut across class and occupation to define the independent, modern individual who was at the heart of the shift from subject to citizen associated with the English Civil War of the mid-seventeenth century.

could include women, such as "scot and lot voters," were rarely taken to do so, even though commentators agreed that women paid such taxes. The 1832 Reform Bill, notably termed "The Representation of the People Act," at the same time as explicitly excluding women through inserting the word "male" for the first time in a British constitutional document, preserved the voting rights of scot and lot voters. Rights attached to the "people" were framed to document women's lack of the parliamentary franchise.[11]

It is necessary, then, to be careful when utilizing vaguely inclusive language as an argument one way or the other about women's political rights or obligations. Sometimes inclusive nouns and pronouns included women, but much more often they were assumed or interpreted to exclude, in the particular, what they seemed to include in the abstract. While political realities, the operations of the British legal system, and women's specific place within the household all contributed to their being seen as non-political beings, one should not overlook the power of falsely universal language in excusing and obscuring women's exclusion from the political realm. Most scholars have simply ignored this reality, moving easily from instances where the word "people" referred only to men to instances (such as population statistics) where the word clearly included members of both sexes. Peter Laslett in *The World We Have Lost* offers one of the few explicit acknowledgments of women's omission from the nation when he writes, "almost no woman ever belonged to England as an individual except it be a queen regnant." It is thus this "falsely universal" inclusion, rather than stated exclusion, or even masculine and feminine qualities, that lay at the heart of women not being viewed as legally competent, as citizens, or as adults who functioned as independent individuals.[12]

---

[11] In the discussion of qualifications for the borough franchise, The Representation of the People Act, 1832 includes all persons who are freeholders of a residence worth at least ten pounds, and "have been rated in respect of such Premises to all Rates for the Relief of the Poor in such Parish ... not subject to any legal Incapacity." This clearly included female householders and was comparable to the scot and lot enfranchisement of *Olive v. Ingram*, yet the act specifies that these provisions apply only to "every Male Person of full Age" (H. J. Hanham, ed., *The 19th Century Constitution: Comments & Commentary*, Cambridge: Cambridge University Press, 1969, 262–68). Anna Clark discusses the broader implications of this exclusion following 1832 in her essay, "Gender, Class and the Nation: Franchise Reform in England, 1832–1928," *Re-reading the Constitution: New Narratives in the Political History of England's Long Nineteenth Century*, ed. James Vernon (Cambridge: Cambridge University Press, 1996), 239–53.

[12] Peter Laslett, *The World We Have Lost* (New York: Charles Scribner's Sons, 1965), 20. It is difficult to select particular references to the false universal since it was so endemic to early modern writings, but perhaps its two most wide-ranging literary and intellectual inscriptions were "the seven ages of man" which appeared widely as a literary trope and "the great chain of being" which encompassed the spectrum of living

In *Olive v. Ingram*, the justices of the court of King's Bench and the lawyers appearing before them, time and again, reflected their attachment to such values by using as precedents for women's exclusion cases that never mentioned such exclusion. Thus cases involving "householder," "rate payer," etc., terms that could easily refer to women, were interpreted to deny women's right to vote. For example, in a dispute between Justices Page and Probyn over whether women could vote for a lesser office such as sexton or the greater political office of member of Parliament, Probyn notes that "the best rule seems to be, that they who pay have a right to nominate whom they will pay to" and that this held for sexton and MP as well. Yet, the general principle stood for the church office but not for the political one because the latter "choice requires an improved understanding, which women are not supposed to have." Page, on the other hand, stated categorically, "I see no disability in a woman from voting for a Parliament-man." Thus without using clear legal or statutory precedent, members of the court fought not over whether women were rate payers, or as such could vote, but whether their supposed lack of "an improved understanding" undercut precedent, even given their inclusion within the relevant category of voters. Also, acts that were taken to verify men's political standing, such as the appointment of deputies to a particular office, did not, they determined, confer comparable standing on women. It is only through assessing the court's use of precedents within a normative linguistic and cultural system that universalized male experience that we can fully understand how and why they utilized particular arguments to support their case.

Women's earlier political roles were denied or supported according to different standards and sorts of evidence. On the one hand, those who denied any female role most often used evidence that employed universal, seemingly non-gendered, language and extrapolated from general principles to women's standing. Or they used bald and unsupported statements by earlier legal commentators (especially Coke) who argued that women could not vote or hold a particular office. On the

beings in the universe and was captured definitively in Arthur Lovejoy's classic, *The Great Chain of Being* (Cambridge, Mass.: Harvard University Press, 1936). The "seven ages of man" appeared most prominently in Shakespeare's *As You Like It* (Act II, sc. vii) where he began "All the world's a stage,/And all the men and women merely players:/They have their exits and their entrances;/And one man in his time plays many parts,/His acts being seven ages." Those ages are infant, boyhood, lover, soldier, justice, pantaloon, and old man. While both men and women are players, only men progress through life's stages. Lovejoy's *Great Chain* offers manifold examples of great chain imagery from the sixteenth through the eighteenth centuries, and the examples for the human link in the chain are drawn from male experience and characteristics and are consistently called "man." Women do not occupy the link, nor do they stand for the species.

other side, those who supported women holding office used as evidence individual cases that risked being interpreted as isolated incidents. They were less apt to offer broad-based principles. Seldom concerned with the gendered meanings of "rate payer," "people," "person," "house-holder," etc., supporters of women's office holding and enfranchisement relied on individual precedents or claimed women's specific suitability for the post of sexton. Thus each side adduced differing types of legal, historical, and linguistic precedents. Those supporting women never took on, in a direct fashion, the ways in which language and the historical record, and their interpretation by legal commentators, had obscured women's earlier political standing.

During the initial hearing of *Olive v. Ingram* in the Hilary term of January 1738/39 the Chief Justice, Sir William Lee, seemed receptive to women's past standing as parliamentary electors and to the case's broad implications for women's political identity during the eighteenth century. However, something clearly transpired between January and the following May that clouded the court's position because the Chief Justice now resisted any implications that the case might generate wide-ranging precedents. His opening remarks of May, 1739 began: "I thought this might have been a case of great consequence; but as it depends merely on its own circumstances, it cannot be drawn into precedent." The Chief Justice next moved to undercut arguments supporting women's interrelated capacities to hold office, appoint others to an office, utilize a deputy for a post, or vote for public offices. His arguments seem to revolve around a dual axis: first, a woman was incapable of carrying out a particular function, and, second, if she carried it out, it did not demonstrate her basic rights of citizenship.[13]

When Sir John Strange, Solicitor General, in May of 1739 presented the government's case opposing women's voting, he argued that usage was the "only evidence of right" and thus women's failure to vote in parliamentary elections was "evidence of a waiver of their right, if ever they had any." He then introduced a familiar phrase in determining women's legal standing: "that in all acts which concern the public, women are put in the same class with infants." He also added a practical concern, namely that "elections being already too popular, this would open a door to greater confusion."[14]

Thomas Bootle, who represented the defendant, argued, to the contrary, that women "had in general power and capacity to vote" and thus some particular disability must be demonstrated to deprive them of the parliamentary franchise. He also stated, in terms that were to

[13] *Olive v. Ingram*, 1231.   [14] Ibid., 1230.

resonate shortly in the American colonies, "that those who contributed to maintain the elected should be electors." Finally, he disputed the Solicitor General's arguments concerning women's being "non user[s]" (presumably of the parliamentary franchise) and stated that more probing needed to be done along the lines of "the difference between being exempted and being incapacitated."[15]

In analyzing the approximately 110 precedents during the court's three sessions on *Olive v. Ingram*, one is struck by the fuzziness of their significance and their dubious applicability to one side or the other. Beginning in May, 1739 Sir William Lee clearly moved to limit the possibility of women's political standing and to downplay the importance of the office of sexton and of the case. However, a number of the precedents he used could have easily supported the defendant's side. For instance, the Chief Justice referred to the custom of householders taking turns serving as constable or tithingmen and women's exclusion from this custom as evidence against their having the same standing and obligations as male householders. The precedent, Prouse's Case (1635), in which an attorney tried to excuse himself from serving as a tithingman in a district where he owned seven houses, first held that it was the custom for all householders to serve as either constable or tithingman when selected, and that although attorneys generally could seek exemptions, in this instance the custom overrode the privilege of exemption. Yet, the court in 1635 ultimately ruled in behalf of the attorney because it held "it cannot be a good custom; for then a woman being an inhabitant in one of the said houses, it may come to her in course to be constable, which the law will not permit," and thus the custom could not be applied to an attorney whose presence was required elsewhere. On the other hand, the case could serve just as easily to demonstrate that women householders were on the same standing as attorneys who purchased homes and that their situation could be used as a precedent for an exemption to an attorney trying to avoid service. If the women lacked the standing of householders, no exception would be necessary based on their sex.[16]

In the same set of arguments, Chief Justice Lee noted that in a later, related case women were required to and did hire substitutes to replace them as constables. Yet, he contended, this still did not demonstrate that women had political standing. "And this opinion does not thwart the case in Croke [Prouse's case]; for though she may hire one, she is still incapable." That such arguments as hiring a deputy illustrated

---

[15] Ibid., 1231.
[16] *Olive v. Ingram*, 1231; "Prouse's Case," Croke. Car. 390. *English Reports*, vol. 79, 940.

political standing for a man but not for a woman exemplifies the shifting grounds of those denying women's prior voting and office holding. At points, women were excluded because they could not hold such a post or vote in such an instance; at other points, even when attaining the qualifying status, they were denied simply for being women.[17]

Toward the end of the hearing, the Chief Justice elaborated on the principle he believed should direct the court's decision, saying "the nature of the office is the true consideration with respect to the person who is to execute it." This principle led Lee to link the post of sexton to a range of posts that were considered to be private trusts so that sexton "cannot be considered on a higher foot than governor of a house of correction or gaol-keeper." Even so, Campbell's *History of the Chief Justices* offers evidence that Lee linked the holding of this office to greater, and clearly political, posts. He quotes Lee in discussing women's office holding in *Olive v. Ingram*, "I am clearly of opinion that a woman may be sexton of a parish. Women have held much higher offices, and, indeed, almost all the offices of the kingdom; as Queen, Marshal, Great Chamberlain, Great Constable, Champion of England, Commissioner of Sewers, Keeper of a Prison, and Returning Officer for members of parliament."[18] And Lee considered it illogical for women to be able to hold the office but not vote for it. As to women's voting for sexton, since it was a private office "women when sole may vote." But voting for this private post held little relevance to women's political standing and led him to conclude: "It would be a very different consideration in voting for public officers, which concern the Government."[19] This was a clear move from his earlier discussions of precedents for individual women having voted for parliament.

While we might consider it a more controversial step to support women's office holding rather than their voting, Lee did not seem to think so, and Strange, in his report of *Olive v. Ingram*, claimed to

---

[17] For a discussion of the appointment of a deputy as constituting political standing see Sir Edward Coke, *Institutes of the Laws of England*, Part I, 233A–234B (Philadelphia: Johnson and Warner, 1812). This commentary refers to Littleton's *Tenures*, Book II, chap. 5, sec. 378–79. The court's decision here supported a general pattern of utilizing the same act (in this case appointing a deputy) to document both men's standing and women's non-standing.

[18] Lord Campbell, *Lives of the Chief Justices*, III, 108.

[19] *Olive v. Ingram*, 1231–32. This case had much broader implications than suggested here. In the 1868 decision in *Chorlton v. Lings* (*Law Reports*, vol. 4, Court of Common Pleas, Michaelmas term 1868 to Trinity term, 1869, 32 Victoria, reported by John Scott and Henry Bompas, ed. J. R. Bulwer [London: Printed for the Council of Law Reporting by William Close and Sons, 1869], 374–97), and in the *Dictionary of National Biography* (XI, 825), entry for Chief Justice William Lee, it is noted as *the* precedent for women gaining the local franchise, first on poor law commissions and school boards and later city and county councils, in the last decades of the nineteenth century.

support the former, but not the latter. After stating that the two issues before the court were whether women could hold the office of sexton and whether they were able to vote for it, he explains his position as Solicitor General as follows: "As to the first, the Court seemed to have no difficulty about it, nor did I think proper to argue it, there having been many cases where offices of greater consequence have been held by women, and there being many women sextons now in London."[20]

In support of his judgment, he includes a number of the same precedents cited by Chief Justice Lee, including Lady Packington as the returning officer for a parliamentary election. But as to women's voting, he states:

As to the second point, [Coke] 4 Inst. 5 was cited to shew women could not vote for members of Parliament or coroners, and yet they have freeholds and contribute to all publick charges, and even to the wages of knights of the shire ... And though they vote in the monied companies, yet that is by virtue of the Acts which give the right to all persons possessed of so much stock.

He acknowledges that the court also accepted women's voting, but never indicates agreement with the decision, while pointing to the private nature of the post and its separation from "the care and inspection of the morals of the parishioners." He states the basis for the decision as follows: "there was no reason to exclude women, who paid rates, from the privilege of voting," and there was no "usage of excluding them stated."[21] While the issue of usage could be seen as pivotal, it still appears another example of where a particular act – in this instance rate paying – did not qualify for parliamentary suffrage, but did so for this parish post.

Supporters of women's ability to serve as sextons played down its sacred nature, its requiring any skill, and its political significance, while those in opposition noted the greater importance of the post and its unsuitability for the sex. Marsh, counsel for the plaintiff, noted that women should not hold the office not only because it was sacred, but also because "it would be servile work for a woman to dig a grave as sextons do." Women's defenders, on the other hand, contended that "there is no reason to say that women are not qualified to be sextons, since they are qualified to pay scot and lot, and all poor rates, and to maintain a sexton." In addition, "this office is so designed, that a sexton may be of either sex, and the duty of the place being to look after the

---

[20] *Olive v. Ingram*, 2 Strange, 1068.

[21] Ibid. It should be noted, as well, that during the actual hearing of *Olive v. Ingram*, Strange spoke as strongly against the office holding as he did the voting of female parishioners.

parson's surplices and vestments, and to keep the church clean, it will be better performed by a woman."[22]

Finally, in evaluating the citations offered as precedent on either side, one must remember that there was no explicit statute or precedent to deny women's parliamentary franchise or ability to hold or nominate others to office. There are two types of precedents employed: first, cases where women's assumed political standing underscores their ability to vote for or hold public office and those that seem to deny such possibilities; and, second, examples where a legal commentator baldly states his opinion against women's public standing. In assessing such precedents, one is forced, for the most part, to read between the lines, relate facts and analyses which seem to have little bearing on the question, or choose either to accept or reject legal opinions on women's legal and political standing.

Sir Edward Coke is cited for his commentary on Magna Charta passages concerning quarantine for widows. The relevance of such comments seems questionable since Sarah Bly did not claim the post by widow's succession.[23] As noted above, the statement by Coke most often cited in the case was from 4 *Institutes* 5, where he includes women in a list of those who came under parliamentary authority without having a role in its election, yet Coke offers no citations or precedents for women's exclusion: "in many cases multitudes are bound by acts of Parliament which are not parties to the elections of knights, citizens, and burgesses, as all they that have no freehold, or have freehold in ancient demesne, and all women having freehold, or no freehold, and men within the age of one and twenty years."[24]

One is thus left with a series of pronouncements by legal commentators (in particular Sir Edward Coke) either not securely grounded in legal precedent or statute, or of questionable application to the situation of *Olive v. Ingram*, on the one side, and numerous, but not conclusive, examples of women's political actions on the other. It is thus difficult to understand the strongly definitive judgments made by contemporaries, and accepted by later historians, that women lacked political standing and obligations in seventeenth- and eighteenth-century England. The

---

[22] *Olive v. Ingram*, 1231–32.

[23] Sir Edward Coke, *The Second Part of the Institutes of the Laws of England*, London: Printed for E. and R. Brooke, 1797, Chapter 7, 16–17.

[24] Sir Edward Coke, *The Fourth Part of the Institutes of the Laws of England* (London: E. and R. Brooke, 1797), 5. Coke notes that before two statutes, 9 Edward 2, statute 2 and 14 Edward 3, statute 1.c.7, freeholders could elect a sheriff at will; he refers only to the standing of freeholders in these statutes, not to any references of women's exclusion, but draws the wider inference in his commentary. Cited on pages 1230, 1232, and 1235, *Olive v. Ingram*, 7 *Modern Reports*.

individual most skeptical of such assertions, and the one who collected more evidence on the topic than anyone before or since, was the suffragist and literary and legal historian, C. C. Stopes. In her *British Freewomen* of 1894 she searched broadly among documents in British legal history to verify women's political actions in medieval and early modern England. She questioned the nature of the precedents cited, the ignoring of counter-precedents, and the role of Sir Edward Coke in denying women's earlier citizenship. According to Stopes, Coke's views on women's legal standing was tied to his origins: "He was an only son with seven sisters which position probably made him overvalue his own sex," she pointed out. This may have been reflected in his abusing his power as father to force an unsavory match on his daughter. As for Coke's personal role in determination of women's citizenship, Stopes noted that he served on a parliamentary committee with William Hakewill and John Glanville which determined the right of Elizabeth Copley (an Elizabethan Catholic) to return members for Gatton as the inhabitant and to transfer such rights to her heirs. This conclusion was brought before Parliament in 1620 and continued in 1628. Also, Coke was Chief Justice when the decisions of *Holt v. Lyle [Lisle]* and *Catherine v. Surr[e]y* allowing women's parliamentary franchise occurred. Such decisions conflicted with Coke's views in 4 *Institutes* 5, where he stated categorically that women were unable to vote. While Stopes had difficulty with a range of legal commentaries and decisions from the seventeenth through the nineteenth centuries which denied women's early citizenship without sure evidence, she was especially angry with Coke, who she believed offered unsupported, arbitrary (and ultimately dangerous) opinions on the topic.[25]

[25] Stopes, *British Freewomen*, 71–76, 99–107. Although her description of Elizabeth Copley's case is somewhat unclear, she contends that the disputed political standing of the Copley family based on their Catholicism was also intertwined with Elizabeth's standing as a woman. Stopes states, as of 1628: "Mr. William Copley was not inclined tamely to resign the ancient privilege of his family of sending up Burgesses for their own borough; again, in spite of the decision of 1620, and through the adverse decision in his case parliament affirmed, and Sir Edward Coke with it, the right of a woman to vote" (76). There is also discussion of the case in the *Commons Debates*, 1628, II, 37, 108. See also Kishlansky, *Parliamentary Selection*, 42–43, for a discussion of the Copley case. In addition, in volume II of the *Institutes*, where Coke is discussing a lord's inability to make an heir a ward "before that he hath taken of him homage," he includes a note that the relevant statute, 35 H 6.52, means only male heirs though the language, simply "*heres*," shows no such indication, and a modern Latin dictionary notes the meaning to include "an heir, heiress" (*Institutes*, II, chap. 3, 10–11 and Cassell's *New Latin Dictionary*, New York: Funk and Wagnalls, 1968, 274). But Coke seemingly contradicts himself for he previously stated in I *Institute* 65, "*Glanvill* saith, women shall not do homage; but Littleton saith that a woman shall doe homage, but she shall not say, *I become your woman, but I do to you homage*, and so is *Glanvill* to be understood, that she shall not doe complete homage" (Edward Coke, *The First Part of the Institutes*

The remainder of *British Freewomen* provides innumerable examples of women nominating MPs and a range of lesser officials, of men being able to serve in Parliament on the right of their wife's title, of women being listed on borough registers returned for elections, of their holding local courts, and of their holding a range of offices. Women, Stopes claimed, clearly could vote, and had voted and held public office at least till the mid-seventeenth century. At that time began a process whereby lawyers, political writers, and politicians denied either the reality or relevance of such past examples. She gave considerable attention to both *Olive v. Ingram* and *Chorlton v. Lings* as two eighteenth- and nineteenth-century cases which exemplified a misreading and misapplication of the legal and historical record. Up to today, no one has successfully denied the legitimacy of her case for women's early office holding and voting, nor her concern that that record was ignored or distorted by later legal decisions and political practice.[26]

When the legal and political significance of *Olive v. Ingram* is pursued into the suffrage debates of the nineteenth century, questions surrounding linguistic and legal precedent continue. As noted earlier, the Representation of the People Act of 1832 included the first explicit exclusion of women through the insertion of the word "male" before the noun "voters." Yet, by 1868, when the appeal of women voters in *Chorlton v. Lings* was heard concerning the registration of over 5,300 women in Manchester following the Second Reform Bill in 1867, the debates over women's past enfranchisement were no closer to resolution. Following the First Reform Bill, the Court of Common Pleas denied that women were persons and thereby suffragists could not appeal being omitted from registration rolls based on a law of 6 Victoria, c. 18. Also relevant to the debate over women's suffrage, and the subsequent debates of *Chorlton v. Lings*, was Lord Brougham's bill of 1851 which stated that when a masculine pronoun or the word "man" was used it was assumed to mean woman as well, unless women were expressly excluded. Therefore, the Second Reform Bill, which included only "men" and not "male persons," did not exclude women. So the quandary continued. Thus the court, in *Chorlton v. Lings*, had to determine which of these definitional standards held.[27]

---

of the Laws of England; or, A Commentary upon Littleton, 1 (London: J. and W. T. Clarke et al., 1832), L.2.C.I. Sect. 86.65.b, [n.p.].

[26] Stopes's work is just under 200 pages and documents women's early political standing. Most relevant for this chapter are her sections on the rights of noblewomen, county women and freewomen, where she offers examples of their carrying out the same functions as their male counterparts politically as well as being members of guilds, etc.

[27] *Chorlton v. Lings*, 374–97. This was one of the earliest cases where suffragists attempted to gain the vote for women through legal precedent rather than new legislation.

While attorneys supporting women's suffrage, including Richard Pankhurst, husband of the famous suffragette, presented similar (and often the same) precedents as offered for women's voting in *Olive v. Ingram* 130 years earlier, members of the court raised the same doubts about women's past political standing. The issues in *Chorlton v. Lings* were whether women were included in the term "man" in the Representation of the People Act, 1867, and, if they were, whether they could be legitimately excluded by the act's stated qualifications for voting, namely, every man who "is of full age, and not subject to any legal incapacity." In other words, even if women were included in the cumulative noun "man," were they still under a legal incapacity that excluded them?

The prospective female voter in the case, Mary Abbott, who stood for all women attempting to register, met the qualifications for voting and had a similar standing to Sarah Bly and her eighteenth-century female supporters. The facts of the case were thus: "It was admitted that Abbott was a woman, of the age of twenty-one years, and unmarried, and that she had for twelve months previously to the last day of July 1868, occupied the dwelling house stated in the claim within the township, and had in all respects complied with the requirements of the Registration Acts."[28]

The debates in 1868 centered around issues quite similar to those in *Olive v. Ingram*. Those for the appellant (Abbott) argued that although women had not voted for Parliament for a long time, "this disuse will not have destroyed the right, if it really existed," and they contended, as had their earlier counterparts, that the "freedom of England" consists "in the right of representation being joined to the liability of taxation." Here, in contrast to *Olive v. Ingram*, both sides debated openly the meaning of the word "person" and "man" and what significance their usage might hold for women's voting. In discussing the 1832 Act, those supporting women's suffrage noted that in that portion of the act "referring to the old rights, the general word 'person' is used throughout; but the expanded franchise of 1832 is conferred only on every 'male person'" who was qualified. Yet in 1867 the Parliament chose not to employ the words "male persons," thus causing that act to fall within the parameters of Lord Brougham's 1851 statute that included

---

[28] *Chorlton v. Lings*, 374–98. The case is listed under the broad title, "Registration Cases," and is only one example of those efforts on the part of suffrage lawyers to argue women did not have to seek a separate suffrage because they had possessed the parliamentary franchise in the past. The Court of Common Pleas, in grappling with both the reality and significance of individual examples of women voting, nominating MPs, or holding offices, incorporated both legal and linguistic evidence.

women in statutes where they were not explicitly excluded. Suffragists thus contended: "The legislature, however, have used the word 'man,' which, by the express provision of Lord Brougham's Act, includes women. The Act, therefore, in terms confers the franchise upon women who possess the new qualifications, unless they are excluded by the words 'under any legal incapacity.'"[29]

Those opposing women's voting, which ultimately included the Court of Common Pleas which rejected the women's appeal to be reinstated on the registration rolls, denied women's earlier political standing. They, more often than in the deliberations during *Olive v. Ingram*, denied any relevance of women's past enfranchisement or political standing. The court in 1868 stated that usage was the most important consideration, and that examples of women's exercising political rights were too distant in time to be applied to present circumstances. In establishing the relevant law to be applied in this instance, Chief Justice William Bovill stated:

In considering what was the common law, the greatest weight is due to the evidence of [the] modern user ... when the course of conduct has been uniform as far back as living memory goes, the Court will not set it aside for anything less than the strictest demonstration. It is admitted that for three centuries past women have not voted, and this raises the strongest inference that they have had not right to do so by law.[30]

Women's "acquies[cence]" in disenfranchisement "raises a strong presumption of what the law is" and throws the burden of proof on those who claim such rights ever existed. The greatest attention, however, was given to the links between the first and second reform bills, and provisions in the second bill that stated that any pre-existing enfranchisement stands under the 1867 Act. Thus, the 1832 provisions which included "male persons" took precedence over Lord Brougham's later attempt to include women in generic terms that utilized male constructions. While those supporting women's suffrage noted that a number of criminal statutes used the word "man" when both sexes were liable to prosecution, the court stated that one must take into consideration the context. "There is no doubt that, in many statutes, 'men' may be properly held to include women, [so] we must look at the subject-matter as well as to the general scope and language of the provisions of the later Act in order to ascertain the meaning [intention] of the legislature."[31]

Justice James S. Willes concurred with the Chief Justice's views and returned to works by John Selden and others documenting women's status under the ancient constitution. First, after agreeing with Chief

[29] Ibid., 378–79.   [30] Ibid., 380.   [31] Ibid., 386.

Justice Bovill that the common law was irrelevant when long-term usage interceded, he gave considerable attention to disproving any common law evidence for women's suffrage. He argued that earlier actions were only through deputies and, in the case of women religious attending public councils, "the abbesses who signed, if present at the Gemot, were so for the purpose of watching matters affecting the interests of their convents ... without forming part of the regular body." As so often happened in such discussions, in this instance a principle, such as the irrelevance of earlier precedents, was established and used against those contending for women's citizenship, but was allowed to those denying its reality.[32]

Finally, in assessing the uses made in *Chorlton v. Lings* of the debates of *Olive v. Ingram*, one should note that both justices Willes and Byles went into detail about the use and meaning of the words "person" and "man" in past and current case law and statute. The report of *Chorlton v. Lings* makes it clear that the 1739 decision was thought to offer the strongest support for women's earlier political identity, but that even there such citizenship was ultimately rejected. That conclusion, mentioned a number of times, was summarized by Justice Willes: "in the course of the discussion of Olive v. Ingram, Lee, C[hief].J[ustice]., appears to have at last satisfied himself that women could not vote for members of parliament."[33] As for definitional issues, the justices mostly avoided legislation that employed the term "person" and contended that "man," as used in the Second Reform Bill, reflected common understanding of the word. Justice Byles spoke about instances in which individuals might assume a generic understanding of "man", but said that it was not in this law.

No doubt, the word "man," in a scientific treatise on zoology or fossil organic remains, would include men, women, and children, as constituting the highest order of vertebrate animals. It is also used in an abstract and general sense in philosophical or religious disquisitions. But, in almost every other connection, the word "man" is used in contradistinction to "woman."

Certainly, he claimed, this restricted meaning was its ordinary and popular usage. And the use of the latter followed "a well-known rule in the construction of statutes."[34]

By 1868 the court had become more rigid, probably because of the efforts of women suffragists to push it in the direction of granting

---

[32] Ibid., 390. While J. G. A. Pocock and others have written extensively about the use of the ancient constitution to bolster men's political rights during the seventeenth century, except for Stopes, little attention has been paid to the role of gender in analyzing ancient political and legal precedents.

[33] Ibid., 391.   [34] Ibid., 392.

women's parliamentary or local suffrage. All members of the Court of Common Pleas rejected women's right to vote for members of Parliament. But for the purpose of this chapter, the most relevant aspect of the case was the court's focus on language and its use of false universals. The words "persons" or "person," even if terms designating earlier political rights, either did not include women or had no relevance to women's suffrage according to the reform bills of 1832 or 1867. While "man" might sometimes include "woman" in a generic sense, it did not in these instances. And Lord Brougham's law, which stated women were to be included where not explicitly excluded, did not apply, because it was accepted that according to usage women were excluded from the parliamentary franchise.

Thus, the failure to deal directly with falsely universal terms in *Olive v. Ingram* continued, and was exacerbated, in the 1868 case which denied women's right to elect members to Parliament through borough elections. Nineteenth-century suffragists were forced to make sex-based arguments and not link women's rights to vote to long-term arguments for liberty or democracy, since courts either rejected or ignored legal language which presumably included women, categories such as householder, scot and lot voter, person, etc. Certainly, the reality of a pre-seventeenth-century "freewoman" who held a status much closer to her male counterparts than has been assumed by historians requires much more investigation. However, it seems clear that much of the evidence used to deny her existence has been incomplete and contradictory, if not simply fallacious.

This chapter seeks a reassessment of evidence supporting women's past political standing, as well as that denying its likelihood. As a part of such efforts, I also hope scholars will take into consideration how deliberations in cases such as *Olive v. Ingram* and *Chorlton v. Lings* were tied to assumptions about false universals, usually to demonstrate how they omitted women, and to shore up the belief that only men constituted the independent, adult, political community that governed England. Such debates may guide us today, in understanding why, as women overcome the economic, educational, and sexual restrictions of the past, we continue to lack significant political power and do not represent the nation or the community, either symbolically or in reality.

Acknowledgments

I would like to thank Anna Suranyi, my research assistant, and to acknowledge most helpful discussions with Professors Charles Gray and Barbara Todd.

16 "To be some body": married women and *The Hardships of the English Laws*

Barbara J. Todd

In 1735 an anonymous woman published a small volume entitled *The Hardships of the English Laws in Relation to Wives . . . in an Humble address to the Legislature.*[1] Although it has received little attention from scholars,[2] its publication drew sufficient notice at the time to be excerpted as a leading essay in May and June in the *Gentleman's Magazine.*[3] In a mere seventy pages the work addresses the current feminist issues of education, property, maternity, and dependency using arguments based on moral philosophy, political and constitutional theory, scripture and theology. It manages to convey both outraged protest and rational acceptance of the social order, emphasizing the contradictory tension between the human moral responsibility of women and their subordination as wives. The author's interpretational framework might be called "Christian feminist." Women's subordination is the just outcome of Eve's first disobedience; but women have souls, they have the right to control their talents, their fortunes, their children, and most importantly their property in their own bodies and minds. The laws of marriage and

---

[1] Published simultaneously in London and Dublin, but never reprinted. I see no reason to doubt the author's self-identification as a married woman whose husband, unusually, has given her "leave to be some body." The tone and purpose of the work is completely different from treatises on the law by men for women (such as the *Lawes Resolutions of Womens Rights* [London, 1632], *A Treatise of Feme Coverts* [London, 1732], *The Laws Respecting Women* [London, 1777]) and also from works in which a male author has adopted a female persona. Its earnest passion argues for female authorship, while its occasionally haphazard structure (contrasting with the organizational patterns male authors interested in legal issues adopt) suggests self-education in the law. The author's diction and style of argument are not unlike that of "Sophia" in *Woman Not Inferior to Man* (1739), but the Christian framework of analysis central to *Hardships* is pointedly absent from the latter essay. The author of the *Hardships* does not claim a public role for women, focusing instead on remedying obstacles to private moral equality.

[2] Excerpts have been reprinted in Vivien Jones, *Women in the Eighteenth Century* (London: Routledge, 1990), 217–25; Alice Browne (*The Eighteenth-Century Feminist Mind* [Brighton: Harvester, 1987], 131–32) summarizes part of its argument, and it is briefly noted in Margaret Hunt, "Wife Beating, Domesticity and Women's Independence in Eighteenth-Century London," *Gender and History* 4 (1992): 15.

[3] Vol. 5, 241–42, 284.

343

of God may impose subordination, but the subordinate wife retains her full humanity and moral responsibility.

The author articulates no specific program of reform. That will only come from men's willingness to modify the "despotic" powers that the law gives them. Although her anger at the most extreme evidences of husbands' power equals some of the strongest eighteenth-century feminist statements, her Christian analysis is outside the mainstream of the later secular feminist canon. Nonetheless, this author identified repressive aspects of marital law in more detail than any other contemporary feminist writer. Her work provides moving insight into how one woman struggled to inform herself about the implications of her status, and then sought to explain how such a manifestly inequitable state of affairs could have arisen.

This author, of course, was not alone in her project of rethinking the implications of marriage for women. Her work is part of a continuing flow of feminist analysis that bridges the century between Astell and Wollstonecraft. Less well known is the fact that in these same years English jurists were also struggling with the fundamental problem this author raised – the contradictory presence of the independent female human being in the unitary legal fiction of the matrimonial couple. In this chapter I will summarize this female author's argument that the woman's soul, mind, and talent was not absorbed in marriage. Then I will review how the courts of common law and equity addressed the independent contractual capacity of the economically separate wife on issues of property, and also sought a solution to the problems raised by the separate standing of the wife in poor-law settlement. But although eighteenth-century courts moved hesitantly toward recognizing the separate legal persona of the wife, in the nineteenth century this trend was reversed, resulting finally in an even fuller subordination of the wife to the legal identity of the husband.

The Hardships of the English Laws

The argument of the *Hardships* can be divided into three parts. The first brief section asserts the right of the author to publish. Her claim to voice is based, in a long tradition, on the right of the subject to petition (although no specific legislation is proposed nor specific redress from the crown sought). The petition is justified by the vulnerable situation of married women, linked with the claims of maternity: no one is more notoriously without redress than women "when we put ourselves in a condition of adding to his majesty's subjects by becoming wives" (2).

The second section articulates what appears to be the immediate impetus to writing: a series of recent cases which seemed to document how marriage was for women "more disadvantageous than slavery."[4] Although this theme was common in contemporary feminist writing, this author makes no reference to other feminist works. She was inspired instead by a case involving the will of a widow that had been invalidated by her subsequent marriage, the court having ruled that her situation was different from the case of an enslaved man whose previous will revived upon his subsequent freedom.[5] Later passages remind the reader that slavery is not compatible with the condition of a "free-born English subject." The author briefly extends to marriage the implications for the social hierarchy of the revolutions of 1649 and 1689. She defends married women's liberty in terms of the premise that liberty of the subject is always in jeopardy so long as any potential exists that it can be taken away: "that nation is in a state of slavery where any man had it in his power to make them so."[6] Marriage should be, like the English constitution, a balance of authority and subjection. Husbands should learn from the monarch, for whom restraint of prerogative is no diminution of honor.

Other cases are then used to demonstrate that a power "more afflictive . . . than life and death" resides in English husbands. Several address the familiar theme of husbands' control of their wives' financial affairs (in one egregious example "about five years ago" a modest gentlewoman married a tradesman who spent her fortune and then enlisted as a soldier, but denied her permission to become a servant unless her wages were paid to him). Further, "wives may be made prisoners for life at the Discretion of their domestick Governors" without protection of habeas corpus. The case that most outraged the author involved one Corbett Vezey, tried at the Old Bailey in 1732.[7] He had imprisoned his wife in a garret without heat or clothing, denied her decent food and horse-whipped her until she threw herself out of the window. Because a crust of bread was found in the room he was acquitted of murder.

The author also considers how the law gives greater parental rights to

---

[4] *Hardships*, 2. Space and time has not permitted a full search for the sources from which she learned of these cases. Although it is not cited specifically, the tone of the anonymous *Treatise of Feme Coverts* (1732) and particularly the reprinting there of Justice Robert Hyde's opinion in *Manby v. Scott* (see below) may have aroused this author to respond.

[5] *Hardships*, 5–6. R. Burn, *Ecclesiastical Law* (first ed., 1763) s.v. Wills, also cites the case without attribution.

[6] Ibid., 46, quoting an unnamed "late MP."

[7] Ibid., 4–5, 8–10. The author acknowledges (11) that she has learned of this case from the public prints. It was reported in detail in the *Old Bailey Sessions Papers* from which it was later reprinted in the *Select Trials at the Sessions-House in the Old-Bailey*, III (London, 1742), 303–17 and briefly noted in the *Gentleman's Magazine* 2 (1732): 584.

the father. She acknowledges that God's law may justify that so long as the husband is alive, but protests vigorously against a father's capacity to choose another guardian and deprive a mother of access to her children after he dies. The question of guardianship leads to a brief discussion of women's education in which the author adopts the familiar feminist premise that women's poor education, which may disqualify them as parents, is not their fault. Less predictably, she examines the mutual right of couples to each other's sexual persons, citing the case of *Chamberlin v. Hewson*.[8] Mrs. Hewson was awarded damages in the ecclesiastical court from her husband's adulterous lover, but the husband had sole right to release the debt and did so, leaving Mrs. Hewson remedyless.

Toward the end of this section the author moves to aspects of the law that will lead toward her analysis of the bases of wifely subordination.[9] Central to her interpretation is the idea that the law denies intellectual, moral, and spiritual equality to wives. This is far more important than mere matters of property or guardianship. She turns to the moral disqualification that apparently arises from the "privilege" of being excused in criminal actions and civil wrongs. The legal principle that concerns the author is the premise that a wife is not responsible for criminal actions done in presence of the husband. Is this simply an acknowledgment of the husband's physical power? No, argues the author, rather the principle is designed to reinforce the authority of the husband. This is shown by the exception that a wife was liable for treason even if she acted with her husband, for here only did the interests of the body politic surpass the "private royalty of the husband." It is no favor to the "weakness of the sex" to grant immunity so a woman may risk damnation. The case the author uses to drive her point home follows. A couple were found hanged inside a locked room with their baby dead in the cradle. Both husband and wife signed the confessional suicide note. Yet only the husband was held responsible as a suicide; the wife was buried in consecrated ground. The full range of the author's sarcasm is stimulated by this episode. Should we presume the woman hanged herself for fear of being killed, she asks. Should she be allowed "to stand more in awe of a temporary resentment from [her husband]

[8] *Hardships*, 16, citing William Salkeld's *Reports of Cases Adjudged in King's Bench*. Unless otherwise noted cited cases may be found in the more accessible reprinted versions collected in the 174 volumes of the *English Reports* (indicated by added reference, e.g. 1 Salkeld 115 = 91 ER 107).

[9] She also answers (30–46) a series of the commonplace "objections" defending the status quo: women choose to marry; England is a "paradise for women"; a wife can swear the peace against her husband, etc. Another section (27–30) compares English women's status unfavorably with wives under Roman civil law.

than of the eternal resentment of Omnipotence itself"?[10] The "privilege" of not being imprisoned for debt is another infringement of married women's civil existence.

To divest a man of all property and then exempt him from jail in consequence of his debts is ... to divest him of all pleasure and in return to decree that he should feel no pain ... such exception from pleasure and pain would in effect strike him out of being a Man ... cut him off from being a member of civil society. So it is for women divested of debts.[11]

In the last section of her work the author seeks the explanation for the subordination of wives. Her ideas challenge the sympathies of modern secular feminists but no doubt resonated with readers of her day. She considers and rejects William Wollaston's argument that man's authority is based on his stronger reason.[12] She also assesses Hobbes's theory that the first natural dominion belongs to the mother, and although she feels "a great abhorrence of the whole scope and design of his author" and his theoretical state of nature, she rather regretfully rejects his theory: "had we ever been in the state of nature what he says is true."[13] Finally she turns to Scripture.[14] Here her thought is inspired by Patrick Delany's *Revelation Examined*.[15] She concludes that the "curse of female subjection" is so universal in human societies that it must be an expression of the will of God, in fact a strong proof of the truth of God's Revelation.

But a work that begins by defending the rights of freeborn English women could hardly end with passive acceptance of wives' oppression as God's will. Thus this Christian feminist goes on to insist first that God's mercy must temper the justice of husbands' rule and then that the virtue of obedience will be rewarded: "our obligations [are] to obey our husbands ... till the fashion of this world passeth away; then will ... the laws of equality ... forever be set right, and she that humbleth herself shall be exalted." Her admission that women's free will must be subject to some discipline combines a theory of moral sentiments with Christian theology. "Moral virtues are in their very nature the objects of our understandings." Yet a "malignity in the will ... occasions all the evils and disorders of the moral world." But God did not give man authority

---

[10] Ibid., 21–27.   [11] Ibid., 41–42.
[12] *The Religion of Nature Delineated* (London, 1724).
[13] *Hardships*, 56-57, citing the work as "Philosophical Rudiments concerning Government and Society," ch. 9.
[14] *Hardships*, 58ff.
[15] Vols. I and II published 1732–34. She does not name him, but the intimate tone of her fulsome approval suggests she may have been part of the Swift–Delany circle. Mary Pendarvis, later Mrs. Delany, was widowed at this time, and thus does not fit the author's self-description.

over woman to deliver her to rob and murder at her husband's command, or to excuse her from her duty of caring for her children. She cannot transfer her intellectual and personal abilities. "Have we not the right by Nature . . . to do all that good, which God has given us abilities to do?" Or in secular terms: do not all parts of the community have "a degree of liberty and property correspondent to the constitution under which they live?" In the "law of God and the rules of Equity . . . we have a right to it, and must answer for the misapplication of our Liberty . . . to God alone."[16]

The work thus conservatively defends the existing social order while it radically and uncompromisingly imposes on married women a fundamental equality of responsibility. There is nothing here of a so-called "instrumental feminism" that attempts to defend female betterment as advantageous to men. Nor is there much sense of "relational feminism" defending the strengths of female difference. Wifely subordination is accepted as God's will, but only in continuing tension with liberty. For this author moral freedom equals "existence." As she observes of herself, "I have a husband who lets me be alive, and gives me leave to be some body." Other wives by "favour of their husbands are [also] still in a state of existence."[17]

Separation and contractual ability

In the half century before this author considered the moral duties of married women, English jurists (in cases which she did not know or did not choose to discuss) were also considering the consequences of the fact that many wives sought "existence" in contradiction to the legal fiction of "unity of persons" in marriage. From the Restoration to the end of the eighteenth century two strands of law addressed the problem of the independent legal identity of the English wife. On one hand were cases arising from the financial problems of privately separated couples; on the other, poor-law cases raised the problem of the wife whose right to relief on the basis of her "settlement" was separate from that of her husband. Just as the author of *The Hardships* admitted that well-regulated marriage benefitted most women, in these cases the courts also tried to find the balance between the benefits a woman derived in a patriarchal world from being part of a family unit, and those rights which she should be able to hold as an individual member of civil society.[18]

---

[16] *Hardships*, 63, 66, 68–69.   [17] Ibid., 51.

[18] Recent feminist jurisprudence has tended to counterpose the notion of status as a collective or maternal identity against the contractual, liberal traditions of masculine

The former cases have been discussed by Susan Staves in *Players'
Scepters* and *Married Women's Separate Property*[19] and her findings will
be briefly summarized here. In the former work she argues that the
experience of the Interregnum induced an environment in which traditional structures of sovereignty in the family could be questioned. One
issue was whether and on what terms a wife living separately from her
husband was legally responsible for her own debts (and hence a full
member of society). Could she as "one flesh" with her husband privately
contract with him to separate, and could the secular courts enforce such
an interference with the rules of marriage? If so, then who was
responsible for her debts? Without credit a gentlewoman might well
starve. In the much discussed and widely reported case of *Manby v.
Scott* (argued between 1659 and 1663) the wife had left her husband
without any formal separation.[20] Although forbidden by the husband to
supply the wife with necessary goods, a trader did so nonetheless and
then sued the husband for payment. The husband's defense rested on
the sanctity of marriage, scriptural subjection, and the disorder that
would be loosed on society if runaway wives, refusing to cohabit, still
could charge necessities to their husbands. As Justice Hyde observed in
his opinion on the case, if that were true it would give "the power to the
wife (who by the law of God and of the land, is put under the power of
the husband . . .) to rule over the husband. Is such power suitable to the
judgement of almighty God inflicted upon women for being first in the
transgression?" Justice Tyrrell took the merchant plaintiff's side, and so
supported the independent wife. She must not starve; though she could
not compel her husband, yet a third person (the tradesman) might,

individualistic society. See for example S. Sherry, "Civic Virtue and the Feminine Voice
in Constitutional Adjudication," *Virginia Law Review* 72 (1986): 543–616 or M. Minow,
"'Forming Underneath Everything that Grows': Toward a History of Family Law,"
Wisconsin Law Review (1985): 819–98). "Difference" or "relational" feminism dom-
inates one stream of this analysis (for example Robin West, "Jurisprudence and
Gender," *University of Chicago Law Review* 55 (1988): 1–34 and J. C. Williams,
"Deconstructing Gender," *Michigan Law Review* 87 (1989): 797–825).

[19] Lincoln, Nebr.: University of Nebraska Press, 1979, 111, 145–55 and Cambridge,
Mass.: Harvard University Press, 163–95.

[20] 1 Modern 124 = 86 ER 781; Bridgeman, O., 229 = 124 ER 561; 1 Siderfin 109 = 82 ER
1000. This and the following section of this chapter are based on printed law reports.
Legal historians have rightly become skeptical about relying on law reports, arguing
that they are unrepresentative and inaccurate. No doubt there is more to be found in
manuscript material on some of the more important cases, and in the case of
settlement, in the records of Justices of the Peace. But in a preliminary exercise in
assessing the history of ideas as expressed in the law the reports are still a useful place
to begin. After all, it was the *reported* cases, and to a surprising extent just the
"headnotes" on cases, that influenced later development of the law by defining the
terms in which succeeding practitioners could begin to think about the issues
addressed.

otherwise any husband might starve his wife. But he also went further in what Staves reads as a "Protestant" vein: "her will is not so subject to his [the husband's] that if he be unreasonable, yet it must be an uncontrollable law." Tyrrell thus recognized both the wife's individuality and her right to benefit from her relational identity as spouse.[21]

Manby v. Scott was decided for the husband, but the arguments presented on the other side were often quoted in later cases that ruled that in common law a married woman could in some cases act as agent of necessity to make a valid contract binding her husband.[22] Of more interest with reference to *The Hardships* is another series of cases descending from *Manby* that recognized the autonomy and independent contractual capacity of married women living separately: they were responsible for their own debts even though they were married.[23] Chancery led the way, first by enforcing alimony orders of ecclesiastical courts and payments husbands owed by private agreements. The 1717 case of *Williams v. Callow* went further in establishing wives' economic autonomy. The wife of a ne'er-do-well glover who had failed to work and who had fired a pistol at her secured the aid of Chancery to have the income from the £500 she had brought to the marriage paid directly to herself. In 1737, just two years after the *Hardships* appeared, in *Cecil v. Juxon* Chancery protected the income of a deserted wife who had supported herself by a millinery business during her husband's absence.[24]

After the 1770s this development was subject to increasing debate. Common law courts (having previously refused to countenance such a "civil widowhood" of the wife)[25] joined Chancery in acting to enforce separation contracts and for a few years confidently acknowledged that some wives were eligible for full membership in civil society. Several cases decided by Chief Justice Mansfield in the 1780s held that the wife was independently liable.[26] But in 1800, in *Marshall v. Rutton*, the trend was firmly reversed: "confusion and inconvenience . . . must necessarily result from a mixed character of being separately responsible while married."[27] In *Lord St. John v. Lady St. John* (1805) private separation

---

21 *Players'*, 146. Tyrrell had been a parliamentarian supporter. That his last wife Bridget was a strong-willed woman is shown in a remarkable deed she drew up to found a series of charities based on a debt owed to her by the crown (PRO, E 407/96, 95ff.). Much remains to be done to assess the backgrounds of the jurists involved in these cases.

22 See Staves, *Players'*, 150, where she cites *Dyer v. East* (2 Keble 554 = 84 ER 347; 1 Ventris 42 = 86 ER 30; 1 Modern 9 = 86 ER 689).

23 See Staves, *Players'*, 151–2; citing for example *Todd v. Stoakes* (1 Lord Raymond 444 = 91 ER 1195; 12 Modern 245 = 88 ER 1294).

24 Staves, *Married*, 175–76.

25 Ibid., 180, quoting Justice DeGrey in *Lean v. Shutz* (1778).

26 Ibid., 178–79.   27 Ibid., 179–81, quoting Lord Chief Justice Kenyon.

agreements were seen as against constitutional order, individual families "constituting the great family of the public."[28] Nonetheless, separate maintenance remained socially necessary, and nineteenth-century secular courts continued to recognize them, but with one critical difference. Contracts between husband and wife were rejected; only those between husband and trustees for the wife were recognized.[29] While private separation was acknowledged, the wife's separate legal personality was denied; she could not act in her own right to secure her separate existence.

Poor wives and settlement law

At the same time as judges in courts of equity and common law were moving hesitantly toward recognizing the separate capacity of some propertied wives, another group of cases, decided mainly in King's Bench at common law, explored the separate legal identity of poor married women.[30] These cases arose as a result of problems in the rules by which married women claimed poor relief. Every system of state welfare contains within it some means for determining entitlement.[31] The English poor law adopted the premise that each person had a place of "settlement," that is a home place or parish where he or she legally belonged and should return for aid. Used at first only with regard to "vagabonds and rogues" in 1662 the concept of settlement had been applied by statute to the poor generally. "A person or persons, he or they" became liable to be sent to receive relief in their last legal settlement, that is the place they had last lived as a native householder, "sojourner," apprentice, or as servant for the space of forty days.[32]

Like all preceding statutes on poverty this act defined poor persons as independent individuals, who, whether male or female, acquired their own right of settlement by birth, work, or property-holding. Only in 1697[33] did marriage and family dependency begin to be considered, when a system was introduced of allowing poor persons to move on the basis of certificates from their home parishes. The certificate obliged the

---

[28] Lord Eldon, quoted in ibid., 185.   [29] Ibid., 186.
[30] Research for this part of this chapter was carried out with the assistance of Kimberley Kippen, whose energy and insights I gratefully acknowledge.
[31] These comments are based on Paul Slack, *Poverty and Policy in Tudor and Stuart England* (London: Longman, 1988), E. M. Leonard, *The Early History of Poor Relief* (Cambridge: Cambridge University Press, 1900), E. M. Hampson, *The Treatment of Poverty in Cambridgeshire, 1597–1834* (Cambridge: Cambridge University Press, 1934), and P. Styles, "The Evolution of the Law of Settlement" in *Studies in Seventeenth Century West Midlands History* (Kinetone: Roundwood Press, 1978).
[32] 13 & 14 Car II, c. 12.   [33] 8/9 Wm. III c. 30. s. 1.

parish that issued it to receive and provide for "the person mentioned in the said certificate together with his or her family as inhabitants of that parish." Further, "any such Person and his or her Children ... not having otherwise acquired a legal Settlement ... [may] be removed conveyed and settled in the parish or place from whence such certificate was brought."[34] Like other early poor law statutes (and in contrast with most other law) this statute was "gender neutral." "Person" still meant "he or she," and children's settlement apparently could be determined by either parent.

The details of the family relationships in settlement by dependency, sketched so roughly in this statute, were worked out in cases argued in King's Bench between the 1690s and the early 1800s. A case would arise when the overseers of the poor of one parish secured an order from two justices of the peace in petty sessions, sending a person or family to another parish, arguing that the latter was the legal place of settlement for relief. The receiving parish, reluctant to spend more money on relief, commonly appealed to Quarter Sessions, the full bench of JPs. The losing parish then often appealed again to the high court and soon a flood of cases began to move from Quarter Sessions to King's Bench. Many of these cases contested the dependent settlement of wives and children.[35]

Case law by its nature addresses peculiar situations. As a general premise the presumption that ordinarily a married woman acquired her husband's status because she was obliged to live with him and was supported by him was adopted quickly into this new branch of law. Nonetheless, parochial overseers or local justices continued to settle some poor wives separately from their husbands. Whether guided by coherent principles or simple expediency, their orders show that differing views persisted as to the subordinate standing of wives and children of poor men. The resulting cases drew common law judges into defining their views on the status of women in marriage, forced them reluctantly to trespass on the traditional jurisdiction of the church courts over

---

[34] A few years earlier, two statutes, 1 Jas II c. 17 and 3 W&M c. 11, had articulated the idea that incoming heads of households should register both themselves and their families and servants in the new parish.

[35] What follows is a study of case law, not necessarily practice. Who was actually removed was a matter of personality, negotiation, and chance, as much as law. In addition to cases reprinted in the *English Reports* I have used two eighteenth-century collections which were not reprinted: *Cases and Resolutions of Cases Adjudg'd in the Court of King's Bench concerning Settlement and Removals from the first Year of King George I to the Present time* (4th ed., London, 1742) (abbreviated Cases SR below) and Sir James Burrows, *Decisions of the Court of King's Bench upon Settlement Cases from the death of Lord Raymond in March 1732 to June 1776 inclusive* (2nd ed., London, 1786) (abbreviated Burr SC).

marriage, and finally led them to reconsider the autonomy of the female individual in the context of old patriarchal tradition, new liberal individualism, and the practices of an incipient welfare bureaucracy.[36]

Between 1690 and 1730 a conservative pattern was sustained, albeit ambivalently. For example, after briefly suggesting that legitimate children might inherit the mother's settlement (bastard children were settled where they were born), the court followed strict principles of patrilinearity.[37] Legitimate children received their father's settlement, leading poor families to define patterns of inheritance in the same way as people with property. Likewise patriarchal rules persisted with respect to wives whose husbands had a settlement. King's Bench was still loath to interfere with ecclesiastical jurisdiction to separate couples (even though Chancery was by now regularly ruling on alimony cases), so principles of unity of person, originally developed to guide decisions about marital property, quickly also prevailed with regard to poor couples' settlement (which was indeed a form of property). To support an order that sent the husband to his parish of settlement and the wife to hers would be to "cause a separation," even if the couple had already manifestly been separated by the desertion of the husband. Poor couples were "one flesh"; the wife's "maiden settlement" acquired by inheritance or employment – her "existence" in poor law terms – was absorbed and obliterated by her husband's.[38] The loss was permanent. Even as a widow she continued to have her husband's settlement. The widow could be sent to some distant place where she had never lived and where she had no connection.[39] By the time of the *Hardships*, this principle was

---

[36] Historians have recently discussed settlement mainly as an arena for debate about free contractualism for men. See for example James Taylor, "The Impact of Pauper Settlement 1691–1834," *Past and Present* 73 (1976): 42–74, and the vigorous debate on the uses of settlement law between Norma Landau, "The Laws of Settlement and the Surveillance of Immigration in Eighteenth-Century Kent," *Continuity and Change* 3 (1988): 391–420 and "The Eighteenth-Century Context of the Laws of Settlement," *Continuity and Change* 6 (1991): 417–39 and Keith Snell, "Pauper Settlement and the Right to Poor Relief in England and Wales," ibid., 375–415.

[37] In *Whitechapel v. Stepney* (1691; Carthew 433 = 90 ER 851) the judges observed that "a legitimate child gains no settlement by its birth, when the place of the *Parent's* last settlement is known; such child must follow the settlement of the parent." Although in hindsight we may presume that "the Parent" was male, as we have seen, the drafters of the statute of 1697 were not yet ready to privilege the male parent completely.

[38] The leading case in the handbooks on poor law was *R. v. Inhabitants of Oking* (about 1700; 3 Salkeld 256 = 91 ER 809); and see *Oby v. Linsbury* (1721; Cases SR 107) "they are *una caro* and cannot be separated, and the settlement of the husband is the settlement of the wife."

[39] As was determined by the influential 1724 case of *St. Giles (Reading) v. Eversley*. The husband had a settlement by apprenticeship in Eversley. After his death the judges ruled that the widow and her children should be sent to there from Reading, their current home: "tho the Wife had another settlement before she married, yet that was

firmly in place. Thus in 1736 in *R. v. Inhabitants of Mansfield*,[40] for example, the order removing a widow and her children to the husband's last settlement was queried only on the form of the order, not on the widow's status. As a widow, however, a woman could acquire a new settlement in her own right, and even give that settlement to any children still living with her.[41] But if she married again, her new identity would again be obliterated and her children would revert to the settlement they had by her first husband,[42] her status as mother overtaken by her relational identity as wife.

Yet in the decade or so before the author of *Hardships* composed her tract one complicating problem continued to force the judges to reconsider just how completely marriage absorbed a wife's identity. The problem arose when a woman who had a maiden settlement married a man who had none (a vagabond, or more commonly a Scot or Irishman who, like a foreigner, had no parish of settlement in England). These husbands themselves partly lacked legal identity and were to that extent not eligible for the full status of the patriarch. These circumstances were unusual, probably no more common than private separations, and the debate in the courts was a specialized matter, not reported in sources our author would have likely known. Yet this strand of cases tells an interesting story of acknowledgment of the separate legal existence of poor wives, a trend she might have approved. But the conservative nineteenth-century reaction that undermined private separations likewise reversed this interpretation in favor of even fuller subordination.

This aspect of settlement law highlights the contradictions of liberal feminist theory as it applies to poor working women rather than women with wealth and property. An egalitarian feminist perspective leads the historian to privilege the idea that the married woman's maiden settlement should be valued equally with that of her husband. But although some propertied women benefitted from separation, the material

---

lost by her marriage" (8 Modern 169 = 88 ER 124). Cited in both Viner's *Abridgement* (XIX, 375) and in eighteenth-century editions of Dalton's *Justice of the Peace*, sec. 73.

[40] Burr SC 76.

[41] *St. Katherine v. St. George* (1715; Fortescue 219 = 92 ER 825) reflects the lingering propensity to weight the maternal interest more strongly than in later law. Counsel arguing against settling the children with the widow had asserted that "children . . . can't be unsettled by the act of the mother." But Chief Justice Parker's opinion was otherwise: "There is no difference between the father's settlement and the mother's, they are as much the mother's children as the father's, [it is equally reasonable that they be settled] where the mother is, as where the father is . . . It is as unnatural to force a child from the mother as from the father, so that if she gains a settlement, her children must too."

[42] See *Cumner v. Milton* (1703; 2 Salkeld 528 = 91 ER 449): "she cannot gain a Settlement for [her children] in this last parish, because under coverture, and having a settlement there herself only as part of her husband's family, from whom she cannot be sever'd."

interests of poor women (indeed most women) in a patriarchal world were best served by living with their husbands. While compulsory residence with a husband sometimes deprived poor married women of opportunities to be fully economically competitive,[43] it is far from clear that such opportunities would in most circumstances have been of substantial benefit to them. That said, however, it is also clear that imposing the husband's settlement on deserted wives and widows often led to abrupt removals to distant and unknown places and imposed severe economic and emotional hardship on them as well.

These cases show the difficulty some legal thinkers initially experienced in following out the full implications of applying "unity of persons" to the poor. "Parity of reason" led the Bench to query whether marriage in itself could or should deprive a woman of settlement. In *Dunsfold v. Winsborough Green* in 1713 the judges had observed that "although a woman by marriage follows the condition of her husband, yet she shall not be put into a worse condition." If her husband is not a parishioner, they asked, "must she therefore starve?"[44] As the headnote to the printed report of the case announced: "A woman doth not lose her settlement by marrying a man who hath none."[45]

But in these cases the theory of masculine dominance and ecclesiastical tradition in marriage was also in play, presented on the losing side. As counsel for Dunsfold argued, "this is a removal of the wife to a place where the husband cannot be removed which will make a separation." By the old vagrancy law poor Scots were to be sent to the borders, and thus the couple would be legally settled in two separate places which would "have the effect of a divorce." A compromise theory developed. In 1723 in *Shadwell v. St. John's, Wapping* the court held that the woman's settlement was only partially obliterated by marriage: "where the wife had a settlement, it was suspended during coverture, and revived on death of husband."[46] The husband was guardian of her

---

[43] As Sophonisba Breckinridge argued in the twentieth century with regard to domicile, *Marriage and the Civic Rights of Women: Separate Domicil, and Independent Citizenship* (Chicago: University of Chicago Press, 1931), 16–17.

[44] Gilbert Cases 97 = 93 ER 272. This case is also briefly reported as *R. v. Inhabitants of Risborough Green* at Fortescue 315 = 92 ER 868. See also *St. Giles v. St. Margaret* (Cases SR 76).

[45] The same principle applied in widowhood. In *Uppoterce v. Dunswell* (1714; Cases SR 68), a woman with her own settlement in Dunswell had married a "Runnagate" who had no settlement. They moved to Uppoterce, where he died, saying he had been born at Wincanton. The local justices sent her to Dunswell, her settlement, and the judges in King's Bench agreed. If the husband had no settlement: "the marriage shall not put her in a worse condition than she was before ... although the husband might have been settled at Wincanton ... yet his wife having never been there, she cannot be sent thither by a Parity of Reason."

[46] See *R. v. Inhabitants of Norton* (Burr SC 123 and Andrews 307 = 95 ER 410). A vagrant

status, but since he did not qualify for full husbandly status, lacking a settlement himself, he could not absorb it entirely, as would a husband with his own settlement.

Shadwell v. St. John's became an influential precedent only in 1738 when it was cited in the important case of *R. v. the Inhabitants of Norton.*[47] The local justices had ordered that one Ellen Birmingham be moved to Norton, the place of her maiden settlement. Her husband, an Irishman, had deserted her and his whereabouts were unknown. Counsel for the parish of Norton appealing against the order cited the principle enunciated in Shadwell, saying that Birmingham's settlement was suspended while her husband lived. Attorneys arguing in support of the order cited the earlier cases: "it has been determined that a woman who marries a man with no legal settlement . . . may be sent to her last settlement, and so may also the children of the marriage." Here there was no problem of separating husband and wife, because he was already absent. But led by Chief Justice Lee, the judges ruled conservatively that the order removing Ellen Birmingham to her own settlement was bad: "for if the husband has no settlement the wife cannot be sent anywhere because they are but one person, and it is against the law of nature to separate them; and if justices of peace had such power they would have in effect the power of divorcing." In *Norton*, then, King's Bench swung in favor of the traditional subordination of wives, even if the husband was without settlement, and this despite the fact that in this case the husband's authority was not really in place. Since he had deserted and disappeared, Ellen Birmingham was certainly not under his power or within his maintenance. Three years after *Hardships*, *Norton* was a strong affirmation of the predominance of the male individual over the married female in even the most marginal of circumstances.

---

with no settlement married a woman settled in St. John's Wapping, and had four children by her, born in Stepney. Although the children were to be sent to the father's settlement, wherever that would be, she would go to her own parish of settlement. Her independent standing thus divided the family. *Shadwell* was not even reported in print at the time but it was very influential in the long run because it came to be associated with an often quoted broadside lyric that summed up the legal principle involved:

> A woman having a Settlement
> Married a Man with none
> The Question was, he being dead,
> If that she had, was *gone?*
> Quoth Sir John Pratt [then Chief Justice] – Her settlement
> Suspended did remain,
> Living the Husband; But, him dead,
> It doth revive again.

[47] See preceding note. *Norton* was decided in the same term as *Olive v. Ingram* (discussed in chapter 15) began. Lee's opinion provides some context for his views of single women's voting capacity in that case.

Yet despite *Norton* the contrary view persisted that stressed poor wives' separate identity. Twenty years later in *R. v. Inhabitants of St. Botolphs without Bishopsgate*,[48] a case first argued in 1753 and because of its importance re-argued in 1755, King's Bench under Sir Dudley Ryder turned back to emphasizing the married woman's independent settlement. The case involved Eleanor Kinley, wife of James Kinley, an Irish sailor with no settlement who was alive and in touch with his wife (she had heard from him two weeks previous to the order for her removal). Before her marriage she had had a settlement by service in the London parish of St. Botolphs. Eleanor and her daughter (and presumably her husband when ashore) lived in the London suburb of Wapping. The magistrates moved wife and daughter to her last legal settlement in St. Botolphs, and that parish appealed. Counsel arguing for the crown and for the order settling the wife in St. Botolphs, observed that "the Justices are finding great inconvenience in the new established Determination" of *Norton*, since by denying them a settlement of their own it left thousands of wives and children without any legal settlements at all.

The court then ordered research into the whole range of precedents and in 1755 Ryder delivered an opinion in which he attempted to restore an awareness of the weight of the maiden settlement. His opinion is reported at length. He was aware he was overturning an established rule, but he found that St. Botolphs was once Eleanor Kinley's settlement and she could not lose it without gaining another. "There is no Case where a settlement ceases by any other method. A Man [another report says 'person'[49]] can not give away or release or suspend his Settlement." Neither, to Ryder's mind, could a woman by the act of marriage deprive herself of the right of settlement. Ryder had no time for the argument that this decision would amount to a divorce; the husband was not with her anyway. "And indeed since he has no settlement of his own, he may as well go to her in her own Maiden-Settlement as in any other Place." The judgment of the court was that the wife's maiden settlement remained having never been changed, but it was suspended so long as she "continued under the power and Protection of the Husband and was maintained and supported by him." The judges were saying that, in effect, an Irish sailor lost his power over his wife when he did not maintain and support her.

Despite Ryder's determination to settle the matter, different views persisted and two decades later his decision was reversed. In 1775 in *R. v. Carleton*,[50] King's Bench reaffirmed the patriarchal status even of

---

[48] Burr SC 367.
[50] Burr SC 813.

[49] Sayer 198 = 96 ER 851.

men who lacked settlements. Here the husband, one Simon MacOwen, was unquestionably present and under normal circumstances able to support his wife. He was a householder and an employed artisan (a clothworker), a fact which doubtless enhanced his eligibility as head of a family. But as an Irishman MacOwen lacked a legal settlement in England. His wife Johanna had inherited a settlement by certificate at Carleton, although she had lived in Hoylandswain all her life. When Johanna and the children became ill of a fever Simon was forced to apply for relief, triggering an order to move Johanna and their four children to Carleton.

Counsel for Carleton moved to quash the order on the now familiar grounds that it "would occasion separation of Husband and wife and amount to a divorce." The high court agreed. The husband was not dead, nor had he deserted his wife. He was alive, followed a business, and had maintained his family till they were taken ill. "The Man is settled in a House, and carries on Business in this Place. There may be no Business for a Clothdresser at Carleton, at all. Or this Man may have no Acquaintance there. He may starve there, though he could maintain his family at Hoylandswain. It is a cruel Behaviour." In all the reports of settlement cases I have read this is the only instance in which the "cruelty" of the order is mentioned. Simon MacOwen's sex partially qualified him for the legal privileges of headship, his capacity as economic actor completed his claims to the rights of eighteenth-century masculinity.

Nevertheless, overseers of the poor continued to try to find ways of avoiding responsibility for the wives and children of "unsettled" men. In 1804 in *R. v. Eltham*[51] the twin strands of property and poor law regarding married women's separate status finally came together. A parish in Southwark had complained about Mary, wife of Peter Finn, a Scot who had never gained a settlement in England. The local justices examined Mary and Peter, ruled that Eltham, Kent, was the last legal settlement of Mary, and ordered Mary and their three children to be moved there "by the mutual consent of the said Peter and Mary." Eltham appealed the order to King's Bench. Eltham's counsel argued that consent by the husband was not sufficient to allow a separation, based on *Marshall v. Rutton*,[52] in which, as we have seen, it was ruled that private separation contracts were not valid.

But the Chief Justice, Lord Ellenborough, had little patience with these objections. His opinion combined both a sense that the poor are

[51] 5 East 113 = 102 ER 1012.   [52] 8 Term Reports 545 = 101 ER 1583.

different, and the notion that even poor men should be able freely to determine the fates of their families.

What doubt is there in the case? A Scotchman, who has no settlement of his own, and is desirous to give his wife and children the benefit of hers, being unable to maintain them, consents that she should be sent to her parish, to which she herself is willing to go. Why should he not consent? This is nothing like the contract of separation declared to be illegal in Marshall. Servants and other persons of that description, members of the same family, who are to subsist by their labour, must frequently separate for that purpose. Here there is neither a private nor a public injury, and there is no law against it.

The order separating this poor couple was affirmed; the husband's consent was all that mattered. From the glimmer of a sense that the wife's settlement was of weight equal to the husband's, to a sense of suspension and then absorption of her existence the court had moved back to recognizing her legal existence if the husband somehow disqualified himself, while reaffirming her subordination to a qualified male. Now they managed both to enforce further the husband's capacity to determine his wife's residence, while acknowledging her separate legal settlement.

But whatever Ellenborough's views, sensibilities of many in the early nineteenth century were offended by this idea of poor couples separating. In 1819 Parliament enacted a different, more "conservative" solution to the problems created by the unsettled Scottish or Irish husband. 50 Geo III c. 12, s. 33 empowered Justices of the Peace to remove not only the husband but also his wife and his children to the country of the husband's origin. It did not go so far as to send the wife of an unsettled alien out of the United Kingdom, nor did it deprive her of her English nationality – that would come in 1870 – but this statute did strip these female English subjects of their right to live in England so long as the husband was alive.

In 1821 in *R. v. the Inhabitants of Leeds*[53] the judges of King's Bench expressed their palpable relief at thus escaping the dilemma posed by voluntary separation of poor families and the consequent informal acknowledgment of the wife's separate status. They were unanimous in condemning independent settlement for poor wives as "contrary to sound policy." This view was further affirmed in statutes under the new poor law that affirmed that a wife could not be separately removed.[54] In 1861 the husband's settlement was guaranteed even to deserted wives whose separate settlement status was thus utterly dissolved.[55] In human

[53] *Revised Reports* vol. 23, 367.
[54] See 9/10 Vic c. 66 s. 1 (1846) (clarified in 1848: 11/12 Vic c. 111, s. 1).
[55] 24/25 Vic c. 55 s. 3 (1861). For the later history of this policy see P. Thane, "Women and the Poor Law in Victorian and Edwardian England," *History Workshop* 6 (1979): 29–51.

terms the promise of a stable residence for the woman was doubtless usually advantageous to her in a world in which a woman's independent economic capacity was always fragile, but the whole thrust of this century of legal development only served to reinforce married women's legal nullity and economic dependency.

These nineteenth-century poor-law decisions presaged changes both more widely effective and more detrimental to married women's status. From denying the right of poor women married to Scots and Irish to live in England, the law moved on in 1870 to deprive of citizenship all women who married non-British husbands, a profound derogation of married women's civil existence that persisted until 1948.[56] Likewise in the nineteenth century the law of domicile developed along lines that paralleled poor-law settlement in ways very destructive to the status of married women. Domicile is the principle that determines which national rules will govern an individual's affairs when conflicting regimes might apply (for example when a citizen of one country resides in another).[57] One of the most enduring principles of British law of domicile was that a wife's domicile was determined by that of her husband no matter where he or she lived. It was not until 1973 that this rule, so profoundly prejudicial to a wife's separate capacity to use her abilities and control her property, was finally reversed.[58]

The Interregnum initiated a period of reexamination of the social order that for more than a century inspired a reconsideration of some implications of marital law. For feminist authors this involved more or less radical critiques of marriage itself. Most, like the conservative author of the *Hardships of the English Laws*, could not countenance the fundamental upheaval to the social order that real change in the marital relationship seemed to entail. Lawyers, too, were forced to consider exceptions to the basic premise that, as Blackstone put it, "by marriage . . . the very being or legal existence of the woman is suspended."[59] But like the feminist debate, this consideration was often hesitant, and collapsed in the face of the same conservative reaction that engulfed feminist argument after 1800. Doctrines of the "sacred" and "convenient" unity of the family were then extended to theories of domicile and nationality to the detriment of the human rights of married women

[56] 33/34 Vic c. 14.
[57] Many works on domicile discuss this: see for example A. V. Dicey, *A Digest of the Law of England with Reference to the Conflict of Laws* (2nd ed., London: Stevens, 1908) and Norman Bentwich, *The Law of Domicile in its Relation to Succession and the Doctrine of Renvoi* (London: Sweet and Maxwell, 1911).
[58] Domicile and Matrimonial Proceedings Act (1973) c. 45.
[59] *Commentaries on the Laws of England* (1st ed., Oxford, 1765), I, 430.

far into the twentieth century. The rights of married women to "existence," to be "some body," asserted by the author of this early conservative feminist tract were finally at least partly achieved, but the path to that achievement was an uneven one indeed.

Conclusion

Women's writing, women's standing: theory and politics in the early modern period

Carole Pateman

A colleague in political science asked me recently whether women were involved in political activity before they were enfranchised. The question illustrates the importance of this volume, and the need to continue to harp on the same questions (to recall Mary Wollstonecraft's words in 1796)[1] about women and politics, past or present.

Political scientists remain remarkably uninterested in women's contributions to the development of the institutions of the modern state, and the means through which men have managed to monopolize political life for so long. Political theorists pay little attention to women's part in the development of the ideas that helped shape those institutions. Even the womanhood suffrage movement, the very different histories of the enfranchisement of women and men, and the fact that women organized against votes for themselves, have been largely ignored, despite the central place of the study of elections and electoral participation in political science. One has to turn to the work of historians to learn about the rich tradition and variety of women's political activities, during which they pioneered some now familiar tactics.

Their activities range in Britain, for example, from petitions to Parliament in the 1640s, through all the major campaigns, such as anti-slavery, the repeal of the Corn Laws and Chartism, to their part in two world wars. Women were active in trade unionism, the peace movement, the struggle for welfare legislation, in political parties, and anti-feminist movements. Their political endeavors extended to areas not often seen as "political" by political scientists, such as the campaign against the Contagious Diseases Acts, and a range of struggles to gain access to education and employment, to remove the legal power of husbands, to improve private and public safety for women and girls, and for temperance and birth control. Moreover, as Linda Colley has shown, it is not possible to understand the development of patriotism and the creation of the British nation, from the Act of Union in 1707 to the accession of

---

[1] Mary Wollstonecraft, *A Short Residence in Sweden, Norway and Denmark* [1796] (Harmondsworth: Penguin Books, 1987), 171.

Queen Victoria, without giving due weight to the political activities of women.[2] They also contributed to the debate about patriotism in their political writings, such as Catherine Macaulay's *History of England*.

A large number of women, of widely differing political persuasions, wrote about politics in a variety of literary forms, including histories – "through sheer ability" Macaulay was the historian of her generation most capable of dealing with the complexities of the party system (John Pocock, chapter 11) – plays, essays, poems, and pamphlets. Their scientific work, too, raised religious and political issues (see Judith Zinsser, chapter 8). Women discussed central topics in political philosophy, commented on and debated with, and were sometimes closely associated with, famous male theorists. Du Châtelet translated Newton and Mandeville, influenced Voltaire, and followed Leibniz rather than Descartes. Mary Astell, influenced by Descartes, was one of the earliest critics of Locke.[3] Macaulay was a critic of Burke and discussed Hume. Mary Wollstonecraft criticized her favorite author, Rousseau, and wrote the first reply to Burke's *Reflections on the Revolution in France*.

The reception of women's political writings varied – sometimes, like Aphra Behn and Elinor James, they were arrested, and one of the latter's pamphlets was seen as important (or seditious) enough to be preserved by the government of James II. But their work was taken seriously, or at least acknowledged, by their contemporaries. In the political theory of the past fifty years, however, they are not to be found.

The history of political thought is the mainstay of the academic curriculum in political theory, but women writers have been ignored in the authors studied as "the history of political thought." The exclusion of women writers, as Berenice Carroll (chapter 1) notes, is exemplified by the Cambridge University Press series, Texts in the History of Political Thought. For a decade, only texts by male authors were published in the series. Finally, following Christine de Pizan's *Book of the Body Politic*, Mary Wollstonecraft's *Vindication of the Rights of Woman* was issued in 1995. Wollstonecraft is significant because, in the late 1990s, her work is at last beginning to be noticed, no doubt stimulated by Virginia Sapiro's fine study of her political theory.[4]

---

[2] Linda Colley, *Britons: Forging the Nation 1707–1837* (New Haven, Conn.: Yale University Press, 1992).

[3] Patricia Springborg, "Mary Astell (1666–1731), Critic of Locke," *American Political Science Review*, 89, 2 (1995): 621–33.

[4] Virginia Sapiro, *A Vindication of Political Virtue* (Chicago: University of Chicago Press, 1992).

The "history" of political thought to which I was introduced thirty years ago is thus (very slowly) being recognized as truncated and partial.[5] Curiously, although feminist political theory has been flourishing for two decades, albeit to a large degree alongside the standard approaches, few feminist scholars have been concerned with their early predecessors. This is a major reason why the standard history of political thought is only now beginning to be challenged, and why so little is known about women's contribution. Unfortunately, while interest in the early modern writers is growing, an influential development in feminist theory, to which I shall turn later, is obscuring them once more.

But the inclusion of women writers is only one step in a reassessment of the standard history; there is also the question of the relationship of feminist political thought to that history. If a common reaction to mention of a female theorist is that she is unoriginal, a typical view, if she is a feminist, is that she merely takes the principles of famous (male) theorists to their logical conclusion by extending them to women. More narrowly, feminist political thought is seen as beginning with Mary Wollstonecraft, and as an outgrowth of "liberalism," the Enlightenment, and the Declaration of the Rights of Man and the Citizen of 1789.[6]

The work of Christine de Pizan, the earliest writer discussed in this volume, immediately casts doubt on this popular picture. Her views diverged in significant ways from those of her contemporaries; her writings about the state were secular in their form, and closer to Machiavelli than theorists of the late fourteenth and early fifteenth centuries (Berenice Carroll, chapter 1). The example of Christine illustrates that feminist thought cannot simply be slotted into existing classifications of political theory. Feminist political argument has its own history – that still remains to be written – interwoven with, cutting across, and standing outside, the standard accounts. Feminist political theorists criticized and rejected fundamental assumptions and tenets of famous theorists, and arguments that can reasonably be seen as "feminist," on characteristic topics, have been made by women writers of varying, and sometimes surprising, political allegiances. It was not only in the writings of women who gave *critical* support to ideas commonly associated with Enlightenment philosophy that themes, issues, and arguments characteristic of what is now understood by "feminism" are

---

[5] A cynical view would see this as inevitable, given the incessant demand for new areas of research by today's voracious publishing and dissertation industries.

[6] For example: "Feminism emerged in the West as one feature of liberalism, indebted to Enlightenment presuppositions and the doctrine of 'the rights of man' ... an enterprise announced by the publication in 1792 of Mary Wollstonecraft's *A Vindication of the Rights of Woman*" (Jean Elshtain, "Is There a Feminist Tradition on War and Peace?," in *The Ethics of War and Peace*, ed. Terry Nardin [Princeton: Princeton University Press, 1996], 214).

to be found. The same preoccupations are evident in the work of women who were intellectual and political opponents of the famous philosophers of the Enlightenment.

Not all early women writers are feminists, but since so many of them managed the remarkable feat of supporting themselves by their pens, and they were all engaged in "masculine" intellectual and political work, their lives hardly follow the conventional standards for women. In the latter part of the seventeenth century, the Tory royalist Aphra Behn mourned the passing of the age of the rover, the cavalier, constrained only by an aristocratic code of honor, who stood above conventions and customs. There was little hope that women could live as she-rovers, although Aphra Behn came close. She saw marriage as the antithesis of free love, yet to comply with the cavalier's language of love and to marry, seems the best that Behn offers women (Melinda Zook, chapter 4).

Criticism of the rule of husbands as despotic, absolute monarchs over their wives, is one of the central themes in feminist political argument from the early modern period onward; another is criticism of men's monopoly of access to education. Husbands were granted their powers under the English common law doctrine of coverture, and in France under civil and public law that constituted a "marital regime system in governance" (as Sarah Hanley calls it, chapter 13),[7] powers that were reinforced by social opinion.

In the earlier part of the eighteenth century, Mary Astell, another royalist and Tory, engaged in religious debates with Locke and Damaris Masham (Patricia Springborg, chapter 5). But she was also the earliest systematic, and one of the harshest, critics of the tyranny of husbands in marriage. In her *Reflections upon Marriage*, she makes some scathing comments about the language of love used by men before marriage, and the reality of absolute submission facing wives after the knot was tied. The problem with marriage for Mary Astell, a political absolutist and advocate of obedience, was not that husbands were absolute rulers, but that they were arbitrary tyrants, whose demands and power had no rational basis, but rested on their strength and the fact of their sex. As she implies, no woman of intelligence or refinement could reasonably accept the terms of submission demanded of a wife.

Astell is the prime example of early modern women writers who were political conservatives, but who nonetheless present arguments that fall

---

[7] On coverture see Carole Pateman, *The Sexual Contract* (Stanford: Stanford University Press, 1988); and in addition on France, Sarah Hanley, "The Monarchic State in Early Modern France: Marital Regime Government and Male Right," in *Politics, Ideology and the Law in Early Modern Europe*, ed. Adrianna Bakos (Rochester: University of Rochester Press, 1994).

squarely within the themes of feminist political thought. Furthermore, as Hilda Smith showed some years ago in *Reason's Disciples*, these women appeal to the claims of Reason every bit as vigorously as their political opponents. In a caustic and witty manner, Astell exposed the inconsistencies of her radical political opponents, supporters of natural liberty and natural rights, who attacked absolute monarchy in the state but claimed it for themselves in the household. Astell had an exceedingly sharp mind, and, precisely because she advocated hierarchy and submission she was, ironically, more aware of the implications of, and limits to, claims about natural rights than many present-day upholders of the doctrines of the English, American, and French revolutionaries. All of which led her to skate upon some exceedingly thin political ice for an absolutist.

By the end of the seventeenth century, political theories about the state of nature and an original contract, that were based on the premise that men were born free, equal, and rational, had gained wide currency. This was a revolutionary intellectual innovation that swept away all the traditional justifications for relations of power and government.[8] The universal language of these theories held out the promise that a new, equal political standing would be open to all in the modern state. The mere subject, bound by, and governed through, personal loyalty to monarchs and lords, and tied into a network of kinship, would be replaced by equal citizens who consented to be governed, and enjoyed rights, including the right to participate in government. But what was the place of women to be in the world of rights, freedom, equality, and reason? Could women enjoy the new standing and share in freedom as a birthright? Was there, for example, such a creature as a freeborn Englishwoman?

The latter question arose most acutely in the case of married women. Coverture obliterated any independent standing for a wife. However, as Barbara Todd shows (chapter 16), the English courts in the seventeenth and eighteenth centuries had to admit, in a series of cases that concerned separated spouses and the poor law, that a wife was a legal individual. In the early nineteenth century, on the other hand, the doctrine of the "unity" of a married couple was reaffirmed once more.

These legal shifts provide one illustration of the contradictory and ambiguous consequences for women that resulted from the philosophical move from birth as status to new ideas about freedom as a birthright, ideas that helped shape the institutions of the modern state.

---

[8] Carole Pateman, *The Problem of Political Obligation*, 2nd ed. (Berkeley: University of California Press, 1985).

In the old, hierarchical political order, women shared in the power, or subordination, of their status. High-born ladies were used to ruling, as well as to exercising influence, in kingdoms and abbeys, and to managing extensive estates. In the new world of natural rights and freedom, women were declared, in theory and in practice, ineligible to share in government by virtue of their sex. The theorists of natural freedom studied under the rubric of the history of political thought – as Astell pointed out – concluded that only men could govern and enjoy rights.

A great, but unacknowledged, insight of the feminists of the early modern period was that "rights" were two-dimensional. The familiar civil and political rights form the first dimension. The second dimension – as both opponents of natural rights, like Astell, and advocates, like Mary Wollstonecraft in the 1790s, were aware – gave men the power of government over women, whether in marriage or in the state. Men's special rights, as I have called this dimension of "rights," [9] depend on the denial that women were born free, or possessed the requisite form of rationality and other capacities to take part in public and political life. Early feminists recognized and attacked men's special rights, and, from the 1790s onward, their support for "the rights of man" was predicated on the rejection of men's special rights. Their critical two-dimensional understanding of natural rights foreshadows the criticisms of "human rights" by feminists in the 1990s.

The women discussed in this volume thought, wrote, and acted when the institutions of the modern state were first being developed. These institutions – governmental, civic, economic, and familial – were built around the division between the private household and the public sphere, a division constructed philosophically in the famous texts of early modern political theory. But a long political road had to be traveled before the arrangements that seemed so natural for most of the nineteenth and twentieth centuries were firmly in place. The appearance of the "housewife," that emblem of the private sphere, was still a very long way off. Women were incorporated into the political order and not merely excluded (or left in "the state of nature"), but their manner of incorporation was different from that of men, and involved exclusion from major rights of citizenship and, hence, lesser standing. However, in the period discussed in this volume it had not yet become an established "fact" that women were ineligible to be voters, or that women should

[9] See Carole Pateman, "The Rights of Man and Early Feminism," *Swiss Yearbook of Political Science*, 1994; and "Democracy, Freedom and Special Rights," in *Taking Justice Seriously: Perspectives in the Problem of Social Justice*, eds. David Boucher and Paul Kelly (London: Routledge, forthcoming).

not enjoy the new rights, freedoms, and equality promised by the universal language of political theory.

For example, women played a much greater part than we have been led to believe in the emergence of the popular press, the development of freedom of expression, and the "public sphere" so important for democracy (Lois Schwoerer, chapter 3). In the early modern period, women were active in printing, publishing, and other trades. Schwoerer estimates (conservatively) that women published 100 titles on political questions between 1640 and 1700, particularly at times of political crises. In political theory, these publications are unknown, although tracts by their male contemporaries have been discovered and discussed.

Nor was it yet "obvious" that women's economic skills should not be turned to new forms of commerce, such as stockholding in the East India Company and South Sea Company. The constitutions of the companies allowed women to participate in their affairs on the same terms as men, and some attended and voted at shareholder meetings, though none appear to have made a speech, and no woman was elected as a director. At least one woman writer, Susanna Centlivre, understood the vocabulary and workings of the new stock market, and another, Mary Barwell, managed her family's investments, demonstrating great political skill as she "organized interests" by lobbying politicians and female connections (Susan Staves, chapter 12).

None of this is to say that the institutional field was completely open or fluid. The right of men to rule over women, and patriarchal doctrines about the rightful powers of fathers and masters in all fields, had been proclaimed for centuries from pulpits and thrones. Men's power in political, legal, economic, intellectual, and spiritual life was also upheld in the long tradition of outright misogyny. In her *Book of the City of Ladies*, Christine de Pizan battled the prominent *genre* of misogynist literature of the 1300 and 1400s, that declared women not merely inferior in intellect, body, and spirit to men, but a source of pollution and corruption of masculinity. The development of printing and the popular press, Schwoerer emphasizes, meant that such views reached a wider audience, and so did Filmer's patriarchal political theory (Gordon Schochet, chapter 10). Mary Astell used rational argument against the misogynist "wits" of her time, and, ever since, her successors have had tirelessly to reiterate the same case.

Men, that is to say, took vigorous steps to *enforce* their rule, their prerogatives, and their monopoly of power in the modern state, through political philosophy, popular writings, and political action. Men fought hard to consolidate their special rights to government in the state, and to power in the capitalist economy, in science, in education, marriage, the household, and sexuality. This volume illustrates some of the political mechanisms at work in the enforcement of masculine rule, and in the resistance to reasoned arguments. The long tradition of misogynist literature is only one example of men's tactics. For example, by the latter part of the eighteenth century, stockholding, and financial management more generally, was being promoted as a manly activity, part of patriotic masculinity. And although Centlivre makes a comedy out of the exchange of political favors for "places," such preferments were hard for women to come by, notwithstanding their support for parties and candidates, in print and in election campaigns.

Political theories that were, ostensibly, universalist gave women powerful intellectual weapons, but men disregarded the claims of reason where their rule was at stake. In France, for instance, the opponents of women's right to the throne even resorted to outright forgery. The Salic law said nothing about women being precluded from monarchy. Between 1409 and 1413, Jean de Montreuil introduced a forged version that purported to exclude women from the throne. This reached a large audience by 1500, and was the crucial precursor to the laws from the mid-1500s through the eighteenth century, that gave men power in the household, the state, and on the throne (Sarah Hanley, chapter 13).

In England, deep anxieties about women as political actors were revealed in the obscure election for parish sexton and the case of *Olive v. Ingram* (Hilda Smith, chapter 15). The case raised fundamental questions about women's eligibility and competence as voters, whether by virtue of precedence, or because women met the relevant criteria for the suffrage. The answers were avoided in the verdict of 1739, when the office of sexton was declared a private trust and so suitable for electors or office holders to be women. Answers were given, though, half a century later during the French Revolution and again in 1832, when women in France and England were explicitly excluded from the national electorates. These famous landmarks of "democratization" made electoral politics a masculine preserve.

Olive v. Ingram was frequently cited, along with other precedents, in the struggle for womanhood suffrage in Britain in the nineteenth century. By the latter part of the century, when the Fifteenth Amendment in the USA had also confined the franchise to men, the suffragists faced a difficult political problem: what arguments could they use that stood some chance of being effective politically? Demands for citizenship based on democratic universalist arguments had fallen on deaf ears. The suffragists began to place more emphasis on other arguments, to claims focused on the valuable contribution that women, by virtue of their difference from men, brought to the political arena. These arguments had been made since the 1790s by, for example, Mary Wollstone-craft, and by the marquis de Condorcet, who, in the course of his deft demolition of the claims of the opponents of women's citizenship, wrote that women were not guided by "the reason of men, but ... by their own." They "make up their minds on other principles, and aim at a different end."[10]

However, neither of these lines of argument offered a way out of (what I have christened) Wollstonecraft's dilemma.[11] To use either argument left the suffragists impaled on a horn of the dilemma. On the one hand, claims based on women's difference appealed to the very same qualities that were widely held – by the French revolutionaries, many other male radicals, and a large body of men and women anti-suffragists – to show that nature demonstrated the necessity of confining citizenship to men. On the other hand, appeals to universalist, democratic arguments were not effective either, in the face of political institutions and citizenship constructed around "man," interpreted, even in his guise as the legal category of "person," as an exclusively masculine figure.[12]

These arguments were made, and the suffrage campaigns were conducted, in the political context of the developing "liberal" state – the context on which most contemporary feminist theory is focused. Yet in the Holy Roman Empire men took steps to monopolize political power in quite different political circumstances (Merry Wiesner, chapter 14). The example of the Empire is instructive in light of the current popularity of republican and communitarian theories as alternatives to "liberalism." In the cities and rural communes of the Holy Roman Empire women were citizens, and could even pass their citizenship on to their husbands. However, citizenship began to become more masculine around the sixteenth and seventeenth centuries. In the political units of the Holy Roman Empire, as elsewhere when women gained rights, their citizenship was never established on the same footing as that of men. Women, like men, swore an oath when admitted as citizens in the cities

---

[10] "Condorcet's Plea for the Citizenship of Women," reprinted in Susan Bell and Karen Offen, eds., *Women, the Family, and Freedom*, vol. 1 (Stanford: Stanford University Press, 1983), 100.

[11] Carole Pateman, "The Patriarchal Welfare State," in *The Disorder of Women* (Stanford: Stanford University Press, 1989), and in *Democracy and the Welfare State*, ed. Amy Gutmann (Princeton: Princeton University Press, 1988).

[12] On the suffrage see my "Three Questions about Womanhood Suffrage," in *Suffrage and Beyond*, eds. Caroline Daley and Melanie Nolan (New York: New York University Press, 1995). I note that the mobilization of anti-feminist forces in the 1970s to defeat the Equal Rights Amendment in the USA involved arguments remarkably similar to those of the anti-suffragists, and that women's difficulties in being elected to legislatures, and obtaining authoritative positions more generally, illustrates that beliefs and sentiments central to opposition to the suffrage still have political force.

and communes of the Holy Roman Empire, but they did not participate, like non-citizen men, in annual oathing ceremonies. Nor did they swear to uphold the religion of their city; the good Christian, too, became a more civic and masculine figure.

Clearly, a great deal more research is required into the mechanisms through which men consolidated their power in different social and political institutions and contexts of the early modern period. But whatever the processes at work, a similar consequence seems to have ensued in otherwise differing circumstances. Whether the individual began to take precedence over kinship, or whether corporate and communal values remained predominant, male heads of households became seen as citizens *par excellence,* and women's membership and citizenship were seen, properly, to be mediated through their husbands.

The structure of the developing political and economic institutions of the period, and women's (lack of) standing and rights, cannot be understood without taking into account the complex interrelationship between the public world of commerce, industry and politics and the institution of marriage. Unfortunately, the insights offered by early feminists into the connections between women's standing as wives and their civil and political standing are being lost from view once more in contemporary feminist theory. In a very influential development, deriving from "post-modernist" critiques of the Enlightenment, feminist theory is held to repeat all the problems of Enlightenment philosophy.[13] It is presented as a reenactment of the sins of the fathers, a white women's version of the ahistorical, partial, imperialist theories, masquerading as universalism, of "the Enlightenment."[14]

Strangely enough, in contemporary arguments of this kind, feminist writers during the Enlightenment are rarely discussed. Instead, one finds a litany of authorities, Derrida, Lyotard, Wittgenstein, Foucault, Heidegger, Lacan, etc., none of whom, as far as I know, display any interest in women writers of the seventeenth and eighteenth centuries. No mention is made of the fact that the early women writers cannot be

---

[13] This approach is well represented, for example, in two widely used anthologies: Linda Nicholson, ed., *Feminism/Postmodernism* (New York: Routledge, 1990); Judith Butler and Joan Scott, eds., *Feminists Theorize the Political* (New York: Routledge, 1992). *Feminism/Postmodernism* contains contributions by some critics of "postmodernist feminism," and the other volume mentions some writers from the nineteenth century. Neither discusses feminist writers during the Enlightenment.

[14] "Historically," another such critic states, "the custodians of feminism drew discursive legitimacy from the universal civilizing mission of the middle class in extending to their less fortunate sisters a matronizingly appropriative embrace" (Anna Yeatman, "Voice and Representation in the Politics of Difference," in *Feminism and the Politics of Difference,* eds. Sneja Gunew and Anna Yeatman [Boulder, Colo.: Westview Press, 1993], 238).

fitted neatly into standard categories such as "the Enlightenment," or that there were feminist critics who did not share the assumptions held to characterize Enlightenment philosophy. A highly sophisticated approach thus serves to reinforce the popular view of feminism as a mere extension of the famous political philosophies of male authors. The oddity of an "Enlightenment" that makes no mention even of Astell or Wollstonecraft, is now being criticized, but the criticisms have not yet received the attention they deserve.[15]

Two major charges brought against feminist theory are, first, that it is "essentialist," a term of condemnation now so ubiquitous that it has been drained of meaning, but that in essence (if I may) refers to a definitive set of attributes ascribed to "woman." Second, feminism is held to be "foundationalist," resting on the idea that there are principles and categories, such as (natural) rights, that are uncontaminated by power, beyond doubt, and so a basis for wider arguments.[16] These foundations, together with the "subject" of politics (such as "man," or "woman" if she is included) must, it is claimed, be abandoned. According to Judith Butler, when the category "woman" is treated as foundational, it becomes "normative in character, and, hence, exclusionary in principle." Yet Butler also states that such criticism is not a "repudiation" of the subject, but "a way of interrogating its construction as a pregiven or foundational premise." Putting foundations in question is "the permanent risk of the process of democratization."[17]

If this is the case, then the early feminist writers can be seen as the precursors of contemporary criticism. Feminist writers before, during, and after the Enlightenment, challenged and criticized exclusion, attacked men's power, interrogated "man" as a "foundation" of political theories, took issue with an "essentialist" view of women and their alleged natural deficiencies, and showed unequivocally how power was implicated in claims about rights, freedom, and reason. I have no intention of claiming Enlightenment feminism as yet another version of

---

[15] See, especially, Pauline Johnson, *Feminism as Radical Humanism* (Boulder, Colo.: Westview Press, 1994). For earlier discussions see, for example, Margaret Hunt et al., *Women and the Enlightenment* (London: The Haworth Press, 1984); and Dale Spender, *Women of Ideas* (London: Routledge and Kegan Paul, 1982).

[16] Even those who argue that feminist theories are only "quasi-metanarratives" still insist that they "share some of the essentialist and ahistorical features" of grand narratives, and "falsely universalize" from the theorist's own attributes and location (Nancy Fraser and Linda Nicholson, "Social Criticism without Philosophy: An Encounter between Feminism and Postmodernism," in Nicholson, *Feminism/Postmodernism*, 27).

[17] Judith Butler, "Gender Trouble, Feminist Theory, and Psychoanalytic Discourse," in Nicholson, *Feminism/Postmodernism*, 325; and "Contingent Foundations: Feminism and the Question of 'Postmodernism,'" in Butler and Scott, *Feminists Theorize the Political*, 9 and 16.

postmodernism *avant la lettre*. Nonetheless, informed criticism of the Enlightenment is impossible without an adequate understanding of women writers' relationship to the intellectual and political developments of the time, and the history, variety, and complexity of feminist argument.[18] It is ironical, to say the least, that "feminism" is declared ahistorical, when fashionable theory is again burying the rich, diverse, and unwieldy work of the women writers discussed in this volume.

Consider Mary Astell, for example; she used a universal and transcendental conception of reason to expose the arbitrary power of husbands and the limits of natural rights. Is she merely introducing another "essentialist" subject, or is she showing what was excluded by the "foundation" of natural rights? Neither characterization captures Astell's peculiar combination of absolutism and an acute awareness of women's subordination.

And how does the complicated figure of Margaret Cavendish, duchess of Newcastle, fit into the Enlightenment? Another royalist and absolutist, influenced by Hobbes (Anna Battigelli, chapter 2), she also wrote plays with lesbian themes. Critical of social disorder, she nevertheless questioned social hierarchy, and castigated political philosophers "which are call'd Moral Philosophers, or Common-wealth makers . . . as Rebels against Nature . . . Inslaving her with Propriety, whereas all is in Common with Nature."[19] The duchess was also keenly aware of women's subordination and their political exclusion. She made the blunt statement that she knew "no reason we should be subjects to the Commonwealth," since women were not sworn to allegiance, held no offices, and were seen as "neither useful in peace, nor serviceable in war."[20]

Finally, consider Mary Wollstonecraft (Mary Shanley, chapter 7), who, together with Catherine Macaulay, turned the tables on Burke by accusing him of an excess of "sensibility" and lack of manliness in argument (Wendy Gunther-Canada, chapter 6). Wollstonecraft was a political radical who argued that private and public virtue, together with

---

[18] In these discussions there is little consideration of exactly which philosophers, and which interpretations of their philosophy, are part of "the Enlightenment." Consider, for example, the fifth of the list of eight propositions "derived from the Enlightenment" presented by Jane Flax ("Postmodernism and Gender Relations in Feminist Theory," in Nicholson, *Feminism/Postmodernism*, 41): "freedom consists of obedience to laws that conform to the necessary results of the right use of reason." Is this derived from Rousseau? If so, what of the reading of Rousseau that sees him as a critic of the Enlightenment?

[19] Cited in Hilda Smith, "'A Meteor Singly Alone' or 'a Star in a Crowd,' the Intellectual Career of Margaret Cavendish, Duchess of Newcastle," unpublished paper, 1996.

[20] Cited in Angeline Goreau, *The Whole Duty of a Woman: Female Writers in Seventeenth Century England* (New York: The Dial Press, 1984), 185–86.

reason, could only develop in a context of freedom. Women appeared to lack reason and virtue, and were weak and ignorant, not because of any natural deficiencies, but because they were denied their birthright of freedom.[21] Women's defects and their exclusion from citizenship, Wollstonecraft argued, were a consequence of men's special rights.

She insisted, against Rousseau, that domestic tyranny undercut republican political virtue. Men's power corrupted both sexes; neither a domestic despot nor a domestic slave could develop the capacities required for citizenship and the enjoyment of rights. Wollstonecraft argued, therefore, not only for the extension of the rights of man, in the sense of civil and political rights, to women, or for their education, but for wives' economic independence from their husbands and the transformation of marriage and sexuality – in short, for the sweeping social and political changes necessary to eliminate men's special rights. Wollstonecraft even raises the issue, differences between women, that preoccupies so many feminist theorists today.[22] To see her – a writer who "confounded gender categories" (Wendy Gunther-Canada, chapter 6) – as merely adding "woman," another "unitary subject," to "man," does an injustice to her remarkable analyses of, and insights into, the way in which the "subject" of natural rights was constructed through power.

Feminist writers faced a complex philosophical situation from the seventeenth century onward. As I have already emphasized, new political theories based on the premise of natural freedom and equality appeared to justify a universal political standing. Yet it was precisely these theories that exemplify the defects of "the Enlightenment" as portrayed in contemporary feminist theory. Couched in universal language, the theories, save for that of Hobbes, are centered around the ("essentialist") assumption that women, by nature, fall outside the category of "man" who is born free.

---

[21] Despite her lengthy arguments to show that women's qualities and capacities were "artificial," not natural, she is frequently denounced as an "essentialist." She has also been seen as "helping to define" what contemporary historians call republican motherhood (Joan Landes, *Women and the Public Sphere in the Age of the French Revolution* [Ithaca: Cornell University Press, 1988], 129). This is an odd charge, when Wollstonecraft rejected the special rights of men entailed by republican motherhood, and insisted that women could only be good mothers if they enjoyed political rights and citizenship. Indeed, Wollstonecraft, did not view fatherhood in an essentialist fashion either, but as a matter of care and responsibility, not nature (see Mary Shanley, chap. 7).

[22] In *Maria: or the Wrongs of Woman*, the novel she was writing when she died, she shows, in the characters of Jemima and Peggy, that she was aware that men's special rights were exercised differently over women of different classes. On slavery, see Moira Ferguson, "Mary Wollstonecraft and the Problematic of Slavery," in *Feminist Interpretations of Mary Wollstonecraft*, ed. Maria Falco (University Park: Pennsylvania State University Press, 1996).

In the standard history of political thought, theorists of an original contract such as Hobbes and Locke are seen as victors over the patriarchal philosophy of Sir Robert Filmer. If this were the case, then the new doctrines would indeed have provided an unambiguous philosophical weapon for early feminists. Filmer's patriarchal theory explicitly elaborated the prevailing view of the natural order of the sexes of his day (Gordon Schochet, chapter 10). A major issue between Filmer and his philosophical opponents, as Schochet notes, was whether the state was part of the natural (Divine) order of the world or a matter of human contrivance, the artifice of freeborn Englishmen. In order to set political relations on a conventional basis, the premise of natural liberty was necessary, the premise that potentially undercut all claims to power and authority, including the authority of men (husbands) over women (wives). In the seventeenth century, the combatants in the philosophical battles over nature and convention were well aware that the stakes included men's power as a sex.

In this volume, Gordon Schochet and Jane Jaquette focus on my argument about these early modern theorists in *The Sexual Contract*, and I now want to turn to their criticisms.

If I had concluded, as Schochet claims, that Filmer's and Locke's arguments "come to much the same thing," I would not have spent so much time distinguishing Filmer's classic, paternal patriarchy from Locke's modern form. There are no feudal relics in modern patriarchy. Filmer argued that patriarchal relations in kingdom and family were natural, constituted by fathers. Locke responded that public (political) and marital relations were conventional, created through contract by juridically free and equal men, and by men and women. But Locke, as Astell pointed out, drew back from the full implications of this theoretical move. He skillfully secured the separation of the private from the public, and obscured men's government in marriage, by relying on claims about women's natural incapacities, and using the language of natural "paternal" power. That marriage is conventional, *part of* the "civil society" brought into being in Locke's texts, not natural, or carried over from the state of nature, is easily overlooked because marriage, a contractual relation between two adults (husband and wife), is so frequently confused with "the family" (relations between mothers, fathers, and children).

The genius of Filmer's opponents, as I argue in *The Sexual Contract*, was to make it appear that women's subordination was not a political question, but "natural." They thus enabled contemporary political theorists to ignore one dimension of the story of the original contract. The latter discuss the *social* contract, that allows the state to be seen as (if it were) an institution created by contract. They maintain silence about the *sexual* contract that places men's power over women on a modern contractual footing. I retrieved this second dimension of the story of the original contract in my book.

Jaquette (chapter 9) takes issue with my interpretation of the texts, in particular, my reading of Hobbes. This is not the place to reply in detail to her version of my wider argument, but there are three general points that bear on my discussion here.

First, given a bizarre view attributed to me by Jaquette, readers may be surprised by this chapter. She asserts that I see women in the seventeenth century as "passive victims," as mere "objects" in the marriage contract. She can make this assertion only because she has made an invalid inference from my analysis, and has misunderstood a crucial step in my argument.[23] In *The Sexual Contract* I look in some detail, for example, at the implications of the common law of coverture for women's standing. This entails nothing whatsoever either about women's "passivity" or about my own views on women in the early modern period. I was exploring a crucial aspect of the legal and social context within which women's action or inaction took place, a context ignored in political theory. The evidence in the writings that have come down to us is that many women had a pretty shrewd understanding of their position as wives and political actors.

Second, a key point in my argument in *The Sexual Contract* is that the political philosophers of an original contract at one and the same time necessarily affirm and deny women's freedom. They must affirm women's freedom because "civil society" is presented in their theories as a free political order. Therefore, women cannot be merely incorporated like slaves. Women must participate in the practice, contract, that exemplifies freedom, and they do so as one of the parties to the marriage contract. They must thus be granted the capacities (the freedom) required to enter into contracts. The political philosophers must simultaneously deny women's freedom because they uphold men's conjugal power and exclude women from citizenship through claims about women's "natural" attributes. My argument is about the "logic" of these political theories. I am not concerned with marriage practices of the time, best explored by historians.

---

[23] She also bolsters her statements by quoting sentences and phrases from my book as if they were my own views, when they are part of my interpretation of the texts. The sentence in her epigraph refers to the manner in which sexual difference is *constructed* by theorists of the original contract; the phrase "contract and coercion are the same" is taken from my reading of Hobbes. My argument about certain actual contracts is not, as Jaquette seems to believe, concerned with coercion but about the consequences of contract even when entry is *voluntary*.

Third, Jaquette argues that during the seventeenth and eighteenth centuries women became the moral center of the nuclear family. Wives (and mothers) have frequently been seen as guardians of morality – but that does not lessen their lack of political standing. The long history of women's attempts to take political action on the basis of their "morality," a mark of their difference from men, is entangled with Wollstonecraft's dilemma. One cannot wish away coverture, or the steps that men took to make democratization their own preserve, as Jaquette appears to think, by focusing on women's moral status within the family.

And what was their position in Hobbes's argument? Hobbes is remarkable as the theorist who not only proclaims the natural equality of men and women, but also insists that, in the state of nature, mothers, not fathers, are lords. That some women were aware of the significance of this assumption is indicated by the anonymous *The Hardships of the English Laws . . .* (1735). The author writes that "had we ever been in the state of nature what he says is true" (Barbara Todd, chapter 16). In contrast, commentators on Hobbes have generally ignored both the standing that Hobbes gives to women in the natural condition, and the fact that he goes on to assume that wives are subordinate to their husbands in civil society. My essay on Hobbes drew attention to this dramatic shift in his argument and, in the absence of a story from Hobbes about how this change occurred, I filled in the logical gap in his theory.

My argument drew on my essay with Teresa Brennan of almost two decades ago, in which we discussed Jaquette's "different feminist question" about the disappearance of mothers in Hobbes's "family."[24] Jaquette argues that in Hobbes's state of nature almost everyone, men and women alike, become servants. So, she claims, "it is class, not gender, oppression" that is at issue in Hobbes's original contract. She is thus assuming that there are no significant differences in a master's relation to male and female servants. More importantly, while Jaquette appears to agree that there is a "significant ellipsis" in Hobbes's argument, it is no longer clear in her account what is missing.

My argument about the original contract is not, as Jaquette asserts, based on my interpretation of Hobbes,[25] nor on the view that "Hobbes

[24] Teresa Brennan and Carole Pateman, " 'Mere Auxiliaries to the Commonwealth': Women and the Origins of Liberalism," *Political Studies*, 27, 2 (1979): 183–200. I also drew on my account of Hobbes's theory, including his identification of enforced submission with consent, and the problem of forming confederations, in *The Problem of Political Obligation*.

[25] Conquest appears when I fill in the missing step of Hobbes's theory, and when I offer a story to make good the lack in the texts of an account of the genesis of sons who overthrow the political rule of their fathers.

modernises patriarchy." As I argue in *The Sexual Contract*, it is above all Locke, a champion of constitutional, limited government, not absolutism, and who separated conjugal from political relations, who provided that service. I was reading theories that, as Schochet noted in his earlier work on Filmer, involve "genetic" argument.[26] That is to say, they are based on the idea of "an origin," a founding moment – the original contract – that brings modern, civil society into being. My argument is not about a "foundation" at all, except in that sense. I am thus not clear what Schochet means in his criticism that my argument depends on an idea of "historical development that makes it impossible to alter institutions and practices without first rooting out their historical foundations."

Schochet writes that "histories of ideas [should] be informed by social structural history." Quite so; in addition to exploring the "logic" of stories of an original contract (which often include conjectural histories of developments in the state of nature), I looked at the social structural consequence of actual contracts about property in the person, e.g. the marriage and employment contracts. (I was not, as Jaquette maintains, concerned with "contract in the abstract"). My analysis of contracts about property in the person is informed by my reading of the early modern texts, in a manner analogous to Rawls's claim that we can best understand contemporary institutions if we assume that they are based on an original contract. However, that does not mean that, for example, the marriage contract forms a "foundation" in the manner of the idea of an original contract. Rather, my argument is that such contracts are the crucial mechanism through which the structure of (what I call) civil subordination, and the patriarchal relations constituting employment ("the economy") and marriage ("the family"), are reproduced every day by living persons.

I could not have written my book if I thought, as Schochet states, that "sexual oppression ... cannot be overcome." Exactly how it can be overcome is certainly not an easy question to answer, but to assess what kind of changes are needed in the 1990s still requires, I would submit, an appreciation of the theoretical, legal, and political background that I analyze in *The Sexual Contract*. I noted in my concluding pages that patriarchal structures were being destabilized. The heyday of the male "breadwinner" and his dependent wife, and the institutions that supported them, is now past. But the central assumptions of contractarianism are more widely influential than a decade ago when I was writing my book. The entanglement of feminism with contract theory and the

---

[26] Gordon Schochet, *Patriarchalism in Political Thought* (Oxford: Basil Blackwell, 1975).

idea of property in the person have to be confronted if social relations and political institutions are to be reconstructed so that women enjoy full political standing in a genuine democracy.

The theoretical maneuvers of the famous theorists of an original contract, and the continuing silence about their female critics, have been vital for the refusal of political theorists to admit that men's power over women is a *political* problem. But modern patriarchal theory required the premise of natural liberty and equality, which gave an opening for feminist arguments that was then impossible to close. The women's movement put the problem on the practical political agenda, but this could not have been done without the women writers of the early modern period who, whether Tories or radicals, whether agreeing with Filmer or Locke on absolutism and natural liberty, knew that women were men's equals.

Index

Abbadie, Jacques, 119
abbesses, 284, 311–14, 323
Abbott, Mary, 339
Addison, Joseph, 198, 250, 265
Adams, John, 253
Advice to the women and maidens of London, 69
Agrippa, Cornelius, *On the Excellence of Women*, 62
Algarotti, Francesco, 180, 184–85
An Answer to Pereat Papa, 61, 65
Anna Dorothea of Quedlinburg, 313
Anna Sophia of Quedlinburg
    Der treue Seelenfreund Christus Jesus, 313
Anne, Queen, 63, 252, 255, 267
Anne of Bourbon, 299
Anslay, Brian, 26
Arcot, nabob of, 266
Arendt, Hannah, 251
Argyle's Rebellion, 89
Aristotelian theory
    and appropriateness, 98, 122
    and civil society, 238
    and philosophy, 111
    view of women, 63, 295–98, 320
Armstrong, Nancy, 217–18
Arnauld, Antoine, 107
Assembly of Notables, 291
Astell, Mary, 1, 64, 97, 99, 102, 117, 250, 252, 305, 344, 366, 368–70, 371, 375–76
    and authority, 108
    The Christian Religion, 97, 107, 110
    and citizenship, 107
    and education, 97
    and Filmer, 107
    and Hobbes, 108, 112–13
    influence, 124
    Letters Concerning the Love of God, 98, 105–06, 110, 114
    and Locke, 107–08, 112–13, 378
    and Masham, 115–16
    and John Norris, 98, 104, 107, 110–14, 120

and philosophy, 98, 106–07, 110–12
and Platonism, 98, 106, 112
and politics, 105
Reflections upon Marriage, 105, 108, 110
and religion, 98, 105, 107, 110, 112
and science, 122–23
A Serious Proposal to the Ladies, 97, 104–05, 108
and sexual inequality, 108
and social contract, 108
and Whigs, 108
Aubrey, John, 44
Augsburg confession, 312
Augustine, St.
    The City of God, 35
Aylmer, John, 313

B.J., Gent.
    A Poem Occasion'd by the Rise and Fall of South-Sea Stock, 262
Bacon's Rebellion, 90
Baldwin, Abigail, 63
Barker-Benfield, G. J., 127, 217–18
de la Barre, Poullain, *The Woman as good as the man*, 62
Barwell, Mary, 198, 273–78, 371
Barwell, Richard, 273–78
Barwell, William, 273–74
Barwick, Grace, 65
Behn, Aphra, 1, 17, 20–21, 75–93, 366, 368
    arrest, 87
    "Astraea's Book of Songs and Satyrs," 89
    The City Heiress, 78, 82–86
    The Feign'd Courtizans, 79
    Epilogue to Romulus, 87
    and freedom, 78
    health, 89
    and James II, 79–80, 87–88, 93
    Love Letters Between a Nobleman and his Sister, 83–84
    The Lucky Chance, 87–88
    Oroonoko, 78, 83, 90–93
    patronage, 79